Mastering PowerShell Scripting
Fifth Edition

Automate repetitive tasks and simplify complex administrative tasks using PowerShell

Chris Dent

Mastering PowerShell Scripting
Fifth Edition

Senior Publishing Product Manager: Reshma Raman

Acquisition Editor – Peer Reviews: Tejas Mhasvekar

Project Editor: Amisha Vathare

Content Development Editor: Deepayan Bhattacharjee

Copy Editor: Safis Editing

Technical Editor: Kushal Sharma

Proofreader: Safis Editing

Indexer: Tejal Daruwale Soni

Presentation Designer: Ganesh Bhadwalkar

Developer Relations Marketing Executive: Meghal Patel

First published: April 2015

Second edition: October 2017

Third edition: February 2019

Fourth edition: June 2021

Fifth edition: May 2024

Production reference: 1160524

Published by Packt Publishing Ltd.

Grosvenor House

11 St Paul's Square

Birmingham

B3 1RB, UK.

ISBN 978-1-80512-027-8

www.packt.com

Contributors

About the author

Chris Dent is an automation specialist with a deep interest in the PowerShell language. Chris has been learning and using PowerShell since 2007 and is often found answering questions in the Virtual PowerShell User Group.

I would like to thank my wife, Emily, and my children, Lizzy and Thomas, for their continued support.

About the reviewer

Mike Roberts is a PowerShell ninja, both in his profession as well as his blog, where he teaches it: https://gngr.ninja. Through his blog, he hopes to educate and inspire others by demonstrating what different technologies are capable of.

I am eternally grateful for the support of my friends and family. Thank you!

Learn more on Discord

Read this book alongside other users, PowerShell experts, and the author himself. Ask questions, provide solutions to other readers, chat with the author via Ask Me Anything sessions, and much more.

Scan the QR code or visit the link to join the community.

https://packt.link/SecNet

Table of Contents

Preface   **xxiii**

Chapter 1: Introduction to PowerShell   **1**

Technical requirements 2

What is PowerShell? 3

The command line 3

PowerShell editors 4

Getting help 6

  Updatable help • 6

  The Get-Help command • 7

    Syntax • 9

    Examples • 9

    Parameter • 10

    Detailed and Full switches • 11

  Save-Help • 12

  Update-Help • 13

  About_* help files • 14

Command naming and discovery 15

  Verbs • 15

  Nouns • 16

  Finding commands • 16

  Aliases • 17

About profile scripts 19

Parameters, values, and parameter sets 20

  Parameters • 20

    Optional parameters • 20

    Optional positional parameters • 21

    Mandatory parameters • 21

    Mandatory positional parameters • 21

    Switch parameters • 22

  Parameter values • 23

  Parameter sets • 24

  Common parameters • 25

  Confirm and WhatIf • 26

    Confirm and ConfirmPreference • 26

    WhatIf and WhatIfPreference • 29

  Force parameter • 30

PassThru parameter • 31

Introduction to providers 32

Drives and providers • 34

Introduction to splatting 35

Splatting to avoid long lines • 36
Conditional use of parameters • 38
Splatting to avoid repetition • 38
Splatting and positional parameters • 39

Parser modes 40

Experimental features 41

Summary 42

Chapter 2: Modules   45

Introducing modules 46

The Get-Module command • 46
The Import-Module command • 47
The Remove-Module command • 48
PSModulePath in PowerShell • 48
Module content • 49
Using Windows PowerShell modules in PowerShell 7 • 50

Finding and installing modules 52

What is the PowerShell Gallery? • 52
The Find-Module command • 53
The Install-Module command • 54
The Update-Module command • 54
The Save-Module command • 55

Microsoft.PowerShell.PSResourceGet 55

Repositories • 56
Version ranges • 56

PowerShell repositories 57

Creating an SMB repository • 57
NuGet repositories • 58

About snap-ins 58

Summary 59

Chapter 3: Variables, Arrays, and Hashtables   61

Naming and creating variables 61

Provider variables • 63

Variables in strings 63

Variable types 64

Assignment with types on the right • 65
Assignment with types on the left • 66

Value and reference types • 66

Type conversion • 68

Variable commands **69**

Get-Variable • 69

New-Variable • 70

Set-Variable • 72

Remove-Variable • 72

Clear-Variable • 73

Variable provider **73**

Variable scope **74**

Accessing variables • 75

Scope modifiers • 76

Numeric scopes • 77

Private variables • 79

About arrays **80**

Array type • 80

Creation by assignment • 81

Creating an array • 82

Arrays with a type • 83

Adding elements to an array • 83

List and ArrayList • 84

Selecting elements from an array • 86

Changing element values in an array • 89

Removing elements • 89

Removing elements by index • 90

Filling variables from arrays • 90

Multi-dimensional and jagged arrays • 91

About hashtables **92**

Creating a Hashtable • 93

Adding, changing, and removing keys • 93

Using a hashtable to filter • 94

Enumerating a Hashtable • 97

About Ordered **98**

Summary **100**

Chapter 4: Working with Objects in PowerShell   **101**

Pipelines **102**

Standard output • 102

Non-standard output • 103

The Object pipeline • 103

Members **104**

The Get-Member command • 105

Accessing object properties • 106

Access modifiers • 107

Using methods • 110

Return types and argument types • 112

Creating and modifying objects • 113

Using PSCustomObject • 113

The New-Object command • 115

The Add-Member command • 115

Add-Member and custom objects • 116

Enumerating and filtering 118

The ForEach-Object command • 118

Begin and End parameters • 119

The Parallel parameter • 120

The MemberName parameter • 122

The Where-Object command • 122

Selecting and sorting 123

The Select-Object command • 124

Calculated properties • 126

The ExpandProperty parameter • 127

The Unique parameter • 128

Property sets • 129

The Sort-Object command • 130

The Unique parameter • 133

Grouping and measuring 134

The Group-Object command • 134

The Measure-Object command • 137

Comparing 139

Importing, exporting, and converting 141

The Export-Csv command • 141

The Import-Csv command • 143

Export-Clixml and Import-Clixml • 145

The Tee-Object command • 146

Formatting 147

Formatting and exporting • 148

The Format-Table command • 148

The Format-List command • 149

Select-Object, Write-Host, and inline output • 150

Format-only properties • 152

Summary 156

Chapter 5: Operators   157

Precedence, grouping, and sub-expressions 158

Operator precedence • 158

Grouping • 158

Sub-expression operator • 159

Array sub-expression operator • 159

Unary, binary, and ternary operators 160

About the ternary operator • 161

Arithmetic operators 161

Addition operator • 162

Subtraction operator • 163

Multiplication operator • 164

Division operator • 164

Remainder operator • 165

Increment and decrement operators • 165

Comparison operators 167

eq and ne • 167

like and notlike • 168

Greater than and less than • 169

Case sensitivity • 170

Comparison operators and arrays • 170

Comparisons to null • 172

contains and in • 173

Regular expression-based operators 173

match and notmatch • 174

replace • 175

split • 177

Logical operators 179

and • 179

or • 179

not • 179

xor (eXclusive OR) • 180

Bitwise operators 180

band (bitwise AND) • 182

bor (bitwise OR) • 182

bxor (bitwise eXclusive OR) • 182

bnot (bitwise NOT) • 183

shl and shr (shift left and right operators) • 183

Assignment operators 186

Assign, add and assign, and subtract and assign • 186

Multiply and assign, divide and assign, and modulus and assign • 188

Statements can be assigned to a variable • 189

Assignment and other operators • 189

Type operators 190

as • 190

is and isnot • 191

Redirection operators 191

About Write-Host • 192

Redirection to a file • 192

PowerShell and default file encoding • 194

Redirecting streams to standard output • 194

    Only stdout • 194

Redirection to null • 195

Other operators **195**

Comma • 196

Index • 196

Range • 197

Call • 197

Format • 198

join • 200

Null coalescing • 200

    Null coalescing assignment • 201

Null conditional • 202

Pipeline chain • 203

Background • 205

Summary **205**

Chapter 6: Conditional Statements and Loops   **207**

if, else, and elseif 208

Assignment within if statements • 209

Implicit Boolean 209

switch statements 210

switch statements and arrays • 210

switch statements and files • 211

Wildcard and Regex parameters • 211

Script block cases • 212

switch statements and enums • 214

switch, break, and continue 215

Loops 217

foreach loop • 217

    foreach keyword and foreach alias • 217

for loop • 218

do-until and do-while loops • 220

while loop • 221

Loops, break, and continue 222

break and continue outside loops • 224

Loops and labels 224

Loops, queues, and stacks 225

Summary 229

Chapter 7: Working with .NET

231

Assemblies 232

About the GAC • 234

Types 235

Type descriptions are objects in PowerShell • 236

Enumerations • 236

Classes • 236

Namespaces • 237

The using keyword 237

Using namespaces • 238

Using assemblies • 239

Type accelerators 240

About PSCustomObject and Ordered • 240

Members 242

Constructors • 243

Properties • 244

Methods • 246

Fluent interfaces • 247

Static methods • 248

About the new() method • 250

Static properties • 250

Reflection in PowerShell 251

The TypeAccelerators type • 252

The ArgumentTypeConverterAttribute type • 253

About generics 256

Generic classes • 256

Generic methods • 257

Summary 259

Online Chapter 260

Chapter 8: Strings, Numbers, and Dates (Online Chapter)

Chapter 9: Regular Expressions (Online Chapter)

Chapter 10: Files, Folders, and the Registry

261

Working with providers 262

Navigating • 263

Getting items • 264

Drives • 265

Items 265

Paths and .NET • 266

Testing for existing items • 267

     Testing filesystem paths • 268
     Testing registry paths • 268
     Testing path type • 269
  Creating items • 270
  Reading and writing content • 271
     Reading and writing in a pipeline • 271
     Reading all content • 272
     Writing content • 272
     About text file encoding • 273
  Temporary files • 274
  Removing items • 275
  Invoking items • 275
  Item properties • 275
     Properties and the filesystem • 275
     Adding and removing file attributes • 276
     Registry values • 277
     Registry values and environment variables • 279
  Searching for items • 280
Windows permissions 282
  Access and audit • 283
  Rule protection • 283
  Inheritance and propagation flags • 285
  Removing ACEs • 286
  Copying lists and entries • 287
  Adding ACEs • 288
     Filesystem rights • 288
     Registry rights • 290
  Numeric values in the ACL • 290
  Ownership • 292
Transactions 293
File catalog commands 294
  About hashing • 294
  New-FileCatalog • 294
  Test-FileCatalog • 295
Summary 298

Chapter 11: Windows Management Instrumentation   **299**

Working with WMI 299
  WMI classes • 299
  WMI commands • 300
  CIM commands • 301
     Getting instances • 301
     Getting classes • 302
     Calling methods • 303

Creating instances • 306
Removing instances • 307
Working with CIM sessions • 308
Associated classes • 309

The WMI Query Language **310**

Understanding SELECT, WHERE, and FROM • 310

Escape sequences and wildcards • 311

Comparison operators • 312

WQL filters and dates • 312

Logic operators • 313

Quoting values • 313

Associated classes • 314

WMI object paths • 315

Using ASSOCIATORS OF • 316

WMI type accelerators **317**

Getting instances • 317

Working with dates • 318

Getting classes • 319

Calling methods • 319

Creating instances • 321

Associated classes • 321

Permissions **321**

Sharing permissions • 322

Creating a shared directory • 322

Getting a security descriptor • 323

Adding an access control entry • 325

Setting the security descriptor • 326

WMI permissions • 327

Getting a security descriptor • 327

The access mask • 327

WMI and SDDL • 328

Summary **330**

Chapter 12: Working with HTML, XML, and JSON   **331**

ConvertTo-Html **332**

Multiple tables • 332

Adding style • 332

ConvertTo-Html and Send-MailMessage • 333

Windows PowerShell and ConvertTo-Html • 334

Modifying HTML content • 335

XML commands **336**

About XML • 337

Elements and attributes • 337

Namespaces • 337

Schemas • 338

Select-Xml • 338

　Select-Xml and namespaces • 340

ConvertTo-Xml • 341

System.Xml **342**

The XML type accelerator • 342

XPath and XmlDocument • 343

SelectNodes and XPathNodeList • 344

Working with namespaces • 345

Creating XML documents • 346

Modifying element and attribute values • 348

Adding elements • 349

Removing elements and attributes • 350

Copying nodes between documents • 350

Schema validation • 351

Inferring a schema • 353

System.Xml.Linq **356**

Opening documents • 356

Selecting nodes • 357

Creating documents • 358

Working with namespaces • 359

Modifying element and attribute values • 360

Adding nodes • 361

Removing nodes • 361

Schema validation • 362

JSON **363**

ConvertTo-Json • 363

　EnumsAsStrings • 364

　AsArray • 365

　EscapeHandling • 365

ConvertFrom-Json • 366

　AsHashtable • 369

　NoEnumerate • 370

Test-Json • 370

Summary **372**

Chapter 13: Web Requests and Web Services　　　　　　　　　　　　　**375**

Technical requirements **375**

Web requests **376**

HTTP methods • 376

Using Invoke-WebRequest • 377

About parsing web pages • 377

Downloading files • 378

Using the HEAD method • 378

HTTPS • 379

  Security protocols • 379

  Certificate validation • 380

  Windows PowerShell and certificate validation • 380

  Capturing SSL errors • 382

Working with REST **383**

  Simple requests • 384

  Using basic authentication • 385

  Requests with arguments • 385

  Working with paging • 388

  OAuth • 390

    Creating an application • 390

    Getting an authorization code • 390

    Implementing an HTTP listener • 391

    Requesting an access token • 392

    Using a token • 392

Working with SOAP **393**

  Finding a SOAP service • 393

  SOAP in Windows PowerShell • 394

    New-WebServiceProxy • 394

    Methods • 395

    Methods and enumerations • 396

    Methods and SOAP objects • 397

    Overlapping services • 398

  SOAP in PowerShell 7 • 399

    Getting the WSDL document • 399

    Discovering methods and enumerations • 399

    Running methods • 401

Summary **404**

Chapter 14: Remoting and Remote Management   405

Technical requirements **405**

Executing remote commands **405**

  Enter-PSSession • 406

  Invoke-Command • 407

    Parallel execution • 409

    Catching remoting failures • 410

    Local functions and remote sessions • 411

    Using ArgumentList • 412

    The using scope modifier • 413

PS Sessions **414**

  New-PSSession and Get-PSSession • 414

  Disconnected sessions • 415

  Import-PSSession • 416

Export-PSSession • 416
Copying items between sessions • 416

WS-Management **417**
Enabling and configuring remoting • 417
The WSMan drive • 418
Remoting and SSL • 418
User Account Control • 421
Trusted hosts • 422

Remoting on Linux **423**
Remoting over SSH • 424
Connecting from Windows to Linux • 425
Connecting from Linux to Windows • 426

The double-hop problem **428**
CredSSP • 429
Passing credentials • 430

CIM sessions **430**
Get-CimSession • 432
Using CIM sessions • 432

Just Enough Administration **432**
Session configuration • 433
Role capabilities • 434

Summary **435**

Chapter 15: Asynchronous Processing   **437**

Working with jobs **437**
Start-Job, Get-Job, and Remove-Job • 438
Receive-Job • 439
Wait-Job • 440
Jobs and the using scope modifier • 441
The background operator • 442
The ThreadJob module • 443
Batching jobs • 443

Reacting to events **445**
The Register-ObjectEvent and *-Event commands • 446
Action, Event, EventArgs, and MessageData parameters • 447
Get-EventSubscriber and Unregister-Event • 449

Using runspaces and runspace pools **450**
Creating a PowerShell instance • 451
The Invoke and BeginInvoke methods • 452
About Streams and InvocationStateInfo • 455
Running multiple instances • 457
Using the RunspacePool object • 458
About the InitialSessionState object • 459

Adding modules and snap-ins • 460

Adding variables • 461

Adding functions • 462

Using the InitialSessionState and RunspacePool objects • 464

Using thread-safe objects 464

Managing concurrent access 467

Summary 471

Chapter 16: Graphical User Interfaces 473

About Windows Presentation Foundation (WPF) 474

Designing a UI 474

About XAML 474

Displaying the UI 475

Layout 477

Using the Grid control • 477

Using the StackPanel control • 481

Using the DockPanel control • 483

About Margin and Padding • 486

Naming and locating controls 488

Handling events 492

Buttons and the Click event • 494

ComboBox and SelectionChanged • 495

Adding elements programmatically • 496

Sorting a ListView • 498

Responsive interfaces 504

Import-Xaml and runspace support • 504

Errors in the background • 506

Using the Dispatcher • 506

ScriptBlock runspace affinity • 509

Using the Action delegate • 510

Using the Func delegate • 512

Summary 515

Chapter 17: Scripts, Functions, and Script Blocks 517

About style 518

Capabilities of scripts, functions, and script blocks 519

Scripts and using statements • 519

Scripts and the Requires statement • 520

Nesting functions • 520

Script blocks and closures • 521

Parameters and the param block 522

Parameter types • 523

Default values • 523

Cross-referencing parameters • 524

The CmdletBinding attribute 525

Common parameters • 525

CmdletBinding properties • 526

ShouldProcess and ShouldContinue • 527

ShouldProcess • 527

ShouldContinue • 530

The Alias attribute 532

begin, process, end, and clean 532

begin • 533

process • 534

end • 534

clean • 536

Named blocks and return • 537

Managing output 538

The Out-Null command • 540

Assigning to null • 540

Redirecting to null • 541

Casting to void • 541

Working with long lines 542

Line break after a pipe • 543

Line break after an operator • 543

Using the array sub-expression operator to break up lines • 543

Comment-based help 545

Output help • 546

Parameter help • 548

Examples • 551

Summary 552

Chapter 18: Parameters, Validation, and Dynamic Parameters   553

The Parameter attribute 553

Position and positional binding • 555

The DontShow property • 557

The ValueFromRemainingArguments property • 558

The HelpMessage property • 559

Validating input 560

The PSTypeName attribute • 560

Validation attributes • 562

The ValidateNotNull attribute • 563

The ValidateNotNullOrEmpty attribute • 565

The ValidateNotNullOrWhitespace attribute • 565

The ValidateCount attribute • 566

The ValidateLength attribute • 566

The ValidatePattern attribute • 567

The ValidateRange attribute • 570

The ValidateScript attribute • 570

The ValidateSet attribute • 571

The ValidateDrive attribute • 572

The ValidateUserDrive attribute • 573

The Allow attributes • 573

The AllowNull attribute • 573

The AllowEmptyString attribute • 574

The AllowEmptyCollection attribute • 574

PSReference parameters • 575

Pipeline input **576**

About ValueFromPipeline • 576

Accepting null input • 577

Input object types • 578

Using ValueFromPipeline for multiple parameters • 579

About ValueFromPipelineByPropertyName • 581

ValueFromPipelineByPropertyName and parameter aliases • 582

Defining parameter sets **583**

Argument completers **587**

The ArgumentCompleter attribute • 588

Using Register-ArgumentCompleter • 589

About CompletionResult • 590

Non-literal values • 591

Listing registered argument completers • 595

Dynamic parameters **596**

Creating a RuntimeDefinedParameter object • 597

Using RuntimeDefinedParameterDictionary • 599

Using dynamic parameters • 600

PSBoundParameters • 600

RuntimeDefinedParameterDictionary • 602

Conditional parameters • 604

Summary **605**

Chapter 19: Classes and Enumerations   **607**

Defining an enumeration **607**

Enum and underlying types • 608

Automatic value assignment • 609

Enum or ValidateSet • 610

The Flags attribute • 611

Using enumerations to convert a value • 615

Creating a class **616**

Properties • 617

Constructors • 618

Methods • 619

The Hidden modifier • 621

The static modifier • 622

Inheritance • 622

Constructors and inheritance • 624

Calling methods in a parent class • 627

Working with interfaces • 628

    Implementing IComparable • 628

    Implementing IEquatable • 630

Supporting casting • 631

Classes and runspace affinity 634

Transformation, validation, and completion 637

Argument transformation attribute classes • 637

Validation attribute classes • 639

    ValidateArgumentsAttribute • 640

    ValidateEnumeratedArgumentsAttribute • 641

ValidateSet value generator • 643

Argument completers • 644

    IArgumentCompleter • 644

    IArgumentCompleterFactory • 646

Classes and Microsoft Desired State Configuration 648

Implementing Get • 650

Implementing Set • 651

Implementing Test • 652

Using the resource • 653

Summary 657

Online Chapter 658

Chapter 20: Building Modules (Online Chapter)

Chapter 21: Testing   659

Technical requirements 659

Static analysis 660

PSScriptAnalyzer • 660

    Configurable rules • 661

    Suppressing rules • 663

Using AST • 666

    Visualizing the AST • 668

    Searching the AST • 669

Tokenizer • 671

Custom script analyzer rules • 672

    Creating a custom rule • 673

    AST-based rules • 673

    Token-based rules • 675

Testing with Pester **676**

Testing methodologies • 678

What to test • 679

Describing tests • 680

About the Describe and Context keywords • 680

About the It keyword • 680

Should and assertions • 681

Testing for errors • 682

Iteration with Pester • 684

Using the ForEach parameter • 684

ForEach with Describe and Context • 686

Conditional testing • 687

Using Set-ItResult • 687

Using Skip • 688

Pester phases • 689

Before and After blocks • 690

Mocking commands • 690

Parameter variables • 693

Parameter filtering • 694

Overriding mocks • 696

Mocking non-local commands • 699

Mocking objects • 701

Adding methods to PSCustomObject • 702

Disarming .NET types • 702

Mocking CIM objects • 705

InModuleScope • 707

Pester in scripts • 708

Summary **710**

Chapter 22: Error Handling

713

Error types **713**

Terminating errors • 713

Non-terminating errors • 715

Error actions **716**

About Get-Error • 717

Raising errors **718**

Error records • 719

Raising non-terminating errors • 720

Using the WriteError method • 722

Raising terminating errors • 724

Using the ThrowTerminatingError method • 725

Catching errors **726**

ErrorVariable • 726

try, catch, and finally • 727

Rethrowing errors • 730
Inconsistent error handling • 733
throw and ErrorAction • 736
Terminating errors in child scopes • 739
Nesting try, catch, and finally • 740
About trap 742
Using trap • 742
trap, scope, and continue • 743
Summary 744

Chapter 23: Debugging   **747**

Common problems 747
Dash characters • 748
Operator usage • 750
Assignment instead of equality • 750
-or instead of -and • 751
Negated array comparisons • 752
Use of named blocks • 753
Code outside of a named block • 753
Pipeline without process • 755
Problems with variables • 756
About strict mode • 756
Variables and types • 758
Types and reserved variables • 759
Debugging in the console 760
Setting a command breakpoint • 760
Using variable breakpoints • 762
Setting a line breakpoint • 763
Debugging in Visual Studio Code 765
Using the debugger • 765
Viewing CALL STACK • 767
Using launch configurations • 768
Debugging modules • 770
Using WATCH • 771
Debugging other PowerShell processes 772

Other Books You May Enjoy   **779**

Index   **783**

Preface

PowerShell is an object-oriented scripting language aimed at systems administrators that was invented by Jeffrey Snover. PowerShell was first conceived as far back as 2002 and entered mainstream use in 2006. Exchange 2007 was one of the first major systems to adopt it as an administration language.

PowerShell has come a long way over the years. PowerShell 7 smooths over a lot of the rough edges in the original releases of the cross-platform PowerShell Core (PowerShell 6).

Like any good scripting language, PowerShell is the glue that ties automated processes together. It is a vital part of the Microsoft ecosystem and is great in heterogeneous environments.

Who this book is for

This book is for PowerShell developers, system administrators, and script authors, new and old, who wish to explore the capabilities and possibilities of the language.

What this book covers

PowerShell fundamentals are explored in the first five chapters:

Chapter 1, *Introduction to PowerShell*, introduces you to editors, the help system, command naming, and more.

Chapter 2, *Modules*, explores finding, installing, and using modules in PowerShell. Snap-ins are not part of PowerShell 7 but are briefly explored as a legacy feature of PowerShell 5.

Chapter 3, *Variables, Arrays, and Hashtables*, covers an important topic in PowerShell. The chapter explores the use of variables, as well as the capabilities of collections.

Chapter 4, *Working with Objects in PowerShell*, looks at the concept of objects in PowerShell and the generic commands available for selecting, filtering, and manipulating values.

Chapter 5, *Operators*, explores the large variety of operators available in PowerShell.

Then, we move on to working with data in PowerShell:

Chapter 6, *Conditional Statements and Loops*, covers the tools used to make decisions in scripts in PowerShell. This chapter explores keywords like If, and the different loop styles available.

Chapter 7, *Working with .NET*, dives into .NET, which was used to create the PowerShell language and is available within PowerShell.

Chapter 8, Strings, Numbers, and Dates, covers a vital part of any scripting language, and PowerShell is no exception. This chapter explores the different techniques available for working with such values. This chapter can be accessed using `https://static.packt-cdn.com/downloads/9781805120278_Chapter_8_and_9.pdf`.

Chapter 9, Regular Expressions, discusses regular expressions, which are an incredibly useful inclusion in PowerShell. You can use regular expressions to make short work of string parsing tasks. The chapter ends by walking through several practical parsing examples. This chapter can be accessed using `https://static.packt-cdn.com/downloads/9781805120278_Chapter_8_and_9.pdf`.

Chapter 10, File, Folders, and the Registry, explores the use of providers in PowerShell, which are mostly used to access the file system and, in Windows, the registry.

Chapter 11, Windows Management Instrumentation, explores WMI in PowerShell, a significant part of the Windows operating system since Windows NT.

Chapter 12, Working with HTML, XML, and JSON, looks at the PowerShell commands and .NET types that you can use to work with these different text-based formats.

Chapter 13, Web Requests and Web Services, explores basic web requests before diving into using PowerShell to work with REST APIs, using the API for GitHub as an example. Support for SOAP in PowerShell 7 is less complete than in PowerShell 5.1. SOAP is explored by way of a web service project via Visual Studio.

Chapters 14 to 16 explores automating with PowerShell:

Chapter 14, Remoting and Remote Management, examines the configuration and use of PowerShell Remoting in both Windows and Linux.

Chapter 15, Asynchronous Processing, dives into the realm of background jobs in PowerShell before exploring .NET events in PowerShell. The chapter ends with a look at runspaces and runspace pools.

Chapter 16, Graphical User Interfaces, shows you how to implement responsive user interfaces in PowerShell.

For the rest of the book, we learn how to extend PowerShell by adding and implementing new functionalities:

Chapter 17, Scripts, Functions, and Script Blocks, explores the building blocks of larger scripts and modules. The chapter looks at how to define parameters, work in a pipeline, and manage output.

Chapter 18, Parameters, Validation, and Dynamic Parameters, looks at the many options available for defining parameters and validating input in PowerShell.

Chapter 19, Classes and Enumerations, shows off the capabilities of the `class` and `enum` keywords, which were introduced with PowerShell 5. The chapter includes an exploration of class inheritance and implementing .NET interfaces. This chapter includes a brief look at writing class-based DSC resources.

Chapter 20, Building Modules, explores the key concepts of creating a module in PowerShell using PowerShell code. The chapter shows off some of the common approaches available to module authors. This chapter can be accessed using `https://static.packt-cdn.com/downloads/9781805120278_Chapter_20.pdf`.

Chapter 21, Testing, explores static analysis using PSScriptAnalyzer as well as acceptance and unit testing using the Pester framework.

Chapter 22, Error Handling, looks at the complex topic of handling errors in PowerShell, including an exploration of both terminating and non-terminating errors.

Chapter 23, Debugging, uses the built-in debugger in PowerShell and Visual Studio to delve into some of the common problems encountered when debugging scripts.

To get the most out of this book

- Some familiarity with operating systems would be beneficial
- Visual Studio Code (https://code.visualstudio.com/) is used a few times in the book and is a useful tool to have available throughout

Download the example code files

The code bundle for the book is hosted on GitHub at https://github.com/PacktPublishing/Mastering-PowerShell-Scripting-5E/. We also have other code bundles from our rich catalog of books and videos available at https://github.com/PacktPublishing/. Check them out!

Download the color images

We also provide a PDF file that has color images of the screenshots/diagrams used in this book. You can download it here: https://packt.link/gbp/9781805120278.

Conventions used

There are a number of text conventions used throughout this book.

CodeInText: Indicates code words in text, database table names, folder names, filenames, file extensions, pathnames, dummy URLs, user input, and Twitter handles. For example: "By default, Save-Help (and Update-Help) will not download help content more often than once every 24 hours."

A block of code is set as follows:

```
Get-Process |
    Select-Object Name, ID -First 1
```

When we wish to draw your attention to a particular part of a code block, the relevant lines or items are set in bold:

```
Get-Process |
    Select-Object Name, ID
```

Any command-line input or output is written as follows:

```
PS> Get-Process | Select-Object Name, ID -First 1

Name        Id
```

```
Pwsh    5068
```

Bold: Indicates a new term, an important word, or words that you see on the screen. For instance, words in menus or dialog boxes appear in the text like this. For example: "Select **System info** from the **Administration** panel."

Warnings or important notes appear like this.

Tips and tricks appear like this.

Get in touch

Feedback from our readers is always welcome.

General feedback: Email feedback@packtpub.com and mention the book's title in the subject of your message. If you have questions about any aspect of this book, please email us at questions@packtpub.com.

Errata: Although we have taken every care to ensure the accuracy of our content, mistakes do happen. If you have found a mistake in this book, we would be grateful if you reported this to us. Please visit http://www.packtpub.com/submit-errata, click **Submit Errata**, and fill in the form.

Piracy: If you come across any illegal copies of our works in any form on the internet, we would be grateful if you would provide us with the location address or website name. Please contact us at copyright@packtpub.com with a link to the material.

If you are interested in becoming an author: If there is a topic that you have expertise in and you are interested in either writing or contributing to a book, please visit http://authors.packtpub.com.

Share your thoughts

Once you've read *Mastering PowerShell Scripting, Fifth Edition*, we'd love to hear your thoughts! Scan the QR code below to go straight to the Amazon review page for this book and share your feedback.

https://packt.link/r/1805120271

Your review is important to us and the tech community and will help us make sure we're delivering excellent quality content.

Download a free PDF copy of this book

Thanks for purchasing this book!

Do you like to read on the go but are unable to carry your print books everywhere?

Is your eBook purchase not compatible with the device of your choice?

Don't worry, now with every Packt book you get a DRM-free PDF version of that book at no cost.

Read anywhere, any place, on any device. Search, copy, and paste code from your favorite technical books directly into your application.

The perks don't stop there, you can get exclusive access to discounts, newsletters, and great free content in your inbox daily.

Follow these simple steps to get the benefits:

1. Scan the QR code or visit the link below:

https://packt.link/free-ebook/9781805120278

2. Submit your proof of purchase.
3. That's it! We'll send your free PDF and other benefits to your email directly.

1

Introduction to PowerShell

PowerShell is a shell scripting language from Microsoft originally released for Windows in 2006. PowerShell was written to appeal to systems administrators and presents a great deal of its functionality as commands such as `Get-ChildItem`, `Get-Content`, `New-Item`, and so on.

Microsoft Exchange was one of the first systems to embrace PowerShell with the release of Exchange 2007.

Active Directory tools followed a few years later along with tools to manage on-premises virtualization platforms from VMware and Microsoft Hyper-V.

More recently, PowerShell has been offered as a management tool for cloud platforms like Azure and AWS. In addition to modules that can be used to interact with either service, Azure and AWS both offer in-browser shells to directly manage services.

Windows PowerShell, or the Desktop edition, includes the original version through to 5.1, which is the final release of the Windows-specific shell. Windows PowerShell versions are based on .NET Framework.

In 2018, the first version of PowerShell Core was released with PowerShell 6. The move from .NET Framework to .NET Core allows the latest versions of PowerShell to run on Linux and macOS, as well as Windows.

Since then, PowerShell 7 has been released and continues to receive new features and updates. The core edition of PowerShell has seen a move through .NET Core 3.1 to .NET 8 with PowerShell 7.4.

The other significant difference between Windows PowerShell and PowerShell is that PowerShell 6 and above are open source. The project is on GitHub and is open to public contributors: `https://github.com/powershell/powershell`.

A significant number of community contributors have been driving change, making commands more usable and useful, adding new features, and fixing bugs. For example, `Invoke-WebRequest` and `Invoke-RestMethod` were completely overhauled in PowerShell 6, greatly improving how they perform while retaining much in the way of backward compatibility.

Several core commands were removed while these changes were being made. For example, the Get-WmiObject and New-WebServiceProxy commands have been removed. The reasons for this vary; in some cases, the commands are fundamentally incompatible with .NET Core. In a few cases, the commands were under restricted licensing agreements and could not be made open source. These differences are highlighted in this book and alternatives are demonstrated where possible.

Despite all this change, PowerShell still maintains strong backward compatibility, with very few breaking changes between the two editions. Operators and language keywords remain the same, and most changes are new features instead of changes to existing ones. Exceptions to this tend to be edge cases like parameter changes to Get-Content when reading byte content. These differences in behavior are highlighted throughout this book. Lessons learned using Windows PowerShell can be applied to PowerShell 7, and they will continue to be applicable to future versions of PowerShell.

This book is split into several sections. Much of this book is intended to act as a reference. The following topics will be covered:

- Exploring PowerShell fundamentals
- Working with data
- Automating with PowerShell
- Extending PowerShell

While exploring the fundamentals of the language, this first section of the book attempts to cover as many of the building blocks as possible.

This chapter explores a diverse set of topics:

- What is PowerShell?
- The command line
- PowerShell editors
- Getting help
- Command naming and discovery
- About profile scripts
- Parameters, values, and parameter sets
- Introduction to providers
- Introduction to splatting
- Parser modes
- Experimental features

Technical requirements

This chapter makes use of the following on the Windows platform: PowerShell 7.

At the start of this chapter, PowerShell was described as a shell scripting language. But this is perhaps not a complete description.

What is PowerShell?

PowerShell is a mixture of a command-line interface, a functional programming language, and an object-oriented programming language. PowerShell is based on Microsoft .NET, which gives it a level of open flexibility that was not available in Microsoft's scripting languages (such as VBScript or batch) before this.

PowerShell has been written to be highly discoverable. It has substantial built-in help, which is accessible within the console via the Get-Help command. PowerShell has commands such as Get-Member to allow a user to discover the details of any objects it returns.

PowerShell 7 can be installed alongside Windows PowerShell. Windows PowerShell is installed in Windows\System32 by the Windows Management Framework packages, and it cannot be moved elsewhere. PowerShell Core and 7 are both installed in the Program Files folder and do not share any of the files used by Windows PowerShell. Preview versions of PowerShell can be installed alongside the full releases and have separate folder structures.

Command line customization is a popular subject, and several tools are available to help.

The command line

PowerShell 7 comes with a module called PSReadLine. A module is a collection of related commands. Modules are explored in greater detail in *Chapter 2, Modules*.

PSReadLine provides command-line syntax highlighting, preserves history between sessions, and offers completion services when writing commands.

PSReadLine can be configured to offer command completion based on previously typed commands, a useful feature when using similar commands in the console and one that can save searching history for the right command. By default, PSReadline 2.2.6 uses history and a command prediction plugin. The plugin may be explicitly enabled using Set-PSReadLineOption.

```
Set-PSReadLineOption -PredictionSource HistoryAndPlugin
```

Once enabled, PSReadLine will offer suggestions based on typed content that may be completed using Tab as shown in *Figure 1.1*.

Figure 1.1: PSReadLine Predictive completion

By default, *Tab* can be used to complete any command or parameter, and a variety of arguments for parameters. In addition to *Tab* completion, PSReadLine allows the use of *Control* and *Space* to provide menu style completion. For example, entering the following partial command:

```
Get-ChildItem -
```

Then pressing *Control* and *Space* (immediately after the hyphen) will show a menu that can be navigated using the cursor keys, as shown in *Figure 1.2*:

Figure 1.2: PSReadLine List completion

In PowerShell, the prompt displayed is controlled by a function named prompt. A very simple prompt can be set as shown below:

```
function prompt {
    "$env:USERNAME $pwd PS>"
}
```

The default prompt can be restored by restarting PowerShell. A profile script is required to make changes on console restart. See about_profiles for more information:

```
Get-Help about_profiles
```

Several modules and tools exist to help customize prompts in PowerShell:

- PowerLine: https://github.com/Jaykul/PowerLine
- oh-my-posh: https://ohmyposh.dev/
- Starship: https://starship.rs/

PowerShell is a complex language; a good editor can save time finding the right syntax to use in a script.

PowerShell editors

While PowerShell scripts can be written using the Notepad application alone, it is rarely desirable. Using an editor that was designed to work with PowerShell can save a lot of time.

Editors with explicit support for PowerShell, such as Visual Studio Code (VS Code with the PowerShell extension) and the PowerShell Studio editor offer automatic completion (IntelliSense). IntelliSense reduces the amount of cross-referencing help content required while writing code. Finding a comfortable editor early on is a good way to ease into PowerShell; memorizing commands and parameters is not necessary.

In addition to VS Code and PowerShell Studio, Windows PowerShell comes with the PowerShell ISE. The PowerShell ISE has not been updated for PowerShell 6 and higher and will only function correctly for the Windows PowerShell Desktop edition.

PowerShell Studio is not free but includes graphical user interface development features.

VS Code is a highly recommended editor for PowerShell as it is free and supports a wide variety of different languages. VS Code is an open-source editor that was published by Microsoft and can be downloaded from `http://code.visualstudio.com`. VS Code tends to be the editor of choice for many in the PowerShell community.

The functionality of VS Code can be enhanced by using extensions from the marketplace: `https://marketplace.visualstudio.com/VSCode`. The Extension installer is part of the VS Code user interface, and the types of available extensions are shown in *Figure 1.3*:

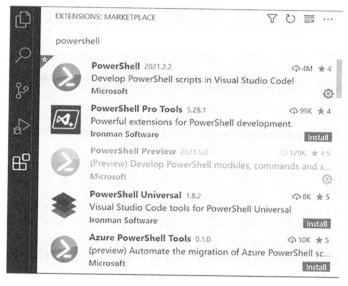

Figure 1.3: PowerShell extensions in VS Code

The icons available on the left-hand side change depending on the extensions installed. A new installation of VS Code will show fewer icons than *Figure 1.3*.

The PowerShell Extension should be installed. Other popular extensions include:

- Bracket Pair Colorizer 2
- Blockman
- Chocolatey
- Error Lens
- Live Share
- Prettify JSON

Paid-for extensions, such as PowerShell Pro Tools, offer us the ability to design user interfaces in VS Code.

The integrated console in VS Code can be used with all installed versions of PowerShell. The following screenshot shows how to change the version of PowerShell used when editing a script. Note the clickable version in the bottom-right corner:

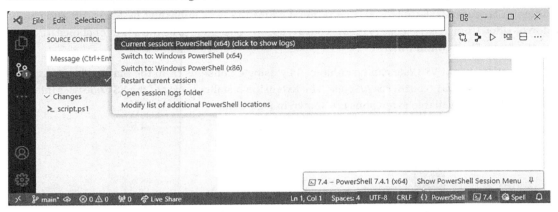

Figure 1.4: Choosing a PowerShell version

The IntelliSense version provided by the editor will list and hint at the possible commands and parameters available. Help content is available to fill in the details.

Getting help

PowerShell includes a built-in help system accessible using the Get-Help command. Help content in PowerShell is often rich and detailed, frequently including multiple examples. Gaining confidence using the built-in help system is an important part of working with PowerShell. Script authors and PowerShell developers can easily write their own help content when working with functions, scripts, and script modules.

Updatable help

The concept of updatable help was added in Windows PowerShell 3. It allows users to obtain the most recent versions of their help documentation outside of PowerShell on a web service. Help content can be downloaded and installed using the Update-Help command in PowerShell.

Which modules support updatable help?

The command below shows a list of modules that support updatable help:

```
Get-Module -ListAvailable | Where-Object HelpInfoURI
```

Help for the core components of PowerShell is not part of the PowerShell 7 installation package. Content must be downloaded before it can be viewed.

The first time Get-Help runs, PowerShell prompts to update help.

Computers with no internet access or computers behind a restrictive proxy server may not be able to download help content directly. The Save-Help command can be used in this scenario, which is discussed later in this section, to work around the problem.

If PowerShell is unable to download help, it can only show a small amount of information about a command; for example, without downloading help, the content for the Out-Null command is minimal, as shown here:

```
PS> Get-Help Out-Null
NAME
    Out-Null

SYNTAX
    Out-Null [-InputObject <psobject>] [<CommonParameters>]

ALIASES
    None

REMARKS
    Get-Help cannot find the Help files for this cmdlet on this computer.
    It is displaying only partial help.
        -- To download and install Help files for the module that
           includes this cmdlet, use Update-Help.
        -- To view the Help topic for this cmdlet online, type:
           "Get-Help Out-Null -Online" or go to
           http://go.microsoft.com/fwlink/?LinkID=113366.
```

The help content in the preceding example is automatically generated by PowerShell. PowerShell inspects the command to determine which parameters are available.

Updatable help as a help file can be viewed using the following command:

```
Get-Help about_Updatable_Help
```

Updateable help is not entirely free from issues. Internet resources change as content moves around over time, which may invalidate HelpInfoUri, the URL stored within the module and used to retrieve help files. For example, help for the Dism module was not available when this chapter was written.

The Get-Help command

When Get-Help is used without parameters, it shows introductory help about the help system. This content is taken from the default help file (Get-Help default); a snippet of this is as follows:

```
PS> Get-Help
TOPIC
  PowerShell Help System
```

```
SHORT DESCRIPTION
  Displays help about PowerShell cmdlets and concepts.

LONG DESCRIPTION
  PowerShell Help describes Windows PowerShell cmdlets, functions,
```

Help content can be long

The help content, in most cases, does not fit on a single screen. The `help` command differs from `Get-Help` in that it pauses (waiting for a key to be pressed) after each page; for example:

`help default`

The previous command is equivalent to running `Get-Help` and piping it into the more command:

```
Get-Help default | more
```

Alternatively, `Get-Help` can be asked to show a window:

```
Get-Help default -ShowWindow
```

The available help content may be listed using either of the following two commands:

```
Get-Help *
Get-Help -Category All
```

Help for a subject can be viewed as follows:

```
Get-Help -Name <Topic>
```

For example, help for the `Get-Variable` command may be shown:

```
Get-Help Get-Variable
```

If a help document includes an online version link, it may be opened in a browser with the `-Online` parameter:

```
Get-Help Get-Command -Online
```

The URL used for online help can be viewed using `Get-Command`:

```
Get-Command Get-Command | Select-Object HelpUri
```

The help content is broken down into several sections: name, synopsis, syntax, description, related links, and remarks.

Name simply includes the name of the command. Synopsis is a short description of the functionality provided by the command, often no more than one sentence. Description often provides much greater detail than synopsis. Related links and remarks are optional fields, which may include links to related content.

Syntax is covered in the following section in more detail as it is the most complex part of the help document. A good understanding of the syntax allows quick evaluation of how to use a command, often removing the need to do more than skim help content.

Syntax

The syntax section lists each of the possible combinations of parameters a command accepts; each of these is known as a parameter set.

A command that has more than one parameter set is shown in this example for the Get-Process command:

```
SYNTAX
    Get-Process [[-Name] <System.String[]>] [-FileVersionInfo] [-Module]
[<CommonParameters>]


    Get-Process [-FileVersionInfo] -Id <System.Int32[]> [-Module]
[<CommonParameters>]
```

The syntax elements written in square brackets are optional; for example, syntax help for Get-Process shows that all its parameters are optional, as the following code shows:

```
SYNTAX
    Get-Process [[-Name] <System.String[]>] [-FileVersionInfo] [-Module]
[<CommonParameters>]
```

As the Name parameter is optional, Get-Process may be run without any parameters. The command may also be run by specifying a value only and no parameter name. Alternatively, the parameter name can be included as well as the value.

Each of the following examples is a valid use of Get-Process:

```
Get-Process
Get-Process pwsh
Get-Process -Name pwsh
```

Get-Command can show syntax

Get-Command may be used to view the syntax for a command. For example, running the following command will show the same output as seen in the *Syntax* section of Get-Help:

```
Get-Command Get-Variable -Syntax
```

The different parameter types and how they are used are explored later in this chapter.

Examples

The Examples section of help provides working examples of how a command may be used. Help often includes more than one example.

In some cases, a command is sufficiently complex that it requires a detailed example to accompany parameter descriptions; in others, the command is simple, and a good example may serve in lieu of reading the help documentation.

PowerShell users can update help

Help documentation for built-in commands is open source. If a cmdlet is missing helpful examples, they can be added.

A link to the PowerShell-Docs repository is available at the bottom of the online help page. It should send you to the en-US version of help:

https://github.com/MicrosoftDocs/PowerShell-Docs.

Examples for a command can be requested by specifying the Examples parameter for Get-Help, as shown in the following example:

```
Get-Help Get-Process -Examples
```

The help information for most cmdlets usually includes several examples of their use, especially if the command has more than one parameter set.

Parameter

Parameters in PowerShell are used to supply named arguments to PowerShell commands.

Help for specific parameters can be requested as follows:

```
Get-Help Get-Command -Parameter <ParameterName>
```

The Parameter parameter allows for the quick retrieval of specific help for a single parameter; for example, help for the Path parameter of the Import-Csv command may be viewed:

```
PS> Get-Help Import-Csv -Parameter Path

-Path [<String[]>]
    Specifies the path to the CSV file to import. You can also
    pipe a path to `Import-Csv`.

    Required? false
    Position? 1
    Default value None
    Accept pipeline input? true (ByValue)
    Accept wildcard characters? false
```

This avoids needing to scroll through a potentially large help file to see how to use just one parameter.

The preceding content describes the parameter, whether the parameter is mandatory (Required), its position, default value, pipeline behavior, and support for wildcards.

Detailed and Full switches

The Detailed switch parameter (a parameter that does not require an argument) asks Get-Help to return the most help content.

The default sections returned by help are Name, Synopsis, Syntax, Description, Related Links, and Remarks.

When Detailed is requested, Parameters and Examples are added. Related Links is excluded.

The Detailed parameter is used as follows:

```
Get-Help Get-Process -Detailed
```

The Full switch parameter includes all the default sections, as well as Parameters, Inputs, Outputs, Notes, and Examples.

The following code shows the sections detailing the input and output types for Get-Process from the full help document; content before those sections has been removed from this example:

```
PS> Get-Help Get-Process -Full
... <content removed> ...
INPUTS
    System.Diagnostics.Process
        You can pipe a process object to Get-Process.
OUTPUTS
    System.Diagnostics.Process
        By default, this cmdlet returns a
        System.Diagnostics.Process object.

    System.Diagnotics.FileVersionInfo
        If you use the FileVersionInfo parameter, this cmdlet
        returns a FileVersionInfo object.

    System.Diagnostics.ProcessModule
        If you use the Module parameter, without the
        FileVersionInfo parameter, this cmdlet returns a
        ProcessModule object.
```

INPUTS is typically used to describe the value types that can be piped to a command. Pipelines are introduced in *Chapter 4, Working with Objects in PowerShell*.

In addition to the extra sections, the Full switch parameter includes metadata in the parameter section, the same parameter metadata seen when using Get-Help Get-Process -Parameter Name.

Help content in PowerShell is extensive and a valuable resource to have on any system running PowerShell.

Save-Help

The Save-Help command can be used with modules that support updatable help. It allows help content for installed modules to be saved to disk.

Help for a module can be downloaded using the following command. The destination folder must exist before running the command:

```
New-Item -Path C:\PSHelp -ItemType Directory
Save-Help -Module Microsoft.PowerShell.Management -DestinationPath C:\PSHelp
```

By default, Save-Help attempts to download help content for the current UI culture; that is, the current user interface language. The Get-UICulture command can be used to view the current culture, as the following example shows:

```
PS> Get-UICulture

LCID            Name                DisplayName
----            ----                -----------
2057            en-GB               English (United Kingdom)
```

If help content is not available for that culture, Save-Help will not do anything and will not raise an error. For UI cultures other than en-US, the C:\PSHelp folder will likely be empty.

Save-Help can be instructed to download help in a specific language by using the UICulture parameter:

```
Save-Help -Module Microsoft.PowerShell.Management -DestinationPath C:\PSHelp
-UICulture en-US
```

If help content is available, it is downloaded as shown in the C:\PSHelp folder here:

Name	Date modified	Type	Size
Microsoft.PowerShell.Management_eefcb906-b326-4e99-9f54-8b4bb6ef3c6d_en-US_HelpContent.cab	04/07/2020 12:07	Cabinet File	122 KB
Microsoft.PowerShell.Management_eefcb906-b326-4e99-9f54-8b4bb6ef3c6d_HelpInfo.xml	04/07/2020 12:07	XML Source File	1 KB

Figure 1.5: Downloaded help content for en-US

By default, Save-Help (and Update-Help) will not download help content more often than once every 24 hours as a rate-limiting control. This can be seen using the Verbose switch parameter:

```
PS> Save-Help -Module Microsoft.PowerShell.Management -DestinationPath C:\
PSHelp -UICulture en-US -Verbose
VERBOSE: Help was not saved for the module Microsoft.PowerShell.Management,
because the Save-Help command was run on this computer within the last 24
hours.
```

The Verbose switch parameter is used to make any verbose messages the command author has included visible in the console.

If help content is available for other cultures, and that content is downloaded immediately after en-US, then the Force parameter must be added:

```
Save-Help -Module Microsoft.PowerShell.Management -DestinationPath C:\PSHelp
-UICulture pl-PL -Force
```

However, as help content for the Microsoft.PowerShell.Management module is only available in en-US, the preceding command displays an error message describing which cultures help is available for.

Help content for all modules supporting updateable help can be saved as follows:

```
Save-Help -DestinationPath C:\PSHelp -UICulture en-US
```

Saved help content can be copied to another computer and imported using Update-Help. This technique is useful for computers that do not have internet access as it means help content can be made available.

Update-Help

The Update-Help command performs two tasks:

- Update help files on the local computer from the internet.
- Updates help files on the local computer from previously saved help files.

To update help from the internet for all modules that support updateable help, run the Update-Help cmdlet with no parameters:

```
Update-Help
```

The Update-Help command includes a Scope parameter, which may be used to make help content available without needing Administrative access:

```
Update-Help -Scope CurrentUser
```

When the Scope parameter is set to CurrentUser, help content is downloaded to and read from (by Get-Help) $home\Documents\PowerShell\help. This path may be affected by folder redirection of the Documents folders, such as with services like OneDrive.

The Scope parameter is not available in Windows PowerShell and administrative rights are required to update help content.

For UI cultures other than `en-US`, the `UICulture` parameter may be required:

```
Update-Help -UICulture en-US
```

Like `Save-Help`, `Update-Help` will not download help for a module more than once every 24 hours by default. This can be overridden by using the `Force` parameter:

```
Update-Help -Name Microsoft.PowerShell.Management -Force -UICulture en-US
```

Help content that was saved using `Save-Help` can be imported from a folder using the `SourcePath` parameter:

```
Update-Help -SourcePath C:\PSHelp
```

If the folder does not contain content for the current UI culture (shown with `Get-UICulture`), an error message will be displayed:

```
PS> Update-Help -Module Microsoft.PowerShell.Management -SourcePath C:\PSHelp
Update-Help: Failed to update Help for the module(s) 'Microsoft.PowerShell.
Management' with UI culture(s) {en-GB} : Unable to retrieve the HelpInfo XML
file for UI culture en-GB. Make sure the HelpInfoUri property in the module
manifest is valid or check your network connection and then try the command
again..
```

The `UICulture` parameter can be used again to update help content from the folder:

```
Update-Help -Module Microsoft.PowerShell.Management -SourcePath C:\PSHelp
-UICulture en-US
```

Help content is not limited to help for specific commands. PowerShell includes many topical help documents.

About_* help files

About_* documents describe features of the language or concepts that apply to more than one command. These items do not fit into help for individual commands.

The list of help files can be viewed by running `Get-Help` with the category set to `HelpFile`, as demonstrated in the following code:

```
Get-Help -Category HelpFile
```

Alternatively, wildcards can be used with the `Name` parameter of `Get-Help`:

```
Get-Help -Name About_*
```

These help files cover a huge variety of topics ranging from aliases to modules to WMI. A number of these are shown here. The list will vary, depending on the modules installed on the computer running the command:

```
Name                          Category  Module  Synopsis
----                          --------  ------  --------
default                       HelpFile          SHORT DESCRIPTION
about_PSReadLine              HelpFile
about_Configuration           HelpFile          The Configuratio...
about_Aliases                 HelpFile
about_Alias_Provider          HelpFile
about_Arithmetic_Operators    HelpFile
about_Arrays                  HelpFile
about_Assignment_Operators    HelpFile
about_Automatic_Variables     HelpFile
about_Break                   HelpFile
```

Using help content is an important part of working with PowerShell. Memorizing content is not necessary where instructions and reference material are easily accessible.

Get-Help may lead to finding a command to help achieve a task; however, it is often quicker to search using Get-Command.

Command naming and discovery

Commands in PowerShell are formed around verb and noun pairs in the form verb-noun.

This feature is useful when finding commands; it allows educated guesses about the names of commands so that there is little need to memorize long lists of commands. Commands use verbs to describe intent, and nouns to describe the target.

Verbs

The list of verbs is maintained by Microsoft. Verbs are words such as Add, Get, Set, and New. This formal approach to naming commands greatly assists in discovery.

The list of verbs can be seen in PowerShell using the following command:

```
Get-Verb
```

Verbs are grouped around different areas, such as data, life cycle, and security. Complementary actions such as encryption and decryption tend to use verbs in the same group; for example, the verb Protect may be used to encrypt something and the verb Unprotect may be used to decrypt something.

More commonly, Get and Set, or New and Remove commands may also be seen as complementary.

Verb descriptions

A detailed list of verbs, along with their use cases, is available on MSDN:

`https://learn.microsoft.com/en-us/powershell/scripting/developer/cmdlet/`
`approved-verbs-for-windows-powershell-commands?view=powershell-7.3&view`
`FallbackFrom=powershell-7.`

It is possible, although not recommended, to use verbs other than those in the approved list. If a command with an unapproved verb is written and included in a module, a warning message will be displayed every time the module is imported.

Verbs are paired with nouns that describe the target of a command.

Nouns

A noun provides a very short description of the object the command is expecting to act on. The noun part may be a single word, as is the case with `Get-Process`, `New-Item`, and `Get-Help`, or more than one word, as seen with `Get-ChildItem`, `Invoke-WebRequest`, and `Send-MailMessage`.

Command names often include a prefix on the noun. The Microsoft AD module uses the `AD` prefix. The Microsoft Graph modules are prefixed with the `Mg` prefix. Commands for managing the network components of the Windows operating system are prefixed with `Net`.

Modules are explored in *Chapter 2, Modules*. As mentioned above, the commands used to manage the networking components of Windows use the `Net` prefix on every noun. This, in turn, allows the use of wildcards to search for commands.

Finding commands

The verb-noun pairing strives to make it easier to find commands without resorting to search engines.

For example, if the goal was to list firewall rules, the following command may be used to show the `Get` commands that might affect the firewall:

```
PS> Get-Command Get-*Firewall*

CommandType Name                              Version Source
----------- ----                              ------- ------
Function    Get-NetFirewallAddressFilter      2.0.0.0 NetSecurity
Function    Get-NetFirewallApplicationFilter  2.0.0.0 NetSecurity
Function    Get-NetFirewallInterfaceFilter    2.0.0.0 NetSecurity
Function    Get-NetFirewallInterfaceTypeFilter 2.0.0.0 NetSecurity
Function    Get-NetFirewallPortFilter         2.0.0.0 NetSecurity
Function    Get-NetFirewallProfile            2.0.0.0 NetSecurity
Function    Get-NetFirewallRule               2.0.0.0 NetSecurity
```

```
Function    Get-NetFirewallSecurityFilter       2.0.0.0 NetSecurity
Function    Get-NetFirewallServiceFilter        2.0.0.0 NetSecurity
Function    Get-NetFirewallSetting              2.0.0.0 NetSecurity
```

A wildcard might be used for the verb or the specific parameters for Verb and Noun might be used with Get-Command:

```
Get-Command -Verb Get, Set -Noun *Firewall*
```

The Get-Help command may also be used to find the list of commands above:

```
Get-Help Get-*Firewall*
```

As Get-Help also searches for help content, it is slower to use to search than Get-Command.

The list of commands returned may vary, depending on the modules installed on the computer.

From the preceding list, Get-NetFirewallRule closely matches the requirement (to see a list of firewall rules) and should be explored. Notice how each of the commands in the list above maintains the same prefix. This is a common naming practice in PowerShell.

Once a potential command has been found, Get-Help can be used to assess whether the command is suitable.

Aliases

An alias in PowerShell is an alternate name for a command. A command may have more than one alias. Unlike languages like Bash, an alias cannot include parameters.

The list of aliases can be viewed by using Get-Alias. The first few aliases are shown in the following example:

```
PS> Get-Alias

CommandType Name
----------- ----
Alias        % -> ForEach-Object
Alias        ? -> Where-Object
Alias        ac -> Add-Content
Alias        cat -> Get-Content
Alias        cd -> Set-Location
```

Get-Alias may be used to find the command behind an alias:

```
Get-Alias dir
```

The aliases available change depending on the operating system. For example, PowerShell on Linux omits aliases such as ac (Add-Content), ls (Get-ChildItem), and cat (Get-Content).

`Get-Alias` may also be used to find the aliases for any command:

```
PS> Get-Alias -Definition Get-ChildItem

CommandType        Name                                Version    Source
-----------        ----                                -------    ------
Alias              dir -> Get-ChildItem
Alias              gci -> Get-ChildItem
Alias              ls -> Get-ChildItem
```

Examples of aliases that are frequently used in examples on the internet include the following:

- `%` for `ForEach-Object`
- `?` for `Where-Object`
- `cd` for `Set-Location`
- `gc` or `cat` for `Get-Content`
- `ls` or `dir` for `Get-ChildItem`
- `irm` for `Invoke-WebRequest`
- `iex` for `Invoke-Expression`

An alias does not change how a command is used. There is no difference in the result of the following two commands:

```
cd $env:TEMP
Set-Location $env:TEMP
```

New aliases are created with the `New-Alias` command. For example, an alias named `grep` for the `Select-String` command can be created as follows:

```
New-Alias grep -Value Select-String
```

Aliases can be removed using the `Remove-Alias` command, including default aliases such as `ls`:

```
Remove-Alias grep
```

Aliases may also be removed using `Remove-Item` as an alternative to `Remove-Alias`:

```
Remove-Item alias:\grep
```

Aliases created in one session are not remembered when a new PowerShell session is started.

More information is available about aliases in the help file `about_Aliases`. The help file is viewed using the following command:

```
Get-Help about_Aliases
```

As mentioned above, aliases do not persist between PowerShell sessions (when the console is restarted). Profile scripts can be used to make an alias (or any other preferences) available when PowerShell is restarted.

About profile scripts

Aliases do not persist across PowerShell sessions. A profile script is often used for user-specific preferences like this.

Profiles are where most user-specific shell customization takes place, from changing prompts and default settings to loading modules to creating aliases.

Shell customization with profile scripts is an enormously involved and highly personal topic. This section provides a brief introduction to the topic only.

PowerShell has four different profile paths – two are user-specific and two are machine-specific. The profile paths are also dependent on the host – one user and one machine path are specific to the terminal that started PowerShell.

The profile paths are described by the built-in variable $profile. The Select-Object * command is used to show all the possible values in the example below:

```
PS> $profile | Select-Object *

AllUsersAllHosts         : C:\Program Files\PowerShell\7\profile.ps1
AllUsersCurrentHost      : C:\Program Files\PowerShell\7\Microsoft.PowerShell_
profile.ps1
CurrentUserAllHosts      : C:\Users\user\Documents\PowerShell\profile.ps1
CurrentUserCurrentHost   : C:\Users\user\Documents\PowerShell\Microsoft.
PowerShell_profile.ps1
```

If the same command is run in the VS Code integrated terminal, the two host-specific paths will differ:

```
PS> $profile | Select-Object *

AllUsersAllHosts         : C:\Program Files\PowerShell\7\profile.ps1
AllUsersCurrentHost      : C:\Program Files\PowerShell\7\Microsoft.VSCode_
profile.ps1
CurrentUserAllHosts      : C:\Users\user\Documents\PowerShell\profile.ps1
CurrentUserCurrentHost   : C:\Users\user\Documents\PowerShell\Microsoft.VSCode_
profile.ps1
```

PowerShell will run each of the profile scripts where the script exists. If the script does not exist, the path is ignored.

Starting PowerShell with the -NoProfile switch avoids loading profile script files, a useful parameter for any scheduled scripts, or for testing to see if the profile is causing a problem.

The paths used above may not exist at all. To create a profile script, create the directory first, if necessary, then save the script file using one of the names and paths above.

The about document for profiles explores this topic further:

```
Get-Help about_profiles
```

A variety of different tools are available to customize the look and feel, which are typically started from a profile script. Customization of the prompt is a common activity:

- PowerLine: https://github.com/Jaykul/PowerLine
- oh-my-posh: https://ohmyposh.dev/
- Sarship: https://starship.rs/

The Windows Terminal customized prompts article makes use of oh-my-posh in an example setup:

https://learn.microsoft.com/en-us/windows/terminal/tutorials/custom-prompt-setup.

Finally, for users with multiple computers, the chezmoi tool might be used to ensure all computers use the same configuration:

https://www.chezmoi.io/.

Commands (and aliases) use parameters to pass arguments into a command.

Parameters, values, and parameter sets

As seen while looking at syntax in Get-Help, commands accept a mixture of parameters. The following sections show how these parameters are described in help and how to use them.

Parameters

When viewing help for a command, several different conventions are used to describe when a parameter is required and how it should be used. These conventions include:

- Optional parameters, where parameter names and arguments are enclosed in a single pair of square brackets.
- Optional positional parameters – the same as an optional parameter but with the parameter name also enclosed in square brackets.
- Mandatory parameters, where the parameter name and argument are not bracketed.
- Mandatory positional parameters, where the parameter name is in square brackets, but the argument is not.

The following sections show each of these conventions in greater detail.

Optional parameters

Optional parameters are surrounded by square brackets. If a parameter is used, a value (or argument) must be supplied. A fragment of the syntax for Get-Help is shown below. It shows that a Category parameter is available and that the parameter is optional.

```
SYNTAX
    Get-Help ... [-Category <string[]>] ...
```

If a value for the Category parameter is to be used, the name of the parameter must also be specified. This is shown in the following example:

```
Get-Help -Category HelpFile
```

The command above filters help documents to help files, the "about" documents.

Optional positional parameters

An optional positional parameter is surrounded by square brackets, like an optional parameter. In addition, the parameter name itself is enclosed in square brackets. This indicates that the parameter is optional and that if it is used, the parameter and value can be supplied, or just the value without the parameter name.

It is not uncommon to see an optional positional parameter as the first parameter:

```
SYNTAX
    Get-Process [[-Name] <string[]>] ...
```

In this example, either of the following may be used:

```
Get-Process -Name pwsh
Get-Process pwsh
```

The output from the two commands is identical. This includes the parameter name, which, even when it is optional, is less ambiguous and therefore a recommended practice.

Mandatory parameters

A mandatory parameter must always be supplied and is written as follows:

```
SYNTAX
    Get-ADUser -Filter <string> ...
```

In this case, the Filter parameter name must be used, and it must be given a value. For example, to supply a Filter for the command, the Filter parameter must be explicitly written:

```
Get-ADUser -Filter 'sAMAccountName -eq "SomeName"'
```

The Get-ADUser command has a second parameter set that uses a different parameter name with a positional value.

Mandatory positional parameters

Mandatory parameters must always be supplied, but in some cases, it is possible to supply the value without using the parameter name. The parameter the value applies to is based on position.

Parameters that are mandatory and accept values based on position are written with the parameter name only in square brackets, as shown here:

```
SYNTAX
    Get-ADUser [-Identity] <ADUser> ...
```

In this case, the Identity parameter name is optional, but the value is not. This command may be used as described by either of the following examples:

```
Get-ADUser -Identity useridentity
Get-ADUser useridentity
```

In both cases, the supplied value fills the Identity parameter.

The Add-Content command has a parameter set that uses more than one mandatory positional parameter. The first part of the syntax for the parameter set is shown here:

```
Add-Content [-Path] <string[]> [-Value] <object[]>
```

In this case, the command may be called using any of the following:

```
Add-Content -Path c:\temp\file.txt -Value 'Hello world'
Add-Content -Value 'Hello world' -Path c:\temp\file.txt
Add-Content 'Hello world' -Path c:\temp\file.txt
Add-Content c:\temp\file.txt -Value 'Hello world'
Add-Content c:\temp\file.txt 'Hello world'
```

The first of these is easiest to read as both parameters are explicitly named and tends to be the better style to use.

Each of the parameters so far has required an argument, a value. PowerShell also allows parameters that do not require arguments.

Switch parameters

A switch parameter does not require an argument. If the switch is present, the value is equivalent to true, while if the switch parameter is absent, it is equivalent to false.

As with the other types of parameters, optional use is denoted by using square brackets around the parameter.

Switch parameters are typically used to toggle a behavior on. For example, Recurse is a switch parameter for Get-ChildItem:

```
SYNTAX
    Get-ChildItem ... [-Recurse] ...
```

Using the switch instructs Get-ChildItem to recurse when listing the content of a directory, as shown here:

```
Get-ChildItem c:\windows -Recurse
```

It is possible to supply a value for a switch parameter from a variable. This might be desirable when writing a script where the presence of a switch parameter is based on another variable. As switch parameters do not normally expect a value, a syntax change is required:

```
# Code which determines if Recurse is required
$recurse = $false
Get-ChildItem c:\windows -Recurse:$recurse
```

In some cases, a switch parameter will default to present, and it may be desirable to stop the parameter from applying. The most common example is the Confirm parameter, which will be explored later in this chapter.

Parameter values

The syntax blocks explored in the preceding sections show the type that is expected when providing a value for a parameter. A type is a .NET concept; it describes what an object is, how it behaves, and what it can do. Types will be covered in greater detail in *Chapter 7, Working with .NET*.

The Get-CimInstance command expects a string as the argument for the ClassName parameter. This is shown in the snippet taken from the syntax block:

```
Get-CimInstance [-ClassName] <String>
```

A string is a sequence of characters. For example, the string Win32_Service can be used as follows:

```
Get-CimInstance -ClassName Win32_Service
```

ClassName must always be a single value. If more than one value is supplied, an error will be displayed:

```
PS> Get-CimInstance -ClassName Win32_Service, Win32_Process
Get-CimInstance: Cannot convert 'System.Object[]' to the type 'System.String'
required by parameter 'ClassName'. Specified method is not supported.
```

Parameters that accept more than one value use [] after the type name. This indicates that the type is an array. The Name parameter for the Get-Service command is shown here:

```
Get-Service [[-Name] <String[]>]
```

In this case, the parameter type is an array of strings. An array may consist of one or more strings separated by a comma:

```
PS> Get-Service -Name WinDefend, WlanSvc

Status    Name          DisplayName
------    ----          -----------
Running   WinDefend     Windows Defender Antivirus Service
Running   WlanSvc       WLAN AutoConfig
```

PowerShell will attempt to coerce any value supplied into the required type. A single string can be used as an argument for the parameter. PowerShell will convert the single value into an array of strings with one element. For example:

```
Get-Service -Name WinDefend
```

Each of the commands used in this section will allow the value to be entered without the parameter name. For example, for Get-Service, the Name parameter can be omitted:

```
Get-Service WinDefend
Get-Service WinDefend, WlanSvc
```

When using positional parameters, PowerShell can use the type to determine which parameter (and which parameter set) should be used.

Parameter sets

In PowerShell, a parameter set is a set of parameters that may be used together when running a command.

Many of the commands in PowerShell have more than one parameter set. This was seen when looking at the Syntax section when using Get-Help.

For example, the Stop-Process command has three parameter sets:

```
SYNTAX
    Stop-Process [-Id] <Int32[]> [-Confirm] [-Force] [-PassThru] [-WhatIf]
[<CommonParameters>]


    Stop-Process [-InputObject] <Process[]> [-Confirm] [-Force] [-PassThru]
[-WhatIf] [<CommonParameters>]


    Stop-Process [-Confirm] [-Force] -Name <String[]> [-PassThru] [-WhatIf]
[<CommonParameters>]
```

PowerShell will attempt to find a matching parameter set based on the parameters and values it is given.

The parameter sets for Stop-Process have two different sets that will accept a value by position:

```
Stop-Process [-Id] <Int32[]>
Stop-Process [-InputObject] <Process[]>
```

The first expects an ID as an integer. The second expects a Process object, an object returned by the Get-Process command.

The variable $PID is an automatic variable that holds the process ID (an integer) of the current PowerShell console. Running the following command will stop the PowerShell process. The first parameter set for Stop-Process is chosen because an integer value is used:

```
Stop-Process $PID
```

The second parameter set expects a value for InputObject. Again, this may be supplied as a positional parameter (or via the pipeline). In this case, PowerShell distinguishes based on its type. The following snippet contains the three possible approaches available when using the InputObject parameter:

```
$process = Start-Process notepad -PassThru
Stop-Process -InputObject $process
Stop-Process $process
$process | Stop-Process
```

Pipeline input

Get-Help shows which parameters accept pipeline input in the help for each parameter. This may be viewed using either of the following commands:

- `Get-Help Stop-Process -Parameter *`
- `Get-Help Stop-Process -Full`

Examples are likely to show how to use the parameters with a pipeline.

If Get-Help is incomplete, Get-Command can be used to explore parameters:

`(Get-Command Stop-Process).Parameters.InputObject.Attributes`

Each of the parameter sets here also shows that the command supports common parameters.

Common parameters

Common parameters are used to control some of the standardized functionality PowerShell provides, such as verbose output and actions to take when errors occur.

When looking at the syntax, most commands will end with a CommonParameters item:

```
SYNTAX
    Get-Process ... [<CommonParameters>]
```

The following is a list of common parameters:

- Debug
- ErrorAction
- ErrorVariable
- InformationAction
- InformationVariable
- OutBuffer
- OutVariable
- PipelineVariable
- Verbose
- WarningAction
- WarningVariable

Each is described in the about_CommonParameters document:

```
Get-Help about_CommonParameters
```

The help document is also available online: https://learn.microsoft.com/en-us/powershell/module/microsoft.powershell.core/about/about_commonparameters.

For example, Stop-Process does not explicitly state that it has a Verbose switch parameter, but since Verbose is a common parameter, it may be used. This can be seen if notepad is started and immediately stopped:

```
PS> Start-Process notepad -Verbose -PassThru | Stop-Process -Verbose
VERBOSE: Performing the operation "Stop-Process" on target "notepad (5592)".
```

Not so verbose

Just because a command supports common parameters does not mean it uses them. For example, Get-Process supports the Verbose parameter, yet it does not write any verbose output when Verbose is specified.

In addition to common parameters, PowerShell also offers specialized parameters for commands that make changes.

Confirm and WhatIf

Confirm and WhatIf can be used with commands that make changes to files, variables, data, and so on. These parameters are often used with commands that use the verbs New, Set, or Remove, but the parameters are not limited to specific verbs.

Confirm and WhatIf have associated preference variables that are used to customize default behavior in PowerShell. Preference variables have an about file, which may be viewed using the following command:

```
Get-Help about_Preference_Variables
```

The Confirm switch parameter is used to control automatic prompting for high impact operations by default.

Confirm and ConfirmPreference

The Confirm switch parameter and the ConfirmPreference variable can be used to decide if a command should prompt. The decision to prompt is based on a comparison of ConfirmPreference with ConfirmImpact when set by a command author.

ConfirmPreference has four possible values:

- High: Prompts when command impact is High (default)
- Medium: Prompts when command impact is Medium or High
- Low: Prompts when command impact is Low, Medium, or High

- None: Never prompts

ConfirmImpact uses the same four values.

In Windows PowerShell, the default value for ConfirmImpact is Medium.

In PowerShell 7, the default value for ConfirmImpact is None. If the command uses SupportsShouldProcess, then the default is Medium. SupportsShouldProcess is explored in greater detail in *Chapter 17, Scripts, Functions, and Script Blocks*.

Finding commands with a specific impact

The following snippet returns a list of all commands that state they have a high impact:

```
Get-Command -CommandType Cmdlet, Function | Where-Object {
    $metadata = [System.Management.Automation.CommandMetadata]$_
    $metadata.ConfirmImpact -eq 'High'
}
```

If the Confirm parameter is explicitly provided, the value of ConfirmPreference within the scope of the command is set to Low, which will trigger any confirmation prompts. Scoping of preference variables is explored in greater detail in *Chapter 17, Scripts, Functions, and Script Blocks*.

The Confirm switch parameter therefore causes a command to prompt before an action is taken; for example, the Confirm switch parameter forces Remove-Item to prompt when a file is to be removed:

```
PS> Set-Location $env:TEMP
PS> New-Item FileName.txt -Force
PS> Remove-Item FileName.txt -Confirm

Confirm
Are you sure you want to perform this action?
Performing the operation "Remove File" on target "C:\Users\whoami\AppData\
Local\Temp\FileName.txt".
[Y] Yes [A] Yes to All [N] No [L] No to All [S] Suspend [?] Help (default is
"Y"):
```

In the previous example, a confirmation prompt was explicitly requested. In a similar manner, confirmation prompts may be suppressed. For example, the value of the Confirm parameter may be explicitly set to false:

```
Set-Location $env:TEMP
New-Item FileName.txt -Force
Remove-Item FileName.txt -Confirm:$false
```

The ability to provide a value for the Confirm parameter is useful for commands that prompt by default; for example, Clear-RecycleBin prompts by default:

```
PS> Clear-RecycleBin

Confirm
Are you sure you want to perform this action?
Performing the operation "Clear-RecycleBin" on target " All of the contents of
the Recycle Bin".
[Y] Yes [A] Yes to All [N] No [L] No to All [S] Suspend [?] Help (default is
"Y"):
```

Setting the Confirm parameter to false for Clear-RecycleBin bypasses the prompt and immediately empties the recycle bin:

```
Clear-RecycleBin -Confirm:$false
```

If the Confirm parameter is not set, whether a prompt is shown is determined by PowerShell. The value of the ConfirmPreference variable is compared with ConfirmImpact on a command.

There is more than one way to prompt

There are two ways of requesting confirmation in PowerShell. These are ShouldProcess and ShouldContinue. These are explored in *Chapter 17, Scripts, Functions, and Script Blocks*.

ShouldProcess is affected by the Confirm parameter and ConfirmPreference variable.

ShouldContinue is a forced prompt and is unaffected by the Confirm parameter and ConfirmPreference variable.

For example, Remove-Item will always prompt when attempting to delete a directory that is not empty without supplying the Recurse parameter.

It is not possible to easily discover commands using forced prompts. Reviewing documentation and testing is vital.

By default, the value of ConfirmPreference is High. This means that prompts will be raised when ConfirmImpact for a command is High. The default value for ConfirmPreference may be viewed as follows:

```
PS> $ConfirmPreference
High
```

Finding ConfirmImpact

In scripts and functions, the ConfirmImpact setting is part of the CmdletBinding attribute:

```
[CmdletBinding(ConfirmImpact = 'High')]
```

 If CmdletBinding or ConfirmImpact is not present, the impact is Medium in Windows PowerShell and None in PowerShell 7.

The impact of a function or cmdlet may be viewed using the ConfirmImpact property of a command's metadata:

```
[System.Management.Automation.CommandMetadata](Get-Command Remove-Item)
```

The use of CmdletBinding is explored in detail in *Chapter 17, Scripts, Functions, and Script Blocks*.

A new value for ConfirmPreference may be set by assigning it in the console; for example, it can be set to Low. When the preference variable is set to Low, prompts may be raised by all commands where ConfirmImpact is Low, Medium, or High:

```
$ConfirmPreference = 'Low'
```

ConfirmPreference and the Confirm parameter

 When ConfirmPreference is set to None to suppress confirmation prompts, confirmation may still be explicitly requested using the Confirm parameter; for example:

```
$ConfirmPreference = 'None'

New-Item NewFile.txt -Confirm
```

Support for confirmation also provides support for WhatIf.

WhatIf and WhatIfPreference

WhatIf is typically used when testing a command. If implemented correctly by a command author, WhatIf should allow a state-changing command to be run without it making the change.

WhatIf is not always implemented as expected

 WhatIf support for a command is defined by a command author. If the author does not correctly handle the preference, an undesirable change may be made.

The Set-ADAccountPassword had a bug for a while where WhatIf was ignored.

Even if a command supports WhatIf, test it on small sets of data before using the parameter to verify a large change.

The `WhatIf` parameter has an associated preference variable, `WhatIfPreference`, which may be set to either `true` or `false`. The default value is `false`.

The `WhatIf` parameter replaces the confirmation prompt with a simple statement describing the action the command would have taken. Using `Remove-Item` as an example again, a message will be displayed, and the file will not be deleted:

```
PS> Set-Location $env:TEMP
PS> New-Item FileName.txt -Force
PS> Remove-Item FileName.txt -WhatIf

What if: Performing the operation "Remove File" on target "C:\Users\whoami\
AppData\Local\Temp\FileName.txt".
```

`WhatIf` can be explicitly set on a per-command basis by supplying a value in the same manner as the `Confirm` parameter. For example, `WhatIf` might be explicitly set to `false`:

```
'Some message' | Out-File $env:TEMP\test.txt -WhatIf:$false
```

Setting `WhatIf` in the manner used here might, for instance, be useful if a log file should be written even if other state-changing commands are ignored.

If the preference variable is set to `true`, all commands that support `WhatIf` act as if the parameter is set explicitly. A new value may be set for the variable, as shown in the following code:

```
$WhatIfPreference = $true
```

The `WhatIf` parameter and `$WhatIfPreference` preference variable take precedence over the `Confirm` parameter. For example, the `WhatIf` dialog is shown when running the following `New-Item`, but the `Confirm` prompt is not:

```
PS> $WhatIfPreference = $true
PS> New-Item NewFile.txt -Confirm
What if: Performing the operation "Create File" on target "Destination: C:\
Users\whoami\AppData\Local\Temp\NewFile.txt".
```

Restarting the console will restore preference variables to their default values.

The behavior of `Confirm` and `WhatIf` is prescribed by PowerShell. Parameters such as `Force` and `PassThru` are commonly used in PowerShell but have less well-defined behavior.

Force parameter

The `Force` parameter is not one of the common parameters with behavior defined by PowerShell itself, but the parameter is frequently used.

`Force` has no fixed usage; the effect of using `Force` is a choice a command author must make. Help documentation should state the effect of using `Force` with a command. For example, the use of `Force` with `Remove-Item` is available:

```
Get-Help Remove-Item -Parameter Force
```

With the Force parameter, New-Item overwrites any existing file with the same path. When used with Remove-Item, the Force parameter allows the removal of files with Hidden or System attributes.

The error that is generated when attempting to delete a Hidden file is shown by running the following code:

```
Set-Location $env:TEMP
New-Item FileName.txt -Force
Set-ItemProperty FileName.txt -Name Attributes -Value Hidden
Remove-Item FileName.txt
```

When Remove-Item is run, the following error will be displayed:

```
Remove-Item: You do not have sufficient access rights to perform
this operation or the item is hidden, system, or read only.
RemoveFileSystemItemUnAuthorizedAccess,Microsoft.PowerShell.Commands.
RemoveItemCommand
```

Adding the Force parameter allows the operation to continue:

```
Remove-Item FileName.txt -Force
```

The Force parameter may be worth exploring if a command is prompting, and the prompts cannot be suppressed using the Confirm parameter or the ConfirmPreference variable.

PassThru parameter

The PassThru parameter, like Force, is frequently used, but the behavior of the parameter is not defined by PowerShell. However, PassThru tends to have predictable behavior.

The PassThru parameter is typically used with commands that do not normally generate output and is used to force the command to return the object it was working with.

For example, the Start-Process command does not normally return any output. If PassThru is used, it will return the process it created:

```
PS> Start-Process notepad -PassThru

NPM(K)    PM(M)    WS(M)   CPU(s)     Id  SI ProcessName
------    -----    -----   ------     --  -- -----------
     9     1.98     6.70     0.05  22636   1 notepad
```

The PassThru parameter is therefore useful if more work is to be done with the object after the first command has finished.

For example, `PassThru` might be used with `Set-Service`, which ordinarily does not return output, allowing a service to be started immediately after another change:

```
Get-Service Audiosrv |
    Set-Service -StartupType Automatic -PassThru |
    Start-Service
```

Parameters in PowerShell are a complex topic but are a vital part of working with the language.

Introduction to providers

A provider in PowerShell is a specialized interface to a service or dataset that presents items to the end user in the same style as a file system.

All operating systems include the following providers:

- **Alias:** PowerShell aliases
- **Environment:** Environment variables (for the process)
- **FileSystem:** Files and folders
- **Function:** Any functions in the session
- **Variable:** Any variables in the session

Windows operating systems also include Windows-specific providers:

- **Registry:** All loaded registry hives
- **Certificate:** The `LocalMachine` and `CurrentUser` certificate stores
- **WSMan:** Windows remoting configuration

Several modules, such as the `ActiveDirectory` and `WebAdministration` modules, add service-specific providers when imported.

A longer description of `Providers` can be seen by viewing the about file:

```
Get-Help about_Providers
```

The available providers can be viewed in the current PowerShell session by running `Get-PSProvider`, as shown in the following example:

```
PS> Get-PSProvider

Name          Capabilities                        Drives
----          ------------                        ------
Registry      ShouldProcess, Transactions         {HKLM, HKCU}
Alias         ShouldProcess                       {Alias}
Environment   ShouldProcess                       {Env}
FileSystem    Filter, ShouldProcess, Credentials  {C, D}
Function      ShouldProcess                       {Function}
```

Variable	ShouldProcess	{Variable}
Certificate	ShouldProcess	{Cert}
WSMan	Credentials	{WSMan}

Each of the previous providers has a help file associated with it. In PowerShell, the help files are named about_<ProviderName>_Provider; for example:

```
Get-Help -Name about_Certificate_Provider
```

A list of all help files for providers in PowerShell 7 can be seen by running the following command:

```
Get-Help -Name About_*_Provider
```

In Windows PowerShell, the help files have a special category and are accessed by name, for example:

```
Get-Help -Name Certificate -Category Provider
```

Or, the provider help files can be listed by category:

```
Get-Help -Category Provider
```

The provider-specific help documents describe the additional parameters added to *-Item and *-ChildItem, as well as Test-Path, Get-Content, Set-Content, Add-Content, Get-Acl, Set-Acl, and so on.

Provider-specific parameters, when added to the preceding commands, allow provider-specific values for filtering, making changes to existing items, and creating new items.

PowerShell offers tab completion for parameters when the Path parameter has been defined. For example, entering the following partial command and then pressing *Tab* will cycle through the parameters available to the certificate provider:

```
Get-ChildItem -Path cert:\LocalMachine\Root -
```

For example, pressing *Tab* several times after the hyphen is entered offers up the CodeSigningCert parameter.

The items within a provider can be accessed by following the name of a provider with two colons. For example, the content of the variable provider can be shown as follows:

```
Get-ChildItem variable::
```

The same approach can be used to view the top-level items available in the Registry provider on Windows:

```
Get-ChildItem registry::
```

Child items can be accessed by adding a name; for example, a variable:

```
Get-Item variable::true
```

The preceding command is equivalent to running Get-Variable true.

The `FileSystem` provider returns an error when attempting to access `FileSystem::` without specifying a path. A child item must be specified, for example:

```
Get-ChildItem FileSystem::C:\Windows
```

While it is possible to access providers directly using the preceding notation, several of the providers are given names and are presented in the same manner as a Windows disk drive.

Drives and providers

Drives are labels used to access data from providers by name. Drives are automatically made available for `FileSystem` based on the drive letters used for mounted partitions in Windows.

The output from `Get-PSProvider` in the previous section shows that each provider has one or more drives associated with it.

Alternatively, the list of drives can be seen using `Get-PSDrive`, as shown in the following example:

```
PS> Get-PSDrive

Name      Used (GB) Free (GB) Provider      Root
----      --------- --------- --------      ----
Alias                         Alias
C             89.13    111.64 FileSystem    C:\
Cert                          Certificate   \
D              0.45     21.86 FileSystem    D:\
Env                           Environment
Function                      Function
HKCU                          Registry      HKEY_CURRENT_USER
HKLM                          Registry      HKEY_LOCAL_MACHINE
Variable                      Variable
WSMan                         WSMan
```

As providers present data in a similar manner to a file system, accessing a provider is like working with a disk drive. This example shows how `Get-ChildItem` changes when exploring the `Cert` drive. The first few certificates are shown:

```
PS C:\> Set-Location Cert:\LocalMachine\Root
PS Cert:\LocalMachine\Root> Get-ChildItem


   Directory: Microsoft.PowerShell.Security\Certificate::LocalMachine\Root


Thumbprint                                Subject
----------                                -------
CDD4EEAE6000AC7F40C3802C171E30148030C072  CN=Microsoft Root Certif...
BE36A4562FB2EE05DBB3D32323ADF445084ED656  CN=Thawte Timestamping C...
A43489159A520F0D93D032CCAF37E7FE20A8B419  CN=Microsoft Root Author...
```

By default, drives are available for the current user, HKEY_CURRENT_USER (HKCU), and local machine, HKEY_LOCAL_MACHINE (HKLM), registry hives.

A new drive named HKCC might be created for HKEY_CURRENT_CONFIG with the following command:

```
New-PSDrive HKCC -PSProvider Registry -Root HKEY_CURRENT_CONFIG
```

After running the preceding command, a new drive may be used to view the content of the hive, as demonstrated by the following example:

```
PS C:\> Get-ChildItem HKCC:


    Hive: HKEY_CURRENT_CONFIG


Name                            Property
----                            --------
Software
System
```

Functions for drive letters

Running C: or D: in the PowerShell console changes to a new drive letter. This is possible because C: is a function that calls the Set-Location command. This can be seen by looking at the definition of one of the functions:

(Get-Command C:).Definition

Every letter of the alphabet (A to Z) has a predefined function (Get-Command *:).

Set-Location must be explicitly used to change to any other drive, for example:

```
Set-Location HKCU:
```

Providers are an important part of PowerShell, especially the FileSystem provider. Providers are explored in greater detail in *Chapter 10*, *Files, Folders, and the Registry*.

Introduction to splatting

Splatting is a way of defining the parameters of a command before calling it. This is an important and often underrated technique that the PowerShell team added to PowerShell 2.

Splatting is often used to solve three potential problems in a script:

- Long lines caused by commands that need many parameters
- Conditional use of parameters
- Repetition of parameters across several commands

Individual parameters are written in a hashtable (@{}), and then the @ symbol is used to tell PowerShell that the content of the hashtable should be read as parameters.

This example supplies the Name parameter for the Get-Process command, and is normally written as Get-Process -Name explorer:

```
$getProcess = @{
    Name = 'explorer'
}
Get-Process @getProcess
```

In this example, getProcess is used as the name of the variable for the hashtable. The name is arbitrary; any variable name can be used.

Splatting can be used with cmdlets, functions, and scripts. Splatting can be used when the call operator is present, for example:

```
$getProcess = @{
    Name = 'explorer'
}
& 'Get-Process' @getProcess
```

The ability to use splatting with the call operator is useful if the command name itself is held in a variable.

The uses of splatting are explored in the following sections.

Splatting to avoid long lines

The benefit of splatting is most obvious when working with commands that expect a larger number of parameters.

This first example uses the module ScheduledTasks to create a basic task that runs once a day at midnight:

```
$taskAction = New-ScheduledTaskAction -Execute pwsh.exe -Argument 'Write-Host
"hello world"'
$taskTrigger = New-ScheduledTaskTrigger -Daily -At '00:00:00'
Register-ScheduledTask -TaskName 'TaskName' -Action $taskAction -Trigger
$taskTrigger -RunLevel 'Limited' -Description 'This line is too long to read'
```

Each of the commands is spread out over multiple lines; it is hard to see where one ends and the next begins.

Commands can also be spread out using a backtick, the escape character in PowerShell, as shown here:

```
$taskAction = New-ScheduledTaskAction `
    -Execute pwsh.exe `
    -Argument 'Write-Host "hello world"'
```

```
$taskTrigger = New-ScheduledTaskTrigger `
    -Daily `
    -At '00:00:00'
Register-ScheduledTask `
    -TaskName 'TaskName' `
    -Action $taskAction `
    -Trigger $taskTrigger `
    -RunLevel 'Limited' `
    -Description 'This line is too long to read'
```

This approach is relatively common, but it is fragile. It is easy to miss a backtick from the end-of-line, or to accidentally add a space after a backtick character. Both break continuation and the command executes but with an incomplete set of parameters; afterward, an error may be displayed, or a prompt may be shown, depending on the parameter (or parameters) it missed.

This problem is shown in the following screenshot, where a space character has been accidentally included after a backtick following the Daily switch parameter:

```
PS> New-ScheduledTaskTrigger   -Daily `

cmdlet New-ScheduledTaskTrigger at command pipeline position 1
Supply values for the following parameters:
At:
```

Figure 1.6: Space after the escape character

Splatting provides a neater, generally easier-to-read, and more robust alternative. The following example shows one possible way to tackle these commands when using splatting:

```
$newTaskAction = @{
    Execute = 'pwsh.exe'
    Argument = 'Write-Host "hello world"'
}
$newTaskTrigger = @{
    Daily = $true
    At    = '00:00:00'
}
$registerTask = @{
    TaskName    = 'TaskName'
    Action      = New-ScheduledTaskAction @newTaskAction
    Trigger     = New-ScheduledTaskTrigger @newTaskTrigger
    RunLevel    = 'Limited'
    Description = 'Splatting is easy to read'
}
Register-ScheduledTask @registerTask
```

Switch parameters may be treated as if they are Boolean when splatting.

The Daily parameter that was defined in the previous example is a switch parameter.

The same approach applies to Confirm, Force, WhatIf, Verbose, and so on.

Conditional use of parameters

Conditional use of parameters is one of the most important ways in which splatting can help.

If a command must be run and the parameters for a command can change based on user input or other circumstances, then it may be tempting to repeat the entire command. For example, a Credential parameter might be conditionally used.

The command may be repeated entirely based on there being a value for the Credential variable:

```
if ($Credential) {
    Get-ADUser 'Enabled -eq $true' -Credential $Credential
} else {
    Get-ADUser 'Enabled -eq $true'
}
```

The disadvantage of this approach is that any change to the command must be repeated in the second version.

Alternatively, a splatting variable may be used, and the Credential parameter added only when it is needed:

```
$params = @{}
if ($Credential) {
    $params['Credential'] = $Credential
}
Get-ADUser 'Enabled -eq $true' @params
```

Using splatting in this manner ensures only one version of the command must be maintained, reducing the risk of introducing a bug when making changes.

Splatting to avoid repetition

Splatting may be used to avoid repetition when a parameter must be optionally passed on to several different commands. It is possible to splat more than one set of parameters.

In this example, the ComputerName and Credential parameters are used by two different commands:

```
# Parameters used to authenticate remote connections
$remoteParams = @{
    Credential   = Get-Credential
    ComputerName = $env:COMPUTERNAME
}
```

```
# Parameters which are specific to Test-WSMan
$testWSMan = @{
    Authentication = 'Default'
    ErrorAction    = 'SilentlyContinue'
}
# By default, do not pass any extra parameters to New-CimSession
$newCimSession = @{}
if (-not (Test-WSMan @testWSMan @remoteParams)) {
    # If WSMan fails, use DCOM (RPC over TCP) to connect
    $newCimSession['SessionOption'] = New-CimSessionOption -Protocol Dcom
}
# Parameters to pass to Get-CimInstance
$getCimInstance = @{
    ClassName   = 'Win32_Service'
    CimSession  = New-CimSession @newCimSession @remoteParams
}
Get-CimInstance @getCimInstance
```

This example takes advantage of several features:

- It is possible to splat no parameters using an empty hashtable (@{}) when all the parameters are conditionally added.
- It is possible to test conditions and dynamically add parameters at runtime (if needed).
- It is possible to splat more than one set of parameters into a command.

As the preceding example shows, it is possible to dynamically choose the parameters that are passed to a command without having to write the command in full more than once in a script.

Splatting and positional parameters

It is possible, although rare and inadvisable in production scripts, to splat positional parameters; that is, to splat a parameter without stating a parameter name.

This can be seen with the Rename-Item command, which has two positional parameters: Path and NewName. Rename-Item may be run as follows:

```
Rename-Item oldname.txt newname.txt
```

An array to splat these positional parameters looks as follows:

```
$renameItem = 'oldname.txt', 'newname.txt'
Rename-Item @renameItem
```

A splatting variable with positional parameters may be used with executable files (.exe files), although it is often difficult to see any difference between splatting and using a normal variable. For example, both of the following commands execute in the same way:

```
$argumentList = '/t', 2
timeout.exe $argumentList
timeout.exe @argumentList
```

Splatting is a powerful technique and can be used to make code more readable by reducing the line length or repetition.

When using splatting, string values in the hashtable must be quoted. Conversely, when using a parameter directly, it is often unnecessary. The parser is responsible for deciding how statements and expressions should be interpreted.

Parser modes

The parser in PowerShell is responsible for taking what is typed into the console, or what is written in a script, and turning it into something PowerShell can execute. The parser has two different modes that explain, for instance, why strings assigned to variables must be quoted, but strings as arguments for parameters only need quoting if the string contains a space.

The parser modes are different modes:

- Argument mode
- Expression mode

Mode switching allows PowerShell to correctly interpret arguments without needing values to be quoted. In the following example, the argument for the Name parameter only needs quoting if the name contains spaces:

```
Get-Process -Name pwsh
```

The parser is running in Argument mode at the point the pwsh value is used and therefore literal text is treated as a value, not something to be executed.

This means that, in the following example, the second command is interpreted as a string and not executed:

```
Set-Content -Path commands.txt -Value 'Get-ChildItem', 'Get-Item'
Get-Command -Name Get-Content commands.txt
```

The second command in the preceding code therefore does not do anything.

To execute the Get-Content command, the argument must be enclosed in parentheses:

```
Set-Content -Path commands.txt -Value 'Get-ChildItem', 'Get-Item'
Get-Command -Name (Get-Content commands.txt)
```

The code in parentheses is executed, and the parser is in Expression mode.

Another example of this can be seen when using an enumeration value. An enumeration is a list of constants described by a .NET type. Enumerations are explored in *Chapter 7, Working with .NET*:

```
PS> Get-Date [DayOfWeek]::Monday
Get-Date: Cannot bind parameter 'Date'. Cannot convert value
"[DayOfWeek]::Monday" to type "System.DateTime". Error: "String
'[DayOfWeek]::Monday' was not recognized as a valid DateTime."
```

If the value for the argument is placed in parentheses, it will run first and expand the value. Once the value is expanded, Get-Date will be able to work with it:

```
Get-Date ([DayOfWeek]::Monday)
```

The help document, about_parsing, explores this topic in greater detail.

Experimental features

PowerShell 7 uses experimental features to make some new functionality available, which are not yet considered to be mainstream features. Features may be added to a later release of PowerShell, or discarded if they are not successful.

Three commands are available for working with experimental features:

- Enable-ExperimentalFeature
- Disable-ExperimentalFeature
- Get-ExperimentalFeature

Get-ExperimentalFeature can be used to view the available features. The list of features changes depending on the version of PowerShell. The following list has been taken from PowerShell 7.3.3.

```
PS> Get-ExperimentalFeature

Name                              Enabled Source   Description
----                              ------- ------   -----------
PSCommandNotFoundSuggestion       False   PSEngine Recommend…
PSLoadAssemblyFromNativeCode      False   PSEngine Expose an API…
PSNativeCommandErrorActionPreferen… False PSEngine Native comman…
PSSubsystemPluginModel            False   PSEngine A plugin mode…
```

In addition to the output shown here, each feature has a description. Format-Table can be used to view these descriptions:

```
Get-ExperimentalFeature | Format-Table Name, Description -Wrap
```

The use of these commands is described in the About_Experimental_Features help file.

If an experimental feature is enabled, PowerShell must be restarted for us to use the feature. For example, PSCommandNotFoundSuggestion can be enabled:

```
Enable-ExperimentalFeature -Name PSCommandNotFoundSuggestion
```

Once enabled, if a command is spelled incorrectly in the console, PowerShell will suggest possible command names alongside the error message:

```
PS> Get-Procss
Get-Procss: The term 'Get-Procss' is not recognized as the name of a cmdlet,
function, script file, or operable program. Check the spelling of the name, or
if a path was included, verify that the path is correct and try again.
Suggestion [4,General]: The most similar commands are: Get-Process, Wait-
Process, Get-Host, Get-DbaProcess.
```

If the feature is no longer wanted, it can be disabled again:

```
Disable-ExperimentalFeature -Name PSCommandNotFoundSuggestion
```

In the past, several experimental features have become permanent features in PowerShell.

Summary

This chapter contained several foundational topics for PowerShell, starting with picking an editor, using help content, and command discovery.

The ability to use the help system and discover commands is vital, regardless of skill level. The availability of help content in the shell allows new commands to be quickly incorporated and used.

Naming plays an important role in PowerShell. Strict use of a reasonably small set of verbs greatly enhances discovery and reasonable assumptions can be made about a command before reaching for help content. PowerShell tends to use longer and more descriptive command names compared with other scripting languages.

Once a command has been found, it is important to understand how to use the help content and the parameters a command offers to use it effectively.

Providers allow access to data in a similar manner to using a file system. Providers play an important role in PowerShell and are explored again later in this book when exploring the file system and registry. Providers are explored in greater detail in *Chapter 10, Files, Folders, and the Registry*.

Splatting was introduced and will be used repeatedly throughout this book. In the context of this book, it is primarily used to reduce line length. Splatting is an incredibly useful technique when scripting. The ability to conditionally use parameters without repeating code reduces complexity and the chance of introducing bugs.

The parser was introduced to explain command syntax, when values must be quoted, and when parentheses are required. The parser is complex and the examples in about_parsing should be reviewed.

Finally, PowerShell 6 introduced the idea of experimental features. This continues into PowerShell 7. Features can be toggled on (or off again) before they become mainstream.

The next chapter moves on to exploring modules and snap-ins, allowing PowerShell users to go beyond the base set of commands and include content published by others.

Learn more on Discord

Read this book alongside other users, PowerShell experts, and the author himself. Ask questions, provide solutions to other readers, chat with the author via Ask Me Anything sessions, and much more.

Scan the QR code or visit the link to join the community.

https://packt.link/SecNet

2

Modules

Modules are packaged collections of commands that may be loaded inside PowerShell, allowing PowerShell to interact with new systems and services. Modules come from a wide variety of different sources.

PowerShell itself is installed with a small number of modules, including `ThreadJob` and `PSReadline`.

Some modules can be installed by adding Windows features or enabling capabilities, for example, the `ActiveDirectory` and `GroupPolicy` modules.

Several applications include modules as part of their installers; for example, Microsoft **Local Administrator Password Solution (LAPS)** includes a PowerShell module that may be used to get passwords and set permissions.

The Windows platform itself includes many modules, for example, the `NetFirewall` module. Most of these have been included since Windows 8 was released.

Modules can be installed from the PowerShell Gallery or another registered repository. The PowerShell Gallery can include updated versions of pre-installed modules.

The PowerShell Gallery is therefore a valuable source of modules published by Microsoft, VMware, Amazon Web Services, and many others.

Finally, many modules are just files and directories in the file system. Modules can often be copied between computers.

Snap-ins were included in PowerShell 1 and largely replaced with modules with the release of PowerShell 2. PowerShell 7 does not support snap-ins; snap-ins are limited to Windows PowerShell.

The chapter covers the following topics:

- Introducing modules
- Installing modules
- Using Windows PowerShell modules in PowerShell 7
- Microsoft.PowerShell.PSResourceGet (formerly PowerShellGet 3)
- PowerShell repositories
- Snap-ins

Modules are a vital part of PowerShell, allowing authors to share sets of commands.

Introducing modules

Modules were introduced with the release of PowerShell version 2.0. A module is a packaged set of commands (binary commands, functions, and aliases) that includes any required supporting content; modules often include help content.

PowerShell 5.1 introduced support for classes written in PowerShell. These are explored in *Chapter 19, Classes and Enumerations*, but while support is present these are rarely directly user-accessible.

Modules tend to target a specific system or focus on a small set of related operations. For example, the `Microsoft.PowerShell.Archive` module contains a small number of commands for interacting with ZIP files.

The modules available on a system can be discovered using the `Get-Module` command.

The Get-Module command

`Get-Module` is used to find the modules either in the current PowerShell session or available on the current system.

PowerShell itself comes with several built-in modules, including `PowerShellGet`, `ThreadJob`, `PSReadLine`, and the commands in the `Microsoft.PowerShell.*` modules.

The Windows platform, especially the most recent versions, comes with a wide variety of modules to manage components of the operating system. These, as well as any other available modules, can be viewed using the `Get-Module -ListAvailable` command.

By default, `Get-Module` returns information about each module that has been imported (either automatically or by using `Import-Module`). For example, if the command is run from PowerShell 7, it shows that the `PSReadLine` module has been loaded:

```
PS C:\> Get-Module


ModuleType Version     PreRelease Name
---------- -------     ---------- ----
Script     2.2.6                  PSReadLine
```

The `ListAvailable` parameter shows the list of modules that are available on the system instead of just those that have been imported:

```
Get-Module -ListAvailable
```

Modules are discovered using the paths in the `PSModulePath` environment variable, which contains a delimited list of paths for PowerShell to search.

Get-Module will show all instances of a module regardless of the path and version when using the All parameter:

```
Get-Module <ModuleName> -All -ListAvailable
```

Modules that are available on a system can be imported either by running Import-Module or by running a command from the module.

The Import-Module command

PowerShell 3 and later attempts to automatically load modules if a command from that module is used and the module is under one of the paths in the $env:PSModulePath environment variable. Explicit use of the Import-Module command is less important than it was before Windows PowerShell 3.

For example, if PowerShell is started and the CimCmdlets module is not imported, running the Get-CimInstance command will cause the module to be automatically imported. This is shown in the following example:

```
PS> Get-Module CimCmdlets
PS> Get-CimInstance Win32_OperatingSystem | Out-Null
PS> Get-Module CimCmdlets
ModuleType Version      PreRelease Name
---------- -------      ---------- ----
Binary     7.0.0.0                 CimCmdlets
```

The autoloader may be disabled using the $PSModuleAutoLoadingPreference variable as shown here:

```
$PSModuleAutoLoadingPreference = 'None'
```

Modules can be explicitly imported in PowerShell using the Import-Module command. Modules may be imported using a name or with a full path, as shown in the following example:

```
Import-Module -Name ThreadJob
Import-Module -Name $PSHome\Modules\ThreadJob\ThreadJob.psd1
```

Importing a module using a path is only required if the module is not in a discoverable path.

Once a module has been imported, the commands within the module may be listed using Get-Command as follows:

```
Get-Command -Module ThreadJob
```

Modules, Get-Command, and autoloading

As the commands exported by a module are only identified by PowerShell importing the module, the previous command will also trigger an automatic import.

If the module autoloading is disabled, the command above will not list any commands (and will not write any errors).

Modules installed in Windows PowerShell 5 and later are placed in a folder named after the module version, for example, `Modules\ModuleName\1.0.0\<ModuleContent>`. This allows multiple versions of the same module to coexist, as shown in the following example:

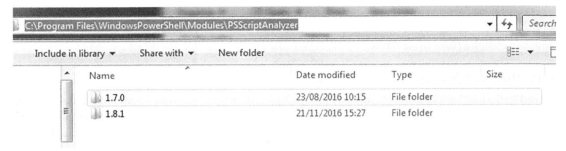

Figure 2.1: Side-by-side versioning

Version 1.8.1 of `PSScriptAnalyzer` will be imported by default, as it is the highest version number. It is possible to import a specific version of a module using the `MinimumVersion` and `MaximumVersion` parameters:

```
Import-Module PSScriptAnalyzer -MaxmimumVersion 1.7.0
```

Modules that have been imported can be removed from a PowerShell session using the `Remove-Module` command.

The Remove-Module command

The `Remove-Module` command removes a previously imported module from the current session.

For binary modules or manifest modules that incorporate a **Dynamic Link Library (DLL)**, commands are removed from PowerShell but DLLs are not unloaded. DLL files used in a PowerShell session cannot be unloaded without restarting the PowerShell process.

`Remove-Module` does not remove or delete the files that make up a module from a computer.

Each of the preceding commands, by default, interacts with modules saved in the `PSModulePath` environment variable.

PSModulePath in PowerShell

`PSModulePath` is a delimited list of paths that can be used to store modules. Modules can import modules in these paths by name and they will be automatically loaded when a command from the module is used.

PowerShell allows the value of `$env:PSModulePath` to be set using user- and machine-scoped environment variables. By default, the machine-scoped variable should include the following paths, which are used by Windows PowerShell and by PowerShell 7 for compatibility:

```
C:\Program Files\WindowsPowerShell\Modules
C:\Windows\System32\WindowsPowerShell\v1.0\Modules
```

If the environment variables do not exist, PowerShell 7 uses the default values:

```
PS> $env:PSModulePath -split [System.IO.Path]::PathSeparator
C:\Users\whoami\Documents\PowerShell\Modules
C:\Program Files\PowerShell\Modules
C:\program files\powershell\7\Modules
C:\WINDOWS\system32\WindowsPowerShell\v1.0\Modules
```

The default values in the preceding list are included regardless of the value of the environment variable.

When using module paths, it is important to note that PowerShell does not search all paths for the latest version of a module. PowerShell searches the list of paths in the order they appear in the PSModulePath environment variable. If a module is listed in more than one path, the most recent version from the first discovered path is used.

For example, if the current user path contains a module with version 1.0.0, and the program files path contains the same module but with version 2.0.0, PowerShell will prefer to load version 1.0.0 because the current user path is searched first. The Version or MinimumVersion parameter must be used with Import-Module if a specific version of a module is required.

If both Windows PowerShell and PowerShell 7 are in use in an environment, care must be taken when updating the PSModulePath environment variable. The behavior described previously differs from Windows PowerShell. In Windows PowerShell:

- If the user environment variable is set, it completely replaces the user value, which defaults to C:\Users\whoami\Documents\WindowsPowerShell\Modules.
- If the machine environment variable is set, it replaces the system32 path: C:\windows\system32\windowspowershell\v1.0\Modules.
- In all cases, the C:\Program Files\WindowsPowerShell\Modules path remains.

The C:\windows\system32\windowspowershell\v1.0\Modules path should be included in the machine environment variable to allow PowerShell 7 to load modules, either directly or using a Windows PowerShell compatibility session.

The value of $env:PSModulePath may be safely modified within all PowerShell versions and all platforms, for example, by using a profile script. Changes made to $env:PSModulePath are scoped to the process and only affect the current PowerShell session and any child processes; the changes do not persist.

As modules are stored in specific places on the file system, it can be said that most modules consist only of files.

Module content

A module is typically made up of several files stored in a directory. For instance, a module might include:

- A manifest, a .psd1 file, which defines metadata like the version, author, and so on.
- A root module, as either a .psm1 file or a .dll file, most often named after the module directory.

- A set of .xml files used to hold help content, formatting data, and so on.
- Any other supporting files required by the module.

These different components are explored in more detail in *Chapter 20, Building Modules*.

In many cases, this means that modules are self-contained and can be copied from one location to another, or from one computer to another, without needing an explicit installation step. This self-contained feature is the basis for the Save-Module command introduced later in this chapter.

Several modules are not self-contained and require content beyond the module directories.

The modules preinstalled by Microsoft as part of the operating system, such as NetAdapter, SmbShare, Storage, and so on, are not portable. They depend on **Windows Management Instrumentation (WMI)** classes installed on the operating system.

Similarly, modules installed as Windows features or components, such as the ActiveDirectory module, are also not portable.

PowerShell 7 can use modules intended for Windows PowerShell either directly or by using a Windows PowerShell compatibility session.

Using Windows PowerShell modules in PowerShell 7

Many modules available to Windows PowerShell are compatible with PowerShell 7 without requiring any changes.

If a module is not compatible with the Core edition (PowerShell 6 and higher), PowerShell 7 will automatically attempt to load the module using the module in a Windows compatibility session. The compatibility session allows PowerShell 7 to communicate with Windows PowerShell somewhat transparently.

The Appx module does not support PowerShell 7; it does not state that it supports the Core edition of PowerShell, as shown by Get-Module:

```
PS> Get-Module Appx -ListAvailable -SkipEditionCheck
Directory:
C:\Windows\System32\WindowsPowerShell\v1.0\Modules
ModuleType Version     PreRelease Name        PSEdition ExportedCommands

---------- -------     ---------- ----        --------- ----------------
Manifest   2.0.1.0                Appx        Desk      {Add-AppxPackag...
```

In Windows 11 and PowerShell 7.4, If a command from the module is used, PowerShell automatically creates a compatibility session and makes the commands accessible. PowerShell 7 will show a different version of the module as a result:

```
PS> Import-Module Appx -UseWindowsPowerShell
PS> Get-Module Appx


ModuleType Version   PreRelease Name  ExportedCommands

---------- -------   ---------- ----  ----------------
Script     1.0                  Appx  {Add-AppxPackage...
```

The compatibility session can be seen using the `Get-PSSession` command after the module has been imported:

```
Get-PSSession -Name WinPSCompatSession
```

In some cases, a module has simply not been tested and marked as compatible with PowerShell 7 by the module author. A module can be explicitly loaded in PowerShell 7 regardless of the stated compatible editions:

```
Import-Module Appx -SkipEditionCheck
```

In the case of the Appx module, the attempt to import the module will fail; the module really does not support PowerShell Core:

```
PS> Import-Module Appx -SkipEditionCheck
Import-Module: Operation is not supported on this platform. (0x80131539)
```

When a module is automatically imported because a command from the module is used, PowerShell does not indicate that the module has been loaded using a compatibility session.

When `Import-Module` is explicitly used, a warning is displayed:

```
PS> Import-Module Appx
WARNING: Module Appx is loaded in Windows PowerShell using WinPSCompatSession
remoting session; please note that all input and output of commands from this
module will be deserialized objects. If you want to load this module into
PowerShell please use 'Import-Module -SkipEditionCheck' syntax.
```

The impact of this warning depends on how the module has been written to work in PowerShell. There is a significant risk that the module's functionality will be impaired, it will likely work in part, or it may work without problem.

Microsoft maintains a list of modules (written by Microsoft) and their compatibility state:

https://learn.microsoft.com/en-us/powershell/windows/module-compatibility.

The effect of an impaired command can be demonstrated by using Get-WmiObject. This is not available in PowerShell 7 and cannot be directly used.

In Windows 11, PowerShell will automatically load the command using the compatibility session.

In Windows 10, the module can be explicitly imported as shown below:

Get-Module Microsoft.PowerShell.Management -ListAvailable |

```
Get-Module Microsoft.PowerShell.Management -ListAvailable |
    Where-Object Version -eq 3.1.0.0 |
    Import-Module -UseWindowsPowerShell
```

A warning will be displayed noting that commands have been skipped, and a second warning describing how the module was loaded in the compatibility session.

Once loaded, the command below will execute successfully:

```
Get-WmiObject Win32_Process -Filter "ProcessID=$PID"
```

If the `Get-WmiObject` command is run in Windows PowerShell, it will have several methods available. Methods are discussed in greater detail in *Chapter 7, Working with .NET*. One of these methods is `GetRelated`, which is typically used as follows when used in Windows PowerShell:

```
$process = Get-WmiObject Win32_Process -Filter "ProcessID=$PID"
$process.GetRelated('Win32_Session')
```

Because PowerShell 7 has a copy of the properties only, the method does not exist, and an error will be displayed. The functionality of the command is impaired because it has been used via the compatibility session.

```
PS> $process = Get-WmiObject Win32_Process -Filter "ProcessID=$PID"
PS> $process.GetRelated('Win32_Session')
InvalidOperation: Method invocation failed because [Deserialized.System.
Management.ManagementObject#root\cimv2\Win32_Process] does not contain a method
named 'GetRelated'.
```

In Windows PowerShell, the command above would successfully return the session associated with the process.

The compatibility feature is incredibly useful but does not replace native compatibility with modern versions of PowerShell.

PowerShell on the Windows platform has a wide variety of modules available, or available through installable applications and features to interact with other systems. New modules can also be installed from resources such as the PowerShell Gallery.

Finding and installing modules

PowerShell includes a module named `PowerShellGet`, which can be used to register repositories and search for and install modules.

By default, `PowerShellGet` searches the PowerShell Gallery.

What is the PowerShell Gallery?

The PowerShell Gallery is a Microsoft-run repository and distribution platform for PowerShell scripts and modules written by Microsoft or other users.

The PowerShell Gallery has parallels in other scripting languages, as shown in the following examples:

- Perl has cpan.org.
- Python has PyPI.
- Ruby has RubyGems.

Support for the gallery is included by default in PowerShell 5 and above. For Windows PowerShell 3 and 4, PowerShellGet must be installed as described in Microsoft Learn:

https://learn.microsoft.com/en-us/powershell/gallery/powershellget/install-on-older-systems.

The PowerShell Gallery may be searched using https://www.powershellgallery.com, as shown in the following screenshot:

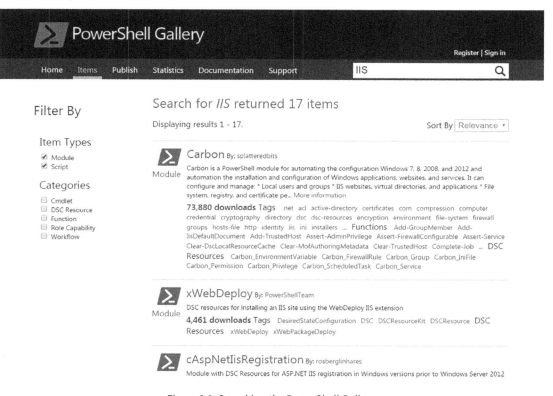

Figure 2.2: Searching the PowerShell Gallery

The Find-Module command can be used to search the PowerShell Gallery, or any registered repository, instead of using the web page.

The Find-Module command

Find-Module is used to search registered PowerShell repositories. Modules are identified by name, as shown in the following example:

```
Find-Module Carbon
Find-Module -Name Carbon
Find-Module -Name Azure*
```

Use the `Filter` parameter when the name alone is not sufficient to find an appropriate module. Supplying a value for the Filter parameter is equivalent to using the search field in the PowerShell Gallery. It expands the search to include tags:

```
Find-Module -Filter IIS
```

The `Find-Module` command cannot filter based on the PowerShell edition, and the result of the search does not state which version the module might work with.

Once found, a module can be installed using the `Install-Module` command.

The Install-Module command

The `Install-Module` command installs modules from the PowerShell Gallery or any other configured repository. By default, `Install-Module` installs modules on the path for `CurrentUser`, at `C:\Users\user\Documents\Modules` on Windows and at `/home/.local/share/share/powershell/Modules` on Ubuntu.

Modules may also be installed in the `AllUsers` scope if a module is to be shared by all users on a system. Installing in the `AllUsers` scope requires administrative access:

```
Install-Module carbon -Scope AllUsers
```

For example, the `posh-git` module may be installed using either of the following two commands:

```
Find-Module -Name posh-git | Install-Module
Install-Module posh-git
```

If the most recent version of a module is already installed, the command ends without providing feedback. If a newer version is available, it will be automatically installed alongside the original.

The `Force` parameter may be used to reinstall a module:

```
Install-Module posh-git -Force
```

`Force` may also be used to install a newer version of a module when the existing version was not installed from a PS repository, or when changing the scope a module is installed in.

The `Install-Module` command does not provide an option to install modules under the `$PSHOME` directory. The `$PSHOME` directory is reserved for modules that are shipped with the PowerShell installer, or for Windows PowerShell, those that are shipped with the Windows operating system.

The Update-Module command

Use the `Update-Module` command to update any module installed using the `Install-Module` command.

In both Windows PowerShell and PowerShell 7, `Update-Module` attempts to update the specified module to the latest or a specified version.

The Save-Module command

The Save-Module command downloads the module from the PowerShell Gallery (or any other registered repository) to a path without installing it.

Installation often only means downloading content to a specific location (one of the paths in $env:PSModulePath); there is rarely a traditional installation step as would be seen by installing an application such as Microsoft Office. The Save-Module command is therefore almost no different from Install-Module. The key difference is that a target path is required when saving module content.

The following example command downloads the Carbon module into a Modules directory in the root of the C: drive:

```
Save-Module -Name Carbon -Path C:\Modules -Force
```

Save-Module will download the module and overwrite any previously saved version in the specified path. The command ignores other downloaded versions of the module.

Each of the preceding commands is part of PowerShellGet 2. PowerShellGet 3 adopts a slightly different approach to the commands.

Microsoft.PowerShell.PSResourceGet

PowerShellGet 2 (for example, PowerShellGet 2.2.4.1) implements the Install-Module, Update-Module, and Save-Module module commands demonstrated at the beginning of this chapter.

Microsoft.PowerShell.PSResourceGet (PSResourceGet), formerly PowerShellGet 3, hopes to replace PowerShellGet version 2 installations. One of the key features is that this new version does not depend on the PackageManagement module, allowing a simpler installation process, and avoiding the need to bootstrap the NuGet provider, making upgrading the module simpler.

The preview version also uses new command names, completely divorcing it from the previous implementations of PowerShellGet. The change in command names means the new version can safely be installed alongside any existing version.

PSResourceGet is included with the PowerShell 7.4 installation.

If not installed, PSResourceGet can be installed as follows:

```
Install-Module Microsoft.PowerShell.PSResourceGet
```

Once installed, the PowerShell Gallery or another repository can be registered using the Register-PSResourceRepository command:

```
Register-PSResourceRepository -PSGallery
```

In PowerShellGet 2.0, there are separate commands to work with modules and scripts. PowerShellGet 3.0 does not differentiate between modules and scripts; all artifacts are termed `PSResource`, and all searches use the `Find-PSResource` command. For example, a module can be found using the following command:

```
Find-PSResource -Name Indented.Net.IP -Type Module
```

The `Type` parameter may be omitted without affecting the search results in this case.

Most of the commands in PowerShellGet 3.0 use the same approach as those in PowerShellGet 2.2.4 and below. Over time, differences between the commands are likely to start to appear; for example, `Install-PSResource` includes a `Reinstall` parameter, which is somewhat like the `Force` parameter for `Install-Module` in PowerShellGet 2.

Repositories

Like older versions of PowerShellGet, repositories are registered on a per-user basis. In PowerShellGet 2.2.4 and below, the repository configuration file is found at the following path:

```
$env:LOCALAPPDATA\Microsoft\Windows\PowerShell\PowerShellGet\PSRepositories.xml
```

The `PSRepositories.xml` file is stored in the CliXml format and may be read using the `Import-CliXml` command. The file is normally read and updated using `Get-PSRepository`, `Register-PSRepository`, and `Unregister-PSRespository`.

PSResourceGet uses a simpler format for the `PSResourceRespository.xml` file. The file may be found at the following path:

```
$env:LOCALAPPDATA\PowerShellGet\PSResourceRepository.xml
```

The `Get-PSResourceRepository`, `Register-PSResourceRepository`, and `Unregister-PSResourceRepository` commands are the expected way of interacting with this file.

As with older versions of PowerShellGet, storing credentials for a repository is not currently supported. If a repository requires authentication, the `Credential` parameter must be used explicitly with each operation.

Version ranges

`Find-PSResource` allows wildcards to be used for the `Version` parameter; using * will return all available versions except pre-releases. The `Prerelease` parameter may be added to include those:

```
Find-PSResource -Name PowerShellGet -Version *
```

A range of versions may be defined using the range syntax used by NuGet, which is described in the following document:

https://learn.microsoft.com/nuget/concepts/package-versioning#version-ranges-and-wildcards.

For example, the highest version of PowerShellGet available between 1.0 (inclusive) and 2.0 (exclusive) may be found using this:

```
Find-PSResource -Name PowerShellGet -Version '[1.0,2.0)'
```

The search can be changed to be inclusive by changing the closing) to]. For example, the following command will find version 2.0.0 of PowerShellGet:

```
Find-PSResource -Name PowerShellGet -Version '[1.0,2.0]'
```

The same syntax will be available when declaring dependencies between modules.

PowerShell repositories

Each of the examples from the previous section uses the PowerShell Gallery as a source for installing modules. This is an important resource, but in a business setting, it may be desirable to restrict access to the gallery. Instead, an internal repository that holds curated or internally developed content may be implemented to share content.

Creating an SMB repository

An SMB file share is a simple way to share PowerShell content. A file share may be registered as a repository as follows:

```
$params = @{
    Name               = 'Internal'
    SourceLocation     = '\\server\share\directory'
    InstallationPolicy = 'Trusted'
}
Register-PSRepository @params
```

Existing modules can be published to the repository using the Publish-Module command. For example, if the module Pester 5.0.2 is installed, it may be published to the newly created internal repository:

```
$params = @{
    Name            = 'pester'
    RequiredVersion = '5.4.0'
    Repository      = 'Internal'
}
Publish-Module @params
```

The RequiredVersion parameter is mandatory if more than one version of the module (in this case, Pester) exists on the system publishing the module. Once published, a nupkg file will appear in the file share. The Pester module is now available for installation by anyone else with the repository registered.

Users installing content from an SMB share must be authenticated and must have at least read access to the share. Guest access may be granted to avoid the authentication requirement.

NuGet repositories

NuGet is a package manager for .NET. PowerShellGet can use a NuGet repository as a source for PowerShell modules. The PowerShell Gallery is a NuGet repository.

NuGet offers greater flexibility when dealing with authentication, or package life cycles, when compared with SMB shares.

At the simple end, the `Chocolatey.Server` package available from `chocolatey.org` may be used to configure an **Internet Information Services (IIS)** website to act as a NuGet repository:

`https://chocolatey.org/packages/chocolatey.server`.

 About Chocolatey

Chocolatey is a package manager for Windows. See `https://chocolatey.org` for further information.

More advanced servers include Sonatype Nexus and ProGet. Both offer free to use servers, which may be locally deployed. These services must be configured, and once configured, packages will typically be published by using an API key to authenticate.

About snap-ins

Snap-ins, and the commands for interacting with snap-ins, are only available in Windows PowerShell; they are not present in PowerShell 7 and the commands used below will not work.

A snap-in is the predecessor to a module. It was the mechanism available to extend the set of commands in PowerShell 1 and was deprecated with the release of PowerShell 2. Unfortunately, a small number of organizations persist in offering PowerShell commands via a snap-in.

The list of installed snap-ins may be viewed using the following command:

```
Get-PSSnapIn -Registered
```

If the `Registered` parameter is excluded, `Get-PSSnapIn` will show the snap-ins that have been imported into the current PowerShell session.

PowerShell does not automatically load commands from a snap-in. All snap-ins must be explicitly imported using the `Add-PSSnapIn` command:

```
Add-PSSnapIn WDeploySnapin3.0
```

Once a snap-in has been installed (registered) and added, `Get-Command` can be used to list the commands as if the snap-in were a module:

```
Get-Command -Module WDeploySnapin3.0
```

The snap-in shown will only be visible if Web Deployment Toolkit 3.0 is installed.

Summary

Modules are a vital part of PowerShell. Modules allow users to extend the commands available within PowerShell, allowing PowerShell to work with many different systems from many different vendors.

The commands explored in this chapter have demonstrated how to discover and use locally available modules along with the commands each module contains. The PowerShell Gallery has been introduced as a public repository of modules, extending PowerShell further still.

PowerShellGet has been a feature of PowerShell since PowerShell 3. With the release of PowerShellGet 3 on the horizon, we demonstrated its new commands and filtering capabilities.

SMB- and NuGet-based repositories were briefly introduced for those looking to establish private repositories for use within an organization. This allows administrators to create private repositories with curated content, reducing exposure to unknown modules.

Snap-ins, an artifact of PowerShell 1 that is limited to Windows PowerShell, were very briefly demonstrated for the products where snap-ins remain important.

The next chapter dives into the commands available to work with objects in PowerShell, including `Where-Object` and `ForEach-Object`.

Learn more on Discord

Read this book alongside other users, PowerShell experts, and the author himself. Ask questions, provide solutions to other readers, chat with the author via Ask Me Anything sessions, and much more.

Scan the QR code or visit the link to join the community.

https://packt.link/SecNet

3

Variables, Arrays, and Hashtables

A variable in a programming language is used to give a name to a piece of information or data. A variable can be used and re-used in the console, script, or function, or any other piece of code.

A variable may be of any .NET type or object instance. It may contain a string such as "Hello World", an integer such as 42, a decimal such as 3.141, an array, a hashtable, a ScriptBlock, and so on. Everything a variable might refer to is an object when used in PowerShell.

This chapter covers the following topics:

- Naming and creating variables
- Variables in strings
- Variable types
- Variable commands
- Variable providers
- Variable scope
- About arrays
- About hashtables
- About Ordered

A variable must be given a name when it is created.

Naming and creating variables

Variables in PowerShell are preceded by the dollar symbol ($), for example:

```
$MyVariable
```

Values are assigned to variables using the assignment operator, =:

```
$MyVariable = 'Hello World'
```

It is possible to assign the same value to several variables in one statement. For example, this creates two variables, `first` and `second`, both with a value of 0:

```
$first = $second = 0
```

The name of a variable may contain numbers, letters, underscores, and question marks. For example, each of the following is a valid name:

- `$123`
- `$x`
- `$my_variable`
- `$variable`
- `$varIABle`
- `$Path_To_File`

The following are invalid names, each includes a character outside of the set above:

- `$a-b`
- `$variable!`
- `$a{b}c`

Variables are frequently written in either camel case or Pascal case. For example:

- `$myVariable` is camel case.
- `$MyVariable` is Pascal case.

PowerShell does not enforce a naming convention, nor does it consistently use a convention in the automatic variables.

One of the most common practices is that variables used as parameters must use Pascal case. Variables used only within a script or a function must use camel case.

All variables should ideally have a descriptive name. In general, PowerShell is a verbose descriptive language.

It is possible to use more complex variable names, such as one containing normally forbidden characters, by surrounding the variable name in curly braces.

For example, the variables below include characters that would not normally be permitted, such as a space and hyphen:

```
${My Variable}
${My-Variable}
```

In general, variables should not include special characters.

The only special character that cannot be used between curly braces, as shown in the example above, is a colon, `:`. When a colon is used, the variable becomes a reference to a provider path.

Provider variables

When a colon is included in a variable, the value, or values, on the left of the colon are read as provider names.

For example, an environment variable is accessed using the env: drive:

```
${env:ProgramFiles(x86)}
```

The braces around the name are necessary here because of the (x86) part of the name.

This type of notation is often seen with environment variables and quite often used to access function definitions. The example below shows the code for the built-in mkdir function:

```
${function:mkdir}
```

It can also be used to change something. In the example below, a function:

```
${function:Write-HelloWorld} = { Write-Host 'Hello world' }
```

This is not a great way to create a function, but it will work.

One far less common use of this approach is to change content on the filesystem. The example below will create a new file in C:\Windows\Temp. Any path can be used:

```
${C:\Windows\Temp\variable.txt} = "New value"
```

While it is relatively common to see this notation for the env and function providers, it is rare to find this used to manage file content.

Curly braces can be used when expanding variables inside double-quoted strings.

Variables in strings

In PowerShell, variables can be included within any double-quoted string. The value of that variable will expand when the string is created.

For example:

```
$count = 5
$string = "There are $count items"
```

Variables will not expand inside single-quoted or literal strings.

Provider-specific values will also expand inside a double-quoted string:

```
"Computer Name: $env:COMPUTERNAME"
```

The example above uses a colon to split the provider name, env, from the variable name, COMPUTERNAME. If a colon is present after a variable name, PowerShell will always interpret it as a provider name.

In the following example, the first variable in the string ends with a colon, which causes a parser error:

```
PS> $computerName = $env:COMPUTERNAME
PS> "$ComputerName: Running PS $PSEdition"
ParserError:
Line |
   1 |    "$ComputerName: Running PS $PSEdition"
     |     ~~~~~~~~~~~~~~~
     |    Variable reference is not valid. ':' was not followed by
     |    a valid variable name character. Consider using ${} to
     |    delimit the name.
```

In both PowerShell 7 and Windows PowerShell, the error message includes the solution to the problem. Surrounding the variable name with curly braces will correctly define the extent of the name:

```
$computerName = $env:COMPUTERNAME
"${ComputerName}: Running PS $PSEdition"
```

A sub-expression would also have been effective in this case:

```
$computerName = $env:COMPUTERNAME
"$($ComputerName): Running PS $PSEdition"
```

The sub-expression is not required in this case. A sub-expression would be required if a more complex expression were included in the string. In the example below, the length of the `ComputerName` string is used in a sub-expression:

```
"${ComputerName}: $($ComputerName.Length) characters long"
```

Sub-expressions may contain any arbitrary code, including their own quoted values (further escaping is not required).

Variable types

Values in PowerShell all have a .NET type. A .NET type describes what a value is. This affects what can be done with or to the value.

In the example below, the .NET type is `System.String`:

```
$variable = "Hello world"
```

This may be seen using the `Get-Member` command:

```
PS> $variable | Get-Member | Select-Object -First 1

   TypeName: System.String

Name  MemberType Definition
```

```
----    ----------  ----------
Clone Method       System.Object Clone(), System.Object ICloneab...
```

The Clone method shown in the example above can be ignored at this point. Methods and .NET in general are explored in more detail in *Chapter 7, Working with .NET*.

One method that is useful at this point is the GetType method. This reveals the .NET type of a value. The method is available on any value that is not null and is used as shown below:

```
PS> $variable.GetType()

IsPublic IsSerial Name       BaseType
-------- -------- ----       --------
True     True     String     System.Object
```

In the output from the example above, the value of Name is the most important. This shows that the value type is string, or the .NET type System.String. The FullName property of the type will show this value:

```
PS> $variable.GetType().FullName
System.String
```

Assigning a numerical value instead will change the value type that is held in the variable:

```
$variable = 1
```

Using Get-Member or the GetType method will show that the value is now System.Int32.

PowerShell is not a statically typed language. When a language is statically typed, the type of a variable cannot be changed as a program, or script, runs. PowerShell allows the value type assigned to a variable to be changed at any point.

It is sometimes necessary to ensure a variable is of a specific type. This is most often done for parameters of functions or scripts.

Creating scripts and functions is explored in *Chapter 17*, *Scripts, Functions, and Script Blocks*. Parameters are explored in *Chapter 18*, *Parameters, Validation, and Dynamic Parameters*.

A type can be given to a value of a variable on either the left- or right-hand side of the assignment.

Assignment with types on the right

When a type is used on the right-hand side of an assignment, the type affects the current value only.

In the example below, an integer value on the right-hand side of an assignment operation is coerced to a string:

```
$variable = [string]1
```

The [string] part of this expression is a type accelerator for System.String. Type accelerators are explored in *Chapter 7, Working with .NET*.

The type used in this assignment affects the value on the right-hand side for the current assignment. It does not prevent different value types from being assigned.

If a script later makes the following assignment, the value type will once again be System.Int32:

```
PS> $variable = 1
PS> $variable.GetType()


IsPublic IsSerial Name           BaseType
-------- -------- ----           --------
True     True     Int32          System.ValueType
```

The type may also be placed on the left of an assignment.

Assignment with types on the left

When a type is used on the left-hand side of an assignment, the type affects the current value and all subsequent assigned values.

For example, the following statement assigns the value 1 to a variable called typedVariable:

```
[string]$typedVariable = 1
```

The integer value will immediately be converted to System.String.

Any other value assigned to the same variable later will also be converted to a string:

```
PS> $typedVariable = 1
PS> $typedVariable.GetType()


IsPublic IsSerial Name           BaseType
-------- -------- ----           --------
True     True     String         System.Object
```

The type assigned persists for the lifetime of a variable, or until a new type is assigned on the left of an assignment. In the following example, the string type is replaced with an int type by the second assignment:

```
[string]$typedVariable = 1
[int]$typedVariable = 1
```

To avoid confusion, if a variable is given a type it should not be re-used to hold values of another type.

As mentioned at the start of this section, the type of a value affects what can be done with the value. This introduces the concept of value types and reference types.

Value and reference types

In .NET languages, a variable may be assigned a value type or a reference type. This is a concept that applies to many different languages and might be considered to describe how the computer holds a value in memory.

It is easiest to explain the difference between the two by looking at reference types first.

A hashtable, which is explored later in this chapter, is a good example of a reference type. When a hashtable is assigned to a variable, the variable maintains a reference to the location in memory of the hashtable:

```
$first = @{ Key = 'value' }
```

If a second variable is created and assigned the value of first, PowerShell will have two variables referencing the same hashtable, the same location in memory:

```
$second = $first
```

The same applies if two variables are created with the same value in a single statement:

```
$first = $second = @{ Key = 'value' }
```

If the second variable is used to make a change to the hashtable, the change will be reflected in the first variable:

```
PS> $second.Key = 'newValue'
PS> $first.Key
newValue
```

The variable holds a reference to the value. Assigning to a new variable does not implicitly create a copy of the value.

Conversely, a variable holding a value type will have an independent copy of the value.

An integer is an example of a value type. Even if two variables are created from the same value, each variable has a distinct instance of that value:

```
$first = $second = 2
```

Strings are not value types but behave in the same way as the value type in practice:

```
$first = $second = 'value'
```

Strings are immutable; a string cannot be changed without creating a new string.

Changing the value of either variable will result in the creation of a new string. The other variable will maintain the current value:

```
PS> $second = 'newValue'
PS> $first
value
```

When a value assigned to a variable must be converted to a different type, PowerShell will attempt several different operations.

Type conversion

PowerShell has an extensive set of operations, which is performed when a value is converted from one type to another.

Type conversion in PowerShell is exceptionally powerful. A great deal of work is hidden behind the simple use of a type against a value. The PowerShell team wrote a short blog post listing the steps taken when PowerShell attempts to cast or coerce a value:

`https://devblogs.microsoft.com/powershell/understanding-powershells-type-conversion-magic/`.

While old, this article is still relevant except for "`Static Create Conversion`," which is no longer in use.

This topic involves concepts that are not explored in more detail until *Chapter 7, Working with .NET*. Terms are used to describe operations, but a deeper exploration must be delayed.

`Trace-Command` can be used to attempt to see how PowerShell is converting a value from one type to another.

For example, converting the string 1/1/1970 to a `DateTime` type implicitly calls the `Parse` method of `DateTime`. `Trace-Command` will show a message stating that the conversion is a `Parse` result:

```
PS> Trace-Command -Expression { [DateTime]'1/1/1970' } -Name TypeConversion
-PSHost
DEBUG: 2024-02-11 13:16:43.5705 TypeConversion Information: 0 : Parse result:
01/01/1970 00:00:00

01 January 1970 00:00:00
```

This, in turn, means it was the result of calling the static `Parse` method with the value – the equivalent of the expression below:

```
[DateTime]::Parse('1/1/1970')
```

Ultimately, this means that PowerShell will try a lot harder to convert from one type to another than a more strongly typed language.

When a variable has been assigned a type on the left, PowerShell will step through the same process of attempting to convert the variable value:

```
[DateTime]$dateTime = Get-Date
Trace-Command -Expression { $dateTime = '1/1/1970' } -Name TypeConversion
-PSHost
```

The command above will show the debug output shown below:

```
DEBUG: 2024-03-24 12:27:29.2837 TypeConversion Information: 0 : Converting
"1/1/1970" to "System.DateTime".
DEBUG: 2024-03-24 12:27:29.2884 TypeConversion Information: 0 :        Parse
result: 01/01/1970 00:00:00
```

The presence of the type converter on a variable can be seen by making use of Get-Variable.

Variable commands

The variable commands may be used to explore and interact with variables defined in PowerShell. However, these commands are rarely used to declare variables when writing scripts or functions.

PowerShell optimizes code when it can, specifically in this section around the use of local variables. Using the *-Variable commands in a script block disables optimization, which will have an impact on the performance of a script.

The following commands are used to work with variables:

- Get-Variable
- New-Variable
- Set-Variable
- Remove-Variable
- Clear-Variable

When using the variable commands, the $ preceding the variable name is not considered part of the name; $ tells PowerShell what follows is a variable name.

Get-Variable

The Get-Variable command provides access to any variable that has been created in the current session as well as the default (automatic) variables created by PowerShell. For further information on automatic variables, refer to Get-Help about_Automatic_Variables.

Default or automatic variables often have descriptions; these may be seen by using the Get-Variable command and selecting the description:

```
Get-Variable | Select-Object Name, Description
```

The following example shows the first few variables with descriptions:

```
PS> Get-Variable | Select-Object Name, Description

Name                      Description
----                      -----------
?                         Status of last command
^
$
args
ConfirmPreference         Dictates when confirmation should...
DebugPreference           Dictates the action taken when a ...
```

One use for `Get-Variable` is to explore attributes of variables. For example, the presence of a type converter on a variable can be seen in an `Attributes` property, as shown below:

```
[string]$variable = 'Hello world'
Get-Variable variable | ForEach-Object Attributes
```

This will show that there is a type converter, the `TypeId` is deliberately shortened from `System.Management.Automation.ArgumentTypeConverterAttribute` in the example below:

```
TransformNullOptionalParameters TypeId
------------------------------- ------
                           True ArgumentTypeConverterAttribute
```

However, while this example shows the attribute is present, it does not show what type an assigned value will be coerced to.

Getting the type is explored here and makes use of an advanced technique called Reflection. This is explored further in *Chapter 7, Working with .NET*.

The following script shows the type associated with the `$variable` variable:

```
[string]$variable = 'Hello world'

$attribute = (Get-Variable variable).Attributes |
    Where-Object TypeId -match 'ArgumentTypeConverterAttribute'

$attribute.GetType().
    GetProperties('Instance,NonPublic').
    GetMethod.Invoke($attribute, @())
```

The example above will show the type below based on the type applied to `$variable`:

```
IsPublic IsSerial Name                      BaseType
-------- -------- ----                      --------
True     True     String                    System.Object
```

Other metadata, such as a variable description, can only be set when creating a variable using the `New-Variable` command.

New-Variable

The `New-Variable` command can be used to create a variable:

```
New-Variable -Name today -Value (Get-Date)
```

The preceding command is the equivalent of using the following assignment:

```
$today = Get-Date
```

In both cases, the outcome is the creation of a variable holding the current date. The format of the date may vary depending on the date-time format settings of the operating system:

```
PS> $today
24 March 2024 12:37:46
```

`Get-Variable` may also be used to review the created variable:

```
PS> Get-Variable today

Name                          Value
----                          -----
today                         24/03/2024 12:37:46
```

`New-Variable` gives more control over the created variable, including adding metadata such as descriptions. For example, it may be used to create a constant, a variable that cannot be changed after creation:

```
New-Variable -Name startTime -Value (Get-Date) -Option Constant
```

The default output for `Get-Variable` will not show that the variable above is a constant, the `Options` for the variable may be shown using `Select-Object *` or, as used in the example below, `Format-List`:

```
PS> Get-Variable startTime | Format-List

Name        : startTime
Description :
Value       : 24/03/2024 12:41:08
Visibility  : Public
Module      :
ModuleName  :
Options     : Constant
Attributes  : {}
```

Any attempt to modify the variable after creation results in an error message, including changing the variable value or its properties, and attempts to remove the variable, as shown here:

```
PS> New-Variable -Name var -Value 1 -Option Constant
PS> $var = 2
WriteError: Cannot overwrite variable var because it is read-only or constant.
```

A variable cannot be changed into a constant after creation. `Set-Variable` may be used to change other variable metadata.

Set-Variable

The `Set-Variable` command allows certain properties of an existing variable to be changed. For example, the following sets the value of an existing variable:

```
$objectCount = 23
Set-Variable objectCount -Value 42
```

It is not common to see `Set-Variable` used in this manner; it is simpler to assign the new value directly, as was done when the variable was created:

Set-Variable may be used to set a description for a variable:

```
Set-Variable objectCount -Description 'The number of objects in the queue'
```

`Set-Variable` can be used to change a variable's scope to `private`:

```
Set-Variable objectCount -Option Private
```

None of the commands above has output, the result of this sequence of changes may be reviewed using `Get-Variable`. `Format-List` is used to see the properties that are not automatically displayed:

```
PS> Get-Variable objectCount | Format-List


Name        : objectCount
Description : The number of objects in the queue
Value       : 42
Visibility  : Public
Module      :
ModuleName  :
Options     : Private
Attributes  : {}
```

`Private` scope is accessible using `$private:objectCount`. Use of the `Set-Variable` command is not required.

Remove-Variable

As the name suggests, the `Remove-Variable` command removes a variable. If this is the only variable referring to an object, the object will be removed from memory shortly afterward.

The `Remove-Variable` command is used as follows:

```
$psProcesses = Get-Process pwsh
Remove-Variable psProcesses
```

If more than one variable refers to an object, the object will not be removed; removal only occurs when all references to the object are removed. For example, the following command shows the name of the first process running (`conhost.exe`, in this case):

```
PS> $object1 = $object2 = Get-Process | Select-Object -First 1
PS> Remove-Variable object1
PS> Write-Host $object2.Name
conhost
```

It is rarely necessary to explicitly remove a variable in a script or function. Variables defined in a block of code fall out of scope at the end of the block in most cases.

Clear-Variable

The Clear-Variable command removes the value from any existing variable. Clear-Variable does not remove the variable itself. For example, the following example calls Write-Host to show the value of the variable:

```
PS> $temporaryValue = "Some-Value"
PS> Write-Host $temporaryValue -ForegroundColor Green
Some-Value
```

Clear-Variable removes the value of the variable. The command below will display a blank line as the output:

```
Clear-Variable temporaryValue
Write-Host $temporaryValue -ForegroundColor Green
```

Get-Variable can be used to show the variable exists:

```
PS> Get-Variable temporaryValue

Name                            Value
----                            -----
temporaryValue
```

Clear-Variable is likely even less common than Remove-Variable. It is far more common to assign null to a variable:

```
$temporaryValue = $null
```

The variable commands are one way of interacting with existing variables; the PowerShell provider for variables is another.

Variable provider

PowerShell includes a provider and a drive, which allows variables to be listed, created, and changed using Get-ChildItem, Test-Path, and so on.

Get-ChildItem may be used to list all the variables in the current scope by running the command shown as follows:

```
Get-ChildItem variable:
```

The first few variables returned by the command above are shown below. This is the same output as would be seen with `Get-Variable`:

```
Name                            Value
----                            -----
?                               True
^                               if
$                               }
args                            {}
ConfirmPreference               High
DebugPreference                 SilentlyContinue
```

The output shown includes the built-in variables, user-created variables, and any added modules that might have been imported.

As the provider behaves much like a filesystem, `Test-Path` may be used to determine whether a variable exists. `Get-Variable` may be used instead, but `Get-Variable` will throw an error if the variable does not exist:

```
Test-Path variable:\VerbosePreference
```

`Set-Item` may be used to change the value of a variable or create a new variable:

```
Set-Item variable:\new -Value variable
```

`Get-Content` can also be used to retrieve the content of any existing variable:

```
PS> Get-Content variable:\PSHome
C:\Program Files\PowerShell\7
```

The backslash character used in the preceding examples is optional. The following command has the same output:

```
PS> Get-Content variable:PSHome
C:\Program Files\PowerShell\7
```

Additional scope modifiers can be included in the variable path. PSHome is globally scoped, and the global scope modifier can be added to the command:

```
PS> Get-Content variable:global:PSHome
C:\Program Files\PowerShell\7
```

Variables are created in local scope by default.

Variable scope

PowerShell uses scopes to limit access to variables (and other items, such as functions). Scopes are layered one on top of another; child scopes inherit from parent scopes. Parent scopes cannot access variables created in child scopes.

Scopes are also used by PowerShell when optimizing blocks. Locally scoped variables can be optimized for performance, but variables from parent scopes cannot be.

There are three named scopes:

- Global
- Script
- Local

Global is the topmost scope; it is the scope the prompt in the console uses and is available to all child scopes.

The Script scope, as the name suggests, is specific to a single script. Script scoped items are available to all child scopes (such as functions) within that script. The Script scope is also available in modules, making it an ideal place to store variables that should be shared within a module.

Local is the current scope and is therefore relative. In the console, the Local scope is also the Global scope. In a script, the Local scope is the Script scope. Functions and script blocks also have a Local scope of their own.

The sections that follow demonstrate how scopes affect variable lookups. More examples are available in the about_Scopes help document.

By default, variables are created in the current scope, the Local scope. However, variables can be accessed from the Local scope or any parent scope.

Accessing variables

When PowerShell retrieves the value for a variable, it starts by looking for the variable in the Local scope. If the variable does not exist in the Local scope, it looks through parent scopes until it either finds the variable or runs out of scopes to search.

The following script uses two variables. The variable $local exists inside the Write-VariableValue function only. The variable $parent exists outside, in the parent scope, but can be used inside the function:

```
function Write-VariableValue {
    $local = 'value from inside the function'
    Write-Host "Local: $local"
    Write-Host "Parent: $parent"
}
$parent = 'value from parent scope'
```

Running the function will show both values:

```
PS> Write-VariableValue
Local: value from inside the function
Parent: value from parent scope
```

If the preceding content is run in the console, the parent scope is the Global scope. If the function and the call to the function are inside a script, the parent scope is Script.

If the parent variable were explicitly added to the Write-VariableValue function, the locally scoped value would be used instead. For example:

```
function Write-VariableValue {
    $local = 'value from inside the function'
    $parent = 'a new value for parent'
    Write-Host "Local: $local"
    Write-Host "Parent: $parent"
}
$parent = 'value from parent scope'
```

The variable $parent inside the function is locally scoped. Assigning a value inside the function has no effect on the value of the variable outside the function. A new variable is created when a value is assigned to a variable for the first time in that scope.

Scope modifiers can be used to explicitly define the scope of a variable.

Scope modifiers

A scope modifier is placed before the variable name and is followed by a colon. For example, the following variable will always be created in the Global scope:

```
$Global:variableName = 123
```

Scope modifiers are available for the scopes defined above, Global, Local, and Script. Scope modifiers may also be used for the private variable option and provider namespaces such as alias, env, function, and variable. The private option is explored later in this topic.

Any child scope accessing the variable may repeat the same scope modifier both to make it clear where the variable is from and to avoid using a variable of the same name in the Local (or another parent) scope.

Non-local scoped variables in scripts and functions

Using user-defined (not automatic) variables from other scopes in scripts and functions can make code very difficult to follow and test. Variable values must be cross-referenced with variable values from elsewhere in a piece of code.

Adding a scope modifier improves the situation as it clearly shows the origin. However, it is still better to avoid out-of-scope variables where possible.

The creation of a child scope is dependent on where the function or script is called, not where it is written.

Numeric scopes

The Get-Variable command allows a numeric value to be used for the Scope parameter. The numeric value describes how far away from the current scope the variable is. Get-Variable may be used when accessing variables in parent scopes, even when a variable of the same name exists in the Local scope.

In the example below, each function defines one unique variable name and re-uses a variable name:

```
function first {
    $first = $name = 'first'
    Write-Host "first: Name: $name; First: $first"
    second
}
function second {
    $second = $name = 'second'
    Write-Host "second: Name: $name; Second: $second"
    third
}
function third {
    $third = $name = 'third'
    Write-Host "third: Name: $name; Third: $third"
}
```

When the function first is called, first will call second, and second will call third. The output from running first is shown below:

```
PS> first
first: Name: first; First: first
second: Name: second; Second: second
third: Name: third; Third: third
```

This shows that the value of the variable $name changes in each case. The $name variable is in the Local scope in each case.

The scopes for these functions are stacked one on top of the other in the order shown in the following list:

- Global or script
- Local scope for first
- Local scope for second
- Local scope for third

Each function can access variables defined in the parent scope. That is, the function third can access variables defined in the function second, variables defined in the function first, as well as any variables in the Global or Script scope.

The variables $first, $second, and $third are unique in the script and are therefore accessible in any child scope. The function third can access the value of $first with no special effort, as shown here:

```
function first {
    $first = $name = 'first'
    second
}
function second {
    $second = $name = 'second'
    third
}
function third {
    "The value of first is $first"
}
first
```

Accessing the value of the $name variable from a specific parent scope requires the Get-Variable command. As described previously, the Scope parameter accepts a numeric value, defined by the number of scopes the given variable is away from the current scope.

In the function third, the value of the variable $name in second is 1 scope away; the value of the variable $name in first is two scopes away. The changes to the function third below, show how Get-Variable can be used to access those variables:

```
function first {
    $first = $name = 'first'
    second
}
function second {
    $second = $name = 'second'
    third
}
function third {
    "The value of name in first is {0}" -f @(
        Get-Variable -Name name -Scope 2 -ValueOnly
    )
    "The value of name in second is {0}" -f @(
        Get-Variable -Name name -Scope 1 -ValueOnly
    )
}
first
```

In the preceding example, if the function second, or third, is run directly, an error will be displayed. For example, running third directly will show the following errors:

```
PS> third
Get-Variable:
Line |
   3 |             Get-Variable -Name name -Scope 2 -ValueOnly
     |             ~~~~~~~~~~~~~~~~~~~~~~~~~~~~~~~~~~~~~~~~~~~~~~
     | The scope number '2' exceeds the number of active scopes. (Parameter
'Scope')
Actual value was 2.
Get-Variable:
Line |
   6 |             Get-Variable -Name name -Scope 1 -ValueOnly
     |             ~~~~~~~~~~~~~~~~~~~~~~~~~~~~~~~~~~~~~~~~~~~~~~
     | Cannot find a variable with the name 'name'.
```

The technique used in the preceding is instructive but is rarely found in production code.

The ability to access variables from parent scopes is affected by the private option, which may be used when creating a variable.

Private variables

A private variable is hidden from child scopes. A private variable may either be created using New-Variable or by using the Private scope modifier, as shown in the following examples:

```
New-Variable -Name thisValue -Option Private
$private:thisValue = "Some value"
```

In the following example, a $name variable is set in the first two functions. The variable is private in the function second:

```
function first {
    $name = 'first'
    second
}
function second {
    $private:name = 'second'
    third
}
function third {
    "In the function third the value of name is $name"
}
```

When the function third uses the $name variable, PowerShell searches through parent scopes since the variable does not exist in the local scope. As the $name variable is private in the function second, that variable value is ignored. PowerShell retrieves the value of the $name variable from the scope for the function first.

The output from calling first is shown below:

```
PS> first
In the function third the value of name is first
```

It is still possible to get the value of the private variable using a numeric scope with the Get-Variable command as demonstrated in the previous section.

Scopes are an important part of PowerShell and are used by more than variables. Certain settings, such as strict mode, are scoped, as are preference variables and functions. Functions are explored in *Chapter 17, Scripts, Functions, and Script Blocks*.

About arrays

An array contains a collection of objects. Each entry in the array is called an element, and each element has an index (position). Indexing in an array starts from 0.

Arrays are an important part of PowerShell. When the return from a command is assigned to a variable, an array will be the result if the command returns more than one object. For example, the following command will yield an array of objects:

```
$processes = Get-Process
```

Arrays created in PowerShell use a non-specific type.

Array type

In PowerShell, arrays are, by default, given the System.Object[] type – an array of objects where [] is used to signify that it is an array.

> **Why System.Object?**
>
> All object instances are derived from a .NET type or class, and, in .NET, every object instance is derived from System.Object (including strings and integers). Therefore, a System.Object array in PowerShell can hold just about anything.

Arrays in PowerShell (and .NET) are immutable (fixed size). The size is declared on creation and cannot be changed. A new array must be created if an element is to be added or removed.

The array operations described next are considered less efficient for large arrays because of the recreation overhead involved in changing the array size.

The following sections explore creating arrays, assigning a type to the array, and selecting elements, as well as adding and removing elements.

When the result of a command is assigned to a variable, and the command returned more than one item, an array is created. For example:

```
$processes = Get-Process
```

This can be seen using the `GetType` method on the variable:

```
PS> $processes.GetType()

IsPublic IsSerial Name      BaseType
-------- -------- ----      --------
True     True     Object[]  System.Array
```

If the command emitted a single value only, the result would be a scalar, a single item of whatever type the command returns:

```
PS> $processes = Get-Process -Id $PID
PS> $processes.GetType()

IsPublic IsSerial Name     BaseType
-------- -------- ----     --------
True     False    Process  System.ComponentModel.Component
```

Enclosing the command in the array sub-expression operator would ensure the value was an array regardless of how many values the command returns (zero, one, or many):

```
$processes = @(Get-Process -Id $PID)
```

Before considering how to explicitly create an array, it is worth considering if it is necessary at all.

Creation by assignment

In PowerShell, all statements can be assigned. It is common to find arrays created and filled as shown below:

```
$array = @()
foreach ($value in 1..5) {
    $array += [PSCustomObject]@{
        Value = $value
    }
}
```

A simpler and more efficient way to write the same statement is shown here:

```
$array = foreach ($value in 1..5) {
    [PSCustomObject]@{
        Value = $value
    }
}
```

Assigning the loop (in this case) immediately avoids the problem of deciding what kind of array to create and how to fill it. The PowerShell engine takes care of that, and the result is assigned when the loop completes.

Loops such as foreach are explored in more detail in *Chapter 6, Conditional Statements and Loops*.

If necessary, it is also possible to create and slowly fill an array.

Creating an array

There are several ways to create arrays. An empty array (containing no elements) can be created by using the array sub-expression operator:

```
$myArray = @()
```

An empty array of a specific size may be created using the new method. Using [ ] after the name of the type denotes that it is an array, and the number following sets the array size:

```
$myArray = [object[]]::new(10)        # 10 objects
$byteArray = [byte[]]::new(100)       # 100 bytes
$ipAddresses = [IPAddress[]]::new(5)  # 5 IP addresses
```

It is typically not necessary to create an array in advance like this.

An array with a few strings in it can be created by assigning values directly to a variable:

```
$myGreetings = "Hello world", "Hello sun", "Hello moon"
```

Alternatively, the array sub-expression operator can be used:

```
$myGreetings = @("Hello world", "Hello sun", "Hello moon")
```

An array may be spread over multiple lines in either the console or a script, which may make it easier to read in a script:

```
$myGreetings = @(
    "Hello world"
    "Hello sun"
    "Hello moon"
)
```

Elements with different types can be mixed in a single array:

```
$myThings = "Hello world", 2, 34.23, (Get-Date)
```

When splitting over lines inside the array sub-expression operator, the parentheses around the Get-Date command are not required:

```
$myThings = @(
    "Hello world"
    2
    34.23
    Get-Date
)
```

If the content of the variable is displayed, it will show that each expression has been executed. Each item in the array is displayed on a new line:

```
PS> $myThings
Hello world
2
34.23

24 March 2024 13:17:34
```

Arrays may be cast to a specific type by including the array type on the left or right of an assignment.

Arrays with a type

An array may be given a type in a similar manner to a variable holding a single value. The difference is that the type name is followed by [ ], as was the case when creating an empty array of a specific size. For example, each of these is an array type that may appear before a variable name:

```
[string[]]      # An array of strings
[ulong[]]       # An array of unsigned 64-bit integers
[xml[]]         # An array of XML documents
```

If a type is set for the array, more care must be taken as regards assigning values. If a type is declared, PowerShell attempts to convert any value assigned to an array element into that type.

In this example, $null will become 0 and 3.45 (a double) will become 3 (normal rounding rules apply when converting integers):

```
[int[]]$myNumbers = 1, 2, $null, 3.45
```

The following example shows an error being thrown, as a string cannot be converted into an integer:

```
PS> [int[]]$myNumbers = 1, 2, $null, "A string"
MetadataError: Cannot convert value "A string" to type "System.Int32". Error:
"Input string was not in a correct format."
```

Elements may be added to an array using the addition operator.

Adding elements to an array

A single item, or another array, can be added to the end of an array using the assignment by addition operator:

```
$myArray = @()
$myArray += 'New value'
```

The preceding command is equivalent to the following:

```
$myArray = $myArray + 'New value'
```

The addition operator can be used to join one array to another, as shown below:

```
$firstArray = 1, 2, 3
$secondArray = 4, 5, 6
$mergedArray = $firstArray + $secondArray
```

Looking at the content of $mergedArray will show it contains all the values from $firstArray and $secondArray:

```
PS> $mergedArray
1
2
3
4
5
6
```

Using the array sub-expression, @( ), around a set of elements or expressions is often the cleanest way to merge values into a single array:

```
$firstArray = 1, 2, 3
$mergedArray = @(
    Get-Date
    'someString'
    $firstArray
)
```

Each of the statements in the array sub-expression will be evaluated. The content of the $mergedArray variable can be shown:

```
PS> $mergedArray

24 March 2024 13:22:24
someString
1
2
3
```

For arrays of a few elements, the cost to add elements like this is trivial and can be ignored. Arrays scaling up to hundreds or thousands of elements may need a different approach.

List and ArrayList

If an array must be created, and it cannot be created by assigning a statement (such as a loop) it is frequently better to make use of a resizable collection. For example, a script might want to separate values into two separate arrays inside a loop.

A List can be created, which holds objects:

```
$list = [System.Collections.Generic.List[object]]::new()
```

Then, elements may be added to this collection using the Add or AddRange methods:

```
$list.Add('New value')
```

This avoids the recreation penalty associated with adding to a fixed-size array.

When using AddRange with a List, the array type being added must be of the same type as the list.

For example, if a list of strings is created, any array being added must be of the same type:

```
$stringList = [System.Collections.Generic.List[string]]::new()
$array = 'one', 'two'
$stringList.AddRange([string[]]$array)
```

If the cast to a string array is omitted from the example above, an error will be raised:

```
PS> $stringList.AddRange($array)
MethodException: Cannot convert argument "collection", with value:
"System.Object[]", for "AddRange" to type "System.Collections.Generic.
IEnumerable`1[System.String]": "Cannot convert the "System.Object[]"
value of type "System.Object[]" to type "System.Collections.Generic.
IEnumerable`1[System.String]"."
```

A popular, but older, alternative to the generic list is an ArrayList:

```
$arrayList = [System.Collections.ArrayList]::new()
```

Elements can be added to the list using the Add or AddRange methods:

```
$arrayList.Add('New value')
```

With the ArrayList, adding an element returns the index of the added element. Therefore, it is often necessary to suppress output. The example below makes use of Out-Null for this, which is a good option in PowerShell 7:

```
$arrayList.Add('New value') | Out-Null
```

Assigning to null or casting to void is another solution, and a fast approach for Windows PowerShell:

```
$null = $arrayList.Add('New value')
[void]$arrayList.Add('New value')
```

Unassigned output from methods like this will otherwise become output from the function or script.

Lists like these do not need to be explicitly created and filled; they can be created when assigning a value. For example, when assigning output from a command:

```
[System.Collections.Generic.List[object]]$processes = Get-Process
```

Or, when assigning the output from a loop:

```
[System.Collections.Generic.List[object]]$list =
    foreach ($value in 1..5) {
        [PSCustomObject]@{
            Value = $value
        }
    }
```

This allows immediate use of the advanced features of these collections.

Get-Member may be used to view the methods available on either collection type. Note that the example below explicitly uses the InputObject parameter. This avoids getting the members of the elements in the collection:

```
Get-Member -InputObject $list
Get-Member -InputObject $arrayList
```

Elements in an array have an index, a zero-based position.

Selecting elements from an array

Individual elements from an array may be selected by index. The first and second elements are available using index 0 and 1:

```
PS> $myArray = 1, 2, 3, 4, 5, 6, 7, 8, 9, 10
PS> $myArray[0]
1
PS> $myArray[1]
2
```

In a similar manner, array elements can be accessed counting backward from the end. The last element is available using -1 as the index, and the penultimate element uses -2 as the index. For example:

```
PS> $myArray[-1]
10
PS> $myArray[-2]
9
```

Ranges of elements may be selected either going forward (starting from 0) or going backward (starting with -1):

```
PS> $myArray[2..4]
3
4
5
```

```
PS> $myArray[-1..-5]
10
9
8
7
6
```

More than one range can be selected in a single statement:

```
PS> $myArray[0..2 + 6..8 + -1]
1
2
3
7
8
9
10
```

This requires some care. The first part of the index set must be an array for the addition operation to succeed; an array cannot be added to an integer. The expression in square brackets is evaluated first and converted into a single array (of indexes) before any elements are selected from the array:

```
PS> $myArray[0 + 6..8 + -1]
InvalidOperation: Method invocation failed because [System.Object[]] does not
contain a method named 'op_Addition'.
```

The same error would be shown when running the expression within square brackets alone:

```
0..2 + 6..8 + -1
```

The following modified command shows three different ways to achieve the intended result:

```
$myArray[@(0) + 6..8 + -1]
$myArray[0..0 + 6..8 + -1]
$myArray[@(0; 6..8; -1)]
```

Each of the examples above will show the output below:

```
1
7
8
9
10
```

As well as selecting elements by index, elements may be selected by value in several different ways.

The IndexOf method may be used to find the position of a value within the array, then the value may be accessed:

```
PS> $index = $myArray.IndexOf(5)
PS> $index
4
PS> $myArray[$index]
5
```

If the value of $index is -1, the value does not exist within the array. For example:

```
PS> $myArray.IndexOf(11)
-1
```

Comparison operators may be used to select elements from the array. For example, using the -gt operator:

```
PS> $myArray -gt 5
6
7
8
9
10
```

Or, using the -lt operator:

```
PS> $myArray -lt 3
1
2
```

Comparisons can be chained together to build more complex expressions provided each part of the expression continues to return an array:

```
PS> $myArray -gt 3 -lt 7
4
5
6
```

For more complex filtering expressions, Where-Object may be used:

```
PS> $myArray | Where-Object { $_ -lt 3 -or $_ -gt 7 }
1
2
8
9
10
```

The Where method may also be used to filter the array. This example has the same output as the Where-Object version:

```
$myArray.Where{ $_ -lt 3 -or $_ -gt 7 }
```

The Where method is faster than Where-Object but will raise an error if the variable is not an array.

Changing element values in an array

Elements within an array may be changed by assigning a new value to a specific index, for example:

```
$myArray = 1, 2, 9, 4, 5
$myArray[2] = 3
```

Elements in an array may be changed within a loop. The following example sets all elements in the array to 9:

```
$myArray = 1, 2, 3, 4, 5
for ($i = 0; $i -lt $myArray.Count; $i++) {
    $myArray[$i] = 9
}
```

Removing elements from a fixed-size array requires recreation of the array.

Removing elements

Elements cannot be removed from a fixed-size array except by recreating the array. This is an extension of selecting elements from an array.

Elements can be removed from List and ArrayList collections by making use of the different Remove methods.

For example, with a list of strings, the Remove method can remove by value:

```
$list = [System.Collections.Generic.List[string]]@('a', 'b', 'c')
$list.Remove('a')
```

Or, the RemoveAt method removes a value at a specific index:

```
$list.RemoveAt(0)
```

After these two operations, the list will only contain the value c.

For fixed-size arrays, it is possible to remove elements by filtering (see *Selecting elements from an array*), or by omitting specific indexes in a copy.

Removing elements by index

Removing elements based on an index requires the creation of a new array and the omission of the value in the element in that index. In each of the following cases, an array with 100 elements will be used as an example; the element at index 49 (with a value of 50) will be removed:

```
$oldArray = 1..100
```

The following example uses indexes to access and add everything we want to keep:

```
$newArray = $oldArray[0..48] + $oldArray[50..99]
```

Using the .NET `Array.Copy` static method. Methods are explored in more detail in *Chapter 7, Working with .NET*.

The example below uses the Copy method to fill a new array with part of the original:

```
$newArray = [Object[]]::new($oldArray.Count - 1)
# Before the index
[Array]::Copy(
    $oldArray,      # Source
    $newArray,      # Destination
    49              # Number of elements to copy
)
# After the index
[Array]::Copy(
    $oldArray,      # Source
    50,             # Copy from index of Source
    $newArray,      # Destination
    49,             # Copy to index of Destination
    50              # Number of elements to copy
)
```

This operation is relatively complex, and it may be better to consider using a resizable collection instead.

Arrays and collections can be used to set the value of multiple variables.

Filling variables from arrays

It is possible to create two (or more) variables by assigning an array to a comma-separated list (an array) of variables:

```
$i, $j = 1, 2
```

Looking at the value of each variable will show it has a value assigned from the array on the right. For example, the value of the variable $i:

```
PS> $i
1
```

Assigning variables from an array can be useful when splitting a string:

```
$firstName, $lastName = -split "First Last"
$firstName, $lastName = "First Last".Split()
```

If the array is longer than the number of variables, all remaining elements are assigned to the last variable. For example, the variable $k will contain 3, 4, and 5, as follows:

```
PS> $i, $j, $k = 1, 2, 3, 4, 5
PS> $k
3
4
5
```

If there are too few elements, the remaining variables will not be assigned a value. In this example, $k will be null:

```
$i, $j, $k = 1, 2
```

If it is desirable to discard part of a split operation, one or more of the variables on the left can be $null:

```
$firstName, $null, $lastName = -split "First A. Last"
```

First and Last can be shown to have values:

```
PS> [PSCustomObject]@{ First = $firstName; Last = $lastName }

First Last
----- ----
First Last
```

The value A. in this example will be assigned to null and therefore discarded.

It is possible to create multi-dimensional arrays in PowerShell.

Multi-dimensional and jagged arrays

Given that an array contains objects, an array can therefore also contain other arrays.

For example, an array that contains other arrays (a multi-dimensional array) might be created as follows:

```
$arrayOfArrays = @(
    @(1, 2, 3),
    @(4, 5, 6),
    @(7, 8, 9)
)
```

Be careful to ensure that the comma following each of the nested arrays (except the last) is in place. If that comma is missing, the entire structure will be flattened, merging the three inner arrays.

Elements in the preceding array are accessed by indexing into each array in turn (starting with the outermost). The element with the value 2 is accessible using the following notation:

```
PS> $arrayOfArrays[0][1]
2
```

This states that we wish to retrieve the first element (which is an array) and the second element of that array.

The element with the value 6 is accessible using the following:

```
PS> $arrayOfArrays[1][2]
6
```

A jagged array is a specific type of multi-dimensional array. An example of a jagged array is as follows:

```
$arrayOfArrays = @(
    @(1,  2),
    @(4,  5,  6,  7,  8,  9),
    @(10, 11, 12)
)
```

As in the first example, it is an array containing arrays. Instead of containing inner arrays, which all share the same size (dimension), the inner arrays have no consistent size (hence, they are jagged).

In this example, the element with the value 9 is accessed as follows:

```
PS> $arrayOfArrays[1][5]
9
```

Multi-dimensional arrays are rarely used in PowerShell. PowerShell tends to flatten arrays, which can make working with complex array structures difficult.

About hashtables

A hashtable is an associative array or an indexed array. Values in the hashtable are added with a unique key. Each key has a value associated with it; this is also known as a key-value pair. Keys cannot be duplicated within the hashtable.

A hashtable is one of several collections broadly known as dictionaries. In each case, the dictionary uses a key to identify a value in the collection.

Hashtables, and dictionaries in general, are incredibly widely used in PowerShell.

For example, *Chapter 1, Introduction to PowerShell,* made use of hashtables when exploring splatting.

They can be used as arguments for parameters by commands such as `Select-Object`, `Sort-Object`, `Group-Object`, `Format-List`, and `Format-Table`. They are also used by many others to accept generic sets of arguments.

Hashtables are used repeatedly throughout this book.

An empty hashtable can be created, or a set of initial values can be set.

Creating a Hashtable

An empty Hashtable is created in much the same way as an empty array. The @ symbol followed by curly braces is used to denote that this is a hashtable:

```
$hashtable = @{}
```

Alternatively, a hashtable may be created with specific keys and values:

```
$hashtable = @{ Key1 = "Value1"; Key2 = "Value2" }
```

Elements in a Hashtable may be spread across multiple lines to make it easier to read:

```
$hashtable = @{
    Key1 = 'Value1'
    Key2 = 'Value2'
}
```

In both cases, the hashtable will display as having names (keys) and values:

```
PS> $hashtable

Name                            Value
----                            -----
Key1                            Value1
Key2                            Value2
```

Unlike fixed-size arrays, hashtables may have keys and values added or removed without penalty.

Adding, changing, and removing keys

The most common way of adding an element to a hashtable is to assign a value to a key. This can make use of the index operator:

```
PS> $hashtable = @{}
PS> $hashtable['Key1'] = 'Value1'
PS> $hashtable

Name                            Value
----                            -----
Key1                            Value1
```

Or, a key can be created using the property dereference operator, a dot:

```
$hashtable = @{}
$hashtable.Key1 = "Value1"
```

In either case, if the key exists in the hashtable, the value will be overwritten.

Alternatively, the Add method may be used:

```
PS> $hashtable = @{}
PS> $hashtable.Add("Key1", "Value1")
PS> $hashtable

Name                              Value
----                              -----
Key1                              Value1
```

If the value already exists, using Add generates an error (as shown here):

```
PS> $hashtable = @{ Existing = "Value0" }
PS> $hashtable.Add("Existing", "Value1")
MethodInvocationException: Exception calling "Add" with "2" argument(s):
"Item has already been added. Key in dictionary: 'Existing'  Key being added:
'Existing'"
```

The Contains or ContainsKey method can be combined with any of the approaches above to control when a value is added, changed, or read:

```
$hashtable = @{
    Key1 = 'Value1'
    Key2 = 'Value2'
}
if (-not $hashtable.Contains('Key3')) {
    $hashtable.Key3 = 'Value3'
}
```

ContainsKey is used in the same way, but while Contains is implemented by a hashtable, ContainsKey is implemented by all dictionary types:

```
if (-not $hashtable.ContainsKey('Key3')) {
    $hashtable.Key3 = 'Value3'
}
```

Keys can be removed from the hashtable using the Remove method:

```
$hashtable.Remove('Key3')
```

Hashtables can be used in PowerShell as an incredibly powerful filtering technique.

Using a hashtable to filter

The lookup of a key in a hashtable is extremely fast; this makes it an exceptional choice for filtering or finding the union of two collections of values.

The snippet below creates two relatively large arrays where a subset of values overlap:

```
$left = 1..10000 | ForEach-Object {
    [PSCustomObject]@{ UserID  = "User$_" }
}
$right = 6400..20000 | ForEach-Object {
    [PSCustomObject]@{ UserID = "User$_" }
}
```

The arrays used here are deliberately large, and the point they overlap is arbitrary.

The goal in this example is to find the overlap between left and right. An inner join.

One simple, but slow, approach is to use Where-Object and the In parameter:

```
$left | Where-Object UserID -in $right.UserID
```

A rough approximation of the time required can be found using Measure-Object. The actual time will depend on the hardware PowerShell has access to:

```
Measure-Command { $left | Where-Object UserID -in $right.UserID }
```

This approach will work, but it is slow. It will easily take several seconds to complete.

Each incoming element from left must be compared against all values from right, until it finds the first match. For User10000, it must search through and reject 9,999 other elements before it finds a match.

More broadly, the operation must loop through the content of $right 10,000 times, once for each value in $left.

This operation can be made significantly faster by making use of a hashtable. First, a lookup hashtable is created from $right:

```
$rightLookup = @{}
$right | ForEach-Object {
    $rightLookup[$_.UserID] = $_
}
```

Then the lookup hashtable is used to test for the value:

```
$left | Where-Object { $rightLookup.Contains($_.UserID) }
```

This has the same result as the version making use of In, but the operation executes in a fraction of the time. This time required should be measurable in a relatively small number of milliseconds.

The speed of this operation is somewhat affected by the loop style. In this case, Where-Object is used to iterate over each element in the array. A keyword loop such as foreach would be faster still. Loops are explored in *Chapter 6, Conditional Statements and Loops*.

A hashtable is not the only collection type that can be used here. Another option is a `HashSet`, which is demonstrated below. The implementation of the hash lookup is the same in either case:

```
$rightLookup = [System.Collections.Generic.HashSet[string]]::new(
    [string[]]$right.UserID,
    [StringComparer]::OrdinalIgnoreCase
)
$left | Where-Object { $rightLookup.Contains($_.UserID) }
```

Hashtables are implicitly case-insensitive in PowerShell, but the `HashSet` used here is not. A case-insensitive comparer must be explicitly provided, making for a more complex solution.

The `HashSet` can also only contain the key, not a value. If the two arrays contained different properties, this would be less useful than a hashtable.

For example, if `$left` and `$right` hold a few unique properties:

```
$left = 1..10000 | ForEach-Object {
    [PSCustomObject]@{
        UserID  = "User$_"
        Country = "UK"
    }
}
$right = 6400..20000 | ForEach-Object {
    [PSCustomObject]@{
        UserID = "User$_"
        City   = "Manchester"
    }
}
```

Assuming the `Country` and `City` values are different for each user, the related values from each set are required to join the sets together.

The example below extends filtering the set to adding a `City` value to each user from `$left`. The matched values are returned as output:

```
$rightLookup = @{}
$right | ForEach-Object {
    $rightLookup[$_.UserID] = $_
}
$left |
    Where-Object { $rightLookup.Contains($_.UserID) } |
    ForEach-Object {
        $_.City = $rightLookup[$_.UserID].City
        $_
    }
```

This allows the two sets to be joined very efficiently.

It is often necessary to enumerate the values within a hashtable.

Enumerating a Hashtable

The content of a hashtable can be enumerated in several different ways. The most common way is to make use of the GetEnumerator method, which turns the keys and values into an array:

```
$hashtable = @{
    Key1 = 'Value1'
    Key2 = 'Value2'
}
```

Using the method on the hashtable above will result in an array of names and values:

```
PS> $hashtable.GetEnumerator()

Name                              Value
----                              -----
Key2                              Value2
Key1                              Value1
```

The Name property may also be referred to as Key. Name is an alias for the Key property.

It is also possible to access the Keys and Values properties of the hashtables to get keys only or values only, respectively:

```
PS> $hashtable.Keys
Key2
Key1
```

The Values property returns values only; the key holding the value is not accessible when using this property:

```
PS> $hashtable.Values
Value2
Value1
```

When using these properties, it is possible to bump into a problem if one of the keys in the hashtable is named Keys, or one of the values is named Values.

For example, consider the following hashtable:

```
$user = @{
    UserID = 'User1'
    Keys   = 'Office', 'Workshop'
}
```

If the Keys property is accessed, PowerShell hides it behind the key in the hashtable itself:

```
PS> $user.Keys
Office
Workshop
```

To work around this problem, the hidden get_Keys method can be used instead:

```
PS> $user.get_Keys()
Keys
UserID
```

At this point, it should be noted that the order of keys in a hashtable is not guaranteed. They appear in hash order, which is not very predictable and should not be depended upon.

If the order of a hashtable is important, then an OrderedDictionary should be used.

About Ordered

OrderedDictionary is made available in PowerShell by using the [Ordered] keyword. This was introduced along with PSCustomObject in PowerShell 3.

An OrderedDictionary preserves the order in which keys were added. For example:

```
$ordered = [Ordered]@{
    One   = 1
    Two   = 2
    Three = 3
}
```

Viewing the value of $ordered will show the keys appear in the same order they were entered:

```
PS> $ordered

Name                           Value
----                           -----
One                            1
Two                            2
Three                          3
```

Conversely, a hashtable may show the keys in a different order:

```
PS> @{ One = 1; Two = 2; Three = 3 }

Name                           Value
----                           -----
Two                            2
Three                          3
One                            1
```

In PowerShell 7, a type accelerator exists for [Ordered], which makes the derivation of the type fairly easy to understand.

In Windows PowerShell, the following code will succeed:

```
[Ordered]@{ One = 1 }
```

But attempting to directly access [Ordered] as a type will fail:

```
PS> [Ordered]
Unable to find type [Ordered].
At line:1 char:1
+ [Ordered]
+ ~~~~~~~~~
    + CategoryInfo          : InvalidOperation: (Ordered:TypeName) [],
RuntimeException
    + FullyQualifiedErrorId : TypeNotFound
```

Ordered is a parser instruction. It can order values only because it sends the parser down a very specific branch of code, which creates things in the order entered. That Windows PowerShell cannot find the type is a symptom of this; it does not need to be able to resolve the type because it is more like a keyword than a type.

Note that the PSCustomObject type accelerator is also a parser instruction and uses much the same code to preserve order.

Beyond the parser specialization, OrderedDictionary may be used in the same way as a hashtable. It is a great way to build up custom objects when the list of properties is not known in advance.

This small example shows that new properties can be added in the order they are listed in the array. The actual values are based on the PowerShell executable path:

```
$properties = @(
    'FullName'
    'Length'
)

$item = Get-Item (Get-Process -Id $PID).Path

$customObject = [Ordered]@{}
$properties | ForEach-Object {
    $customObject.$_ = $item.$_
}
[PSCustomObject]$customObject
```

Ordered is used widely in PowerShell to dynamically build objects where the properties might not be known in advance.

Summary

In this chapter, we explored the creation of and interaction with variables in PowerShell, a fundamental part of any scripting language.

Variables can be used in strings to create dynamic content in code. The use of provider-specific variables in strings was explored.

Variable commands can be used to interact with variables beyond changing the value, such as setting a description, making a variable in a specific scope, or exploring the facets of a variable.

Variable scope was explored, and scope modifiers were introduced, which can affect the scope in which a variable is set.

Arrays and more advanced collections were introduced as a means of storing large sets of data. The idea of assigning statements instead of explicitly building arrays was introduced as the simplest and most performance-friendly approach.

Finally, hashtables and ordered dictionaries were explored. Hashtables are very widely used in PowerShell for multiple purposes and can be used as indexed lookups to build fast comparisons.

The next chapter explores branching and looping in PowerShell.

Learn more on Discord

Read this book alongside other users, PowerShell experts, and the author himself. Ask questions, provide solutions to other readers, chat with the author via Ask Me Anything sessions, and much more.

Scan the QR code or visit the link to join the community.

https://packt.link/SecNet

4

Working with Objects in PowerShell

Everything in PowerShell revolves around working with objects. An object is a representation of a thing, and realistically, that can be anything. However, at this stage, it is better to stick with things PowerShell already does.

The Get-Process command in PowerShell returns objects that represent running processes in the operating system. The processes are broadly described by the Process type.

Type is a term .NET uses to describe the abstract representation of a thing. Abstract because it does not represent any single process (in this case), but how a process should look to the programming language (like PowerShell).

A single specific process is represented by an instance of the Type.

At this point, it can be said that running Get-Process returns instances of the Process Type. Each Process instance is therefore a single object.

Instances of a Type, like the Process object, have what are known as Members. There are different types of Members, two of which are called Properties and Methods (in PowerShell). These are the only two Member types explored in this chapter.

The descriptions of Types and Members started here are explored again and in more detail in *Chapter 7, Working with .NET.*

An object is a representation of a thing, for example, this book might be represented as an object in PowerShell.

A book is an object that can have properties that describe its physical characteristics, such as the number of pages, the weight, or physical size. It has metadata (information about data) properties that describe the author, the publisher, the table of contents, and so on.

The book might also have methods. A method might affect the state of an object. For example, there might be methods to open or close the book or methods to jump to different chapters. A method might also convert an object into a different format. For example, there might be a method to copy a page, or even destructive methods such as one to split or dispose of the book.

Properties are therefore used to describe information about a thing. For example, the Process object includes Properties, which holds the process name, the amount of memory the process is using, and so on.

Methods are used to act, to change something about the object, or to make something new. The Process object includes methods that can be used to Close or Kill the process. It also includes a ToString method to convert the (representation of the) Process object into a string.

PowerShell has a variety of commands to work with objects, either for the purpose of discovery such as Get-Member, or to select, filter, format, and so on. These commands are typically used in a pipeline.

This chapter covers the following topics:

- Pipelines
- Members
- Enumerating and filtering
- Selecting and sorting
- Grouping and measuring
- Comparing
- Importing, exporting, and converting
- Formatting

Pipelines in PowerShell allow output from one command to be passed to another.

Pipelines

The pipeline is one of the most prominent features of PowerShell. The pipeline is used to send output from one command to another command as input.

Most of the output from a command is sent to what is known as standard output, often shortened to stdout.

Standard output

The term standard output is used because there are different kinds of output. Each of these different types of output is sent to a different stream, allowing each to be read separately. In PowerShell, the streams are Standard, Error, Warning, Verbose, Debug, and Information.

When assigning the output of a command to a variable, the assigned value is taken from the standard output (the output stream) of a command. For example, the following command assigns the data from the standard output to a variable:

```
$computerSystem = Get-CimInstance -ClassName Win32_ComputerSystem
```

Non-standard output, such as Verbose, will not be assigned to the variable.

Non-standard output

In PowerShell, each of the streams has a command associated with it:

Stream	Command	Stream number
Standard output	Write-Output	1
Error	Write-Error	2
Warning	Write-Warning	3
Verbose	Write-Verbose	4
Debug	Write-Debug	5
Information	Write-Information	6

Table 4.1: Streams and their associated commands

In PowerShell 5 and later, the `Write-Host` command is a wrapper for `Write-Information`. It sends output to the information stream.

Prior to Windows PowerShell 5, `Write-Host` did not have a dedicated stream; the output could only be captured via a transcript, that is, by using the `Start-Transcript` command to log console output to a file.

For example, if the Verbose switch is added to the preceding command, more information is shown. This extra information is not held in the variable; it is sent to a different stream:

```
PS> $computerSystem = Get-CimInstance Win32_ComputerSystem -Verbose
VERBOSE: Perform operation 'Enumerate CimInstances' with following parameters,
''namespaceName' = root\cimv2,'className' = Win32_ComputerSystem'.
VERBOSE: Operation 'Enumerate CimInstances' complete.
```

The content of the variable can be reviewed afterward, showing it does not contain the Verbose message:

```
PS> $computerSystem

Name   PrimaryOwnerName   Domain      TotalPhysicalMemory   Model
----   ----------------   ------      -------------------   -----
NAME   Username           WORKGROUP   17076875264           Model
```

PowerShell is not limited to sending strings between commands in a pipeline.

The Object pipeline

Languages such as batch script (on Windows) or tools on Linux and Unix often use a pipeline to pass text between commands. When the output from one command is piped to another, it is up to the next command in the pipeline to figure out what the text from the input pipeline means.

PowerShell, on the other hand, sends objects from one command to another when using the pipeline.

The pipe (|) symbol is used to send the standard output between commands.

In the following example, the output of Get-Process is sent to the Where-Object command, which applies a filter. The filter used in the example below returns only processes that are using more than 50 MB of memory according to the WorkingSet64 property:

```
Get-Process | Where-Object WorkingSet64 -gt 50MB
```

Any number of commands can be added to the pipeline, each command filtering, selecting, sorting, or changing the output from the command before it.

As pipelines can be long, it can be useful to add a line break between commands:

```
Get-Process |
    Where-Object WorkingSet64 -gt 50MB |
    Select-Object -Property Name, ID
```

Or, in PowerShell 7, the pipe may be placed at the start of the following line within a script or script block. To demonstrate in the console, hold *Shift* and press *Return* at the end of each line; the prompt will change to >> for each subsequent line:

```
Get-Process
    | Where-Object WorkingSet64 -gt 50MB
    | Select-Object Name, ID
```

When the pipe is placed at the end of a line, the command can be pasted or typed in the console as-is. When using a pipe at the beginning of a new line, *Shift + Return* must be used in the console to add the new line without ending the code block.

No special action is required in a script or function to use the pipe at the beginning of the line.

Two generalized rules can be applied to any pipeline created in PowerShell:

- Filter as far left in a pipeline as possible.
- Format as far right in a pipeline as possible.

If the first command in a pipeline can filter, then filtering should be done there if possible. Otherwise, a command like Where-Object, explored in more detail later in this chapter, might be added as the second command in a pipeline.

In the example above, the WorkingSet64 name is a Property, one of the members of the object returned by the Get-Process command.

Members

Members, as described at the beginning of this chapter, are used to interact with an object.

Members of objects in PowerShell have several possible origins:

- Members are defined by a .NET type.
- Members can be added by PowerShell (essentially by the PowerShell team).

- Members can be added by a user or developer in PowerShell.

The Get-Member command is one of the most important discovery tools available in PowerShell.

The Get-Member command

The Get-Member command can be used to view the different members of an object. For example, it can be used to list the members of a Process object returned by Get-Process. The $PID automatic variable holds the process ID of the current PowerShell process:

```
PS> Get-Process -Id $PID | Get-Member


    TypeName: System.Diagnostics.Process


Name            MemberType     Definition
----            ----------     ----------
Handles         AliasProperty  Handles = Handlecount
Name            AliasProperty  Name = ProcessName
NPM             AliasProperty  NPM = NonpagedSystemMemorySize64
PM              AliasProperty  PM = PagedMemorySize64
SI              AliasProperty  SI = SessionId
```

In this case, the first few members are AliasProperty. This is an example of a member that has been added by the command developer.

Get-Member offers filters using its parameters (MemberType, Static, and View). For example, to view the properties of the PowerShell process object, the following can be used:

```
Get-Process -Id $PID | Get-Member -MemberType Property
```

The first few lines of output are shown below again. This time, each of the members is a Property:

```
    TypeName: System.Diagnostics.Process


Name                MemberType Definition
----                ---------- ----------
BasePriority        Property   int BasePriority {get;}
Container           Property   System.ComponentModel.IContai...
EnableRaisingEvents Property   bool EnableRaisingEvents {get...
ExitCode            Property   int ExitCode {get;}
ExitTime            Property   datetime ExitTime {get;}
```

Wildcards can be used with the MemberType parameter. Using *Property* would have included the original AliasProperty members in the result.

The Static parameter is covered in *Chapter 7, Working with .NET*.

The View parameter is set to All by default. It has three additional values:

- Base: This shows properties that are derived from a .NET object, omitting members defined by PowerShell (such as the AliasProperty members).
- Adapted: This shows members handled by the **Adapted Type System (ATS)** in PowerShell, which is often the same as the Base properties.
- Extended: This shows members added by the **Extended Type System (ETS)** in PowerShell. AliasProperty members will, for example, are shown here.

ATS and ETS

ATS and ETS make it easy to work with object frameworks other than .NET in PowerShell, for example, objects returned by ADSI, COM, WMI, or XML. Each of these frameworks is discussed later in this book.

Microsoft published an article on ATS and ETS in 2011 that is still relevant today:

https://learn.microsoft.com/en-us/archive/blogs/besidethepoint/psobject-and-the-adapted-and-extended-type-systems-ats-and-ets.

Every object in PowerShell includes additional properties provided by the type systems above, which are typically not visible. These include PSBase, PSObject, and PSTypeNames. These properties may be displayed by adding the Force parameter to Get-Member, which causes the command to display all hidden members:

```
Get-Process -Id $PID | Get-Member PS* -Force
```

These hidden properties are used in more than one chapter in this book as objects are used in increasingly complex ways.

Properties of objects can be directly accessed using a dot or period.

Accessing object properties

The properties of an object in PowerShell may be accessed by writing the property name after a period. For example, the Name property of the current PowerShell process may be accessed by using the following code:

```
$process = Get-Process -Id $PID
$process.Name
```

PowerShell also allows us to access these properties by enclosing a command in parentheses:

```
(Get-Process -Id $PID).Name
```

The properties of an object are objects themselves. For example, the StartTime property of a process is a DateTime object. Get-Member can be used to show information about the property:

```
PS> Get-Process -Id $PID | Get-Member -Name StartTime


    TypeName: System.Diagnostics.Process


Name       MemberType Definition
----       ---------- ----------
StartTime Property    datetime StartTime {get;}
```

The DateTime object in turn has properties and methods. Get-Member can be used again:

```
(Get-Process -Id $PID).StartTime | Get-Member -MemberType Property
```

One of the properties shown is DayOfWeek. The value of DayOfWeek may be accessed using the following example:

```
$process = Get-Process -Id $PID
$process.StartTime.DayOfWeek
```

The variable assignment step may be skipped if parentheses are used:

```
(Get-Process -Id $PID).StartTime.DayOfWeek
```

The examples above will show the current day. As this content was written on a Sunday, it shows that value:

```
Sunday
```

The ability to assign a property or assign a new value to a property is governed by the accessor for a property.

Access modifiers

An accessor for a property has two possible values: Get, indicating that the property can be read; and Set, indicating that the property can be written to (changed).

Depending on the type of object, properties may be read-only or read/write. These may be identified using Get-Member and by inspecting the accessor.

In the following example, the value in curly braces at the end of each line is the accessor:

```
PS> $File = New-Item NewFile.txt
PS> $File | Get-Member -MemberType Property


    TypeName: System.IO.FileInfo


Name            MemberType      Definition
----            ----------      ----------
Attributes      Property        System.IO.FileAttributes Attributes {get;set;}
CreationTime    Property        datetime CreationTime {get;set;}
```

```
CreationTimeUtc      Property      datetime CreationTimeUtc {get;set;}
Directory            Property      System.IO.DirectoryInfo Directory {get;}
DirectoryName        Property      string DirectoryName {get;}
Exists               Property      bool Exists {get;}
```

When the accessor is {get;}, the property value is read-only; attempting to change the value results in an error:

```
PS> $File = New-Item NewFile.txt -Force
PS> $File.Name = 'NewName'
InvalidOperation: 'Name' is a ReadOnly property.
```

When the modifier is {get;set;}, the property value may be read and changed. In the preceding example, CreationTime has the set accessor. The value can be changed; in this case, it may be set to any date after January 1, 1601:

```
$File = New-Item NewFile.txt -Force
$File.CreationTime = Get-Date -Day 1 -Month 2 -Year 1692
```

The result of the preceding command can be seen by reviewing the properties for the file in PowerShell:

```
Get-Item NewFile.txt | Select-Object -ExpandProperty CreationTime
```

This command will show the date that was assigned above:

```
01 February 1692 09:14:27
```

The value displayed will change depending on the date and time formatting configuration of the operating system.

Alternatively, File Explorer can be used to view the properties of a file, as shown in *Figure 4.1*:

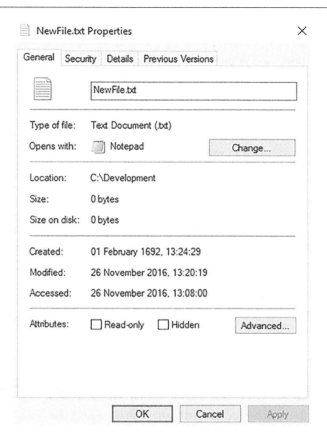

Figure 4.1: Changing the created date

In the preceding example, the change made to CreationTime is passed from the object representing the file to the file itself. The object used here, based on the .NET System.IO.FileInfo class, is written in such a way that it supports the change. A property may indicate that it can be changed (by supporting the set access modifier in Get-Member) and still not pass the change back to whatever the object represents.

Using methods

Methods perform an action, such as creating something new or effecting a change in state.

Methods are called using the following notation in PowerShell:

```
<Object>.Method()
```

The methods available on an object are specific to that object type. For example, a string has several methods that can be used to create a new string based on the current string.

The methods available for a String can be seen using the Get-Member command:

```
'any string' | Get-Member -MemberType Method
```

For example, a method can be used to convert an uppercase or mixed-case string to a lowercase string. This causes the creation of a new string:

```
'CaT'.ToLower()
```

Methods often accept arguments. For example, the Replace method on a string can be given arguments to describe an old value to find, and a new value to insert:

```
'My pet is a cat'.Replace('cat', 'dog')
```

This results in the following string:

```
My pet is a dog
```

The result of this operation can be considered somewhat like using the -replace operator. The most notable difference with this simple replacement is that the Replace method is case-sensitive and the -replace operator is not:

```
'My pet is a cat' -replace 'cat', 'dog'
```

There are more differences between the two approaches and the -replace operator is discussed in more detail in *Chapter 5, Operators*.

Methods often allow more than one set of arguments. When a method is called without parentheses, PowerShell will show the overload definitions. Overloading a method is a .NET concept; it comes into play when two or more methods share the same name but have different arguments and implementations.

The example below shows the possible arguments for the Substring method:

```
PS> 'thisString'.Substring

OverloadDefinitions
-------------------
string Substring(int startIndex)
string Substring(int startIndex, int length)
```

It is possible to use Substring to get characters from a starting point to the end:

```
'My cat'.Substring(3)
```

Which returns the word "cat", starting from the third character of the string.

Or Substring can be used with both startIndex and length, where indexing starts at 0:

```
'My cat is gray'.Substring(3, 3)
```

This also returns the word "cat", but this time by finding the third character, it can get the following 3 characters.

One very common use of methods in PowerShell comes when working with dates. The Get-Date command can be used to get a date. If no parameters are used it gets the current date and time:

```
$date = Get-Date
```

The DateTime object returned by this command has properties and methods that can be used to change the value. As with the string examples above, the Get-Member command may be used to show the available properties. In this example, it just shows the Date property:

```
PS> Get-Date | Get-Member -Name Date -MemberType Property


    TypeName: System.DateTime


Name MemberType Definition
---- ---------- ----------
Date Property   datetime Date {get;}
```

The Date property can be used to go to the start of the day:

```
$date = Get-Date
$date.Date
```

DateTime also includes methods that can be used to move backward or forward in time:

```
PS> $date | Get-Member -Name Add* -MemberType Method


    TypeName: System.DateTime


Name               MemberType Definition
----               ---------- ----------
Add                Method     datetime Add(timespan value)
AddDays            Method     datetime AddDays(double value)
AddHours           Method     datetime AddHours(double value)
AddMicroseconds    Method     datetime AddMicroseconds(double value)
AddMilliseconds    Method     datetime AddMilliseconds(double value)
```

```
AddMinutes       Method      datetime AddMinutes(double value)
AddMonths        Method      datetime AddMonths(int months)
AddSeconds       Method      datetime AddSeconds(double value)
AddTicks         Method      datetime AddTicks(long value)
AddYears         Method      datetime AddYears(int value)
```

These methods accept positive numerical values to go forward in time and negative numeric values to go backward:

```
$date.Date.AddDays(1)
$date.Date.AddDays(-1)
```

The output from Get-Member above shows both the value type returned by the method and the permissible types for the arguments.

Return types and argument types

The output from Get-Member also shows the type of object returned by the method:

```
PS> Get-Date | Get-Member -Name AddDays -MemberType Method

    TypeName: System.DateTime

Name              MemberType Definition
----              ---------- ----------
AddDays           Method      datetime AddDays(double value)
```

The same information is visible by using AddDays on a DateTime object without using parentheses and arguments:

```
PS> (Get-Date).AddDays

OverloadDefinitions
-------------------
datetime AddDays(double value)
```

In the definitions above:

- datetime is the type of the value that the method returns.
- AddDays is the name of the method.
- double (System.Double) is the type name of the argument. Double allows values with a decimal point such as 1.5, 9.8, and so on. Whole numbers may be used as well, 1.0 or 1 for example.

The return value, datetime, in this case means that it is possible to use more than one method (or property) in a single statement. Each method used returns a new DateTime instance.

For example, the command below finds the start date (the Date property), then goes back one second (using AddSeconds with a negative value), then forward one and a half days:

```
$date = Get-Date
$date.Date.AddSeconds(-1).AddDays(1.5)
```

The result will be 11:59:59 tomorrow.

Objects in PowerShell may be created or changed either directly or within a pipeline.

Creating and modifying objects

Creating objects is explored again in more detail in *Chapter 7, Working with .NET*. This section focuses on creating custom objects and includes an exploration of approaches used in the past that still find their way into modern code. New-Object and Add-Member are briefly introduced in relation to custom object creation.

A custom object is one where the properties shown are defined by the author of a piece of code (a script, a function, or just something in the console). Custom objects are frequently used to create output from commands, for instance, to generate a report.

The [PSCustomObject] type accelerator is frequently used to create a custom object.

Using PSCustomObject

PowerShell 3 introduced the ability to create a custom object using the [PSCustomObject] type in front of a hashtable (@{}). Hashtables were introduced in *Chapter 3, Variables, Arrays, and Hashtables*. A hashtable contains key and value pairs. For example, the command below creates a custom object with a single property, Email:

```
[PSCustomObject]@{
    Email = 'name@domain.com'
}
```

The resulting object can be used with any of the commands in this chapter.

PSCustomObject is parser magic

The [PSCustomObject] statement, and the [Ordered] statement used later in this section, are instructions to the parser.

PowerShell does include a type accelerator for PSCustomObject, which resolves to System. Management.Automation.PSObject when running:

[PSCustomObject].FullName

Type accelerators are explored in *Chapter 7, Working with .NET*.

However, the statement below will create a custom object from a hashtable:

[PSCustomObject]@{ Name = 'Value' }

Using the apparent full name will not change the hashtable into a custom object at all:

```
[System.Management.Automation.PSObject]@{

    Name = 'Value'

}
```

Any number of properties can be defined within the hashtable, a second property is shown below:

```
[PSCustomObject]@{
    Username = 'username'
    Email    = 'name@domain.com'
}
```

The order the properties are displayed in the console is the same as the order in which they were written. The outcome is shown below:

```
Username  Email
--------  -----
username  name@domain.com
```

In the example above, all properties are expected to be known in advance. Properties can be set (or changed) after the object has been created:

```
$customObject = [PSCustomObject]@{
    Username = 'username'
    Email    = ''
}
$customObject.Email = 'name@domain.com'
```

Properties can be filled based on conditions or other decisions made by the script.

If the properties that should be added cannot be known in advance, an OrderedDictionary can be created first. Conditional statements can be used to test if a property should be added, then once the object is complete it can be converted into a PSCustomObject:

```
$customObject = [Ordered]@{
    Username = 'username'
}
if ($email) {
    $customObject.Email = $email
}
$customObject = [PSCustomObject]$customObject
```

Custom objects can also be created using the New-Object command.

The New-Object command

The New-Object command in PowerShell can be used to create instances of .NET objects and COM objects. These features are explored in greater detail in *Chapter 7, Working with .NET*.

Custom object creation using New-Object was added in PowerShell 2 and effectively deprecated by the introduction of [PSCustomObject] and [Ordered] in PowerShell 3.

Custom objects can be created with New-Object, as shown below:

```
New-Object -TypeName PSObject -Property @{
    Username = 'username'
    Email    = 'name@domain.com'
}
```

A limitation of this approach is that the order in which properties have been written may not be reflected in the resulting object. The example below shows the possible output from the command:

```
Email           Username
-----           --------
name@domain.com username
```

In PowerShell 3 and above it is possible to add the [Ordered] type to the hashtable to maintain order. However, if PowerShell 3 or above is available, [PSCustomObject] should be used instead.

Another common approach is to create an empty object, then add properties (members) to the object afterward using the Add-Member command.

The Add-Member command

Add-Member allows new members (including Properties and Methods) to be added to existing objects.

The creation of Methods and ScriptProperty members with Add-Member is explored in *Chapter 7, Working with .NET*.

Add-Member can be useful if the object type must be preserved. Select-Object can often be used to a similar effect, but it changes the object type when doing so. Select-Object is explored later in this chapter.

Add-Member can be used to add arbitrary properties to an existing object. The example below takes the output of Get-ChildItem and then adds a property called ComputerName to each item:

```
$dir = Get-ChildItem
$dir | Add-Member -NotePropertyName ComputerName -NotePropertyValue
$env:COMPUTERNAME
```

The new property can be seen using Get-Member based on the example above:

```
PS> $dir | Get-Member ComputerName


    TypeName: System.IO.DirectoryInfo


Name          MemberType   Definition
----          ----------   ----------
ComputerName NoteProperty string ComputerName=PSTEST


    TypeName: System.IO.FileInfo


Name          MemberType   Definition
----          ----------   ----------
ComputerName NoteProperty string ComputerName=PSTEST
```

Because the Get-ChildItem command, in this case, finds both files and directories, two entries are seen in the output from Get-Member.

Add-Member and custom objects

The Add-Member command was popularized as part of a way of creating custom objects when it was released with PowerShell 2. In some cases, it was used to overcome the ordering problem when using New-Object.

Using the custom object example above, Add-Member might be used as follows:

```
$customObject = New-Object Object
$customObject | Add-Member -Name Username -Value 'username' -MemberType
NoteProperty
$customObject | Add-Member -Name Email -Value 'name@domain.com' -MemberType
NoteProperty
$customObject
```

Alternatively, the `NotePropertyName` and `NotePropertyValue` parameters might be used:

```
$customObject = New-Object Object
$customObject | Add-Member -NotePropertyName Username -NotePropertyValue
'username'
$customObject | Add-Member -NotePropertyName Email -NotePropertyValue 'name@
domain.com'
$customObject
```

This series of commands results in an object with the requested properties:

```
Username Email
-------- -----
username name@domain.com
```

`Add-Member` also has a `PassThru` parameter, which allows the statements above to be used in a pipeline:

```
New-Object Object |
    Add-Member -NotePropertyName Username -NotePropertyValue 'username'
-PassThru |
    Add-Member -NotePropertyName Email -NotePropertyValue 'name@domain.com'
-PassThru
```

The named parameters can be replaced with positional parameters to reduce the length of the statements above:

```
New-Object Object |
    Add-Member Username 'username' -PassThru |
    Add-Member Email 'name@domain.com' -PassThru
```

As with the previous series of commands, this creates an object with each property:

```
Username Email
-------- -----
username name@domain.com
```

As with the `New-Object` style of creating a custom object, the approach should be replaced with [PSCustomObject] as it is simpler and faster.

`Add-Member` has uses beyond custom objects. It can add arbitrary members to an existing object, which is useful if the object type must be preserved.

As well as being used to present information to an end user, the properties and methods of an object are used when enumerating and filtering collections of objects.

Enumerating and filtering

Enumerating, or listing, the objects in a collection in PowerShell does not need a specialized command. For example, if the results of Get-PSDrive were assigned to a variable, enumerating the content of the variable is as simple as writing the variable name and pressing *Return*, allowing the values to be viewed:

```
PS> $drives = Get-PSDrive
PS> $drives

Name     Used (GB)    Free (GB)    Provider       Root

----     ---------    ---------    --------       ----

Alias                              Alias
C          319.37       611.60     FileSystem     C:\
Cert                               Certificate    \
Env                                Environment
...
```

ForEach-Object may be used to work on an existing collection or objects or used to work on the output from another command in a pipeline.

Where-Object may be used to filter an existing collection or objects, or it may be used to filter the output from another command in a pipeline.

The ForEach-Object command

ForEach-Object is used to work on each object in an input pipeline. For example, the following command works on each of the results from Get-Process in turn by running the specified script block (enclosed in { }):

```
Get-Process | ForEach-Object {
    Write-Host $_.Name -ForegroundColor Green
}
```

The script block, an arbitrary block of code, is used as an argument for the Process parameter. The preceding command may explicitly include the Process parameter name shown here:

```
Get-Process | ForEach-Object -Process {
    Write-Host $_.Name -ForegroundColor Green
}
```

The script block executes once for each object in the input pipeline, that is, once for each object returned by Get-Process. The special $_ variable is used to access the current object.

The $PSItem variable may be used in place of $_ if desired. There is no difference between the two variable names. $_ is the more commonly used name.

The Process parameter is accompanied by the Begin and End parameters. Begin and End are used to run script blocks before the first value is sent to the Process script block, and after the last value has been received.

Begin and End parameters

If ForEach-Object is given a single script block as an argument, it is passed to the Process parameter. The Process script block runs once for each object in the input pipeline.

ForEach-Object also supports Begin and End parameters. Begin runs once before the first value in the pipeline is passed. End runs once after the last value has been received from the input pipeline.

The behavior of these parameters is shown in the following example:

```
1..5 | ForEach-Object -Begin {
    Write-Host "Starting the pipeline. Creating value."
    $value = 0
} -Process {
    Write-Host "Adding $_ to value."
    $value += $_
} -End {
    Write-Host "Finished the pipeline. Displaying value."
    $value
}
```

The command above will generate the following output:

```
Starting the pipeline. Creating value.
Adding 1 to value.
Adding 2 to value.
Adding 3 to value.
Adding 4 to value.
Adding 5 to value.
Finished the pipeline. Displaying value.
15
```

The trailing 15 is the value of the variable $value from the End block.

The parameters above match the names of named blocks used by other commands acting in a pipeline and are explored in greater detail in *Chapter 17, Scripts, Functions, and ScriptBlocks*.

Positional parameters

The ForEach-Object command is written to allow all parameters to be passed based on position. The first positional parameter is Process. However, ForEach-Object will switch parameters around based on the number of arguments:

```
1 | ForEach-Object { "Process: $_" }
```

If more than one script block is passed, the first position is passed to the Begin parameter:

```
1 | ForEach-Object { "Begin" } { "Process: $_" }
```

 If a third script block is added, it will be passed to the End parameter:

```
1 | ForEach-Object {

    "Begin"

} {

    "Process: $_"

} {

    "End"

}
```

The parallel parameter was added to ForEach-Object in PowerShell 7 as a convenient way of running operations in parallel.

The Parallel parameter

In PowerShell 7, ForEach-Object gains a Parallel parameter. This, as the name suggests, can be used to run process blocks in parallel rather than one after another.

By default, ForEach-Object runs 5 instances of the process block at a time; this is controlled by the ThrottleLimit parameter. The limit may be increased (or decreased) depending on where the bottleneck is with a given process.

Running a simple ForEach-Object command with a Start-Sleep statement shows how the output is grouped together as each set of jobs completes:

```
1..10 | ForEach-Object -Parallel {
    Start-Sleep -Seconds 2
    $_
}
```

When using ForEach-Object without the Parallel parameter, variables created before the command are accessible without any special consideration:

```
$string = 'Hello world'
1 | ForEach-Object {
    # The string variable can be used as normal
    $string
}
```

When using `Parallel`, each parallel script block runs in a separate thread. Variables created outside the `ForEach-Object` command must be accessed by prefixing the variable name with the `using` scope modifier, as shown here:

```
$string = 'Hello world'
1 | ForEach-Object -Parallel {
    # The $string variable is only accessible if using is used.
    $using:string
}
```

For the most part, the `using` scope modifier is one-way. That is, values may be read from the scope, but new values cannot be set. For example, the following attempt to write a value to `$using:newString` will fail:

```
1 | ForEach-Object -Parallel {
    $using:newString = $_
}
```

This example causes the following error:

```
ParserError:
Line |
   2 |        $using:newString = $_
     |        ~~~~~~~~~~~~~~~~~~~~~
     | The assignment expression is not valid. The input to an
     | assignment operator must be an object that is able to
     | accept assignments, such as a variable or a property.
```

Advanced array types and hashtables can be changed; however, parentheses are required around the variable name, or the value must be assigned to another variable first. For example:

```
$values = @{}
1..5 | ForEach-Object -Parallel {
    ($using:values).Add($_, $_)
}
$values
```

While it is possible to access the hashtable like this, a hashtable is not built to be changed from multiple threads (it is not thread-safe).

Output from a parallel ForEach-Object should ideally be sent to the output pipeline. For example:

```
$output = 1..5 | ForEach-Object -Parallel { $_ }
```

ForEach-Object is most often used to add complexity when processing the output from another command, or when working on a collection. ForEach-Object may also be used to read a single property or execute a method of every object in a collection.

The MemberName parameter

ForEach-Object may also be used to get a single property or execute a single method on each of the objects. For example, ForEach-Object may be used to return only the Path property when using Get-Process:

```
Get-Process | ForEach-Object -MemberName Path
```

Or ForEach-Object may be used to run the ToString method on a set of dates:

```
@(
    Get-Date '01/01/2019'
    Get-Date '01/01/2020'
) | ForEach-Object ToString('yyyyMMdd')
```

This will result in strings based on each date:

```
20190101
20200101
```

ForEach-Object is frequently used alongside Where-Object.

The Where-Object command

Filtering the output from commands may be performed using Where-Object. For example, processes might be filtered for those started after 9 am today. If there are no processes started after 9 am, then the statement will not return anything:

```
Get-Process | Where-Object StartTime -gt (Get-Date 9:00:00)
```

The syntax shown in help for Where-Object does not quite match the syntax used here. The help text is as follows:

```
Where-Object [-Property] <String> [[-Value] <Object>] -GT ...
```

In the preceding example, we see the following:

- StartTime is the argument for the Property parameter (first argument by position).
- The comparison is greater than, as signified by the gt switch parameter.
- The date (using the Get-Date command) is the argument for the Value parameter (second argument by position).

Based on the points above the example might be written as follows:

```
Get-Process |
    Where-Object -Property StartTime -Value (Get-Date 9:00:00) -GT
```

However, it is arguably easier to read "StartTime is greater than <some date>," so most examples tend to follow that pattern.

Where-Object also accepts filters using the FilterScript parameter. FilterScript is often used to describe more complex filters and filters where more than one term is used:

```
Get-Service | Where-Object {
    $_.StartType -eq 'Manual' -and
    $_.Status -eq 'Running'
}
```

In this example, a list of services satisfying the filter will be shown. The services listed will depend on those available on the computer running the command. The output will be like this partial example:

```
Status    Name              DisplayName

------    ----              -----------
Running   Appinfo           Application Information
Running   AppXSvc           AppX Deployment Service (AppXSVC)
Running   BluetoothUserServ… Bluetooth User Support Service_535639
Running   BTAGService       Bluetooth Audio Gateway Service
```

When a filter like this is used, the conditions are evaluated in the order they are written. This can be used to avoid conditions that may otherwise cause errors.

In the following example, Test-Path is used before Get-Item, which is used to test the last time a file was written on a remote computer (via the administrative share):

```
$date = (Get-Date).AddDays(-90)
'Computer1', 'Computer2' | Where-Object {
    (Test-Path "\\$_\c$\temp\file.txt") -and
    (Get-Item "\\$_\c$\temp\file.txt").LastWriteTime -lt $date
}
```

If Test-Path is removed, the snippet will throw an error if either the computer or the file does not exist.

Selecting and sorting

Select-Object acts on an input pipeline, either an existing collection of objects or the output from another command. Select-Object can be used to select a subset of properties, to change properties, or to add new properties. Select-Object also allows a user to limit the number of objects returned.

Sort-Object can be used to perform both simple and complex sorting based on an input pipeline.

Using `Select-Object` is a key part of working with PowerShell, output can be customized to suit circumstances in several ways.

The Select-Object command

`Select-Object` is an extremely versatile command as shown by each of the following short examples, which demonstrate some of the simpler uses of the command.

`Select-Object` can be used to explore what is available on an object by using a wildcard for the `Property` parameter:

```
Get-Process -Id $PID | Select-Object *
```

This can be a handy way of viewing all available properties and sometimes a useful alternative to `Get-Member`.

`Select-Object` may be used to limit the properties returned by a command by name:

```
Get-Process | Select-Object -Property Name, Id
```

In this case, output will be formatted as shown below, although the process names and IDs will differ:

```
Name                                           Id
----                                           --
Aac3572DramHal_x86                           9904
Aac3572MbHal_x86                            11868
AacKingstonDramHal_x64                       5144
AacKingstonDramHal_x86                      11724
AcPowerNotification                         11752
```

`Select-Object` can limit the properties returned from a command using wildcards:

```
Get-Process | Select-Object -Property Name, *Memory*
```

As more than one property is matched by the `Memory` wildcard and there are more than 4 selected properties, the output from the command above will be displayed as a list instead of a table.

The first result is shown below. The result will depend on locally executing processes:

```
Name                         : Aac3572DramHal_x86
NonpagedSystemMemorySize64   : 10728
NonpagedSystemMemorySize     : 10728
PagedMemorySize64            : 1572864
PagedMemorySize              : 1572864
PagedSystemMemorySize64      : 103744
PagedSystemMemorySize        : 103744
PeakPagedMemorySize64        : 2154496
PeakPagedMemorySize          : 2154496
```

```
PeakVirtualMemorySize64        : 77770752
PeakVirtualMemorySize          : 77770752
PrivateMemorySize64            : 1572864
PrivateMemorySize              : 1572864
VirtualMemorySize64            : 51818496
VirtualMemorySize              : 51818496
```

Select-Object can list everything but a few properties:

```
Get-Process | Select-Object -Property * -ExcludeProperty *Memory*
```

The first few properties of the output from the command above are shown below:

```
Name                 : Aac3572DramHal_x86
Id                   : 9904
PriorityClass        :
FileVersion          :
HandleCount          : 195
WorkingSet           : 10051584
TotalProcessorTime   :
```

Select-Object can get the first few objects in a pipeline:

```
Get-ChildItem C:\ -Recurse | Select-Object -First 2
Or Select-Object can select the last few objects in a pipeline:
```

```
Get-ChildItem C:\ | Select-Object -Last 3
```

Select-Object can Skip items at the beginning, in this example, the fifth item:

```
Get-ChildItem C:\ | Select-Object -Skip 4 -First 1
```

Or it can Skip items at the end. This example returns the third from the end:

```
Get-ChildItem C:\ | Select-Object -Skip 2 -Last 1
```

Select-Object can get an object from a pipeline by index:

```
Get-ChildItem C:\ | Select-Object -Index 3, 4, 5
```

In PowerShell 7 and above, Select-Object can omit certain indexes:

```
Get-ChildItem C:\ | Select-Object -SkipIndex 3, 4, 5
```

Select-Object also offers several more advanced uses. The following sections describe calculated properties, the ExpandProperty parameter, the Unique parameter, and property sets.

Calculated properties are perhaps one of the most used features of Select-Object.

Calculated properties

`Select-Object` can be used to add new properties to or rename existing properties on objects in an input pipeline.

Calculated properties are described using a hashtable with specific key names. The format is described in the help for `Select-Object`. In addition to names, the following hashtable formats are acceptable for the Property parameter:

```
@{ Name = 'PropertyName'; Expression = { 'PropertyValue' } }
@{ Label = 'PropertyName'; Expression = { 'PropertyValue' } }
@{ n = 'PropertyName'; e = { 'PropertyValue' } }
@{ l = 'PropertyName'; e = { 'PropertyValue' } }
```

The expression is most often a script block, which allows other commands to be executed, mathematical operations to be performed, substitutions to be made, and so on.

If a property is being renamed, a quoted string can be used instead of the script block. The following two examples have the same result:

```
Get-Process | Select-Object @{ Name = 'ProcessID'; Expression = 'ID' }
Get-Process | Select-Object @{ Name = 'ProcessID'; Expression = { $_.ID } }
```

If the list of properties is long, it can be better to enclose the list in @(), the array operator, allowing the properties to be spread across different lines:

```
Get-Process | Select-Object -Property @(
    'Name'
    @{Name = 'ProcessId'; Expression = 'ID' }
    @{Name = 'FileOwner'; Expression = {
        (Get-Acl $_.Path).Owner
    }}
)
```

Any number of properties might be added in this manner. The preceding example includes the output from `Get-Acl`. If more than one property were required, `ForEach-Object` might be added to the command:

```
Get-Process | Where-Object Path | ForEach-Object {
    $acl = Get-Acl $_.Path
    Select-Object -InputObject $_ -Property @(
        'Name'
        @{Name = 'ProcessId'; Expression = 'ID' }
        @{Name = 'FileOwner'; Expression = { $acl.Owner }}
        @{Name = 'Access';   Expression = { $acl.AccessToString }}
    )
}
```

When Select-Object is used with the Property parameter, a new custom object is always created. If the existing object type must be preserved, Add-Member should be used instead. For example, if the object includes methods that must be accessible later in a script, the Property parameter of Select-Object should not be used.

The following example shows that the object type is preserved if the Property parameter is not used. The following command shows that the type is Process, which allows any of the methods, such as WaitForExit, to be used later in a script:

```
(Get-Process | Select-Object -First 1).GetType()
```

If the Property parameter is used, the output is the PSCustomObject type. The resulting object will not have any of the methods specific to the Process type:

```
(Get-Process | Select-Object -Property Path, Company -First 1).GetType()
```

Calculated properties are extremely flexible, allowing an object to be modified, or a more complex object to be created with a relatively small amount of code.

The ExpandProperty parameter

The ExpandProperty parameter of Select-Object may be used to expand a single property of an object. This might be used to expand a property containing a string, leaving the output as an array of strings:

```
Get-Process | Select-Object -First 5 -ExpandProperty Name
```

If ExpandProperty is omitted, the returned object will be a PSCustomObject object with a Name property rather than the simpler array of strings.

Expanding a single property containing a string, or a numeric value, or an array of either, is the most common use of the ExpandProperty parameter.

Occasionally, it may be desirable or necessary to expand a property containing a more complex object. The members of the expanded property are added to the custom object:

```
Get-ChildItem $env:SYSTEMROOT\*.dll |
    Select-Object FullName, Length -ExpandProperty VersionInfo |
    Format-List *
```

Conflicting property names will cause an error to be raised; the conflicting name is otherwise ignored.

It is possible, if unusual, to use this technique to build up a single custom object based on the output from multiple commands:

```
$computerInfo = Get-CimInstance Win32_ComputerSystem |
    Select-Object -Property @(
        @{n='ComputerName';e={ $_.Name }}
        'DnsHostName'
        @{n='OSInfo';e={ Get-CimInstance Win32_OperatingSystem }}
    ) |
```

```
Select-Object * -ExpandProperty OSInfo |
Select-Object -Property @(
    'ComputerName'
    'DnsHostName'
    @{n='OperatingSystem';e='Caption'}
    'SystemDirectory'
)
```

The resulting object will contain two properties from Win32_ComputerSystem and two properties from Win32_OperatingSystem. The values shown will depend on the current system and are expected to be similar to those shown below:

```
PS> $computerInfo | Format-List

ComputerName    : NAME
DnsHostName     : Name.domain.com
OperatingSystem : Microsoft Windows 11 Pro
SystemDirectory : C:\WINDOWS\system32
```

A common requirement is to make a list of objects unique; Select-Object has a parameter to help with this.

The Unique parameter

Select-Object returns unique values from arrays of simple values with the Unique parameter:

```
1, 1, 1, 3, 5, 2, 2, 4 | Select-Object -Unique
```

About Get-Unique

Get-Unique may also be used to create a list of unique elements. When using Get-Unique, a list must be sorted first, for example:

```
1, 1, 1, 3, 5, 2, 2, 4 | Sort-Object | Get-Unique
```

In the following example, an object is created with one property called Number. The value for the property is 1, 2, or 3. The result is two objects with a value of 1, two with a value of 2, and so on:

```
1, 2, 3, 1, 2, 3 | ForEach-Object {
    [PSCustomObject]@{
        Number = $_
    }
}
```

This statement creates an array of custom objects as shown below:

```
Number
------
```

```
1
2
3
1
2
3
```

Select-Object can remove the duplicates from the set in this example using the Unique parameter if a list of properties (or a wildcard for the properties) is set:

```
1, 2, 3, 1, 2, 3 | ForEach-Object {
    [PSCustomObject]@{
        Number = $_
    }
} | Select-Object -Property * -Unique
```

This causes the removal of any instance where all properties match:

```
Number
------
    1
    2
    3
```

Select-Object builds up a collection of unique objects by comparing each property of each object to every unique object that came before it in a pipeline. This allows Select-Object to work without relying on an ordered collection (as Get-Unique requires).

When working with strings, the comparison used by Select-Object is case-sensitive. In the statement below, the two occurrences of Mouse will be retained.

```
'dog', 'dog', 'cat', 'cat', 'mouse', 'Mouse' |
    Select-Object -Unique
```

Select-Object may be used to select property sets, although this is rarely used in practice.

Property sets

A property set is a pre-defined list of properties that might be used when exploring an object. The property set is stored with the object itself. Select-Object can be used to select the properties within a specified property set.

In the following example, Get-Member is used to view the property sets available on the objects returned by Get-Process:

```
PS> Get-Process -Id $PID | Get-Member -MemberType PropertySet

    TypeName: System.Diagnostics.Process
```

```
Name                    MemberType        Definition
----                    ----------        ----------
PSConfiguration         PropertySet       PSConfiguration {Name, Id, ...
PSResources             PropertySet       PSResources {Name, Id, Hand...
```

Select-Object may then be used to display one of the property sets, PSConfiguration:

```
PS> Get-Process -Id $PID | Select-Object -Property PSConfiguration

Name    Id PriorityClass FileVersion
----    -- ------------- -----------
pwsh 2220          Normal 7.4.1.500
```

Objects, including selected objects, may be sorted using the Sort-Object command.

The Sort-Object command

The Sort-Object command allows objects to be sorted. By default, Sort-Object will sort objects in ascending order:

```
PS> 5, 4, 3, 2, 1 | Sort-Object
1
2
3
4
5
```

Strings are sorted in ascending order, irrespective of uppercase or lowercase:

```
PS> 'ccc', 'BBB', 'aaa' | Sort-Object
aaa
BBB
ccc
```

When dealing with more complex objects, Sort-Object may be used to sort based on a named property. For example, processes may be sorted based on the Id property:

```
Get-Process | Sort-Object -Property Id
```

Objects may be sorted on multiple properties; for example, a list of files may be sorted on LastWriteTime and then on Name:

```
Get-ChildItem C:\Windows\System32 |
    Sort-Object LastWriteTime, Name
```

In the preceding example, items are first sorted on `LastWriteTime`. Items that have the same value for `LastWriteTime` are then sorted based on `Name`.

`Sort-Object` is not limited to sorting on existing properties. A script block (a fragment of script, enclosed in curly braces) can be used to create a calculated value for sorting. For example, it is possible to order items based on a word, as shown in this example:

```
$examResults = @(
    [PSCustomObject]@{ Exam = 'Music';   Result = 'N/A';  Mark = 0 }
    [PSCustomObject]@{ Exam = 'History'; Result = 'Fail'; Mark = 23 }
    [PSCustomObject]@{ Exam = 'Biology'; Result = 'Pass'; Mark = 78 }
    [PSCustomObject]@{ Exam = 'Physics'; Result = 'Pass'; Mark = 86 }
    [PSCustomObject]@{ Exam = 'Maths';   Result = 'Pass'; Mark = 92 }
)
$examResults | Sort-Object {
    switch ($_.Result) {
        'Pass' { 1 }
        'Fail' { 2 }
        'N/A'  { 3 }
    }
}
```

The result of sorting the objects is shown here:

```
Exam        Result    Mark
----        ------    ----
Maths       Pass        92
Physics     Pass        86
Biology     Pass        78
History     Fail        23
Music        N/A         0
```

In the preceding example, when `Sort-Object` encounters a Pass result it is given the lowest numerical value (1) to sort on. As `Sort-Object` defaults to ascending order, this means exams with a result of Pass appear first in the list. This process is repeated to give a numeric value to each of the other possible results.

Sorting within each result set varies depending on the version of PowerShell. Windows PowerShell changes the order of the elements within each set, listing Maths, Physics, then Biology. PowerShell 6 and above, on the other hand, maintains the original order, listing Biology, then Physics, then Maths within the pass set.

As Sort-Object is capable of sorting on more than one property, the preceding example can be taken further to sort by mark next. This makes the output order entirely predictable, regardless of the version of PowerShell:

```
$examResults | Sort-Object {
    switch ($_.Result) {
        'Pass' { 1 }
        'Fail' { 2 }
        'N/A'  { 3 }
    }
}, Mark
```

The result is a table sorted by Result, then by Mark:

```
Exam       Result    Mark
----       ------    ----
Biology    Pass       78
Physics    Pass       86
Maths      Pass       92
History    Fail       23
Music      N/A         0
```

Adding the Descending parameter to Sort-Object will reverse the order of both fields:

```
$examResults | Sort-Object {
    switch ($_.Result) {
        'Pass' { 1 }
        'Fail' { 2 }
        'N/A'  { 3 }
    }
}, Mark -Descending
```

The output from the command is sorted again, this time in descending order for both Result and Mark:

```
Exam       Result    Mark
----       ------    ----
Music      N/A         0
History    Fail       23
Maths      Pass       92
Physics    Pass       86
Biology    Pass       78
```

The ordering behavior can be made property-specific using the notation that is shown in the following example. @() is used to try and make the property list easier to read:

```
$examResults | Sort-Object @(
```

```
    {
        switch ($_.Result) {
            'Pass' { 1 }
            'Fail' { 2 }
            'N/A'  { 3 }
        }
    }
    @{ Expression = { $_.Mark }; Descending = $true }
)
```

This example shows different sorting for the two properties:

```
Exam       Result      Mark

----       ------      ----

Maths      Pass         92
Physics    Pass         86
Biology    Pass         78
History    Fail         23
Music      N/A           0
```

The hashtable, @{}, is used to describe an expression (a calculated property; in this case, the value for Mark) and the sorting order, which is either ascending or descending.

In the preceding example, the first sorting property, based on the Result property, is sorted in ascending order as this is the default. The second property, Mark, is sorted in descending order.

Like Select-Object, Sort-Object can be used to find unique values.

The Unique parameter

Sort-Object can be used to make a set of values unique, but unlike Select-Object, comparisons between objects are not case-sensitive:

```
'dog', 'dog', 'cat', 'cat', 'mouse', 'Mouse' |
    Sort-Object -Unique
```

Of course, unlike Select-Object, the resulting collection will be sorted as shown below:

```
cat
dog
mouse
```

Once a set of data has been prepared by selecting and sorting, grouping, and measuring can be used to work on the collection.

Grouping and measuring

Group-Object is a powerful command that allows objects to be grouped together under a single property name or an expression.

Measure-Object supports several simple mathematical operations, such as counting the number of objects, calculating an average, calculating a sum, and so on. Measure-Object also allows characters, words, or lines to be counted in text fields.

The Group-Object command

The Group-Object command shows a Group and Count for each occurrence of a value in a collection of objects.

Given the sequence of numbers shown, Group-Object creates a Name that holds the value it is grouping, a Count as the number of occurrences of that value, and a Group property as the set of similar values:

```
PS> 6, 7, 7, 8, 8, 8 | Group-Object

Count    Name                  Group
-----    ----                  -----
    1    6                     {6}
    2    7                     {7, 7}
    3    8                     {8, 8, 8}
```

The Group property may be removed using the NoElement parameter, which simplifies the output of the command:

```
PS> 6, 7, 7, 8, 8, 8 | Group-Object -NoElement

Count    Name
-----    ----
    1    6
    2    7
    3    8
```

Group-Object can group based on a specific property. For example, it might be desirable to list the number of occurrences of a file in an extensive folder structure. In the following example, the C:\Windows\Assembly folder contains different versions of DLLs for different versions of packages, including the .NET Framework:

```
Get-ChildItem C:\Windows\Assembly -Filter *.dll -Recurse |
    Group-Object Name
```

Combining Group-Object with commands such as Where-Object and Sort-Object allows reports about the content of a dataset to be generated extremely quickly, for example, a report on the names of the top five files that appear more than once in a file tree:

```
Get-ChildItem C:\Windows\Assembly -Filter *.dll -File -Recurse |
    Group-Object Name -NoElement |
    Where-Object Count -gt 1 |
    Sort-Object Count, Name -Descending |
    Select-Object Name, Count -First 5
```

The output from the preceding command will vary from one computer to another; it depends on the installed software, development kits, .NET Framework version, and so on. The output from the preceding command might be like the following example:

Name	Count
Microsoft.Web.Diagnostics.resources.dll	14
Microsoft.Web.Deployment.resources.dll	14
Microsoft.Web.Deployment.PowerShell.resources.dll	14
Microsoft.Web.Delegation.resources.dll	14
Microsoft.Web.PlatformInstaller.resources.dll	13

As was seen with Sort-Object, Group-Object can group on more than one property. For example, we might group on both a filename and the size of a file (the Length property of a file):

```
Get-ChildItem C:\Windows\Assembly -Filter *.dll -Recurse |
    Group-Object Name, Length -NoElement |
    Where-Object Count -gt 1 |
    Sort-Object Name -Descending |
    Select-Object Name, Count -First 5
```

As with the previous example, the output from the command will vary from one computer to another:

Name	Count
WindowsFormsIntegration.Package.ni.dll, 100352	2
Templates.Editorconfig.Wizard.resources.ni.dll, 9216	13
Templates.Editorconfig.Wizard.resources.ni.dll, 8192	13
System.Web.ni.dll, 16939008	2
System.Web.ni.dll, 14463488	2

In the preceding example, System.Web.ni.dll is listed twice (with a count of two in each case). Each pair of files has the same file size.

Like Sort-Object, Group-Object is not limited to properties that already exist. Calculated properties can be used to create a new value to group on. For example, grouping on an email domain in a list of email addresses might be useful. The domain is obtained by splitting on the @ character:

```
'one@one.example', 'two@one.example', 'three@two.example' |
    Group-Object { ($_ -split '@')[1] }
```

The created groups are shown below:

```
Count    Name                Group
-----    ----                -----
    2    one.example         {one@one.example, two@one.example}
    1    two.example         {three@two.example}
```

In this example, the split operator is used to split on the @ character; everything to the left is stored in index 0, while everything to the right is stored in index 1.

By default, Group-Object returns the collection of objects shown in each of the preceding examples. Group-Object can also return a hashtable using the AsHashtable parameter.

When using the AsHashTable parameter, the AsString parameter can be added, which ensures that keys in the resulting hashtable are always strings. This parameter ensures that a group can be accessed after the grouping operation is complete. For example:

```
$hashtable = @(
    [IPAddress]'10.0.0.1'
    [IPAddress]'10.0.0.2'
    [IPAddress]'10.0.0.1'
) | Group-Object -AsHashtable -AsString
```

AsString allows the use of a string instead of an IPAddress instance to access values:

```
PS> $hashtable['10.0.0.1']

AddressFamily      : InterNetwork
ScopeId            :
IsIPv6Multicast    : False
IsIPv6LinkLocal    : False
IsIPv6SiteLocal    : False
IsIPv6Teredo       : False
IsIPv6UniqueLocal  : False
IsIPv4MappedToIPv6 : False
Address            : 16777226
IPAddressToString  : 10.0.0.1

AddressFamily      : InterNetwork
ScopeId            :
IsIPv6Multicast    : False
IsIPv6LinkLocal    : False
IsIPv6SiteLocal    : False
IsIPv6Teredo       : False
IsIPv6UniqueLocal  : False
```

```
IsIPv4MappedToIPv6 : False
Address            : 16777226
IPAddressToString  : 10.0.0.1
```

If the AsString parameter was excluded from the preceding example, the value used to access the key would have to be an IPAddress type. For example:

```
$hashtable = @(
    [IPAddress]'10.0.0.1'
    [IPAddress]'10.0.0.2'
    [IPAddress]'10.0.0.1'
) | Group-Object -AsHashtable
```

Then the key used to access the value must also match the type:

```
$hashtable[[IPAddress]'10.0.0.1']
```

In the preceding example, attempting to access the key without the [IPAddress] type will fail; no value will be returned, and no error will be shown.

By default, Group-Object is not case sensitive. The strings one, ONE, and One are all considered equal when grouping. The CaseSensitive parameter forces Group-Object to differentiate between items where cases differ:

```
PS> 'one', 'ONE', 'One' | Group-Object -CaseSensitive

Count Name                Group
----- ----                -----
    1 one                 {one}
    1 ONE                 {ONE}
    1 One                 {One}
```

Group-Object can be used to count occurrences of a value within a collection of objects. Measure-Object is useful when it is necessary to analyze the values, such as when determining the average of a specific property.

The Measure-Object command

When used without any parameters, Measure-Object returns a value for Count, which is the number of items passed in using the pipeline, for example:

```
PS> 1, 5, 9, 79 | Measure-Object

Count   : 4
Average :
Sum     :
```

```
Maximum   :
Minimum   :
Property  :
```

Each of the remaining properties is empty, unless requested using their respective parameters. For example, Sum may be requested:

```
PS> 1, 5, 9, 79 | Measure-Object -Sum
Count     : 4
Average   :
Sum       : 94
Maximum   :
Minimum   :
Property  :
```

Adding the remaining parameters adds values to the rest of the fields (except Property):

```
PS> 1, 5, 9, 79 | Measure-Object -Average -Maximum -Minimum -Sum

Count     : 4
Average   : 23.5
Sum       : 94
Maximum   : 79
Minimum   : 1
Property  :
```

The value for Property is added when Measure-Object is asked to work against a particular property (instead of a set of numbers). For example:

```
PS> Get-Process | Measure-Object WorkingSet -Average

Count     : 135
Average   : 39449395.2
Sum       :
Maximum   :
Minimum   :
Property  : WorkingSet
```

When working with text, Measure-Object can count characters, words, or lines. For example, it can be used to count the number of lines, words, and characters in a text file:

```
Get-Content C:\Windows\WindowsUpdate.log |
    Measure-Object -Line -Word -Character
```

This time, an object is shown that describes the content of the text file:

```
Lines    Words    Characters    Property
-----    -----    ----------    --------
    3       32           268
```

`Group-Object` and `Measure-Object` are essential parts of a PowerShell toolkit. They can significantly simplify analyzing collections of data for repetition or performing simple mathematical operations. Each of these commands is used against a single collection of objects; when working with more than one collection of objects, it may be necessary to compare.

Comparing

The `Compare-Object` command can be used to compare two collections of objects with one another.

`Compare-Object` must be supplied with values for the `ReferenceObject` and `DifferenceObject` parameters, which are normally collections or arrays of objects. If either value is null, then an error will be displayed. If both values are equal, `Compare-Object` does not return anything by default. For example, the reference and difference objects in the following example are identical:

```
Compare-Object -ReferenceObject 1, 2 -DifferenceObject 1, 2
```

If there are differences, `Compare-Object` displays the results, as shown here:

```
PS> Compare-Object -ReferenceObject 1, 2, 3, 4 -DifferenceObject 1, 2

InputObject SideIndicator
----------- -------------
          3 <=
          4 <=
```

This shows that `ReferenceObject` (the collection on the left, denoted by the direction of the `<=` arrow) has the values, but `DifferenceObject` (the collection on the right) does not.

`Compare-Object` has several other parameters that may be used to change the output. The `IncludeEqual` parameter adds values that are present in both collections to the output:

```
$params = @{
    ReferenceObject  = 1, 2, 3, 4
    DifferenceObject = 1, 2
    IncludeEqual     = $true
}
Compare-Object @params
```

The result from this command will show the values that are equal as requested:

```
InputObject SideIndicator
----------- -------------
          1 ==
          2 ==
          3 <=
          4 <=
```

ExcludeDifferent will omit the results that differ. This parameter makes sense if IncludeEqual is also set; without this, the command will always return nothing.

The PassThru parameter is used to return the original object instead of the representation showing the differences. In the following example, it is used to select values that are common to both the reference and difference objects:

```
$params = @{
    ReferenceObject  = 1, 2, 3, 4
    DifferenceObject = 1, 2
    ExcludeDifferent = $true
    IncludeEqual     = $true
    PassThru         = $true
}
Compare-Object @params
```

This example shows the values only:

```
1
2
```

Compare-Object can compare based on properties of objects, as well as the simpler values in the preceding examples. This can be a single property or a list of properties. For example, the following command compares the contents of C:\Windows\System32 with C:\Windows\SysWOW64, returning files that have the same name and are the same size in both:

```
$params = @{
    ReferenceObject  = Get-ChildItem C:\Windows\System32 -File
    DifferenceObject = Get-ChildItem C:\Windows\SysWOW64 -File
    Property         = 'Name', 'Length'
    IncludeEqual     = $true
    ExcludeDifferent = $true
}
Compare-Object @params
```

By default, `Compare-Object` writes an error if either the reference or difference objects are null. If `Compare-Object` is used when there is a chance of either being empty, the following technique can be used to avoid an error being generated provided neither contains an explicit null value:

```
$reference = Get-ChildItem C:\Windows\System32\tcpmon*.ini
$difference = Get-ChildItem C:\Windows\SysWOW64\tcpmon*.ini
Compare-Object @($reference) @($difference) -Property Name
```

The array operator (`@()`) around each parameter value will be discarded by PowerShell. If `$difference` is empty, it will be treated as an empty array instead of it being a null value.

Collections of objects generated by any of the preceding commands might be exported to move data outside of PowerShell. The result of any of these operations might be exported to a file for another user, system, or program to use.

Importing, exporting, and converting

Getting data in and out of PowerShell is a critical part of using the language. There are several commands dedicated to this task, including:

- `Export-Csv`
- `Import-Csv`
- `Export-CliXml` and `Import-CliXml`
- `Tee-Object`

Other PowerShell modules, such as the `ImportExcel` module, available in the PowerShell Gallery can be used to extend the output formats available. Commands such as `ConvertTo-Html`, `ConvertTo-Json`, and `ConvertFrom-Json` are explored in later chapters.

The Export-Csv command

The `Export-Csv` command writes data from objects to a text file, for example:

```
Get-Process | Export-Csv processes.csv
```

By default, `Export-Csv` writes a comma-delimited file using UTF8 encoding and completely overwrites any file using the same name.

`Export-Csv` may be used to add lines to an existing file using the `Append` parameter. When the `Append` parameter is used, the input object must have each of the fields listed in the CSV header or an error will be thrown, unless the `Force` parameter is used.

If this a CSV file is created using the command below:

```
Get-Process -ID $PID |
    Select-Object Name, Id |
    Export-Csv .\Processes.csv
```

Then a second command, with a different set of properties is run to add to the CSV:

```
Get-Process explorer |
    Select-Object Name |
    Export-Csv .\Processes.csv -Append
```

Then the following error will be shown:

```
Export-Csv: Cannot append CSV content to the following file: .\Processes.csv.
The appended object does not have a property that corresponds to the following
column: Id. To continue with mismatched properties, add the -Force parameter,
and then retry the command.
```

If the Append parameter is used and the input object has more fields than the CSV, the extra fields are silently dropped when writing the CSV file. For example, the value held in Id is ignored when writing the results to the existing CSV file:

```
Get-Process pwsh |
    Select-Object Name | Export-Csv .\Processes.csv
Get-Process explorer |
    Select-Object Name, Id |
    Export-Csv .\Processes.csv -Append
```

Export-Csv in Windows PowerShell writes a header line to each file, which details the .NET type it has just exported. If the preceding example was used in Windows PowerShell, the header line would be as follows:

```
#TYPE Selected.System.Diagnostics.Process
```

This header is only included in PowerShell 7 (and PowerShell Core) when explicitly using the IncludeTypeInformation parameter.

Export-Csv in Windows PowerShell can be instructed to exclude this header using the NoTypeInformation parameter:

```
Get-Process | Export-Csv processes.csv -NoTypeInformation
```

ConvertTo-Csv in Windows PowerShell is like Export-Csv, except that instead of writing content to a file, content is written as command output:

```
PS> Get-Process powershell | Select-Object Name, Id | ConvertTo-Csv
#TYPE Selected.System.Diagnostics.Process
"Name","Id"
"pwsh","404"
```

Both Export-Csv and ConvertTo-Csv are limited in what they can do with arrays of objects in properties. For example, ConvertTo-Csv is unable to display the values that are in an array:

```
[PSCustomObject]@{
    Name = "Numbers"
    Value = 1, 2, 3, 4, 5
} | ConvertTo-Csv -NoTypeInformation
```

PowerShell will write Numbers as System.Object[], as shown below:

```
"Name","Value"
"Numbers","System.Object[]"
```

The value of the Value property in the CSV content is taken from the ToString method, which is called on the property named Value; for example:

```
$object = [PSCustomObject]@{
    Name = "Numbers"
    Value = 1, 2, 3, 4, 5
}
$object.Value.ToString()
```

This will display the text System.Object[].

If a CSV file is expected to hold the content of an array, code must be written to convert it into a suitable format. For example, the content of the array can be written after converting it to a string:

```
[PSCustomObject]@{
    Name  = "Numbers"
    Value = 1, 2, 3, 4, 5
} | ForEach-Object {
    $_.Value = $_.Value -join ', '
    $_
} | ConvertTo-Csv -NoTypeInformation
```

Creating the joined string allows the value to be represented in the CSV content:

```
"Name","Value"
"Numbers","1, 2, 3, 4, 5"
```

In the preceding example, the value of the property is joined using a comma followed by a space. The modified object (held in $_) is passed on to the ConvertTo-Csv command.

The Import-Csv command

Comma-Separated Value (CSV) files are structured text. Applications such as Microsoft Excel can work with CSV files without changing the file format, although Excel's advanced features cannot be saved to a CSV file.

By default, Import-Csv expects the input to have a header row, be comma-delimited, and use ASCII file encoding. If any of these items are different, the command parameters may be used. For example, a tab may be set as the delimiter:

```
Import-Csv TabDelimitedFile.tsv -Delimiter `t
```

A tick (grave accent) followed by t (`t) is used to represent the tab character in PowerShell.

Data imported using Import-Csv will always be formatted as a string. If Import-Csv is used to read a file containing the following text, each of the numbers will be treated as a string:

```
Name,Position
Jim,35
Matt,3
Dave,5
```

Attempting to use Sort-Object on the imported CSV file results in values being sorted as if they were strings, not numbers:

```
PS> Import-Csv .\positions.csv | Sort-Object Position

Name      Position
----      --------
Matt      3
Jim       35
Dave      5
```

Sort-Object can use an expression in a script block to coerce the value of the Position property to an integer:

```
PS> Import-Csv .\positions.csv | Sort-Object { [Int]$_.Position }

Name Position
---- --------
Matt 3
Dave 5
Jim  35
```

This conversion problem exists regardless of whether the data in a CSV file is numerical, a date, or any type other than a string.

The ConvertFrom-Csv command is like Import-Csv in that it reads CSV content and creates custom objects from that content. The difference is that ConvertFrom-Csv reads strings from standard input instead of a file. In the following example, a string is converted into a custom object using the ConvertFrom-Csv command with the Header parameter:

```
PS> "powershell,404" | ConvertFrom-Csv -Header Name, Id

Name            Id
----            --
powershell      404
```

`ConvertFrom-Csv` expects either an array of strings or a single string with line-breaks. The following example includes a header in the string:

```
"Name,Id
Powershell,404" | ConvertFrom-Csv
```

CSV is a simple and accessible format. However, CSV is a pure-text format; it cannot express different value types (such as numbers and dates) – all data is a string. The `CliXml` format is at the other end of the spectrum: it can be used to store complex data types.

Export-Clixml and Import-Clixml

`Export-Clixml` creates representations of objects in XML files. The CLI acronym stands for Common Language Infrastructure, a technical standard developed by Microsoft. `Export-Clixml` is extremely useful where type information about each property must be preserved.

For example, the following object may be exported using `Export-Clixml`:

```
[PSCustomObject]@{
    Integer = 1
    Decimal = 2.3
    String  = 'Hello world'
} | Export-Clixml .\object.xml
```

The resulting XML file shows the type for each of the properties it has just exported:

```
PS> Get-Content object.xml
<Objs Version="1.1.0.1" xmlns="http://schemas.microsoft.com/
powershell/2004/04">
  <Obj RefId="0">
    <TN RefId="0">
      <T>System.Management.Automation.PSCustomObject</T>
      <T>System.Object</T>
    </TN>
    <MS>
      <I32 N="Number">1</I32>
      <Db N="Decimal">2.3</Db>
      <S N="String">Hello world</S>
    </MS>
  </Obj>
</Objs>
```

In the preceding example, I32 is a 32-bit integer (Int32). Db is a double-precision floating-point number (double). S is a string.

With this extra information in the file, PowerShell can rebuild the object, including the different types, using Import-Clixml, as follows:

```
$object = Import-Clixml .\object.xml
```

Once imported, the value types can be inspected using the GetType method:

```
PS> $object.Decimal.GetType()

IsPublic   IsSerial   Name      BaseType
--------   --------   ----      --------
    True       True   Double    System.ValueType
```

The ability to rebuild the original object allows Export-CliXml to convert credential objects to text. When it does so, password values are encrypted using the **Data Protection API (DPAPI)** on Windows. For example, providing a username and password when prompted will create an XML file holding the encrypted password:

```
Get-Credential | Export-CliXml -Path secret.xml
```

The file can be opened in a text editor to view the encrypted password. The credential can be imported again using Import-CliXml:

```
$credential = Import-CliXml -Path secret.xml
```

And from there, the password may be viewed by making use of the GetNetworkCredential method:

```
$credential.GetNetworkCredential().Password
```

The password for the credential is encrypted using the current user account (protected by the login password). The key used is held in the user profile; the resulting file can only be decrypted on the computer it was created on (without a roaming profile).

Note that while the command above can be used on Linux and Mac operating systems, the password value in the XML file will be in plain text.

The Tee-Object command

The Tee-Object command is used to send output to two places at the same time. Tee-Object is used to write output to a console and a file or variable.

For example, the following command both displays the output of Get-Process on the screen and writes the content to a $processes variable:

```
Get-Process | Tee-Object -Variable processes
```

The first few values from the `$processes` variable are shown below:

```
PS> $processes

NPM(K)  PM(M)    WS(M)   CPU(s)      Id  SI ProcessName
------  -----    -----   ------      --  -- -----------
    10   1.50     9.59     0.00    9904   0 Aac3572DramHal_x86
    13   2.38    10.60     0.00   11868   0 Aac3572MbHal_x86
    10   1.70     8.63     0.00    5144   0 AacKingstonDramHal_x64
    11   1.64     9.63     0.00   11724   0 AacKingstonDramHal_x86
    32  33.48    10.23     0.06   11752   1 AcPowerNotification
```

`Tee-Object` writes file output as the console sees it (table or list) rather than writing in CSV or another format:

```
Get-Process | Tee-Object -FilePath .\processes.txt
```

The first few lines of the file are shown in *Figure 4.3*:

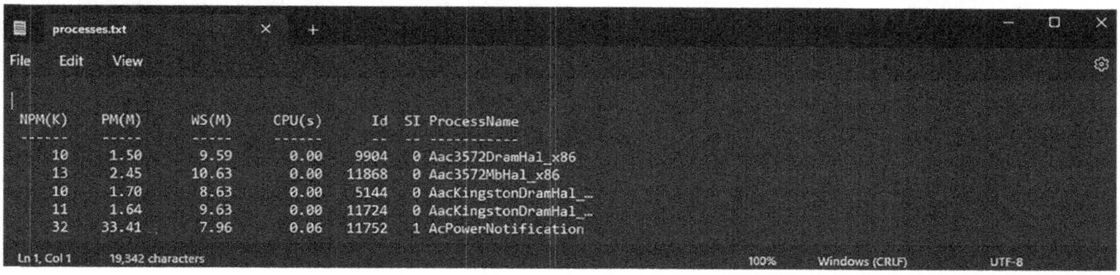


```
NPM(K)    PM(M)      WS(M)     CPU(s)      Id  SI ProcessName
------    -----      -----     ------      --  -- -----------
    10     1.50       9.59       0.00    9904   0 Aac3572DramHal_x86
    13     2.45      10.63       0.00   11868   0 Aac3572MbHal_x86
    10     1.70       8.63       0.00    5144   0 AacKingstonDramHal_…
    11     1.64       9.63       0.00   11724   0 AacKingstonDramHal_…
    32    33.41       7.96       0.06   11752   1 AcPowerNotification
```

Figure 4.3: Tee-Object file formatting

It is important to note here that some of the lines end with ellipses (...). The output format `Tee-Object` generates is governed by the width of the console. This can be good for debugging or even some logging, but it is not a good thing if something else is supposed to act on this file output.

The output shown above is part of the larger topic on formatting in PowerShell.

Formatting

Formatting in PowerShell encompasses the use of the `Format-` and `Out-` commands from the built-in `Microsoft.PowerShell.Utility` module.

PowerShell includes a complex formatting system that allows command authors to dictate the default appearance of objects in the console. Objects shown in the console almost always have more properties available than are displayed by default.

Formatting and exporting

It is important to note that format commands shown in this section should not be used alongside commands like Export-Csv. Formatting commands completely change the objects they receive into a set of formatting instructions.

This can be seen by combining Format-Table and ConvertTo-Csv in the example pipeline below:

```
Get-Process |
    Select-Object Name, ID, WorkingSet -First 2 |
    Format-Table |
    ConvertTo-Csv
```

This example will generate output like that shown below:

```
"ClassId2e4f51ef21dd47e99d3c952918aff9cd","pageHeaderEntry","pageFooterEntry",
"autosizeInfo","shapeInfo","groupingEntry"
"033ecb2bc07a4d43b5ef94ed5a35d280",,,,"Microsoft.PowerShell.Commands.Internal.
Format.TableHeaderInfo",
"9e210fe47d09416682b841769c78b8a3",,,,,,
"27c87ef9bbda4f709f6b4002fa4af63c",,,,,,
"27c87ef9bbda4f709f6b4002fa4af63c",,,,,,
"4ec4f0187cb04f4cb6973460dfe252df",,,,,,
"cf522b78d86c486691226b40aa69e95c",,,,,,
```

The output from the format commands can be used alongside commands such as Out-String and Out-File, but not with Add-Content, Set-Content, and Out-GridView (which can be used to display a user interface).

As shown above, Format-Table can be used to create tabular formats.

The Format-Table command

Format-Table can be used in a pipeline to request the table format of an object. As this is the default for Get-Process it has no significant effect on the output below:

```
PS> Get-Process -Id $PID | Format-Table

 NPM(K)    PM(M)     WS(M)    CPU(s)      Id  SI ProcessName
 ------    -----     -----    ------      --  -- -----------
    107   120.85    201.59      2.30    5512   1 pwsh
```

Format-Table, much like Select-Object, can request specific properties to display:

```
PS> Get-Process -Id $PID | Format-Table ProcessName, Path

ProcessName Path
----------- ----
pwsh        C:\Program Files\PowerShell\7\pwsh.exe
```

Wildcards may be used for the property name. If a wildcard is used and table format is requested PowerShell will fit as many properties in the table as it is able to fit in the console:

```
Get-Process | Format-Table *
```

Format-Table allows custom properties to be defined in much the same way as Select-Object:

```
Get-Process | Format-Table -Property @(
    'Name'
    @{ Name = 'Started'; Expression = { $_.StartTime } }
)
```

However, as Format-Table is writing something to display it includes several additional keys that may be defined in the custom property.

For example, the Width option can be added:

```
Get-Process | Format-Table -Property @(
    @{ Expression = 'Name'; Width = 30 }
    @{ Name = 'Started'; Expression = 'StartTime' }
)
```

It is also possible to dictate a format for fields using the FormatString key, which applies a specific format to a value:

```
Get-Process | Format-Table -Property @(
    @{ Expression = 'Name'; Width = 30 }
    @{ Expression = 'StartTime'; FormatString = '{0:HH:mm}' }
)
```

The format string used above is a composite format, commonly used with the -f operator. Composite formatting and the -f operator are explored in *Chapter 5*, *Operators*, and *Chapter 8*, *Strings, Numbers, and Dates*.

Additional parameters, such as AutoSize and Wrap, may be used to further affect the format.

Format-List can be used to generate a vertical view instead of a horizontal, tabular, view.

The Format-List command

The Get-Process command includes both table (the default) and list views. If run in a pipeline with no arguments, Format-List requests that any list format that may exist is applied:

```
PS> Get-Process -Id $PID | Format-List


Id      : 5512
Handles : 1062
CPU     : 9.859375
SI      : 1
Name    : pwsh
```

Because list formats do not have a width constraint, using a wildcard for the property can be used to display all properties of an object:

```
Get-Process -Id $PID | Format-List *
```

Like both `Select-Object` and `Format-Table`, custom properties may be created using a hashtable. As `Format-List` is generating a vertical view it does not support defining a `Width`.

`FormatString` is supported by `Format-List` in the same way as `Format-Table`:

```
Get-Process | Format-List -Property @(
    'Name'
    @{ Expression = 'StartTime'; FormatString = '{0:HH:mm}' }
)
```

Formatted output, often created using `Select-Object`, is frequently mixed with informational output in interactive scripts: scripts that prompt for user input or write informational messages for the user to read.

Select-Object, Write-Host, and inline output

Because PowerShell wants to make informed decisions about how to display something a 300 ms (millisecond) delay is implemented before something is displayed in the console.

If the example below is run in the console, the output will not be displayed in the order the commands imply:

```
& {
    $counter = @{ index = 0 }

    Write-Host 'Item picker'
    Write-Host '==========='
    $process = Get-Process | Select-Object -First 3
    $process | Select-Object -Property @(
        @{ Name = 'Option'; Expression = { ($counter.index++) }}
        'ProcessName'
        'ID'
        'StartTime'
    )
    [int]$picked = Read-Host 'Please select an item'

    Write-Host 'Thank you, you picked:'
    $process[$picked - 1]
}
```

Instead of showing the process list before the prompt to pick an item, the prompt is shown first, and the result of the Select-Object command is shown at the end:

```
Item picker
===========


Please select an item: 1
Thank you, you picked:
Option ProcessName     Id StartTime
------ -----------     -- ---------
     1 powershell    5768 01/05/2023 11:17:38
     2 pwsh          5512 01/05/2023 09:31:20
     3 pwsh         12384 01/05/2023 11:02:04
       powershell    5768 01/05/2023 11:17:38
```

There are several ways to prevent this problem.

Out-Host might be added to the Select-Object pipeline to immediately display values in the console rather than allowing PowerShell to delay this:

```
& {
    $counter = @{ index = 0 }

    Write-Host 'Item picker'
    Write-Host '==========='
    $process = Get-Process -Name pwsh, powershell
    $process | Select-Object -Property @(
        @{ Name = 'Option'; Expression = { ($counter.index++) }}
        'ProcessName'
        'ID'
        'StartTime'
    ) | Out-Host
    [int]$picked = Read-Host 'Please select an item'

    Write-Host 'Thank you, you picked:'
    $process[$picked - 1] | Out-Host
}
```

Or Select-Object in this case can be substituted with Format-Table, which will also immediately write to the console:

```
& {
    $counter = @{ index = 0 }
```

```
Write-Host 'Item picker'
Write-Host '==========='
$process = Get-Process -Name pwsh, powershell
$process | Format-Table -Property @(
    @{ Name = 'Option'; Expression = { ($counter.index++) }}
    'ProcessName'
    'ID'
    'StartTime'
) | Out-Host
[int]$picked = Read-Host 'Please select an item'

Write-Host 'Thank you, you picked:'
$process[$picked - 1] | Out-Host
}
```

With either change, the output from the script displays content in the right order:

```
Item picker
===========


Option ProcessName    Id StartTime
------ -----------    -- ---------
     1 powershell  27572 10/03/2024 11:22:08
     2 pwsh         2296 10/03/2024 08:43:21
     3 pwsh         5600 10/03/2024 08:43:04


Please select an item: 1
Thank you, you picked:

 NPM(K)    PM(M)      WS(M)     CPU(s)      Id  SI ProcessName
 ------    -----      -----     ------      --  -- -----------
     38   142.37     159.36       0.47   27572   1 powershell
```

This feature of formatted output is a relatively common problem for those writing menus and other interactive prompts.

Formats can be used to present a human-friendly view of something that is often a lot more complicated. As a by-product of this, what is shown by a format may differ from what is available.

Format-only properties

One of the more frustrating features of PowerShell is that authors can create properties that exist for the purposes of a formatted view only.

The ability to do this is useful, but where it hides the origin of a value it is detrimental to discovery and an unfriendly practice.

The Get-Process command has been used in many of the examples in this chapter. The Get-Process command outputs Process objects; the Process objects are subject to a format as shown below:

```
PS> Get-Process -Id $PID

 NPM(K)    PM(M)     WS(M)    CPU(s)      Id  SI ProcessName
 ------    -----     -----    ------      --  -- -----------
     92    75.65    114.28      1.41    5512   1 pwsh
```

Looking at the output above, it is reasonable to expect that it should be possible to select two of those columns:

```
Get-Process -Id $PID | Select-Object ProcessName, 'NPM(K)'
```

However, while ProcessName will show, NPM(K) will not. The NPM(K) column is added by a format and the value is derived from the value in the NPM property.

In this case, it does not take much to figure out that the (K) is just a divisor, a unit (KB) applied to the value. Get-Process is not the only command that exhibits this behavior. Modules such as UpdateServices use this feature extensively and the link between the displayed field and actual data is much less obvious.

Unfortunately, format-only values are not shown by Get-Member, and it is therefore not possible to use this as a tool to explore the origin of a value.

Advanced examples

The examples that follow are the most complex in this chapter. They follow the nested objects that are derived from PSControl:

https://learn.microsoft.com/en-us/dotnet/api/system.management.automation.pscontrol.

It is possible to explore these fully using tools like Get-Member, but doing so is a multi-stage process. Properties at every level must be expanded and explored. These examples are left without that deep explanation but may be used as-is.

The formats used can be found using the Get-FormatData along with the type of the object being formatted command. The easiest way to access the Type name is by using the hidden PSTypeNames property of all objects in PS:

```
$process = Get-Process -Id $PID
$format = Get-FormatData -TypeName $process.PSTypeNames
```

In this case, multiple formats are available, but only the Table and List formats will be explored in the code that follows.

The format definitions are nested under a FormatViewDefinition property. Then the Control property is used to describe each format.

To make this more complicated, a Process object (returned by Get-Process) has more than one table format. These are the values used with the View parameter of Format-Table.

For example, the command below shows the table formats:

```
$format.FormatViewDefinition | Where-Object {
    $_.Control.GetType().Name -eq 'TableControl'
}
```

One of those definitions is called Priority, which can be used with Format-Table:

```
Get-Process | Format-Table -View Priority
```

Only the process view definition is of interest. This is the default view displayed when looking at the output from Get-Process:

```
$tableFormat = $format.FormatViewDefinition | Where-Object {
    $_.Control.GetType().Name -eq 'TableControl' -and
    $_.Name -eq 'process'
}
```

Because this is a table format the Control property defines Headers and Rows, which describe how the table is formed.

A header is associated with a specific entry in a row by position in an array. A loop with a counter can be used to link these together:

```
$tableFormat | ForEach-Object {
    $viewName = $_.Name
    $viewType = $_.Control.GetType().Name

    $index = 0
    $columns = $_.Control.Rows.Columns

    $_.Control.Headers | ForEach-Object {
        [PSCustomObject]@{
            ViewName = $viewName
            ViewType = $viewType
            Label    = $_.Label
            Entry    = $columns[$index].DisplayEntry
        }
        $index++
    }
}
```

The output from this process is shown below:

```
ViewName ViewType       Label  Entry
-------- --------       -----  -----
process  TableControl NPM(K) script: [long]($_.NPM / 1024)
process  TableControl PM(M)  script: "{0:N2}" -f [float]($_.PM / 1MB)
process  TableControl WS(M)  script: "{0:N2}" -f [float]($_.WS / 1MB)
process  TableControl CPU(s) script: "{0:N2}" -f [float]($_.CPU)
process  TableControl        property: Id
process  TableControl        property: SI
process  TableControl        property: ProcessName
```

This shows that the NPM(K) property is created by taking the NPM property, dividing it by 1,024, and casting it to [long] (a 64-bit number).

A Process object does not have a List view defined, but a module returned by the Get-Module command does.

List views are slightly simpler and require slightly less work to extract. List views are described as a list of entries; there is no need to try and link up an array of headers to an array of values in rows.

The example below finds the format data for a PSModuleInfo object, the object type returned by the Get-Module command. It filters and expands the format data to create a short set of objects describing the composition of that format. This example combines several of the commands used in this chapter to dig into the output from Get-FormatData:

```
$module = Get-Module | Select-Object -First 1
Get-FormatData -TypeName $module.PSTypeNames |
    ForEach-Object FormatViewDefinition |
    Where-Object {
        $_.Control.GetType().Name -eq 'ListControl'
    } |
    ForEach-Object {
        $viewName = $_.Name
        $viewType = $_.Control.GetType().Name

        $_.Control.Entries.Items | Select-Object -Property @(
            @{ Name = 'ViewName'; Expression = { $viewName }}
            @{ Name = 'ViewType'; Expression = { $viewType }}
            'Label'
            @{ Name = 'Entry'; Expression = 'DisplayEntry' }
        )
    }
```

Formatting is a relatively small but complex and critical part of PowerShell. Like much of PowerShell, there is an opportunity to delve into the details, often without ever leaving the console.

Formatting is itself a small part of this much broader topic, which explores many of the capabilities of these generic commands for working in pipelines in PowerShell.

Summary

The pipeline is a key component of PowerShell. It allows data, as objects, to be sent from one command to another. Each command can act on the data it has received and, in many cases, return more data.

PowerShell includes a variety of commands for working with objects in a pipeline.

The Get-Member command allows the members (properties, methods, and so on) to be explored, which can be used to understand what an object is capable of.

[PSCustomObject] and [Ordered] can be used to create a new custom object. Historically, New-Object and Add-Member have had a significant part to play in creating custom objects but their usage has now been deprecated.

ForEach-Object is a common command that's used to run arbitrary code against objects in a pipeline. Where-Object may be used to filter a pipeline, returning only relevant objects.

The Select-Object command is used to define what properties should be returned. Select-Object can be used to include or remove objects from a pipeline, for example, by selecting the first few objects from a pipeline. The Sort-Object command takes pipeline input and allows it to be sorted based on property names, or more complex criteria described by a script block.

Comparisons of collections of objects are made possible using the Compare-Object command.

Content in PowerShell can be exported to and imported from files in a variety of different ways. This chapter explored exporting and importing content using the Export-Csv and Import-Csv commands, as well as the more complex output created by Export-CliXml.

Finally, formatting in PowerShell was briefly explored, as well as common issues with integrating commands into interactive sequences.

The next chapter, *Chapter 5, Operators*, explores the wide variety of operators available in PowerShell, ranging from arithmetic and comparison operators to binary and redirection operators.

Learn more on Discord

Read this book alongside other users, PowerShell experts, and the author himself. Ask questions, provide solutions to other readers, chat with the author via Ask Me Anything sessions, and much more.

Scan the QR code or visit the link to join the community.

https://packt.link/SecNet

5

Operators

In programming, an operator is a keyword that is used to manipulate an item of data. An operator might be used to compare values, add or subtract, perform replacements, split or join values, and so on. An operator is a fundamental part of any programming language, and PowerShell is no exception.

PowerShell has a wide variety of operators; each is explored within this chapter.

Many of the operators in PowerShell are binary, requiring two arguments (operands), such as `-eq`, `-like`, and so on.

Unary operators require a single argument (on the right-hand side), such as the `-not` and `-bnot` operators.

Ternary operators, which are new in PowerShell 7, require three arguments.

A small number of operators can be used as both unary and binary, including `-join` and `-split`.

This chapter covers the following topics:

- Precedence, grouping, and sub-expressions
- Unary, binary, and ternary operators
- Arithmetic operators
- Comparison operators
- Regular expression-based operators
- Logical operators
- Bitwise operators
- Assignment operators
- Type operators
- Redirection operators
- Other operators

Precedence and grouping are topics that apply to all operators.

Precedence, grouping, and sub-expressions

Each operator in PowerShell is given a precedence, an order in which it will be evaluated.

The operators used in this section are explored during this chapter.

Operator precedence

Operations are executed in a specific order depending on the operator used. For example, consider the following two simple calculations:

```
3 + 2 * 2
2 * 2 + 3
```

The result of both preceding expressions is 7 (2 multiplied by 2, and then add 3) because the multiplication operator has higher precedence than the addition operator.

Where operator precedence is equal, the expression is evaluated from left to right.

PowerShell includes a help document describing the precedence for each operator. The precedence list is long and not duplicated in this chapter:

```
Get-Help about_Operator_Precedence
```

The online version of the same document is available at Microsoft Learn:

https://learn.microsoft.com/en-us/powershell/module/microsoft.powershell.core/about/about_operator_precedence.

The help topic lists the operators in the order they are evaluated. The multiplication operator, *, has higher precedence (higher in the list) than addition, +; therefore, in an operation using both operators, * is calculated first.

The grouping operator can be used to affect the order in which terms in an expression are evaluated.

Grouping

Expressions in brackets or parentheses have the highest precedence and are, therefore, always calculated before any other.

Brackets may, therefore, be used to group expressions together in cases where the default operator precedence would give an incorrect result.

For example, if the intent of the expression below were to add together 3 and 2, and then multiply that by 2, the default operator precedence would cause an incorrect result:

```
3 + 2 * 2
```

Because the multiplication operator has a higher precedence, 2 * 2 is executed first, and then 3 is added to the result.

Adding brackets around the expression will make it match the intent stated above:

```
(3 + 2) * 2
```

The result of the preceding calculation is 10; the expression in brackets is calculated first, giving 5, and the result of that is multiplied by 2.

Sub-expression operator

Sub-expressions in PowerShell are somewhat like grouping operators in appearance.

PowerShell includes two sub-expression operators:

- Sub-expression: $( )
- Array sub-expression: @( )

The sub-expression operator is almost exclusively used in double-quoted strings to expand the properties of objects for inclusion in the string. For example, the Length property of a string is included in the double-quoted string below:

```
$word = 'one'
"Length: $($word.Length)"
```

The sub-expression is evaluated before the value is inserted into the string. If the sub-expression is omitted, PowerShell will expand $word; .Length is a literal value:

```
PS> $word = 'one'
PS> "Length: $word.Length"
Length: one.Length
```

The sub-expression operator can also be used when calling executables that use /Name:Value style parameters.

For example, if an object has a Path property containing a path to search, a sub-expression is required to pass that value to the /D parameter of FindStr:

```
$dir = [PSCustomObject]@{ Path = (Get-Item ~).FullName }
FindStr /D:$($dir.Path) SomeValue *.txt
```

The sub-expression is used here because PowerShell expands values in arguments as if they were double-quoted strings. If the sub-expression is omitted, FindStr will be handed the value of $dir converted to a string, followed by the literal value .Path.

The array sub-expression operator is not used inside strings, except perhaps inside a sub-expression.

Array sub-expression operator

The array sub-expression operator will always create an array regardless of the number of items enclosed by the operator.

It can, therefore, be used to create an array out of a single object:

```
$processes = @(Get-Process -ID $PID)
```

Piping the array to Get-Member will not show that it is an array because the pipeline enumerates array values. Get-Member, therefore, would show information about the Process object element inside the array.

If the value is directly used with the InputObject parameter, it can be shown to be an array, denoted by the TypeName:

```
PS> $processes = @(Get-Process -ID $PID)
PS> Get-Member -InputObject $Processes


   TypeName: System.Object[]
...
```

The array sub-expression operator can include any number of commands or elements, and even complex statements:

```
$myArray = @(
    Get-Process | Where-Object ProcessName -in @(
        'pwsh'
        'powershell'
    )
    Get-Process notepad
)
```

The examples above have made some simple use of the arithmetic operators.

Unary, binary, and ternary operators

As mentioned at the start of this chapter, operators can expect different numbers of arguments.

A unary operator requires a single argument (acting on a single item), and in PowerShell, this argument is normally placed on the right-hand side of the operator. For example, the -not operator is a unary operator used as shown below:

```
-not $false
```

Several operators can be used as either unary or binary. The addition operator, +, and subtraction operators can be used as unary operators:

```
+1
-1
```

Addition and subtraction operators may also be used as binary operators (acting on two items), that is, an operator that expects two arguments, one on the left and one on the right:

```
1 + 1
1 - 1
```

A third type of operator is one that expects three arguments, a ternary operator (acting on three items).

PowerShell only has one operator that is strictly classed as ternary. It is used to express a logical condition.

About the ternary operator

The ternary operator is a conditional operator that performs a comparison and returns one of two values.

The ternary operator can be used to replace the following statement:

```
$result = if ($value) {
    1
} else {
    2
}
```

When the ternary operator is used, the statement can be simplified to the following:

```
$result = $value ? 1 : 2
```

If $value is true, PowerShell sets $result to 1. If $value is false, PowerShell sets $result to 2.

As the ternary operator acts on a Boolean value, the values 0 and null, empty strings, and empty arrays are all considered to be false.

Complex expressions are those that might affect precedence, or commands that can be used with the ternary operator if the expression is enclosed in parentheses, for example:

```
(Get-Process notepad -ErrorAction Ignore) ? 'Running' : 'Not running'
```

The ternary operator is very concise and a useful addition for code targeting PowerShell 7 and above.

Arithmetic operators

Arithmetic operators are used to perform numeric calculations. The arithmetic operators in PowerShell are as follows:

- Addition: +
- Subtraction: -
- Multiplication: *
- Division: /
- Remainder: %

As well as its use in numeric calculations, the addition operator may also be used with strings, arrays, and hashtables. The multiplication operator may also be used with strings and arrays.

The addition operator attempts to add two values together.

Addition operator

The addition operator may be used to add values together, or any object type that supports addition.

For example, the following simple addition operation will result in the value 5.14159:

```
2.71828 + 3.14159
```

The addition operator may also be used to concatenate strings:

```
'good' + 'bye'
```

This style of concatenation can be applied to the example used with a sub-expression:

```
$word = 'one'
"Length: " + $word.Length
```

If an attempt is made to concatenate a string with a number, the number will be converted into a string:

```
'hello number ' + 1
```

The addition operator can be used as a unary operator, for example:

```
+1
```

Practically, this value is the same as writing 1 alone. The utility of + as a unary operator comes when converting string values to numeric values:

```
# Read-Host will read a string
$number = Read-Host 'Please enter a number'
# + can be used to convert this to a number
$number = +$number
```

The result of the operation can be demonstrated by using Get-Member to view the type name:

```
PS> $number | Get-Member


    TypeName: System.Int32
...
```

This approach will work even if the user responds to the prompt with a negative number. However, if the user responds with a string, an error will be shown – the same error as would be seen when running:

```
PS> +'string'
InvalidArgument: Cannot convert value "string" to type "System.Int32". Error:
"The input string 'string' was not in a correct format."
```

The same error is seen when an explicit attempt is made to add a string to a number.

PowerShell expects the entire expression to be numeric if the left-hand side of the expression is numeric:

```
PS> 1 + ' is the number I like to use'
InvalidArgument: Cannot convert value "is the number I like to use" to type
"System.Int32". Error: "Input string was not in a correct format."
```

PowerShell will try and coerce the value on the right-hand side into a number; therefore, a string containing a number is acceptable and will complete without error:

```
1 + '4'
```

The addition operator may be used to add single elements to an existing array. As arrays are of fixed size, a new array will be created containing 1, 2, and 3:

```
@(1, 2) + 3
```

Joining arrays with the addition operator is simple. Each of the following three examples creates an array, and each array contains the values 1, 2, 3, and 4:

```
@(1, 2) + @(3, 4)
(1, 2) + (3, 4)
1, 2 + 3, 4
```

The last example is an array containing 1, 2, 3, and 4 because the array operator has higher precedence than addition. Therefore, two arrays are added together.

The attempt to add like this will fail if the left of + is a scalar, a single value:

```
PS> 1 + 3, 4
InvalidOperation: Method invocation failed because [System.Object[]] does not
contain a method named 'op_Addition'.
```

Hashtables may be joined in a similar manner:

```
@{key1 = 1} + @{key2 = 2}
```

The addition operation fails if keys are duplicated as part of the addition operation:

```
PS> @{key1 = 1} + @{key1 = 2}
OperationStopped: Item has already been added. Key in dictionary: 'key1'  Key
being added: 'key1'Subtraction operator
```

Like the addition operator, the subtraction operator can be used as both a binary and unary operator.

Subtraction operator

The subtraction operator may only be used for numeric expressions. The results of the following expressions are 3 and -18, respectively:

```
5 - 2
2 - 20
```

Used as a unary operator, - is often used to represent negative numbers (numbers below 0):

```
-5
```

Subtraction is a simple but important operation used in everyday calculations. The following sections explore the multiplication, division, and remainder operators.

Multiplication operator

The multiplication operator can perform simple numeric operations. For example, the result of the following expression is 5:

```
2.5 * 2
```

The multiplication operator can be used to duplicate strings. The following example results in hellohellohello:

```
'hello' * 3
```

As with the addition operator, the multiplication operator will throw an error if a number is on the left of the expression. PowerShell will expect the entire expression to be numeric if the value on the left-hand side is numeric:

```
PS> 3 * 'hello'
InvalidArgument: Cannot convert value "hello" to type "System.Int32". Error:
"Input string was not in a correct format."
```

The multiplication operator may also be used to duplicate arrays. Each of the following examples creates an array containing one, two, one, and two:

```
@('one', 'two') * 2
('one', 'two') * 2
'one', 'two' * 2
```

The division operator complements the multiplication operator.

Division operator

The division operator performs numeric division:

```
PS> 20 / 5
4
```

Division by any non-zero numeric value is permitted, as shown in the simple example above.

An error will be thrown if an attempt to divide by 0 is made:

```
PS> 1 / 0
RuntimeException: Attempted to divide by zero.
```

Division using negative numbers is permitted in PowerShell. When a positive number is divided by a negative number, the result is negative.

Remainder operator

The remainder operator returns the remainder of the whole-number (integer) division. For example, the result of the following operation is 1:

```
3 % 2
```

One possible use of the remainder operator is alternating, that is, swapping between two values repeatedly. This can be used to perform an action on every second, third, fourth, and nth increment in an iteration. For example:

```
1..20 | ForEach-Object {
    if ($_ % 2 -eq 0) {
        $foregroundColor = 'Cyan'
    } else {
        $foregroundColor = 'White'
    }
    Write-Host $_ -ForegroundColor $foregroundColor
}
```

The preceding example alternates the color of the text.

Increment and decrement operators

The ++ and -- operators are used to increment and decrement numeric values. The increment and decrement operators are split into pre-increment and post-increment versions.

Post-increment and decrement operators are written after a value, for example:

```
$i = 0
$i++     # Post-increment
$i--     # Post-decrement
```

The pre-increment operators are written before a value, for example:

```
$i = 0
++$i     # Pre-increment
--$i     # Pre-decrement
```

In the examples above, nothing is shown in the console when these values run. Extra lines can be added to show the value after each operation:

```
$i = 0
Write-Host "i starts at $i"
$i++
Write-Host "i is now $i"
$i--
Write-Host "i is now $i"
```

The output of the example above is identical whether the pre- or post-versions of the operators are used.

These operators have output if they are enclosed in brackets (parentheses) or used as an argument for another operator. The post-increment operator is shown below; the values are only changed after the current value is displayed.

```
$i = 0
($i++)     # Post-increment
($i--)     # Post-decrement
```

And here is the pre-increment version, which shows that the values change before display:

```
$i = 0
(++$i)     # Pre-increment
(--$i)     # Pre-decrement
```

The post-increment operators are frequently seen in for loops, which are explored in more detail in *Chapter 6, Conditional Statements and Loops*. The value for $i is used and then incremented by one after use. In the case of the for loop, the value is incremented after the statements inside the loop block have executed:

```
for ($i = 1; $i -le 15; $i++) {
    Write-Host $i -ForegroundColor $i
}
```

The post-decrement operator reduces the value by one after use:

```
for ($i = 15; $i -ge 0; $i--) {
    Write-Host $i -ForegroundColor $i
}
```

Post-increment and post-decrement operators are often seen when iterating through an array – in this case, a while loop, which is also explored in more detail in *Chapter 6, Conditional Statements and Loops*:

```
$array = 1..15
$i = 0
while ($i -lt $array.Count) {
    # $i will increment after this statement has completed.
    Write-Host $array[$i++] -ForegroundColor $i
}
```

Pre-increment and pre-decrement operators are rarely seen. Instead of incrementing or decrementing a value after use, the change happens before the value is used. For example:

```
$array = 1..5
$i = 0
while ($i -lt $array.Count - 1) {
    # $i is incremented before use, 2 will be the first printed.
```

```
    Write-Host $array[++$i]
}
```

The post-increment operator, ++, is common and is typically used in looping scenarios like those above.

Comparison operators

Comparison operators can be used to compare two values. PowerShell has a wide variety of comparison operators, which are as follows:

- Equal to and not equal to: -eq and -ne
- Like and not like: -like and -notlike
- Greater than and greater than or equal to: -gt and -ge
- Less than and less than or equal to: -lt and -le
- Contains and not contains: -contains and -notcontains
- In and not in: -in and -notin

Values can be directly compared to one another in PowerShell using the equality operators.

eq and ne

The -eq (equal to) and -ne (not equal to) operators perform exact (and, by default, case-insensitive) comparisons. In the following example, true is returned for each of the comparisons:

```
1 -eq 1
'string' -eq 'string'
```

Similarly, -ne (not equal) will return true for each of the following:

```
20 -ne 100
'this' -ne 'that'
```

When working with comparison expressions, it is important to consider the left-hand side of the expression.

PowerShell will always attempt to convert the value on the right-hand side to match the type on the left. For example, in the following statement, the value on the right is converted to match the left (an int):

```
1 -eq '1'
```

Reversing the statement will return the same result:

```
'1' -eq 1
```

If PowerShell cannot convert the value, it will try a direct comparison. For example, PowerShell cannot convert the value on the right below to an integer:

```
1 -eq 'one'
```

Because PowerShell will always attempt to coerce values, a comparison of a Boolean value to a string is possible:

```
$true -eq 'True'
```

However, this style of comparison should be discouraged, as it suggests that the following is also possible:

```
$false -eq 'False'
```

In both cases, PowerShell takes the value on the right-hand side of the expression and coerces it directly to a Boolean value. As neither string is empty, the result of the conversion is always true:

```
[bool]'True'
[bool]'False'
```

The comparison of the Boolean value $false with the not-empty string 'False', therefore, will always show that the values differ.

Not all comparisons can be exact; a different operator is required for a wildcard-based comparison.

like and notlike

The -like and -notlike operators support wildcard terms on the right-hand side of the expression. The most obvious of these wildcards is the * character. * matches a string of any length, zero or more characters long:

```
'The cow jumped over the moon' -like '*moon*'
'' -like '*'
```

Individual characters may be represented by the ? character. This wildcard is exactly one character long.

```
'Hello world' -like '?ello ?orld'
'Hello world' -like '??llo w*'

'' -notlike '?*'
```

Extending this, a string containing one or more characters can be matched:

```
'Hello world' -like '?*'
'Hello world' -like '*?'
```

If the string is empty, the result of the comparison will be false.

```
'' -like '?*'
```

In addition to * and ?, a range of characters can be defined using square brackets:

```
'Hello world' -like '[f-k]*'
```

If a wildcard expressions should be literal, then the wildcard must escape. For example:

```
'*.txt' -like '`*.txt'
'*.txt' -like '`*.*'
```

The ` character escapes the special meaning of *. PowerShell can help provide a pattern with wildcard characters escaped. The command below escapes all the wildcard expressions in the string:

```
[WildcardPattern]::Escape('* [a-z] ?')
```

This will escape each character used to express a wildcard with a grave accent character:

```
`* `[a-z`] `?
```

When comparing numbers, or ordering values, the greater than and less than operators are used.

Greater than and less than

When comparing numbers, each of the operators -ge (greater than or equal to), -gt (greater than), -le (less than or equal to), and -lt (less than) is simple to use:

```
1 -ge 1        # Returns true
2 -gt 1        # Returns true
1.4 -lt 1.9    # Returns true
1.1 -le 1.1    # Returns true
```

String comparison with operators places 0 first, and then each lowercase and uppercase character in turn. For example, from least to greatest, 0123456789aAbBcCdD...xXyYzZ. Also, it is important to note the following:

- **Cultural variants of characters:** For example, the a A and b should be styled as code.
- **Other alphabets:** For example, Cyrillic and Greek come after the Roman alphabet (after Z).

Comparisons can be made in a specific culture when using commands such as Sort-Object with the Culture parameter. Comparisons are always based on en-US when using the operators:

```
'apples' -lt 'pears'    # Returns true
'Apples' -lt 'pears'    # Returns true
```

```
'bears' -gt 'Apples'     # Returns true
'å' -gt 'a'              # Returns true
```

When a case-sensitive operator, such as -clt, is used, B can be seen to fall between b and c:

```
'bat' -clt 'Bat'    # True, b before B
'Bat' -clt 'cat'    # True, B before c
```

The use of greater than and less than with strings may often be difficult to apply. Careful testing is recommended.

Case sensitivity

The comparison operators are not case-sensitive by default. Each of the comparison operators has two additional variants, one that explicitly states it is case-sensitive and another that explicitly states it is case-insensitive.

For example, the following statement returns true:

```
'Trees' -eq 'trees'
```

Adding a c prefix in front of the name of the operator forces PowerShell to make a case-sensitive comparison. The following statement returns false:

```
'Trees' -ceq 'trees'
```

In addition to the case-sensitive prefix, PowerShell also has an explicit case-insensitive modifier. In the following example, the statement returns true:

```
'Trees' -ieq 'trees'
```

However, as case-insensitive comparison is the default, it is extremely rare to see examples of the i prefix.

These behaviour prefixes can be applied to all the comparison operators.

The behavior of comparison operators used changes again when the left-hand side of the comparison is an array.

Comparison operators and arrays

When comparison operators are used with scalar values (a single item as opposed to an array), the comparison results in true or false.

When a comparison operator is used with an array or collection, the result of the comparison is all matching elements, that is, the array is enumerated, and all successfully compared values are returned. For example:

```
1, $null -ne $null              # Returns 1
1, 2, 3, 4 -ge 3                # Returns 3, 4
'one', 'two', 'three' -like '*e*'   # Returns one, three
```

This array comparison behavior does not apply when using -contains, -notcontains, -in, or -notin.

A little care is required when using comparisons with arrays as conditional expressions. For example, take the condition below in an if statement:

```
$value = 'one'
if ($value -notlike 't*') {
    'two or three not found'
}
```

In this example, the left is a scalar; -notlike will return a true or false value.

The condition can be removed to explore the output from -like and -notlike:

```
$value = 'one'
$value -like 't*' # Will be true
$value -notlike 't*' # Will be false
```

When the value on the left is an array, the outcome can yield a less obvious result:

```
$value = 'one', 'two', 'three'
If ($value -notlike 't*') {
    'two or three not found'
}
```

This happens because the comparison no longer returns a true or false value; instead, it returns the values that satisfy the condition:

```
$value = 'one', 'two', 'three'
$value -notlike 't*'    # Returns the value "one"
```

To establish the absence of a thing in an array when using a wildcard comparison, the -not operator and a positive comparison must be used instead:

```
$value = 'one', 'two', 'three'
If (-not ($value -like 't*')) {
    'two and three not found'
}
```

The variable $value is tested to see if it contains any value matching the wildcard expression t*. Extra parentheses are required to stop -not acting only on $value. Then, the whole expression returns true if none of those values are found.

These steps are broken down below:

```
$value = 'one', 'two', 'three'

# Will find the values two and three
$value -like 't*'
```

```
# True because the array of results is not empty
[bool]($value -like 't*')

# Negates the result above, simulating -notlike on a single value
-not ($values -like 't*')
```

The ability to compare against an array is why it is suggested that $null is placed on the left of a comparison expression.

Comparisons to null

Returning each matching value from an array can be problematic if a comparison is used to test whether a variable holding an array exists.

In the following example, -eq is successfully used to test that a value has been assigned to a variable called array:

```
$array = 1, 2
if ($array -eq $null) { Write-Host 'Variable not set' }
```

This test is valid if the array does not hold two or more null values. When two or more values are present, the condition unexpectedly returns true:

```
PS> $array = 1, 2, $null, $null
PS> if ($array -eq $null) { Write-Host 'No values in array' }
No values in array
```

This happens because the result of the comparison is an array with two null values. PowerShell returns matching values from the array, not just true or false.

If the value of $array were a single null value, PowerShell would flatten the array for the comparison. With two values, PowerShell cannot do that. The effect of two null values can be seen when casting each to a Boolean:

```
[bool]@($null)              # Returns false
[bool]@($null, $null)       # Returns true
```

To avoid this problem, $null must be on the left-hand side of the expression. For example, the following Write-Host statement does not execute; the array variable is not null:

```
$array = 1, 2, $null, $null
if ($null -eq $array) { Write-Host 'Variable not set' }
```

In this case, the array is not enumerated; null is compared with the entire array. The result will be false; the array variable is set.

contains and in

The -contains, -notcontains, -in, and -notin operators are used to test the content of arrays. Each comparison is exact; wildcards cannot be used on the right-hand side of the operator.

When using -contains or -notcontains, the array must be on the left-hand side of the operator:

```
1, 2 -contains 2       # Returns true
1, 2, 3 -contains 4    # Returns false
```

When using -in or -notin, the array must be on the right-hand side of the operator:

```
1 -in 1, 2, 3     # Returns true
4 -in 1, 2, 3     # Returns false
```

-contains or -in?

When using comparison operators, I tend to write the subject (the item I want to compare) on the left and the object on the right.

Comparisons to null are an exception to this rule: null is placed on the left.

The subject is the variable or property I am testing; the object is the thing I am testing against. For example, I might set the subject to a user in Active Directory:

```
$subject = Get-ADUser -Identity $env:USERNAME -Properties @(
    'department'
    'memberOf'
)
```

I use -contains where the subject is an array and the object is a single value:

```
$subject.MemberOf -contains 'CN=Group,DC=domain,DC=example'
```

I use -in where the subject is a single value and the object is an array:

```
$subject.Department -in 'Department1', 'Department2'
```

The -contains and -in operators are used for literal comparisons against arrays. For partial or wildcard matching, -like or a regular expression operator might be used.

Regular expression-based operators

Regular expressions are an advanced form of pattern matching. In PowerShell, some operators have direct support for regular expressions. Regular expressions themselves are covered in much greater detail in *Chapter 9, Regular Expressions*.

The following operators use regular expressions:

- Match: -match
- Not match: -notmatch
- Replace: -replace
- Split: -split

The -match operator tests a string, or array of strings, against a pattern.

match and notmatch

The -match and -notmatch operators test whether a string matches a regular expression. If so, the operators will return $true or $false:

```
'The cow jumped over the moon' -match 'cow'   # Returns true
'The       cow' -match 'The +cow'             # Returns true
```

In the preceding example, the + symbol is reserved; it indicates that The is followed by one or more spaces before cow.

Match is a comparison operator

Like the other comparison operators, if -match (or -notmatch) is used against an array, it returns each matching element instead of true or false. The following comparison returns the values one and three:

```
"one", "two", "three" -match 'e'
```

When -match is used against an array, the $matches variable is not set.

In addition to returning a true or false value about the state of the match, a successful match adds values to a reserved variable, $matches. For example, the following regular expression uses a character class (a set of values enclosed in square brackets) to indicate that it should match any character from 0 to 4, repeated 0 or more times:

```
'1234567689' -match '[0-4]*'
```

Once the match has been executed, the $matches variable (a hashtable) is populated with the part of the string that matched the expression:

```
PS> $matches

Name                           Value
----                           -----
0                              1234
```

Regular expressions use parentheses to denote groups. Groups may be used to capture interesting elements of a string:

```
PS> 'Group one, Group two' -match 'Group (.*), Group (.*)'
True
PS> $matches
Name                            Value
----                            -----
2                               two
1                               one
0                               Group one, Group two
```

The captured value, one, is held in the group named 1, and it is accessible using either of the following statements:

```
$matches[1]
$matches.1
```

The $matches variable is an automatically filled hashtable; in the preceding example, the value 1 is used as a key to access a capture group.

replace

The -replace operator performs string replacement based on a regular expression. For example, it can be used to replace several instances of the same thing:

```
PS> 'abababab' -replace 'a', 'c'
cbcbcbcb
```

In the example, a is the regular expression that dictates what must be replaced. c is the value any matching values should be replaced with.

The syntax for the -replace operator can be generalized as follows:

```
<Value> -replace <Match>, <Replace-With>
```

If the Replace-With value is omitted, the matches are replaced with nothing (that is, they are removed):

```
PS> 'abababab' -replace 'a'
bbbb
```

Regular expressions use parentheses to capture groups (a sub-string of the original). The -replace operator can use those groups. Each group may be used in the Replace-With argument. For example, a set of values can be reversed:

```
'value1,value2,value3' -replace '(.*),(.*),(.*)', '$3,$2,$1'
```

In the preceding regular expression, .* matches zero or more of any character. Each capture group is expected to be separated by a comma value.

The values $1, $2, and $3 are references to each of the capture groups in the order they appear in the expression. These tokens or references are only substituted if the match includes a group to replace them with. For example:

```
'1' -replace '.', 'No groups, $1 is not substituted'
```

If a literal value of $1 is required in the Replace-With text, the value can escape using an additional $ character:

```
'1' -replace '(1)', 'The value of group $$1 is $1'
```

The extra $ will be removed by -replace regardless of whether the pattern contains the group.

When performing the operations above, the Replace-With argument uses single quotes to prevent PowerShell from evaluating the group references as if they were variables. This problem is shown in the following example. The first attempt works as expected; the second shows an expanded Power-Shell variable instead:

```
PS> 'value1,value2,value3' -replace '(.*),(.*),(.*)', '$3,$2,$1'
value3,value2,value1
PS> $1 = $2 = $3 = 'Oops'
PS> 'value1,value2,value3' -replace '(.*),(.*),(.*)', "$3,$2,$1"
Oops,Oops,Oops
```

Capture groups are explored in greater detail in *Chapter 9, Regular Expressions*.

Finally, the -replace operator can use a script block as the Replace-With argument. In the example below, -replace is used on an array of strings. Each string contains a ProcessID. The Get-Process command is used on each value to replace the ID with a process name:

```
'0', '4', $PID -replace '.+', { (Get-Process -Id $_.Value).Name }
```

The script block, enclosed in { }, uses the variable $_, which holds a System.Text.RegularExpressions. Match object. This object in turn has a Value, which includes the matched value:

```
@(
    'Process: 0'
    'Process: 4'
    "Process: $PID"
) -replace '\d+', {
    (Get-Process -ID $_.Value).Name
}
```

The output from this example is:

```
Process: Idle
Process: System
Process: pwsh
```

The `Match` object used here is explored in *Chapter 9, Regular Expressions*.

The `-replace` operator is incredibly useful and widely used.

split

The `-split` operator splits a string into an array based on a regular expression.

The following example splits a string into an array containing a, b, c, and d, based on each of the numbers in the string:

```
PS> 'a1b2c3d4' -split '[0-9]'
a
b
c
d
```

The `-split` operator can be used as a unary operator to split up a string based on contiguous white space. The example below will return an array of a, b, and c:

```
-split "a`tb       c"
```

The syntax for the `-split` operator can be generalized as follows. Only the `Match` argument is mandatory:

```
<Value> -split <Match>, <Maximum-Number>, <Split-Options>
```

The results of a split can be assigned to one or more variables. For example:

```
$first, $second, $third = '1,2,3,4,5' -split ','
```

The string 1 will be assigned to `$first` and 2 to `$second`. The variable `$third` will contain the strings 3, 4, and 5 as an array. Using `$null` instead would discard 3, 4, and 5:

```
$first, $second, $null = '1,2,3,4,5' -split ','
```

`Maximum-Number` can be used to limit the number of split operations performed on the string on the left-hand side.

The default value of `Maximum-Number` is 0, meaning an unlimited number of split operations. The following example will result in an array containing two elements: the first element will be the string 1, and the second element will be 2,3,4,5:

```
PS> $split = '1,2,3,4,5' -split ',', 2
PS> $split
1
2,3,4,5
```

Maximum-Number can negatively index. This changes the expression to match right to left (instead of the default left to right). For example, the first element in this example will be 1,2,3,4, and the second will be 5:

```
PS> $split = '1,2,3,4,5' -split ',', -2
PS> $split
1,2,3,4
5
```

If -3 is used instead, three elements will be created, splitting from the end of the string:

```
PS> $split = '1,2,3,4,5' -split ',', -3
PS> $split
1,2,3
4
5
```

The Split-Options field is used to change how the match is performed. It includes several options:

*   SimpleMatch
*   RegexMatch
*   CultureInvariant
*   IgnorePatternWhitespace
*   Multiline
*   Singleline
*   IgnoreCase
*   ExplicitCapture

The .NET reference has descriptions of each of these possible values:

https://learn.microsoft.com/en-gb/dotnet/api/system.management.automation.splitoptions.

These values are also explored in *Chapter 9, Regular Expressions*.

For example, the SimpleMatch option changes -split to be explicit instead of using a regular expression, as shown in the following example:

```
'a?b?c?d?' -split 'b?', 0, 'SimpleMatch'
```

The preceding example splits the string in two; the first value will be a?, and the second c?d?. If SimpleMatch is taken away, the result will be very different. In a regular expression, the ? character makes the preceding character optional.

Multiple options can be used as a comma-separated list. For example:

```
'axbxcxd' -csplit ' X ', 0, 'IgnoreCase, IgnorePatternWhiteSpace'
```

The -csplit variant of the -split operator makes the match case-sensitive; setting the IgnoreCase option switches back to case-insensitive.

Logical operators

Logical operators evaluate two or more comparisons or other operations that produce a `Boolean` (true or false) result.

The following logic operators are available:

- And: `-and`
- Or: `-or`
- Exclusive or: `-xor`
- Not: `-not` and `!`

and

The `-and` operator returns true if the values on the left-hand and right-hand sides are both true.

For example, each of the following returns `$true`:

```
$true -and $true
1 -lt 2 -and "string" -like 's*'
1 -eq 1 -and 2 -eq 2 -and 3 -eq 3
(Test-Path C:\Windows) -and (Test-Path 'C:\Program Files')
```

The `-and` operator is often combined with the `-or` operator.

or

The `-or` operator returns true if the value on the left, the value on the right, or both are `true`.

For example, each of the following returns `$true`:

```
$true -or $true
2 -gt 1 -or "something" -ne "nothing"
1 -eq 1 -or 2 -eq 1
(Test-Path C:\Windows) -or (Test-Path D:\Windows)
```

The `-and` and `-or` operators are very frequently used, and often in combination with the `-not` operator.

not

The `-not` (or `!`) operator, a unary operator, is used to negate the expression that follows it.

For example, each of the following returns true:

```
-not $false
-not (Test-Path X:\)
-not ($true -and $false)
!($true -and $false)
```

The `-not` operator will always coerce the value on the right-hand side to a Boolean value. The result of the two examples below is false because the string has a value:

```
-not 'string'
!'string'
```

It is rare but entirely possible to use the `-not` operator next to another `-not` operator. For example, the expression below returns true:

```
$string = 'string'
-not -not $string
```

This is slightly contrary, and is more often found to be used with the `!` variant of the operator:

```
$string
!!$string
```

The result is always a Boolean value – true if the string is not empty and false if the string is empty.

The `-xor` operator is perhaps the least common of the logic operators.

xor (eXclusive OR)

The `-xor` operator will return true if either the value on the left is true or the value on the right is true, but not both.

For example, each of the following returns `$true`:

```
$true -xor $false
1 -le 2 -xor 1 -eq 2
(Test-Path C:\Windows) -xor (Test-Path D:\Windows)
```

The `-xor` operator is perhaps one of the most rarely used in PowerShell.

Bitwise operators

Bitwise operators are used to perform operations based around the bits that make up a numeric value. Each operator returns the numeric result of a bitwise operation.

The available operators are:

*   Binary and: `-band`
*   Binary or: `-bor`
*   Binary exclusive or: `-bxor`
*   Binary not: `-bnot`
*   Shift left: `-shl`
*   Shift right: `-shr`

All numeric values can be broken down into bytes and, in turn, bits, a base 2 value.

A byte is made up of 8 bits. Each bit in the byte has a value based on its position, with the highest value (or most significant) first. These bits can be combined to make up any number between 0 and 255.

The possible bit values for a byte in base 10 can be represented as a table:

Bit position	1	2	3	4	5	6	7	8
Bit value	128	64	32	16	8	4	2	1

Table: 5.1: Bit (base 2) values of a base 10 byte

This is not to say that the bitwise operators only work on byte values. The examples in this section use a single byte as the easiest to describe as a table.

Bitwise operators are perhaps not all that frequently used in PowerShell. In this book, they are used when exploring permissions in *Chapter 10, Files, Folders, and the Registry*, and again in *Chapter 19, Classes and Enumerations*, while looking at flag enumerations.

The bitwise operators demonstrated here will often return a 32-bit integer (int or System.Int32) value. When both values are numerically smaller (in maximum absolute value) than a 32-bit integer, the result will be a 32-bit integer.

A 32-bit integer can have a minimum value of -2147483648 and a maximum value of 2147483647. This is comprised of one signing bit and 31 bits that can be used to define the number:

Get-Member can be used to show this in action:

```
# Both sides are int, result is System.Int32
1 -band 1 | Get-Member
```

In this case, both sides of the expression are an int, so the result will also be int.

Similarly, if the input value is a byte, the result will be an int. A byte has a minimum value of 0 and a maximum of 255:

```
# Both sides are byte, result is Int32
[byte]1 -band [byte]1 | Get-Member
```

The output type only changes when the value type on either side can possibly exceed the capacity of 32 bits. At that point, the largest of the types is used.

A 64-bit integer (System.Int64) is made up of 8 bytes and has a maximum value of 9223372036854775807. This value, therefore, cannot possibly be represented as a 32-bit integer. If the value used on either side is a 64-bit integer, the result will be a 64-bit integer.

Both statements below show that the operator creates a System.Int64 value:

```
[Int64]1 -band 1 | Get-Member
1 -band [Int64]1 | Get-Member
```

Each of the examples above has made use of the bitwise AND operator.

band (bitwise AND)

The result of -band is a number where each of the bits in both the value on the left and the value on the right is set.

In the following example, the result is 2:

```
11 -band 6
```

This bitwise AND operation can be shown in a table. Each value is shown in binary:

Bit value		8	4	2	1
Left-hand side	11	1	0	1	1
Right-hand side	6	0	1	1	0
-band	2	0	0	1	0

Table 5.2: 11 -band 6

The result of -band is a number where both the value on the left-hand side and the value on the right-hand side include the bit.

bor (bitwise OR)

The result of -bor is a number where the bits are set in either the value on the left or right.

In the following example, the result is *15*:

```
11 -bor 12
```

This operation can be shown in a table:

Bit value		8	4	2	1
Left-hand side	11	1	0	1	1
Right-hand side	12	1	1	0	0
-band	15	1	1	1	1

Table 5.3: 11 -bor 12

The result is a number made up of the bits from each number where either number has the bit set.

bxor (bitwise eXclusive OR)

The result of -bxor is a number where the bits are set in either the value on the left or the value on the right, but not both.

In the following example, the result is 11:

```
6 -bxor 13
```

This operation can be shown in a table:

Bit value		8	4	2	1
Left-hand side	6	0	1	1	0
Right-hand side	13	1	1	0	1
-band	11	1	0	1	1

Table 5.4: 6 -bxor 13

The -bxor operator is useful for toggling bit values. For example, -bxor might be used to toggle the AccountDisable bit of UserAccountControl in Active Directory:

```
512 -bxor 2 # Result is 514 (Disabled, 2 is set)
514 -bxor 2 # Result is 512 (Enabled, 2 is not set)
```

The exclusive OR operator is useful to toggle bits in a value; to reverse the bits in a value, -bnot must be used.

bnot (bitwise NOT)

The -bnot operator is applied before a numeric value; it does not use a value on the left-hand side. The result is a value that's composed of all bits that are not set.

The -bnot operator works with signed and unsigned 32-bit and 64-bit integers (Int32, UInt32, Int64, and UInt64). When working with 8-bit or 16-bit integers (SByte, Byte, Int16, and UInt16), the result is always a signed 32-bit integer (Int32).

In the following example, the result is -123:

```
-bnot 122
```

As the preceding result is a 32-bit integer (Int32), it is difficult to show the effect in a small table. If this value were an SByte, the operation could be expressed in a table, as follows:

Bit value		Signing	64	32	16	8	4	2	1
Before -bnot	122	0	1	1	1	1	0	1	0
After -bnot	-123	1	0	0	0	0	1	0	1

Table 5.5: -bnot 122

As shown in the preceding table, the -bnot operator reverses the value for each bit. The signing bit is not treated any differently.

shl and shr (shift left and right operators)

The -shl and -shr operators were introduced with PowerShell 3.0. These operators perform bit-shifting.

The `-shl` and `-shr` operators have the lowest precedence and are only executed after all other operators. For example, the result of the following calculation is 128; the multiplication and addition operators are evaluated before `-shl`:

```
2 * 4 -shl 2 + 2
```

The effect of shift operators is best demonstrated by representing numeric values in binary. For the value of 78, the following bits must be set:

Bit value	128	64	32	16	8	4	2	1
On or off	0	1	0	0	1	1	1	0

Table 5.6: Bit values

When a left-shift operation is performed, every bit is moved a defined number of places to the left; in the following example, it is one bit to the left:

```
78 -shl 1
```

The result is 156, which is expressed in this bit table:

Bit value	128	64	32	16	8	4	2	1
Before shift	0	1	0	0	1	1	1	0
After shift	1	0	0	1	1	1	0	0

Table 5.7: Shift left

Shifting one bit to the right reverses the operation:

```
PS> 156 -shr 1
78
```

When the shift-left (`-shl`) operator converts values using left or right shifting, bits that are set and right-shifted past the rightmost bit (bit value 1) become 0. For example:

```
PS> 3 -shr 1
1
```

This is expressed in the following table. Bits that end up in the rightmost column are discarded; they are outside of the range of bits used by the numeric value:

Bit value	128	64	32	16	8	4	2	1	Out of range
Before shift	0	0	0	0	0	0	1	1	
After shift	0	0	0	0	0	0	0	1	1

Table 5.8: Shift right – discarded bits

If the numeric value is of a specific numeric type, the resulting number cannot exceed the maximum value for that type. For example, a byte has a maximum value of 255; if the value of 255 is shifted one bit to the left, the resulting value will be 254:

```
PS> [byte]255 -shl 1
254
```

Shifting out of range is shown in this table:

Bit value	Out of range	128	64	32	16	8	4	2	1
Before shift		1	1	1	1	1	1	1	1
After shift	1	1	1	1	1	1	1	1	0

Table 5.9: Shift left – discarded bits

If the value were capable of being larger, such as a 16- or 32-bit integer, the value would be allowed to increase, as it would no longer fall out of range:

```
PS> [Int16]255 -shl 1
510
```

Bit shifting like this is easiest to demonstrate with unsigned types such as Byte, UInt16, UInt32, and UInt64. Unsigned types cannot support values lower than 0 (negative numbers), as they have no way of describing a negative value.

Signed types, such as SByte, Int16, Int32, and Int64, use the highest-order bit to indicate whether the value is positive or negative. For example, this table shows the bit positions for a signed byte (SByte):

Bit position	1	2	3	4	5	6	7	8
Bit value	Signing	64	32	16	8	4	2	1

Table 5.10: Signed byte

The preceding bit values may be used to express numbers between 127 and -128. The binary forms of 1 and -1 are shown as an example in the following table:

Bit value	Signing	64	32	16	8	4	2	1
1	0	0	0	0	0	0	0	1
-1	1	1	1	1	1	1	1	1

Table 5.11: Positive and negative in bits

For a signed type, each bit (except for signing) adds to a minimum value:

- When the signing bit is not set, add each value to 0
- When the signing bit is set, add each value to -128

When applying this to left shift, if the value of 64 is shifted one bit to the left, it becomes -128:

```
PS> ([SByte]64) -shl 1
-128
```

The shift left into the signing bit is expressed in the following table:

Bit value	Signing	64	32	16	8	4	2	1
Before shift	0	1	0	0	0	0	0	0
After shift	1	0	0	0	0	0	0	0

Table 5.12: Shift into signing bit

Shift operations such as these are common in the networking world. For example, the IP address 192.168.4.32 may be represented in several different ways:

- In hexadecimal: C0A80420
- As an unsigned 32-bit integer: 3232236576
- As a signed 32-bit integer: -1062730720

The signed and unsigned versions of an IP address are calculated using left shift. For example, the IP address 192.168.4.32 may be written as a signed 32-bit integer (Int32):

```
(192 -shl 24) + (168 -shl 16) + (4 -shl 8) + 32
```

Shift operations such as these can be useful but are not common. The next section explores the assignment operator.

Assignment operators

Assignment operators are used to give values to variables. The assignment operators that are available are as follows:

- Assign: =
- Add and assign: +=
- Subtract and assign: -=
- Multiply and assign: *=
- Divide and assign: /=
- Remainder and assign: %=

As with the arithmetic operators, add and assign may be used with strings, arrays, hashtables, and many more. Multiply and assign may be used with strings and arrays.

Assign, add and assign, and subtract and assign

The assignment operator (=) is used to assign values to variables and properties; for example, it may be used to assign a value to a variable:

```
$variable = 'some value'
```

Alternatively, the PowerShell console window title (or **Windows Terminal** tab title) might be changed by assigning a new value to the WindowTitle property:

```
$host.UI.RawUI.WindowTitle = 'PowerShell window'
```

The add and assign operator (+=) operates in a similar manner to the addition operator. The following example assigns the value 1 to a variable, and then += is used to add 20 to that value:

```
$i = 1
$i += 20
```

The preceding example is equivalent to writing the following:

```
$i = 1
$i = $i + 20
```

The add-and-assign operator, +=, can be used to concatenate strings:

```
$string = 'one'
$string += 'one'
```

As with the addition operator, attempting to add a numeric value to an existing string is acceptable. Attempting to add a string to a variable containing a numeric value is not:

```
PS> $variable = 1
PS> $variable += 'one'
InvalidArgument: Cannot convert value "one" to type "System.Int32". Error:
"Input string was not in a correct format."
```

The += operator may be used to add elements to an existing array:

```
$array = 1, 2
$array += 3
```

The += operator can be used to add another array:

```
$array = 1, 2
$array += 3, 4
```

The += operator may be used to join two hashtables:

```
$hashtable = @{key1 = 1}
$hashtable += @{key2 = 2}
```

As seen when using the addition operator, the operation fails if one of the keys already exists.

The subtract and assign operator (-=) is intended for numeric operations, as shown in the following examples:

```
$i = 20
$i -= 2
```

After this operation has been completed, $i has a value of 18.

Multiply and assign, divide and assign, and modulus and assign

Numeric assignments using the multiply and assign operator may be performed using *=. The value held by the variable i is 4:

```
$i = 2
$i *= 2
```

The multiply and assign operator may be used to duplicate a string held in a variable:

```
$string = 'one'
$string *= 2
```

The value on the right-hand side of the *= operator must be numeric or able to convert to a number. For example, a string containing the number 2 is acceptable:

```
$string = 'one'
$string *= '2'
```

Using a string that PowerShell cannot convert to a number will result in an error, as follows:

```
PS> $variable = 'one'
PS> $variable *= 'one'
InvalidArgument: Cannot convert value "one" to type "System.Int32". Error:
"Input string was not in a correct format."
```

The multiply and assign operator may be used to duplicate an array held in a variable. In the following example, the variable holds the value 1, 2, 1, 2 after this operation:

```
$variable = 1, 2
$variable *= 2
```

The divide-and-assign operator is used to perform numeric operations. The variable holds a value of 1 after the following operation:

```
$variable = 2
$variable /= 2
```

The remainder-and-assign operator will assign the result of the remainder operation to a variable:

```
$variable = 10
$variable %= 3
```

After the preceding operation, the variable holds a value of 1, which is the remainder when dividing 10 by 3.

Statements can be assigned to a variable

In PowerShell, statements can be assigned to variables. All output from that statement will be captured in the variable.

The most common use for this is capturing arrays of results. The following example creates a custom object that includes output from both the `Win32_Service` CIM class and the `Get-Process` command. All the generated objects are assigned to the `$serviceInfo` variable:

```
$services = Get-CimInstance Win32_Service -Filter 'State="Running"'
$serviceInfo = foreach ($service in $services) {
    $process = Get-Process -ID $service.ProcessID
    [PSCustomObject]@{
        Name        = $service.Name
        ProcessName = $process.Name
        ProcessID   = $service.ProcessID
        Path        = $process.Path
        MemoryUsed  = $process.WorkingSet64 / 1MB
    }
}
```

Assigning statements such as loops in PowerShell is the most efficient way of gathering a set of results into a variable.

The assignment of statements such as loops in PowerShell will be discussed in *Chapter 6, Conditional Statements and Loops*.

Assignment and other operators

Assigning a value to a variable is a useful step in simplifying a piece of code. It can be used to break up a complex statement into multiple parts, and it acts as a point that can be inspected if debugging code.

For example, the `if` statement below might be considered unclear and too complex:

```
$value = 1, 2, 3
if ($value -and $value.Count -eq 3 -and $value -contains 2 -and -not ($value
-gt 4)) {
    <# Script statements #>
}
```

Assigning a value before the `if` condition can make it easier to read the condition:

```
$value = 1, 2, 3
$isValidValue = $value -and $value.Count -eq 3 -and $value -contains 2 -and
-not ($value -gt 4)
```

```
if ($isValidValue) {
    <# Script statements #>
}
```

Adding line breaks to the comparison might improve how readable the expression is:

```
$isValidValue = $value -and
    $value.Count -eq 3 -and
    $value -contains 2 -and
    -not ($value -gt 4)

if ($isValidValue) {
    <# Script statements #>
}
```

Combining operators and assigning the result is a useful technique that can be used to simplify code without sacrificing readability.

Type operators

Type operators are designed to work with and test .NET types. The following operators are available:

- As: -as
- Is: -is
- Is not: -isnot

These operators may be used to convert an object of one type into another, or to test whether an object is of a given type.

as

The -as operator is used to attempt to convert a value into an object of a specified type. The operator returns null (without throwing an error) if the conversion cannot be completed.

For example, the operator may be used to perform the following conversions:

```
"1" -as [Int32]
'String' -as [Type]
```

If the attempt to convert the value fails, nothing is returned, and no error is raised:

```
$true -as [DateTime]
```

The -as operator can be useful for testing whether a value can be cast to a specific type, or whether a specific type exists.

For example, the System.Windows.Forms assembly is not imported by default, and the System.Windows.Forms.Form type does not exist in the current PowerShell session.

The -as operator may be used to test if it is possible to find the System.Windows.Forms.Form type:

```
if (-not ('System.Windows.Forms.Form' -as [Type])) {
    Write-Host 'Adding assembly' -ForegroundColor Green
    Add-Type -Assembly System.Windows.Forms
}
```

If the System.Windows.Forms assembly has not been imported, attempting to turn the string, System.Windows.Forms.Form, into a type will fail. The failure to convert will not generate an error.

is and isnot

The -is and -isnot operators test whether a value is of a specified type.

For example, each of the following returns true:

```
'string' -is [String]
1 -is [Int32]
[String] -is [Type]
123 -isnot [String]
```

The -is and -isnot operators are especially useful for testing the exact type of a value, often in an if statement when the action taken depends on the value type.

Redirection operators

Chapter 4, Working with Objects in PowerShell, started exploring the different output streams that PowerShell utilizes.

Information from a command may be redirected using the redirection operator, >. Information may be sent to another stream or a file.

For example, the output from a command can be directed to a file. The file contains the output as it would have been displayed in the console:

```
PS> Get-Process -Id $pid > process.txt
PS> Get-Content process.txt

 NPM(K)    PM(M)     WS(M)    CPU(s)      Id  SI ProcessName
 ------    -----     -----    ------      --  -- -----------
     78   144.69    186.91     12.69   15284   1 pwsh
```

Each of the streams in PowerShell has a number associated with it. These are shown in the following table:

Stream name	Stream number
Standard out	1
Error	2
Warning	3
Verbose	4
Debug	5
Information	6

Table 5.13: PowerShell streams

Each of the preceding streams can be redirected. In most cases, PowerShell provides parameters for commands, which can be used to capture the streams when used. For example, the ErrorVariable , InformationVariable, and WarningVariable parameters.

About Write-Host

Before PowerShell 5, the output written using the Write-Host command could not be captured, redirected, or assigned to a variable. In PowerShell 5, Write-Host became a wrapper for Write-Information; the message is sent to the information stream.

Information written using Write-Host is unaffected by the InformationPreference variable and the InformationAction parameter, except when either is set to Ignore.

When InformationAction for the Write-Host command is set to Ignore, the output will be suppressed. When Ignore is set for the InformationPreference variable, an error is displayed, stating that it is not supported.

Redirection to a file

Output from a specific stream may be directed by placing the stream number on the left of the redirect operator.

For example, the output written by Write-Warning can be directed to a file:

```
function Test-Redirect{
    'This is standard out'
    Write-Warning 'This is a warning'
}
$output = Test-Redirect 3> 'warnings.txt'
```

The $output variable will contain the string This is standard out. The warning message from stream 3 is redirected to the warnings.txt file.

When using the Redirect operator, any file of the same name is overwritten. If data is to be appended to a file, the operator is changed to >>:

```
function Test-Redirect{
    Write-Warning "Warning $i"
}
$i = 1
Test-Redirect 3> 'warnings.txt'    # Overwrite

$i++
Test-Redirect 3>> 'warnings.txt'   # Append
```

It is possible to redirect additional streams, for example, warnings and errors, by adding more Redirect statements. The following example redirects the error and warning streams to separate files:

```
function Test-Redirect{
    'This is standard out'

    Write-Error 'This is an error'
    Write-Warning 'This is a warning'
}
Test-Redirect 3> 'warnings.txt' 2> 'errors.txt'
```

The wildcard character * may be used to represent all streams if all content was to be sent to a single file:

```
$verbosePreference = 'continue'
function Test-Redirect {
    'This is standard out'

    Write-Information 'This is information'
    Write-Host 'This is information as well'
    Write-Error 'This is an error'
    Write-Verbose 'This is verbose'
    Write-Warning 'This is a warning'
}
Test-Redirect *> 'alloutput.txt'
```

The preceding example starts by setting the verbosePreference variable. Without this, or the addition of the verbose parameter to the Write-Verbose command, the output from Write-Verbose will not be shown at all.

PowerShell and default file encoding

The encoding of a file, including text files, can be optionally described using a **Byte-Order Mark** (**BOM**). The BOM is written to the first few bytes of a file and describes the encoding used by the content that follows, that is, how to interpret the bytes in the file to represent characters to display. The BOM is not hidden by most editors.

The different BOM values are described on Wikipedia:

https://wikipedia.org/wiki/Byte_order_mark.

The BOM is optional; files without a BOM that are opened in a text editor are generally assumed to be UTF8 (depending on the editor).

In Windows PowerShell, files written using redirection are encoded using **UTF-16LE**. In PowerShell 7, files are written using **UTF8** without a BOM at the beginning of the file.

If PowerShell 7 uses >> to append to a file created using > in Windows PowerShell, the result will be a file with mixed encoding. The presence of the Unicode BOM renders the content unreadable in most cases.

Streams can be redirected to other streams rather than a file.

Redirecting streams to standard output

Streams can be redirected to **standard output** (**Stdout**) in PowerShell. The destination stream is written on the right-hand side of the redirect operator (without a space). Stream numbers on the right-hand side are prefixed with an ampersand (&) to distinguish the stream from a filename.

Only stdout

Each of the following examples shows redirection to stdout, &1. It is not possible to redirect to streams other than stdout.

For example, the output from Write-Information, stream 6, is redirected:

```
PS> function Test-Redirect{
>>     'This is standard out'
>>     Write-Information 'This is information'
>> }
```

The redirection operator is used to send output from stream 6 to stdout, stream 1.

```
PS> $stdOut = Test-Redirect 6>&1
PS> $stdOut
This is standard out
This is information
```

It is possible to redirect additional streams, for example, warnings and errors, by adding more Redirect statements. The following example redirects the error and warning streams to stdout:

```
function Test-Redirect {
    'This is standard out'
    Write-Error 'This is an error'
    Write-Warning 'This is a warning'
}
$stdOut = Test-Redirect 2>&1 3>&1
```

The wildcard character * may be used to represent all streams if all streams were to be sent to another stream:

```
$verbosePreference = 'Continue'
function Test-Redirect {
    'This is standard out'
    Write-Information 'This is information'
    Write-Host 'This is information as well'
    Write-Error 'This is an error'
    Write-Verbose 'This is verbose'
    Write-Warning 'This is a warning'
}
$stdOut = Test-Redirect *>&1
```

The preceding example starts by setting the verbosePreference variable. Without this, the output from Write-Verbose will not be shown at all.

Redirection to null

Redirecting output to null can be used as a technique to drop unwanted output. The $null variable takes the place of the filename:

```
Get-Process > $null
```

Dropping unwanted output is explored further in *Chapter 17, Scripts, Functions, and Script Blocks*.

The stream number or * may be included to the left of the Redirect operator. For example, warnings and errors might be redirected to null:

```
.\somecommand.exe 2> $null 3> $null
.\somecommand.exe *> $null
```

Redirection like this is often used with native executables; redirection is rarely necessary with PowerShell commands.

Other operators

PowerShell has a wide variety of operators, a few of which do not easily fall into a specific category:

- Comma: ,
- Index: [ ]

- Range: ..
- Call: &
- Format: -f
- Increment and decrement: ++ and --
- Join: -join
- Null coalescing
- Null conditional
- Pipeline chain
- Background

Each of these operators is in common use. The range operator is often used with the index operator and arrays, the call operator can run a command based on a string, the format operator can be used to build up complex strings, and so on.

Comma

The comma operator may be used to separate elements in an array. For example:

```
$array = 1, 2, 3, 4
```

If the comma operator is used before a single value (as a unary operator), it creates an array containing one element:

```
$array = ,1
```

The use of unary commas is explored again in *Chapter 17, Scripts, Functions, and Script Blocks*.

The index operator can be used to access the elements of an array.

Index

The index operator is used to access elements in an array by position, numbering from 0. For example, the first element in the array below:

```
$array = 1, 2, 3, 4, 5
$array[0]
```

More than one index can be accessed using the comma operator:

```
$array = 1, 2, 3, 4, 5
$array[0, 1]
```

Using negative values accesses values in an array from the end. The example below will return the values 5 (-1) and 4 (-2):

```
$array = 1, 2, 3, 4, 5
$array[-1, -2]
```

The index operator can be used with any value that is indexable. For example, the index operator can be used with a string:

```
$name = 'Andrew'
$firstLetter = $name[0]
```

The index operator can be combined with the range operator.

Range

The range operator, as the name suggests, can be used to create a range of values. For example, the statement below creates an array of numbers from 1 to 10:

```
1..10
```

The start and end values are arbitrary and do not have to be written in ascending order. For example, a descending array of numbers can be created:

```
90..75
```

In PowerShell 7 (but not in Windows PowerShell), the same notation can be used to create an array of characters:

```
'a'..'f'
```

The range operator can be used with the index operator to select a range of values from an array.

```
$array = 1, 2, 3, 4, 5
$array[2..4]
```

The range operator might be quickly used to loop a fixed number of times. In the example below, we make use of the ForEach-Object command in a pipeline:

```
1..10 | ForEach-Object { Start-Sleep -Seconds 1 }
```

The range operator is widely used both to create ranges of numbers and as a simple means of iterating a fixed number of times.

Call

The call operator (&) is used to execute a string or script block. The call operator is particularly useful when running commands (executables or scripts) that have spaces in the path.

The following example runs pwsh.exe, using a full path held in a string:

```
& 'C:\Program Files\PowerShell\7\pwsh.exe'
```

The path to pwsh.exe is normally in the PATH environment variable, so using the full path as in the example above should not be necessary.

The call operator is also useful if the command name changes based on circumstances, such as the operating system running a command. For example, if a command is described by a variable, we use the call operator as follows:

```
$pwsh = 'C:\Program Files\PowerShell\7\pwsh.exe'
& $pwsh
```

This technique can be applied to any command, including PowerShell commands, scripts, and other Windows executables.

Any arguments required by the command can be written in-line, as if the call operator were not present. For example:

```
$pwsh = 'C:\Program Files\PowerShell\7\pwsh.exe'
& $pwsh -NoProfile -NoLogo -Command "Write-Host 'Hello world'"
```

Alternatively, arguments can be supplied as an array, a technique that is useful for commands expecting many arguments:

```
$pwsh = 'C:\Program Files\PowerShell\7\pwsh.exe'
$argumentList = @(
    '-NoProfile'
    '-NoLogo'
    '-Command'
    'Write-Host "Hello world"'
)
& $pwsh $argumentList
```

The call operator may also be used to execute script blocks:

```
$scriptBlock = { Write-Host 'Hello world' }
& $scriptBlock
```

Parameters and arguments can be passed to the script block either in-line, as shown in the previous examples, or by using splatting. Splatting was introduced in *Chapter 1, Introduction to PowerShell*.

Format

The -f operator can be used to create complex formatted strings.

The format operator is often used as an alternative to including variables in strings or using sub-expressions.

The string format is known as a composite format. Microsoft maintains detailed examples and format references for numeric, DateTime, and Timespan types. Check this link, which will provide more information on this:

```
https://learn.microsoft.com/en-us/dotnet/standard/base-types/composite-formatting.
```

The -f operator uses a placeholder, a number in curly braces ({<number>}), in a string on the left of the operator. The number is the index of a value in an array on the right. For example:

```
PS> '1: {0}, 2: {1}, 3: {2}' -f 'one', 'two', 'three'
1: one, 2: two, 3: three
```

At the start of this chapter, the following example was used:

```
$word = 'one'
"Length: $($word.Length)"
```

If the format operator were used instead, the example would become:

```
$word = 'one'
'Length: {0}' -f $word.Length
```

The format operator is one possible way to assemble complex strings in PowerShell. In addition, -f may be used to simplify some string operations. For example, a decimal may be formatted as a percentage:

```
'The pass mark is {0:P}' -f 0.8
```

An integer may be formatted as a hexadecimal string:

```
'244 in Hexadecimal is {0:X2}' -f 244
```

A number may be written as a culture-specific currency; in the UK, it will use the £ symbol, in the US, $, and so on:

```
'The price is {0:C2}' -f 199
```

A date may be formatted as a string, which is useful if parts of the date are used in several places in the string:

```
'Today is {0:dddd} the {0:dd} of {0:MMMM}' -f (Get-Date)
```

When using the -f operator, curly braces are considered reserved characters. If a curly brace is to be included in a string as a literal value, it can escape:

```
'The value in {{0}} is {0}' -f 1
```

The array sub-expression operator may be used on the right-hand side of -f for longer or more complex lists of values. For example, to set up a window title for PowerShell:

```
$host.UI.RawUI.WindowTitle = '{0}{1} - PowerShell {2}' -f @(
    [Environment]::UserName
    [IntPtr]::Size -eq 4 ? ' (32-bit)' : ''
    $PSVersionTable.PSVersion
)
```

The example above also makes use of the Ternary operator, demonstrated later in this section.

Any array on the right-hand side of -f must at least have as many elements as there are placeholders. However, PowerShell will also accept arrays that contain more elements:

```
'{0}, {1}' -f 'one', 'two', 'three', 'four'
```

This means that a common set of values can be used with different format strings:

```
$errorDetails = @(
    'Error!'
    'My error message'
    'At line 1, character 30'
)
$shortFormat = '{0} {1}'
$longFormat = '{0} {1}: {2}'
```

Then, each format string can be used with the $errorDetails variable:

```
$shortFormat -f $errorDetails
$longFormat -f $errorDetails
```

The format operator is a potential alternative to embedding variables and sub-expressions into strings or using the + operator to concatenate.

join

The -join operator joins arrays using a string. In the following example, the string is split based on a comma, and then it is joined based on a tab (`t):

```
PS> 'a', 'b', 'c', 'd' -join "`t"
a       b       c       d
```

The -join operator may also be used in front of an array (used as a unary operator) when there is no need for a separator. For example:

```
PS> -join ('hello', 'world')
helloworld
```

If the parentheses are excluded from the example, the statement will be considered incomplete and will not execute.

Null coalescing

The null coalescing operator in PowerShell 7 may be used to define a default for a value when the subject is null.

For example, null coalescing is useful if the value for a variable is dependent on another. This operation might be performed using an if statement:

```
$valueA = $null
if ($null -eq $valueA) {
```

```
      $valueB = 'Default value'
} else {
      $valueB = $valueA
}
```

The null coalescing operator can simplify this expression:

```
$valueA = $null
$valueB = $valueA ?? 'Default value'
```

If $valueA is given a non-null value, it will be returned as the result of the expression:

```
$valueA = 'Supplied value'
$valueA ?? 'Default value'
```

Null coalescing operators can be chained to build up a more complex expression. In the following example, the value of the variable will be set to the first of the functions that returns a non-null value:

```
function first { }
function second { 'second' }
function third { 'third' }


(first) ?? (second) ?? (third)
```

The preceding expression will return the value 'second', as the function first does not return a value. The function third will not be called in this case.

If the value were removed from the second function, the result of the expression would be 'third' as the only non-null value in the expression:

```
function first { }
function second { }
function third { 'third' }
(first) ?? (second) ?? (third)
```

A default value might be added to the end to always ensure the result is never null:

```
(first) ?? (second) ?? (third) ?? 'default'
```

The null coalescing operator allows a complex conditional expression to be defined with a very concise statement. The operator may also be used in an assignment operation.

Null coalescing assignment

The null coalescing assignment operator can be used to simplify the use of the null coalescing operator when assigning values.

In the following example, $value will only become 1 if it is null:

```
$value = $null
if ($null -eq $value) {
    $value = 1
}
```

The expression can be simplified by using the null coalescing assignment operator:

```
$value = $null
$value ??= 1
```

In the preceding example, because $value is already set, it will not be changed by the second assignment:

```
$value = 1
$value ??= 2
```

The value must be explicitly null (not false, 0, or an empty string) for the assignment to complete.

This approach might be used to ensure an object exists, for example, a specific process:

```
$process = Get-Process notepad -ErrorAction SilentlyContinue
$process ??= Start-Process notepad -PassThru
```

In the preceding example, Notepad will only start if the process does not already exist.

Null conditional

The null conditional operator can be used to avoid errors when a property or method is used on an object, and the object itself is null.

The behavior of the operator is best described with an example. The following command will raise an error if the variable has not been set or the value is null:

```
PS> $someObject.ToString()
InvalidOperation: You cannot call a method on a null-valued expression.
```

The null conditional operator can be used so that the method is only run if the object is not null:

```
${someObject}?.ToString()
```

As the ? character can be part of a normal variable name, curly braces must be used to separate the variable name from the null conditional operator.

The same technique can be used for properties of objects that may not be set. As the ? character is not normally part of a property name, curly braces are not required:

```
$someOtherObject = [PSCustomObject]@{
    Value = $null
}
```

```
$someOtherObject.Value?.ToString()
```

If a value for the Value property is set, the method executes and returns as normal. This operator avoids the need for conditional statements to test the property value:

```
$someOtherObject = [PSCustomObject]@{
    Value = $null
}
if ($someOtherObject.Value) {
    $someOtherObject.Value.ToString()
}
```

If the value was created in a way that means it includes a ? character, the curly braces can again be used to describe the extent of the property name:

```
$someOtherObject = [PSCustomObject]@{
    'Value?' = $null
}
$someOtherObject.{Value?}?.ToString()
```

This operator cannot be used to avoid errors from accessing non-existent properties when strict mode is enabled.

For example, because the Value property does not exist in $someOtherObject below, an error will be displayed when strict mode is enabled.

```
& {
    Set-StrictMode -Version Latest
    $someOtherObject = [PSCustomObject]@{}
    $someOtherObject.Value?.ToString()
}
```

See Get-Help Set-StrictMode to explore the features and functionality of strict mode in PowerShell.

Pipeline chain

The pipeline chain operators allow conditional execution of commands based on the success (or failure) of another command. Two operators are available, && and ||.

These operators are present in cmd.exe and are also implemented in Bash on Linux.

Evaluating success or failure is based on the value of the $? variable.

To demonstrate these operators, two commands are used. The following command gets the current directory and should, therefore, always succeed:

```
Get-Item .
```

Write-Host is used to show when the right-hand side runs.

When the && operator is used, the command on the right-hand side only runs if the command on the left-hand side is successful:

```
PS> Get-Item . && Write-Host 'Exists'


        Directory: C:\


Mode                 LastWriteTime         Length Name
----                 -------------         ------ ----
d----            21/01/2024     12:53             workspace
Exists
```

The statement above is, therefore, the equivalent of the example below, which will have the same output:

```
Get-Item .
if ($?) {
    Write-Host 'Exists'
}
```

If the left-hand side command were to fail, the right-hand side command would not run. The ErrorAction parameter is added to the example below to hide the error and demonstrate that the right-hand side still runs:

```
Get-Item DoesNotExist -ErrorAction Ignore &&
    Write-Host 'Exists'
```

In this example, there will be no output.

The || operator causes the right-hand side to run only when the left-hand side fails. As before, failure is determined by the value of the $? variable:

```
Get-Item DoesNotExist -ErrorAction Ignore ||
    Write-Host 'Does not exist'
```

This time, the command will show the 'Does not exist' message and no other output.

This is equivalent to the example below:

```
Get-Item DoesNotExist -ErrorAction Ignore
if (-not $?) {
    Write-Host 'Does not exist'
}
```

Fixing the path will cause the directory object to display and not the message:

```
PS> Get-Item . -ErrorAction Ignore || Write-Host 'Does not exist'


        Directory: C:\
```

```
Mode                LastWriteTime      Length Name
----                -------------      ------ ----
d----      21/01/2024     12:53               workspace
```

These pipeline chain operators may be useful if installing and then running an application, for example, using the made-up commands shown here:

```
installApplication.exe && application.exe
```

These operators are a small addition to PowerShell and may help users approaching PowerShell from other languages or shells.

Background

The background operator may be used to send the command preceding the operator into a job. For example, running the following command creates a background job:

```
$job = Get-Process &
```

The background job is visible using the Get-Job command, as shown in the following example:

```
PS> Get-Job

Id  Name  PSJobTypeName   State    HasMoreData  Location  Command
--  ----  -------------   -----    -----------  --------  -------
1   Job1  BackgroundJob   Running  True         localhost  Micro...
```

Any output from the job may be retrieved using the Receive-Job command:

```
$job = Get-Process &
$job | Receive-Job
```

The job commands are explored in detail in *Chapter 15, Asynchronous Processing*.

Summary

This chapter covered many of the operators PowerShell has to offer, including operators for performing arithmetic, assignment, and comparison.

Several specialized operators that use regular expressions were introduced for matching, replacing, and splitting. Regular expressions are explored in *Chapter 9, Regular Expressions*. Binary, logical, and type operators were demonstrated.

Finally, several other significant operators were introduced, including the call, format, increment, decrement, and join operators, along with the new ternary, null-coalescing, pipeline chain, and background operators.

Chapter 6, Conditional Statements and Loops, explores how to test and react to values and how to make use of loops in PowerShell.

Learn more on Discord

Read this book alongside other users, PowerShell experts, and the author himself. Ask questions, provide solutions to other readers, chat with the author via Ask Me Anything sessions, and much more.

Scan the QR code or visit the link to join the community.

`https://packt.link/SecNet`

6

Conditional Statements and Loops

Conditional statements and loops are the backbone of any programming or scripting language. Being able to react to a state and choose a path to take or to repeat instructions is vital.

Each conditional statement or loop creates a branch in a script or piece of code. The branch represents a split in the instruction set. Branches can be conditional, such as one created by an `if` statement, or unconditional, such as a `foreach` loop. As the number of branches increases, so does the complexity. The paths through the script spread out in the same manner as the limbs of a tree.

Statements or lines of code may be executed when certain conditions are met. PowerShell provides `if` and `switch` statements for this purpose. Loops allow code to be repeated for a set of elements or until a specific condition is met.

Loops can be combined with components such as collections like queues and stacks to perform even more advanced operations – for example, to perform recursion-like operations on file systems.

In this chapter, the following topics are covered:

- if, else, and elseif
- Implicit Boolean
- switch statements
- switch, break, and continue
- Loops
- Loops, break, and continue
- Loops and labels
- Loops, queues, and stacks

The `if` statement is a vital keyword and is used in most scripts.

if, else, and elseif

An if statement is used to execute an action when a condition is met. The following shows the syntax for an if statement; the statements enclosed by the if statement execute if the condition evaluates to true:

```
if (<condition>) {
    <statements>
}
```

The else statement is optional and runs if all previous conditions evaluate as false:

```
if (<first-condition>) {
    <first-statements>
} else {
    <second-statements>
}
```

The elseif statement allows several conditions to be tested in order:

```
if (<first-condition>) {
    <first-statements>
} elseif (<second-condition>) {
    <second-statements>
} elseif (<last-condition>) {
    <last-statements>
}
```

The else statement may be added after any number of elseif statements.

Execution of a block of conditions stops as soon as a single condition is true. For example, both the first and second condition would evaluate to true, but only the first executes:

```
$value = 1
if ($value -eq 1) {
    Write-Host 'value is 1'
} elseif ($value -lt 10) {
    Write-Host 'value is less than 10'
} else {
    Write-Host 'value is not equal to 1'
}
```

When the example above runs, and because the value is 1, the first Write-Host statement runs. The output from the example is shown below:

```
value is 1
```

If the `if` statement structure becomes too complicated, a `switch` statement might be used instead. This is explored later in this chapter.

Assignment within if statements

Values may be assigned to variables inside `if` statements, as shown here:

```
if ($i = 1) {
    Write-Host "The variable i is $i"
}
```

The condition will be true if the value of the variable evaluates to true.

This is most used when testing for the existence of a value in a variable, for example:

```
if ($interface = Get-NetAdapter | Where-Object Status -eq 'Up') {
    Write-Host "$($interface.Name) is up"
}
```

In the previous example, the statement to the right of the assignment operator (=) is executed, assigned to the `$interface` variable, and then the value in the variable is treated as an implicit Boolean.

Supporting this type of assignment means PowerShell does not alert the author of a script if an assignment operation is used instead of a comparison. This is most often a problem when the assignment was intended instead to be a comparison.

Implicit Boolean

Implicit Boolean is a feature that allows conditions to be simplified. A value that is not Boolean but is tested as if it were true or false is an implicit Boolean. For example, the following `if` statement tests the output from a command:

```
if (Get-ChildItem c:\users\a*) {
    # If statement body
}
```

The condition evaluates as true when the `Get-ChildItem` command finds one or more files or folders. The condition evaluates as false when no files or folders are found.

An explicit version of the same comparison is shown here:

```
if ($null -ne (Get-ChildItem c:\users\c*)) {
    # If statement body
}
```

The explicit statement above is more complex and arguably more difficult to read.

A condition with no comparison operator implicitly evaluates to false if it is any of the following:

- $null
- An empty string

- An empty array
- The numeric value 0

A variable containing a single object, or an array containing one or more elements, and so on, evaluates to true.

switch is a common alternative to if, elseif, and else statements; let's look at that next.

switch statements

A switch statement executes statements where a case evaluates as true. The case can be a number, a string, or any other value. A switch statement is similar in some respects to an if, elseif, and else statement. The key difference is that in switch, more than one condition can run for the value being tested.

A switch statement uses the following generalized notation:

```
switch [-regex|-wildcard|-exact][-casesensitive] (<value>) {
    <case>   { <statements> }
    <case>   { <statements> }
    default  { <statements> }
}
```

The value is the "subject" of the switch statement; it is compared to each of the cases in turn.

The casesensitive parameter applies when the cases are strings. The regex and wildcard parameters are explored later in this section.

Each case is evaluated in turn and, by default, all matching cases will execute. The default case is optional and will only be executed if no other case matches, as shown here:

```
$value = 2
switch ($value) {
    1       { Write-Host 'value is 1' }
    default { Write-Host 'No conditions matched' }
}
```

Within the switch statement, the variable $_ or $PSItem may be used to refer to the value. If switch is enclosed in ForEach-Object, for example, the value of $_ may differ from the value ForEach-Object holds in the process block.

switch statements and arrays

The switch statement can be used on both scalar (single) values and arrays of values. If the value is an array, then each case will be tested against each element of the array:

```
$arrayOfValues = 1..3
switch ($arrayOfValues) {
    1 { 'One' }
```

```
    2 { 'Two' }
    3 { 'Three' }
}
```

The switch statement executes once for each item in an array of items. The statement does not execute at all if given an empty array (such as @()). In the following example, an empty array is the value. As switch has no values to compare, it does not execute any cases:

```
switch (@()) {
    default { 'this default case will not run' }
}
```

The switch statement will execute if an explicit $null value is used. For example:

```
switch ($null) {
    default { 'this default case will run' }
}
```

The ability to act on an array allows switch to act on file content.

switch statements and files

The switch statement can be used to work on the content of a file using the following notation:

```
switch [-regex|-wildcard] [-casesensitive] -File <Name> {
    <condition> { <statements> }
    <condition> { <statements> }
}
```

The File parameter can be used to select from a text file (line by line); the content of the file is read as an array.

Wildcard and Regex parameters

The Wildcard and Regex parameters are used when matching strings.

The Wildcard parameter allows the use of the characters ? (any single character) and * (any string of zero or more characters) in a condition, and ranges defined in square brackets. For example:

```
switch -Wildcard ('cat') {
    'c*'        { Write-Host 'The word begins with c' }
    '???'       { Write-Host 'The word is 3 characters long' }
    '*t'        { Write-Host 'The word ends with t' }
    '*[aeiou]*' { Write-Host 'The word contains a vowel' }
}
```

In the example above, the wildcards used will cause each of the four cases to display as shown below:

```
The word begins with c
The word is 3 characters long
The word ends with t
The word contains a vowel
```

The Regex parameter allows for the use of regular expressions to match patterns. Regular expressions are explored in much greater detail in *Chapter 9, Regular Expressions*. For example:

```
switch -Regex ('cat') {
  '^c'      { Write-Host 'The word begins with c' }
   '^.{3}$' { Write-Host 'The word is 3 characters long' }
   't$'      { Write-Host 'The word ends with t' }
}
```

When the example above runs, all three of the cases match. The output is shown below:

```
The word begins with c
The word is exactly 3 characters long
The word ends with t
```

The switch statement also allows the cases to be defined as a script block.

Script block cases

The switch statement allows a script block to be used in place of the simpler direct comparisons. The script block is executed, and the result determines whether the case is matched. For example:

```
switch (Get-Date) {
    { $_ -is [DateTime] } { Write-Host 'This is a DateTime type' }
    { $_.Year -ge 2020 }  { Write-Host 'It is 2020 or later' }
}
```

Script block cases like those used above may be mixed with other values. The following example uses a single ScriptBlock expression as well as a comparison with the value 5:

```
$Value = 5
switch ($Value) {
    { $_ -is [int] } { Write-Host 'This is a Int32 type' }
    5                { Write-Host 'The value is five' }
}
```

Expressions like the example above might replace a more complex if-elseif statement or may be used to perform more complex comparison combinations.

For example, shared code might be established to use with more than one case:

```
function Set-FileState {
    param (
        [Parameter(Mandatory)]
        [ValidateSet('Update', 'Create', 'Delete')]
        [string]$Action
    )
    $params = @{
        Path = '~\test.txt'
    }
    switch ($Action) {
        { $_ -in 'Update', 'Create' } {
            $params['Value'] = 'File content'
        }
        'Update' { Set-Content @params }
        'Create' { New-Item @params -ItemType File }
        'Delete' { Remove-Item @params }
    }
}
Set-FileState -Action Update
```

Inside a switch statement, $_ is the value that is being tested. It is possible to re-assign the value of $_ in one case, allowing a second case (or any other cases) to be applied:

```
function Set-FileState {
    param (
        [Parameter(Mandatory)]
        [ValidateSet('Update', 'Create', 'Delete')]
        [string]$Action
    )
    $params = @{
        Path = '~\test.txt'
        ItemType = 'File'
        Value    = 'File content'
    }
    switch ($Action) {
        { $_ -in 'Delete', 'Update' } {
            if (Test-Path -Path $params.Path) {
                Remove-Item -Path $params.Path
            }
            if ($_ -eq 'Update') {
                $_ = 'Create'
```

```
        }
    }
    'Create' {
        New-Item @params
    }
    }
}
}
Set-FileState -Action Update
```

One common issue with the switch statement is that cases are converted into strings.

switch statements and enums

An enum, or enumeration, is a list of constant values where each value is given a name.

Enumerations are explored in more detail in *Chapter 7, Working with .NET*, and in *Chapter 19, Classes and Enumerations*.

The DayOfWeek enumeration, as the name suggests, describes the names of each day in the week and gives each day a numeric value. This enumeration is used with the DateTime type. An instance of DateTime is returned by the Get-Date command.

A single value in the enumeration can be accessed as follows:

```
[DayOfWeek]::Monday
```

If a switch statement uses an enumeration value as a case, it is tempting to write the case as shown below:

```
switch ((Get-Date).DayOfWeek) {
    [DayOfWeek]::Monday    { 'Monday' }
    [DayOfWeek]::Tuesday   { 'Tuesday' }
    [DayOfWeek]::Wednesday { 'Wednesday' }
    [DayOfWeek]::Thursday  { 'Thursday' }
    [DayOfWeek]::Friday    { 'Friday' }
    [DayOfWeek]::Saturday  { 'Saturday' }
    [DayOfWeek]::Sunday    { 'Sunday' }
    default { 'It is not a week day at all' }
}
```

However, this will not act as might be expected. The switch statement turns each of the cases into a literal string. Using Monday as an example, the first case will only match if the subject is the same string (not the enumeration value):

```
switch ('[DayOfWeek]::Monday') {
    [DayOfWeek]::Monday { 'This case matched' }
}
```

Where the value is an enumeration like this, there are two possible solutions. The name of the enumeration value can be used, with the first two days shown below:

```
switch ((Get-Date).DayOfWeek) {
    'Monday'  { 'Monday' }
    'Tuesday' { 'Tuesday' }
}
```

Or, each case can be enclosed in brackets; the first two days are shown below:

```
switch ((Get-Date).DayOfWeek) {
    ([DayOfWeek]::Monday)  { 'Monday' }
    ([DayOfWeek]::Tuesday) { 'Tuesday' }
}
```

The same applies if the case is a static property. Static properties are accessed using the same notion as was used with the enumeration. For example, the DateTime type has a Today static property. In this case, the only option is to use brackets around the case:

```
switch ((Get-Date).Date) {
    ([DateTime]::Today) { 'It is still today' }
}
```

The switch statement will run every case that matches the value in turn until the last is reached. The break and continue keywords may be used to affect how a switch statement ends.

switch, break, and continue

By default, switch executes every case where the case evaluates as true when compared with the value.

The break and continue keywords may be used within the switch statement to control when testing should stop:

- When break is used in a case, the switch statement ends.
- When continue is used and the value is a scaler, the switch statement ends.
- When continue is used and the value is an array, it moves to the next element.

break is often most appropriate if the value is a scalar, and continue when the value is an array. However, either may be used as needed.

The switch statement will not stop testing conditions unless the break keyword is used. In the example below, all conditions are tested:

```
$value = 1
switch ($value) {
    1 { Write-Host 'value is 1' }
    1 { Write-Host 'value is still 1' }
}
```

The example above will show the following output:

```
value is 1
value is still 1
```

In the following example, where switch is acting on an array, both statements will execute:

```
switch (1, 2) {
    1 { Write-Host 'Equals 1' }
    2 { Write-Host 'Equals 2' }
}
```

In the example above, both statements will be displayed as shown here:

```
Equals 1
Equals 2
```

If the break keyword is included, as shown here, only the first executes and then the switch statement stops:

```
switch (1, 2) {
    1 { Write-Host 'Equals 1'; break }
    2 { Write-Host 'Equals 2' }
}
```

The output from the example above is shown below:

```
Equals 1
```

The first example in this section has two cases that match the value 1. If continue is used, the second matching statement is skipped, and switch continues to the next element in the array:

```
switch (1, 2) {
    1 { Write-Host 'Equals 1'; continue }
    1 { Write-Host 'value is still 1' }
    2 { Write-Host 'Equals 2' }
}
```

The second condition in the example above is skipped; the result is shown below:

```
Equals 1
Equals 2
```

Finally, break and continue can be mixed if necessary. In the following example, the condition for the value 3 will never be reached if the array contains the value 2:

```
switch (1, 2, 3) {
    1 { Write-Host 'One'; continue }
    1 { Write-Host 'One again' }
```

```
    2 { Write-Host 'Two'; break }
    3 { Write-Host 'Three' }
}
```

The output from the example above is shown below:

```
One
Two
```

The switch statement is incredibly flexible and allows relatively complex condition structures to be described in a concise manner.

PowerShell has several other loop keywords that may be used to repeat statements.

Loops

Loops may be used to iterate through collections, perform an operation against each element in the collection, or repeat an operation (or series of operations) until a condition is met.

The following loops will be demonstrated in this section:

- foreach
- for
- do
- while

The foreach loop is perhaps the most common of these loops.

foreach loop

The foreach loop executes against each element of a collection using the following notation:

```
foreach (<element> in <collection>) {
    <statements>
}
```

For example, the foreach loop may be used to iterate through each of the processes returned by Get-Process:

```
foreach ($process in Get-Process) {
    Write-Host $process.Name
}
```

If the collection is empty, the body of the loop will not execute.

foreach keyword and foreach alias

PowerShell comes with the alias foreach for the ForEach-Object command. When this alias acts depends on the context.

If `foreach` is first in a statement, then the loop keyword is used:

```
$array = 1..3
foreach ($value in $array) {
    'Will repeat three times!'
}
```

If `foreach` is placed after a pipe and then the alias is used, the `ForEach-Object (foreach)` is used:

```
$array = 1..3
$array | foreach {
    'Will repeat three times!'
}
```

Because this can cause confusion, it is rarely a good idea to use the `foreach` alias.

for loop

The `for` loop is typically used to step through a collection using the following notation:

```
for (<initial>; <condition>; <repeat>){
    <body-statements>
}
```

Each of the three blocks can include arbitrary code, which makes the `for` loop one of the most complex available.

`<initial>` runs before the loop starts and is normally used to set the initial state; this is normally the variables used within the loop. Typically, a counter of some kind.

The loop continues to run if `<condition>` evaluates to true.

The `<repeat>` block is executed after each iteration of the loop. This is most often used to increment a value set in the initial block.

Much like the `foreach` loop, the `for` loop can be used to loop over the content of a variable:

```
$processes = Get-Process
for ($i = 0; $i -lt $processes.Count; $i++) {
    Write-Host $processes[$i].Name
}
```

The `for` loop provides a significant degree of control over the loop. It is useful where the increment, or the actions inside the loop, need to be completed in an order other than a simple ascending order. The examples that follow show some of the possible ways in which the `for` loop can be used.

For example, the `<repeat>` criteria can be used to execute the body for every third element:

```
for ($i = 0; $i -lt $processes.Count; $i += 3) {
    Write-Host $processes[$i].Name
}
```

Or, the <initial> parameter can be set to start at the end and work toward the beginning of an array:

```
for ($i = $processes.Count - 1; $i -ge 0; $i--) {
    Write-Host $processes[$i].Name
}
```

As the body of the loop in the preceding example has access to the index, it can easily access elements adjacent or relative to the current element. The following example reads two characters at a time from $encodedString:

```
$encodedString = '68656C6C6F20776F726C64'
[char[]]$characters = for ($i = 0; $i -lt $encodedString.Length; $i += 2) {
    $hex = '0x{0}{1}' -f @(
        $encodedString[$i]
        $encodedString[$i + 1]
    )
    +$hex
}
[string]::new($characters)
```

The example above will show the decoded string content. The output from this loop is shown below:

```
hello world
```

Running the preceding example will allow PowerShell to convert each pair of characters into a hexadecimal number based on $i incrementing two at a time. The result is a single string.

This technique can be used to parse any string containing hexadecimal character pairs (nibbles). The loop acts to convert each pair of nibbles into an integer value between 0 and 255. Common cases might include some certificate formats or other values commonly written as strings such as RGB colors.

Each element in the for loop is optional; the following loop only ends because the body contains break:

```
for (;;) {
    break
}
```

Any of the three elements, initial, condition, and repeat, may be included individually or in any combination to describe how the loop should act.

The for loop can also act on more than one variable at a time, although it is incredibly rare to find this used in practice – generally, the kind of code that might be found as solutions to coding challenges rather than code used in a practical setting.

In the following example, two variables are given an initial state and two variables are incremented after each iteration of the loop:

```
for (($i = 0), ($j = 0); $i -le 10 ; $i++, ($j += 2)) {
    Write-Host "$i :: $j"
}
```

The preceding condition only tests the state of one variable in the preceding example, but a more complex expression might have been used, for example:

```
$i -le 10 -and $j -le 20
```

The preceding example works because the different elements of the for loop, initial, condition, and repeat, are arbitrary blocks of code.

do and while loops are more commonly used than the for loop.

do-until and do-while loops

do-until and do-while each execute the body of the loop at least once. The condition to see if the loop should continue is at the end of the statement. Loops based on do-until will exit when the condition evaluates as true; loops based on do-while will exit when the condition evaluates as false.

do loops are written using the following notation:

```
do {
    <body-statements>
} <until | while> (<condition>)
```

A do-until loop is suited to exit conditions that are expected to be positive. Using until avoids the need to test for a false value in the condition. For example, a script might wait for a computer to respond to a ping:

```
do {
    Write-Host "Waiting for boot"
    Start-Sleep -Seconds 5
} until (Test-Connection 'SomeComputer' -Quiet -Count 1)
```

A do-until loop can also be a good choice when validating user input via the Read-Host command:

```
do {
    $yesOrNo = Read-Host 'Continue?'
} until ($yesOrNo -in 'y', 'n')

if ($yesOrNo -eq 'n') {
    return
}
Write-Host "Continuing"
```

The do-while loop is more suitable for exit conditions that are negative. For example, a loop might wait for a remote computer to stop responding to a ping:

```
do {
    Write-Host "Waiting for shutdown"
    Start-Sleep -Seconds 5
} while (Test-Connection 'SomeComputer' -Quiet -Count 1)
```

Or, a do-while loop might be used to work on paged responses from a web service. The example below will not run as the URI is not valid, but the pattern used is common:

```
$uri = 'https://somewebservice'
do {
    $response = Invoke-WebRequest -Uri $uri
    $response.Value
    $uri = $response.Next
} while ($uri)
```

Looping with web requests will be explored again in *Chapter 13, Web Requests and Web Services*.

As noted above, the do loop will execute at least once before testing the condition at the end. The while loop, on the other hand, places the condition first.

while loop

As the condition for a while loop comes first, the body of the loop will only execute if the condition evaluates to true:

```
while (<condition>) {
    <body-statements>
}
```

A while loop may be used to wait for something to happen. In the following example, the loop continues until a file exists:

```
while (-not (Test-Path $env:TEMP\test.txt -PathType Leaf)) {
    Start-Sleep -Seconds 10
}
```

A while loop is a good choice for operations like generating usernames:

```
$baseUsername = $username = 'chris'
$i = 1
while (Get-ADUser -Filter "SamAccountName -eq '$username'") {
    $username = '{0}{1:D2}' -f $baseUsername, $i
    $i++
}
```

The first time the loop runs, it tests the original value of $username. Then, each iteration of the loop changes a number at the end. The following values are tested:

1. chris
2. chris01
3. chris02
4. chris03

And so on, until a name that does not exist in Active Directory (in this case) is found.

It is often desirable to stop a loop earlier than a condition at the start or end of the loop might allow, or to stop a loop that does not have an explicit exit condition, such as foreach. Loops can make use of the break and continue keywords; let's see how.

Loops, break, and continue

The break and continue keywords can be used to control the flow within a loop, typically to exit earlier than a condition at the start or end of the loop would normally permit.

In the example below, a set of random numbers is created, then the foreach loop is used to find the first instance of any number greater than 10:

```
$randomNumbers = Get-Random -Count 30 -Minimum 1 -Maximum 30
foreach ($number in $randomNumbers) {
    if ($number -gt 10) {
        break
    }
}
$number
```

The loop in the following example would continue until the value of $i is 20. break is used to stop the loop when $i reaches 10:

```
for ($i = 0; $i -lt 20; $i += 2) {
    Write-Host $i
    if ($i -eq 10) {
        break     # Stop this loop
    }
}
```

The break keyword acts on the loop it is nested inside. In the following example, the do loop breaks early when the variable $i is less than or equal to 2 and the variable $k is greater than or equal to 3:

```
$i = 1 # Initial state for i
do {
    Write-Host "i: $i"
    $k = 1 # Reset k
    while ($k -lt 5) {
        Write-Host "  k: $k"
        $k++ # Increment k
        if ($i -le 2 -and $k -ge 3) {
            break
        }
```

```
    }
    $i++ # Increment i
} while ($i -le 3)
```

The output from the loop in the example above is shown below:

```
i: 1
   k: 1
   k: 2
i: 2
   k: 1
   k: 2
i: 3
   k: 1
   k: 2
   k: 3
   k: 4
```

The continue keyword may be used to move on to the next iteration of a loop immediately. For example, the following loop executes a subset of the loop body when the value of the $i variable is less than 2:

```
for ($i = 0; $i -le 5; $i++) {
    Write-Host $i
    if ($i -lt 2) {
        continue     # Continue to the next iteration
    }
    Write-Host "Remainder when $i is divided by 2 is $($i % 2)"
}
```

The output from the example above is shown below:

```
0
1
2
Remainder when 2 is divided by 2 is 0
3
Remainder when 3 is divided by 2 is 1
4
Remainder when 4 is divided by 2 is 0
5
Remainder when 5 is divided by 2 is 1
```

The break and continue keywords are meant to be used inside loops (or within the switch statement).

break and continue outside loops

If break is used outside a loop, PowerShell will look through any parent scopes (to the global scope) until it finds a loop to stop or runs out of scopes to search.

In the following example, break is erroneously used to end a function early:

```
function Test-Value {
    [CmdletBinding()]
    param (
        [int]$Value
    )
    if ($Value -eq 7) {
        break
    }
    $true
}
```

A casual test may suggest that break is only stopping the function, and everything is working as it should. However, if the function is used within a loop, break will affect that loop. This happens no matter how many scopes (or other functions) there are between the scope below and the function scope:

```
foreach ($value in 1..10) {
    Write-Verbose "Working on $value" -Verbose
    if ($value -gt 5) {
        if (Test-Value $value) {
            Write-Host "$value is OK"
        }
    }
}
```

The script should repeat the Write-Host statement for 6, 8, 9, and 10. However, because break is used in the function, the foreach loop stops as soon as it reaches 7.

The continue keyword has the same problem, although this will continue to the next iteration of the loop in the parent scope instead of terminating the loop.

break and continue in loops can make use of labels to identify a specific loop.

Loops and labels

In PowerShell, a loop can be given a label. The label may be used with break and continue to define a specific point loop to act on.

The label is written before the loop keyword (for, while, do, or foreach) and is preceded by a colon character. For example:

```
:ThisIsALabel foreach ($value in 1..10) {
    $value
}
```

The label may be placed directly before the loop keyword or on the line above. For example:

```
:ThisIsALabel
foreach ($value in 1..10) {
    $value
}
```

The example above will work when saved as a script, but if it is pasted into the label, it will be split from the loop. Holding *Shift* and *Return* between the label and loop is required when typing the example into the console.

White space may appear between the label and the loop keyword.

The label is used with break or continue and can be useful when one loop is nested inside another. The label name is written after the break or continue keyword without the colon:

```
:outerLoop for ($i = 1; $i -le 5; $i++) {
    :innerLoop foreach ($value in 1..5) {
        Write-Host "$i :: $value"
        if ($value -eq $i) {
            continue outerLoop
        }
    }
}
```

The break statement may be used in a similar manner to end a labeled loop.

Loops, especially do or while, can be combined with queues (a First In, First Out collection) or stacks (a First In, Last Out collection) to perform operations that behave like recursion.

Loops, queues, and stacks

The file system is an example of a tree-like structure that can be traversed by making use of a loop and a queue or stack.

Consider the following directory tree:

```
Project
  | - A
  |   | - B
  |       | - C
  |       | - Large
  |               | - Tree
  | - D
```

```
  | - Large
      | - Tree
```

The `Get-ChildItem -Recurse` command may be used to find items in this path and all child paths.

However, if there was a requirement to avoid looking inside folders named `Large`, then the `Recurse` parameter is not particularly efficient. Any filtering would have to happen after the command had run, and the command would still visit those directories.

The snippet below may be used to create this directory tree, allowing the loop below to be tested. The folders are created in the current working directory:

```
New-Item Project\A\B\C -ItemType Directory
New-Item Project\A\B\Large\Tree -ItemType Directory
New-Item Project\D\Large\Tree -ItemType Directory
```

To achieve this, the functionality provided by the `Recurse` parameter of `Get-ChildItem` must be replaced.

It is possible to write recursive functions in PowerShell – that is, a function that calls itself repeatedly. Recursive functions are beyond the scope of this chapter but will be explored in *Chapter 17, Scripts, Functions, and Script Blocks*.

Using a loop with a queue or stack is generally more efficient than implementing a recursive function. The loop is required to visit directories. The loop will continue if there are items to visit.

Both `Stack` and `Queue` can be used for this. The choice affects the order of items in the output from this code. This first variant uses `Queue`. The queue is created before the loop starts, and the `Project` directory, the starting point, is enqueued:

```
$path = Get-Item Project
$queue = [System.Collections.Generic.Queue[object]]$path
```

A loop is created to process items in the queue. The loop will end when there are no more items to process. The `Count` property can be used to see if the queue is empty, and a `while` loop can be used to check the state before the iteration starts.

Each time the loop finds a child directory, the child directory gets added to the queue.

The version below does not have assignable output and just shows how items are added and removed from the queue. This version does not avoid the `Large` folder:

```
$path = Get-Item Project
$queue = [System.Collections.Generic.Queue[object]]$path
while ($queue.Count) {
    $current = $queue.Dequeue()
    Write-Host "Taking $current from the queue"
    foreach ($child in Get-ChildItem -Path $current -Directory) {
        Write-Host "Adding $child to the queue"
```

```
        $queue.Enqueue($child)
    }
}
```

To make this loop have output, the value of $current may be emitted. The loop is assigned to a variable to capture that output:

```
$path = Get-Item Project
$queue = [System.Collections.Generic.Queue[object]]$path
$output = while ($queue.Count) {
    $current = $queue.Dequeue()
    $current
    foreach ($child in Get-ChildItem -Path $current -Directory) {
        $queue.Enqueue($child)
    }
}
$output.Name
```

The example above will show each of the directories it visits. The names of those are shown below:

```
Project
A
D
B
Large
C
Large
Tree
Tree
```

To make this ignore the content of the Large folder, an if statement is needed within the foreach loop:

```
$path = Get-Item Project
$queue = [System.Collections.Generic.Queue[object]]$path
$output = while ($queue.Count) {
    $current = $queue.Dequeue()
    $current
    foreach ($child in Get-ChildItem -Path $current -Directory) {
        if ($current.Name -eq 'Large') {
            continue
        }
        $queue.Enqueue($child)
    }
}
$output.Name
```

With the change in the example above, the folders nested under each Large folder are no longer included in the output, as shown below:

```
Project
A
D
B
Large
C
Large
```

Using a Stack instead of a Queue is a very small change:

```
$path = Get-Item Project
$stack = [System.Collections.Generic.Stack[object]]$path
$output = while ($stack.Count) {
    $current = $stack.Pop()
    $current
    foreach ($child in Get-ChildItem -Path $current -Directory) {
        if ($current.Name -eq 'Large') {
            continue
        }
        $stack.Push($child)
    }
}
$output.Name
```

The only effective difference is the order in which folders in the tree are visited. The output from the example above is shown below:

```
Project
D
Large
A
B
Large
C
```

The loop demonstrated here may be enhanced to allow it to return files in the folder, or it may make use of faster methods to enumerate folder content than Get-ChildItem. It might allow control search depth, and so on.

Summary

This chapter explored the different conditional and looping statements available in PowerShell.

The `if` statement allows statements to be run when a condition is met and may be extended to test several conditions with `elseif`.

The `switch` statement has similarities with `if`, a comparison of one value against another. However, `switch` can test many individual cases expressed in a concise manner, allows more than one case to apply to a value, and can operate on an array.

Looping is a vital part of any programming language and PowerShell is no exception. The `foreach` loop is perhaps the most used, allowing repeated code to be enclosed and executed against several objects. The `foreach` loop keyword can often be replaced with the `ForEach-Object` command (or vice versa) depending on circumstances, but the two should not be confused.

`for` loops are more complex but offer a great deal of flexibility for any operation based on a numeric sequence. `while` and `do` loops can be used to carry on working until a condition is met, for example, waiting for a timeout, or an item is created.

The next chapter explores how .NET Framework (and .NET Core) are used in PowerShell.

Learn more on Discord

Read this book alongside other users, PowerShell experts, and the author himself. Ask questions, provide solutions to other readers, chat with the author via Ask Me Anything sessions, and much more.

Scan the QR code or visit the link to join the community.

`https://packt.link/SecNet`

7

Working with .NET

Microsoft .NET is an extensive library of **Application Program Interfaces (APIs)** or pre-created code that can be used by developers when writing applications, or scripters when writing scripts. Microsoft has created several different versions of .NET over the years starting with .NET Framework 1.0 released in 2002. .NET Framework is limited to the Windows operating system.

Windows PowerShell is built using .NET Framework. The .NET Framework version depends on the local installation and the PowerShell version. PowerShell 5.1 was built using .NET 4.5 and can make use of .NET 4.8 if it is installed: https://learn.microsoft.com/dotnet/api/?view=netframework-4.8.

In 2016, Microsoft released .NET Core, a release of .NET that could be run across different platforms, including Windows, Linux distributions, and macOS.

PowerShell 6 and PowerShell 7.0 were built using .NET Core, that is, .NET Core 3.1 for PowerShell 7.0. PowerShell 7.0 can therefore make use of many of the APIs in .NET Core 3.1: https://learn. microsoft.com/dotnet/api/?view=netcore-3.1.

In November 2020, Microsoft released .NET 5, which extends on .NET Core. "Core" was removed from the name to indicate a merging of the two distinct releases of .NET. Going forward, there is no more .NET Framework (Windows only) and .NET Core (cross-platform); there is just .NET, and that is cross-platform.

PowerShell 7.3.5 was built using .NET 7 and can make use of the APIs in .NET 7: https://learn. microsoft.com/dotnet/api/?view=net-7.0.

The ability to consume .NET APIs adds a tremendous amount of flexibility to PowerShell over and above the commands provided by PowerShell itself or any modules that can be installed.

The concept of working with objects was introduced in *Chapter 4, Working with Objects in PowerShell*. This chapter extends on working with objects, moving from objects created by commands to objects created from .NET classes.

Working directly with .NET is important because, as a PowerShell developer, you do not want to be limited to the things that have been turned into neat commands. Being able to directly use these types opens the possibility of using third-party assemblies, such as those on nuget.org: `https://www.nuget.org/packages`.

It is important to understand that .NET is vast; it is not possible to cover everything about .NET in a single chapter. This chapter aims to show how .NET may be used within PowerShell based on the .NET reference: `https://learn.microsoft.com/dotnet/api/?view=net-7.0`.

Therefore, the goal is not to learn everything about .NET but to learn enough know-how to find out more.

This chapter covers the following topics:

- Assemblies
- Types
- Enumerations
- Classes
- Namespaces
- The using keyword
- Type accelerators
- Members
- Fluent interfaces
- Reflection in PowerShell

Assemblies are the starting point; they contain the types that can be used in PowerShell.

Assemblies

An assembly is a collection of types and any other supporting resources. .NET objects are implemented within assemblies. An assembly may be static (based on a file) or dynamic (created in memory).

The assembly type load locations can be seen by exploring the `Assembly` property of the type. For example, the `String` type is loaded from `System.Private.CoreLib.dll` in PowerShell 7:

```
PS> [System.String].Assembly.Location
C:\Program Files\PowerShell\7\System.Private.CoreLib.dll
```

In PowerShell 7, the assemblies that are loaded by default or those that can be loaded by name are in the `$PSHome` directory.

The list of currently loaded assemblies by PowerShell in the current session can be viewed using the following statement:

```
[System.AppDomain]::CurrentDomain.GetAssemblies()
```

The list can be quite extensive and can grow as different modules (which might depend on other .NET types) are loaded. The first few lines are shown here:

```
GAC     Version     Location
---     -------     --------
False   v4.0.30319  C:\Program Files\PowerShell\7\System.Private.CoreLib.dll
False   v4.0.30319  C:\Program Files\PowerShell\7\pwsh.dll
False   v4.0.30319  C:\Program Files\PowerShell\7\System.Runtime.dll
False   v4.0.30319  C:\Program Files\PowerShell\7\Microsoft.PowerShell.Co...
False   v4.0.30319  C:\Program Files\PowerShell\7\System.Management.Autom...
False   v4.0.30319  C:\Program Files\PowerShell\7\System.Threading.Thread...
False   v4.0.30319  C:\Program Files\PowerShell\7\System.Runtime.InteropS...
False   v4.0.30319  C:\Program Files\PowerShell\7\System.Threading.dll
```

The ClassExplorer module from the PowerShell Gallery may be used to simplify the previous command:

```
Install-Module ClassExplorer
Get-Assembly
```

Assemblies can be explicitly loaded with the Add-Type command. For example, PowerShell 7 includes the System.Windows.Forms.dll file in the $PSHome folder but will only load it if told to. The DLL is used to write graphical user interfaces. You can therefore load it using the name alone (instead of a full path to the DLL):

```
Add-Type -AssemblyName System.Windows.Forms
```

Once an assembly and the types it contains have been loaded into a session, they cannot be unloaded without restarting the PowerShell session. This might affect an upgrade to an existing module based on a DLL; PowerShell cannot unload the DLL and load a newer version. When a DLL is in use by an application, it is locked; attempting to delete the DLL file would fail.

Much of PowerShell itself is implemented in the System.Management.Automation DLL. You can view details of the DLL using the following statement:

```
[System.Management.Automation.PowerShell].Assembly
```

In this statement, the PowerShell type is used to get information about the System.Management.Automation assembly. The PowerShell type will be used in *Chapter 15, Asynchronous Processing*.

Any other type in the same assembly may be used to get the same Assembly property. The PowerShell type could be replaced with any other type implemented as part of PowerShell itself:

```
[System.Management.Automation.PSCredential].Assembly
[System.Management.Automation.PSObject].Assembly
```

In Windows PowerShell, assemblies are often loaded from the **Global Assembly Cache (GAC)**. PowerShell 7 (and other .NET Core applications) cannot use the GAC, which is why the GAC property in each of the assemblies in use by PowerShell 7 is False.

About the GAC

In Windows PowerShell, most types exist in DLL files stored in `$env:SystemRoot\Assembly`. This folder stores what is known as the GAC. The DLL files registered here can be used by any .NET Framework application on the computer. Each DLL may be used by name, rather than an application needing to know the exact path to a DLL.

The `Gac` module from the PowerShell Gallery may be used to list assemblies in the GAC. The versions of an assembly in the GAC will vary depending on the installed versions of .NET Framework and any other installed components, such as **Software Development Kits (SDKs)**:

```
PS> Install-Module Gac -Scope CurrentUser
PS> Get-GacAssembly System.Windows.Forms


Name                    Version      Culture PublicKeyToken   PrArch
----                    -------      ------- --------------   ------
System.Windows.Forms 2.0.0.0                b77a5c561934e089 MSIL
System.Windows.Forms 1.0.5000.0             b77a5c561934e089 None
System.Windows.Forms 4.0.0.0                b77a5c561934e089 MSIL
```

If a specific version of an assembly is required, the full name of the assembly may be used. It uniquely identifies the assembly:

```
Add-Type -AssemblyName 'System.Windows.Forms, Version=4.0.0.0, Culture=neutral,
PublicKeyToken=b77a5c561934e089'
```

Note that multiple versions of the same assembly cannot be loaded in a single session.

You can use the `Gac` module to show the `FullName` value used in the previous code. The values displayed depend on the installed versions of .NET Framework:

```
Get-GacAssembly System.Windows.Forms |
    Select-Object FullName
```

The output from the command above will look like the following:

```
FullName
--------
System.Windows.Forms, Version=2.0.0.0, Culture=neutral,
PublicKeyToken=b77a5c561934e089
System.Windows.Forms, Version=1.0.5000.0, Culture=neutral,
PublicKeyToken=b77a5c561934e089
System.Windows.Forms, Version=4.0.0.0, Culture=neutral,
PublicKeyToken=b77a5c561934e089
```

An assembly typically contains several different types.

Types

A type is used to represent the generalized functionality of an object. This description is vague but a .NET type can be used to describe anything; it is hard to be more specific. To use this book as an example, it could have several types, including the following:

*   PowerShellBook
*   TextBook
*   Book

Each of these types describes how an object can behave.

In PowerShell, types are written between square brackets. The [System.AppDomain] and [System.Management.Automation.PowerShell] statements, used when discussing previous assemblies, are types.

The type of an object can be revealed by the Get-Member command (the following output is truncated):

```
PS> 1 | Get-Member


   TypeName: System.Int32


Name        MemberType Definition
----        ---------- ----------
CompareTo   Method     int CompareTo(System.Object value), int ...
Equals      Method     bool Equals(System.Object obj), bool Equ...
GetHashCode Method     int GetHashCode()
```

The GetType() method may also be used – for example, by using the method on a variable:

```
PS> $variable = 1
PS> $variable.GetType()


IsPublic IsSerial Name                                     BaseType
-------- -------- ----                                     --------
True     True     Int32                                    System.ValueType
```

For numeric values, GetType() may also be used when the value is in parentheses:

```
PS> (1).GetType()


IsPublic IsSerial Name                                     BaseType
-------- -------- ----                                     --------
True     True     Int32                                    System.ValueType
```

Methods are explored later in this chapter.

Type descriptions are objects in PowerShell

[System.AppDomain] is a type but the syntax used to describe the type is itself an object. The object has properties and methods and a type of its own (RuntimeType).

This can be seen by running the following command:

```
[System.AppDomain].GetType()
```

Types can be created in languages such as C# using several different keywords, including class, enum, interface, and struct. Of these, PowerShell itself can create class and enum, which are explored along with the use of interfaces in *Chapter 19, Classes and Enumerations*. A more detailed description of struct is beyond the scope of this book.

Enumerations

An enumeration is a specialized type that is used to express a list of constants. Enumerations are used throughout .NET and PowerShell.

PowerShell itself makes use of enumerations for many purposes. For example, the possible values for the $VerbosePreference variable are described in an enumeration:

```
PS> $VerbosePreference.GetType()


IsPublic IsSerial Name                 BaseType
-------- -------- ----                 --------
True     True     ActionPreference     System.Enum
```

Notice that BaseType is System.Enum, indicating that this type is an enumeration.

The possible values for an enumeration can be listed in several different ways. The most convenient of these is to use the GetEnumValues() method on the enumeration type:

```
PS> $VerbosePreference.GetType().GetEnumValues()
SilentlyContinue
Stop
Continue
Inquire
Ignore
Suspend
Break
```

Enumerations are relatively simple types. They contain a list of constants that you can use in your code. A class is more complex.

Classes

A class is a set of instructions that dictates how a specific instance of an object behaves, including how it can be created and what it can do. A class is, in a sense, a recipe.

In the case of this book, a class might include details of authoring, editorial processes, and publication steps. These steps are, hopefully, invisible to anyone reading this book; they are part of the internal implementation of the class. Following these steps will produce an instance of the `PowerShellBook` object.

Once a class has been compiled, it is used as a type. The members of the class are used to interact with the object. Members are explored later in this chapter.

Classes (and types) are arranged and categorized into namespaces.

Namespaces

A namespace is used to organize types into a hierarchy, grouping types with related functionality together. A namespace can be considered like a folder in a filesystem.

PowerShell is, for the most part, implemented in the `System.Management.Automation` namespace. This namespace has associated documentation: `https://learn.microsoft.com/dotnet/api/system.management.automation?view=powershellsdk-7.0.0`.

Similarly, types used to work with the filesystem are grouped together in the `System.IO` namespace: `https://learn.microsoft.com/dotnet/api/system.io`.

For the following given type name, the namespace is everything before the final label. The namespace value is accessible as a property of the type:

```
PS> [System.IO.File].Namespace
System.IO
```

In PowerShell, the `System` namespace is implicit. The `System.AppDomain` type was used at the start of the chapter to show which assemblies PowerShell is currently using. This can be shortened to:

```
[AppDomain]::CurrentDomain.GetAssemblies()
```

The same applies to types with longer names, such as `System.Management.Automation.PowerShell`, which can be shortened to:

```
[Management.Automation.PowerShell].Assembly
```

PowerShell automatically searches the System namespace for these types. The `using` keyword can be used to look up types in longer namespaces.

The using keyword

The `using` keyword simplifies the use of namespaces and can be used to load assemblies or PowerShell modules. The `using` keyword was introduced with PowerShell 5.0.

The `using` keyword can be used in a script, a module, or in the console. In a script, the `using` keyword can only be preceded by comments.

The `using module` statement is used to access PowerShell classes created within a PowerShell module. The `using module` statement is explored in *Chapter 19, Classes and Enumerations*.

In the context of working with .NET, namespaces and assemblies are of interest.

Using namespaces

The using namespace statement instructs PowerShell to look for any type names used in an additional namespace. For example, by default, attempting to use System.IO.File without a full name will result in an error:

```
PS> [File]
InvalidOperation: Unable to find type [File].
```

PowerShell looked for the type in the System namespace and did not find it.

If using namespace System.IO is added, first, PowerShell will search the System.IO namespace for the type (in addition to the top-level namespace System):

```
PS> using namespace System.IO
PS> [File]


IsPublic IsSerial Name                    BaseType
-------- -------- ----                    --------
True     False    File                    System.Object
```

In the console, PowerShell only recognizes the last using namespace statement that was entered. In the following example, the first using namespace statement is replaced by the second when typed into the console:

```
using namespace System.IO
using namespace System.Data.SqlClient
```

PowerShell will be able to find the type System.Data.SqlClient.SqlConnection by name only, as the following code shows:

```
PS> [SqlConnection]

IsPublic IsSerial Name                 BaseType
-------- -------- ----                 --------
True     False    SqlConnection        System.Data.Common.DbConnection
```

But PowerShell will fail to find the [File] type again because the previous using namespace statement is no longer valid:

```
PS> [File]
InvalidOperation: Unable to find type [File].
```

A script file allows multiple using namespace statements. Each is processed when the script is parsed. In the console, it is only possible to have more than one using namespace statement if they are separated by a semi colon:

```
using namespace System.IO; using namespace System.Data.SqlClient
```

After this, PowerShell will search System.Data.SqlClient, System.IO, and System when a type is entered by name only.

The namespace value used with a using namespace statement does not have to exist and PowerShell does not attempt to validate the value. This means that an assembly that implements the types in a namespace can be loaded after the using namespace statement.

For example, if a new PowerShell session is started and the System.Windows.Forms DLL has not yet loaded, the following commands can be executed and PowerShell will find types by name from the loaded assembly:

```
PS> using namespace System.Windows.Forms
PS> Add-Type -AssemblyName System.Windows.Forms
PS> [Button]

IsPublic IsSerial Name          BaseType
-------- -------- ----          --------
True     False    Button        System.Windows.Forms.ButtonBase
```

It is possible to load assemblies (before or after using namespace) with the using assembly statement.

Using assemblies

The using assembly statement is used to load assemblies into the PowerShell session.

In PowerShell 7, using assembly can only load assemblies using a path (full or relative). In Windows PowerShell, assemblies can either be loaded using a path or from the GAC.

For example, the System.Windows.Forms assembly can be loaded in Windows PowerShell with the following command:

```
using assembly System.Windows.Forms
```

In PowerShell 7, you must use the full path. The path would have to be written in full as variables are not permitted in the statement:

```
using assembly 'C:\Program Files\PowerShell\7\System.Windows.Forms.dll'
```

PowerShell 7 may only be able to load by name in the future, but a GitHub issue about this has been open for 2 years.

PowerShell allows you to run the using assembly statement any number of times in a script, and more than one assembly can be loaded in a single script.

Before using namespace became available with PowerShell 5, the only way to shorten a type name was to use a type accelerator.

Type accelerators

A type accelerator is an alias for a type. At the beginning of this chapter, the System.Management.Automation.PowerShell type was used; this type has an accelerator available. The name of the type accelerator is simply PowerShell. The type accelerator allows the following to be used:

```
[PowerShell].Assembly
```

Another commonly used example is the ADSI accelerator. This represents the System.DirectoryServices.DirectoryEntry type. This means that the following two commands are equivalent:

```
[System.DirectoryServices.DirectoryEntry]"WinNT://$env:COMPUTERNAME"
[ADSI]"WinNT://$env:COMPUTERNAME"
```

The full type name behind a type accelerator can be seen using the FullName property:

```
PS> [ADSI].FullName
System.DirectoryServices.DirectoryEntry
```

PowerShell includes a lot of type accelerators; these accelerators are documented in about_Type_Accelerators:

```
Get-Help about_Type_Accelerators
```

Getting and adding type accelerators in code is explored later in this chapter.

The two accelerators mentioned above are arguably not the most frequently used.

About PSCustomObject and Ordered

PSCustomObject and Ordered are both type accelerators in PowerShell 7.

PSCustomObject and Ordered were both introduced in PowerShell 3. The type accelerator for Ordered is a very recent addition and is not available in PowerShell 5.1.

Unlike the type accelerators demonstrated at the start of this section, PSCustomObject and Ordered affect the parser rather than being intended for direct use as an accelerator.

When either is placed on the left of a hash table, the parser interprets these as an instruction to create a particular thing based on the hash table.

The difference between these can be demonstrated by making use of the -as operator.

If the following code is run in PowerShell, the result will be an integer value in both cases:

```
[int]"1"
"1" -as [int]
```

The int type accelerator is used to coerce the string value into an integer and, in both cases, the result is the integer 1.

PSCustomObject instances are typically created by prefixing a hash table with the [PSCustomObject] type:

```
[PSCustomObject]@{ Name = 'Value' }
```

Get-Member may be used to show this creates a custom object:

```
PS> [PSCustomObject]@{ Name = 'Value' } | Get-Member


    TypeName: System.Management.Automation.PSCustomObject


Name        MemberType   Definition
----        ----------   ----------
Equals      Method       bool Equals(System.Object obj)
GetHashCode Method       int GetHashCode()
GetType     Method       type GetType()
ToString    Method       string ToString()
Name        NoteProperty string Name=Value
```

If this were a regular type, then the following statement would yield the same value type:

```
@{ Name = 'Value' } -as [PSCustomObject]
```

However, because PSCustomObject (and Ordered) are parser instructions, the result is unexpected. The output below is truncated; the TypeName value at the top is the most significant:

```
PS> @{ Name = 'Value' } -as [PSCustomObject] | Get-Member


    TypeName: System.Collections.Hashtable


Name       MemberType         Definition
----       ----------         ----------
Add        Method             void Add(System.Obje…
Clear      Method             void Clear(), void I…
Clone      Method             System.Object Clone(…
```

A similar result will show if the full type name for PSCustomObject is used on the left:

```
PS> [PSCustomObject].FullName
System.Management.Automation.PSObject


PS> [System.Management.Automation.PSObject]@{ Name = 'Value' } | Get-Member


    TypeName: System.Collections.Hashtable
```

```
Name                    MemberType              Definition
----                    ----------              ----------
Add                     Method                  void Add(System.Obje…
Clear                   Method                  void Clear(), void I…
Clone                   Method                  System.Object Clone(…
```

Attempting the operation using [Ordered] will show a similar disparity, again, with truncated output:

```
PS> [Ordered]@{ Name = 'Value' } | Get-Member


    TypeName: System.Collections.Specialized.OrderedDictionary

Name                    MemberType              Definition
----                    ----------              ----------
Add                     Method                  void Add(System.Obje…
AsReadOnly              Method                  ordered AsReadOnly()
Clear                   Method                  void Clear(), void I…
```

Using -as, the result will be null as the cast is not valid.

Casting directly using the full type name will reveal the problem when converting:

```
[System.Collections.Specialized.OrderedDictionary]@{
    Name = 'Value'
}
```

When using the example above, the error below will be displayed:

```
InvalidArgument: Cannot create object of type "System.Collections.Specialized.
OrderedDictionary". The property 'Name' was not found for the 'System.
Collections.Specialized.OrderedDictionary' object. There is no settable
property available.
```

Therefore, PSCustomObject and Ordered retain their specialized use case and do not extend beyond that despite the presence of the type accelerators. It can be observed that these will continue to work on the left of a hash table even if the type accelerators are removed.

Types have members; the members available depend on the type. Types derived from classes are likely to have several different members, including constructors, properties, and methods.

Members

All types have members. Members represent data or dictate the behavior of the object represented by a type.

In .NET, the members are described in the C Sharp (C#) programming guide in the .NET reference: https://learn.microsoft.com/dotnet/csharp/programming-guide/classes-and-structs/members.

PowerShell also adds members; these member types are also described in the .NET reference: `https://learn.microsoft.com/dotnet/api/system.management.automation.psmembertypes`.

This section focuses on a small number of members used when working with .NET types:

- Constructors
- Properties
- Methods

The `Event` member is explored in *Chapter 15, Asynchronous Processing*.

The `ScriptProperty` and `ScriptMethod` property types are specific to PowerShell and may be added with the Add-Member command. These member types are outside of the scope of this chapter.

Constructors are one possible way of creating an instance of a type.

Constructors

A constructor is used to create an instance of a type. For example, the `System.Text.StringBuilder` type can be used to build complex strings.

The `StringBuilder` class is documented in the .NET reference: `https://learn.microsoft.com/dotnet/api/system.text.stringbuilder`.

The **StringBuilder Constructors** section of the `StringBuilder` class documentation has several constructors, as shown in *Figure 7.1*:

StringBuilder Constructors

Namespace: System.Text
Assembly: System.Runtime.dll

Initializes a new instance of the <u>StringBuilder</u> class.

Overloads

StringBuilder()	Initializes a new instance of the <u>StringBuilder</u> class.
StringBuilder(Int32)	Initializes a new instance of the <u>StringBuilder</u> class using the specified capacity.
StringBuilder(String)	Initializes a new instance of the <u>StringBuilder</u> class using the specified string.
StringBuilder(Int32, Int32)	Initializes a new instance of the <u>StringBuilder</u> class that starts with a specified capacity and can grow to a specified maximum.
StringBuilder(String, Int32)	Initializes a new instance of the <u>StringBuilder</u> class using the specified string and capacity.
StringBuilder(String, Int32, Int32, Int32)	Initializes a new instance of the <u>StringBuilder</u> class from the specified substring and capacity.

Figure 7.1: Constructors for StringBuilder

Each constructor has a different list of arguments. These are known as overloads, where one member has different possible sets of arguments. The class distinguishes between the overloads to call based on the number and types of the arguments supplied.

In PowerShell, there are two different ways to use a constructor. The `New-Object` command can be used:

```
New-Object System.Text.StringBuilder
```

Or the static method `new()` can be used. The `new()` method was introduced with PowerShell 5:

```
[System.Text.StringBuilder]::new()
```

Static methods are explored in more detail later in this section.

In either case and because no arguments were supplied, the first overload from *Figure 7.1* will be used. If a string were used as an argument (and it were the only argument), the third overload in the list would be used (one argument with type `String`):

```
[System.Text.StringBuilder]::new(
    'This is the start of the string'
)
```

When the constructor in the example above is used, an instance of the `StringBuilder` type is returned, which shows the properties of the class. The result is shown below:

```
Capacity   MaxCapacity   Length
--------   -----------   ------
      31    2147483647       31
```

A property holds data about the object.

Properties

A property describes some aspect of the object. The last example shows the `Capacity`, `MaxCapacity`, and `Length` properties of the `StringBuilder` object.

Each of the properties is described in the .NET reference: `https://learn.microsoft.com/dotnet/api/system.text.stringbuilder?view=net-7.0#properties`.

Figure 7.2 shows the properties from the .NET reference:

Properties

Capacity	Gets or sets the maximum number of characters that can be contained in the memory allocated by the current instance.
Chars[Int32]	Gets or sets the character at the specified character position in this instance.
Length	Gets or sets the length of the current StringBuilder object.
MaxCapacity	Gets the maximum capacity of this instance.

Figure 7.2: Properties for StringBuilder

Clicking on each property will show further details. For example, clicking on Capacity will describe the property and the property's use in far more detail. The Capacity property documentation also includes an example that uses that property. Examples tend to be available in C#, VB, or C++. Few, if any, examples are available in PowerShell.

.NET classes also list fields as member types. Fields are indistinguishable from properties in PowerShell. In .NET, a property will implement a get or set (or both) accessor to access a value. Accessors were demonstrated in *Chapter 4, Working with Objects in PowerShell*.

The class created in the following C# snippet includes both a field and a property. The property uses get and set accessors, while the field does not:

```
Add-Type -TypeDefinition '
public class MyClass
{
    public string thisIsAField;
    public string thisIsAProperty { get; set; }
}
'
```

Once the MyClass type has been added to the PowerShell session, you can create an instance and use Get-Member to show the members of the class:

```
PS> [MyClass]::new() | Get-Member


    TypeName: MyClass


Name            MemberType Definition
----            ---------- ----------
Equals          Method     bool Equals(System.Object obj)
GetHashCode     Method     int GetHashCode()
GetType         Method     type GetType()
ToString        Method     string ToString()
thisIsAField    Property   string thisIsAField {get;set;}
thisIsAProperty Property   string thisIsAProperty {get;set;}
```

It is possible to show that the thisIsAField member is indeed a field by using the GetMembers() method of the type:

```
PS> [MyClass].GetMembers() | Select-Object Name, MemberType


Name                   MemberType
----                   ----------
get_thisIsAProperty    Method
set_thisIsAProperty    Method
```

```
GetType              Method
ToString             Method
Equals               Method
GetHashCode          Method
.ctor                Constructor
thisIsAProperty      Property
thisIsAField         Field
```

The GetMembers() method is part of a broader topic known as reflection, which is explored to a limited extent later in this chapter.

The fact that this is a field does not really matter to PowerShell; it can be used in the same way as a property.

To continue to add to the string in StringBuilder, the class methods can be used.

Methods

A method enacts some change on an object. Methods can be used to change the internal state of an object, such as the Append() method in the StringBuilder type. Or methods can be used to return something different from the object, such as the ToString() method.

The methods available to the StringBuilder type are documented after the properties in the .NET reference: https://learn.microsoft.com/dotnet/api/system.text.stringbuilder?view=net-7.0#methods.

Figure 7.3 shows the first few methods:

Methods

Append(Boolean)	Appends the string representation of a specified Boolean value to this instance.
Append(Byte)	Appends the string representation of a specified 8-bit unsigned integer to this instance.
Append(Char)	Appends the string representation of a specified Char object to this instance.
Append(Char*, Int32)	Appends an array of Unicode characters starting at a specified address to this instance.
Append(Char, Int32)	Appends a specified number of copies of the string representation of a Unicode character to this instance.
Append(Char[])	Appends the string representation of the Unicode characters in a specified array to this instance.

Figure 7.3: Methods for StringBuilder

Several of the preceding methods have the same name but different arguments. As with the constructor, these methods with the same name are overloaded. The method that will be used is based on the number and types of the arguments.

For example, running the following will use the first of the methods in *Figure 7.3*:

```
$stringBuilder = [System.Text.StringBuilder]::new()
$stringBuilder.Append($true)
```

Running the same method name with a byte will use the second method:

```
$stringBuilder.Append([Byte]1)
```

In the case of the StringBuilder type, each of the methods used to append to the string returns an instance of the same StringBuilder type.

One possible strategy for dealing with this is to pipe each statement to Out-Null. If the output from the method call is not interesting, then this is a perfectly valid approach:

```
$stringBuilder = [System.Text.StringBuilder]::new()
$stringBuilder.Append('Hello') | Out-Null
$stringBuilder.AppendLine() | Out-Null
$stringBuilder.AppendLine('World') | Out-Null
```

Once the string is complete, the ToString method may be called to show the final string:

```
PS> $stringBuilder.ToString()
Hello
World
```

If a method name is used without brackets at the end, PowerShell will show the overloads for that method instead of executing the method:

```
PS> $stringBuilder.ToString

OverloadDefinitions
-------------------
string ToString()
string ToString(int startIndex, int length)
```

Methods returning the instance of the type, as shown by StringBuilder, are known as fluent interfaces.

Fluent interfaces

A fluent interface is a particular pattern where each method call returns the instance of the object the method is affecting.

Fluent interfaces are intended to allow a sequence of methods to be called in turn to build a complex statement that is still easy for a human to read.

In the StringBuilder type, this can be used to assemble a relatively complex string:

```
$string = [System.Text.StringBuilder]::new().
    AppendLine('Hello').
```

```
    AppendLine('World').
    ToString()
```

The preceding example is a simple one; however, you can use `StringBuilder` to build far more complex and elaborate strings. PowerShell itself includes another example of a fluent interface:

```
[PowerShell]::Create().
    AddCommand('Get-Process').
    AddCommand('Where-Object').
    AddParameter('Property', 'Name').
    AddParameter('Value', 'pwsh').
    AddParameter('EQ', $true).
    Invoke()
```

The preceding snippet creates a PowerShell runspace, and then runs a command in that runspace. It is equivalent to the following command:

```
Get-Process | Where-Object -Property Name -Value pwsh -EQ
```

PowerShell runspaces are explored in *Chapter 15, Asynchronous Processing*.

In the previous example, `Create()` is a static method. The example before used `new()`, which is also a static method; however, the `new()` method is added by PowerShell itself.

Static methods

Static methods can be used without creating an instance of the object. Static methods are used in a wide variety of different contexts.

`Get-Member` can be used to explore the static methods of a type in PowerShell, for example, the static methods on the `DateTime` type:

```
[DateTime] | Get-Member -MemberType Method -Static
```

`IsLeapYear` is one of the static methods on the `System.DateTime` type. It will return `True` when the year used as an argument is a leap year:

```
PS> [DateTime]::IsLeapYear(2020)
True
```

Another example of a static method is the `Reverse()` method on the `System.Array` type. This method is notable because it does not return anything. It acts on an existing instance of an array:

```
$array = 1, 2, 3
[Array]::Reverse($array)
```

The change is directly applied to the array referenced by the `$array` variable. The array content will be reversed:

```
PS> $array
3
2
1
```

The list of methods on the .NET reference does not distinguish between static and non-static methods. For example, the Reverse method from the Methods section in the .NET reference is shown in *Figure 7.4*:

Reverse(Array)   Reverses the sequence of the elements in the entire one-
                                        dimensional Array.

Reverse(Array, Int32, Int32)   Reverses the sequence of a subset of the elements in the one-
                                        dimensional Array.

Reverse<T>(T[])   Reverses the sequence of the elements in the one-dimensional
                                        generic array.

Reverse<T>(T[], Int32, Int32)   Reverses the sequence of a subset of the elements in the one-
                                        dimensional generic array.

Figure 7.4: Reverse method from the Methods section

Clicking into the documentation for a specific overload (for example, the first in the list above) shows that the method is static: https://learn.microsoft.com/dotnet/api/system.array.reverse?view=net-7.0#System_Array_Reverse_System_Array.

This is shown in *Figure 7.5*:

Reverse(Array)

Reverses the sequence of the elements in the entire one-dimensional Array.

```
C#                                                                                          Copy

public static void Reverse (Array array);
```

Figure 7.5: Reverse method of System.Array

Note the static keyword in *Figure 7.5*.

The new() method used in a few of the examples in this chapter was added in PowerShell 5 and will not appear in the documentation in the .NET reference.

About the new() method

The new static method is added to .NET types by PowerShell. The method is visible when using Get-Member. Because PowerShell adds the method, it does not show in the .NET reference.

The new() method can be used with any of the constructors of a class. The new() method was used when exploring constructors to create an instance of a StringBuilder:

```
[System.Text.StringBuilder]::new()
```

Omitting the brackets from the end of the static method will show the overloads instead of creating the object:

```
PS> [System.Text.StringBuilder]::new

OverloadDefinitions
-------------------
System.Text.StringBuilder new()
System.Text.StringBuilder new(int capacity)
System.Text.StringBuilder new(string value)
System.Text.StringBuilder new(string value, int capacity)
System.Text.StringBuilder new(string value, int startIndex, int...
System.Text.StringBuilder new(int capacity, int maxCapacity)
```

While the previous list is not as detailed as the .NET reference, it can serve as a useful reminder in the console.

Properties can also be static as well as methods.

Static properties

Static properties are used to return values that are related to the type but do not require an instance of the type to be created.

Like static methods, static properties can be listed using the Get-Member command:

```
PS> [DateTime] | Get-Member -MemberType Property -Static

   TypeName: System.DateTime

Name       MemberType Definition
----       ---------- ----------
MaxValue   Property   static datetime MaxValue {get;}
MinValue   Property   static datetime MinValue {get;}
Now        Property   datetime Now {get;}
Today      Property   datetime Today {get;}
UnixEpoch  Property   static datetime UnixEpoch {get;}
UtcNow     Property   datetime UtcNow {get;}
```

Like static methods, the .NET reference does not differentiate between static and non-static properties in the property list, only in the detail of a specific property, as shown in *Figure 7.6*:

DateTime.Now Property

Namespace: System

Assemblies: mscorlib.dll, System.Runtime.dll

Gets a DateTime object that is set to the current date and time on this computer, expressed as the local time.

C#   📋 Copy

```C#
public static DateTime Now { get; }
```

Figure 7.6: System.DateTime Now static property

Static properties are used as shown here:

```
[DateTime]::Now
```

The preceding property is like using the Get-Date command with no parameters.

The types and members used above are public – that is, they are accessible outside of the assembly they were defined in.

Reflection in PowerShell

Types, properties, and methods can be marked as internal or private. Internal types and members are only accessible by other types and members within the same assembly. Private members are only accessible within the same class or type. Collectively, these can be described as non-public types and members.

Non-public types and members are accessible using what is known as reflection. The .NET reference describes reflection in the dynamic programming guide: https://learn.microsoft.com/dotnet/ framework/reflection-and-codedom/reflection.

PowerShell can make use of reflection to explore and use non-public types and members. Doing so introduces a risk; such types and members are not part of a public-supported API. As the code is updated, these non-public types and members may disappear or change behavior. Therefore, it is not recommended to make code that is to be used in production dependent on a non-public implementation.

Even if it might not be supported, exploring is interesting and the ability to use reflection in Power-Shell is handy.

Type accelerators in PowerShell are defined in a non-public type.

The TypeAccelerators type

The `TypeAccelators` type is used to list and add type accelerators to the PowerShell session.

The `TypeAccelerators` type is not public and, therefore, cannot be so easily accessed. The type may be found by using the `GetType()` method on an `Assembly` object. The type is part of the `System.Management.Automation` namespace. The following command uses the PowerShell type to get the assembly:

```
[PowerShell].Assembly
```

The `Assembly` object may be used to run the `GetType()` method, which will find a type within an assembly:

```
[PowerShell].Assembly.GetType(
    'System.Management.Automation.TypeAccelerators'
)
```

The statement above returns the `TypeAccelerators` type, as shown below:

```
IsPublic IsSerial Name                             BaseType
-------- -------- ----                             --------
False    False    TypeAccelerators                 System.Object
```

The name used with the `GetType()` method is case-sensitive; the type name must be written exactly as above.

The `IsPublic` property indicates that this type is not public and, therefore, cannot be accessed by putting the name in square brackets.

You can use the `GetType()` method on the assembly object to list all of the types within that assembly.

The type can be assigned to a variable to make it easier to work with:

```
$typeAccelerators = [PowerShell].Assembly.GetType(
    'System.Management.Automation.TypeAccelerators'
)
```

The `TypeAccelerators` type has two relevant public methods and one relevant public property. These members, along with the `Equals` and `ReferenceEquals` methods inherited from `System.Object`, are shown in the following code:

```
PS> $typeAccelerators | Get-Member -Static


   TypeName: System.Management.Automation.TypeAccelerators

Name            MemberType Definition
----            ---------- ----------
Add             Method     static void Add(string typeName, ty...
```

```
Equals           Method      static bool Equals(System.Object ob...
ReferenceEquals  Method      static bool ReferenceEquals(System....
Remove           Method      static bool Remove(string typeName)
Get              Property    System.Collections.Generic.Dictiona...
```

As the property and the two methods are static, they are accessed using the static member operator, ::. For example, the Get property can be used to list the type accelerators:

```
$typeAccelerators::Get
```

A new type accelerator can be added with the Add method. In the following example, a type accelerator is added to make accessing this TypeAccelerators type easier:

```
$typeAccelerators::Add(
    'TypeAccelerators',
    $typeAccelerators
)
```

Once done, the new type accelerator can be used in place of the variable:

```
[TypeAccelerators]::Get
```

The newly added type accelerator will go away when PowerShell is closed.

The properties and methods used on the TypeAccelators type are public and are therefore easy to use once an instance of the type is available. Non-public members may also be listed and used with reflection.

When a variable is assigned a type in PowerShell, an attribute is created to handle conversions when values are assigned.

The ArgumentTypeConverterAttribute type

The ArgumentTypeConverterAttribute attribute is used by PowerShell when casting a variable value. The attribute is added to a variable when the type is on the left-hand side of an assignment.

For example, any values assigned to the following variable will be cast to a string:

```
[string]$variable = 'value'
```

Once the variable has been created, the presence of the attribute can be seen using Get-Variable, but the type it casts to is not visible:

```
PS> (Get-Variable variable).Attributes | Format-List
TransformNullOptionalParameters : True
TypeId                          : System.Management.Automation.Arg...
```

Discovering the type used by the variable means exploring the non-public members of the attribute.

The attribute type itself is non-public, but an existing variable can be used to get an instance of the type itself. In the following example, [0] is used to access the attribute; the Attributes property is a collection (a PSVariableAttributeCollection):

```
[string]$variable = 'value'
$typeConverter = (Get-Variable variable).Attributes[0]
$typeConverterType = $typeConverter.GetType()
```

The type the attribute converts values to is held in a non-public member of the attribute. The possible members, both public and non-public, can be listed using the GetMembers() method on the type. Without any arguments, GetMembers() will only show public members the same information that the Get-Member command shows:

```
PS> $typeConverterType.GetMembers() |
>>      Select-Object Name, MemberType, IsPublic
```

You can see the non-public members by using an overload for the GetMembers() method. The overload accepts a System.Reflection.BindingFlags value. As a Flags enumeration, BindingFlags allows more than one value to be used. The values are supplied as a comma-separated string in the following example:

```
$typeConverterType.GetMembers('NonPublic,Instance') |
    Select-Object Name, MemberType, IsPublic
```

The statement above will show the members in the example below:

```
Name                                 MemberType IsPublic
----                                 ---------- --------
get_TargetType                           Method    False
Transform                                Method    False
TransformInternal                        Method    False
MemberwiseClone                          Method    False
Finalize                                 Method    False
.ctor                               Constructor    False
TargetType                             Property
_convertTypes                             Field    False
```

The output from the command shows two members, which may show the target type of any value assigned to the variable. The property TargetType, however, looks the most promising.

The Instance flag used in the previous example indicates that members that are present on instances of the type should be returned. If the Static flag was used instead, only static members would be returned. If Static was used in addition to Instance, both static and non-static members would be displayed.

The following example shows the impact of changing the flag to Static:

```
$typeConverterType.GetMembers('NonPublic, Static') |
    Select-Object Name, MemberType, IsPublic, IsStatic
```

The non-public members from the statement above are shown below:

```
Name                                    MemberType IsPublic IsStatic
----                                    ---------- -------- --------
CheckBoolValue                              Method    False     True
ThrowPSInvalidBooleanArgumentCaE...         Method    False     True
```

The IsPublic property is empty for the TargetType property. Properties allow more complex definitions of when the value can be read or written. The following snippet gets the property definition and then shows whether the Get method for the property is public or not:

```
$typeConverterType.GetProperty(
    'TargetType',
    [System.Reflection.BindingFlags]'Instance,NonPublic'
).GetMethod | Select-Object Name, IsPublic
```

The example above shows the existence of a get_TargetType get method, as shown below:

```
Name              IsPublic
----              --------
get_TargetType     False
```

You can call the GetValue() method on the preceding property definition to get the value. When calling the GetValue() method, the instance of the attribute from Get-Variable must be passed as an argument. The original variable definition is included in the following to make the example complete:

```
[string]$variable = 'value'
$typeConverter = (Get-Variable variable).Attributes[0]
$typeConverterType = $typeConverter.GetType()
$targetTypeProperty = $typeConverterType.GetProperty(
    'TargetType',
    [System.Reflection.BindingFlags]'Instance,NonPublic'
)
$targetTypeProperty.GetValue($typeConverter)
```

The last line returns the type values assigned to the variable:

```
PS> $targetTypeProperty.GetValue($typeConverter)

IsPublic IsSerial Name           BaseType
-------- -------- ----           --------
True     True     String         System.Object
```

Reflection, as demonstrated, is complex, even when the scope is as small as this single property.

The `ImpliedReflection` module can be used to simplify the process. Unfortunately the `ImpliedReflection` module does not currently work in PowerShell 7.4 and above. Hopefully this bug will be fixed soon. Once the module is installed, enable it by using the `Enable-ImpliedReflection` command:

```
Install-Module ImpliedReflection
Enable-ImpliedReflection
```

A confirmation message will be displayed, which should be accepted to enable the module functionality. Once enabled, the `TargetType` property will display on the attribute via `Get-Variable`, as the following shows:

```
PS> [string]$variable = 'value'
PS> (Get-Variable variable).Attributes[0] | Format-List


TransformNullOptionalParameters : True
TypeId                          : System.Management.Automation...
_convertTypes                   : {System.String}
TargetType                      : System.String
```

`ImpliedReflection` cannot be disabled in a session; PowerShell must be restarted to return to normal.

About generics

.NET has a concept called generics and PowerShell, as a .NET language, can make use of generic types and methods.

Microsoft describes this as follows in an article with the same name as this section:

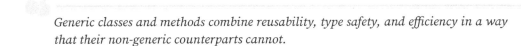

> *Generic classes and methods combine reusability, type safety, and efficiency in a way that their non-generic counterparts cannot.*

(Source: `https://learn.microsoft.com/en-us/dotnet/csharp/fundamentals/types/generics`)

The use of generic classes, or types, is common in the modern use of PowerShell.

Generic classes

.NET has the concept of a generic class; some of these are very common such as `System.Collections.Generic.List<T>`, where T is a type that must be declared when the instance is created. For example:

```
[System.Collections.Generic.List[string]]::new()
```

Generic types avoid the cost of what is known as boxing. This is where a value is wrapped in an instance of `System.Object` before it is stored.

The cost of boxing is unlikely to be noticeable in the vast majority of PowerShell code. Explicitly avoiding boxing is not the reason for introducing this topic. It is present simply because it is often desirable to use generic classes and methods in PowerShell code.

The ArrayList type is an older style of collection that must box each element when it is added, and unbox each one when it is accessed:

```
$listOfObjects = [System.Collections.ArrayList]::new()
# Box the string value
$listOfObjects.Add('hello world')
# Unbox the string value
$value = $listOfObjects[0]
```

The ArrayList stores the string as System.Object and there is a cost associated with doing this.

Conversely, the generic collection System.Collections.Generic.List does not need this extra internal step. When it is created, it must be given a type – [string] in the example below:

```
$listOfStrings = [System.Collections.Generic.List[string]]::new()
```

If required, the List above can be declared using a less specific type. For example:

```
using namespace System.Collections.Generic

$listOfObject = [List[object]]::new()
```

The List shown above is a generic type, but the methods it implements do not require special handling in PowerShell; none of the methods are explicitly generic.

Generic methods

The ability to easily invoke generic methods is new in PowerShell 7.3. To show this in action, a generic method is needed.

The assemblies implementing PowerShell include several types that implement generic methods.

The ClassExplorer module may be used to search for these:

```
Find-Type -Namespace System.Management.Automation |
    Find-Member -GenericParameter System.Object
```

For example, the LanguagePrimitives class is used by PowerShell to convert one type to another. The class has a ConvertTo static method that may be shown with Get-Member:

```
[System.Management.Automation.LanguagePrimitives] |
    Get-Member ConvertTo -Static
```

This method has several overloads available:

```
PS> [System.Management.Automation.LanguagePrimitives]::ConvertTo
```

```
OverloadDefinitions
-------------------
static System.Object ConvertTo(System.Object valueToConvert, type resultType)
static System.Object ConvertTo(System.Object valueToConvert, type resultType,
System.IFormatProvider formatProvider)
static T ConvertTo[T](System.Object valueToConvert)
```

If the ClassExplorer module is imported, the view of these overloads is less messy:

```
OverloadDefinitions
-------------------
public static object ConvertTo(object valueToConvert, Type resultType);
public static object ConvertTo(object valueToConvert, Type resultType,
IFormatProvider formatProvider);
public static T ConvertTo<T>(object valueToConvert);
```

The last of these is a generic method and will be used as an example. The type name in this method represents the desired output type.

As mentioned above, PowerShell 7.3 made invoking generic methods easy. The method may be invoked simply by including the type name before the method arguments:

```
using namespace System.Management.Automation
# A value to convert
$value = Get-Date
[LanguagePrimitives]::ConvertTo[string]($value)
```

This can be compared to the code required to invoke the method in PowerShell 7.2 below:

```
using namespace System.Management.Automation

# Find the method based on the arguments it expects
$genericMethod = [LanguagePrimitives].GetMethod(
    'ConvertTo',
    [Type[]][object]
)
# Convert the generic method to a typed method
$method = $genericMethod.MakeGenericMethod([string])

# A value to convert
$value = Get-Date

# Invoke the method
$method.Invoke($null, $value)
```

The code above makes use of reflection to find the method based on the arguments it is expected to accept, and then uses the `MakeGenericMethod()` to create an object representing the constructed method.

The first argument of `$method.Invoke` is `$null` because this is a `static` method rather than an `instance` method. If this were an `instance` method, the first argument would be the instance the method is being invoked on.

The code above is complex and requires a much deeper understanding of .NET and reflection. It is easy to see the value of the new feature in 7.3.

Summary

Delving into .NET significantly increases the flexibility of PowerShell over using built-in commands and operators. .NET is made up of hundreds of classes and enumerations, many of which can be easily used in PowerShell.

.NET types are arranged in namespaces, grouping types with similar purposes together. For example, the `System.Data.SqlClient` namespace contains types for connecting to and querying Microsoft SQL Server instances.

The `using` keyword, introduced with PowerShell 5.1, allows types to be used by name only, instead of the full name that includes the namespace.

Type accelerators have been in PowerShell since its release. PowerShell provides many built-in type accelerators allowing types to be used by a short name. Examples include `Xml` for `System.Xml.XmlDocument`, and `ADSI` for `System.DirectoryServices.DirectoryEntry`.

Types in .NET have members, including constructors, properties, and methods. These are used to hold information or enact change on an object.

Static methods and properties are used throughout .NET to expose methods associated with a type – for example, the `Reverse` method of `System.Array` – or data that may be referenced, such as the `Now` property of `DateTime`.

Reflection is an advanced set of types and methods used to access information about types and members of types. Reflection exposes access to non-public members and types. While working with non-public members and types is not necessarily suitable for production code, reflection remains a valuable tool for exploring both the inner workings of PowerShell and .NET in general.

Finally, generic classes and methods were explored, and the improvements to invoking generic methods were demonstrated.

The next chapter shows you how to work with different data types.

Online Chapter

Chapters 8 and 9 are online-only chapters covering strings, numbers, dates, and using regular expressions in PowerShell.

Scan this QR code or visit the link to access these chapters:

https://static.packt-cdn.com/downloads/9781805120278_Chapter_8_and_9.pdf

Learn more on Discord

Read this book alongside other users, PowerShell experts, and the author himself. Ask questions, provide solutions to other readers, chat with the author via Ask Me Anything sessions, and much more.

Scan the QR code or visit the link to join the community.

https://packt.link/SecNet

10

Files, Folders, and the Registry

In PowerShell, providers are the most obvious subsystem for working with the filesystem and registry. A provider presents access to a data store as a hierarchy consisting of container or leaf objects. Using the filesystem as an example, a folder or directory is a container; a file is a leaf. Conversely, the Registry provider only supports containers or keys.

PowerShell offers common commands to interact with a provider hierarchy. The commands available to a provider differ depending on the features the provider supports. For example, supporting navigation makes `Get-ChildItem`, `Get-Item`, `New-Item`, and so on available.

PowerShell can also make use of .NET types. The `System.IO` namespace contains classes for working with the filesystem. The `Microsoft.Win32` namespace contains classes for working with the registry.

It is important to note that PowerShell is a generalized toolbox, the provider commands it offers are not specialized high performance tools. For example, large filesystem copy operations in Windows are frequently best performed using the `robocopy` utility instead of `Copy-Item`. Commands such as `robocopy` are out of scope of this chapter as the focus here is PowerShell, but use should not be dismissed as a bad practice.

A provider is therefore a way to access arbitrary data that has been arranged to somewhat represent a filesystem.

This chapter covers the following topics:

- Working with providers
- Items
- Windows permissions
- Transactions
- File catalog commands

The commands used to work with data within a provider, such as a filesystem, are common to all providers.

Working with providers

Each provider shares a common set of commands, such as Set-Location, Get-Item, and New-Item.

The full list of commands that you can use when interacting with a provider can be seen by running the following snippet:

```
$params = @{
    Name = @(
        '*-Item*'
        '*-ChildItem'
        '*-Content'
        '*-Acl'
        '*-Location'
        '*-Path'
    )
    Module = @(
        'Microsoft.PowerShell.Management'
        'Microsoft.PowerShell.Security'
    )
}
Get-Command @params
```

Each group of commands (such as the *-Content commands) is used when a provider supports a certain behavior. This is indicated by the .NET type it inherits, and the interfaces it implements.

For example, a provider that supports navigation allows the use of Get-Item, Get-ChildItem, Set-Location, and so on. This is possible because FileSystemProvider inherits from a NavigationCmdletProvider type:

```
PS> (Get-PSProvider FileSystem).ImplementingType.BaseType

IsPublic IsSerial Name                      BaseType
-------- -------- ----                      --------
True     False    NavigationCmdletProvider  System.Management...
```

A provider that has content may allow the use of Get-Content, Set-Content, and so on. This is indicated by a provider supporting the IContentCmdletProvider interface:

```
PS> (Get-PSProvider FileSystem).ImplementingType.ImplementedInterfaces

IsPublic IsSerial Name                      BaseType
-------- -------- ----                      --------
True     False    IResourceSupplier
True     False    IContentCmdletProvider
```

```
True        False       IPropertyCmdletProvider
True        False       ISecurityDescriptorCmdletProvider
True        False       ICmdletProviderSupportsHelp
```

The preceding output also shows that the FileSystem provider implements the ISecurityDescript orCmdletProvider interface. This indicates support for Get-Acl and Set-Acl.

In addition to the commands each provider supports, a provider can add dynamic parameters to a command. For example, in the certificate provider (the cert: drive), the Get-ChildItem command gains parameters for CodeSigningCert, DocumentEncryptionCert, SSLServerAuthentication, and so on.

These dynamic parameters are described in the help files for each provider. The help files are all in the HelpFile category along with all other about_ files. The following command may be used to list available help:

```
Get-Help about_*_provider
```

The name of the provider is taken from Get-PSProvider. The most common operation, especially with a provider like FileSystem, is navigating.

Navigating

Set-Location, which has the alias cd, is used to navigate around a provider hierarchy, for example:

```
Set-Location \                 # The root of the current drive
Set-Location Windows           # A child container named Windows
Set-Location ..                # Navigate up one level
Set-Location ..\..             # Navigate up two levels
Set-Location Cert:             # Change to a different drive
Set-Location HKLM:\Software    # Change to a container under a drive
```

Set-Location may only be used to switch to a container object, such as a FileSystem folder or registry key.

The print working directory ($PWD) variable shows the current location across all providers:

```
PS> $PWD

Path
----
HKLM:\Software\Microsoft\Windows\CurrentVersion
```

The Set-Location command changes the working directory to a new location. PowerShell also offers two commands that allow movement into and out of locations.

Push-Location will change the current location:

```
Push-Location c:\windows
```

Pop-Location returns to the previous location:

```
Pop-Location
```

In PowerShell 7, Push-Location and Pop-Location include a StackName parameter, which allows movement across several different lists of locations.

PowerShell 7 simplifies and enhances this by adding two special arguments to Set-Location. PowerShell tracks the locations visited with Set-Location. Using the - symbol for the path will move backward in the list of visited locations (somewhat equivalent to Pop-Location):

```
Set-Location c:\windows
# Return to the previous location
Set-Location -Path -
```

Using the + symbol for the path will move forward in the list of visited paths. Running the following example assumes - has been used beforehand, otherwise there will not be a location to move forward to:

```
Set-Location -Path +
```

These two values are synonymous with the back and forward buttons available in any web browser.

Getting items

The Get-Item command is used to get an instance of an object represented by a path:

```
Get-Item -Path \                        # The root container
Get-Item -Path .                        # The current container
Get-Item -Path ..                       # The parent container
Get-Item -Path C:\Windows\regedit.exe   # A leaf item
Get-Item -Path Cert:\LocalMachine\Root  # A container item
```

If a wildcard is used with the Get-Item command and the Path parameter, all matching items will be returned.

When working with the filesystem, a container is a directory, or folder, and a leaf is a file. In the registry, a key is a container and there are no leaves. In a certificate provider, a store or store location is a container, and a certificate is a leaf.

The Get-ChildItem command, which has the dir, ls, and gci aliases, is used to list the children of the current item.

Get-ChildItem and Get-Item will not show hidden files and folders by default. The following error will be returned for a hidden item:

```
PS> Get-Item $env:USERPROFILE\AppData
Get-Item: Could not find item C:\Users\Chris\AppData.
```

The Force parameter may be added to access hidden items:

```
PS> Get-Item $env:USERPROFILE\AppData -Force


    Directory: C:\Users\Someone


Mode                 LastWriteTime          Length Name
----                 -------------          ------ ----
d--h--        23/09/2016      18:22                AppData
```

Any path may be "provider qualified," most often where a specific drive does not exist or the path might otherwise be ambiguous. For example, the HKEY_USERS registry hive can be accessed without a specific drive by prefixing the key name with the provider:

```
Get-ChildItem Registry::HKEY_USERS
```

Items are typically made available under a drive, the most common entry point for a provider hierarchy.

Drives

PowerShell will automatically create a drive for any disk with a drive letter, any existing shared drive, the HKEY_LOCAL_MACHINE and HKEY_CURRENT_USER registry hives, the certificate store, and so on.

Additional drives may be added using New-PSDrive; for example, a network drive can be created:

```
New-PSDrive -Name X -PSProvider FileSystem -Root \\Server\Share
```

Or a drive may be added using the Registry provider to present access to HKEY_CLASSES_ROOT:

```
$params = @{
    Name = 'HKCR'
    PSProvider = 'Registry'
    Root       = 'HKEY_CLASSES_ROOT'
}
New-PSDrive @params
```

Existing drives may be removed using Remove-PSDrive. PowerShell allows filesystem drives to be removed; however, this is not a destructive operation, and it only removes the reference to the drive from PowerShell.

The FileSystem provider supports the use of credentials when creating a drive, allowing network shares to be mapped using specific credentials.

Items

Support for each of the *-Item and *-Path commands varies from one provider to another. The FileSystem provider supports all the commands, while the Registry provider supports a smaller number.

Items accessed using a provider also expose access to .NET methods associated with an item.

Provider commands offer convenience and reduced complexity at the cost of speed. In many cases provider commands have .NET equivalents that are significantly faster at the cost of extra complexity.

One point of extra complexity is handling relative paths.

Paths and .NET

PowerShell allows relative paths to be used with many commands including the provider commands.

For example, the following command will write content to a file in the current directory in PowerShell:

```
Set-Content file.txt -Value 'Some content'
```

An equivalent .NET method for the command above is the Exists method of the System.IO.Path type:

```
[System.IO.File]::Exists('file.txt')
```

However, when the method above is used, the path used is considered relative to the process directory, not the current directory in PowerShell. This value may be shown using the Environment type:

```
[Environment]::CurrentDirectory
```

It may be that the process directory and the current path in PowerShell are the same, in which case the relative path above will work as intended. However, changing directory in PowerShell will not change the process directory. If the two values differ then the .NET method will not behave as expected with a relative path.

One simple solution is to make use of the $pwd variable to complete the path:

```
[System.IO.File]::Exists("$pwd\file.txt")
```

The disadvantage of this approach is where a path is supplied by a user and where it may be either a full path or relative.

PowerShell includes two commands that may be used to change a relative path into a full path.

Convert-Path returns the path as a string:

```
$path = 'file.txt'
$path = Convert-Path $path
```

Resolve-Path returns a PathInfo object, which can in most circumstances treated as a string:

```
$path = 'file.txt'
$path = Resolve-Path $path
```

The limitation of these two commands is that the path must exist, or an error will be raised.

If the file does not already exist a more complex method is available, the GetUnresolvedProvider PathFromPSPath method. This method makes a full path from a path; it will not change a full path.

The example below converts a relative path into a full path based on the current location in PowerShell:

```
$path = 'file.txt'
$path = $ExecutionContext.SessionState.
    Path.
    GetUnresolvedProviderPathFromPSPath($path)
```

Scripts and functions may use the built-in `$PSCmdlet` variable to access the method:

```
$path = 'file.txt'
$path = $PSCmdlet.GetUnresolvedProviderPathFromPSPath($path)
```

The use of this method in scripts and functions will be explored again in *Chapter 18, Parameters, Validation, and Dynamic Parameters*.

This usage of the method above expects a single argument. Two additional arguments may be used to update variables with the provider and drive for the path at the same time:

```
$path = 'file.txt'
$provider = $null
$drive = $null
$ExecutionContext.SessionState.
    Path.
    GetUnresolvedProviderPathFromPSPath(
        $path,
        [ref]$provider,
        [ref]$drive
    )
```

After the statement has run the `$provider` and `$drive` variables will be filled. However, the most common use of this method is using the path alone.

A string describing a path can be tested to see if the path exists.

Testing for existing items

The `Test-Path` command may be used to test for the existence of a specific item under a drive:

```
Test-Path C:\Temp
```

Or using the `Registry` provider:

```
Test-Path HKLM:\Software\Microsoft
```

.NET methods may also be used in place of either provider.

Testing filesystem paths

For the filesystem, the preceding command may be replaced with a .NET static method on Windows. The following method is relatively new and does not exist in .NET versions used before PowerShell 7.3:

```
[System.IO.Path]::Exists('C:\Temp')
```

When using the Exists method above, care must be taken to ensure a full path is provided.

If code testing for the existence of a path was expected to run on both Windows and Linux (or Mac), the directory separator character would become important. Windows uses \ as the directory separator, while Linux uses /, but Test-Path and the FileSystem provider in general can use either separator on either platform.

For example, on Windows the following is valid:

```
Test-Path C:/Temp
```

On Windows, the Path.Exists method used above will continue to work:

```
[System.IO.Path]::Exists('C:/Temp')
```

And on Linux using the wrong separator with Test-Path is also permissible and the command below can be expected to return True:

```
Test-Path \tmp
```

However, on Linux the Path.Exists method will return False when the wrong separator character is used:

```
[System.IO.Path]::Exists('\tmp')
```

The operating system-specific directory separator character is available using:

```
[System.IO.Path]::DirectorySeparatorChar
```

Testing for a path using the Registry provider requires a different approach.

Testing registry paths

Testing if a registry key exists can be done simply with the command below:

```
Test-Path HKLM:\Software\Microsoft
```

Using .NET requires a more complex approach. First a BaseKey must be opened, in this case HKEY_LOCAL_MACHINE:

```
[Microsoft.Win32.RegistryKey]::OpenBaseKey(
    'LocalMachine',
    'Registry64'
)
```

The command is forced to view the 64-bit version of the registry by defining `RegistryView` as `Registry64`.

Once the Hive is opened, an attempt can be made to open a sub-key:

```
# Attempt to open the key
$null -eq [Microsoft.Win32.RegistryKey]::OpenBaseKey(
    'LocalMachine',
    'Registry64'
).OpenSubKey(
    'Software\Microsoft'
)
```

The comparison with `null` will cause the statement to return `True` or `False` based on the existence of the key. The command will not raise an error if the subkey does not exist.

Alternatively, the `GetSubKeyNames` method can be used:

```
# Or enumerate subkeys of the parent
[Microsoft.Win32.RegistryKey]::OpenBaseKey(
    'LocalMachine',
    'Registry64'
).OpenSubKey(
    'Software'
).GetSubKeyNames() -contains 'Microsoft'
```

It can often be best to mix provider commands with .NET methods to achieve a reasonable mix of performance versus complexity. Mixing approaches results in:

```
(Get-Item HKLM:\Software).GetSubKeyNames() -contains 'Microsoft'
```

The provider command can therefore be used to abstract a much more complex statement.

This mixed approach makes more sense in the context of testing registry values rather than paths.

The `Registry` provider supports container objects only, but for the `FileSystem` provider and many others, a path may be a container or leaf.

Testing path type

`Test-Path` distinguishes between item types with the `PathType` parameter. The container and leaf terms are used across providers to broadly classify items.

The following commands test for items of differing types:

```
Test-Path C:\Windows -PathType Container
Test-Path C:\Windows\System32\cmd.exe -PathType Leaf
```

Conversely, testing a path that is a file (leaf) with the container `PathType` will return false:

```
Test-Path C:\Windows\System32\cmd.exe -PathType Container
```

A .NET approach uses different types for each test:

```
[System.IO.Directory]::Exists('C:\Windows')
[System.IO.File]::Exists('C:\Windows\System32\cmd.exe')
```

A second approach creates an instance of DirectoryInfo or FileInfo then tests the Exists property:

```
[System.IO.DirectoryInfo]::new('C:\Windows').Exists
[System.IO.FileInfo]::new('C:\Windows\System32\cmd.exe').Exists
```

Any of these approaches is valid whether the path exists or not.

The Test-Path command is often used in an if statement prior to creating a file or directory to determine if creating the object is necessary:

```
if (-not (Test-Path C:\Temp\NewDirectory -PathType Container)) {
    New-Item C:\Temp\NewDirectory -ItemType Directory
}
```

In the preceding example, if a C:\Temp\NewDirectory file exists, the New-Item command will fail. PathType validation is perhaps more useful when validating parameters in functions and scripts than as an existence check before creating an object.

Creating items

The New-Item command can create files, directories, keys, and so on depending on the provider:

```
New-Item $env:Temp\newfile.txt -ItemType File
New-Item $env:Temp\newdirectory -ItemType Directory
New-Item HKLM:\Software\NewKey -ItemType Key
```

When creating a file using New-Item in PowerShell, the file is empty (0 bytes).

In PowerShell 5, New-Item gained the ability to create symbolic links, junctions, and hard links:

- A symbolic link is a link to another file or directory. Creating a symbolic link requires administrator privileges (run as administrator).
- A hard link is a link to another file on the same drive.
- A junction is a link to another directory on any local drive. Creating a junction does not require administrative privileges.

A link can be created as shown below:

```
New-Item LinkName -ItemType SymbolicLink -Value \\Server\Share
New-Item LinkName.txt -ItemType HardLink -Value OriginalName.txt
New-Item LinkName -ItemType Junction -Value C:\Temp
```

For example, a junction may be used to link together the user directories for each edition of PowerShell. Any existing Windows Powershell folder would need to be deleted before creating the junction:

```
$params = @{
    Path = '~\Documents\WindowsPowerShell'
    ItemType = 'Junction'
    Value = '~\Documents\PowerShell'
}
New-Item @params
```

With this change, items like modules installed into CurrentUser scope could be shared between PowerShell editions.

When New-Item is used to create a file, the command will fail if parent directories do not exist. Adding the Force parameter causes the command to create any missing intermediate directories:

```
New-Item $env:Temp\folder\newfile.txt -ItemType File -Force
```

This extra parameter is not required when ItemType is Directory.

New items are also implicitly created when using Set-Content or Add-Content on a path that does not exist. However, the *-Content commands will not create missing directories in a path.

Reading and writing content

The Get-Content command is the provider command used to read content from leaf objects such as files. The Get-Content command is not used with the Registry provider.

For example, Get-Content may be used to read a file:

```
Get-Content C:\windows\win.ini
```

Get-Content can be used with other providers such as the function provider:

```
Get-Content function:prompt
```

By default, Get-Content emits individual lines from a file as they are read. This raises the problem that reading from and writing to the same file in a pipeline will fail.

Reading and writing in a pipeline

Get-Content emits lines as they are read and maintains an open file until the end. Set-Content starts writing lines as they are accepted from the pipeline.

If a file is created as shown below:

```
Set-Content file.txt -Value first, second
```

Then an attempt is made to update the file in a pipeline, in this case to keep one line only, and an error will be displayed:

```
Get-Content file.txt |
    Where-Object { $_ -eq 'first' } |
    Set-Content file.txt
```

The command above will raise the error shown below because Get-Content is still reading the file:

```
Set-Content: The process cannot access the file 'C:\temp\file.txt' because it
is being used by another process.
```

This can be avoided by ensuring that all content is read before the pipeline starts. This can be achieved by enclosing the first command in the pipeline in brackets:

```
(Get-Content file.txt) |
    Where-Object { $_ -eq 'first' } |
    Set-Content file.txt
```

As shown above, Get-Content reads one line at a time and sends the line immediately to the next command in the pipeline.

Reading all content

The Get-Content command allows the use of a Raw parameter when reading from the filesystem. This parameter reads the entire file as a single string, which includes any line-break characters.

The Get-Content command is slow when reading from large files without the Raw parameter. Each line it emits is decorated with additional note properties that describe the source file. The example below shows these:

```
Set-Content file.txt -Value 'Hello world'
Get-Content file.txt | Select-Object PS*
```

The command above will show the note properties added to each line as shown below:

```
PSPath        : C:\temp\file.txt
PSParentPath : C:\temp
PSChildName  : file.txt
PSDrive       : C
PSProvider    : Microsoft.PowerShell.Core\FileSystem
```

A much faster way to read the lines from a file is to use a .NET method:

```
[System.IO.File]::ReadAllLines("$pwd\file.txt")
```

As with the other .NET methods used with the filesystem a full path is required, the $pwd variable is used to get the current path from PowerShell.

Writing content

Set-Content and Add-Content commands may be used to write content using a supported provider.

Set-Content will overwrite an existing file, Add-Content will append content to an existing item. In both cases, if the item does not exist, it will be created if the parent path exists.

For example, it is possible to use Set-Content to create functions:

```
Set-Content function:Write-HelloWorld -Value {
    Write-Host "Hello World"
}
```

Or Set-Content may be used to set an environment variable for the current process:

```
Set-Content env:HelloWorld -Value 'Hello world'
```

For the filesystem, content may also be written using .NET methods. For example:

```
[System.IO.File]::WriteAllLines('file.txt', ('first', 'second'))
```

When writing file content, file encoding can be important.

About text file encoding

Encoding in text files describes how the bytes in a file should be interpreted. ASCII files contain only bytes between 0 and 127 where each byte represents a single character.

UTF8 encoding supports a larger character set and allows characters to be represented by more than one byte.

For example, the following string includes a smiley, a Unicode character that in UTF8 is written across three bytes:

```
Set-Content file.txt 'Hello World ☺'
```

The smiley is represented by the bytes 0xe2, 0x98, and 0xba.

In PowerShell 7, if a file does not explicitly indicate an encoding it will assume UTF8 when reading a file. The commands below will both write and read the same value:

```
Set-Content file.txt 'Hello World ☺'
Get-Content file.txt
```

If content cannot be copied from the text above the character may be recreated from the bytes for testing:

```
Set-Content file.txt ('Hello World {0}' -f
    [System.Text.Encoding]::UTF8.GetString((0xe2, 0x98, 0xba))
)
```

Windows PowerShell is a good example of an application that does not assume UTF8 encoding. Windows PowerShell will assume ASCII content and therefore incorrectly parse the three-byte character:

```
PS> Get-Content file.txt
Hello World â˜º
```

If Get-Content in Windows PowerShell is expressly told the file encoding, it will interpret the character correctly:

```
PS> Get-Content file.txt -Encoding UTF8
Hello World ☺
```

This behaviour becomes important when working with scripts in Windows PowerShell that contain non-ASCII characters.

Text files, including PowerShell script files, can optionally include a **Byte Order Mark (BOM)** at the start of the file, which instructs the reader which encoding should be used to parse the file content.

The following command may be used in PowerShell 7 to rewrite the file so that it contains a BOM:

```
(Get-Content file.txt) | Set-Content file.txt -Encoding utf8BOM
```

Text editors will read the BOM, but not show it. The Format-Hex command may be used to look for the value. For UTF8, this is written to the first three bytes of the file:

```
PS> Format-Hex -Path file.txt | Select-Object HexBytes

HexBytes
--------
EF BB BF 48 65 6C 6C 6F 20 57 6F 72 6C 64 20 E2
98 BA 0D 0A
```

The first three bytes, 0xEF, 0xBB, and 0xBF, are the UTF8 BOM, they will not be visible when the file is opened in a text editor.

Scripts often need to temporarily write to the filesystem.

Temporary files

If a script needs a file to temporarily store data, the New-TemporaryFile command may be used. For example:

```
$tempFile = New-TemporaryFile
```

This command was introduced with PowerShell 5. Earlier versions of PowerShell may use the Path.GetTempFileName static method:

```
$tempFile = [System.IO.Path]::GetTempFileName()
```

Both commands create an empty file. The resulting file may be used with Set-Content, Out-File, or any commands or methods that write data to a file.

Removing items

The Remove-Item command may be used to remove an existing item under a provider, for example:

```
$file = New-TemporaryFile
Set-Content -Path $file -Value 'Temporary: 10'
Remove-Item $file
```

Providers such as FileSystem and Registry are reasonably flexible about removing items. When removing a directory or key with children, the recurse parameter should be used.

The certificate provider restricts the use of Remove-Item to certificates; certificate stores cannot be added or removed.

Invoking items

Invoke-Item (which has an alias, ii) will open or execute an object using the default settings for that object:

```
# Open the current directory in explorer
Invoke-Item .
# Open test.ps1 in the default editor
Invoke-Item test.ps1
# Open cmd
Invoke-Item $env:windir\system32\cmd.exe
# Open the certificate store MMC for the current user
# Windows PowerShell only
Invoke-Item Cert:
```

The Registry provider does not support Invoke-Item.

Items in each of the different providers may have one or more properties.

Item properties

The Get-ItemProperty and Set-ItemProperty commands allow individual properties to be modified.

What is meant by an item property varies from one provider to another. In the FileSystem provider, this can be an attribute of the file, such as Hidden or System. For the Registry provider, an item property is a value under a registry key.

Properties and the filesystem

When working with the FileSystem provider, Get-ItemProperty and Set-ItemProperty are rarely needed. For example, Set-ItemProperty might be used to make a file read-only. The following example assumes that the somefile.txt file already exists:

```
Set-ItemProperty .\somefile.txt -Name IsReadOnly -Value $true
```

The same property may be set from a file object retrieved using Get-Item (or Get-ChildItem):

```
(Get-Item 'somefile.txt').IsReadOnly = $true
```

The IsReadOnly property affects the attributes of the file object, adding the ReadOnly attribute.

Adding and removing file attributes

The attributes of the file are used to describe if a file is hidden, or a system file, and so on.

The attributes property of a file object is a bit field presented as a number and given an easily understandable value by the System.IO.FileAttributes enumeration.

The System.IO.FileAttributes value is a 32-bit integer that contains 16 flags. The names of the flags may be viewed using:

```
[System.IO.FileAttributes].GetEnumValues()
```

Each individual flag is represented by a single bit value in the number. Several of the possible attributes are shown in Table 10.1:

Name	Compressed	Archive	System	Hidden	Read-only
Bit value	2048	32	4	2	1

Table 10.1: Attribute values

A complete list can be shown using the example below:

```
[System.IO.FileAttributes].GetEnumValues() | ForEach-Object {
    [PSCustomObject]@{
        Name   = $_
        Value  = [int]$_
        Binary = [Convert]::ToString([int]$_, 2).PadLeft(32, '0')
    }
}
```

For instance, if an item is Hidden and ReadOnly it will have a numeric value of 3. PowerShell will show this as ReadOnly, Hidden.

While the value is numeric, the use of the enumeration means words can be used to describe each property:

```
PS> [System.IO.FileAttributes]'ReadOnly, Hidden' -eq 3
True
```

Because PowerShell will coerce the right of a comparison to match the type on the left, the following comparison will also succeed:

```
[System.IO.FileAttributes]'ReadOnly, Hidden' -eq 'Hidden, ReadOnly'
```

This opens several possible ways to set attributes on a file.

Attributes may be replaced entirely:

```
(Get-Item 'somefile.txt').Attributes = 'ReadOnly, Hidden'
```

Attributes may be toggled:

```
$file = Get-Item 'somefile.txt'
$file.Attributes = $file.Attributes -bxor 'ReadOnly'
```

Attributes may be added:

```
$file = Get-Item 'somefile.txt'
$file.Attributes = $file.Attributes -bor 'ReadOnly'
```

The +, -, +=, and -= operators may be used, as this is a numeric operation. Addition or subtraction operations are not safe, as they do not account for existing flags. For example, if a file is already read-only and += was used to attempt to make the file read-only, the result would be a hidden file:

```
PS> $file = Get-Item 'somefile.txt'
PS> $file.Attributes = 'ReadOnly'
PS> $file.Attributes += 'ReadOnly'
PS> $file.Attributes
Hidden
```

This change can be undone by setting attributes back to ReadOnly:

```
$file.Attributes = 'ReadOnly'
```

Finally, regardless of whether a flag is present, attributes may be written as a string. The -Force parameter is added to this example to allow it to find the file if it is still hidden:

```
$file = Get-Item 'somefile.txt' -Force
$file.Attributes = "$($file.Attributes), ReadOnly"
```

This is a feasible approach because casting to the enumeration type will ignore any duplication:

```
PS> [System.IO.FileAttributes]'ReadOnly, Hidden, ReadOnly'
ReadOnly, Hidden
```

Unlike the filesystem the registry consists of keys, or container objects, which may have arbitrary properties.

Registry values

Get-ItemProperty, Get-ItemPropertyValue, Set-ItemProperty, and New-ItemProperty are most useful when manipulating registry values.

The following method may be used to get values from the registry:

```
Get-ItemProperty -Path HKCU:\Environment
Get-ItemProperty -Path HKCU:\Environment -Name Path
Get-ItemProperty -Path HKCU:\Environment -Name Path, Temp
```

Individual values may be written back to the registry under an existing key:

```
Set-ItemProperty -Path HKCU:\Environment -Name NewValue -Value 'New'
```

A registry value may be subsequently removed:

```
Remove-ItemProperty -Path HKCU:\Environment -Name NewValue
```

When the Set-ItemProperty command creates a value, it does not directly allow the value type to be influenced. The command will do as much as it can to fit the value into the existing type. For a property with type REG_SZ, numbers will be converted to a string.

If a value does not already exist, a registry type will be created according to the value type:

- Int32: REG_DWORD
- Int64: REG_QWORD
- String: REG_SZ
- String[]: REG_MULTI_SZ (must use "[String[]]@('value', 'value')")
- Byte[]: REG_BINARY
- Any other type: REG_SZ

If a value of a specific type is required, the New-ItemProperty command should be used instead, for instance, if an expanding string must be created:

```
$params = @{
    Path         = 'HKCU:\Environment'
    Name         = 'Expand'
    Value        = 'User: %USERNAME%'
    PropertyType = 'ExpandString'
}
New-ItemProperty @params
```

New-ItemProperty will throw an error if a property already exists. The Force parameter may be used to overwrite an existing value with the same name.

A common use for Get-ItemProperty is reading values from the uninstall keys to determine if something is installed in Windows. The Get-ItemProperty command can get properties for multiple path items, and it supports wildcards used in the path.

The Software key in the registry has two views, a 32-bit view and a 64-bit view.

When accessing from a 64-bit process, HKLM:\Software will show the 64-bit packages, and HKLM:\Software\Wow6432Node the 32-bit packages.

When accessing from a 32-bit process, HKLM:\Software will show the 32-bit packages, and HKLM:\Software\Wow6432Node the 64-bit packages.

The static property `Is64BitProcess` of the `Environment` type can be used to determine which the current process is:

```
[Environment]::Is64BitProcess
```

In addition to the `LocalMachine` view, individual users can have software installed. That can be explored by searching loaded user hives under `HKEY_USERS`.

Keys are defined using a trailing wildcard to expand each key that might contain uninstall information. Results are filtered to only keys that have a `DisplayName` property, and a few properties are selected, and a property is added to show if a package is 32- or 64-bit:

```
$keys = @(
    'HKLM:\Software'
    'HKLM:\Software\Wow6432Node'
    'Registry::HKEY_USERS\S-1-*\Software'
    'Registry::HKEY_USERS\S-1-*\Software\Wow6432Node'
) | Join-Path -ChildPath (
    'Microsoft\Windows\CurrentVersion\Uninstall\*'
)

Get-ItemProperty -Path $keys -ErrorAction Ignore |
    Where-Object DisplayName |
    Select-Object -Property @(
        @{
            Name       = 'Is64Bit'
            Expression = {
                [Environment]::Is64BitProcess -and
                $_.PSPath -notmatch 'Wow6432Node'
            }
        }
        'DisplayName'
        'DisplayVersion'
        'Publisher'
        'InstallLocation'
    )
```

When values are read from the registry using `Get-ItemProperty`, environment variables will be expanded.

Registry values and environment variables

When `Get-ItemProperty` reads a registry value that contains an environment variable, the environment variable is implicitly expanded.

For example, if a registry value is created as follows:

```
$params = @{
    Path = 'HKCU:\Environment'
    Name = 'TestValue'
    Value = '%USERPROFILE%\TestValue'
    Type = 'ExpandString'
}
New-ItemProperty @params
```

When this value is read again, the environment variable will be expanded:

```
PS> Get-ItemPropertyValue -Path $params['Path'] -Name $params['Name']
C:\Users\chris\TestValue
```

To access the raw value, .NET methods must be used:

```
using namespace Microsoft.Win32

$key = Get-Item 'HKCU:\Environment'
$key.GetValue(
    'TestValue',
    $null,
    [RegistryValueOptions]::DoNotExpandEnvironmentNames
)
```

The PowerShell commands do not provide the ability to retrieve the value without expansion.

The value created above may be removed using:

```
Remove-ItemProperty -Path $params['Path'] -Name $params['Name']
```

This limitation is critical when updating values in the registry where the value might contain an environment variable, such as when updating the PATH environment variable in the registry.

Searching for items

The Get-ChildItem command implements a provider-specific item search. This search process can be quite slow, and it is possible to use .NET types to search more quickly.

In *Chapter 6, Conditional Statements and Loops*, a loop utilizing a queue and a stack was shown to traverse a filesystem.

The following command will typically take a few seconds to execute as a non-elevated user depending on disk speed. Inaccessible directories are written as a warning:

```
$files = Get-Childitem c:\windows -File -Recurse -ErrorVariable failures
$failures | Write-Warning
```

A faster variant is to make use of the Enumerate methods of a DirectoryInfo object. Get-Item can be used to get the starting point for this search:

```
$directory = Get-Item c:\windows
$files = $directory.EnumerateFiles(
    '*',
    [System.IO.EnumerationOptions]@{
        RecurseSubdirectories = $true
    }
) | Write-Output
```

The command should be completed more quickly than Get-ChildItem.

The EnumerationOptions type used in the example above includes a flag that indicates that inaccessible files should be ignored. However, the Get-ChildItem command used a variable to track errors and write warnings for those.

If EnumerationOptions is changed as shown below so it does not ignore that condition, the statement will fail on the first inaccessible directory:

```
$files = $directory.EnumerateFiles(
    '*',
    [System.IO.EnumerationOptions]@{
        IgnoreInaccessible    = $false
        RecurseSubdirectories = $true
    }
) | Write-Output
```

To allow the operation to continue, the enumerator can be directly controlled in PowerShell:

```
$directory = Get-Item c:\windows
$enumerator = $directory.EnumerateFiles(
    '*',
    [System.IO.EnumerationOptions]@{
        IgnoreInaccessible    = $false
        RecurseSubdirectories = $true
    }
).GetEnumerator()

$files = while ($true) {
    try {
        if (-not $enumerator.MoveNext()) {
            break
        }
        $enumerator.Current
```

```
    } catch {
        Write-Warning $_.Exception.GetBaseException().Message
    }
}
```

If the enumerator encounters an inaccessible directory or file, the MoveNext method will raise an exception. MoveNext is enclosed in try to allow that error to be trapped and rewritten as a warning. When there are no more items available, MoveNext will return False, and the otherwise-infinite loop will come to an end.

Access to items in the filesystem or registry are governed by permissions in Windows.

Windows permissions

Security descriptors in Windows are used to describe permissions in Windows. The security descriptor contains an **Access Control List (ACL)**.

For example, an NTFS ACL is used to describe who or what can access which file or folder.

Individual rights in an ACL are described using a set of **Access Control Entries (ACEs)**.

The FileSystem and Registry providers support Get-Acl and Set-Acl, which allow the different ACLs to be modified.

Working with permissions in PowerShell involves a mixture of PowerShell commands and .NET objects and methods.

Alternatives to .NET classes

The NtfsSecurity module found in the PowerShell Gallery may be an easier alternative to the native methods discussed in this section.

While some values and classes differ between the different providers, many of the same concepts apply.

The following snippet creates a set of files and folders in C:\Temp. These files and folders are used in the examples that follow:

```
New-Item C:\Temp\ACL -ItemType Directory -Force
1..5 | ForEach-Object {
    New-Item C:\Temp\ACL\$_ -ItemType Directory -Force
    'content' | Out-File "C:\Temp\ACL\$_\$_.txt"
    New-Item C:\Temp\ACL\$_\$_ -ItemType Directory -Force
    'content' | Out-File "C:\Temp\ACL\$_\$_\$_.txt"
}
```

The Get-Acl command is used to retrieve an existing ACL for an object. Set-Acl is used to apply an updated ACL to an object.

If Get-Acl is used against a directory, the ACL type is DirectorySecurity; for a file, the ACL type is FileSecurity, and for a registry key, the ACL type is RegistrySecurity.

Access and audit

Access lists come with two different types of access controls.

The **Discretionary Access Control List (DACL)** is used to grant (or deny) access to a resource. The DACL is referred to as Access in PowerShell.

The **System Access Control List (SACL)** is used to define which activities should be audited. The SACL is referred to as Audit in PowerShell.

Reading and setting the audit ACL requires administrator privileges (run as administrator). Get-Acl will only attempt to read the audit ACL if it is explicitly requested. The -Audit switch parameter is used to request the list:

```
Get-Acl C:\Temp\ACL\1 -Audit | Format-List
```

As none of the folders created have audit ACLs at this time, the -Audit property will be blank.

ACEs may be inherited from a parent container or may be explicitly defined. Inheritance is controlled by "rule protection."

Rule protection

ACLs, by default, inherit rules (ACEs) from parent container objects. Access rule protection blocks the propagation of rules from a parent object.

Rule protection can be enabled for the access ACL using the SetAccessRuleProtection method or for the audit ACL using the SetAuditRuleProtection method on the ACL.

Setting rule protection has the same effect as disabling inheritance in the GUI.

Each of the methods expects two arguments. The first argument, isProtected, dictates whether the list should be protected. The second argument, named preserveInheritance, dictates what should be done with existing inherited entries. Inherited entries can either be copied or discarded.

In the following example, access rule protection is enabled (inheritance is disabled) and the previously inherited rules are copied into the ACL:

```
$acl = Get-Acl C:\Temp\ACL\2
$acl.SetAccessRuleProtection($true, $true)
Set-Acl C:\Temp\ACL\2 -AclObject $acl
```

Copied rules will only appear on the ACL (as explicit rules) after Set-Acl has been run.

If access rule protection is subsequently re-enabled, copied rules are not removed. The resulting ACL will contain both inherited and explicit versions of each of the rules. Inheritance can be re-enabled as follows:

```
$acl = Get-Acl C:\Temp\ACL\2
$acl.SetAccessRuleProtection($false, $false)
Set-Acl C:\Temp\ACL\2 -AclObject $acl
```

The ACL will have doubled in length:

```
Get-Acl C:\Temp\ACL\2 |
    Select-Object -ExpandProperty Access |
    Select-Object FileSystemRights, IsInherited, IdentityReference
```

The output from the command above is expected to be like the output below:

```
          FileSystemRights IsInherited IdentityReference
          ---------------- ----------- -----------------
                -536805376       False NT AUTHORITY\Authentica…
     Modify, Synchronize         False NT AUTHORITY\Authentica…
               FullControl       False NT AUTHORITY\SYSTEM
               FullControl       False BUILTIN\Administrators
  ReadAndExecute, Synchronize    False BUILTIN\Users
               FullControl        True BUILTIN\Administrators
               FullControl        True NT AUTHORITY\SYSTEM
  ReadAndExecute, Synchronize     True BUILTIN\Users
          Modify, Synchronize     True NT AUTHORITY\Authentica…
                -536805376        True NT AUTHORITY\Authentica…
```

Discarding access rules will result in an empty ACL:

```
$acl = Get-Acl C:\Temp\ACL\3
$acl.SetAccessRuleProtection($true, $false)
Set-Acl C:\Temp\ACL\3 -AclObject $acl
```

Once this operation completes, any attempt to access the directory will result in access being denied:

```
PS> Get-ChildItem C:\Temp\ACL\3
Get-ChildItem: Access to the path 'C:\Temp\ACL\3' is denied.
```

Access to the folder can be restored provided the current user has the `SeSecurityPrivilege` privilege. The list of privileges held by the current account may be viewed using the `whoami` command in Windows:

```
whoami /priv
```

The privilege is granted when a process is run as administrator. Re-enabling inheritance is the simplest way to restore access:

```
$acl = Get-Acl C:\Temp\ACL\3
$acl.SetAccessRuleProtection($false, $false)
Set-Acl C:\Temp\ACL\3 -AclObject $acl
```

In the previous example, the second argument for SetAccessRuleProtection, preserveInheritance, is set to false. This value has no impact; it only dictates behavior when access rule protection is enabled.

Inheritance and propagation flags

Inheritance and propagation flags dictate how individual ACEs are pushed down to child objects.

Inheritance flags are described by the System.Security.AccessControl.InheritanceFlags enumeration. The possible values are as follows:

- None: Objects will not inherit this ACE.
- ContainerInherit: Only container objects (such as directories) will inherit this entry.
- ObjectInherit: Only leaf objects (such as files) will inherit this entry.

Propagation flags are described by the System.Security.AccessControl.PropagationFlags enumeration. The possible values are as follows:

- None: Propagation of inheritance is not changed.
- NoPropagateInherit: Do not propagate inheritance flags.
- InheritOnly: This entry does not apply to this object, only children.

These two flag fields are used to build the Applies To option shown in the GUI when setting security on a folder. Table 10.2 shows how each option is created:

Option	Flags
This folder only	Inheritance: None
	Propagation: None
This folder, subfolders, and files	Inheritance: ContainerInherit, ObjectInherit
	Propagation: None
This folder and subfolders	Inheritance: ContainerInherit
	Propagation: None
This folder and files	Inheritance: ObjectInherit
	Propagation: None
Subfolders only	Inheritance: ContainerInherit
	Propagation: InheritOnly
Files only	Inheritance: ObjectInherit
	Propagation: InheritOnly

Table 10.2: GUI names and flag values

The NoPropagateInherit propagation flag comes into play when the Only apply these permissions to objects and/or containers within this container tick box is checked. The tick box is available regardless of the object type and the flag is only applicable on container objects.

Removing ACEs

Individual rules may be removed from an ACL using several different methods:

- RemoveAccessRule: Matches IdentityReference and AccessMask
- RemoveAccessRuleAll: Matches IdentityReference
- RemoveAccessRuleSpecific: Exact match

Access mask is a generic term used to refer to specific rights granted (filesystem rights for a file or directory and registry rights for a registry key).

To demonstrate rule removal, explicit entries might be added to the DACL. Enabling and then disabling access rule protection will add new rules: the original inherited set and an explicitly set copy of the same rules.

To enable access rule protection and copy inherited rules, do the following:

```
$acl = Get-Acl C:\Temp\ACL\3
$acl.SetAccessRuleProtection($true, $true)
Set-Acl C:\Temp\ACL\3 -AclObject $acl
```

When disabling protection, once committed, the inherited rules will appear alongside the copied rules:

```
$acl = Get-Acl C:\Temp\ACL\3
$acl.SetAccessRuleProtection($false, $true)
Set-Acl C:\Temp\ACL\3 -AclObject $acl
```

The rules in the DACL may be viewed using Get-Acl:

```
$acl = Get-Acl C:\Temp\ACL\3
$acl.Access |
    Select-Object FileSystemRights, IsInherited, IdentityReference
```

The output from the command above is shown below:

```
          FileSystemRights IsInherited IdentityReference
          ---------------- ----------- -----------------
                -536805376       False NT AUTHORITY\Authentica…
      Modify, Synchronize        False NT AUTHORITY\Authentica…
              FullControl        False NT AUTHORITY\SYSTEM
              FullControl        False BUILTIN\Administrators
ReadAndExecute, Synchronize      False BUILTIN\Users
              FullControl         True BUILTIN\Administrators
              FullControl         True NT AUTHORITY\SYSTEM
```

```
ReadAndExecute, Synchronize        True  BUILTIN\Users
         Modify, Synchronize        True  NT AUTHORITY\Authentica…
                  -536805376        True  NT AUTHORITY\Authentica…
```

The following example finds each explicit rule and removes it from the DACL:

```
$acl = Get-Acl C:\Temp\ACL\3
$acl.Access |
    Where-Object IsInherited -eq $false |
    ForEach-Object {
        $acl.RemoveAccessRuleSpecific($_)
    }
Set-Acl C:\Temp\ACL\3 -AclObject $acl
```

Security descriptors and individual ACEs can be copied from one item to another.

Copying lists and entries

Access lists can be copied from one object to another; for example, a template ACL might have been prepared:

```
$acl = Get-Acl C:\Temp\ACL\4
$acl.SetAccessRuleProtection($true, $true)
$acl.Access |
    Where-Object IdentityReference -like '*\Authenticated Users' |
    ForEach-Object { $acl.RemoveAccessRule($_) }
Set-Acl C:\Temp\ACL\4 –AclObject $acl
```

The ACL from one object can be applied to another object:

```
$acl = Get-Acl C:\Temp\ACL\4
Set-Acl C:\Temp\ACL\5 -AclObject $acl
```

If the ACL contains a mixture of inherited and explicit entries, the inherited entries will be discarded.

Access control rules may be copied in a similar manner:

```
# Get the ACE to copy
$ace = (Get-Acl C:\Temp\ACL\3).Access | Where-Object {
    $_.IdentityReference -like '*\Authenticated Users' -and
    $_.FileSystemRights -eq 'Modify, Synchronize' -and
    $_.IsInherited
}
# Get the target ACL
$acl = Get-Acl C:\Temp\ACL\5
# Add the entry
$acl.AddAccessRule($ace)
```

```
# Apply the change
Set-Acl C:\Temp\ACL\5 -AclObject $acl
```

ACEs may be created from scratch instead of being copied.

Adding ACEs

ACEs must be created before they can be added to an ACL.

Creating an ACE for the filesystem or the registry, and for access or audit purposes, uses a set of .NET classes:

- `System.Security.AccessControl.FileSystemAccessRule`
- `System.Security.AccessControl.FileSystemAuditRule`
- `System.Security.AccessControl.RegistryAccessRule`
- `System.Security.AccessControl.RegistryAuditRule`

There are several different ways to use these classes; this section focuses on the most common one.

Filesystem rights

The filesystem ACE uses the `System.Security.AccessControl.FileSystemRights` enumeration to describe the different rights that might be granted.

PowerShell can list each right name using the `GetEnumValues` (or `GetEnumNames`) static methods:

```
[System.Security.AccessControl.FileSystemRights].GetEnumValues()
```

PowerShell might be used to show the names, numeric values, and even the binary values associated with each. Several of these rights are composites, such as write, which summarizes `CreateFiles`, `AppendData`, `WriteExtendedAttributes`, and `WriteAttributes`:

```
using namespace System.Security.AccessControl

[FileSystemRights].GetEnumNames() | ForEach-Object {
    $value = $_ -as [FileSystemRights]
    [PSCustomObject]@{
        Name    = $_
        Value   = [int]$value
        Binary  = [Convert]::ToString(
            [int]$value , 2
        ).PadLeft(32, '0')
    }
}
```

The list generated by the command above includes several duplicate values. Flags with the same value can have a different meaning depending on the target. A right of `ReadData` is contextually correct for a file, compared with the right of `ListDirectory` for a folder; the two rights are described using the same bit position.

The .NET reference is a better place to find a descriptive meaning of each of the different flags: https://learn.microsoft.com/dotnet/api/system.security.accesscontrol.FileSystemrights.

FileSystemRights is a bit field and can therefore be treated in the same way as FileAttributes earlier in this chapter. The simplest way to present rights is in a comma-separated list. There are many possible combinations; the GUI shows a small number of these before heading into advanced options. Table 10.3 shows the main options:

GUI option	Filesystem rights
Full control	FullControl
Modify	Modify, Synchronize
Read and execute	ReadAndExecute, Synchronize
List folder contents	ReadAndExecute, Synchronize
Read	Read, Synchronize
Write	Write, Synchronize

Table 10.3: GUI options

Table 10.3 shows that both "Read and execute" and "List folder contents" have the same value. This is because the access mask is the same; the difference is in the inheritance flags:

GUI option	Inheritance flags
Read and execute	ContainerInherit, ObjectInherit
List folder contents	ContainerInherit

Table 10.4: Inheritance flags

In all other cases, the inheritance flags are set to ContainerInherit and ObjectInherit. Propagation flags are set to None for all examples.

The rights, inheritance, and propagation values above can be used to create a Full Control ACE using one of the constructors for FileSystemAccessRule:

```
$ace = [System.Security.AccessControl.FileSystemAccessRule]::new(
    'DOMAIN\User',                      # Identity reference
    'FullControl',                      # FileSystemRights
    'ContainerInherit, ObjectInherit',  # InheritanceFlags
    'None',                             # PropagationFlags
    'Allow'                             # ACE type (allow or deny)
)
```

If the ACE is changed to use a valid user, the ACE can be applied to the ACL:

```
$acl = Get-Acl C:\Temp\ACL\5
$acl.AddAccessRule($ace)
Set-Acl C:\Temp\ACL\5 -AclObject $acl
```

Registry access is granted in a similar way.

Registry rights

Creating ACEs for registry keys follows the same pattern as for filesystem rights. The rights are defined in the `System.Security.AccessControl.RegistryRights` enumeration.

PowerShell can list these rights but not the descriptions. The descriptions in the .NET reference are more useful: https://learn.microsoft.com/dotnet/api/system.security.accesscontrol. registryrights.

A rule is created in the same way as a filesystem rule:

```
$ace = [System.Security.AccessControl.RegistryAccessRule]::new(
    'DOMAIN\User',                      # Identity reference
    'FullControl',                      # RegistryRights
    'ContainerInherit, ObjectInherit',  # InheritanceFlags
    'None',                             # PropagationFlags
    'Allow'                             # ACE type (allow or deny)
)
```

The rule can be applied to a key (in this case, a newly created key):

```
$key = New-Item HKCU:\TestKey -ItemType Key -Force
$acl = Get-Acl $key.PSPath
$acl.AddAccessRule($ace)
Set-Acl $key.PSPath -AclObject $acl
```

Each of the access rights, such as `FullControl` used above, is described by an enumeration – in the previous example, the `RegistryRights` enumeration.

Numeric values in the ACL

The `FileSystemRights` enumeration used when creating a filesystem ACE does not cover all the possible values one might see when inspecting an ACL. In some cases, the rights will be shown as numeric values rather than names. The `-536805376` and `268435456` values were both shown when removing ACEs. The missing values are part of the generic portion of the ACE, which is described in the more broadly applicable access mask documentation: https://learn.microsoft.com/windows/ win32/secauthz/access-mask-format.

This generic portion is not accounted for by the `FileSystemRights` enumeration. These generic values, in turn, represent summarized rights: https://learn.microsoft.com/windows/win32/fileio/ file-security-and-access-rights.

Converting each of the values to binary goes a long way in showing their composition:

```
foreach ($value in -536805376, 268435456) {
    '{0,-10}: {1}' -f @(
        $value
```

```
            [Convert]::ToString($value, 2).PadLeft(32, '0')
    )
}
```

The command above will display the binary values shown below:

```
-536805376: 11100000000000010000000000000000
268435456 : 00010000000000000000000000000000
```

This script uses a `GenericAccessRights` enumeration to show how these values may be deconstructed:

```
using namespace System.Security.AccessControl

# Define an enumeration which describes the generic access mask (only)
[Flags()]
enum GenericAccessRights {
    GenericRead    = 0x80000000
    GenericWrite   = 0x40000000
    GenericExecute = 0x20000000
    GenericAll     = 0x10000000
}
# For each value to convert
foreach ($value in -536805376, 268435456) {
    # For each enum that describes might describe a bit
    $accessRights = foreach ($enum in [GenericAccessRights],
[FileSystemRights]) {
        # Find values from the enum where the value with
        # the exact bit set.
        [Enum]::GetValues($enum) | Where-Object {
            ($value -band $_) -eq $_
        }
    }
    # Output the original value and the values from the enum (as a string)
    '{0} : {1}' -f $value, ($accessRights -join ', ')
}
```

The two values discussed are therefore the following:

- -536805376: GenericExecute, GenericWrite, GenericRead, and Delete
- 268435456: GenericAll

These rights are mapped by the operating system to the rights applicable to the securable object as shown in the following table:

GenericRight	Item right
GenericAll	FullControl
GenericExecute	Execute
GenericRead	Read
GenericWrite	Write

Table 10.5: Generic rights

The security descriptor describes the owner of the object. This owner can be changed.

Ownership

Ownership of a file or directory may be changed using the SetOwner method of the ACL object. Changing the ownership of a file requires administrative privileges.

The owner of the C:\Temp\ACL\1 file is the current user:

```
PS> Get-Acl C:\Temp\ACL\1 | Select-Object Owner

Owner
-----
COMPUTER\Chris
```

The owner may be changed (in this case, to the Administrator account) using the SetOwner method:

```
$acl = Get-Acl C:\Temp\ACL\1
$acl.SetOwner(
    [System.Security.Principal.NTAccount]'Administrator'
)
Set-Acl C:\Temp\ACL\1 -AclObject $acl
```

This is not taking ownership

Setting ownership when the current user already has full control is one thing. Specific privileges are required to take ownership without existing permissions: SeRestorePrivilege, SeBackupPrivilege, and SeTakeOwnershipPrivilege.

The takeown.exe tool is a better choice for forcefully taking ownership.

Managing security in PowerShell can be complicated without the use of modules dedicated to the task. However, an understanding of how to work with ACLs in this manner is important as many different systems utilize the same generalized security objects and not all will have friendly modules.

Transactions

A transaction allows a set of changes to be grouped together and committed at the same time. Transactions are only supported under Windows PowerShell. This section briefly explores this feature with no expectation that it will return in more recent editions of PowerShell.

The Registry provider supports transactions in Windows, as shown in the following code:

```
PS> Get-PSProvider

Name          Capabilities                          Drives
----          ------------                          ------
Registry      ShouldProcess, Transactions           {HKLM, HKCU}
Alias         ShouldProcess                         {Alias}
Environment   ShouldProcess                         {Env}
FileSystem    Filter, ShouldProcess, Credentials    {B, C, D}
Function      ShouldProcess                         {Function}
Variable      ShouldProcess                         {Variable}
```

A transaction can be created using the Start-Transaction command, then each subsequent command can use that transaction:

```
Start-Transaction
$path = 'HKCU:\TestTransaction'
New-Item $path -ItemType Key -UseTransaction
Set-ItemProperty $path -Name 'Name' -Value 'Transaction' -UseTransaction
Set-ItemProperty $path -Name 'Length' -Value 20 -UseTransaction
```

At this point, the transaction can be undone:

```
Undo-Transaction
```

Alternatively, the transaction may be committed:

```
Complete-Transaction
```

A list of the commands that support transactions may be viewed, although not all of these may be used with the Registry provider:

```
Get-Command -ParameterName UseTransaction
```

Transactions are an interesting feature, but they are only supported by the Registry provider and were not available in the earliest versions of .NET Core. The latest versions of .NET Core (and .NET 5 and higher) do provide support, but the commands used above are not part of PowerShell 7 and may never return.

File catalog commands

The file catalog commands were added in Windows PowerShell 5.1. A file catalog is a reasonably light-weight form of **File Integrity Monitoring (FIM)**. The file catalog generates and stores SHA1 hashes for each file within a folder structure and writes the result to a catalog file.

About hashing

Hashing is a one-way process; a hash is not an encryption or encoding. A hash algorithm converts data of any length to a fixed-length value. The length of the value depends on the hashing algorithm used.

MD5 hashing is one of the more common algorithms; it produces a 128-bit hash that can be repre-sented by a 32-character string.

SHA1 is rapidly becoming the default; it produces a 160-bit hash that can be represented by a 40-char-acter string.

PowerShell has a Get-FileHash command that can be used to calculate the hash for a file.

As the catalog is the basis for determining integrity, it should be maintained in a secure location, away from the set of files being analyzed.

A small set of directories and files can be created to help demonstrate the commands in the following subsections:

```
New-Item C:\Temp\FileCatalog -ItemType Directory -Force
1..5 | ForEach-Object {
    New-Item C:\Temp\FileCatalog\$_ -ItemType Directory -Force
    'content' | Out-File "C:\Temp\FileCatalog\$_\$_.txt"
    New-Item C:\Temp\FileCatalog\$_\$_ -ItemType Directory -Force
    'content' | Out-File "C:\Temp\FileCatalog\$_\$_\$_.txt"
}
```

You will modify these files to demonstrate how the FileCatalog commands show changes.

New-FileCatalog

The New-FileCatalog command is used to generate (or update) a catalog:

```
New-FileCatalog -Path <ToWatch> -CatalogFilePath <StateFile>
```

A hash can only be generated for files that are larger than 0 bytes. However, filenames are recorded irrespective of the size.

The following command creates a file catalog from the files and folders created when exploring permissions:

```
$params = @{
    Path             = 'C:\Temp\FileCatalog'
    CatalogFilePath = 'C:\Temp\Security\example.cat'
```

```
}
New-FileCatalog @params
```

The only output from this command is an object representing the catalog file. The Security folder used above will be created if it does not already exist.

If the CatalogFilePath had been a directory instead of a file, New-FileCatalog would have automatically created a file named catalog.cat.

Test-FileCatalog

The Test-FileCatalog command compares the content of the catalog file to the filesystem. Hashes are recalculated for each file.

If none of the content has changed, Test-FileCatalog will return Valid; this can be seen by running the following command:

```
$params = @{
    Path            = 'C:\Temp\FileCatalog'
    CatalogFilePath = 'C:\Temp\Security\example.cat'
}
Test-FileCatalog @params
```

If a file has been added, removed, or changed, the Test-FileCatalog command will return ValidationFailed:

```
Set-Content C:\Temp\FileCatalog\3\3.txt -Value 'New content'
$params = @{
    Path            = 'C:\Temp\FileCatalog'
    CatalogFilePath = 'C:\Temp\Security\example.cat'
}
Test-FileCatalog @params
```

At this point, the Detailed parameter can be used to see what has changed.

Is it faster without Detailed?

The Detailed parameter does not change the amount of work Test-FileCatalog must do. If the result is to be used, it might be better to use the Detailed parameter right away. This saves the CPU cycles and I/O operations required to list the content of a directory and generate the hashes a second time.

The command does not provide a summary of changes; instead, it returns all files and hashes from the catalog and all files and hashes from the path being tested:

```
Set-Content C:\Temp\FileCatalog\3\3.txt -Value 'New content'
$params = @{
```

```
    Path            = 'C:\Temp\FileCatalog'
    CatalogFilePath = 'C:\Temp\Security\example.cat'
    Detailed        = $true
}
Test-FileCatalog @params
```

The output from the command above is shown below:

```
Status        : ValidationFailed
HashAlgorithm : SHA1
CatalogItems  : {[1\1.txt, 3AC201172677076A818A18EB1E8FEECF1A04722A...}
PathItems     : {[1\1.txt, 3AC201172677076A818A18EB1E8FEECF1A04722A...}
Signature     : System.Management.Automation.Signature
```

Before exploring the output, a few more changes should be made:

```
Set-Content C:\Temp\FileCatalog\3\3-1.txt -Value 'New file'
Remove-Item C:\Temp\FileCatalog\1\1.txt
```

The catalog can be used to find changes between the two folders. First the result of a detailed catalog test is assigned to a variable:

```
$params = @{
    Path            = 'C:\Temp\FileCatalog'
    CatalogFilePath = 'C:\Temp\Security\example.cat'
    Detailed        = $true
}
$result = Test-FileCatalog @params
```

The PathItems and CatalogItems properties are dictionary objects that contain the relative file path as a key, and the hash as the value. For example:

```
PS> $result.PathItems

Key         Value
---         -----
2\2.txt     3AC201172677076A818A18EB1E8FEECF1A04722A
3\3-1.txt   74A5D5EBDB364E61A6FB15090A2009937473312F
3\3.txt     0E2126C909E867CD180E140CA501CE52533C381F
4\4.txt     3AC201172677076A818A18EB1E8FEECF1A04722A
5\5.txt     3AC201172677076A818A18EB1E8FEECF1A04722A
1\1\1.txt   3AC201172677076A818A18EB1E8FEECF1A04722A
2\2\2.txt   3AC201172677076A818A18EB1E8FEECF1A04722A
3\3\3.txt   3AC201172677076A818A18EB1E8FEECF1A04722A
```

```
4\4\4.txt 3AC201172677076A818A18EB1E8FEECF1A04722A
5\5\5.txt 3AC201172677076A818A18EB1E8FEECF1A04722A
```

The $result variable may now be used to describe the changes. Files that have been added can be listed with the following code:

```
$result.PathItems.Keys | Where-Object {
    -not $result.CatalogItems.ContainsKey($_)
}
```

This will show that the file 3\3-1.txt has been created. The hash of that file can be seen from PathItems as shown here:

```
PS> $result.PathItems['3\3-1.txt']
74A5D5EBDB364E61A6FB15090A2009937473312F
```

Files that have been removed are listed with the following:

```
$result.CatalogItems.Keys | Where-Object {
    -not $result.PathItems.ContainsKey($_)
}
```

If the file was removed above, then 1\1.txt will show in the output. Since PathItems does not contain that file, the hash must be retrieved from CatalogItems if it is important:

```
PS> $result.CatalogItems['1\1.txt']
3AC201172677076A818A18EB1E8FEECF1A04722A
```

Files that have been added or modified are listed with the following code:

```
$result.PathItems.Keys | Where-Object {
    $result.CatalogItems[$_] -ne $result.PathItems[$_]
}
```

This command should show both 3\3-1.txt and 3\3.txt. To find changes only, the key must be present in both CatalogItems and PathItems:

```
$result.PathItems.Keys | Where-Object {
    $result.CatalogItems.ContainsKey($_) -and
    $result.CatalogItems[$_] -ne $result.PathItems[$_]
}
```

Running this command will show that the only changed file is 3\3.txt.

As the file catalog only stores hashes, the command is unable to describe exactly what has changed about a file, only that something has.

Summary

This chapter looked at working with providers, focusing on the FileSystem and Registry providers.

Providers use a common set of commands to access data arranged in a hierarchy. Providers may choose to add extra functionality with dynamic parameters for each of the commands, for example, by adding parameters to provide filtering.

Provider implementations can choose to support a variety of different operations, from reading and writing content to management ACLs.

In Windows PowerShell, the Registry provider supports transactions, allowing a sequence of changes to be prepared, then either committed or undone as applicable.

PowerShell 5 added commands to work with file catalogs. You can use a file catalog to see how a set of files changes over time or to validate a copied folder.

The next chapter explores how to work with WMI using the CIM commands built into Windows PowerShell and PowerShell Core.

Learn more on Discord

Read this book alongside other users, PowerShell experts, and the author himself. Ask questions, provide solutions to other readers, chat with the author via Ask Me Anything sessions, and much more.

Scan the QR code or visit the link to join the community.

https://packt.link/SecNet

11

Windows Management Instrumentation

Windows Management Instrumentation (**WMI**) was introduced as a downloadable component with Windows 95 and NT. Windows 2000 had WMI pre-installed, and it has since become a core part of the operating system.

WMI is how Microsoft chose to implement a **Common Information Model** (**CIM**).

WMI can be used to access a huge amount of information about the computer system. This includes printers, device drivers, user accounts, ODBC, and so on; there are hundreds of classes to explore.

This chapter covers the following topics:

- Working with WMI
- The WMI Query Language
- WMI type accelerators
- Permissions

Let's start with WMI, which is made up of a large collection of classes.

Working with WMI

The scope of WMI is vast, which makes it a fantastic resource for automating processes. WMI classes are not limited to the core operating system; it is not uncommon to find classes created after software or device drivers have been installed.

Given the scope of WMI, finding an appropriate class can be difficult. PowerShell can be used to explore the available classes.

WMI classes

PowerShell, as a shell for working with objects, presents WMI classes in a similar manner to .NET classes or any other object. There are several parallels between WMI classes and .NET classes.

A WMI class is used as the recipe to create an instance of a WMI object. The WMI class defines properties and methods. The `Win32_Process` WMI class is used to gather information about running processes in a similar manner to the `Get-Process` command.

The `Win32_Process` class has properties such as `ProcessId`, `Name`, and `CommandLine`. `Win32_Process` has a `Terminate` method that can be used to kill a process, as well as a `Create` static method that can be used to spawn a new process.

Each WMI class resides within a WMI namespace, which is much like a folder structure for WMI classes. The default namespace is `root\cimv2`, which includes classes such as `Win32_OperatingSystem` and `Win32_LogicalDisk`.

WMI commands

PowerShell has two different sets of commands dedicated to working with WMI.

`Get-WmiObject` is included with PowerShell 1.0 to 5.1 but is not present in PowerShell 6 and above.

The CIM cmdlets, including `Get-CimInstance`, were introduced with PowerShell 3.0. They are compatible with the **Distributed Management Task Force (DMTF)** standard **DSP0004**. A move toward compliance with open standards is critical as the Microsoft world becomes more diverse.

WMI itself is a proprietary implementation of the CIM server, using the **Distributed Component Object Model (DCOM)** API to communicate between the client and server.

Standards compliance and differences in approach aside, there are solid, practical reasons to consider when choosing which one to use.

Some properties of CIM commands are as follows:

- Available in both Windows PowerShell and PowerShell Core
- Automatically handle date conversion
- Can make use of WSMan (Windows remoting) for remote connections by default but can be configured to use DCOM over RPC
- Can be used for all WMI operations

Some properties of WMI cmdlets are as follows:

- Only available in Windows PowerShell and not in PowerShell Core
- Do not automatically convert dates
- Use DCOM over RPC exclusively
- Can be used for all WMI operations
- Have been superseded by the CIM cmdlets

The `Get-WmiObject` command is not part of PowerShell 7, but it can be used to a limited extent. If `Get-WmiObject` is used, PowerShell 7 will attempt to make the command available using the compatibility PS session. Compatibility sessions were introduced in *Chapter 2, Modules*.

Using `Get-WmiObject` in the compatibility session will allow queries to execute, but methods that might effect change cannot be used.

The use of `Get-WmiObject` should be replaced with `Get-CimInstance` and the other CIM commands.

CIM commands

As mentioned in the previous section, the CIM cmdlets were introduced with PowerShell 3 and are the only commands available to access WMI in PowerShell 6 and above.

This section explores the following commands from the `CimCmdlets` module. There are more commands than those listed, but those are less common and thus not demonstrated here:

- `Get-CimInstance`
- `Get-CimClass`
- `Get-CimAssociatedInstance`
- `Get-CimSession`
- `Invoke-CimMethod`
- `New-CimInstance`
- `New-CimSession`
- `New-CimSessionOption`
- `Remove-CimInstance`

Each of these CIM cmdlets uses either the `ComputerName` or `CimSession` parameters to target the operation at another computer.

Getting instances

The `Get-CimInstance` command is used to execute queries for instances of WMI objects, as the following code shows:

```
Get-CimInstance -ClassName Win32_OperatingSystem
Get-CimInstance -ClassName Win32_Service
Get-CimInstance -ClassName Win32_Share
```

Several different parameters are available when using `Get-CimInstance`. The command can be used with a filter, as follows:

```
Get-CimInstance Win32_Directory -Filter "Name='C:\\Windows'"
Get-CimInstance Win32_Service -Filter "State='Running'"
```

Each command will return instances matching the filter. In the case of `Win32_Directory`, a single object is returned, as the following output shows:

```
Name            Hidden  Archive  Writeable  LastModified
----            ------  -------  ---------  ------------
C:\Windows      False   False    True       20/02/2021 09:25:20
```

The filter format is **WMI Query Language**, or **WQL**, and is explored later in this chapter.

When returning large amounts of information, the Property parameter can be used to reduce the number of fields returned by a query:

```
Get-CimInstance Win32_UserAccount -Property Name, SID
```

The Query parameter may be used in place of the ClassName, Property, and Filter parameters:

```
Get-CimInstance -Query "SELECT * FROM Win32_Process"
Get-CimInstance -Query "SELECT Name, SID FROM Win32_UserAccount"
```

CIM can be queried for more detail of the classes used above.

Getting classes

The Get-CimClass command is used to return the details of a WMI class:

```
PS> Get-CimClass Win32_Process


    NameSpace: ROOT/cimv2


CimClassName        CimClassMethods              CimClassProperties
-----------         ---------------              ------------------
Win32_Process       {Create, Terminate, Get...}  {Caption, Description...}
```

The class object describes the capabilities of that class. By default, Get-CimClass lists classes from the root\cimv2 namespace.

The Namespace parameter will fill using tab completion, meaning if the following partial command is entered, pressing *Tab* repeatedly will cycle through the possible root namespaces.

The child namespaces of a given namespace are listed in a __Namespace class instance. For example, the following command returns the namespaces under root:

```
Get-CimInstance __Namespace -Namespace root
```

The first few namespaces returned by the command above are shown below:

```
Name                PSComputerName
----                --------------
subscription
DEFAULT
CIMV2
msdtc
Cli
```

Extending this technique, it is possible to recursively query __Namespace to find all the possible namespace values. Certain WMI namespaces are only available to administrative users (**run as administrator**); the following function may display errors for some namespaces:

```
function Get-CimNamespace {
    param (
        $Namespace = 'root'
    )

    $children = Get-CimInstance __Namespace -Namespace $Namespace
    foreach ($child in $children) {
        $childNamespace = Join-Path $Namespace -ChildPath $child.Name
        $childNamespace

        Get-CimNamespace -Namespace $childNamespace
    }
}
Get-CimNamespace
```

CIM class objects describe the methods available for a class. These methods are used to change objects.

Calling methods

The Invoke-CimMethod command is used to call a method on either CIM instances or CIM classes. The CIM class can be used to find details of the methods that a class supports:

```
PS> (Get-CimClass Win32_Process).CimClassMethods

Name          ReturnType  Parameters          Qualifiers
----          ----------  ----------          ----------
Create        UInt32      {CommandLine...}    {Constructor...}
Terminate     UInt32      {Reason}            {Destructor...}
GetOwner      UInt32      {Domain...}         {Implemented...}
GetOwnerSid   UInt32      {Sid}               {Implemented...}
```

The method with the Constructor qualifier can be used to create a new instance of Win32_Process.

The Parameters property of a specific WMI method can be explored to find out how to use a method:

```
PS> (Get-CimClass Win32_Process).CimClassMethods['Create'].Parameters

Name                          CimType   Qualifiers
----                          -------   ----------
CommandLine                   String    {ID, In, MappingStrings}
```

CurrentDirectory	String	{ID, In, MappingStrings}
ProcessStartupInformation	Instance	{EmbeddedInstance, ID...}
ProcessId	UInt32	{ID, MappingStrings, Out}

If an argument has the In qualifier, it can be passed as an argument when creating an object. If an argument has the Out qualifier, it will be returned once the instance has been created. Arguments are passed in using a hashtable.

When creating a process, the CommandLine argument is required; the rest can be ignored until later:

```
$params = @{
    ClassName  = 'Win32_Process'
    MethodName = 'Create'
    Arguments  = @{
        CommandLine = 'notepad.exe'
    }
}
$return = Invoke-CimMethod @params
```

The return object holds three properties in the case of the Create method of Win32_Process. This includes ProcessId and ReturnValue. PowerShell adds a PSComputerName property to these:

```
PS> $return

ProcessId    ReturnValue    PSComputerName
---------    -----------    --------------
    15172              0
```

PSComputerName is blank when a request is local. ProcessId is the Out property listed under the Create method parameters. ReturnValue indicates whether the operation succeeded, and 0 indicates that it was successful.

Any return value other than zero indicates that something went wrong, but the values are not translated in PowerShell.

The return values for each class are described by the WMI reference documentation for that class. For example, documentation on Win32_Process can be found at:

https://learn.microsoft.com/windows/win32/cimwin32prov/create-method-in-class-win32-process.

The Create method used here creates a new instance. The other methods for Win32_Process act against an existing instance (an existing process).

Extending the preceding example, a process can be created and then terminated:

```
$invokeParams = @{
    ClassName  = 'Win32_Process'
    MethodName = 'Create'
```

```
    Arguments  = @{
        CommandLine = 'notepad.exe'
    }
}
$return = Invoke-CimMethod @invokeParams

pause

$getParams = @{
    ClassName = 'Win32_Process'
    Filter    = 'ProcessId={0}' -f $return.ProcessId
}
Get-CimInstance @getParams |
    Invoke-CimMethod -MethodName Terminate
```

The pause command will wait for *return* to be pressed before continuing, showing that Notepad was opened before it was terminated.

The Terminate method has an optional argument that is used as the exit code for the termination process. This argument may be added using a hashtable; in this case, a (made-up) value of 5 is set as the exit code:

```
$invokeParams = @{
    ClassName  = 'Win32_Process'
    MethodName = 'Create'
    Arguments  = @{
        CommandLine = 'notepad.exe'
    }
}
$return = Invoke-CimMethod @invokeParams

$getParams = @{
    ClassName = 'Win32_Process'
    Filter    = 'ProcessId={0}' -f $return.ProcessId
}
Get-CimInstance @getParams |
    Invoke-CimMethod -MethodName Terminate -Arguments @{
        Reason = 5
    }
```

The return values associated with the Terminate method of Win32_Process are documented in the WMI reference:

https://learn.microsoft.com/windows/win32/cimwin32prov/terminate-method-in-class-win32-process.

Some methods require or can use instances of CIM classes as arguments. In some cases, these instances must be created.

Creating instances

The arguments for Win32_Process include a ProcessStartupInformation parameter. ProcessStartupInformation is described by a WMI class, Win32_ProcessStartup.

There are no existing instances of Win32_ProcessStartup. Querying the current computer for instances of Win32_ProcessStartup will not find anything. The Win32_ProcessStartup class does not have a Create method (or any other constructor) that can be used to create an instance either.

The New-CimInstance command can be used to create an instance of the class:

```
$class = Get-CimClass Win32_ProcessStartup
$startupInfo = New-CimInstance -CimClass $class -ClientOnly
```

It is also possible to use New-Object:

```
$class = Get-CimClass Win32_ProcessStartup
$startupInfo = New-Object CimInstance $class
```

Finally, the new method may be used:

```
$class = Get-CimClass Win32_ProcessStartup
$startupInfo = [CimInstance]::new($class)
```

Once the instance has been created, properties can be set to define how a process should be started. The effect of each property is documented in the WMI reference: https://learn.microsoft.com/windows/win32/cimwin32prov/win32-processstartup.

In the following example, properties are set to dictate the position and title of a pwsh.exe window:

```
$class = Get-CimClass Win32_ProcessStartup
$startupInfo = New-CimInstance -CimClass $class -ClientOnly
$startupInfo.X = 50
$startupInfo.Y = 50
$startupInfo.Title = 'This is the window title'
$params = @{
    ClassName  = 'Win32_Process'
    MethodName = 'Create'
    Arguments  = @{
        CommandLine               = 'pwsh.exe'
        ProcessStartupInformation = $startupInfo
    }
}
$returnObject = Invoke-CimMethod @params
```

If the process starts successfully, $returnObject will have a return value of 0.

Removing instances

Removal of an instance is typically a destructive operation. Remove-CimInstance is most used where a class does not explicitly have a specific method to destroy the instance, such as a Delete method.

For example, if a process is started using New-CimInstance, then Get-CimInstance is used to get that process based on the ProcessID:

```
$params = @{
    ClassName  = 'Win32_Process'
    MethodName = 'Create'
    Arguments  = @{
        CommandLine = 'notepad.exe'
    }
}
$returnObject = Invoke-CimMethod @params
$params = @{
    ClassName = 'Win32_Process'
    Filter    = 'ProcessID={0}' -f $returnObject.ProcessID
}
$process = Get-CimInstance @params
```

Then the Remove-CimInstance command will cause the process to forcefully close:

```
$process | Remove-CimInstance
```

It may have been better to use the Terminate method of the Win32_Process class, but removal of the instance is also a valid approach.

One very common use of Remove-CimInstance is cleaning up user profiles. Removal of a Win32_UserProfile object causes deletion of a profile directory on a computer.

```
$params = @{
    ClassName = 'Win32_UserProfile'
    Filter    = 'Special=FALSE'
}
Get-CimInstance @params |
    Where-Object LastUseTime -lt (Get-Date).AddDays(-90) |
    Remove-CimInstance -WhatIf
```

This example above includes the -WhatIf parameter; the parameter should be removed after testing that it targets the right objects.

The preceding example is explored again later in this chapter when looking at the WMI Query Language.

Working with CIM sessions

As mentioned earlier in this chapter, a key feature of the CIM cmdlets is their ability to change how connections are formed and used.

The Get-CimInstance command has a ComputerName parameter, and when it is used, the command automatically creates a session to a remote system using WSMAN. The connection is destroyed as soon as the command is completed.

PowerShell remoting and WSMan are explored in much more detail in *Chapter 14, Remoting and Remote Management*.

The Get-CimSession, New-CimSession, New-CimSessionOption, and Remove-CimSession commands are optional commands that can be used to define the behaviour of remote connections.

The New-CimSession command creates a connection to a remote server. An example is as follows:

```
PS> $cimSession = New-CimSession -ComputerName Remote1
PS> $cimSession


Id          : 1
Name        : CimSession1
InstanceId  : 1cc2a889-b649-418c-94a2-f24e033883b4
ComputerName : Remote1
Protocol    : WSMAN
```

Alongside the other parameters, New-CimSession has a Credential parameter that can be used in conjunction with Get-Credential to authenticate a connection.

If the remote system does not allow access to WSMAN, it is possible to switch the protocol down to DCOM by using the New-CimSessionOption command:

```
PS> $option = New-CimSessionOption -Protocol DCOM
PS> $cimSession = New-CimSession -ComputerName Remote1 –SessionOption $option
PS> $cimSession


Id          : 2
Name        : CimSession2
InstanceId  : 62b2cb56-ec84-472c-a992-4bee59ee0618
ComputerName : Remote1
Protocol    : DCOM
```

DCOM connections use RPC, the same connection method used by the older Get-WmiObject command.

The New-CimSessionOption command is not limited to protocol switching; it can affect many of the other properties of the connection, as shown in the help and the examples for the command.

Once a session has been created, it exists in memory until it is removed. The Get-CimSession command shows a list of connections that have been formed, and the Remove-CimSession command permanently removes connections.

Associated classes

Classes in WMI can be related to other classes. For example, each instance of Win32_NetworkAdapter has an associated Win32_NetworkAdapterConfiguration instance, associating the hardware information with the configuration information.

The Get-CimAssociatedClass command allows queries to return information from related classes.

The following command gets the class instances associated with Win32_NetworkAdapterConfiguration. As the arguments for the Get-CimInstance command are long strings, splatting is used to pass the parameters into the command:

```
$params = @{
    ClassName = 'Win32_NetworkAdapterConfiguration'
    Filter    = 'IPEnabled=TRUE AND DHCPEnabled=TRUE'
}
Get-CimInstance @params | Get-CimAssociatedInstance
```

The following example uses Get-CimAssociatedClass to get the physical interface associated with the IP configuration:

```
$params = @{
    ClassName = 'Win32_NetworkAdapterConfiguration'
    Filter    = 'IPEnabled=TRUE AND DHCPEnabled=TRUE'
}
Get-CimInstance @params | ForEach-Object {
    $adapter = $_ | Get-CimAssociatedInstance -ResultClassName Win32_
NetworkAdapter

    [PSCustomObject]@{
        NetConnectionID = $adapter.NetConnectionID
        Speed           = [Math]::Round($adapter.Speed / 1MB, 2)
        IPAddress       = $_.IPAddress
        IPSubnet        = $_.IPSubnet
        Index           = $_.Index
        Gateway         = $_.DefaultIPGateway
    }
}
```

The preceding command returns details of every IP and DHCP-enabled network adapter, merging the results of two different CIM classes into a single object.

Similarly, `Win32_LogonSession` is associated with both the `Win32_UserAccount` and `Win32_Process` classes. The following example gets a list of running processes for a named user starting with a username:

```
Get-CimInstance Win32_UserAccount -Filter "Name='$env:USERNAME'" |
    Get-CimAssociatedInstance -ResultClassName Win32_LogonSession |
    Get-CimAssociatedInstance -ResultClassName Win32_Process
```

Many classes express relationships with one another and the `Get-CimAssociatedInstance` command can be used to explore those.

The WMI Query Language

WMI Query Language, or WQL, is used to query WMI in a similar style to SQL.

WQL implements a subset of **Structured Query Language (SQL)**. The keywords are traditionally written in uppercase; however, WQL is not case-sensitive.

The WMI reference describes the keywords available: `https://learn.microsoft.com/windows/win32/wmisdk/wql-sql-for-wmi`.

Certain products like Microsoft **System Center Configuration Manager (SCCM)** extend WQL. The extended keywords may only be used with WMI classes defined by SCCM: `https://learn.microsoft.com/mem/configmgr/develop/core/understand/extended-wmi-query-language`.

Both the CIM and the older WMI commands support the `Filter` and `Query` parameters, which accept WQL queries.

Understanding SELECT, WHERE, and FROM

The `SELECT`, `WHERE`, and `FROM` keywords are used with the `Query` parameter of either `Get-CimInstance` or `Get-WmiObject`.

The generalized syntax for the `Query` parameter is as follows:

```
SELECT <Properties> FROM <WMI Class>
SELECT <Properties> FROM <WMI Class> WHERE <Condition>
```

The wildcard * may be used to request all available properties, or a list of known properties may be used:

```
Get-CimInstance -Query "SELECT * FROM Win32_Process"
Get-CimInstance -Query "SELECT ProcessID, CommandLine FROM Win32_Process"
```

The `WHERE` keyword is used to filter results returned by `SELECT`; for example, see the following:

```
Get-CimInstance -Query "SELECT * FROM Win32_Process WHERE ProcessID=$PID"
```

The command above will return information about the current PowerShell process, like the example below:

ProcessId	Name	HandleCount	WorkingSetSize	VirtualSize
78684	pwsh.exe	1344	98746368	2481049194496

WQL cannot filter array-based properties; for example, the capabilities property of Win32_DiskDrive.

Escape sequences and wildcards

The backslash character, \, is used to escape the meaning of characters in a WMI query. It can be used to escape a wildcard character, quotes, or itself. For example, the following WMI query uses a path; each instance of "\" in the path must be escaped:

```
Get-CimInstance Win32_Process -Filter "ExecutablePath='C:\\Windows\\Explorer.
exe'"
```

The preceding command returns any instances of the explorer.exe process, as shown below:

ProcessId	Name	HandleCount	WorkingSetSize	VirtualSize
8320	explorer.exe	3412	198606848	2204322111488

The properties shown will vary from one computer to another.

About Win32_Process and the Path property

The Path script property is added to the output from the Win32_Process class by PowerShell. While it appears in the output, the property cannot be used to define a filter, nor can Path be selected using the Property parameter of either Get-CimInstance or Get-WmiObject.

Get-Member shows that it is a ScriptProperty, as follows:

Get-CimInstance Win32_Process -Filter "ProcessId=$pid" |

    Get-Member -Name Path

Get-WmiObject Win32_Process -Filter "ProcessId=$pid" |

    Get-Member -Name Path

WQL defines two wildcard characters that can be used with string queries:

- The % (percentage) character matches any number of characters and is equivalent to using * in a filesystem path or with the -like operator.
- The _ (underscore) character matches a single character and is equivalent to using ? in a filesystem path or with the -like operator.

The following query filters the results of Win32_Service, including services with paths starting with a single drive letter and ending with .exe:

```
Get-CimInstance Win32_Service -Filter 'PathName LIKE "_:\\%.exe"'
```

LIKE is an example of a comparison operator.

Comparison operators

Comparison operators may be used with the Filter and Query parameters to restrict the items the query finds.

The examples in the table below are based on the following command:

```
Get-CimInstance Win32_Process -Filter "Name='pwsh.exe'"
```

Filters will return instances based on the current state of the system.

Description	Operator	Example
Equal to	=	Name='powershell.exe' AND ProcessId=0
Not equal to	<>	Name<>'powershell.exe'
Greater than	>	WorkingSetSize>$(100MB)
Greater than or equal to	>=	WorkingSetSize>=$(100MB)
Less than	<	WorkingSetSize<$(100MB)
Less than or equal to	<=	WorkingSetSize<=$(100MB)
Is	IS	CommandLine IS NULL CommandLine IS NOT NULL
Like	LIKE	CommandLine LIKE '%.exe'

Table 11.1: WQL comparison operators

WQL filters and dates

A WQL filter may include dates in the filter string provided the date is correctly formatted.

The expected format date format is complicated:

```
$date = (Get-Date).AddDays(-90).ToString('yyyyMMddHHmmss.fK')
```

But this can be simplified slightly by making use of a built-in converter:

```
using namespace System.Management

$date = [ManagementDateTimeConverter]::ToDmtfTime(
    (Get-Date).AddDays(-90)
)
```

Then the date can be directly included in the filter instead of deferring that part of the filtering to `Where-Object`:

```
$params = @{
    ClassName = 'Win32_UserProfile'
    Filter    = 'Special=FALSE AND LastUseTime<{0}' -f
        $date
}
Get-CimInstance @params | Remove-CimInstance -WhatIf
```

Both methods are sufficiently complicated that it is rare to see dates presented in `filter` strings.

Filters may be combined using logic operators to build a more complex query.

Logic operators

Logic operators can be used to combine conditions or, in the case of the `NOT` operator, to reverse the result of a comparison. Logic operators can be used with the `Filter` and `Query` parameters.

For example, the following is a filter that might find different web browser processes:

```
$params = @{
    ClassName = 'Win32_Process'
    Filter    = 'Name="msedge.exe" OR ' +
        'Name="firefox.exe" OR ' +
        'Name="chrome.exe"'
}
Get-CimInstance @params
```

The table below describes the available logic operators.

Description	Operator	Syntax	Example
Logical and	AND	`<Condition1> AND <Condition2>`	`ProcessID=$pid AND Name='powershell.exe'`
Logical or	OR	`<Condition1> OR <Condition2>`	`ProcessID=$pid OR ProcessID=0`
Logical not	NOT	`NOT <Condition>`	`NOT ProcessID=$pid`

Table 11.2: WQL logical operators

When building filters, values may need to be quoted.

Quoting values

When building a WQL query, string values must be quoted; numeric and Boolean values do not need quotes.

As the filter is also a string, this often means nesting quotes within one another. For filters or queries containing fixed string values, use either of the following styles. Use single quotes outside and double quotes inside:

```
Get-CimInstance Win32_Process -Filter 'Name="pwsh.exe"'
```

Alternatively, use double quotes outside and single quotes inside:

```
Get-CimInstance Win32_Process -Filter "Name='pwsh.exe'"
```

For filters or queries containing PowerShell variables or sub-expressions, use double quotes around the filter. Variables within single-quoted strings will not expand:

```
Get-CimInstance Win32_Process -Filter "ProcessId=$PID"
Get-CimInstance Win32_Process -Filter "ExecutablePath LIKE '$($PSHome -replace
'\\', '\\')%'"
```

The "\" character is also an escape character for regular expressions. The expression "\\" represents a single literal "\". Each "\" in the $PSHome path is replaced with "\\" to account for WQL using "\" as an escape character as well.

In the previous example, the filter extends over a single line. If a filter is long or contains several conditions, consider using the format operator to compose the filter string:

```
$params = @{
    ClassName = 'Win32_Process'
    Filter    = "ExecutablePath LIKE '{0}%'" -f @(
        $PSHOME -replace '\\', '\\'
    )
}
Get-CimInstance @params
```

The format operator is used to add the escaped version of the path to the string. Running the command above will show any instances of PowerShell that are running, as shown below:

ProcessId	Name	HandleCount	WorkingSetSize	VirtualSize
14868	pwsh.exe	1114	243924992	2204239736832
10952	pwsh.exe	1513	180326400	2204260892672

WQL filters are especially useful when working with CIM classes that contain many instances.

Associated classes

WMI classes often have several different associated or related classes; for example, each instance of Win32_Process has an associated class, CIM_DataFile.

Associations between two classes are expressed by a third class. In the case of Win32_Process and CIM_DataFile, the relationship is expressed by the CIM_ProcessExecutable class.

The relationship is defined by using the antecedent and dependent properties, as shown in the following example:

```
Get-CimInstance CIM_ProcessExecutable |
    Where-Object Dependent -match $PID |
    Select-Object -First 1
```

The example above returns an instance of CIM_ProcessExecutable, as shown below:

```
Antecedent          : CIM_DataFile (Name = "C:\Program Files\PowerShell\7\pwsh.
exe")
Dependent           : Win32_Process (Handle = "86864")
BaseAddress         : 140697581191168
GlobalProcessCount  :
ModuleInstance      : 3042508800
ProcessCount        : 0
PSComputerName      :
```

This CIM_ProcessExecutable class does not need to be used directly; it is only used to express the relationship between two other classes.

WMI object paths

A WMI path is required to find classes associated with an instance. The WMI object path uniquely identifies a specific instance of a WMI class.

The object path is made up of several components:

```
<Namespace>:<ClassName>.<KeyName>=<Value>
```

The namespace can be omitted if the class is under the default namespace, root\cimv2.

The KeyName for a given WMI class can be discovered in several ways. In the case of Win32_Process, the key name might be discovered by using any of the following methods.

It can be discovered by using the CIM cmdlets:

```
(Get-CimClass Win32_Process).CimClassProperties |
    Where-Object { $_.Flags -band 'Key' }
```

It can be discovered by using the WMI reference, which provides descriptions of each property (and method) exposed by the class: https://learn.microsoft.com/windows/win32/cimwin32prov/win32-process.

Having identified a key, only the value remains to be found. In the case of Win32_Process, the key (handle) has the same value as the process ID. The object path for the Win32_Process instance associated with a running PowerShell console is, therefore, as follows:

```
root\cimv2:Win32_Process.Handle=$PID
```

The namespace does not need to be included if it uses the default, root\cimv2; the object path can be shortened to the following:

```
Win32_Process.Handle=$PID
```

Get-CimInstance and Get-WmiObject do not retrieve an instance from an object path, but the wmi type accelerator can:

```
PS> [wmi]"Win32_Process.Handle=$PID" | Select-Object Name, Handle


Name       Handle
----       ------
pwsh.exe 11672
```

The preceding object is somewhat equivalent to using a filter for Handle when querying Win32_Process.

Using ASSOCIATORS OF

Queries using ASSOCIATORS OF are used to find instances of classes that are related to a specific object.

The ASSOCIATORS OF query may be used for any given object path; for example, using the preceding object path results in the following command:

```
Get-CimInstance -Query "ASSOCIATORS OF {Win32_Process.Handle=$PID}"
```

This query will return objects from three different classes: Win32_LogonSession, Win32_ComputerSystem, and CIM_DataFile. The classes that are returned are shown in the following example:

```
$params = @{
    Query = "ASSOCIATORS OF {Win32_Process.Handle=$PID}"
}
Get-CimInstance @params | Select-Object CimClass -Unique
```

The command above gets the associated CIM classes shown below:

```
CimClass
--------
root/cimv2:Win32_ComputerSystem
root/cimv2:Win32_LogonSession
root/cimv2:CIM_DataFile
```

The query can be refined to filter a specific resulting class; an example is as follows:

```
Get-CimInstance -Query "ASSOCIATORS OF {Win32_Process.Handle=$PID} WHERE
ResultClass = CIM_DATAFILE"
```

The value in the ResultClass condition is deliberately not quoted.

The result of this operation is a long list of files that are used by the PowerShell process. A snippet of this is shown below:

```
$params = @{
    Query = "ASSOCIATORS OF {Win32_Process.Handle=$PID} " +
        "WHERE ResultClass = CIM_DATAFILE"
}
Get-CimInstance @params | Select-Object Name
```

The first few results from the query are shown below:

```
Name
----
C:\Program Files\PowerShell\7\pwsh.exe
C:\WINDOWS\SYSTEM32\ntdll.dll
C:\WINDOWS\System32\KERNEL32.DLL
C:\WINDOWS\System32\KERNELBASE.dll
C:\WINDOWS\System32\USER32.dll
C:\WINDOWS\System32\win32u.dll
```

While the older Get-WmiObject command has not been continued into PowerShell 6, the WMI type accelerators remain.

WMI type accelerators

The WMI cmdlets were removed in PowerShell 6 and are not going to be reinstated.

The following type accelerators remain and can still be used:

- wmi: System.Management.ManagementObject
- wmiclass: System.Management.ManagementClass
- wmisearcher: System.Management.ManagementObjectSearcher

When necessary, these accelerators may be used to simulate the functionality provided by the older WMI cmdlets.

Both the wmi and wmiclass type accelerators can be written to use a remote computer by including the computer name. An example is as follows:

```
[wmi]"\\RemoteComputer\root\cimv2:Win32_Process.Handle=$PID"
[wmiclass]"\\RemoteComputer\root\cimv2:Win32_Process"
```

These type accelerators may be used in PowerShell 6 and higher.

Getting instances

The wmisearcher type accelerator may be used to execute queries and retrieve results:

```
([wmisearcher]"SELECT * FROM Win32_Process").Get()
```

The returned object is identical to the object that would have been returned by the Get-WmiObject command.

Working with dates

WMI instances retrieved using type accelerators do not convert date-time properties into the `DateTime` type. Querying the `Win32_Process` class for the creation date of a process returns the date-time property as a long string:

```
$query = '
SELECT Name, CreationDate
FROM Win32_Process
WHERE ProcessId={0}
' -f $PID
([wmisearcher]$query).Get() | Select-Object Name, CreationDate
```

The query used above will show the instance of the current PowerShell process and the creation date of that process, as shown below:

```
Name        CreationDate
----        ------------
pwsh.exe 20200510090416.263973+060
```

The .NET namespace, `System.Management`, includes a class called `ManagementDateTimeConverter`, dedicated to converting date and time formats found in WMI. This method is added to WMI objects in PowerShell as a `ConvertToDateTime` script method.

The string in the preceding example may be converted as follows:

```
$query = '
SELECT Name, CreationDate
FROM Win32_Process
WHERE ProcessId={0}
' -f $PID
([wmisearcher]$query).Get() | Select-Object @(
    'Name'
    @{
        Name = 'CreationDate'
        Expression = {
            $_.ConvertToDateTime($_.CreationDate)
        }
    }
)
```

WMI classes may be used via the `wmiclass` accelerator.

Getting classes

An instance of a class may be created using the wmiclass accelerator, as the following code shows:

```
PS> [wmiclass]'Win32_Process'


   NameSpace: ROOT\cimv2


Name              Methods            Properties
----              -------            ----------
Win32_Process    {Create, Terminate,… {Caption, CommandLine, Creat…}
```

The class describes the methods and properties that can be used.

Calling methods

Calling a method on an existing instance of an object found using wmisearcher is like using any other .NET method call.

The following example gets and restarts the Print Spooler service. The following operation requires administrative access:

```
$query = '
  SELECT *
  FROM Win32_SERVICE
  WHERE DisplayName="Print Spooler"
'
$service = ([WmiSearcher]$query).Get()
$service.StopService()      # Call the StopService method
$service.StartService()     # Call the StartService method
```

The WMI class can be used to find the details of a method; for example, the Create method of Win32_ Share, as follows:

```
PS> ([WmiClass]'Win32_Share').Methods['Create']

Name          : Create
InParameters  : System.Management.ManagementBaseObject
OutParameters : System.Management.ManagementBaseObject
Origin        : Win32_Share
Qualifiers    : {Constructor, Implemented, MappingStrings, Static}
```

When the Invoke-CimMethod command accepts a hashtable, methods invoked on a WMI object expect arguments to be passed in a specific order. The order is described in the WMI reference for the class, found here: https://learn.microsoft.com/windows/win32/cimwin32prov/create-method-in-class-win32-share.

The documentation shows which arguments are mandatory (not optional) in the syntax element at the top.

Alternatively, the order arguments must be written like so:

```
PS> ([WmiClass]'Win32_Share').Create.OverloadDefinitions -split '(?<=,)'

System.Management.ManagementBaseObject Create(System.String Path,
 System.String Name,
 System.UInt32 Type,
 System.UInt32 MaximumAllowed,
 System.String Description,
 System.String Password,
 System.Management.ManagementObject#Win32_SecurityDescriptor Access)
```

To create a share, the argument list must contain an argument for Access, then Description, then MaximumAllowed, and so on. If the argument is optional, it can be ignored, or a null value may be provided:

```
([wmiclass]'Win32_Share').Create(
    'C:\Temp\Share1', # Path
    'Share2',         # Name
    0                 # Type (Disk Drive)
)
```

The Description argument follows the MaximumAllowed argument. If Description were to be set (but not MaximumAllowed), a null value can be added for that argument:

```
([wmiclass]'Win32_Share').Create(
    'C:\Temp\Share1', # Path
    'Share3',         # Name
    0,                # Type (Disk Drive),
    $null,            # MaximumAllowed
    'Description'     # Description
)
```

ReturnValue describes the result of the operation; a ReturnValue of 0 indicates success. As this operation requires administrator privileges (**run as administrator**), a ReturnValue of 2 is used to indicate that it was run without sufficient rights.

If the folder used in the previous example does not exist, ReturnValue will be set to 24.

A less well-known alternative is available compared to passing arguments in an array. You can pass arguments by setting the values of an object. The object is retrieved using the GetMethodParameters method on a WMI class:

```
$class = [WmiClass]'Win32_Share'
$params = $class.GetMethodParameters('Create')
$params.Name = 'Share1'
$params.Path = 'C:\Temp\Share1'
$params.Type = 0
$class.InvokeMethod('Create', $params)
```

Creating an object to represent the parameters has a clear advantage in that each property has a clear name, rather than being reliant on discovering and using positional arguments.

Creating instances

An instance of a WMI class can be created using the CreateInstance method of the class. The following example creates an instance of Win32_Trustee:

```
([WmiClass]'Win32_Trustee').CreateInstance()
```

This is similar in effect to the New-CimInstance approach used earlier in this chapter.

Associated classes

Objects returned by Wmisearcher have a GetRelated method that can be used to find associated instances.

The GetRelated method accepts arguments that can be used to filter the results. The first argument, relatedClass, is used to limit the instances that are returned to specific classes, as shown here:

```
using namespace System.Management

([wmisearcher]'SELECT * FROM Win32_LogonSession').Get() | ForEach-Object {
    [PSCustomObject]@{
        LogonName      = $_.GetRelated('Win32_Account').Caption
        SessionStarted = [ManagementDateTimeConverter]::ToDateTime(
            $_.StartTime
        )
    }
}
```

In general, it is simpler to use the CIM commands than the type accelerators above. The type accelerators provide an avenue to replace Get-WmiObject without completely rewriting into the newer CIM style.

Permissions

Working with permissions in WMI is more difficult than in .NET as the values in use are not given friendly names. However, the .NET classes can still be used, even if not quite as intended.

The following working examples demonstrate configuring the permissions.

Sharing permissions

Get-Acl and Set-Acl are fantastic tools for working with filesystem permissions, or permissions under other providers. However, these commands cannot be used to affect SMB share permissions.

The SmbShare module

The SmbShare module has commands that affect share permissions. This example uses WMI classes to modify permissions. It might be used if the SmbShare module cannot be.

The Get-SmbShareAccess command might be used to verify the outcome of this example.

The following operations require administrative privileges; use PowerShell as an administrator when attempting to use these examples.

Creating a shared directory

The following snippet creates a directory and shares that directory:

```
$path = 'C:\Temp\WmiPermissions'
New-Item $path -ItemType Directory
$params = @{
    ClassName = 'Win32_Share'
    MethodName = 'Create'
    Arguments = @{
        Name = 'WmiPerms'
        Path = $path
        Type = 0u
    }
}
Invoke-CimMethod @params
```

The Create method used here will fail if the argument for Type is not correctly defined as a UInt32 value. PowerShell will set the type to Int32 if the value of 0 is used without the numeric literal, "u".

The requirement for UInt32, in this case, may be viewed by exploring the parameters required for the method:

```
(Get-CimClass Win32_Share).
    CimClassMethods['Create'].Parameters |
    Where-Object Name -eq Type
```

The output describing the Type parameter is shown below:

Name	CimType	Qualifiers	ReferenceClassName
Type	UInt32	{ID, In, MappingStrings}	

Now that the share exists, the security descriptor can be retrieved.

Getting a security descriptor

When Get-Acl is used, the object that it gets is a security descriptor. The security descriptor includes a set of control information (ownership and so on), along with the discretionary and system access control lists.

The WMI class Win32_LogicalShareSecuritySetting is used to represent the security for each of the shares on a computer:

```
$params = @{
    ClassName = 'Win32_LogicalShareSecuritySetting'
    Filter    = "Name='WmiPerms'"
}
$security = Get-CimInstance @params
```

The returned object has a limited number of properties, as shown below:

```
Caption         : Security settings of WmiPerms
Description     : Security settings of WmiPerms
SettingID       :
ControlFlags    : 32772
Name            : WmiPerms
PSComputerName  :
```

This instance is important as it is required to use the GetSecurityDescriptor method:

```
$return = $security |
    Invoke-CimMethod -MethodName GetSecurityDescriptor
$aclObject = $return.Descriptor
```

The security descriptor held in the aclObject variable is different from the result returned by Get-Acl:

```
PS> $aclObject

ControlFlags    : 32772
DACL            : {Win32_ACE}
Group           :
Owner           :
SACL            :
TIME_CREATED    :
PSComputerName  :
```

The ControlFlags value states that a DACL is present and that the security descriptor information is stored in a contiguous block of memory. These values are described in the security reference: https://learn.microsoft.com/windows/win32/secauthz/security-descriptor-control.

The DACL, or discretionary access control list, is used to describe the permission levels for each security principal (a user, group, or computer account). Each entry in this list is an instance of Win32_ACE:

```
PS> $aclObject.DACL

AccessMask              : 1179817
AceFlags                : 0
AceType                 : 0
GuidInheritedObjectType :
GuidObjectType          :
TIME_CREATED            :
Trustee                 : Win32_Trustee
PSComputerName          :
```

The Win32_ACE object has a Trustee property that holds the Name, Domain, and SID properties of the security principal (in this case, the Everyone principal):

```
PS> $aclObject.DACL.Trustee

Domain         :
Name           : Everyone
SID            : {1, 1, 0, 0...}
SidLength      : 12
SIDString      : S-1-1-0
TIME_CREATED   :
PSComputerName :
```

AceFlags describes how an **Access Control Entry** (ACE) is to be inherited. As this is a share, the AceFlags property will always be 0. Nothing can, or will, inherit this entry; .NET can be used to confirm this:

```
PS> [System.Security.AccessControl.AceFlags]0
None
```

AceType is either AccessAllowed (0) or AccessDenied (1). Again, .NET can be used to confirm this:

```
PS> [System.Security.AccessControl.AceType]0
AccessAllowed
```

Finally, the AccessMask property can be converted into a meaningful value with .NET as well. The access rights that can be granted on a share are a subset of those that might be assigned to a file or directory:

```
PS> [System.Security.AccessControl.FileSystemRights]1179817
ReadAndExecute, Synchronize
```

Putting this together, the entries in a shared DACL can be made much easier to understand:

```
using namespace System.Security.AccessControl

$aclObject.DACL | ForEach-Object {
    [PSCustomObject]@{
        Rights   = [FileSystemRights]$_.AccessMask
        Type     = [AceType]$_.AceType
        Flags    = [AceFlags]$_.AceFlags
        Identity = $_.Trustee.Name
    }
}
```

In the preceding example, the domain of the trustee is ignored. If the trustee is something other than Everyone, the domain should be included.

Adding an access control entry

To add an ACE to an existing list, you must create Win32_ACE. Creating an ACE requires Win32_Trustee. The following trustee is created from the current user:

```
$trustee = New-CimInstance (Get-CimClass Win32_Trustee) -ClientOnly
$trustee.Domain = $env:USERDOMAIN
$trustee.Name = $env:USERNAME
```

SID does not need to be set on the trustee object. If the security principal is invalid, attempting to apply the change to security will fail.

Once Win32_Trustee has been created, Win32_ACE may be created to grant the trustee full control of the share:

```
using namespace System.Security.AccessControl

$ace = New-CimInstance (Get-CimClass Win32_ACE) -ClientOnly
$ace.AccessMask = [UInt32][FileSystemRights]'FullControl'
$ace.AceType = [UInt32][AceType]'AccessAllowed'
$ace.AceFlags = [UInt32]0
$ace.Trustee = $trustee
```

The ACE can be added to the DACL using the += operator:

```
$aclObject.DACL += $ace
```

With the DACL updated, the security descriptor can be applied.

Setting the security descriptor

Once the ACL has been changed, the modified security descriptor must be set. The instance returned by `Win32_LogicalShareSecuritySetting` contains a `SetSecurityDescriptor` method:

```
$params = @{
    MethodName = 'SetSecurityDescriptor'
    Arguments  = @{
        Descriptor = $aclObject
    }
}
$security | Invoke-CimMethod @params
```

A return value of 0 indicates that the change to the ACL has been successfully applied. You can view this change by looking at the properties of the share in File Explorer, as shown in the following example:

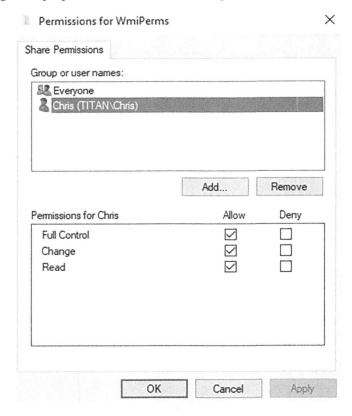

Figure 11.1: Modified share permissions

In early versions of PowerShell (and earlier versions of Windows), WMI was the only option for changing configurations like share permissions. The `SmbShare` module is an easier-to-use set of commands than the convoluted process used here. It is also able to show the assigned share permissions:

```
PS> Get-SmbShareAccess -Name WmiPerms

Name        ScopeName   AccountName   AccessControlType   AccessRight
----        ---------   -----------   -----------------   -----------
WmiPerms    *           Everyone      Allow               Read
WmiPerms    *           TITAN\Chris   Allow               Full
```

While share permissions have better commands available, the preceding process provides a good basis for modifying any security presented via WMI. One of these is the permissions defined on namespaces in WMI.

WMI permissions

Getting and setting WMI security in PowerShell uses the same approach as share security. WMI permissions might be set using wmimgmt.msc if the GUI is used. The content of the DACL differs slightly.

The __SystemSecurity class is used to access the security descriptor. Each WMI namespace has its own instance of the __SystemSecurity class; an example is as follows:

```
Get-CimClass __SystemSecurity -Namespace root
Get-CimClass __SystemSecurity -Namespace root\cimv2
```

Getting the security descriptor is like working with Win32_LogicalShareSecuritySettings.

Getting a security descriptor

The security descriptor for a given namespace can be retrieved from the __SystemSecurity class. By default, administrator privileges are required to get the security descriptor:

```
$security = Get-CimInstance __SystemSecurity -Namespace root\cimv2
$return = $security | Invoke-CimMethod -MethodName GetSecurityDescriptor
$aclObject = $return.Descriptor
```

Each ACE in the DACL has an access mask.

The access mask

The access mask defines which rights are assigned by the ACE. The values of an access mask in the DACL are documented as access right constants in the WMI reference: https://learn.microsoft.com/windows/win32/wmisdk/namespace-access-rights-constants.

The standard access rights, ReadSecurity and WriteSecurity, are also relevant. The access mask is a composite of the values listed here:

- EnableAccount: 1
- ExecuteMethods: 2
- FullWrite: 4
- PartialWrite: 8

- WriteProvider: 16
- RemoteEnable: 32
- ReadSecurity: 131072
- WriteSecurity: 262144

These values can be used to add a new ACE and set the security descriptor in exactly the same way as was done with sharing permissions.

The WMI methods used in this subsection also allow a security descriptor to be exported to and imported from a **Security Descriptor Definition Language (SDDL)** string.

WMI and SDDL

SDDL is used to describe the content of a security descriptor as a string. The string format is described in the following *Authorization* reference: https://learn.microsoft.com/windows/win32/secauthz/security-descriptor-string-format.

A security descriptor returned by Get-Acl has a method that can convert the entire security descriptor into a string, as follows:

```
PS> (Get-Acl C:\).GetSecurityDescriptorSddlForm('All')
O:S-1-5-80-956008885-3418522649-1831038044-1853292631-2271478464G:S-1-5-
80-956008885-3418522649-1831038044-1853292631-2271478464D:PAI(A;;LC;;;AU)
(A;OICIIO;SDGXGWGR;;;AU)(A;;FA;
;;SY)(A;OICIIO;GA;;;SY)(A;OICIIO;GA;;;BA)(A;;FA;;;BA)(A;OICI;0x1200a9;;;BU)
```

A security descriptor defined using SDDL can also be imported. If the sddlString variable is assumed to hold a valid security descriptor, then you can use the following command:

```
$acl = Get-Acl C:\
$acl.SetSecurityDescriptorSddlForm($sddlString)
```

The imported security descriptor will not apply to the directory until Set-Acl is used.

WMI security descriptors can be converted to and from different formats, including SDDL. WMI has a specialized class for this: Win32_SecurityDescriptorHelper. The methods for this class are shown here:

```
PS> (Get-CimClass Win32_SecurityDescriptorHelper).CimClassMethods

Name                 ReturnType  Parameters              Qualifiers
----                 ----------  ----------              ----------
Win32SDToSDDL        UInt32      {Descriptor, SDDL}      {implemented, static}
Win32SDToBinarySD    UInt32      {Descriptor, BinarySD}  {implemented, static}
SDDLToWin32SD        UInt32      {SDDL, Descriptor}      {implemented, static}
SDDLToBinarySD       UInt32      {SDDL, BinarySD}        {implemented, static}
BinarySDToWin32SD    UInt32      {BinarySD, Descriptor}  {implemented, static}
BinarySDToSDDL       UInt32      {BinarySD, SDDL}        {implemented, static}
```

A WMI security descriptor might be converted into SDDL to create a backup before making a change, as follows:

```
$security = Get-CimInstance __SystemSecurity -Namespace root\cimv2
$return = $security |
    Invoke-CimMethod -MethodName GetSecurityDescriptor
$aclObject = $return.Descriptor

$params = @{
    ClassName = 'Win32_SecurityDescriptorHelper'
    MethodName = 'Win32SDToSDDL'
    Arguments  = @{
        Descriptor = $aclObject
    }
}
$return = Invoke-CimMethod @params
```

If the operation succeeds (when ReturnValue is 0), the security descriptor in SDDL form will be available:

```
PS> $return.SDDL
O:BAG:BAD:AR(A;CI;CCDCWP;;;S-1-5-21-2114566378-1333126016-908539190-1001)
(A;CI;CCDCLCSWRPWPRCWD;;;BA)(A;CI;CCDCRP;;;NS)(A;CI;CCDCRP;;;LS)
(A;CI;CCDCRP;;;AU)
```

An SDDL string can be imported as a security descriptor:

```
$params = @{
    ClassName = 'Win32_SecurityDescriptorHelper'
    MethodName = 'SDDLToWin32SD'
    Arguments  = @{
        SDDL =
'O:BAG:BAD:AR(A;CI;CCDCWP;;;S-1-5-21-2114566378-1333126016-908539190-1001)
(A;CI;CCDCLCSWRPWPRCWD;;;BA)(A;CI;CCDCRP;;;NS)(A;CI;CCDCRP;;;LS)
(A;CI;CCDCRP;;;AU)'
    }
}
$return = Invoke-CimMethod @params
$aclObject = $return.Descriptor
```

If ReturnValue is 0, the aclObject variable will contain the imported security descriptor:

```
PS> $aclObject

ControlFlags   : 33028
```

```
DACL            : {Win32_ACE, Win32_ACE, Win32_ACE, Win32_ACE...}
Group           : Win32_Trustee
Owner           : Win32_Trustee
SACL            :
TIME_CREATED    :
PSComputerName  :
```

The ACL object, like much of WMI, is not particularly descriptive. The raw information is there, and the descriptor can be set. Reading the descriptor requires work, as you must translate all the values into their human-readable equivalents.

Summary

This chapter explored working with WMI classes, the different available commands, and the WMI Query Language.

The CIM commands are the best way of working with WMI in PowerShell 3 and above.

Since Get-WmiObject has been removed from PowerShell, the WMI type accelerators were explored as an alternative means of working with WMI in the same style as Get-WmiObject. This may be useful for the few rare classes that do not work using the CIM cmdlets.

Managing permissions is one of the more advanced WMI operations, and SMB shares and WMI permissions were used to demonstrate this.

The next chapter explores working with and generating and consuming data from a variety of different text-based formats.

Learn more on Discord

Read this book alongside other users, PowerShell experts, and the author himself. Ask questions, provide solutions to other readers, chat with the author via Ask Me Anything sessions, and much more.

Scan the QR code or visit the link to join the community.

https://packt.link/SecNet

12

Working with HTML, XML, and JSON

PowerShell has several commands for working with the HTML, XML, and **JavaScript Object Notation** (**JSON**) formats. These commands, combined with some of the available .NET classes, provide a rich set of tools for creating or modifying these formats.

HTML is often used for generating user-consumable reports.

PowerShell includes the ConvertTo-Html command, which can generate HTML content.

The PSWriteHtml module can be used to create more complex HTML documents. The module is available in the PowerShell Gallery. PSWriteHtml uses a **Domain-Specific Language** (**DSL**) to describe HTML documents in PowerShell.

What is a Domain-Specific Language?

A Domain-Specific Language or DSL is a specialized language used to describe something, in this case, an HTML document. Keywords are used to describe individual elements of the document. In this case, those keywords are hierarchically arranged.

Other DSLs frequently used in PowerShell include **Desired State Configuration** (**DSC**) and Pester.

XML is a popular data format, although it tends to be less fashionable. Web services may still use XML, although these are less common as time goes on. XML content is still frequently used to store configuration information from a systems administrator perspective. The ability to work with complex documents is a useful skill.

JSON has become more prominent over the years with the rise of REST-based web services that almost always use JSON to send complex information as a string.

Web services are explored in *Chapter 13, Web Requests and Web Services*.

This chapter covers the following topics:

- HTML
- XML commands
- `System.Xml`
- `System.Xml.Linq`
- JSON

ConvertTo-Html

`ConvertTo-Html` generates an HTML document with a table based on an input object. The following example generates a table based on the output from `Get-Process`:

```
Get-Process | ConvertTo-Html -Property Name, Id, WorkingSet
```

The preceding code generates a table format by default. Table is the default value for the `As` parameter. The `As` parameter also accepts a list as an argument to generate output like `Format-List`.

Multiple tables

`ConvertTo-Html` can be used to build more complex documents by making use of the `Fragment` parameter. The `Fragment` parameter generates an HTML table or list only (instead of a full document). Tables can be combined to create a larger document:

```
# Create the body
$body = @(
    '<h1>Services</h1>'
    Get-Service |
        Where-Object Status -eq 'Running' |
        ConvertTo-Html -Property Name, DisplayName -Fragment
    '<h1>Processes</h1>'
    Get-Process |
        Where-Object WorkingSet -gt 50MB |
        ConvertTo-Html -Property Name, Id, WorkingSet -Fragment
) | Out-String
# Create a document with the merged body
ConvertTo-Html -Body $body -Title Report |
    Set-Content report.html
```

HTML content generated by `ConvertTo-Html` is raw and does not include any information to make it visually appealing to the user.

Adding style

HTML content can be enhanced by adding a **Cascading Style Sheet (CSS)** to the header. When CSS is embedded in an HTML document, it is added between style tags in the head element.

The following style uses CSS to change the font, color the table headers, define the table borders, and justify the table content:

```
$css = @'
<style>
    body { font-family: Arial; }
    table {
        width: 100%;
        border-collapse: collapse;
    }
    table, th, td {
        border: 1px solid Black;
        padding: 5px;
    }
    th {
        text-align: left;
        background-color: LightBlue;
    }
    tr:nth-child(even) {
        background-color: GainsBoro;
    }
</style>
'@
```

The `Head` parameter of `ConvertTo-Html` is used to add the element to the document:

```
Get-Process |
    ConvertTo-Html -Property Name, Id, WorkingSet -Head $css |
    Set-Content report.html
```

The CSS language is complex and very capable. The elements that are used in the preceding code, and many more, are documented with examples on the W3Schools website: https://www.w3schools.com/css/.

Different browsers support different parts of the CSS language, and email clients tend to support a yet smaller set. Testing how a document renders in the expected client is an important part of developing HTML content.

The `ConvertTo-Html` command can be used to build HTML documents very quickly; these can be sent as email content or used as web pages.

ConvertTo-Html and Send-MailMessage

`ConvertTo-Html` outputs an array of strings, while `Send-MailMessage` will only accept a body as a string. Attempting to use the output from `ConvertTo-Html` with `Send-MailMessage` directly will raise an error.

Send-MailMessage is obsolete

The Send-MailMessage command is obsolete because it cannot support modern encryption used by modern mail services.

If Send-MailMessage is being used to send an email in plain text using an internal mail relay this is not important.

If it is being used to send via a public service, alternatives should be considered.

Several modules on the PowerShell gallery implement drop-in substitute commands based on the MailKit library, which supports modern encryption: https://www.powershellgallery.com/packages?q=MailKit.

The Out-String command may be added to ensure the output from ConvertTo-Html is a string:

```
$messageBody = Get-Process |
    ConvertTo-Html Name, Id, WorkingSet -Head $css |
    Out-String
```

When ConvertTo-Html is asked to convert content that includes special characters, those special characters will be replaced.

Windows PowerShell and ConvertTo-Html

In Windows PowerShell, the ConvertTo-Html command incorrectly handles single-property objects when writing HTML content.

For example, in PowerShell 7 the following command will generate a small HTML fragment:

```
Get-Process pwsh, powershell -ErrorAction Ignore |
    Select-Object Name -First 2 |
    ConvertTo-Html
```

The table header in the resulting document will be written as shown below:

```
<tr><th>Name</th></tr>
```

When the same command is used in Windows PowerShell, the table header is incorrectly written as:

```
<tr><th>*</th></tr>
```

The problem in Windows PowerShell would have to be fixed after the HTML content is generated:

```
(Get-Process pwsh, powershell |
    Select-Object Name -First 2 |
    ConvertTo-Html) -replace '\*', 'Name'
```

A similar technique can be used to modify HTML content after it has been generated.

Modifying HTML content

At times it is necessary to modify generated HTML content so that it displays as intended.

The object created by the snippet below includes an array of values:

```
[PSCustomObject]@{
    Name   = 'Name'
    Values = 'First', 'Second'
}
```

If this is converted to HTML, the Values column will contain the string System.Object[]. This value might be joined before generating the HTML content. For example, the value might be joined using a comma:

```
[PSCustomObject]@{
    Name   = 'Name'
    Values = 'First', 'Second'
} | Select-Object Name, @{
    Name = 'Values'; Expression = { $_.Values -join ', ' }
} | ConvertTo-Html
```

Joining the value using a line break is slightly more complicated. The expression above can be modified to use:

```
@{
    Name = 'Values'; Expression = { $_.Values -join "`n" }
}
```

However, the browser will not render a newline character as a line break. The values will appear joined by a space:

Name   Values

Name First Second

Figure 12.1: Missing line break

The <br /> token is required to make a line break, but this cannot be inserted into the string before ConvertTo-Html as it will be encoded by the command. This problem is shown below:

```
[PSCustomObject]@{
    Name   = 'Name'
    Values = 'First', 'Second'
} | Select-Object Name, @{
    Name = 'Values'; Expression = { $_.Values -join '<br />' }
} | ConvertTo-Html |
    Set-Content file.html
```

If the file content is viewed in a browser, it will include <br /> as a literal value.

Name   Values

Name First
Second

*Figure 12.2: Literal
*

If the file is viewed as text, it can be shown to contain an escaped version of the line break token:

```
<tr><td>Name</td><td>First&lt;br /&gt;Second</td></tr>
```

To work around this problem, a placeholder can be added to the HTML content, and that placeholder replaced after the content is generated:

```
$content = [PSCustomObject]@{
    Name   = 'Name'
    Values = 'First', 'Second'
} | Select-Object Name, @{
    Name = 'Values'; Expression = { $_.Values -join '%BR%' }
} | ConvertTo-Html
$content -replace '%BR%', '<br />' |
    Set-Content file.html
```

This time the content will render with an HTML line break in the browser:

Name Values

Name First
         Second

Figure 12.3: Replaced token

Replacing fragments of content in a generated document is a great way to add additional styling and formatting, especially when combined with a style element.

HTML is one of several text-based formats supported by PowerShell and XML is another (working with XML content is a common requirement within PowerShell).

XML commands

Extensible Markup Language (XML) is a plain text format that is used to store structured data. XML is written to be both human and machine readable.

PowerShell includes the Select-Xml and ConvertTo-Xml commands to work with XML content.

Before exploring the commands, it is useful to understand the basic structure of an XML document.

About XML

XML documents often begin with a declaration, as shown here:

```
<?xml version="1.0" encoding="utf-8"?>
```

This declaration has three possible attributes. The *version* attribute is mandatory when a declaration is included:

- *version*: The XML version, 1.0 or 1.1.
- *encoding*: The file encoding, most frequently utf-8 or utf-16.
- *standalone*: Whether the XML file uses an internal or external **Document Type Definition (DTD)**; permissible values are yes or no.

The use of the standalone directive with DTD is beyond the scope of this chapter.

Elements and attributes

XML is similar in appearance to HTML. Elements begin and end with a tag name. The tag name describes the name of an element, such as in the following example:

```
<?xml version="1.0"?>
<rootElement>value</rootElement>
```

An XML document can only have one root element, but an element may have many descendants:

```
<?xml version="1.0"?>
<rootElement>
    <firstChild>1</firstChild>
    <secondChild>2</secondChild>
</rootElement>
```

An element may also have attributes. The rootElement element in the following example has an attribute named attr:

```
<?xml version="1.0"?>
<rootElement attr="value">
    <child>1</child>
</rootElement>
```

Any XML document may include references to one or more schemas. When more than one schema is in use, the schemas are applied to a document (or parts of a document) using a namespace attribute.

Namespaces

XML documents can use one or more namespaces. A namespace is normally used to associate a node or set of nodes with a specific XML schema.

XML namespaces are declared in an attribute with a name prefixed by `xmlns:`, as in the following example:

```
<?xml version="1.0"?>
<rootElement xmlns:item="http://namespaces/item">
    <item:child>1</item:child>
</rootElement>
```

The XML namespace uses a URL as a unique identifier. The identifier is used to describe an element as belonging to a schema.

Schemas

An XML schema can be used to describe and constrain the elements, attributes, and values within an XML document.

About DTDs

A document type definition, or DTD, may be used to constrain the content of an XML file. As DTDs have little bearing on the use of XML in PowerShell, they are considered beyond the scope of this book.

XML schema definitions are saved with an XSD extension. Schema files can be used to validate the content of an XML file.

The following is a simple schema that defines the elements and values permissible in the `item` namespace of the previous XML document:

```
<?xml version="1.0"?>
<xs:schema xmlns:xs="http://www.w3.org/2001/XMLSchema"
           targetNamespace="http://namespaces/item"
           xmlns="https://www.w3schools.com"
           elementFormDefault="qualified">
    <xs:element name="rootElement">
        <xs:element name="child" type="xs:string" />
    </xs:element>
</xs:schema>
```

Schemas are explored again later in this chapter when validating a document or inferring a schema from an existing document.

Select-Xml

The `Select-Xml` command may be used to search XML documents using the XPath query language. PowerShell (and .NET) uses `XPath 1.0`.

More about XPath

The structure and format of XPath queries are beyond the scope of this chapter. However, web resources are available, including the XPath reference:

```
https://learn.microsoft.com/en-us/previous-versions/dotnet/
netframework-4.0/ms256115(v=vs.100).
```

Function names, element names, and values used in XPath queries, and XML in general, are case-sensitive.

Given the following XML snippet, Select-Xml might use an XPath expression to select the engines of green cars:

```
$string = @"
<?xml version="1.0"?>
<cars>
    <car type="Saloon">
        <colour>Green</colour>
        <doors>4</doors>
        <transmission>Automatic</transmission>
        <engine>
            <size>2.0</size>
            <cylinders>4</cylinders>
        </engine>
    </car>
</cars>
"@
```

The XPath parameter and the result are shown here:

```
PS> Select-Xml -XPath '//car[colour="Green"]/engine' -Content $string |
    Select-Object -ExpandProperty Node

size    cylinders
----    ---------
2.0     4
```

The XPath query breaks down as follows:

- //car: Find car elements anywhere in the document.
- [colour="Green"]: Filter where the colour element is green.
- /engine: Find engine elements directly under the car element.

When the XML document includes namespaces, Select-Xml must include the Namespace parameter.

Select-Xml and namespaces

Each of the namespaces used in an XPath expression used to search a document must be included in the Namespace parameter as a hashtable when performing a search:

```
[Xml]$xml = @"
<?xml version="1.0"?>
<cars xmlns:c="http://example/cars">
    <car type="Saloon">
        <c:colour>Green</c:colour>
        <c:doors>4</c:doors>
        <c:transmission>Automatic</c:transmission>
        <c:engine>
            <size>2.0</size>
            <cylinders>4</cylinders>
        </c:engine>
    </car>
</cars>
"@
Select-Xml '//car' -Xml $xml -Namespace @{
    c = 'http://example/cars'
}
```

In the preceding example, the document uses the prefix "c" to refer to the http://example/cars namespace. This prefix is repeated in the XPath search, and in the Namespace parameter for Select-Xml.

The prefix itself is, in this context, unimportant. The ID, or the **Uniform Resource Identifier (URI)**, is the critical part. The prefix value can therefore be changed in the search, provided that the new prefix value uses the same URI.

```
[Xml]$xml = @"
<?xml version="1.0"?>
<cars xmlns:c="http://example/cars">
    <car type="Saloon">
        <c:colour>Green</c:colour>
        <c:doors>4</c:doors>
        <c:transmission>Automatic</c:transmission>
        <c:engine>
            <size>2.0</size>
            <cylinders>4</cylinders>
        </c:engine>
    </car>
</cars>
"@
```

```
Select-Xml '//car' -Xml $xml -Namespace @{
    x = 'http://example/cars'
}
```

The result of the search will show the prefix used in the search, not the prefix from the XML document as shown below:

```
Node    Path         Pattern
----    ----         -------
engine  InputStream  //car/x:engine
```

Select-Xml is useful for finding content within an XML document. The ConvertTo-Xml command may be useful when creating an XML representation of an object.

ConvertTo-Xml

The ConvertTo-Xml command creates an XML representation of an object as an XmlDocument. For example, the current PowerShell process object might be converted into XML:

```
Get-Process -Id $pid | ConvertTo-Xml
```

The command used in the previous example creates an XML representation of the object. All numeric values are stored as strings. For example:

```
$xml = Get-Process -Id $pid |
    Select-Object Name, WorkingSet |
    ConvertTo-Xml
```

The resulting formatted XML document is shown below:

```
<?xml version="1.0" encoding="utf-8"?>
<Objects>
    <Object Type="System.Management.Automation.PSCustomObject">
        <Property Name="Name" Type="System.String">pwsh</Property>
        <Property Name="WorkingSet" Type="System.Int32">190771200</Property>
    </Object>
</Objects>
```

Because the format is XML, all values are stored as a string:

```
$property = $xml.Objects.Object.Property |
    Where-Object Name -eq WorkingSet
$property.'#text'.GetType()
```

The example above shows that the WorkingSet property is represented in the XML document as a string, shown below:

```
IsPublic IsSerial Name                 BaseType
-------- -------- ----                 --------
True     True     String               System.Object
```

The type names expressed in the XML document have no special meaning in PowerShell. A converter would have to be written if they were to be used.

The ConvertTo-Xml command is very rarely seen. It does not generate a particularly useful document. There is no complementary ConvertFrom command that can be used to bring the object back into PowerShell.

Bespoke XML formats are more common, while for detailed serialization, the ConvertTo-CliXml and ConvertFrom-CliXml commands might be used. The *-CliXml commands were introduced in *Chapter 7, Working with .NET*.

When changing documents, the System.Xml.XmlDocument type is frequently used.

System.Xml

PowerShell primarily uses the System.Xml.XmlDocument type to work with XML content. This type is part of the System.Xml namespace. The documentation for the types available in this namespace is available in the .NET reference: https://learn.microsoft.com/en-gb/dotnet/api/system.xml.

The System.Xml.XmlDocument type is normally used via a type accelerator, [Xml].

The XML type accelerator

The XML type accelerator can be used to create instances of XmlDocument, as shown in the following code:

```
[Xml]$xml = @"
<?xml version="1.0"?>
<cars>
    <car type="Saloon">
        <colour>Green</colour>
        <doors>4</doors>
        <transmission>Automatic</transmission>
        <engine>
            <size>2.0</size>
            <cylinders>4</cylinders>
        </engine>
    </car>
</cars>
"@
```

Elements and attributes of an XmlDocument object may be accessed as if they were properties. This is a feature of the PowerShell language rather than the .NET object:

```
PS> $xml.cars.car

type            : Saloon
```

```
colour        : Green
doors         : 4
transmission  : Automatic
engine        : engine
```

If the document contains more than one car element, each of the instances will be returned. Content may be filtered using Where-Object if required, as in the following example:

```
[Xml]$xml = @"
<?xml version="1.0"?>
<cars>
    <car type="Saloon">
        <colour>Green</colour>
    </car>
    <car type="Saloon">
        <colour>Blue</colour>
    </car>
</cars>
"@
$xml.cars.car | Where-Object type -eq 'Saloon'
```

Treating the XML document as a PowerShell object makes opening the document very convenient and requires no specialist knowledge of the XmlDocument type.

Searching large documents using Where-Object can be slow. For larger documents, XPath is more appropriate.

XPath and XmlDocument

The Select-Xml command introduced earlier in this chapter is one way of searching a document. If the document is held in a variable with the expectation that changes are to be made, then you can use the SelectNodes and SelectSingleNodes methods.

The following SelectNodes method is used with an XPath expression to find the engine node for all car elements where the value of the colour element is Green:

```
[Xml]$xml = @"
<?xml version="1.0"?>
<cars>
    <car type="Saloon">
        <colour>Green</colour>
        <doors>4</doors>
        <transmission>Automatic</transmission>
        <engine>
            <size>2.0</size>
            <cylinders>4</cylinders>
```

```
        </engine>
    </car>
</cars>
"@
$xml.SelectNodes('//car[colour="Green"]/engine')
```

The SelectNodes method is appropriate when more than one element might be returned (or an un-known number is expected).

SelectNodes and XPathNodeList

If the SelectNodes method is called, and there are no results, an empty XPathNodeList object is returned. The following condition is flawed:

```
$nodes = $xml.SelectNodes('//car[colour="Blue"]')
if ($nodes) {
    Write-Host "A blue car record exists"
}
```

In this case, using the Count property is a better approach. The condition below will only succeed if the document contains at least one matching node:

```
if ($nodes.Count -ge 1) {
    Write-Host "A blue car record exists"
}
```

If a single element is expected from a search, the SelectSingleNodes method can be used instead:

```
[Xml]$xml = @"
<?xml version="1.0"?>
<cars>
    <car type="Saloon">
        <numberPlate>abcd</numberPlate>
        <colour>Green</colour>
        <doors>4</doors>
        <transmission>Automatic</transmission>
        <engine>
            <size>2.0</size>
            <cylinders>4</cylinders>
        </engine>
    </car>
</cars>
"@
$xml.SelectSingleNode('//car[numberPlate="abcd"]')
```

This is useful when retrieving an element with a specific identity, where the match will be unique.

XML documents often use namespaces to indicate that certain elements belong to a specific schema. These namespaces must be provided when searching the content of a document.

Working with namespaces

If an XML document includes a namespace, then queries for elements within the document are more difficult. Not only must the namespace tag be included, but XmlNamespaceManager must be defined. XmlNamespaceManager is used to describe the different namespaces in use in the document.

The document below includes a default namespace statement that will affect how the SelectSingleNode and SelectNodes methods can be used:

```
[Xml]$xml = @"
<?xml version="1.0"?>
<cars xmlns="http://example/cars">
    <car type="Saloon">
        <numberPlate>abcd</numberPlate>
        <colour>Green</colour>
        <doors>4</doors>
        <transmission>Automatic</transmission>
        <engine>
            <size>2.0</size>
            <cylinders>4</cylinders>
        </engine>
    </car>
</cars>
"@
```

Unlike the example used when exploring Select-Xml, this namespace is a default and is implicitly applicable to all elements (nodes and attributes).

Attempting to search the document using SelectNodes with a filter for a specific element name will return no results:

```
$xml.SelectNodes('//engine')
```

Using Select-Xml would also show no results:

```
Select-Xml -Xml $xml -XPath '//engine'
```

When using the SelectNodes method, XmlNamespaceManager must be built first and passed as an argument. XmlNamespaceManager itself requires the NameTable property from the XML document as an argument.

```
$namespaceManager = [System.Xml.XmlNamespaceManager]::new(
    $xml.NameTable
)
```

Each namespace used by the document is added to the namespace manager. Default namespaces can be given an arbitrary prefix name if the prefix is included in the XPath query.

```
$namespaceManager.AddNamespace('any', 'http://example/cars')
```

Viewing the namespace manager variable will just list the namespaces it knows:

```
PS> $namespaceManager
xmlns
xml
any
```

Then the namespace manager can be used to search the document. Note that the XPath query includes the prefix on each element name.

```
$xml.SelectNodes(
    '//any:car[any:colour="Green"]/any:engine',
    $namespaceManager
)
```

The preceding code will find the engine node from the document, as shown below:

```
size cylinders
---- ---------
2.0  4
```

It is unfortunately not possible to omit the made-up prefix in this example where a default namespace is used.

XML documents, such as group policy reports, are difficult to work with as they often contain many different namespaces. Each of the possible namespaces must be added to a namespace manager for a search using those namespaces to be successful.

Creating XML documents

PowerShell can be used to create XML documents from scratch. One possible way to do this is by using the XmlWriter class. An instance of the XmlWriter class is created using the Create static method:

```
$writer = [System.Xml.XmlWriter]::Create("$pwd\newfile.xml")
$writer.WriteStartDocument()
$writer.WriteStartElement('cars')
$writer.WriteStartElement('car')
$writer.WriteAttributeString('type', 'Saloon')
$writer.WriteElementString('colour', 'Green')
$writer.WriteEndElement()
$writer.WriteEndElement()
$writer.Flush()
$writer.Close()
```

Methods from the `XmlWriter` are called in turn to add content to the newly created document:

- `WriteStartDocument` – Adds the XML declaration.
- `WriteStartElement` – Adds a new element as a child of any current element.
- `WriteAttributeString` – Adds an attribute to the current element.
- `WriteElementString` – Writes text data for the element.
- `WriteEndElement` – Closes the current element and moves up to a parent.
- `Flush` – Writes all pending content back to the file stream.
- `Close` – Closes the stream and allows the file to be used by other processes.

The use of the `Create` method of this type is described in the .NET reference: https://learn.microsoft.com/dotnet/api/system.xml.xmlwriter.create.

Elements opened by `WriteStartElement` must be closed to maintain a consistent document.

The `XmlWriter` class is a buffered writer; content is not immediately written, it is held in a buffer and periodically flushed or pushed to the underlying file (or stream). The `Flush` method is called at the end to ensure all content of the buffer has been written to the file.

The format of the generated XML can be changed by supplying an `XmlWriterSettings` object when calling the `Create` method. For example, it might be desirable to write line breaks and indent elements, as shown in the following example:

```
$writerSettings = [System.Xml.XmlWriterSettings]@{
    Indent = $true
}
$writer = [System.Xml.XmlWriter]::Create(
    "$pwd\newfile.xml",
    $writerSettings
)
$writer.WriteStartDocument()
$writer.WriteStartElement('cars')
$writer.WriteStartElement('car')
$writer.WriteAttributeString('type', 'Saloon')
$writer.WriteElementString('colour', 'Green')
$writer.WriteEndElement()
$writer.WriteEndElement()
$writer.Flush()
$writer.Close()
```

The preceding example creates a short XML document in a file named `newfile.xml`. The following shows the content of the file:

```
<?xml version="1.0" encoding="utf-8"?>
<cars>
```

```
<car type="Saloon">
  <colour>Green</colour>
</car>
</cars>
```

Modifying an existing document is a common requirement. A document can be changed in several ways.

Modifying element and attribute values

Existing elements in an XML document can be modified by assigning a new value. For example, the misspelling of `Appliances` could be corrected:

```
[Xml]$xml = @"
<?xml version="1.0"?>
<items>
    <item name='Fridge'>
        <category>Appliances</category>
    </item>
    <item name='Cooker'>
        <category>Appliances</category>
    </item>
</items>
"@
($xml.items.item | Where-Object name -eq 'Fridge').category = 'Appliances'
```

Attributes may be changed in the same way; the interface does not distinguish between the two value types.

A direct assignment of a new value cannot be used if the XML document contains more than one element or attribute with the same name (at the same level). For example, the following XML snippet has two values with the same name:

```
[Xml]$xml = @"
<?xml version="1.0"?>
<list>
    <name>one</name>
    <name>two</name>
</list>
"@
```

The first value may be changed if it is uniquely identified and selected:

```
$xml.list.SelectSingleNode('./name[.="one"]').'#text' = 'three'
```

The following example shows a similar change being made to the value of an attribute:

```
[Xml]$xml = @"
<?xml version="1.0"?>
    <list name='letters'>
    <name>1</name>
</list>
"@
$xml.SelectSingleNode('/list[@name="letters"]').
    SetAttribute('name', 'numbers')
```

The @ symbol preceding name in the XPath expression denotes that the value type is an attribute. If the attribute referred to by the SetAttribute method does not exist, it will be created.

Adding elements

Elements must be created before they can be added to an existing document. Elements are created in the context of a document:

```
[Xml]$xml = @"
<?xml version="1.0"?>
<list type='numbers'>
    <name>1</name>
</list>
"@
$newElement = $xml.CreateElement('name')
$newElement.InnerText = 2
$null = $xml.list.AppendChild($newElement)
```

The example above creates a new element called name, sets the value (InnerText) to 2, and then adds it as a child of the existing list element.

When AppendChild is used, the added element is returned as output. This output is suppressed by assigning the statement to null.

The command below saves the XML document to a file and then displays the file. The file is used to format the document for display in this example:

```
PS> $xml.Save("$pwd\newelement.xml")
PS> Get-Content newelement.xml
<?xml version="1.0"?>
<list type="numbers">
  <name>1</name>
  <name>2</name>
</list>
```

Complex elements may be built up by repeatedly using the Create method of the XmlDocument (held in the $xml variable).

If the new node is substantial, it may be easier to treat the new node set as a separate document and merge one into the other.

Removing elements and attributes

Elements may be removed from a document by selecting the node, then calling the RemoveChild method on the parent:

```
[Xml]$xml = @"
<?xml version="1.0"?>
<list type='numbers'>
    <name>1</name>
    <name>2</name>
    <name>3</name>
</list>
"@
$node = $xml.SelectSingleNode('/list/*[.="3"]')
$null = $node.ParentNode.RemoveChild($node)
```

The RemoveAll method is also available; however, this removes all children (and attributes) of the selected node.

Attributes are also easy to remove from a document:

```
$xml.list.RemoveAttribute('type')
```

The result of these two changes to the document can be viewed. A file is used to format the XML content for this example:

```
PS> $xml.Save("$pwd\remove.xml")
PS> Get-Content remove.xml
<?xml version="1.0"?>
<list>
  <name>1</name>
  <name>2</name>
</list>
```

At times it is necessary to copy content between two different XML documents. Let's look at this now.

Copying nodes between documents

Nodes (elements, attributes, and so on) can be copied and moved between different XML documents. To bring a node from an external document into another, it must first be imported.

The following example creates two simple XML documents. The first (the xml variable) is the intended destination. The newNodes variable contains a set of elements that should be copied:

```
[Xml]$xml = @"
<?xml version="1.0"?>
<list type='numbers'>
    <name>1</name>
</list>
"@
[Xml]$newNodes = @"
<root>
    <name>2</name>
    <name>3</name>
    <name>4</name>
</root>
"@
```

Copying the name nodes requires each node to be selected in turn, imported into the original document, and added to the desired node:

```
foreach ($node in $newNodes.SelectNodes('/root/name')) {
    $newNode = $xml.ImportNode($node, $true)
    $null = $xml.list.AppendChild($newNode)
}
```

The ImportNode method requires two parameters: the node from the foreign document (newNodes) and the specification of whether the import is deep (one level or fully recursive).

The resulting XML can be viewed by inspecting the OuterXml property of the xml variable:

```
PS> $xml.OuterXml
<?xml version="1.0"?><list type="numbers"><name>1</name><name>2</name><name>3</
name><name>4</name></list>
```

The structure and content of an XML document may be described by a schema, as we'll see next.

Schema validation

XML documents that reference a schema can be validated against that schema. The schema defines which elements and attributes may be present, the values and value types, and even the order in which elements can appear.

Windows PowerShell comes with several XML files with associated schema in the help files. For example, here's the help file for ISE:

```
PS> Get-Item $env:windir\System32\WindowsPowerShell\v1.0\modules\ISE\en-US\ISE-
help.xml
```

```
        Directory: C:\Windows\System32\WindowsPowerShell\v1.0\modules\ISE\en-US


Mode                    LastWriteTime          Length Name
----                    -------------          ------ ----
-a----          29/11/16      07:57             33969 ISE-help.xml
```

This file has been chosen as it will fail schema validation.

The schema documents used by the help content are saved in C:\Windows\System32\WindowsPowerShell\ v1.0\Schemas\PSMaml.

The following snippet may be used to load the schema files and then test the content of the document:

```
$path = 'C:\Windows\System32\WindowsPowerShell\v1.0\modules\ISE\en-US\ISE-help.
xml'
$schemaPath = 'C:\Windows\System32\WindowsPowerShell\v1.0\Schemas\PSMaml\maml.
xsd'

$document = [Xml]::new()
$document.Load($path)
$document.Schemas.XmlResolver = [System.Xml.XmlUrlResolver]::new()
$document.Schemas.Add(
    'http://schemas.microsoft.com/maml/2004/10',
    $schemaPath
)
$document.Validate({
    param ($sender, $eventArgs)
    if ($eventArgs.Severity -in 'Error', 'Warning') {
        Write-Host $eventArgs.Message
    }
})
```

The results of the validation are written to the console in the preceding example. The following shows the first message:

```
The element 'details' in namespace 'http://schemas.microsoft.com/maml/dev/
command/2004/10' has invalid child element 'verb' in namespace 'http://schemas.
microsoft.com/maml/dev/command/2004/10'. List of possible elements expected:
'description' in namespace 'http://schemas.microsoft.com/maml/2004/10'.
```

The XML document refers to several schema documents; MAML content is complex. The schema set will only correctly load in .NET Core if XmlSchemaSet ($document.Schemas) is given an XmlUrlResolver to use to process the schema references in the document. This property is mandatory in .NET Core and optional in .NET Framework. The documentation describing this type is available in the .NET reference: https://learn.microsoft.com/dotnet/api/system.xml.xmlurlresolver.

The argument for Validate is a script block that is executed each time an error is encountered. Write-Host is used to print a message to the console. A value cannot be directly returned as the script block is executed in response to an event. A global variable can be used to collect the results for later reference:

```
$path = 'C:\Windows\System32\WindowsPowerShell\v1.0\modules\ISE\en-US\ISE-help.
xml'
$schemaPath = 'C:\Windows\System32\WindowsPowerShell\v1.0\Schemas\PSMaml\maml.
xsd'

$document = [Xml]::new()
$document.Load($path)
$document.Schemas.XmlResolver = [System.Xml.XmlUrlResolver]::new()
$document.Schemas.Add(
    'http://schemas.microsoft.com/maml/2004/10',
    $schemaPath
)
$validateResult = [System.Collections.Generic.List[object]]::new()
$document.Validate({
    param ($sender, $eventArgs)
    if ($eventArgs.Severity -in 'Error', 'Warning') {
        $validateResult.Add($eventArgs)
    }
})
```

The `$validateResult` list will include each of the failure messages from the validation process. The following shows the first of these:

```
PS> $validateResult[0]

Severity  Exception
--------  ---------
   Error  System.Xml.Schema.XmlSchemaValidationException: The e...
```

The line number and line position information are not available using this technique.

Inferring a schema

Normally, a schema is created before writing an XML document. It is possible to take an existing XML document and create (or infer) a schema from the document.

Schema documents can be inferred from an existing XML document using the XmlSchemaInference type.

The following document is based on an example used earlier in this chapter:

```
$xml = [Xm"]@"
<?xml versi"n="".0"?>
<cars>
    <car ty"e="Sal"on">
        <colour>Green</colour>
    </car>
</car">
"@
```

XmlReader or XmlNodeReader is required for the InferSchema method. These reader types can be created from the previous XML document we created:

```
$reader = [System.Xml.XmlNodeReader]$xml
```

In the preceding example, XmlSchema is created from an existing XmlDocument in memory. XmlReader can be created using any of the options provided by the Create static method of the XmlReader class, such as providing a full path to an existing XML file: https://learn.microsoft.com//dotnet/api/system.xml.xmlreader.create.

XmlReader is passed to the InferSchema method of the XmlSchemaInference type to create a SchemaSet.

```
$xmlSchemaInference = [System.Xml.Schema.XmlSchemaInference]::new()
$schemaSet = $xmlSchemaInference.InferSchema($reader)
```

In the preceding example, the SchemaSet will contain a single document that can be written to a stream or XmlWriter. StringWriter is used to write the schema in the proceeding code; the ToString method used at the end retrieves the schema that has been created.

The following shows the complete example with all the preceding steps:

```
$xml = [Xml]@"
<?xml version="1.0"?>
<cars>
    <car type="Saloon">
        <colour>Green</colour>
    </car>
</cars>
"@
$reader = [System.Xml.XmlNodeReader]$xml
$xmlSchemaInference = [System.Xml.Schema.XmlSchemaInference]::new()
$schemaSet = $xmlSchemaInference.InferSchema($reader)
$writer = [System.IO.StringWriter]::new()
$schemaSet.Schemas()[0].Write($writer)
$writer.ToString()
```

The result is an XML schema document describing the structure of the XML document as shown below:

```
<?xml version="1.0" encoding="utf-16"?>
<xs:schema attributeFormDefault="unqualified" elementFormDefault="qualified"
xmlns:xs="http://www.w3.org/2001/XMLSchema">
  <xs:element name="cars">
    <xs:complexType>
      <xs:sequence>
        <xs:element name="car">
          <xs:complexType>
            <xs:sequence>
              <xs:element name="colour" type="xs:string" />
            </xs:sequence>
            <xs:attribute name="type" type="xs:string" use="required" />
          </xs:complexType>
        </xs:element>
      </xs:sequence>
    </xs:complexType>
  </xs:element>
</xs:schema>
```

If the XML document contains namespace declarations, a schema will be created for each namespace.

The reader can focus on a smaller part of the document by selecting an element and creating an XmlNodeReader at that point in the document. For example, the following snippet creates a schema for the car element only:

```
$reader = [System.Xml.XmlNodeReader]$xml.SelectSingleNode('//car')
$schemaSet = $xmlSchemaInference.InferSchema($reader)
$writer = [System.IO.StringWriter]::new()
$schemaSet.Schemas()[0].Write($writer)
$writer.ToString()
```

The smaller inferred schema from the example above is shown below:

```
<?xml version="1.0" encoding="utf-16"?>
<xs:schema attributeFormDefault="unqualified" elementFormDefault="qualified"
xmlns:xs="http://www.w3.org/2001/XMLSchema">
  <xs:element name="car">
    <xs:complexType>
      <xs:sequence>
        <xs:element name="colour" type="xs:string" />
      </xs:sequence>
      <xs:attribute name="type" type="xs:string" use="required" />
    </xs:complexType>
```

```
    </xs:element>
  </xs:schema>
```

The resultant schema can be modified as appropriate to meet the needs of the document it is intended to validate.

The System.Xml namespace contains the classes that are most used in PowerShell. .NET also includes an alternative set of classes to work with XML documents.

System.Xml.Linq

The System.Xml.Linq namespace was added with .NET 3.5. This is known as **LINQ** to XML. **Language Integrated Query (LINQ)** is used to describe a query in the same language as the rest of a program. Therefore, interacting with a complex XML document does not require the use of XPath queries.

System.Xml.Linq is loaded by default in PowerShell 7. Windows PowerShell can make use of System.Xml.Linq once the required assembly has been added:

```
Add-Type -AssemblyName System.Xml.Linq
```

As a newer interface, System.Xml.Linq tends to be more consistent. The same syntax is used to create a document from scratch that is used to add elements and so on.

Opening documents

The Xdocument class is used to load or parse a document. XML content may be cast to Xdocument in the same way that content is cast using the [Xml] type accelerator:

```
[System.Xml.Linq.Xdocument]$xDocument = @"
<?xml version="1.0"?>
<cars>
    <car type="Saloon">
        <colour>Green</colour>
        <doors>4</doors>
        <transmission>Automatic</transmission>
        <engine>
            <size>2.0</size>
            <cylinders>4</cylinders>
        </engine>
    </car>
</cars>
"@
$xDocument.Save("$pwd\cars.xml")
```

If the content has been saved to a file, the Load method may be used with a filename:

```
PS> $xDocument = [System.Xml.Linq.Xdocument]::Load("$pwd\cars.xml")
PS> $xDocument.ToString()

<cars>
  <car type="Saloon">
    <colour>Green</colour>
    <doors>4</doors>
    <transmission>Automatic</transmission>
    <engine>
      <size>2.0</size>
      <cylinders>4</cylinders>
    </engine>
  </car>
</cars>
```

The Xdocument object may also be searched.

Selecting nodes

LINQ to XML uses PowerShell to query the content of XML files. This is achieved by combining the methods that are made available through XDocument (or XContainer or XElement). Methods are available to find attributes and elements, either as immediate children or deeper within a document:

```
$xDocument = [System.Xml.Linq.XDocument]::Load("$pwd\cars.xml")
$xDocument.Descendants('car').
    Where( { $_.Element('colour').Value -eq 'Green' } ).
    Element('engine')
```

As the query script block encapsulated by the Where method is native PowerShell, the comparison operation (-eq) is case-insensitive. The selection of the element by name is case-sensitive.

Although it is not the preferred approach, XPath can still be used by calling the XPathSelectElements static method, as shown here:

```
[System.Xml.XPath.Extensions]::XPathSelectElements(
    $xDocument,
    '//car[colour="Green"]/engine'
)
```

Document creation using XDocument is must more succinct than using XmlWriter.

Creating documents

`System.Xml.Linq` can be used to create a document from scratch, as in the following example:

```
using namespace System.Xml.Linq

$xDocument = [XDocument]::new(
    [XDeclaration]::new('1.0', 'utf-8', 'yes'),
    [XElement]::new('list', @(
        [XAttribute]::new('type', 'numbers'),
        [XElement]::new('name', 1),
        [XElement]::new('name', 2),
        [XElement]::new('name', 3)
    ))
)
```

Using the System.Xml.Linq namespace

`using namespace System.Xml.Linq` is assumed in the remainder of the examples to reduce repetition of the namespace.

Converting the `XDocument` object into a string shows the document without the declaration:

```
PS> $xDocument.ToString()

<list type="numbers">
    <name>1</name>
    <name>2</name>
    <name>3</name>
</list>
```

The `Save` method may be used to write the document to a file:

```
$xDocument.Save("$pwd\test.xml")
```

Reviewing the document shows the declaration:

```
PS> Get-Content test.xml
<?xml version="1.0" encoding="utf-8" standalone="yes"?>
<list type="numbers">
    <name>1</name>
    <name>2</name>
    <name>3</name>
</list>
```

Like the types in the System.Xml namespace, System.Xml.Linq must be told about any namespaces in use.

Working with namespaces

LINQ to XML handles the specification of namespaces by adding an XNamespace object to an XName object, as in the following example:

```
PS> [XNameSpace]'http://example/cars' + [XName]'engine'

LocalName     Namespace            NamespaceName
---------     ---------            -------------
engine        http://example/cars  http://example/cars
```

As XNamespace expects to have XName added to it, casting to that type can be skipped, simplifying the expression:

```
[XNamespace]'http://example/cars' + 'engine'
```

A query for an element in a specific namespace will use the following format:

```
[XDocument]$xDocument = @"
<?xml version="1.0"?>
<cars xmlns:c="http://example/cars">
    <car type="Saloon">
        <c:colour>Green</c:colour>
        <c:doors>4</c:doors>
        <c:transmission>Automatic</c:transmission>
        <c:engine>
            <size>2.0</size>
            <cylinders>4</cylinders>
        </c:engine>
    </car>
</cars>
"@

$xNScars = [XNameSpace]'http://example/cars'
$xDocument.Descendants('car').ForEach( {
    $_.Element($xNScars + 'engine')
} )
```

Selected elements and attributes may be modified, as we'll see next.

Modifying element and attribute values

Modifying an existing node, whether it is an attribute or an element value, can be done by assigning a new value. In the following example, the category value is used to correct a typo in the Fridge item of the XML document:

```
[XDocument]$xDocument = @"
<?xml version="1.0"?>
<items>
    <item name='Fridge'>
        <category>Appliances</category>
    </item>
    <item name='Cooker'>
        <category>Appliances</category>
    </item>
</items>
"@
$xDocument.Element('items').
    Elements('item').
    Where( { $_.Attribute('name').Value -eq 'Fridge' } ).
    ForEach( { $_.Element('category').Value = 'Appliances' } )
```

Modifying the value of an attribute uses the same syntax:

```
[XDocument]$xDocument = @"
<?xml version="1.0"?>
<list name='letters'>
    <name>1</name>
</list>
"@
$xDocument.Element('list').Attribute('name').Value = 'numbers'
```

If the attribute does not exist, an error will be thrown:

```
PS> $xDocument.Element('list').Attribute('other').Value = 'numbers'
InvalidOperation: The property 'Value' cannot be found on this object. Verify
that the property exists and can be set.
```

The changes made by the preceding assignments may be viewed in the xDocument variable:

```
PS> $xDocument.ToString()
<list name="numbers">
  <name>1</name>
</list>
```

New nodes (elements and attributes) may be added to an existing document.

Adding nodes

Nodes can be added to an existing document by using the Add methods, which include Add, AddAfterSelf, AddBeforeSelf, and AddFirst. Consider the following example:

```
using namespace System.Xml.Linq

[XDocument]$xDocument = @"
<?xml version="1.0"?>
<list type='numbers'>
    <name>1</name>
</list>
"@
$xDocument.Element('list').
    Element('name').
    AddAfterSelf(@(
        [XElement]::new('name', 2),
        [XElement]::new('name', 3),
        [XElement]::new('name', 4)
    ))
```

The different Add methods afford a great deal of flexibility over the content of a document; in this case, the new elements appear after the <name>1</name> element:

```
PS> $xDocument.ToString()
<list type="numbers">
  <name>1</name>
  <name>2</name>
  <name>3</name>
  <name>4</name>
</list>
```

Content can also be removed from an XDocument, as we'll see next.

Removing nodes

The Remove method of XElement or XAttribute is used to remove the current node.

In the following example, the first name element is removed from the document:

```
[XDocument]$xDocument = @"
<?xml version="1.0"?>
<list type='numbers'>
    <name>1</name>
    <name>2</name>
    <name>3</name>
```

```
</list>
"@
$xDocument.Element('list').FirstNode.Remove()
```

Documents that use a schema may be validated against that schema, as we'll cover in the next section.

Schema validation

LINQ to XML can be used to validate an XML document against a schema file.

The ISE-help.xml XML document is validated against its schema in the following example:

```
using namespace System.Xml.Linq

$path = 'C:\Windows\System32\WindowsPowerShell\v1.0\modules\ISE\en-US\ISE-help.
xml'
$schemaPath = 'C:\Windows\System32\WindowsPowerShell\v1.0\Schemas\PSMaml\maml.
xsd'
$xDocument = [XDocument]::Load(
    $path,
    [LoadOptions]::SetLineInfo
)


$xmlSchemaSet = [System.Xml.Schema.XmlSchemaSet]::new()
$xmlSchemaSet.XmlResolver = [System.Xml.XmlUrlResolver]::new()
$null = $xmlSchemaSet.Add(
    'http://schemas.microsoft.com/maml/2004/10',
    $schemaPath
)
[System.Xml.Schema.Extensions]::Validate(
    $xDocument,
    $xmlSchemaSet,
    {
        param ($sender, $eventArgs)

        if ($eventArgs.Severity -in 'Error', 'Warning') {
            Write-Host $eventArgs.Message
            Write-Host ('  At {0} column {1}' -f
                $sender.LineNumber,
                $sender.LinePosition
            )
        }
    }
)
```

Positional information is made available by loading XDocument with the SetLineInfo option in the example above.

XML parsing and editing is an important feature in PowerShell. XML remains a popular data format.

JSON

JavaScript Object Notation (JSON) is a lightweight format used to store and transport data.

JSON is like XML in some respects. It is intended to be both human and machine readable. Additionally, like XML, JSON is written in plain text.

JSON is a form of serialization. Data can be converted to and from a string that represents that data. Like a hashtable, JSON-formatted objects are made up of key-value pairs, as in the example:

```
{
    "key1": "value1",
    "key2": "value2"
}
```

PowerShell 3 introduced the ConvertTo-Json and ConvertFrom-Json commands.

Newtonsoft JSON is native in PowerShell 7

PowerShell 7 (and PowerShell 6) use the JSON library from NewtonSoft to serialize and deserialize JSON content.

Advanced JSON serialization and deserialization are available using the classes in the Newtonsoft namespace. The capabilities are documented on the Newtonsoft website:

https://www.newtonsoft.com/json/help/html/Introduction.htm.

In PowerShell 7, the ConvertTo-Json and ConvertFrom-Json commands gain several new parameters. The parameters are explored in the following sections.

ConvertTo-Json

The ConvertTo-Json command can be used to convert a PowerShell object (or hashtable) into JSON:

```
Get-Process -Id $PID |
    Select-Object Name, Id, Path |
    ConvertTo-Json
```

The command above generates a JSON string like the example below:

```
{
    "Name":  "pwsh",
    "Id":  3944,
    "Path":  " C:\\Program Files\\PowerShell\\7\\pwsh.exe"
}
```

By default, ConvertTo-Json will convert objects into a depth of two. Running the following code will show how the value for three is simplified as a string:

```
@{
    one = @{     # 1st iteration (depth 1)
        two = @{     # 2nd iteration (depth 2)
            three = @{
                four = 'value'
            }
        }
    }
} | ConvertTo-Json
```

The three property is present, but the value is listed as System.Collections.Hashtable, as acquiring the value would need a third iteration. Setting the Depth parameter of ConvertTo-Json to 3 allows the properties under the key three to convert.

Going too deep

JSON serialization is a recursive operation. The depth may be increased, which is useful when converting a complex object.

Some value types may cause ConvertTo-Json to apparently hang. This is caused by the complexity of those value types. Such value types may include circular references.

A ScriptBlock object, for example, cannot be efficiently serialized as JSON. The following command takes over 15 seconds to complete and results in a string that's over 50 million characters long:

```
Measure-Command { { 'ScriptBlock' } |
    ConvertTo-Json -Depth 6 -Compress }
```

Increasing the recursion depth to 7 results in an error as keys (property names) begin to duplicate.

EnumsAsStrings

When ConvertTo-Json encounters an enumeration value, it writes that value as a numeric value by default. For example, DayOfWeek is written as a numeric value in the following:

```
@{ Today = (Get-Date).DayOfWeek } | ConvertTo-Json
```

For example, if it is Sunday, the value of Today will be 0, as shown below:

```
{
  "Today": 0
}
```

Conversely, running (Get-Date).DayOfWeek alone will return the name of the day. This change occurs because the DayOfWeek value is taken from the System.DayOfWeek enumeration.

In PowerShell 7, the switch parameter EnumsAsStrings may be used to write the value as a string instead of a number.

```
PS> @{ Today = (Get-Date).DayOfWeek } | ConvertTo-Json -EnumsAsStrings
{
  "Today": "Sunday"
}
```

This option is not available in Windows PowerShell.

In Windows PowerShell, the ConvertTo-Json command is unable to create an array when a single object is piped. This is where AsArray comes in handy.

AsArray

The ConvertTo-Json command is normally used as part of a pipeline. In a pipeline, the command is unable to determine whether the input object was originally an array.

In the following example the input is an array, but only one value is sent to the input pipeline for ConvertTo-Json.

```
@(Get-Process -ID $PID | Select-Object Name, ID) | ConvertTo-Json
```

To create a JSON array in Windows PowerShell, the value must be explicitly passed to the InputObject parameter:

```
ConvertTo-Json -InputObject @(
    Get-Process -ID $PID | Select-Object Name, ID
)
```

In PowerShell 7, the AsArray parameter can be used instead:

```
Get-Process -ID $PID |
    Select-Object Name, ID |
    ConvertTo-Json -AsArray
```

PowerShell 7 also offers control over how certain characters should be escaped by using the EscapeHandling parameter.

EscapeHandling

PowerShell 7 includes greater control over escape characters. By default, only JSON control characters are escaped in content. Additional options are included to escape all non-ASCII content (EscapeNonAscii), and to escape HTML control characters (EscapeHtml).

Support for these new values is provided by the Newtonsoft library: https://www.newtonsoft.com/json/help/html/T_Newtonsoft_Json_StringEscapeHandling.htm.

For example, the following string contains an accent over one character. The accent is preserved when converting to JSON:

```
PS> @{ String = 'Halló heimur' } | ConvertTo-Json
{
  "String": "Halló heimur"
}
```

If the `EscapeNonAscii` value for the `EscapeHandling` parameter is used, the resulting string will include a Unicode character sequence instead:

```
@{ String = 'Halló heimur' } |
    ConvertTo-Json -EscapeHandling EscapeNonAscii
```

This time the non-ASCII character is written as a Unicode character sequence, as shown below:

```
{
  "String": "Hall\u00f3 heimur"
}
```

This adds flexibility, allowing PowerShell to generate JSON content for a wider variety of other languages and applications.

PowerShell will correctly interpret either format when reading in content with the `ConvertFrom-Json` command.

ConvertFrom-Json

The `ConvertFrom-Json` command is used to turn a JSON document into an object, as in the following example:

```
'{ "Property": "Value" }' | ConvertFrom-Json
```

This creates a `PSCustomObject` with a single property as shown below:

```
Property
--------
Value
```

`ConvertFrom-Json` creates a `PSCustomObject` from the JSON content by default.

JSON understands several different data types, and each of these types is converted into an equivalent .NET type. The following example shows how each different type might be represented:

```
$object = @"
{
    "Decimal": 1.23,
    "String": "string",
    "Int32": 1,
```

```
    "Int64": 2147483648,
    "Boolean": true
}
"@ | ConvertFrom-Json
```

Once converted, the result is a custom object as the following shows:

```
PS> $object

Decimal : 1.23
String  : string
Int32   : 1
Int64   : 2147483648
Boolean : True
```

Inspecting individual elements after conversion reflects the type, as demonstrated in the following example:

```
PS> $object.Int64.GetType()

IsPublic IsSerial Name                     BaseType
-------- -------- ----                     --------
True     True     Int64                    System.ValueType

PS> $object.Boolean.GetType()

IsPublic IsSerial Name                     BaseType
-------- -------- ----                     --------
True     True     Boolean                  System.ValueType
```

JSON serialization within PowerShell is useful, but it is not perfect. For example, consider the result of converting Get-Date:

```
PS> Get-Date | ConvertTo-Json
{
    "value":  "\/Date(1489321529249)\/",
    "DisplayHint":  2,
    "DateTime":  "12 March 2017 12:25:29"
}
```

The value includes a DisplayHintNoteProperty and a DateTimeScriptProperty, added to the DateTime object. These add an extra layer of properties when converting back from JSON:

```
PS> Get-Date | ConvertTo-Json | ConvertFrom-Json
```

```
value                        DisplayHint    DateTime
-----                        -----------    --------
12/03/2017 12:27:25                    2    12 March 2017 12:27:25
```

The DateTime property can be removed using the following code:

```
Get-TypeData System.DateTime | Remove-TypeData
```

Dates without type data

Get-Date will appear to return nothing after running the previous command. The date is still present; this is an aesthetic problem only. Without the type data, PowerShell does not know how to display the date, which is ordinarily composed as follows:

```
$date = Get-Date
'{0} {1}' -f $date.ToLongDateString(), $date.ToLongTimeString()
```

DisplayHint is added by Get-Date, and therefore the command cannot be used when creating a date object for use in a JSON string.

Any extraneous members such as this would have to be tested for invalid members prior to conversion, which makes the solution more of a problem:

```
Get-TypeData System.DateTime | Remove-TypeData
[DateTime]::Now |
    ConvertTo-Json |
    ConvertFrom-Json |
    Select-Object *
```

The command above will show the properties of the new custom object as shown below:

```
Date        : 12/03/2017 00:00:00
Day         : 12
DayOfWeek   : Sunday
DayOfYear   : 71
Hour        : 12
Kind        : Utc
Millisecond : 58
Minute      : 32
Month       : 3
Second      : 41
Ticks       : 636249187610580000
TimeOfDay   : 12:32:41.0580000
Year        : 2017
```

By default, PowerShell converts JSON data into a custom object. In some cases, it may be preferable to read JSON content as a hashtable.

AsHashtable

By default, `ConvertFrom-Json` creates a `PSCustomObject` from the JSON content. This conversion includes nested objects in the JSON content.

In PowerShell 7, you can use the `AsHashtable` parameter to create a hashtable instead of a `PSCustomObject`:

```
$hashtable = @"
{
    "Decimal": 1.23,
    "String": "string",
    "Int32": 1,
    "Int64": 2147483648,
    "Boolean": true
}
"@ | ConvertFrom-Json -AsHashtable
```

The resulting hashtable can be viewed below:

```
PS> $hashtable

Name                             Value
----                             -----
Decimal                          1.23
String                           string
Int32                            1
Int64                            2147483648
Boolean                          True
```

If the JSON content includes nested objects, they are also converted into hashtables:

```
$hashtable = @"
{
    "Key": "Value",
    "Nested": {
        "Key": "NestedValue"
    }
}
"@ | ConvertFrom-Json -AsHashtable
```

In PowerShell, hashtable keys are not case-sensitive by default when created using @{}. hashtables created by `ConvertFrom-Json` have case-sensitive keys.

NoEnumerate

The NoEnumerate parameter is relevant when the root element in a document is an array, and that array contains only one element.

By default, ConvertFrom-Json will squash the array, returning a scalar value:

```
$content = @"
[
    { "Element": 1 }
]
"@ | ConvertFrom-Json
```

The output this command creates can be shown to be a scalar, a single value:

```
PS> $content.GetType()

IsPublic IsSerial Name                          BaseType
-------- -------- ----                          --------
True     False    PSCustomObject                System.Object
```

If NoEnumerate is used, the resulting type will be an array, Object[].

```
$content = @"
[
    { "Element": { "Value": 1 } }
]
"@ | ConvertFrom-Json -NoEnumerate
```

Inspecting the object type again will show that the result is an array.

```
PS> $content.GetType()

IsPublic IsSerial Name                          BaseType
-------- -------- ----                          --------
True     True     Object[]                      System.Array
```

JSON is an incredibly useful format, as it is available in many other languages and used by many other systems. It is an excellent way of drawing data into PowerShell or passing data along to another application or language.

Like XML, JSON content can be constrained or described using a schema.

Test-Json

The Test-Json command in PowerShell 7 allows JSON content to be validated against a schema.

The layout of a JSON schema is documented on the https://json-schema.org/ site. PowerShell 7 uses the draft-7 schema version.

A simple schema is created in a file as shown below:

```
Set-Content item.json -Value @'
{
    "$schema": "http://json-schema.org/draft-07/schema#",
    "$id": "item",
    "type": "object",
    "properties": {
        "name": { "type": "string" }
    },
    "required": [ "name" ],
    "additionalProperties": false
}
'@
```

This schema has the following features:

- The JSON document must include a name property.
- The name property must be a string.
- Additional properties are not permitted.

It can therefore be used to validate the following content:

```
PS> Test-Json -Json '{ "name": "first" }' -SchemaFile item.json
True
```

If an extra property is added to the JSON content, validation will fail:

```
PS> $json = '{ "name": "first", "position": 1 }'
PS> Test-Json -Json $json -SchemaFile item.json
Test-Json: The JSON is not valid with the schema: All values fail against the
false schema at '/position'
False
```

This error indicates that the position property is not permitted, and the content is no longer valid according to the schema.

If a Boolean result is required, the error can be ignored:

```
Test-Json -Json $json -SchemaFile item.json -ErrorAction Ignore
```

Schema documents can become quite complex. For example, the item.json schema above might be a small part of a larger schema. A parent object might be defined as follows:

```
Set-Content items.json -Value @'
{
    "$schema": "http://json-schema.org/draft-07/schema#",
```

```
    "$id": "items",
    "type": "object",
    "properties": {
        "items": {
            "anyOf": [
                { "$ref": "item.json" },
                {
                    "type": "array",
                    "minItems": 1,
                    "items": {
                        "$ref": "item.json"
                    }
                }
            ]
        }
    },
    "required": [ "items" ]
}
'@
```

This parent schema includes the `anyOf` keyword, which will successfully validate the following examples:

```
PS> $json = '{ "items": { "name": "first" } }'
PS> Test-Json -Json $json -SchemaFile .\items.json
True
```

Or an array of items:

```
PS> $json = '{"items": [ { "name": "first" }, { "name": "second" } ] }'
PS> Test-Json -Json $json -SchemaFile .\items.json
True
```

Note that the `items.json` schema references the `item.json` schema. This can be referenced by a relative or absolute file path.

If a schema ID is a URL, such as `http://example.com/items.json`, PowerShell will attempt to retrieve the schema from the specified URL. This is not desirable for schemas on the local file system.

Summary

This chapter took a brief look at working with HTML content and how HTML content is formatted.

Working with XML content is a common requirement. This chapter introduced the structure of XML, along with the use of `Select-Xml`, the `System.Xml` .NET types, and the `System.Xml.Linq` .NET types for working with XML content.

Finally, JSON serialization was introduced, along with the ConvertTo-Json and ConvertFrom-Json commands. JSON schemas were introduced as a means of validating the structure of a JSON document.

The next chapter explores working with **Representational State Transfer (REST)** and **Simple Object Access Protocol (SOAP)**-based web services in PowerShell.

Learn more on Discord

Read this book alongside other users, PowerShell experts, and the author himself. Ask questions, provide solutions to other readers, chat with the author via Ask Me Anything sessions, and much more.

Scan the QR code or visit the link to join the community.

https://packt.link/SecNet

13

Web Requests and Web Services

Representational State Transfer (REST) and **Simple Object Access Protocol (SOAP)** are often used as labels to refer to two different approaches to implementing a web-based **Application Programming Interface (API)**.

This chapter explores the client-side of this process, acting as the consumer of a web service rather than the author.

REST is extremely popular nowadays, and most web services seem to use this approach. From the developer's perspective, a REST-based service can be created very quickly, and a great deal can be done to automatically generate clients for such services. REST is stateless, meaning that each request is independent from other requests.

SOAP services are quite difficult to find, especially services that can be demonstrated. SOAP APIs are not stateless; the contract between the client and server is stricter, which can make using the services more complicated.

The growth of cloud-based services in recent years has pushed the chances of working with such interfaces from rare to almost certain.

This chapter covers the following topics:

- Web requests
- Working with REST
- Working with SOAP

This chapter has some technical requirements to consider.

Technical requirements

In addition to PowerShell and PowerShell Core, Visual Studio 2019 Community Edition or later is used to follow the SOAP service example.

SOAP interfaces typically use the `New-WebServiceProxy` command in Windows PowerShell. This command is not available in PowerShell 7, as the assembly it depends on is not available. The command is unlikely to be available in PowerShell Core unless it is rewritten.

Web requests, such as getting content from a website or downloading files, are a common activity in PowerShell, and this is the first topic we will cover.

Web requests

A background in web requests is valuable before delving into interfaces that run over the top of the **Hypertext Transfer Protocol (HTTP)**.

Each web request sent to a web server has an HTTP method.

HTTP methods

HTTP supports several different methods, including the following:

- GET
- HEAD
- POST
- PUT
- DELETE
- CONNECT
- OPTIONS
- TRACE
- PATCH

These methods are defined in the HTTP 1.1 specification in RFC 2616: `https://www.rfc-editor.org/rfc/rfc2616.html#section-9`.

It is common to find that a web server only supports a subset of these. In many cases, supporting too many methods is deemed to be a security risk.

GET is the most common method which is used to retrieve information from a server. After that, the POST method is the most common, which is used to send information from a client back to a server—for example, when entering values into a web form.

PUT and DELETE methods are sometimes supported by web APIs but less often by websites intended for users to view.

The HEAD method is less frequently used but is useful for getting a minimal response from a site. This method is explored again later in this section.

The OPTIONS method can sometimes be used to ask for the capabilities of a site. However, this method is rarely permitted by publicly accessible sites.

PowerShell uses either Invoke-WebRequest or Invoke-RestMethod to interact with web servers. Invoke-RestMethod is explored in more detail later in this chapter; it has a lot in common with Invoke-WebRequest.

Using Invoke-WebRequest

PowerShell can use `Invoke-WebRequest` to send HTTP requests to websites and receive responses. For example, the following command will return the response to a GET request to the **PowerShell Community** blog:

```
Invoke-WebRequest https://devblogs.microsoft.com/powershell-community/
```

The first few lines of output from the command above are shown below:

```
StatusCode        : 200
StatusDescription : OK
Content           : <!DOCTYPE html>
                    <html lang="en-US"  theme = "light">
                    <head>
                        <meta charset="UTF-8">
                        <script>
```

Since this attempt to show the content of a web page, the output is extensive.

When using PowerShell 7, a relatively simple parser is used to expose the content of the site. The response is split into different properties, including *Content*, *Headers*, *Images*, *Links*, and so on.

About parsing web pages

The properties of the response allow access to some of the simpler elements of the page. However, getting a simple list of articles, for example, is not easy from this response. Pages like this are written for users to consume in a browser, not for scripts to pull apart or scrape.

The parsed response from the website above can be termed basic parsing.

Windows PowerShell offers a more advanced form of parsing that is based on it using the Internet Explorer engine to interact with a web page and parse a response. PowerShell 7 does not do this, so in Windows PowerShell, the equivalent of the above command is:

```
Invoke-WebRequest https://devblogs.microsoft.com/powershell-community/
-UseBasicParsing
```

It is possible to attempt to get Windows PowerShell to perform more advanced parsing. However, since this is dependent on Internet Explorer, which is far too old, it is relatively common for it to struggle with modern content. The command may hang entirely.

Ultimately, getting website content from a page intended to be rendered in a browser for an end user is a complex topic. Websites including dynamic content often require the execution of client-side JavaScript code. This is far more advanced than `Invoke-WebRequest` alone can offer.

A more advanced approach is to make use of browser automation tools such as Selenium. Selenium is often used to test website functionality, and because of this, it needs to know how to parse web responses.

The selenium-powershell module is available on the PowerShell Gallery and has a GitHub project page that offers an introduction: https://github.com/adamdriscoll/selenium-powershell.

The use of this module is beyond the scope of this book. When a problem arises that requires interaction with a web page or service, it is always best to first explore if the service provides an API using REST or SOAP.

REST and SOAP are explored later in this chapter.

The GET method can also be used to download files from a web server.

Downloading files

Invoke-WebRequest can be used to download a file by making use of the OutFile parameter. The example below attempts to download the PowerShell 7.3.6 installer from GitHub to the current directory ($pwd):

```
$uri = 'https://github.com/PowerShell/PowerShell/releases/download/v7.3.6/
PowerShell-7.3.6-win-x64.msi'
Invoke-WebRequest $uri -OutFile (Split-Path $uri -Leaf)
```

The OutFile parameter used here expects a path that includes a filename; the filename is not inferred from the request. If a directory is used in the path, the directory must exist.

Invoke-WebRequest has often been criticized for showing progress while downloading files, especially in Windows PowerShell. Progress is perhaps useful feedback to a user, but writing progress can slow down a command and is, therefore, not helpful in non-interactive scenarios. This can be suppressed using preference variables:

```
$ProgressPreference = 'SilentlyContinue'
$uri = 'https://github.com/PowerShell/PowerShell/releases/download/v7.3.6/
PowerShell-7.3.6-win-x64.msi'
Invoke-WebRequest $uri -OutFile (Split-Path $uri -Leaf)
```

PowerShell will immediately start to download the file specified by the URL, which is, of course, useful if the intent is to run the file.

A slightly different case is where it might be desirable to test if a download link is going to work, or to request the size of a file before downloading.

Using the HEAD method

The HEAD method can be used to get some metadata about a URI. This information is typically part of the Headers in the response.

The last example downloaded the PowerShell installer. If the goal were to test if the link is valid, or to determine the size of a file before downloading, HEAD can be used. Note that the OutFile parameter is not used in this example:

```
$uri = 'https://github.com/PowerShell/PowerShell/releases/download/v7.3.6/
PowerShell-7.3.6-win-x64.msi'
$response = Invoke-WebRequest $uri -Method HEAD
$response.Headers['Content-Length']
```

The example above will display the size of the file in bytes without downloading content.

The URLs used in each of the preceding examples make use of HTTPS to secure the connection to the web server.

HTTPS

Connecting to a site using **HTTPS (HTTP over Secure Sockets Layer (SSL))** has two potential challenges to overcome. The client and server must negotiate a security protocol to use, and the certificate must be validated.

PowerShell 7 and Windows PowerShell have slightly different default security protocols because of the versions of .NET each uses.

Security protocols

Windows PowerShell, as it uses an older version of .NET, defaults to older security protocols and must be explicitly instructed to use a newer protocol. This is done using the ServicePointManager: https:// learn.microsoft.com/dotnet/api/system.net.servicepointmanager?view=netframework-4.8.

TLS 1.2 and 1.3 are not enabled by default; the command below enables them for the current session:

```
using namespace System.Net


[ServicePointManager]::SecurityProtocol =
[ServicePointManager]::SecurityProtocol -bor 'Tls12' -bor 'Tls13'
```

Alternatively, the list of protocols may be set in full:

```
using namespace System.Net


[ServicePointManager]::SecurityProtocol = 'Tls, Tls11, Tls12, Tls13'
```

TLS 1.2 requires a minimum of .NET Framework 4.7. TLS 1.3 requires a minimum of .NET Framework 4.8. Because of the .NET dependency, this kind of protocol change cannot be used in very old versions of PowerShell (such as PowerShell v2).

The change to security protocols will revert if PowerShell is restarted. Newer security protocols for Windows PowerShell can be enabled by default by setting SchUseStrongCrypto in the registry, as described in the .NET reference: https://learn.microsoft.com/dotnet/framework/network-programming/ tls#configure-security-via-the-windows-registry.

Certificate validation also differs between PowerShell 7 and Windows PowerShell.

Certificate validation

The bad SSL site can be used to test how PowerShell might react to different SSL scenarios: https://badssl.com/.

For example, when attempting to connect to a site with an expired certificate (using Invoke-WebRequest), the following message will be displayed in Windows PowerShell:

```
PS> Invoke-WebRequest https://expired.badssl.com/
Invoke-WebRequest: The remote certificate is invalid because of errors in the
certificate chain: NotTimeValid
```

Invoke-WebRequest and Invoke-RestMethod in PowerShell 7 can ignore problems with web server certificates by using the SkipCertificateCheck. The web commands were overhauled with the release of PowerShell 6, making them significantly easier to work with.

SkipCertificateCheck is a switch parameter and simply accepts the certificate from the server:

```
Invoke-WebRequest https://expired.badssl.com/ -SkipCertificateCheck
```

Because the certificate is ignored, the example above will successfully get content from the site. The first few lines of output from the command are shown below:

```
StatusCode        : 200
StatusDescription : OK
Content           : <!DOCTYPE html>
                    <html>
                    <head>
                      <meta charset="utf-8">
                      <meta name="viewport" content="width=device-width,
initial-scale=1">
                      <link rel="shortcut icon" href="/icons/favicon-red.ico"/>
                      <link rel="a…
RawContent        : HTTP/1.1 200 OK
```

It may be necessary to ignore an SSL error when making a web request – for example, the certificate might be self-signed. SSL errors in PowerShell 7 can be bypassed using the parameter demonstrated above.

Ignoring certificate errors in Windows PowerShell is much more involved.

Windows PowerShell and certificate validation

In Windows PowerShell, Invoke-WebRequest cannot bypass or ignore an invalid certificate on its own (using a parameter). Certificate validation behavior may be changed by adjusting the CertificatePolicy on the ServicePointManager.

The CertificatePolicy is a process-specific policy control affecting web requests in .NET made by that process. The policy is applied using the ServicePointManager, which manages HTTP connections.

If a service has an invalid certificate, the best response is to fix the problem. When it is not possible or practical to address the real problem, a workaround can be created.

The approach described here applies to Windows PowerShell only. PowerShell Core does not include the IcertificatePolicy type.

This modification applies to the current PowerShell session and will reset to default behavior every time a new PowerShell session is opened.

The current policy may be saved in a variable to allow the policy change to be reverted:

```
$default = [System.Net.ServicePointManager]::CertificatePolicy
```

The certificate policy used by the ServicePointManager can be replaced with a customized handler by writing a class (PowerShell version 5) that implements the CheckValidationResult method.

Note that the following example uses two different namespaces. If the example is pasted into the console, then these using statements must appear on a single line, separated by a semicolon:

```
using namespace System.Net
using namespace System.Security.Cryptography.X509Certificates

class AcceptAllPolicy: ICertificatePolicy {
    [bool] CheckValidationResult(
        [ServicePoint] $servicePoint,
        [X509Certificate] $certificate,
        [WebRequest] $webRequest,
        [int] $problem
    ) {
        return $true
    }
}
[ServicePointManager]::CertificatePolicy = [AcceptAllPolicy]::new()
```

With this policy in place, a request to a site with an expired or invalid certificate will succeed.

```
PS> Invoke-WebRequest "https://expired.badssl.com/"

StatusCode        : 200
StatusDescription : OK
...
```

If the default policy was saved to a variable, it may be restored:

```
[System.Net.ServicePointManager]::CertificatePolicy = $default
```

Alternatively, restarting the PowerShell console will revert to the default policy.

In some cases, it may be useful to capture errors with certificates.

Capturing SSL errors

The SslStream type (System.Net.Security.SslStream) can be used to capture detailed certificate validation information. The approach used in the following example works in both Windows PowerShell and PowerShell Core.

This example converts certificate validation information using Export-CliXml. Assigning the parameters to a global variable is possible, but certain information is discarded when the callback ends, including the elements of the certificate chain:

```
using namespace System.Security.Cryptography.X509Certificates
using namespace System.Net.Security
using namespace System.Net.Sockets

$path = @{
    Path = '.\CertValidation.xml'
}

$remoteCertificateValidationCallback = {
    param (
        [object] $sender,
        [X509Certificate2] $certificate,
        [X509Chain] $chain,
        [SslPolicyErrors] $sslPolicyErrors
    )
    $PSBoundParameters | Export-CliXml @path
    # Always indicate SSL negotiation was successful
    $true
}
try {
    [Uri]$uri = 'https://expired.badssl.com/'
    $tcpClient = [TcpClient]::new()
    $tcpClient.Connect($Uri.Host, $Uri.Port)
    $sslStream = [SslStream]::new(
        $tcpClient.GetStream(),
        # LeaveInnerStreamOpen: Close when complete
        $false,
        $remoteCertificateValidationCallback
    )
    $sslStream.AuthenticateAsClient($Uri.Host)
} catch {
```

```
        throw
    } finally {
        if ($tcpClient.Connected) {
            $tcpClient.Close()
        }
    }
    $certValidation = Import-CliXml @path
```

Once the content of the XML file has been loaded, the content may be investigated. For example, the certificate that was exchanged can be viewed:

```
PS> $certValidation.Certificate


Thumbprint                                Subject
----------                                -------
404BBD2F1F4CC2FDEEF13AABDD523EF61F1C71F3  CN=*.badssl.com,...
```

Alternatively, the response can be used to inspect all the certificates in the key chain:

```
$certValidation.Chain.ChainElements | ForEach-Object Certificate
```

The ChainStatus property exposes details of any errors during chain validation:

```
$certValidation.Chain.ChainStatus
```

ChainStatus is summarized by the SslPolicyErrors property.

The HTTP methods demonstrated in this section can be used with **Representational State Transfer (REST)**.

Working with REST

A REST-compliant web service allows a client to interact with the service using a set of predefined stateless operations. REST is not a protocol; it is an architectural style.

Whether or not an interface is truly REST-compliant is not particularly relevant when the goal is to use one in PowerShell. Interfaces must be used according to any documentation that has been published.

Invoke-RestMethod is the default command most often used when interacting with REST services. Invoke-RestMethod automatically parses responses, typically JSON responses, into an object that can be directly used in PowerShell.

Invoke-RestMethod is occasionally also useful if the content of a site is interesting. The command automatically expands content instead of returning information about the web request.

For example, Invoke-RestMethod can be used to get the weather:

```
Invoke-RestMethod -Uri wttr.in
```

It can also be used with any service that returns JSON content, such as the PowerShell Reddit:

```
$ps = Invoke-RestMethod  https://www.reddit.com/r/powershell.json
$ps.data.children.data |
     Select-Object author, created, title -First 1
```

The pinned post in the subreddit from the response is shown below:

```
author                 created title

------                 ------- -----
AutoModerator 1711972834.0 What have you done with PowerShell ...
```

`Invoke-RestMethod` is frequently used with documented APIs.

Simple requests

The REST API provided by GitHub can be used to list repositories made available by the PowerShell team, by making use of the `Invoke-RestMethod` command.

The API entry point, the common URL that all REST methods share, is `https://api.github.com`, as documented in the GitHub reference: `https://docs.github.com/rest`.

When working with REST, documentation is important. The way an interface is used is common, but the way it may respond is not (as this is an architectural style, not a strict protocol).

The specific method being called is documented on a different page of the following reference: `https://docs.github.com/rest/reference/repos#list-user-repositories`.

The name of the user forms part of the URI; there are no arguments for this method. Therefore, the following command will execute the method and return detailed information about the repositories owned by the PowerShell user (or organization):

```
Invoke-RestMethod -Uri https://api.github.com/users/powershell/repos
```

As GitHub has grown, API requests have more often needed authentication. There are many authentication systems that can be used when working with web services.

For services that expect to use the current user account to authenticate, the `UseDefaultCredential` parameter can be used to pass authentication tokens without explicitly passing a username and password. A service integrated into an Active Directory domain, expecting to use Kerberos authentication, is an example of such a service.

REST interfaces written to provide automation access tend to offer reasonably simple approaches to automation, often including basic authentication.

GitHub offers several different authentication methods, including basic and OAuth. These are shown here when attempting to request the email addresses of a user that requires authentication.

Using basic authentication

Basic authentication with a username and password is the simplest method available. For the GitHub API, the password must be a personal access token; basic authentication with a username and password was discontinued in November 2020.

Personal access tokens can be generated by visiting account settings, and then developer settings. This process is documented by GitHub: https://docs.github.com/authentication/keeping-your-account-and-data-secure/managing-your-personal-access-tokens.

The examples below assume the token has user scope.

Once generated, the personal access token cannot be viewed again. The personal access token is used in place of a password.

The examples below assume a credential has been created and assigned to a variable, either from Get-Credential or by making a PSCredential, as shown below:

```
$credential = [PSCredential]::new(
    'your-github-username',
    (ConvertTo-SecureString 'xxxx' -AsPlainText -Force)
)
```

Where the username and xxxx values are replaced to make a valid credential. Then, the credential can be used with Invoke-RestMethod:

```
$params = @{
    Uri            = 'https://api.github.com/user/emails'
    Credential     = $credential
    Authentication = 'Basic'
}
Invoke-RestMethod @params
```

In Windows PowerShell, the Authentication parameter does not exist and should be omitted.

OAuth is an alternative to using a personal access token and will be explored later in this section.

The simple request above does not require any arguments.

Requests with arguments

The search code method of the **GitHub REST API** is used to demonstrate how arguments can be passed to a REST method.

The documentation for the method is found in the following API reference: https://docs.github.com/rest/search/search#search-code.

The following example uses the search code method by building a query string and appending that to the end of the URL. The search looks for occurrences of the Get-Content term in PowerShell language files in the PowerShell repository. The search term is, therefore, as follows (the search string here should not be confused with a PowerShell command):

```
Get-Content language:powershell repo:powershell/powershell
```

Converting the example from the documentation for the search method, the URL required is as follows. Spaces can be replaced by + when encoding the URL: https://api.github.com/search/code?q=Get-Content+language:powershell+repo:powershell/powershell. Note that the URL cannot be used in a browser, API authentication is required as demonstrated in the example which follows.

The task of encoding the URL can be simplified by making use of the ParseQueryString method of the HttpUtility type:

```
Add-Type -AssemblyName System.Web

$queryString = [System.Web.HttpUtility]::ParseQueryString('')
$queryString.Add(
    'q',
    'Get-Content language:powershell repo:powershell/powershell'
)
$params = @{
    Uri            = 'https://api.github.com/search/code?{0}' -f
        $queryString
    Credential     = $credential
    Authentication = 'Basic'
}
Invoke-RestMethod @params
```

Note that the example makes use of the $credential variable from the previous section on authentication. GitHub does not allow anonymous code searches.

The result is a custom object that includes the search results:

```
PS> Invoke-RestMethod @params

total_count incomplete_results items
----------- ------------------ -----
         91              False {@{name=UpdateDotnetRuntime.ps1...
```

Running $queryString.ToString() shows that the colon character has been replaced by %3, and the forward slash in the repository name has been replaced by %2. The %3 and %2 are URL encodings of the colon and forward-slash characters.

The arguments for the search do not necessarily have to be passed as a query string. Instead, a body for the request may be set, as shown here:

```
$params = @{
    Uri                = 'https://api.github.com/search/code'
    Body               = @{
        q = 'Get-Content language:powershell repo:powershell/powershell'
    }
    Credential      = $credential
    Authentication = 'Basic'
}
Invoke-RestMethod @params
```

Invoke-RestMethod converts the body (a hashtable) and handles any encoding required. The result of the search is the same whether the body or a query string is used.

In both cases, details of the files found are held within the items property of the response. The following example shows the filename and path:

```
$params = @{
    Uri = 'https://api.github.com/search/code'
    Body = @{
        q = 'Get-Content language:powershell repo:powershell/powershell'
    }
    Credential      = $credential
    Authentication = 'Basic'
}
Invoke-RestMethod @params |
    Select-Object -ExpandProperty items |
    Select-Object name, path
```

This pattern, where the actual results are nested under a property in the response, is frequently seen with REST interfaces. Exploration is often required.

It is critical to note that REST interfaces are case-sensitive; using a parameter named Q would result in the following error message:

```
Invoke-RestMethod: {"message":"Validation
Failed","errors":[{"resource":"Search","field":"q","code":"missing"}],
"documentation_url":"https://docs.github.com/v3/search"}
```

The GitHub API returns an easily understood error message in this case. This will not be true of all REST APIs; it is common to see a generic error returned by an API. An API may return a simple HTTP 400 error and leave it to the user or developer to figure out what went wrong.

Working with paging

Many REST interfaces will return large result sets from searches in pages, a subset of the results. The techniques used to retrieve each subsequent page can vary from one API to another. This section explores how those pages can be retrieved from the web service.

The GitHub API exposes the link to the next page in the HTTP header. This is consistent with RFC 5988: https://tools.ietf.org/html/rfc5988#page-6.

In PowerShell 7, it is easy to retrieve and view the header when using Invoke-RestMethod, allowing the next links to be inspected:

```
$params = @{
    Uri                     = 'https://api.github.com/search/issues'
    Body                    = @{
        q = 'documentation state:closed repo:powershell/powershell'
    }
    ResponseHeadersVariable = 'httpHeader'
    Credential              = $credential
    Authentication          = 'Basic'
}
Invoke-RestMethod @params | Select-Object -ExpandProperty items
```

Once run, the link field of the header can be inspected via the httpHeader variable:

```
PS> $httpHeader['link']
 <https://api.github.com/search/
issues?q=documentation+state%3Aclosed+repo%3Apowershell%2Fpowershell&page=2>;
rel="next",
 <https://api.github.com/search/
issues?q=documentation+state%3Aclosed+repo%3Apowershell%2Fpowershell&page=34>;
rel="last"
```

PowerShell 7 can also automatically follow this link by using the FollowRelLink parameter. This might be used in conjunction with the MaximumFollowRelLink parameter to ensure that a request stays within any rate limit imposed by the web service: https://docs.github.com/rest/overview/resources-in-the-rest-api#rate-limiting.

The following request searches for closed documentation issues, following the paging link twice:

```
$params = @{
    Uri                  = 'https://api.github.com/search/issues'
    Body                 = @{
        q = 'documentation state:closed repo:powershell/powershell'
    }
    FollowRelLink        = $true
    MaximumFollowRelLink = 2
```

```
    Credential          = $credential
    Authentication      = 'Basic'
}
Invoke-RestMethod @params | Select-Object -ExpandProperty items
```

Windows PowerShell, unfortunately, cannot automatically follow this link. Nor does the `Invoke-RestMethod` command expose the header from the response. When working with complex REST interfaces in Windows PowerShell, it is often necessary to fall back to the `Invoke-WebRequest` or even `HttpWebRequest` classes.

The example that follows uses `Invoke-WebRequest` in Windows PowerShell to follow the next link, similar to `Invoke-RestMethod` in PowerShell 7:

```
# Used to limit the number of times "next" is followed
$followLimit = 2
# The initial set of parameters, describes the search
$params = @{
    Uri = 'https://api.github.com/search/issues'
    # PowerShell will convert this to JSON
    Body = @{
        q = 'documentation state:closed repo:powershell/powershell'
    }
    Credential  = $credential
    ContentType = 'application/json'
}
# Just a counter, works in conjunction with followLimit.
$followed = 0
do {
    # Get the next response
    $response = Invoke-WebRequest @params
    # Convert and leave the results as output
    $response.Content |
        ConvertFrom-Json |
        Select-Object -ExpandProperty items
    # Retrieve the links from the header and find the next URL
    if ($response.Headers['link'] -match '<([^>]+?)>;\s*rel="next"') {
        $next = $matches[1]
    } else {
        $next = $null
    }
    # Parameters which will be used to get the next page
    $params = @{
        Uri = $next
```

```
        }
        # Increment the followed counter
        $followed++
    } until (-not $next -or $followed -ge $followLimit)
```

Because of the flexible nature of REST, implementations of page linking may vary. For example, links may appear in the body of a response instead of the header. Exploration is a requirement when working around a web API.

Each of the commands above has made use of basic authentication with a PAT token. OAuth is a more advanced approach.

OAuth

OAuth is offered by a wide variety of web services. The details of this process will vary slightly between different APIs. The GitHub documentation describes the process that must be followed: https://docs. github.com/apps/oauth-apps/building-oauth-apps/authorizing-oauth-apps#web-application-flow.

Implementing OAuth requires a web browser, or a web browser and a web server. As the browser will likely need to run JavaScript, this cannot be done using Invoke-WebRequest alone.

Creating an application

Before starting with code, an application must be registered with GitHub. This is done by visiting **Settings**, then **Developer settings**, and finally, **OAuth Apps**.

A new OAuth app must be created to acquire a clientId and clientSecret. Creating the application requires a homepage URL and an authorization callback URL. Both should be set to http:// localhost:40000 for this example. This URL is used to acquire the authorization code.

The values from the web page will fill the following variables. The client secret must be generated by clicking **Generate a new client secret**. The secret must be regenerated if lost:

```
$clientId = 'FromGitHub'
$clientSecret = 'FromGitHub'
```

These values are used with the commands below to carry out authentication.

Getting an authorization code

Once an application is registered, an authorization code is required. Obtaining the authorization code gives the end user the opportunity to grant the application access to a GitHub account. If the user is not currently logged into GitHub, it will also prompt them to log on.

A URL must be created that will prompt for authorization:

```
$authorizeUrl = 'https://github.com/login/oauth/authorize?client_
id={0}&scope={1}' -f @(
    $clientId
```

```
        'user:email'
)
```

The user:email scope describes the rights the application would like to have. The web API guide contains a list of possible scopes: https://docs.github.com/apps/oauth-apps/building-oauth-apps/scopes-for-oauth-apps.

It is possible to implement a web browser control using a UI framework such as WPF. However, these are difficult to implement and place an operating system dependency on code.

Instead, it would be better to implement an HTTP listener and use a user-preferred browser to visit a page.

Implementing an HTTP listener

Implementing the web server has two advantages:

*   Implementing a web server does not need additional libraries.
*   The web server can potentially be used on platforms other than Windows.

Note that the example makes use of the $clientId variable.

The HttpListener is configured with the callback URL as a prefix. The prefix must end with a forward slash. The operating system gets to choose which browser should be used to complete the request:

```
$httpListener = [System.Net.HttpListener]::new()
$httpListener.Prefixes.Add('http://localhost:40000/')
$httpListener.Start()
$authorizeUrl = 'https://github.com/login/oauth/authorize?client_
id={0}&scope={1}' -f @(
    $clientId
    'user:email'
)
# Let the operating system choose the browser to use for this request
Start-Process -FilePath $authorizeUrl
$context = $httpListener.GetContext()
$buffer = [byte[]][char[]]"<html><body>OAuth complete! Please return to
PowerShell!</body></html>"
$context.Response.OutputStream.Write(
    $buffer,
    0,
    $buffer.Count
)
$context.Response.OutputStream.Close()
$httpListener.Stop()
$authorizationCode = $context.Request.QueryString['code']
```

In either case, the result of the process is code held in the $authorizationCode variable. This code can be used to request an access token.

Requesting an access token

The next step is to create an access token. The access token is valid for a limited time.

The $clientSecret and $clientId are sent with this request; if this were an application that was given to others, keeping the secret would be a challenge to overcome:

```
$params = @{
    Uri = 'https://github.com/login/oauth/access_token'
    Method = 'POST'
    Body = @{
        client_id     = $clientId
        client_secret = $clientSecret
        code          = $authorizationCode
    }
}
$response = Invoke-RestMethod @params
$token = [System.Web.HttpUtility]::ParseQueryString($response)['access_token']
```

The previous request used the HTTP method POST. The HTTP method, which should be used with a REST method, is documented for an interface in the Developer Guides.

Each of the requests that follow will use the access token from the previous request. The access token is placed in an HTTP header field named Authorization.

Using a token

REST methods that require authentication can be called by adding a token to the HTTP header. The format of the Authorization header field is as follows:

```
Authorization: token OAUTH-TOKEN
```

OAUTH-TOKEN is replaced, and the Authorization head is constructed as follows:

```
$headers = @{
    Authorization = 'token {0}' -f $token
}
```

The token can be used in subsequent requests for the extent of its lifetime:

```
$headers = @{
    Authorization = 'token {0}' -f $token
}
Invoke-RestMethod 'https://api.github.com/user/emails' -Headers $headers
```

Each REST API for each different system or service tends to take a slightly different approach to authentication, authorization, calling methods, and even details like paging. However, despite the differences there, the lessons learned using one API are still useful when attempting to write code for another.

REST is an extremely popular style these days. Before REST became prominent, services built using SOAP were common.

Working with SOAP

Unlike REST, which is an architectural style, SOAP is a protocol. It is perhaps reasonable to compare working with SOAP to importing a .NET assembly (DLL) to work with the types inside. As a result, a SOAP client is much more strongly tied to a server than is the case with a REST interface.

SOAP uses XML to exchange information between the client and server.

In Windows PowerShell, the command `New-WebServiceProxy` was made available to make it easier to work with SOAP services. Using a SOAP service in Windows PowerShell is more like using .NET types. The calls made to the web service are hidden from the user.

`New-WebServiceProxy` is not available in PowerShell 6 and higher; this section explores writing SOAP requests directly based on a **Web Services Description Language** (**WSDL**) document, which describes the XML requests and responses that the service expects.

Finding a SOAP service

SOAP-based web APIs have become quite rare, and they are much less popular than REST. REST services are easy to write, which makes them very convenient. The examples in this section are based on a simple SOAP service written for this book.

This SOAP service is available on GitHub as a Visual Studio solution. The solution is also available in the GitHub repository containing the code examples used in this chapter: `https://github.com/indented-automation/SimpleSOAP`.

The solution should be downloaded and opened in Visual Studio (2019, Community Edition, or better), and debugging should be started by pressing *F5*. A browser page will open, which will show the port number that the service operates on. A 403 error may be displayed; this can be ignored.

Localhost and a port

Throughout this section, localhost and a port are used to connect to the web service. The port is set by Visual Studio while debugging the simple SOAP web service and must be updated to use these examples.

This service is not well-designed; it has been contrived to expose similar patterns in its method calls to those seen in real SOAP services.

A `ReadMe` file accompanies the project. Common problems when running the project will be noted there.

The discovery-based approaches explored in this section should be applicable to any SOAP-based service.

SOAP in Windows PowerShell

The New-WebServiceProxy examples that follow apply to Windows PowerShell only. The New-WebServiceProxy command is not available in PowerShell 7.

New-WebServiceProxy

The New-WebServiceProxy command is used to connect to a SOAP web service. This can be a service endpoint, such as a .NET service.asmx URL or a WSDL document.

The web service will include methods and can also include other object types and enumerations.

The command accesses a service anonymously by default. If the current user should be passed on, the UseDefaultCredential parameter should be used. If explicit credentials are required, the Credential parameter can be used.

By default, New-WebServiceProxy creates a dynamic namespace. This is as follows:

```
$params = @{
    Uri = 'http://localhost:62369/Service.asmx'
}
$service = New-WebServiceProxy @params
$service.GetType().Namespace
```

The automatically generated namespace value created by the command above is shown below:

```
Microsoft.PowerShell.Commands.NewWebserviceProxy.AutogeneratedTypes.
WebServiceProxy4__localhost_62369_Service_asmx
```

The dynamic namespace is useful, as it avoids problems when multiple connections are made to the same service in the same session.

To simplify exploring the web service, a fixed namespace might be defined:

```
$params = @{
    Uri       = 'http://localhost:62369/Service.asmx'
    Namespace = 'SOAP'
}
$service = New-WebServiceProxy @params
```

The $service object returned by New-WebServiceProxy describes the URL used to connect, the timeout, the HTTP user agent, and so on. The object is also the starting point for exploring the interface; it is used to expose web services' methods.

Methods

The methods available can be viewed in several ways. The URL used can be visited in a browser or `Get-Member` can be used. A subset of the output from `Get-Member` follows:

```
PS> $service | Get-Member


Name                  MemberType  Definition
----                  ----------  ----------
GetElement            Method      SOAP.Element GetElement(string Name)
GetAtomicMass         Method      string GetAtomicMass(string Name)
GetAtomicNumber       Method      int GetAtomicNumber(string Name)
GetElements           Method      SOAP.Element[] GetElements()
GetElementsByGroup    Method      SOAP.Element[] GetElementsByGroup(SOAP.Group
group)
GetElementSymbol      Method      string GetElementSymbol(string Name)
SearchElements        Method      SOAP.Element[] SearchElements(SOAP.
SearchCondition[] searchConditions)
```

The preceding `GetElements` method requires no arguments and can be called immediately, as shown here:

```
PS> $service.GetElements() | Select-Object -First 5 | Format-Table

AtomicNumber  Symbol  Name      AtomicMass   Group
------------  ------  ----      ----------   -----
           1  H       Hydrogen  1.00794(4)   Nonmetal
           2  He      Helium    4.002602(2)  NobleGas
           3  Li      Lithium   6.941(2)     AlkaliMetal
           4  Be      Beryllium 9.012182(3)  AlkalineEarthMetal
           5  B       Boron     10.811(7)    Metalloid
```

Methods requiring string or numeric arguments can be similarly easy to call, although the value the method requires is often open to interpretation. In this case, the Name argument may be either an element name or an element symbol:

```
PS> $service.GetAtomicNumber('oxygen')
8
PS> $service.GetAtomicMass('H')
1.00794(4)
```

Whether the web service is SOAP or REST, using the service effectively is dependent on being able to locate the service documentation.

Methods and enumerations

The `GetElementsByGroup` method shown by `Get-Member` requires an argument of type `SOAP.Group`, as the following shows:

```
PS> $service | Get-Member -Name GetElementsByGroup


Name                MemberType Definition
----                ---------- ----------
GetElementsByGroup  Method     SOAP.Element[] GetElementsByGroup(SOAP.Group…
```

`SOAP.Group` is an enumeration, as indicated by the `BaseType`:

```
PS> [SOAP.Group]


IsPublic    IsSerial     Name     BaseType
--------    --------     ----     --------
True        True         Group    System.Enum
```

The values of the enumeration can be shown by running the `GetEnumValues` method:

```
PS> [SOAP.Group].GetEnumValues()
Actinoid
AlkaliMetal
AlkalineEarthMetal
Halogen
Lanthanoid
Metal
Metalloid
NobleGas
Nonmetal
PostTransitionMetal
TransitionMetal
```

PowerShell will help cast to enumeration values; a string value is sufficient to satisfy the method:

```
PS> $service.GetElementsByGroup('Nonmetal') | Format-Table


AtomicNumber    Symbol    Name        AtomicMass      Group
------------    ------    ----        ----------      -----
           1    H         Hydrogen    1.00794(4)      Nonmetal
           6    C         Carbon      12.0107(8)      Nonmetal
           7    N         Nitrogen    14.0067(2)      Nonmetal
           8    O         Oxygen      15.9994(3)      Nonmetal
          15    P         Phosphorus  30.973762(2)    Nonmetal
```

```
    16    S      Sulfur      32.065(5)    Nonmetal
    34    Se     Selenium    78.96(3)     Nonmetal
```

If the real value of the enumeration must be used, it can be referenced as a static property of the enumeration:

```
$service.GetElementsByGroup([SOAP.Group]::Nonmetal) | Format-Table
```

It is relatively common for a method to require an instance of an object provided by the SOAP interface.

Methods and SOAP objects

When working with SOAP interfaces, it is common to encounter methods that need instances of objects presented by the SOAP service. The SearchElements method is an example of this type.

The SearchElements method requires an array of SOAP.SearchCondition as an argument. This is shown in the following by accessing the definition of the method:

```
PS> $service.SearchElements

OverloadDefinitions
-------------------
SOAP.Element[] SearchElements(SOAP.SearchCondition[] searchConditions)
```

An instance of SearchCondition may be created as follows:

```
$searchCondition = [SOAP.SearchCondition]::new()
```

Exploring the object with Get-Member shows that the operator property is another type from the SOAP service. This is an enumeration, as shown here:

```
PS> [SOAP.ComparisonOperator]

IsPublic    IsSerial    Name                BaseType
--------    --------    ----                --------
True        True        ComparisonOperator  System.Enum
```

A set of search conditions can be constructed and passed to the method:

```
$searchConditions = @(
    [SOAP.SearchCondition]@{
        PropertyName = 'AtomicNumber'
        Operator     = 'ge'
        Value        = 1
    }
    [SOAP.SearchCondition]@{
        PropertyName = 'AtomicNumber'
        Operator     = 'lt'
```

```
        Value        = 6
    }
)
$service.SearchElements($searchConditions)
```

Using a hardcoded namespace can present a challenge when testing.

Overlapping services

When testing a SOAP interface, it is easy to get into a situation where New-WebServiceProxy has been called several times against the same web service. This can be problematic if the Namespace parameter is used.

Consider the following example, which uses two instances of the web service:

```
$params = @{
    Uri = 'http://localhost:62369/Service.asmx'
    Namespace = 'SOAP'
}
# Original version
$service = New-WebServiceProxy @params
# New version
$service = New-WebServiceProxy @params
$searchConditions = @(
    [SOAP.SearchCondition]@{
        PropertyName = 'Symbol'
        Operator     = 'eq'
        Value        = 'H'
    }
)
```

In theory, there is nothing wrong with this example. In practice, the SOAP.SearchCondition object is created based on the original version of the service created, using New-WebServiceProxy. The method, on the other hand, executes against the newer version.

As the method called and the type used are in different assemblies, an error is shown; this is repeated in the following:

```
PS> $service.SearchElements($searchConditions)
Cannot convert argument "searchConditions", with value: "System.Object[]", for
"SearchElements" to type
"SOAP.SearchCondition[]": "Cannot convert the "SOAP.SearchCondition" value of
type "SOAP.SearchCondition" to type
"SOAP.SearchCondition"."
```

```
At line:1 char:1
+ $service.SearchElements($searchConditions)
+ ~~~~~~~~~~~~~~~~~~~~~~~~~~~~~~~~~~~~~~~~~~~~
    + CategoryInfo       : NotSpecified: (:) [], MethodException
    + FullyQualifiedErrorId : MethodArgumentConversionInvalidCastArgument
```

It is still possible to access the second version of SearchCondition by searching for the type, and then creating an instance of it:

```
$searchCondition = ($service.GetType().Module.GetTypes() |
    Where-Object Name -eq 'SearchCondition')::new()
$searchCondition.PropertyName = 'Symbol'
$searchCondition.Operator = 'eq'
$searchCondition.Value = 'H'
$searchConditions = @($searchCondition)
$service.SearchElements($searchConditions)
```

However, it is generally better to avoid the problem by allowing New-WebServiceProxy to use a dynamic namespace, at which point, an instance of the SearchCondition can be created, as the following shows:

```
('{0}.SearchCondition' -f $service.GetType().Namespace -as [Type])::new()
```

PowerShell 7 cannot use the New-WebServiceProxy command.

SOAP in PowerShell 7

Windows PowerShell can use the New-WebServiceProxy command. In PowerShell 7, requests can be manually created and sent using Invoke-WebRequest by writing XML directly.

Getting the WSDL document

The WSDL document for the web service contains details of the methods and enumerations it contains. The document can be requested as follows:

```
$params = @{
    Uri = 'http://localhost:62369/Service.asmx?wsdl'
}
[Xml]$wsdl = Invoke-WebRequest @params | Select-Object -ExpandProperty Content
```

The document shows the methods that can be executed and the arguments for those methods. Obtaining a list requires a bit of correlation.

Discovering methods and enumerations

The WSDL document can be used to discover the methods available from the SOAP service. The default view of the document presents a list of methods. Clicking on a method will show an example of the expected header and body values.

It is possible to retrieve the methods in PowerShell dynamically as well. Two SOAP versions are presented by the service. SOAP 1.2 is used in the following example, although both will show the same information in this case:

```powershell
$xmlNamespaceManager = [System.Xml.XmlNamespaceManager]::new($wsdl.NameTable)
# Load everything that looks like a namespace
$wsdl.definitions.PSObject.Properties |
    Where-Object Value -match '^http' |
    ForEach-Object {
        $xmlNamespaceManager.AddNamespace(
            $_.Name,
            $_.Value
        )
    }
$wsdl.SelectNodes(
    '/*/wsdl:binding[@name="ServiceSoap12"]/wsdl:operation',
    $xmlNamespaceManager
) | ForEach-Object {
    [PSCustomObject]@{
        Name        = $_.name
        Inputs      = $wsdl.SelectNodes(
            ('//s:element[@name="{0}"]/*/s:sequence/*' -f
                $_.name),
            $xmlNamespaceManager
        ).ForEach{
            [PSCustomObject]@{
                ParameterName = $_.name
                ParameterType = $_.type -replace '.+:'
            }
        }
        Outputs     = $wsdl.SelectNodes(
            ('//s:element[@name="{0}Response"]/*/*/s:element/@type' -f
                $_.name),
            $xmlNamespaceManager
        ).'#text' -replace '.+:'
        SoapAction = $_.operation.soapAction
    }
}
```

The preceding script shows a rough list of the parameters required and value types returned for each of the methods. For example, the GetElement method expects a string argument and will return an Element object:

Name	Inputs	Outputs
GetElement	{@{ParameterName=Name; ParameterType=string}}	Element

Enumeration values are also exposed in the WSDL. Continuing from the previous example, they can be retrieved using the following:

```
$wsdl.SelectNodes(
    '/*/*/*/s:simpleType[s:restriction/s:enumeration]',
    $xmlNamespaceManager
) | ForEach-Object {
    [PSCustomObject]@{
        Name   = $_.name
        Values = $_.restriction.enumeration.value
    }
}
```

The Group and ComparisonOperator enumerations will be displayed.

Running methods

Invoke-WebRequest can be used to execute methods by providing a SOAP envelope in the body of the request. The response is an XML document that includes the results of the method. The envelope includes the web service URI, http://tempuri.org:

```
$params = @{
    Uri         = 'http://localhost:62369/Service.asmx'
    ContentType = 'text/xml'
    Method      = 'POST'
    Header      = @{
        SOAPAction = 'http://tempuri.org/GetElements'
    }
    Body        = '
        <soapenv:Envelope
                xmlns:soapenv="http://schemas.xmlsoap.org/soap/envelope/">
            <soapenv:Body>
                <GetElements />
            </soapenv:Body>
        </soapenv:Envelope>
    '
}
$webResponse = Invoke-WebRequest @params
$xmlResponse = [Xml]$webResponse.Content
$body = $xmlResponse.Envelope.Body
$body.GetElementsResponse.GetElementsResult.Element
```

As the preceding code shows, the response content is specific to the method that was executed.

If a method requires arguments, these must be passed in the body of the request. In the following example, the argument is a single string:

```
$params = @{
    Uri         = 'http://localhost:62369/Service.asmx'
    ContentType = 'text/xml'
    Method      = 'POST'
    Header      = @{
        SOAPAction = 'http://tempuri.org/GetElement'
    }
    Body        = '
        <soapenv:Envelope
                xmlns:soapenv="http://schemas.xmlsoap.org/soap/envelope/"
                xmlns="http://tempuri.org/">
            <soapenv:Body>
                <GetElement>
                    <Name>Oxygen</Name>
                </GetElement>
            </soapenv:Body>
        </soapenv:Envelope>
    '
}
$webResponse = Invoke-WebRequest @params
$xmlResponse = [Xml]$webResponse.Content
$body = $xmlResponse.Envelope.Body
```

The body shows the object returned by the method:

```
PS> $body.GetElementResponse.GetElementResult

AtomicNumber : 8
Symbol       : O
Name         : Oxygen
AtomicMass   : 15.9994(3)
Group        : Nonmetal
```

The name of the argument used above correlates with the name and value shown in the WSDL:

```
<s:element minOccurs="0" maxOccurs="1" name="Name" type="s:string"/>
```

The preceding method expects a string. If an enumeration value is required, it can be described as a string in the XML envelope.

More complex types can be built based on following the expected structure of the arguments, or by following the examples provided when browsing the Service.asmx file. The following example includes two SearchCondition objects:

```
$params = @{
    Uri          = 'http://localhost:62369/Service.asmx'
    ContentType = 'text/xml'
    Method       = 'POST'
    Body         = '
        <soapenv:Envelope
                xmlns:soapenv="http://schemas.xmlsoap.org/soap/envelope/"
                xmlns="http://tempuri.org/">
            <soapenv:Body>
                <SearchElements>
                    <searchConditions>
                        <SearchCondition>
                            <PropertyName>AtomicNumber</PropertyName>
                            <Value>1</Value>
                            <Operator>ge</Operator>
                        </SearchCondition>
                        <SearchCondition>
                            <PropertyName>AtomicNumber</PropertyName>
                            <Value>6</Value>
                            <Operator>lt</Operator>
                        </SearchCondition>
                    </searchConditions>
                </SearchElements>
            </soapenv:Body>
        </soapenv:Envelope>
    '
}
$webResponse = Invoke-WebRequest @params
$xmlResponse = [Xml]$webResponse.Content
$body = $xmlResponse.Envelope.Body
$body.SearchElementsResponse.SearchElementsResult.Element
```

New-WebServiceProxy in Windows PowerShell took away some of the difficulty of defining the SOAP envelope, but in most cases, it is not difficult to create.

Summary

This chapter explored the use of `Invoke-WebRequest` and how to work with and debug SSL negotiation problems.

`Invoke-WebRequest` is used to send requests to web services and get responses. The command makes a raw request available to work with.

`Invoke-RestMethod` is frequently used in place of `Invoke-WebRequest` and is written to make it easy to work with REST-based services.

Working with REST, we explored simple method calls, authentication, and OAuth negotiation, before exploring REST methods that require authenticated sessions.

SOAP is hard to find these days; it is not as quick or convenient for a developer to create a SOAP-based API. A sample project was used to show how the capabilities of a SOAP service might be discovered and used.

The next chapter explores remoting and remote management.

Learn more on Discord

Read this book alongside other users, PowerShell experts, and the author himself. Ask questions, provide solutions to other readers, chat with the author via Ask Me Anything sessions, and much more.

Scan the QR code or visit the link to join the community.

`https://packt.link/SecNet`

14

Remoting and Remote Management

Windows remoting came to PowerShell with the release of version 2.0. Windows remoting is a powerful feature that allows administrators to move away from RPC-based remote access.

This chapter covers the following topics:

- Executing remote commands
- PS Sessions
- WS-Management
- Remoting on Linux
- The double-hop problem
- CIM sessions
- Just Enough Administration

The examples in this chapter have additional technical requirements to follow along.

Technical requirements

This chapter makes use of a remote Windows system named PSTest, which runs on Windows 10, Windows PowerShell 5.1, and PowerShell 7.

Remoting between Windows and Linux is demonstrated using a system that runs CentOS 7, PowerShell 7, and the **PowerShell Remoting Protocol (PSRP)** package.

The most obvious first use of PowerShell remoting is to run commands on remote systems.

Executing remote commands

PowerShell remoting can be described as a client-server service. The client is responsible for sending requests and, beyond PowerShell itself, has no mandatory configuration. The server is responsible for receiving and processing requests and requires the remoting service to be enabled.

The term server in this context does not describe the role of a computer in a network; it means nothing more than "a computer receiving a request." The server is therefore the remote computer on which commands are run. The server runs the winrm service to listen for requests.

Enabling and performing the initial configuration of the remoting service to allow a computer to receive requests can be done with a single command:

```
Enable-PSRemoting
```

The command performs the initial configuration of the remoting service and adds Windows Firewall exceptions for the Private and Domain profiles. The SkipNetworkProfileCheck parameter can be used to enable limited access to remoting when using a Public profile.

If using both Windows PowerShell and PowerShell 7, the Enable-PSRemoting command should be run in both editions.

More advanced remoting configuration is explored later in this chapter.

If a single computer is being used to work with examples where the client and server are the same machine, PowerShell must be running as administrator.

The client makes use of two commands to send commands to execute:

- Enter-PSSession
- Invoke-Command

In addition to these, several other commands exist that either aid troubleshooting or allow for more complex scenarios:

- Test-WSMan
- New-PSSession and Get-PSSession
- Import-PSSession and Export-PSSession
- Copy-Item

Enter-PSSession is a good starting point, arguably the simplest of the available commands.

Enter-PSSession

The Enter-PSSession command is used to create an interactive console session with a remote system. The command cannot be used as part of a script to execute commands on a remote system.

If a remote computer is available, a connection can be made by providing a computer name:

```
Enter-PSSession PSTest
```

If the console is running as administrator and the local computer has remoting enabled, a connection can be made to localhost:

```
Enter-PSSession localhost
```

Alternatively, the EnableNetworkAccess parameter can be used with the remoting commands:

```
Enter-PSSession localhost -EnableNetworkAccess
```

When running this command from PowerShell 7 the connection will, by default, be made to a Windows PowerShell session as shown below:

```
PS> $PSVersionTable.PSEdition
Core
PS> Enter-PSSession localhost
[localhost] PS> $PSVersionTable.PSEdition
Desktop
```

This happens because the default configuration used by the connection is Microsoft.PowerShell. A PowerShell 7 configuration is accessible via the PowerShell.7 configuration. To connect to PowerShell 7 on a remote system, PowerShell 7 must be installed and the Enable-PSRemoting command must have been run within the PowerShell 7 console.

This configuration can be provided in one of two ways. It can be explicitly provided:

```
Enter-PSSession localhost -ConfigurationName PowerShell.7
```

Or a preference variable can be set that applies to all remoting commands used in the PowerShell session. This preference will revert when PowerShell is restarted:

```
$PSSessionConfigurationName = 'PowerShell.7'
Enter-PSSession localhost -EnableNetworkAccess
```

Setting the variable in a profile script can be used to make this setting a default next time PowerShell starts.

Session configuration is explored in more detail later in this chapter.

Once a session is open commands may be run interactively on the remote computer.

Invoke-Command uses the same connection method and the same session names, but allows commands or scripts to be immediately executed.

Invoke-Command

Invoke-Command can immediately run a script on a remote computer. It is not interactive. For example:

```
Invoke-Command -ComputerName localhost -ScriptBlock {
    Get-Process
}
```

The example above expects the current user on the client to be able to log on to the remote computer, and the current user must be an administrator on the remote computer.

The script that is run on the remote computer can be as complex as required; it is not limited to a single command. For example, the command below combines the output of three different commands and creates a custom object as output:

```
Invoke-Command -ComputerName localhost -ScriptBlock {
    $os = (Get-CimInstance Win32_OperatingSystem).Caption

    $params = @{
        AddressFamily = 'IPv4'
        PrefixOrigin  = 'Dhcp'
    }
    Get-NetIPAddress @params | ForEach-Object {
        $adapter = $_ | Get-NetAdapter

        [PSCustomObject]@{
            ComputerName    = $env:COMPUTERNAME
            OperatingSystem = $os
            InterfaceName   = $adapter.Name
            IPAddress       = $_.IPAddress
            MacAddress      = $adapter.MacAddress
            LinkSpeed       = $adapter.LinkSpeed
        }
    }
}
```

The output from the command above is shown below:

```
ComputerName    : COMPUTERNAME
OperatingSystem : Microsoft Windows 11 Pro
InterfaceName   : Ethernet
IPAddress       : 192.168.1.1
MacAddress      : AA-AB-AC-AD-AE-AF
LinkSpeed       : 1 Gbps
PSComputerName  : localhost
RunspaceId      : 775b79de-2f56-4835-8aa6-64cd903fd27a
```

Note that the command must either be run in an administrative console or the `-EnableNetworkAccess` parameter must be added. This applies to any subsequent examples running against the local computer.

The script executed can be as complex as necessary.

When `Invoke-Command` is given an array of computer names to act on, it will run the script block in parallel.

Parallel execution

Parallel execution is a built-in feature of Invoke-Command. For example, a list of computers might be found in Active Directory and used as the target of an operation, in this case, the members of a group that contains computer accounts:

```
$computerNames = Get-ADGroupMember GroupName |
    Get-ADComputer -Properties DnsHostName |
    Select-Object -ExpandProperty DnsHostName
Invoke-Command -ComputerName $computerNames -ScriptBlock {
    Get-Service dnscache
}
```

When using an array of computer names, Invoke-Command will run the script block on up to 32 computers at once by default. The number is controlled by the ThrottleLimit parameter and may be increased or decreased as appropriate. For example, this value might be increased:

```
$params = @{
    ComputerName  = $computerNames
    ThrottleLimit = 200
    ScriptBlock   = {
        Get-Service dnscache
    }
}
Invoke-Command @params
```

Sample output from the command above is shown below:

```
Status    Name       DisplayName         PSComputerName
------    ----       -----------         --------------
Running   dnscache   DNS Client          Computer1
Running   dnscache   DNS Client          Computer2
Running   dnscache   DNS Client          Computer3
Stopped   dnscache   DNS Client          Computer4
```

This command will return the results of the command for each host that responds. The output of Invoke-Command has several properties added to each object:

*   PSComputerName
*   PSShowComputerName
*   RunspaceId

A result can therefore be attributed to a single machine using the PSComputerName property. This might be used to replace the use of $env:COMPUTERNAME in an earlier example. These properties are always added, even if the output from the command is a string or a number.

This command run against localhost shows the presence of the properties:

```
PS> $output = Invoke-Command localhost { 1 }
PS> $output
1
PS> $output.PSComputerName
localhost
```

These extra properties only show when one of the parameters indicates that the command is being used on a remote computer (even `localhost`). For example, the properties will not show in the output from the following command.

```
Invoke-Command { Get-Process -ID $PID }
```

When `Invoke-Command` is used on a set of computers, it is often necessary to report on which computers failed to respond.

Catching remoting failures

In the scenario where a subset of computers may fail, it can be tempting to use ICMP, for instance with a command like `Test-Connection`.

This `ping` approach tends to reflect how scripts in older languages might approach the problem of assessing availability. However, this approach has two problems:

- It requires more work to make it run in parallel: Parallel execution is not natively supported by `Test-Connection`.
- It tests if the remote computer responds to "ping", not to a PS remoting request.

It is often better to let `Invoke-Command` get on with the job and capture the errors.

Using a `try` statement with the error action set to `Stop` is not appropriate as any single failure will cause the command to end, even if all the rest were successful. Error handling with `try` and `catch` is discussed in *Chapter 22, Error Handling*.

An `ErrorAction` of `SilentlyContinue` and the `ErrorVariable` parameter can be used to capture failures:

```
$params = @{
    ComputerName  = $computerNames
    ThrottleLimit = 200
    ScriptBlock   = {
        Get-Service dnscache
    }
    ErrorAction   = 'SilentlyContinue'
    ErrorVariable = 'failure'
}
$success = Invoke-Command @params
```

Once complete, the $success variable will contain the output from everything that completed. The $failure variable will include the errors for each that did not.

The ErrorRecord created by Invoke-Command includes the target of the operation allowing the names of failing computers to be extracted:

```
$failure | Select-Object -Property @(
    @{ Name = 'ComputerName'; Expression = 'TargetObject' }
    @{ Name = 'Error'; Expression = { $_.ToString() } }
)
```

Note that the script block to be executed on a remote computer is not limited to a single command as in the examples above.

Local functions and remote sessions

All of the code to be executed on a remote computer, and any commands called, must be available on that computer. Using a complex script block with the command is one possible approach.

It is also possible to use the body of a function as the script block. For example, if a function is created to get network information:

```
function Get-NetInformation {
    $params = @{
        AddressFamily = 'IPv4'
        PrefixOrigin  = 'Dhcp'
    }
    Get-NetIPAddress @params | ForEach-Object {
        $adapter = $_ | Get-NetAdapter

        [PSCustomObject]@{
            InterfaceName   = $adapter.Name
            IPAddress       = $_.IPAddress
            MacAddress      = $adapter.MacAddress
            LinkSpeed       = $adapter.LinkSpeed
        }
    }
}
```

This function can be used as the script block for Invoke-Command via the function provider.

```
Invoke-Command ${function:Get-NetInformation} -ComputerName localhost
```

This technique succeeds because the body of the function is declared as a script block.

If the function depends on other locally defined functions, the attempt will fail.

Remotely executed code often requires arguments from the client to complete.

Using ArgumentList

The ArgumentList parameter allows values to be passed to a remotely executed script block using positional binding.

The script below gets free space from specific drives using units based on two arguments for the script block that are passed using ArgumentList:

```
$params = @{
    ComputerName = 'localhost'
    ArgumentList = 'C', 'GB'
    ScriptBlock  = {
        param (
            $Name,
            $Units
        )
        Get-PSDrive -Name $Name | ForEach-Object {
            [PSCustomObject]@{
                Name      = $_.Name
                FreeSpace = [Math]::Round($_.Free / "1$Units", 2)
            }
        }
    }
}
Invoke-Command @params
```

If multiple drives were desired, then the array sub-expression operator could be used in ArgumentList:

```
$params['ArgumentList'] = @('C', 'D'), 'GB'
```

However, because it uses positional binding, ArgumentList cannot practically deal with optional parameters (except by order) or Switch parameters.

It is possible to work around this by encapsulating the script to execute inside another script:

```
$definition = {
    param ( $Name, $Units )
    Get-PSDrive -Name $Name | ForEach-Object {
        [PSCustomObject]@{
            Name      = $_.Name
            FreeSpace = [Math]::Round($_.Free / "1$Units", 2)
        }
    }
}

$params = @{
```

```
        ComputerName = 'localhost'
        ArgumentList = @(
            $definition
            @{
                Name  = 'C'
                Units = 'GB'
            }
        )
        ScriptBlock  = {
            param ($definition, $arguments)

            & ([ScriptBlock]::Create($definition)) @arguments
        }
    }
}
Invoke-Command @params
```

This approach has the advantage that it can deal with complex parameters passed to a script block with Invoke-Command. But the clear disadvantage is that the approach is very complicated.

The script block definition is serialized as a string when it is sent to the remote computer, and the script block must be recreated before anything can be executed.

The using scope modifier can be used as an alternative to this approach.

The using scope modifier

The using scope modifier can be used to access variables created outside of a script block when used with Invoke-Command, Start-Job, and Start-ThreadJob. The Job commands are explored in *Chapter 15, Asynchronous Processing*.

For example, the value of the $hello variable can be accessed inside Invoke-Command as shown below:

```
$hello = 'Hello world'
Invoke-Command { $using:hello } -ComputerName localhost
```

This approach can be extended to the free space script, which previously required arguments to be passed:

```
$params = @{
    ComputerName = 'localhost'
    ScriptBlock  = {
        Get-PSDrive -Name $using:Name | ForEach-Object {
            [PSCustomObject]@{
                Name      = $_.Name
                FreeSpace = [Math]::Round(
                    $_.Free / "1$using:Units",
```

```
                    2
                )
            }
        }
    }
}

$Name = 'C'
$Units = 'GB'

Invoke-Command @params
```

The variables must be defined before Invoke-Command is called, but this can be anywhere in the script.

Each of the commands demonstrated so far has accepted a computer name or array of computer names to execute. PowerShell offers greater control if a PSSession is explicitly created and used.

PS Sessions

When Enter-PSSession and Invoke-Command were used with the ComputerName parameter, a PSSession was implicitly created and destroyed for each remote computer.

Creating the session outside of Invoke-Command is less convenient but allows sessions to be reused and offers greater control of the session lifespan.

New-PSSession and Get-PSSession

Sessions are created using the New-PSSession command. In the following example, a session is created on a computer named PSTEST:

```
PS> New-PSSession -ComputerName PSTEST

Id   Name       ComputerName State  ConfigurationName       Availability
--   ----       ------------ -----  -----------------       ------------
1    Session1   PSTEST       Opened Microsoft.PowerShell    Available
```

Sessions created using New-PSSession persist until the PSSession is removed (by Remove-PSSession) or the PowerShell session ends.

The following example returns sessions created in the current PowerShell session:

```
PS> Get-PSSession | Select-Object Id, ComputerName, State

Id ComputerName State
-- ------------ -----
 1 PSTEST       Opened
```

If the ComputerName parameter is supplied, Get-PSSession will show sessions created on that computer. For example, imagine a session is created in one PowerShell console:

```
$session = New-PSSession -ComputerName PSTest -Name Example
```

A second administrator console session will be able to view details of that session:

```
Get-PSSession -ComputerName PSTest |
    Select-Object Name, ComputerName, State
```

The output from the command above is shown below:

```
Name      ComputerName   State

----      ------------   -----

Example   PSTest         Disconnected
```

The session above shows as disconnected. Invoke-Command has a specific use for disconnected sessions.

Disconnected sessions

The InDisconnectedSession of Invoke-Command starts the requested script and immediately disconnects the session. This allows a script to be started and collected from a different console session or a different computer.

The session parameter cannot be used with InDisconnectedSession; Invoke-Command creates a new session for a specified computer name. The session is returned by the following command:

```
Invoke-Command {
    Start-Sleep -Seconds 120
    'Done'
} -ComputerName PSTest -InDisconnectedSession
```

A second PowerShell session or computer can connect to the disconnected session to retrieve the results. The following command assumes that only one session exists with the PSTest computer:

```
Get-PSSession -ComputerName PSTest |
    Connect-PSSession |
    Receive-PSSession
```

Once the session has been created and disconnected, the PowerShell console can be closed. A second PowerShell console can find and connect to the existing session:

```
$session = Get-PSSession -ComputerName PSTest -Name 'Example'
Connect-PSSession $session
```

Reviewing the details of the session can show that it is busy running Start-Sleep:

```
Get-PSSession |
    Select-Object Name, ComputerName, State, Availability
```

Expected output from the command above is shown below:

```
Name          ComputerName    State     Availability
----          ------------    -----     ------------
Example       PSTest          Opened    Busy
```

PS Sessions are also used to make commands defined on one computer available on another.

Import-PSSession

Import-PSSession brings commands from a remote computer into the current session. Microsoft Exchange uses this technique to provide remote access to the Exchange Management Shell, and PowerShell 7 uses this technique to provide access to modules compatible with Windows PowerShell only.

The following example imports the NetAdapter module from a remote server into the current session:

```
$computerName = 'PSTest'
$session = New-PSSession -ComputerName $computerName
Import-PSSession -Session $session -Module NetAdapter
```

Any commands used within this module are executed against the session target, not against the local computer.

If the session is removed, the imported module and its commands will be removed from the local session.

Export-PSSession

In the preceding example, Import-PSSession is used to immediately import commands from a remote system into a local session. Export-PSSession writes a persistent module that can be used to achieve the same goal.

The following example creates a module in the current user's module path:

```
$computerName = 'PSTest'
$session = New-PSSession -ComputerName $computerName
Export-PSSession -Session $session -Module NetAdapter -OutputModule
"NetAdapter-$computerName"
```

Once the module has been created, it can be imported by name:

```
Import-Module "NetAdapter-$computerName"
```

This process replaces the need to define and import a session and is useful for remote commands that are used on a regular basis.

Copying items between sessions

PowerShell 5 introduced the ability to copy between sessions using the Copy-Item command.

The FromSession parameter is used to copy a file to the local system:

```
$session1 = New-PSSession PSTest1
Copy-Item -Path C:\temp\doc.txt -Destination C:\Temp -FromSession $session1
```

In the preceding example, Path is on PSTest1.

The ToSession parameter is used to copy a file to a remote system:

```
$session2 = New-PSSession PSTest2
Copy-Item -Path C:\temp\doc.txt -Destination C:\Temp -ToSession $session2
```

In the previous example, the path used for the destination parameter is on PSTest2.

The FromSession and ToSession parameters cannot be specified together; two separate commands are required to copy a file between two remote sessions.

Before a server can accept requests using PowerShell remoting it must be enabled and configured. At the start of this chapter, Enable-PSRemoting was used to achieve this, but it is not the only option.

WS-Management

Windows remoting uses WS-Management as its communication protocol. Support for WS-Management and remoting was introduced with PowerShell 2.0. WS-Management uses **Simple Object Access Protocol (SOAP)** to pass information between the client and the server.

PowerShell Remoting Protocol (PSRP) uses WS-Management as a means of communicating with a remote PowerShell instance.

Enabling and configuring remoting

Before remoting can be used on a desktop operating system, it must be enabled. In a domain environment, remoting can be enabled using a group policy:

- **Policy name:** Allow remote server management through WinRM
- Path: Computer configuration\Administrative Templates\Windows Components\Windows Remote Management (WinRM)\WinRM Service

If remoting is enabled using a group policy, a firewall rule should be created to allow access to the service:

- **Policy name:** Define inbound port exceptions
- **Path:** Computer Configuration\Administrative Templates\Network\Network Connections\ Windows Firewall\Domain Profile
- Port exception example: 5985:TCP:*:enabled:WSMan

PowerShell remoting can be enabled on a per-machine basis using the Enable-PSRemoting command.

Remoting may be disabled in PowerShell using `Disable-PSRemoting`. Disabling remoting will show the following warning:

```
PS> Disable-PSRemoting
WARNING: Disabling the session configurations does not undo all the changes
made by the Enable-PSRemoting or Enable-PSSessionConfiguration cmdlet. You
might have to manually undo the changes by following these steps:
1. Stop and disable the WinRM service.
2. Delete the listener that accepts requests on any IP address.
3. Disable the firewall exceptions for WS-Management communications.
4.Restore the value of the LocalAccountTokenFilterPolicy to 0, which restricts
remote access to members of the Administrators group on the computer.
```

If `Enable-PSRemoting` is run in the PowerShell 7 console, additional session configurations will be created that allow a choice of either Windows PowerShell (the default) or PowerShell 7.

The `ConfigurationName` parameter of `Invoke-Command` and the `PSSession` commands or `$PSSessionConfigurationName` preference variable can be set to `PowerShell.7` to access the Power-Shell 7 configuration.

The WSMan drive

The content of the WSMan drive is accessible when PowerShell is running as the administrator. The drive can be used to view and change the configuration of remoting.

For example, the provider can be used to update settings such as `MaxEnvelopeSize`, which affects the maximum permissible size of SOAP messages sent and received by WSMan:

```
Set-Item WSMan:\localhost\MaxEnvelopeSizekb 8KB
```

The `MaxEnvelopeSize` property is defined in the WSMan protocol extension specification: https://learn.microsoft.com/en-gb/openspecs/windows_protocols/ms-wsman/8a6b1967-ff8e-4756-9a3b-890b4b439847.

The property is often referenced in relation to Exchange and IIS, which can require the size to be increased above the default value of `1024` bytes. The value must be a multiple of `1024`; the previous example uses `8 KB`, a commonly used size in response to a message where the request has exceeded the configured quota.

The `WinRM` service may need to be restarted for changes to take effect:

```
Restart-Service winrm
```

The WSMan provider can also be used to configure SSL.

Remoting and SSL

By default, Windows remoting requests are unencrypted. An HTTPS listener can be created to support encryption. Before attempting to create an HTTPS listener, a certificate is required.

Using a self-signed certificate is often the first step when configuring SSL. Windows 10 and 11 come with a PKI module that can be used to create a certificate. In the following example, a self-signed certificate is created in the computer personal store:

```
PS> New-SelfSignedCertificate -DnsName $env:COMPUTERNAME


    PSParentPath: Microsoft.PowerShell.Security\Certificate::LocalMachine\MY


Thumbprint                                Subject
----------                                -------
D8D2F174EE1C37F7C2021C9B7EB6FEE3CB1B9A41  CN=SSLTEST
```

Once the certificate has been created, an HTTPS listener can be created using the WSMan drive. Replace the thumbprint in the following code with the thumbprint of a valid certificate, such as one created using the command in the previous example:

```
$params = @{
    Path                  = 'WSMan:\localhost\Listener'
    Address               = '*'
    Transport             = 'HTTPS'
    CertificateThumbprint = 'D8D2F174EE1C37F7C2021C9B7EB6FEE3CB1B9A41'
    Force                 = $true
}
New-Item @params
```

The Force parameter is used to suppress a confirmation prompt.

If Windows Firewall is running, a new rule must also be created to allow inbound connections to TCP port 5986:

```
$params = @{
    DisplayName = $name = 'Windows Remote Management (HTTPS-In)'
    Name        = $name
    Profile     = 'Any'
    LocalPort   = 5986
    Protocol    = 'TCP'
}
New-NetFirewallRule @params
```

Any created HTTPS listeners may be viewed as follows:

```
Get-ChildItem WSMan:\localhost\Listener\* |
    Where-Object {
        (Get-Item "$($_.PSPath)\Transport").Value -eq 'HTTPS'
    }
```

The command above will show the listener container displayed below. The name of the listener will vary:

```
WSManConfig: Microsoft.WSMan.Management\WSMan::localhost\Listener


Type         Keys                              Name
----         ----                              ----
Container {Transport=HTTPS, Address=*} Listener_1305953032
```

The example below rewrites the output so the keys can be viewed as properties:

```
Get-ChildItem WSMan:\localhost\Listener | ForEach-Object {
    $listener = [Ordered]@{
        Name = $_.Name
    }
    Get-ChildItem $_.PSPath | ForEach-Object {
        $listener[$_.Name] = $_.Value
    }
    [PSCustomObject]$listener
} | Where-Object Transport -eq 'HTTPS'
```

The self-signed certificate can be assigned in this manner, but for an SSL connection to succeed, the client must trust the certificate. Without trust, the following error is shown:

```
PS> Invoke-Command -ScriptBlock { Get-Process } -ComputerName $env:COMPUTERNAME
-UseSSL

[SSLTEST] Connecting to remote server SSLTEST failed with the following error
message : The server certificate on the destination computer (SSLTEST:5986) has
the following errors:
The SSL certificate is signed by an unknown certificate authority. For more
information, see the about_Remote_Troubleshooting Help topic.
+ CategoryInfo : OpenError: (SSLTEST:String) [], PSRemotingTransportException
+ FullyQualifiedErrorId : 12175,PSSessionStateBroken
```

Two options are available to bypass this option:

- Disable certificate verification.
- Add the certificate from the remote server to the local root certificate store.

Disabling certificate verification can be achieved by configuring the options of PSSession:

```
$options = New-PSSessionOption -SkipCACheck
$session = New-PSSession $env:COMPUTERNAME -SessionOption $options
```

Either of the preceding options will allow the connection to complete. This can be verified using the `Test-WSMan` command:

```
Test-WSMan -UseSSL
```

If a new certificate is obtained, you can replace the certificate for the listener using `Set-Item`. The listener ID and certificate thumbprint should be updated with locally relevant values:

```
$params = @{
    Path  = 'WSMan:\localhost\Listener\Listener_1305953032\
CertificateThumbprint'
    Value = 'D8D2F174EE1C37F7C2021C9B7EB6FEE3CB1B9A41'
}
Set-Item @params
```

Windows systems, even without using SSL, will still encrypt traffic using remoting.

User Account Control

User Account Control (UAC) restricts local (not domain) user accounts that log on using a remote connection. By default, the remote connection will be made as a standard user account, that is, a user without administrative privileges.

The `Enable-PSRemoting` command disables UAC remote restrictions. If another method has been used to enable remoting, and a local account is being used to connect, it is possible that remote restrictions are still in place.

The current value can be viewed using the following:

```
$params = @{
    Path = 'HKLM:\SOFTWARE\Microsoft\Windows\CurrentVersion\Policies\System'
    Name = 'LocalAccountTokenFilterPolicy'
}
Get-ItemProperty @params
```

The command above will show the current value of the property. If only the value is needed, `Get-ItemProperty` can be substituted for `Get-ItemPropertyValue`. The output of the command is shown below:

```
LocalAccountTokenFilterPolicy : 1
PSPath                        : Microsoft.PowerShell.Core\Registry
                                ::HKEY_LOCAL_MACHINE\SOFTWARE\Micr
                                osoft\Windows\CurrentVersion\Polic
                                ies\System
PSParentPath                  : Microsoft.PowerShell.Core\Registry
                                ::HKEY_LOCAL_MACHINE\SOFTWARE\Micr
```

```
                            osoft\Windows\CurrentVersion\Polic
                            ies
PSChildName              : System
PSDrive                  : HKLM
PSProvider               : Microsoft.PowerShell.Core\Registry
```

If the key or value is missing, an error will be thrown. The impact of this is described in the help article linked below. UAC remote restrictions can be disabled as follows. Using the Force parameter will allow the creation of both the key and the value:

```
$params = @{
    Path  = 'HKLM:\SOFTWARE\Microsoft\Windows\CurrentVersion\Policies\System'
    Name  = 'LocalAccountTokenFilterPolicy'
    Value = 1
    Force = $true
}
Set-ItemProperty @params
```

The change used previously, and the UAC remote restrictions, is described in the Windows troubleshooting reference: https://learn.microsoft.com/troubleshoot/windows-server/windows-security/user-account-control-and-remote-restriction.

When the client is not part of the same domain as the server, the trusted hosts setting is important.

Trusted hosts

If either the client or server is not part of a domain, or is part of an untrusted domain, an attempt to connect using remoting may fail. The remote system must either be listed in trusted hosts or use SSL.

The use of trusted hosts also applies when connecting to another computer using a local user account.

Trusted hosts are set on the client, that is, the system making the connection. The following command gets the current value:

```
Get-Item WSMan:\localhost\Client\TrustedHosts
```

The list is empty by default and the value will be blank, as shown below:

```
   WSManConfig: Microsoft.WSMan.Management\WSMan::localhost\Client

Type            Name           SourceOfValue    Value
----            ----           -------------    -----
System.String   TrustedHosts
```

The value is a comma-delimited list. Wildcards are supported in the list. The following function may be used to add a value to the list:

```
function Add-TrustedHost {
```

```
    param (
        [string]$Hostname
    )

    $item = Get-Item WSMan:\localhost\Client\TrustedHosts
    $trustedHosts = @($item.Value -split ',')
    $trustedHosts = $trustedHosts + $Hostname |
        Where-Object { $_ } |
        Select-Object -Unique

    $item | Set-Item -Value ($trustedHosts -join ',')
}
```

Adding a trusted host will raise a confirmation prompt:

```
PS> Add-TrustedHost '192.168.1.*'

WinRM Security Configuration.
This command modifies the TrustedHosts list for the WinRM client. The computers
in the TrustedHosts list might not be
authenticated. The client might send credential information to these computers.
Are you sure that you want to modify
this list?
[Y] Yes  [N] No  [S] Suspend  [?] Help (default is "Y"):
```

If the prompt is accepted the entry will be added and will show when Get-Item is run again:

```
PS> Get-Item WSMan:\localhost\Client\TrustedHosts

   WSManConfig: Microsoft.WSMan.Management\WSMan::localhost\Client

Type          Name           SourceOfValue    Value
----          ----           -------------    -----
System.String TrustedHosts                    192.168.1.*
```

PowerShell remoting is not limited to Windows. PowerShell on Linux can also be configured to support remoting, as we'll see next.

Remoting on Linux

Microsoft provides instructions for installing PowerShell on Linux; these should be followed before attempting to configure remoting: https://learn.microsoft.com/powershell/scripting/install/installing-powershell-on-linux.

Once installed, it is possible to make PowerShell the default shell. This is optional and does not affect remoting. First, check that PowerShell is listed in the `shells` file:

```
Get-Content /etc/shells    # Use cat or less in Bash
```

The native `chsh` (change shell) command can be used to change the default shell for the current user, as shown in the following example:

```
chsh -s /usr/bin/pwsh
```

To configure remoting using `WSMan`, the `OMI` and `PSRP` packages must be installed. The following example uses yum since the operating system in use is CentOS 7:

```
yum install omi.x86_64 omi-psrp-server.x86_64
```

By default, CentOS has a firewall configured. The network interface in use, in this case, `eth0`, must be added to an appropriate zone, and WinRM must be allowed:

```
firewall-cmd --zone=home --change-interface=eth0
firewall-cmd --zone=home --add-port=5986/tcp
```

Once configured, it should be possible to connect to the remote host. SSL is required to form the connection. The certificate is self-signed so certificate validity tests must be skipped at this stage:

```
$params = @{
    ComputerName   = 'LinuxSystemNameOrIPAddress'
    Credential     = Get-Credential
    Authentication = 'Basic'
    UseSsl         = $true
    SessionOption  = New-PSSessionOption -SkipCACheck -SkipCNCheck
}
Enter-PSSession @params
```

The state of the certificate leaves the identity of the host in question, but it does ensure that traffic is encrypted. If SSL is to be used beyond testing, a valid certificate chain should be established.

At this point, the remote computer should be accessible using both Windows PowerShell and PowerShell Core.

Remoting over SSH

PowerShell Core introduced the concept of remoting over SSH. This provides a useful alternative to remoting over HTTPS, avoiding the burden of managing certificates: https://learn.microsoft.com/powershell/scripting/learn/remoting/ssh-remoting-in-powershell-core.

The SSH transport for remoting cannot be used from Windows PowerShell, only PowerShell 6 and 7.

This section explores the use of SSH between a Windows and Linux client, but SSH can also be used between two Windows systems.

Connecting from Windows to Linux

If connecting from Windows, an SSH client must be installed.

In Windows 10 and Windows Server 2019, you can enable OpenSSH as an optional feature. For example:

```
Add-WindowsCapability -Online -Name OpenSSH.Client~~~~0.0.1.0
```

The feature is documented in the Windows Server reference: https://learn.microsoft.com/en-gb/windows-server/administration/openssh/openssh_install_firstuse.

Alternatively, the openssh package can be installed using the Chocolatey package manager (http://chocolatey.org):

```
choco install openssh
```

Depending on the desired configuration, public key authentication may be enabled in the SSH daemon configuration file. A subsystem must be added to the file.

To enable public key authentication, set PubkeyAuthentication:

```
PubkeyAuthentication yes
```

An existing subsystem entry will likely exist toward the end of the file; this new entry can be added beneath the existing entry (the value in the following code is a single configuration line):

```
Subsystem        powershell    /opt/microsoft/powershell/7/pwsh -sshs -NoLogo
-NoProfile
```

The sshd service should be restarted after changing the configuration file:

```
service sshd restart
```

The connection in this example uses SSH key authentication. This requires an SSH key on Windows. If an existing key is not available, the ssh-keygen command can be used to create a new key pair. The command will prompt for any information it requires.

The private key created by this command will be used when connecting to a remote host. The public key is used to authorize a user and will be placed on the Linux system.

The public key can be obtained by running the following command on the system on which it was generated. This command assumes default filenames were used when generating the key:

```
Get-Content ~\.ssh\id_rsa.pub | Set-Clipboard
```

~ is home

The tilde character may be used as shorthand for the path to the home directory. On Linux it is typically /home/<username>, and on Windows it is typically like C:\users\<username>.

~ may be replaced with the $home variable, or the $env:USERPROFILE environment variable on Windows, if desired.

The public key should be added to the `authorized_keys` files on Linux:

```
$publicKey = 'ssh-rsa AAAABG...'
New-Item ~/.ssh -ItemType Directory
Set-Content -Path ~/.ssh/authorized_keys -Value $publicKey
```

Once complete, a session can be created and used to interact with the Linux system:

```
$params = @{
    HostName     = 'LinuxSystemNameOrIPAddress'
    UserName     = $env:USERNAME
    SSHTransport = $true
    KeyFilePath  = '~\.ssh\id_rsa'
}
Enter-PSSession @params
```

As remoting is encapsulated in exchanged XML requests, interactive commands such as vi will not work in the remoting session.

Connecting from Linux to Windows

Connecting from Linux to Windows is a harder path; it is clearly undergoing rapid change and is much less mature than connections in the other direction.

Before moving on to configuring SSH, verify that WSMan functions. An HTTPS listener must be set up; HTTP connections are prohibited by the PSRP package. If HTTPS is not already available, a self-signed certificate may be created and used as shown in the *Remoting and SSL* section.

If remoting is not yet configured for PowerShell 7, run the Enable-PSRemoting command in the Core console (as an administrator). Once enabled, find the name of the configuration entry using the Get-PSSessionConfiguration command.

You can use the configuration name to create a session to PowerShell Core that runs on the Windows system:

```
$params = @{
    HostName          = 'WindowsSystemNameOrIPAddress'
    Credential        = (Get-Credential)
    Authentication    = 'Basic'
    UseSSL            = $true
    ConfigurationName = 'PowerShell.6.1.1'
}
Enter-PSSession @params
```

At the time of writing, attempting to connect from Linux to a PowerShell 5.1 session results in an access denied error message.

The OpenSSH package must be installed on Windows to continue. The OpenSSH server feature can be installed using the following command:

```
Add-WindowsCapability -Online -Name OpenSSH.Server~~~~0.0.1.0
```

Alternatively, if the Chocolatey package was used, the server can be enabled:

```
& "C:\Program Files\OpenSSH-Win64\install-sshd.ps1"
```

Windows Firewall must also be opened if it is in use:

```
$params = @{
    DisplayName = 'OpenSSH Server (sshd)'
    Name        = 'sshd'
    Enabled     = 'True'
    Direction   = 'Inbound'
    LocalPort   = 22
    Protocol    = 'TCP'
    Action      = 'Allow'
}
New-NetFirewallRule @params
```

Once this step is complete, it should be possible to create an SSH connection from Linux to Windows:

```
ssh user@WindowsSystemNameOrIPAddress
```

As with configuring Linux, public key authentication may be allowed, and a subsystem must be configured, this time on the Windows system. The C:\ProgramData\ssh\sshd_config file must be edited.

To enable public key authentication, set PubkeyAuthentication:

```
PubkeyAuthentication yes
```

Add a subsystem to the file. This may be specified in addition to any existing subsystem:

```
Subsystem       powershell      C:/progra~1/PowerShell/7/pwsh.exe -sshs -NoLogo
-NoProfile
```

PowerShell 7 may be configured as the default shell for incoming SSH connections:

```
$params = @{
    Path = 'HKLM:\SOFTWARE\OpenSSH'
    Name = 'DefaultShell'
    Value = Join-Path -Path $pshome -ChildPath 'pwsh.exe'
    Force = $true
}
New-ItemProperty @params
```

The sshd service should be restarted after changing the configuration file or the default shell:

```
Restart-Service sshd
```

At this point, it will be possible to create a remoting session using SSH by entering a password when prompted:

```
$params = @{
    HostName       = 'WindowsSystemNameOrIPAddress'
    UserName       = $env:USERNAME
    SSHTransport = $true
}
Enter-PSSession @params
```

Public key authentication may be configured in the same way as was done for Linux. A key can be generated on Linux using the ssh-keygen command.

The public key, by default ~/.ssh/id_rsa.pub, may be added to an authorized_keys file on Windows. The following command, when run on Linux, displays the public key:

```
Get-Content ~/.ssh/id_rsa.pub
```

This public key may be added to an authorized_keys file for a user on the Windows system:

```
$publicKey = 'ssh-rsa AAAABG...'
Set-Content -Path ~/.ssh/authorized_keys -Value $publicKey
```

At this point, the Linux system will be able to use public key authentication to access the Windows system:

```
$params = @{
    HostName       = 'WindowsSystemNameOrIPAddress'
    UserName       = 'username'
    SSHTransport = $true
    KeyFilePath  = '~\.ssh\id_rsa'
}
Enter-PSSession @params
```

Extending this further, Windows systems running PowerShell 7 and the SSH daemon may use SSH as a remoting transport to access other Windows systems.

One of the most common problems when using remoting is accessing remote resources from within a remoting session.

The double-hop problem

The double-hop problem describes a scenario in PowerShell where remoting is used to connect to a host and the remote host tries to connect to another resource. In this scenario, the second connection, the second hop, fails because authentication cannot be implicitly passed.

The command below would cause a double-hop problem:

```
Invoke-Command -ComputerName WEB01 -ScriptBlock {
    Get-Content \\FS01\share\somefile.txt
}
```

The connection from the client to the server WEB01 is the first hop and the credentials of the current user are acceptable for this. The connection from WEB01 to FS01 (using an SMB file share) is a second hop and will fail.

The same can be seen for any service that requires an authenticated request. For example, the Microsoft Active Directory module:

```
Invoke-Command -ComputerName FS01 -ScriptBlock {
    $adUser = Get-ADUser -Identity username
}
```

This time the second hop is from FS01 to the Active Directory web services gateway.

Over the years, there have been numerous articles that discuss this problem. Ashley McGlone published a blog post in 2016 that describes the problem and the possible solutions: https://learn. microsoft.com/en-gb/archive/blogs/ashleymcglone/powershell-remoting-kerberos-double-hop-solved-securely.

The delegation methods described by the article are the preferred fix for unavoidable double-hop scenarios, but the setup required for these goes beyond the scope of this chapter.

This section briefly explores using CredSSP, as well as how to pass explicit credentials to a remote system. Neither of these options is considered secure, but they require the least amount of work to implement.

These two options are useful in the following situations:

- The remote endpoint is trusted and has not been compromised.
- Critical authentication tokens can be extracted by an administrator on the remote system.
- They are not used for wide-scale regular or scheduled automation, as the methods significantly increase exposure.

CredSSP must be configured on both the server and client.

CredSSP

Credentials passed using CredSSP are sent in clear text. CredSSP is not considered secure.

A session can be created using CredSSP as the authentication provider:

```
$params = @{
    ComputerName    = 'PSTest'
    Credential      = Get-Credential
```

```
      Authentication = 'CredSSP'
}
New-PSSession @params
```

CredSSP must be enabled on the client to support passing credentials to a remote system. The DelegateComputer parameter can be used with either a specific name or a wildcard (*):

```
Enable-WSManCredSSP -Role Client -DelegateComputer PSTest
```

CredSSP must also be enabled on the server to receive credentials:

```
Enable-WSManCredSSP -Role Server
```

If this approach is used as a temporary measure, the CredSSP roles might be removed afterward.

On the server making the connection, the Client role can be disabled:

```
Disable-WSManCredSSP -Role Client
```

On the remote system, the Server role can be disabled:

```
Disable-WSManCredSSP -Role Server
```

An alternative workaround is to pass explicit credentials to a remote session.

Passing credentials

Passing credentials into a remote session means the second hop can authenticate without being dependent on authentication tokens from the original system.

In this example, the using scope modifier is used to access a credential variable. The credential is used to run a query against Active Directory from a remote system:

```
$Credential = Get-Credential
Invoke-Command -ComputerName FS01 -ScriptBlock {
    Get-ADUser -Filter * -Credential $using:Credential
}
```

Passing credentials in this manner works around the problem but cannot be considered a secure solution. The article quoted at the beginning of this session properly explores the alternatives available.

PS Sessions are not the only thing to use Windows remoting. **Common Information Model (CIM)** sessions also use Windows remoting but are only used to access WMI.

CIM sessions

CIM sessions are used to work with CIM services, predominantly WMI or commands that base their functionality on WMI. Such commands include those in the NetAdapter and Storage modules available on Windows 2012 and Windows 8. A list of commands that support CIM sessions may be viewed by entering the following:

```
Get-Command -ParameterName CimSession
```

The list will only include commands from modules that have been imported.

The CIM commands are only available in Windows installations of PowerShell. The CIM implementation is specific to the Microsoft platform and is not implemented only in .NET.

```
New-CimSession
```

CIM sessions are created using the New-CimSession command. The following example creates a CIM session using the current system as the computer name and using WSMan as the protocol:

```
PS> New-CimSession -ComputerName $env:COMPUTERNAME

Id           : 1
Name         : CimSession1
InstanceId   : bc03b547-1051-4af1-a41d-4d16b0ec0402
ComputerName : PSTEST
Protocol     : WSMAN
```

If the computer name parameter is omitted, the protocol will be set to DCOM:

```
PS> New-CimSession

Id           : 2
Name         : CimSession2
InstanceId   : 804595f4-0144-4590-990a-92b2f22f894f
ComputerName : localhost
Protocol     : DCOM
```

New-CimSession can be used to configure operation timeout settings and whether an initial network test should be performed.

The protocol used by New-CimSession can be changed using New-CimSessionOption. Changing the protocol can be useful if there is a need to interact with systems where WinRM is not running or configured:

```
$params = @{
    ComputerName = $env:COMPUTERNAME
    SessionOption = New-CimSessionOption -Protocol DCOM
}
New-CimSession @params
```

The session created by the command above is shown below:

```
Id           : 3
Name         : CimSession3
InstanceId   : 29bba117-c899-4389-b874-5afe43962a1e
ComputerName : PSTEST
Protocol     : DCOM
```

Sessions created using New-CimSession can be viewed using Get-CimSession.

Get-CimSession

Sessions created using New-CimSession persist until the CIM session is removed (by Remove-CimSession) or the PowerShell session ends:

```
PS> Get-CimSession | Select-Object Id, ComputerName, Protocol

Id   ComputerName Protocol
--   ------------ --------
1    PSTEST       WSMAN
2    localhost    DCOM
3    PSTEST       DCOM
```

CIM sessions can be used by different calls to Get-CimInstance or other CIM commands.

Using CIM sessions

Once a CIM session has been created, it can be used for one or more CIM requests. In the following example, a CIM session is created and then used to gather disk and partition information:

```
$ErrorActionPreference = 'Stop'
try {
    $session = New-CimSession -ComputerName $env:COMPUTERNAME
    Get-Disk -CimSession $session
    Get-Partition -CimSession $session
} catch {
    throw
}
```

In the preceding script, if the attempt to create the session succeeds, the session will be used to get disk and partition information.

If a single command in the block fails, the block will stop running. If the attempt to create a new session fails, Get-Disk and Get-Partition will not run.

Just Enough Administration

Just Enough Administration (JEA) leverages PowerShell remoting to allow administrative delegation via a remoting session.

JEA consists of:

- A session configuration file that describes the commands to be made available and language modes.
- A registered PSSession configuration that is created based on that file.

- Access control that is set on the PSSession configuration.

JEA documentation can be found in the PowerShell reference: https://learn.microsoft.com/powershell/scripting/learn/remoting/jea/overview.

JEA configuration is defined in a session configuration file. The file is saved as a PowerShell data file (a PSSC file, the same format as psd1 files) and is used to define and register the JEA remoting endpoint.

Microsoft has a couple of small archived examples that can be viewed on GitHub: https://github.com/PowerShell/JEA.

JEA can be configured manually, as shown in the following sections, or using a DSC configuration in Windows PowerShell.

Session configuration

Session configuration files can be created using the New-PSSessionConfigurationFile command.

The session configuration file determines which commands are available to anyone importing the session.

A session configuration file should be restrictive. Commands such as Invoke-Expression and Add-Type should not be permitted; they allow arbitrary code execution, which defeats the point of a restricted endpoint. The language mode will ideally be set to restricted or none.

The following example is a simple session configuration that allows access to the Get-ComputerInfo command. Each of the commands is executed in an administrative session in PowerShell 7:

```
if (-not (Test-Path c:\jea)) {
    New-Item c:\jea -ItemType Directory
}
$params = @{
    Path          = 'c:\jea\jea.pssc'
    LanguageMode  = 'NoLanguage'
    SessionType   = 'RestrictedRemoteServer'
    VisibleCmdlets = @(
        'Get-ComputerInfo'
        'Export-Csv'
    )
}
New-PSSessionConfigurationFile @params
```

Once the configuration file has been created, the session configuration can be registered:

```
$params = @{
    Name = 'JEATest'
    Path = 'c:\jea\jea.pssc'
}
Register-PSSessionConfiguration @params
```

The file that describes the session can be deleted once the session is registered.

You can use the new session immediately, for example, by entering the possession:

```
Enter-PSSession -ComputerName localhost -ConfigurationName JEATest
```

By default, the session configuration allows administrators or members of the local group **Remote Management Users**. Additional rights may be granted as seen when exploring remoting permissions.

Once inside the session, several default commands will be available, such as Get-Command. These are permitted because of the SessionType. Export-Csv and Get-ComputerInfo are available because they have been explicitly permitted.

If the endpoint is no longer required, it can be removed as shown in the following code:

```
Unregister-PSSessionConfiguration -Name 'JEATest'
```

Careful consideration should be given to which commands are exposed by JEA. The default account configuration used in the preceding example grants administrative rights to the system hosting the endpoint.

Role capabilities

Role capabilities add a lot of flexibility to the endpoint. Different commands can be made available via an endpoint depending on the user, or the group the user belongs to. If a user belongs to more than one role the user will be granted access to the commands from each role.

Role capabilities must be maintained in a file. A role capabilities file can be created using the New-PSRoleCapabilityFile command:

```
$params = @{
    Path             = 'c:\jea\group.psrc'
    VisibleCmdlets   = @(
        'Get-ComputerInfo'
        'Export-Csv'
    )
}
New-PSRoleCapabilityFile @params
```

The command above has no output; it creates the .psrc file, which is a PowerShell data file containing a hashtable.

The content of the .psrc file can be viewed, with the first few lines shown below:

```
PS> Get-Content C:\jea\group.psrc
@{

# ID used to uniquely identify this document
GUID = '37cfe0e6-6011-47f1-b3f2-13438baa2a4b'
```

```
# Author of this document
Author = 'chris'
...
```

This file may be used when creating a session configuration in place of the simple list of commands:

```
$params = @{
    Path            = 'c:\jea\jea.pssc'
    LanguageMode    = 'NoLanguage'
    SessionType     = 'RestrictedRemoteServer'
    RoleDefinitions = @{
        'DOMAIN\Group' = @{
            RoleCapabilityFiles = 'c:\jea\group.psrc'
        }
    }
}
New-PSSessionConfigurationFile @params
```

As is the case when creating the capability file, this command does not have any output.

The pssc file is also a PowerShell data file and can be viewed as text. Here's a part of it:

```
PS> Get-Content c:\jea\jea.pssc
@{

# Version number of the schema used for this document
SchemaVersion = '2.0.0.0'

# ID used to uniquely identify this document
GUID = '4f2e442e-446b-4832-920f-716a0472b271'
...
```

The role capability file must be retained after the session has been registered.

With careful consideration, JEA can be an effective delegation tool. Thought must be given to the permitted language features and the permissions assigned to accounts.

Summary

This chapter delved into remoting in PowerShell, starting with a look at Enter-PSSession and Invoke-Command, the backbone of any code making use of remoting.

PS Sessions were explored, which allow greater flexibility and enable the use of the ToSession and FromSession parameters of Copy-Item.

WS-Management was explored, along with the more advanced configuration scenarios for PowerShell remoting it offers, before looking at configuring PS remoting on Linux.

The double-hop problem was briefly considered, and remains a common problem for remoting users.

CIM sessions will, by default, make use of PS remoting and therefore implicitly depend on the service. CIM can be explicitly made to use DCOM instead if required.

Just Enough Administration offers the ability to provide delegated access to PowerShell content via a remoting session.

The next chapter explores asynchronous processing.

Learn more on Discord

Read this book alongside other users, PowerShell experts, and the author himself. Ask questions, provide solutions to other readers, chat with the author via Ask Me Anything sessions, and much more.

Scan the QR code or visit the link to join the community.

https://packt.link/SecNet

15

Asynchronous Processing

PowerShell prefers to run things synchronously, that is, sequentially, or one after another. However, it is frequently necessary to run many things simultaneously, without waiting for another command to complete. This is called an asynchronous operation.

Operations of this nature may be local to the current machine or might run queries or code against remote systems. *Chapter 14, Remoting and Remote Management,* showed how Invoke-Command can be used to run a script simultaneously against a set of remote computers.

PowerShell includes several different commands and classes that can be used to do more than one thing at a time. The most obvious of these are the job commands.

In addition to the job commands, PowerShell can react to .NET events and use runspaces and runspace pools.

This chapter explores the following topics:

- Working with jobs
- Reacting to events
- Using runspaces and runspace pools
- Using thread-safe objects
- Managing concurrent access

PowerShell jobs, using commands like Start-Job, are the simplest starting point for executing code asynchronously.

Working with jobs

The Start-Job command in PowerShell provides a means of executing code asynchronously by creating a new PowerShell process for each job.

As each job executes within a new process, data cannot be implicitly shared between jobs. Any required modules, functions, and variables all need to be imported into each job.

Additionally, jobs might be considered resource heavy as each job must start a new PowerShell process.

PowerShell provides several commands to create and interact with jobs. In addition to the specific job commands, commands such as Invoke-Command offer an AsJob parameter.

The lifecycle of a job is most often controlled by Start-Job and Remove-Job.

Start-Job, Get-Job, and Remove-Job

You can use the Start-Job command to execute a script block in a similar manner to Invoke-Command, as shown in *Chapter 14, Remoting and Remote Management*. Also, you can use Start-Job to execute a script using the FilePath parameter.

When Start-Job is executed, a job object, System.Management.Automation.PSRemotingJob, is created. The job object continues to be available using the Get-Job command regardless of whether the output from Start-Job is assigned.

```
PS> Start-Job -ScriptBlock { Start-Sleep -Seconds 10 }

Id   Name   PSJobTypeName   State     HasMoreData   Location    Command
--   ----   -------------   -----     -----------   --------    -------
 1   Job1   BackgroundJob   Running          True   localhost   Start-Sleep -Seconds
10
```

Running Get-Job will show the same job returned by Start-Job:

```
PS> Get-Job

Id   Name   PSJobTypeName   State     HasMoreData   Location    Command
--   ----   -------------   -----     -----------   --------    -------
 1   Job1   BackgroundJob   Running          True   localhost   Start-Sleep -Seconds
10
```

When working with a script using jobs, a good practice is to capture the jobs created instead of relying entirely on Get-Job. This avoids problems if any other content used in the PowerShell session also creates jobs. The state of the job is reflected on the job object; Get-Job is not required to update the status.

By default, job objects and any data the job has returned remain available until removed using the Remove-Job command. The Receive-Job command, explored later in this section, can also cause the removal of jobs with the AutoRemoveJob parameter.

The command below will remove all jobs from the current session:

```
Get-Job | Remove-Job
```

Alternatively, only completed jobs can be removed:

```
Get-Job -State Completed | Remove-Job
```

Start-Job includes a RunAs32 parameter to run code on the 32-bit version of PowerShell if required.

In PowerShell 7, Start-Job also includes a PSVersion parameter that allows a job to be run using PowerShell 5.1:

```
Start-Job -PSVersion 5.1 -ScriptBlock { $PSVersionTable } |
    Receive-Job -Wait
```

The parameter also exists in PowerShell 5.1 and below, but there it is documented as being able to run in PowerShell 2 or PowerShell 3. Using a PSVersion of 3.0 can be interpreted as running in the current version of Windows PowerShell. Describing it as running in PowerShell 3 is due to a lack of updates to the documentation.

Start-Job does not offer a throttling capability, that is, limiting the number of concurrent activities. PowerShell will simultaneously execute every job. Each job will compete for system resources. A while or do loop may be implemented to maintain a pool of running jobs:

```
$listOfJobs = 1..50
foreach ($job in $listOfJobs) {
    while (@(Get-Job -State Running).Count -gt 10) {
        Start-Sleep -Seconds 10
    }
    Start-Job {
        Start-Sleep -Seconds (Get-Random -Minimum 10 -Maximum 121)
    }
}
```

The jobs created here do not return any data and can therefore be removed as soon as they have been completed. Data must be retrieved from a job before it is removed.

Receive-Job

Receive-Job is used to retrieve data from a job. Receive-Job may be used when a job is being executed, or when the job is finished. If Receive-Job is run before a job is finished, any existing values will be returned. Running Receive-Job again will get any new values that have been added since it was last run. This is shown in the following example:

```
$job = Start-Job {
    1..10 | ForEach-Object {
        $_
        Start-Sleep -Seconds 2
    }
}
Write-Host 'Sleeping 2'
Start-Sleep -Seconds 2
$job | Receive-Job
Write-Host 'Sleeping 5'
Start-Sleep -Seconds 5
$job | Receive-Job
```

The results from the script above are received as they become available, as shown below:

```
Sleeping 2
1
2
Sleeping 5
3
4
```

The remaining results will be available to Receive-Job as they are returned, or when the job has been completed.

The Wait parameter of Receive-Job will receive data from the job as it becomes available and send it to the output pipeline.

As noted above, the Receive-Job command also includes an AutoRemoveJob parameter, avoiding a need to explicitly use Remove-Job.

Receive-Job can be combined with the Wait-Job command.

Wait-Job

The Wait-Job command waits for all the jobs in the input pipeline to be completed. Wait-Job supports a degree of filtering and offers a timeout parameter to determine the length of time to wait for a job to complete before the job is run in the background.

In some cases, it is desirable to pull output from jobs as they complete. This can be solved by creating a while or do loop in PowerShell, reacting to jobs as the state changes:

```
while (Get-Job -State Running) {
    $jobs = Get-Job -State Completed
    $jobs | Receive-Job
    $jobs | Remove-Job
    Start-Sleep -Seconds 1
}
```

A while loop does not have an output pipeline; if output is to be piped to another command, it would need to be piped within the loop. For example, if the job output were filling a CSV file, Export-Csv would be added inside the loop and the Append parameter would be used:

```
while (Get-Job -State Running) {
    $jobs = Get-Job -State Completed
    $jobs | Receive-Job | Export-Csv output.csv -Append
    $jobs | Remove-Job
    Start-Sleep -Seconds 1
}
```

This technique is useful if the job is returning a large amount of data. Streaming output to a file as jobs complete will potentially help manage memory usage across a larger number of jobs.

This approach can be combined with the snippet, which limits the number of concurrent jobs. The tweak is shown as follows:

```
$listOfJobs = 1..50
$jobs = foreach ($job in $listOfJobs) {
    while (@(Get-Job -State Running).Count -gt 10) {
        Start-Sleep -Seconds 10
    }
    Start-Job {
        Start-Sleep -Seconds (Get-Random -Minimum 10 -Maximum 121)
    }
    Get-Job -State Completed |
        Receive-Job |
        Export-Csv output.csv -Append
}
$jobs |
    Wait-Job |
    Receive-Job |
    Export-Csv output.csv -Append
```

The final line is required to wait for and then receive the jobs that were still running when the last job was started.

Jobs and the using scope modifier

The using scope modifier was introduced in *Chapter 4, Working with Objects in PowerShell*, with ForEach-Object -Parallel, and used again in *Chapter 14, Remoting and Remote Management*, with Invoke-Command.

All commands that use jobs can make use of the using scope modifier to access variables created in the job creator's scope.

For example, the following job uses the value of a variable from the scope that started the job:

```
$message = 'Hello world'
Start-Job -ScriptBlock { Write-Host $using:message } |
    Receive-Job -Wait
```

Once the job above has finished, and the output has been received, it will display the message shown below:

```
Hello world
```

The using scope modifier can be combined with other scope modifiers, for example, a variable explicitly created in the global scope:

```
function Test-UsingScope {
    # A variable in the functions local scope
    $Variable = 2
    Start-Job -ScriptBlock {
        $using:Global:Variable
    }
}
# A variable in global scope
$Variable = 1
Test-UsingScope | Receive-Job -Wait
```

The using scope modifier acts in one direction only. Jobs can read from it but never use it to create variables. This limitation is deliberately applied when calling methods on existing variables:

```
$hashtable = @{}
Start-Job { $using:hashtable.Add('newValue', 1) } |
    Receive-Job -Wait
```

The attempt to use the Add method above causes a parser error, as shown below:

```
ParserError:
Line |
   1 |  Start-Job { $using:hashtable.Add('newValue', 1) } |
     |              ~~~~~~~~~~~~~~~~~~~~~~~~~~~~~~~~~~~~~
     |  Expression is not allowed in a Using expression.
```

It is possible to circumvent this error by enclosing the expression in parentheses or assigning the value to another variable first. However, this will be ineffective when using Start-Job as it is running in an isolated process.

```
$hashtable = @{}
Start-Job { ($using:hashtable).Add('newValue', 1) } |
    Receive-Job -Wait
```

Values returned from a job should use the output pipeline and be retrieved using Receive-Job.

The background operator

PowerShell 7 introduces the background operator feature. To use this, an ampersand (&) character is placed after the end of a statement. The placement of the operator is important. If placed at the beginning of a statement, & is the call operator. & must be the last thing in the statement; it cannot be used as an intermediate step in a pipeline, for example.

The following statement places the preceding statement into a job:

```
Get-Process &
```

The preceding command is therefore equivalent to the following Start-Job command:

```
Start-Job -ScriptBlock { Get-Process }
```

In both cases, the jobs are started in the current PowerShell working directory.

When using Start-Job, the working directory is implicitly inherited from the session starting the job.

When using the background operator, the working directory is explicitly set, as the following shows:

```
PS> $job = Get-Process &
PS> $job.Command
Microsoft.PowerShell.Management\Set-Location -LiteralPath $using:pwd ; Get-
Process
```

The preceding example shows that assignments can be used to capture the job object; they are not part of the background job.

The ThreadJob module

The ThreadJob module is shipped with PowerShell 7. Start-ThreadJob provides a faster alternative to Start-Job. It leverages PowerShell runspaces, which are explored at the end of this chapter to execute scripts.

Start-ThreadJob is used in much the same way as Start-Job. Once a job has started, the remaining job commands can be used to interact with it. For example, Receive-Job will be used to retrieve output:

```
Start-ThreadJob { Write-Host 'Hello world' } | Receive-Job -Wait
```

The Start-ThreadJob command allows a user to define an initialization script; this script runs in the runspace before the rest of the command starts. The initialization script cannot make use of the using scope modifier at this time.

The initialization script may be useful to split separate content but otherwise runs in the same runspace.

Batching jobs

When working with the preceding commands, as well as runspaces, explored at the end of this chapter, it is important to consider what constitutes a job.

For example, if the task involves running a single command on 100 remote hosts using Invoke-Command, then there may be little harm in allowing 100 to run at once. The system hosting the jobs only must connect to the remote system and instruct it to get on with things.

If, on the other hand, the task is local and needs access to local resources (such as CPU or disk), it may be more appropriate to run a smaller number of jobs, often aligned with the number of available cores.

The same consideration applies to jobs that have expensive setup steps, such as connecting to a remote service. It may be better to create batches of content rather than pushing everything into a job of its own. More is not always better.

Given an array of objects to process, batches can be created using a for loop:

```
$objects = foreach ($value in 1..1000) {
    [PSCustomObject]@{ Value = $value }
}
$batchSize = 100
$ScriptBlock = {
    # Long job set-up step
    Start-Sleep -Seconds 120
    foreach ($object in $using:batch) {
        # Perform action and create output
        $object
    }
}
for ($i = 0; $i -lt $objects.Count; $i += $batchSize) {
    $batch = $objects[$i..($i + $batchSize)]
    Start-Job -ScriptBlock $ScriptBlock
}
```

In PowerShell 7, as it is built on .NET 7, a Chunk method from Linq can be used instead:

```
using namespace System.Linq

$objects = foreach ($value in 1..1000) {
    [PSCustomObject]@{ Value = $value }
}
$batchSize = 100
$ScriptBlock = {
    # Long job set-up step
    Start-Sleep -Seconds 120
    foreach ($object in $using:batch) {
        # Perform action and create output
        $object
    }
}
$batches = [Enumerable]::Chunk[object]($objects, $batchSize)
foreach ($batch in $batches) {
    Start-Job -ScriptBlock $ScriptBlock
}
```

If each job is created using $batch, then each will act on 100 elements; a total of 10 jobs are created in this example.

Throttling might be added to ensure that the host is not overloaded by the request. Throttling techniques outside of the ThrottleLimit parameter were demonstrated earlier in this section.

Jobs provide a means of proactively executing code in an asynchronous manner. It is also possible to react to events.

Reacting to events

Events in .NET occur when something of interest happens to an object. For instance, System. IO.FileSystemWatcher can be used to monitor a file system for changes; when something changes, an event will be raised.

Many different types of objects raise events when changes occur. Get-Member can be used to explore an instance of an object for Event members. For example, a Process object returned by the Get-Process command includes several events, shown as follows:

```
PS> Get-Process | Get-Member -MemberType Event


    TypeName: System.Diagnostics.Process


Name                MemberType  Definition
----                ----------  ----------
Disposed            Event       System.EventHandler Disposed(Syst...
ErrorDataReceived   Event       System.Diagnostics.DataReceivedEv...
Exited              Event       System.EventHandler Exited(System...
OutputDataReceived  Event       System.Diagnostics.DataReceivedEv...
```

PowerShell can react to these events, executing code when an event occurs.

This section uses the events raised by FileSystemWatcher to demonstrate working with events. FileSystemWatcher can react to several different events. The event names can be viewed using Get-Member:

```
[System.IO.FileSystemWatcher]::new() |
    Get-Member -MemberType Event |
    Select-Object -ExpandProperty Name
```

The statement above will show the event names below:

```
Changed
Created
Deleted
Disposed
Error
Renamed
```

The following examples will use the Changed and Created events.

The Register-ObjectEvent and *-Event commands

Register-ObjectEvent is used to register interest in an event raised by a .NET object. The command creates a PSEventSubscriber object.

The Register-ObjectEvent command expects at least the name of the object that will be raising the event and the name of the event.

The following FileSystemWatcher instance watches the C:\Data folder. By default, the watcher will only watch for changes at that level; the IncludeSubDirectories property might be changed if this must change. Subscribers are created for the Changed and Created events in the following example:

```
$watcher = [System.IO.FileSystemWatcher]::new('C:\Data')
Register-ObjectEvent -InputObject $watcher -EventName Changed
Register-ObjectEvent -InputObject $watcher -EventName Created
```

If a file is created in the folder specified, an event will be raised. The Get-Event command can be used to view the event data:

```
PS> New-Item C:\Data\new.txt | Out-Null
PS> Get-Event

ComputerName      :
RunspaceId        : 46d2a562-2d07-4c58-9416-f82a3e9da5b8
EventIdentifier   : 3
Sender            : System.IO.FileSystemWatcher
SourceEventArgs   : System.IO.FileSystemEventArgs
SourceArgs        : {System.IO.FileSystemWatcher, new.txt}
SourceIdentifier  : ff0784dc-1f0f-4214-b5e7-5d5516eaa13e
TimeGenerated     : 19/02/2019 17:29:53
MessageData       :
```

The SourceEventArgs property contains a FileSystemEventArgs object. This object includes the type of change, the path, and the filename.

The event remains until it is removed using Remove-Event, or the PowerShell session is closed. If another event is raised, it will be returned by Get-Event in addition to the existing event.

Depending on the operation performed, FileSystemWatcher may return more than one event. When using Add-Content, a single event will be raised, as follows:

```
PS> Get-Event | Remove-Event
PS> Add-Content C:\Data\new.txt -Value value
PS> Get-Event | Select-Object -ExpandProperty SourceEventArgs
```

```
ChangeType        FullPath                Name
----------        --------                ----
   Changed        C:\Data\new.txt         new.txt
```

Set-Content is used when two events are raised. Set-Content makes two changes to the file, directly or indirectly. This will often be the case, depending on how an application interacts with the filesystem, which is shown as follows:

```
PS> Get-Event | Remove-Event
PS> Set-Content C:\Data\new.txt -Value value
PS> Get-Event | Select-Object -ExpandProperty SourceEventArgs

ChangeType        FullPath                Name
----------        --------                ----
   Changed        C:\Data\new.txt         new.txt
   Changed        C:\Data\new.txt         new.txt
```

Whether an event will trigger once or twice depends on the type in use, the event raised, and the subsystem that caused the event to be raised in the first place. Repeated events can potentially be ignored.

The Get-Event and Wait-Event process can be put inside a loop. In this case, events are raised asynchronously but handled synchronously.

```
while ($true) {
    Wait-Event | Get-Event | ForEach-Object {
        $_.SourceEventArgs
        $_ | Remove-Event
    }
}
```

The advantage of responding to an event synchronously is that writing the results of an event to the console or a file, or any other single-threaded resource, is trouble free.

If the response to the event should execute asynchronously, the Action parameter may be used.

Action, Event, EventArgs, and MessageData parameters

The Action parameter of Register-ObjectEvent allows a script block to be automatically executed when an event is raised.

Script blocks used with the Action parameter should avoid making calls to resources that are implicitly single threaded. For example, an Action block should avoid using Write-Host as it will add a delay while attempting to access the PowerShell host. Similarly, care should be taken around writing to external resources like log files if it is possible for events to be raised simultaneously.

The script block can use a reserved variable, $event, which is equivalent to the output from Get-Event. In the following example, the event subscriber includes an action, which creates a log message. The log messages are written to file in a different folder; if they were written to the same folder, a loop would be created:

```
New-Item C:\Audit -ItemType Directory
$watcher = [System.IO.FileSystemWatcher]::new('C:\Data')
$params = @{
    InputObject = $watcher
    EventName   = 'Changed'
    Action      = {
        $event.SourceEventArgs |
            Export-Csv C:\Audit\DataActivity.log -Append
    }
}
Register-ObjectEvent @params
```

If a file is created in the C:\Data folder, an event will be raised, and an entry will be created in C:\Audit\DataActivity.log:

```
PS> Set-Content C:\Data\new.txt -Value new
PS> Import-Csv C:\Audit\DataActivity.log

ChangeType      FullPath             Name
----------      --------             ----
Changed         C:\Data\new.txt      new.txt
Changed         C:\Data\new.txt      new.txt
```

Additional information can be passed to the Action script block using the MessageData parameter. MessageData is an arbitrary object that contains user-defined information. Before continuing to the example, the event subscriber that was just created should be removed. The log file is also deleted as the format of the file will be changed:

```
Get-EventSubscriber | Unregister-Event
Remove-Item C:\Audit\DataActivity.log
```

The following example adds a date stamp to the log entry and a custom message, which is supplied via MessageData. The values passed in using the MessageData parameter are made available as a MessageData property on the $event variable:

```
$watcher = [System.IO.FileSystemWatcher]::new('C:\Data')
$params = @{
    InputObject = $watcher
    EventName   = 'Changed'
    Action      = {
```

```
            $user = $event.MessageData |
                Where-Object {
                    $event.SourceEventArgs.Name -match $_.Expression
                } |
                Select-Object -ExpandProperty User -First 1
            $event.SourceEventArgs |
                Select-Object -Property @(
                    @{Name = 'Date'; Expression = {
                        Get-Date -Format u
                    }}
                    'ChangeType'
                    'FullPath'
                    @{Name = 'User'; Expression = { $user }}
                ) |
                Export-Csv C:\Audit\DataActivity.log -Append
        }
        MessageData = @(
            [PSCustomObject]@{ Expression = '\.txt$'; User = 'Sarah' }
            [PSCustomObject]@{ Expression = '\.mdb';  User = 'Phil' }
        )
    }
}
Register-ObjectEvent @params
```

Setting the content of a file in the C:\Data folder will trigger the event subscriber. An entry will be written to the log file using the entry from MessageData:

```
PS> Set-Content C:\Data\test.mdb 1
PS> Import-Csv C:\Audit\DataActivity.log


Date                    ChangeType  FullPath         User
----                    ----------  --------         ----
2024-04-20 10:43:04Z    Changed     C:\Data\test.mdb Phil
```

Event subscribers are globally scoped; they should be removed if they are no longer required. Closing the PowerShell session will remove all event subscribers.

Get-EventSubscriber and Unregister-Event

The Get-EventSubscriber command may be used to view any existing event handlers created using Register-ObjectEvent. For example, Get-EventSubscriber will display the subscribers created for FileSystemWatcher:

```
PS> Get-EventSubscriber
```

```
SubscriptionId    : 4
SourceObject      : System.IO.FileSystemWatcher
EventName         : Changed
SourceIdentifier  : 6516aebc-d191-44b5-a38f-60314f606102
Action            :
HandlerDelegate   :
SupportEvent      : False
ForwardEvent      : False
SubscriptionId    : 5
SourceObject      : System.IO.FileSystemWatcher
EventName         : Created
SourceIdentifier  : ff0784dc-1f0f-4214-b5e7-5d5516eaa13e
Action            :
HandlerDelegate   :
SupportEvent      : False
ForwardEvent      : False
```

If the subscribers are no longer required, they can be removed using the Unregister-Event command. The following command removes all registered event subscribers:

```
Get-EventSubscriber | Unregister-Event
```

Whether running jobs or reacting to events, the commands demonstrated in the previous sections are a great part of any PowerShell developer's toolkit. However useful they are, the commands lack fine control of the sessions they create and use. When greater control is required, PowerShell runspaces and runspace pools can be used directly via .NET types.

Using runspaces and runspace pools

Runspaces and runspace pools are an efficient way of asynchronously executing PowerShell code. Runspaces are far more efficient than jobs created by Start-Job as they execute in the same process. The main disadvantage is complexity: PowerShell does not include native commands to simplify working with these classes.

These days, the lack of native tooling is less of a problem. PowerShell 7 includes several alternatives that execute code in efficient runspaces, including ForEach-Object with the Parallel parameter, and the Start-ThreadJob command.

In addition to these, the (now older) PoshRSJob module remains available on the PowerShell Gallery: https://www.powershellgallery.com/packages/PoshRSJob.

The PoshRSJob module is very mature and has a rich set of features. It was the most frequently recommended module, providing an alternative to the Start-Job command.

When more flexibility or efficiency is needed, it is helpful to understand how PowerShell can use runspaces directly.

Creating a PowerShell instance

PowerShell instances, runspaces in which PowerShell code can be executed, are created using the Create static method of the System.Management.Automation.PowerShell type. A type accelerator exists for this type and the name can be shortened:

```
$psInstance = [PowerShell]::Create()
```

References to instances of System.Management.Automation.PowerShell as PowerShell are highlighted in this section.

The object created by the Create method has a fluent interface. Methods can be chained one after another without assigning a value. The following example adds a single command and a parameter, and then runs the command:

```
[PowerShell]::Create().
    AddCommand('Get-Process').
    AddParameter('Name', 'powershell').
    Invoke()
```

A complex script can be built in this manner. If two commands are chained together, they are assumed to be part of the same statement, implementing a pipeline. The AddStatement method is used to start a new statement, ending the current command pipeline:

```
[PowerShell]::Create().
    AddCommand('Get-Process').AddParameter('ID',$PID).
    AddStatement().
    AddCommand('Get-Service').
    AddCommand('Select-Object').AddParameter('First', 1).
    Invoke()
```

The example above will immediately run the two commands and will display output like the below:

```
NPM(K)      PM(M)       WS(M)      CPU(s)      Id  SI ProcessName
------      -----       -----      ------      --  -- -----------
   123     143.61      240.43        2.33    9472   2 pwsh

Status      : Stopped
Name        : Service name
DisplayName : Service display name
```

The result of the preceding example is equivalent to the following script:

```
Get-Process -Name powershell
Get-Service | Select-Object -First 1
```

The `AddCommand`, `AddParameter`, and `AddStatement` methods demonstrated so far are particularly useful when assembling a script programmatically. If the script content is already known, the script can be added using the `AddScript` method:

```
$script = @'
    Get-Process -Name powershell
    Get-Service | Select-Object -First 1
'@
[PowerShell]::Create().AddScript($script).Invoke()
```

The script is added as a string, not as a script block; however, it is common to see a script block being used. The block will be cast to a string, but it allows syntax highlighting when editing the block:

```
$script = {
    Get-Process -Name powershell
    Get-Service | Select-Object -First 1
}
[PowerShell]::Create().AddScript($script).Invoke()
```

The `AddScript` method can be used in conjunction with any of the other methods used here to build a complex set of commands.

The Invoke and BeginInvoke methods

The Invoke method used with each of the following examples executes the code immediately and synchronously. The `BeginInvoke` method is used to execute asynchronously, that is, without waiting for the last operation to complete.

Both the PowerShell instance object and the `IASyncResult` returned by `BeginInvoke` must be captured. Assigning the values allows continued access to the instances and is required to retrieve output from the commands:

```
$psInstance = [PowerShell]::Create().
    AddCommand('Start-Sleep').AddParameter('Seconds', 300)
$asyncResult = $psInstance.BeginInvoke()
```

While the job is running, the `InvocationStateInfo` property of the `PowerShell` object will show as Running:

```
PS> $psInstance.InvocationStateInfo


State      Reason
-----      ------
Running
```

This state is reflected on the IASyncResult object held in the $asyncResult variable:

```
PS> $asyncResult | Format-List

CompletedSynchronously : False
IsCompleted            : False
AsyncState             :
AsyncWaitHandle        : System.Threading.ManualResetEvent
```

When the command completes, both objects will reflect that state:

```
PS> $psInstance.InvocationStateInfo.State
Completed
PS> $asyncResult.IsCompleted
True
```

Setting either (or both) of these variables to null does not stop the script from executing in the PowerShell instance. Doing so only removes the variables assigned, making it impossible to interact with the runspace:

```
$psInstance = [PowerShell]::Create().AddScript('
    1..60 | ForEach-Object {
        Add-Content -Path c:\temp\output.txt -Value $_
        Start-Sleep -Seconds 1
    }
')
$asyncResult = $psInstance.BeginInvoke()
$psInstance = $null
$asyncResult = $null
```

The script continues to execute, filling the output file. The following file may be using Get-Content:

```
Get-Content c:\temp\output.txt -Wait
```

EndInvoke is one of two possible ways to get output from a PowerShell instance. The EndInvoke method may be called as follows:

```
$psInstance = [PowerShell]::Create()
$asyncResult = $psInstance.AddScript('1..10').BeginInvoke()
$psInstance.EndInvoke($asyncResult)
```

If the invocation has not finished, EndInvoke will block execution until it has completed.

The second, less common, method involves passing a PSDataCollection object to the BeginInvoke method:

```
using namespace System.Management.Automation

$instanceInput = [PSDataCollection[object]]::new()
$instanceOutput = [PSDataCollection[object]]::new()
$psInstance = [PowerShell]::Create()
$asyncResult = $psInstance.AddScript('
    1..10 | ForEach-Object {
        Start-Sleep -Seconds 1
        $_
    }
').BeginInvoke(
    $instanceInput,
    $instanceOutput
)
```

The $psInstance and $asyncResult variables are still used to determine whether the script has completed. Results are available in $instanceOutput as they become available. Attempting to access $instanceOutput in the console will block execution until the script completes. New values added to the collection will be displayed as they are added.

The unused $instanceInput variable in the preceding example may be populated with values for an input pipeline if required, for example:

```
using namespace System.Management.Automation

$instanceInput = [PSDataCollection[object]]@(1..10)
$instanceOutput = [PSDataCollection[object]]::new()
$psInstance = [PowerShell]::Create()
$asyncResult = $psInstance.
    AddCommand('ForEach-Object').
    AddParameter('Process', { $_ }).
    BeginInvoke(
        $instanceInput,
        $instanceOutput
    )
```

The AddCommand method was used in the preceding example as ForEach-Object will act on an input pipeline. A script can accept pipeline input within a process block; pipeline input is not implicitly passed to the commands within the script. The following example implements an input pipeline and uses the built-in $_ variable to repeat the numbers from the input pipeline:

```
using namespace System.Management.Automation

$instanceInput = [PSDataCollection[PSObject]](1..10)
$instanceOutput = [PSDataCollection[PSObject]]::new()
$asyncResult = $psInstance.AddScript('
    process {
        $_
    )
').BeginInvoke(
    $instanceInput,
    $instanceOutput
)
```

If the work of the script is no longer required, the Stop method can be called:

```
$psInstance = [PowerShell]::Create()
$asyncResult = $psInstance.
    AddCommand('Start-Sleep').
    AddParameter('Seconds', 120).
    BeginInvoke()
$psInstance.Stop()
```

A terminating error is raised when the Stop method is called. Any attempt to get output from the instance after Stop has been used will cause an error to be displayed:

```
PS> $psInstance.EndInvoke($asyncResult)
MethodInvocationException: Exception calling "EndInvoke" with "1" argument(s):
"The pipeline has been stopped."
```

The final output from the $psInstance can be collected using EndInvoke, but access to the other output streams is also available.

About Streams and InvocationStateInfo

Each instance of the PowerShell type used above includes a Streams property. This property exposes direct access to each of the output streams other than standard output.

For example, a runspace can be set up to write a verbose message then go to sleep, then write a second message:

```
$instance = [PowerShell]::Create()
$instance.AddScript({
    Write-Verbose Start -Verbose
    Start-Sleep -Seconds 30
    Write-Verbose End -Verbose
}).BeginInvoke()
```

Notice that the script used above explicitly uses the Verbose parameter. The $VerbosePreference might be used instead.

Immediately after the script starts by calling BeginInvoke, the verbose message can be seen:

```
PS> $instance.Streams.Verbose
Start
```

Then, once the Start-Sleep command has completed, the second message is added:

```
PS> $instance.Streams.Verbose
Start
End
```

In a similar way, any non-terminating errors raised during the execution of the script block are stored in the Error stream. *Chapter 22, Error Handling,* takes a much longer look at the different types of errors in PowerShell.

The example below writes a non-terminating error:

```
$instance = [PowerShell]::Create()
$instance.AddScript({
    Write-Error 'Something went wrong'
}).BeginInvoke()
```

And that error record is visible in the Error stream:

```
PS> $instance.Streams.Error

Write-Error: Something went wrong
```

When an error is raised, the HadErrors property is also set:

```
PS> $instance.HadErrors
True
```

Terminating errors are not written to the error stream. Those affect the state of the entire invocation and are therefore displayed under the InvocationStateInfo property. The throw keyword is used to raise a terminating error in the example below:

```
$instance = [PowerShell]::Create()
$instance.AddScript({
    throw 'Something went wrong'
}).BeginInvoke()
```

This time, the Error stream is empty, but InvocationStateInfo shows the error:

```
$instance.InvocationStateInfo.Reason
```

The Reason property is detailed and presents access to the error record as well as stack trace information.

As well as exposing information via output streams, runspaces can also be debugged. Debugging runspaces using the Debug-Runspace command is explored in *Chapter 23, Debugging*.

Each of the examples so far has concerned itself with running a single script or a set of commands.

Running multiple instances

As an individual instance is executing asynchronously with BeginInvoke, several may be started. In each case, both the PowerShell object and the IASyncResult object should be preserved:

```
$jobs = 1..5 | ForEach-Object {
    $instance = [PowerShell]::Create().AddScript('
        Start-Sleep -Seconds (Get-Random -Minimum 10 -Maximum 120)
    ')
    [PSCustomObject]@{
        Id          = $instance.InstanceId
        Instance    = $instance
        AsyncResult = $instance.BeginInvoke()
    } | Add-Member State -MemberType ScriptProperty -PassThru -Value {
        $this.Instance.InvocationStateInfo.State
    }
}
```

Each job will continue for a random number of seconds and then complete. As each job completes, the State property created by Add-Member will change to reflect that:

```
PS> $jobs | Select-Object Id, State


Id                                     State
--                                     -----
de79dcc3-8092-4592-a89e-271fc2b8b65e   Completed
85de5d4d-f754-461d-88da-ac5c7948c546   Running
eb8e0b84-2a47-4379-bd89-e7e523201033   Running
6357a4c3-b6d1-4a9f-8f88-ee3ac0891eb1   Running
3dc050fe-8ff9-4f93-afa9-86768bd3b407   Completed
```

The following snippet might be used to wait for all the jobs to complete:

```
while ($jobs.State -contains 'Running') {
    Start-Sleep -Milliseconds 100
}
```

Each of the runspaces created is also visible from the Get-Runspace command:

```
PS> Get-Runspace
 Id Name       ComputerName  Type   State   Availability
 -- ----       ------------  ----   -----   ------------
  1 Runspace1  localhost     Local  Opened  Busy
  2 Runspace2  localhost     Local  Opened  Available
  3 Runspace3  localhost     Local  Opened  Busy
  4 Runspace4  localhost     Local  Opened  Busy
  5 Runspace5  localhost     Local  Opened  Busy
  6 Runspace6  localhost     Local  Opened  Available
```

In the output shown above, Runspace1 is the runspace associated with the console, the interactive session.

If the number of jobs is significantly larger, the system running the jobs might well become overwhelmed.

Using the RunspacePool object

RunspacePool can be used to overcome the problem of overwhelming a system. The pool can be configured with a minimum and maximum number of threads to execute at any point in time.

The RunspacePool object is created using the RunspaceFactory type, as follows:

```
[RunspaceFactory]::CreateRunspacePool(1, 5)
```

RunspacePool must be opened before it can be used. The same pool is set for each of the PowerShell instances that expect to use the pool:

```
$runspacePool = [RunspaceFactory]::CreateRunspacePool(1, 2)
$runspacePool.Open()
$jobs = 1..10 | ForEach-Object {
    $instance = [PowerShell]::Create().AddScript(
        'Start-Sleep -Seconds 10'
    )
    $instance.RunspacePool = $runspacePool
    [PSCustomObject]@{
        Id          = $instance.InstanceId
        Instance    = $instance
        AsyncResult = $instance.BeginInvoke()
    } | Add-Member State -MemberType ScriptProperty -PassThru -Value {
        $this.Instance.InvocationStateInfo.State
    }
}
```

Each of the jobs will show as running, but only two will complete at a time, based on the maximum set for the pool in the following example. After 10 seconds, the state of the jobs will be like the following:

```
PS> $jobs | Select-Object Id, State

Id                                      State
--                                      -----
63e2ab2d-613a-4c9c-8f21-d93c8a126008    Completed
781e4a08-04d6-4927-986a-e116fb16a852    Completed
1d80c45d-326b-423b-93d9-21703e747a93    Running
6840dfb1-f47d-4977-868f-697fcbb8af7e    Running
6f3aa668-f680-40b6-8a94-c9d04693b1ad    Running
868f324c-7ba5-4913-83a9-345d8f356aec    Running
318a44ec-b390-45a5-a2cc-0272c1e2ad20    Running
ced0f017-1a1c-42d0-9c53-9e09f9c8ace9    Running
9d003c91-6a2b-4d6f-820e-975fffeb57d8    Running
71818997-b55e-41d6-bdf2-e62426036863    Running
```

When all processing is finished, all objects should be explicitly disposed of to ensure they are closed:

```
$jobs.Instance | ForEach-Object Dispose
$runspacePool.Dispose()
```

After Dispose has been run, the variables might be set to null. Objects that are no longer referenced will be removed by garbage collection. Garbage collection can be run immediately using the following command if a large amount of memory was committed when running the jobs:

```
[GC]::Collect()
```

Runspace pools are incredibly useful. To improve the utility of the pool, it can be seeded with modules, functions, and variables before the pool is opened.

About the InitialSessionState object

InitialSessionState is used by Runspace or RunspacePool to describe a starting point. The InitialSessionState object may have modules, functions, or variables added.

PowerShell provides several different options for creating InitialSessionState. This is achieved using a set of static methods. The most used are CreateDefault and CreateDefault2. For example, CreateDefault2 is used as follows:

```
$initialSessionState = [InitialSessionState]::CreateDefault2()
```

The difference between CreateDefault and CreateDefault2 is that CreateDefault includes engine snap-ins, while CreateDefault2 does not.

PowerShell Core does not include support for snap-ins. The difference between the two methods is therefore not apparent with PowerShell Core.

CreateDefault2 is slightly more lightweight and is more appropriate for more recent versions of PowerShell, that is, PowerShell 6 and greater.

In Windows PowerShell, the difference may be shown by creating and comparing the list of snap-ins in each case:

```
[PowerShell]::Create([InitialSessionState]::CreateDefault()).
    AddCommand('Get-PSSnapIn').Invoke().Name
```

The snap-in names will be listed as shown below:

```
Microsoft.PowerShell.Diagnostics
Microsoft.PowerShell.Host
Microsoft.PowerShell.Core
Microsoft.PowerShell.Utility
Microsoft.PowerShell.Management
Microsoft.PowerShell.Security
Microsoft.WSMan.Management
```

In Windows PowerShell, CreateDefault2 only adds the Microsoft.PowerShell.Core snap-in. The statement below can be used to show this:

```
[PowerShell]::Create([InitialSessionState]::CreateDefault2()).
    AddCommand('Get-PSSnapIn').Invoke().Name
```

Items can be added to InitialSessionState before Runspace (or RunspacePool) is opened.

Adding modules and snap-ins

Modules are added to an InitialSessionState using the ImportPSModule method:

```
$initialSessionState = [InitialSessionState]::CreateDefault2()
$initialSessionState.ImportPSModule('Pester')
```

Several modules can be added with the same method. Modules can be specified by name, in which case the most recent will be used. A module can be specified using a hashtable that describes the name and version information:

```
$initialSessionState.ImportPSModule(@(
    'NetAdapter'
    @{ ModuleName = 'Pester'; ModuleVersion = '4.6.0' }
))
```

A MaximumVersion or RequiredVersion may also be used with the hashtable.

A snap-in may be imported in Windows PowerShell using the ImportPSSnapIn method. The method requires the name of a single snap-in, and a reference to a variable to hold any warnings raised during import:

```
Using namespace System.Management.Automation.Runspaces

$warning = [PSSnapInException]::new()
$initialSessionState.ImportPSSnapIn(
    'WDeploySnapin3.0',
    [ref]$warning
)
```

If multiple snap-ins are required, you must call the ImportPSSnapIn method once for each snap-in.

Adding variables

InitialSessionState objects created using CreateDefault2 will include all the built-in variables with default values. The value of these variables cannot be changed before the session is opened.

Additional variables can be added using the Add method of the Variables property. Variables are defined as a SessionStateVariableEntry object. An example of adding a variable is shown here:

```
using namespace System.Management.Automation.Runspaces

$variableEntry = [SessionStateVariableEntry]::new(
    'Variable',
    'Value',
    'Optional description'
)
$initialSessionState = [InitialSessionState]::CreateDefault2()
$initialSessionState.Variables.Add($variableEntry)
```

The Variables collection of the InitialSessionState can be viewed to prove that the variable was added:

```
PS> $initialSessionState.Variables | Where-Object Name -eq Variable

Value       : Value
Description : Optional description
Options     : None
Attributes  : {}
Visibility  : Public
Name        : Variable
PSSnapIn    :
Module      :
```

Several overloads are available, each allowing the variable to be defined in greater detail. For example, a variable with the Private scope may be created by using one of the values of the System.Management. Automation.ScopedItemOptions enumeration:

```
using namespace System.Management.Automation.Runspaces

$variableEntry = [SessionStateVariableEntry]::new(
    'PrivateVariable',
    'Value',
    'Optional description',
    'Private'
)
$initialSessionState.Variables.Add($variableEntry)
```

Defining a fixed type for a variable is more difficult; the ArgumentTypeConverterAttribute needed to do this is private and difficult to create in PowerShell. To work around this problem, you can create a variable with the required attributes, then SessionStateVariableEntry can be created from the variable:

```
using namespace System.Management.Automation.Runspaces

[ValidateSet('Value1', 'Value2')][string]$ComplexVariable = 'Value1'
$variable = Get-Variable ComplexVariable
$variableEntry = [SessionStateVariableEntry]::new(
    $variable.Name,
    $variable.Value,
    $variable.Description,
    $variable.Options,
    $variable.Attributes
)
$initialSessionState.Variables.Add($variableEntry)
```

Using this approach allows complex variables to be defined within the session.

Adding functions

Functions and other commands can be added to the InitialSessionState object in much the same way as variables. If a function is within a module, the module should be imported instead.

Functions, as SessionStateFunctionEntry objects, are added to the Commands property of the InitialSessionState object.

Simple functions can be added by defining the body of the function inline, as follows:

```
using namespace System.Management.Automation.Runspaces

$functionEntry = [SessionStateFunctionEntry]::new(
    'Write-Greeting',
    'Write-Host "Hello world"'
)
$initialSessionState.Commands.Add($functionEntry)
```

Commands (including functions) in the initial session state can be listed using the Commands property:

```
$initialSessionState.Commands |
    Where-Object Name -eq 'Write-Greeting'
```

This will display the function that was added by the command above, as shown below:

```
Definition  : Write-Host "Hello world"
Options     : None
HelpFile    :
CommandType : Function
Visibility  : Public
Name        : Write-Greeting
PSSnapIn    :
Module      :
```

Functions with scope options can be added in the same way as with variables. Scoping is rarely used with functions.

If the function already exists in the current session, the output of Get-Command might be used to fill the SessionStateFunctionEntry object:

```
using namespace System.Management.Automation.Runspaces

function Write-Greeting {
    Write-Host 'Hello world'
}
$function = Get-Command Write-Greeting
$functionEntry = [SessionStateFunctionEntry]::new(
    $function.Name,
    $function.Definition
)
$initialSessionState.Commands.Add($functionEntry)
```

Once the InitialSessionState object is filled with the required objects, it may be used to create a PowerShell instance or a RunspacePool.

Using the InitialSessionState and RunspacePool objects

The RunspacePool object can be created using RunspaceFactory. RunspacePool can be created with either the minimum and maximum number of concurrent threads, or an InitialSessionState object.

Creating the pool using an InitialSessionState object is shown here:

```
$initialSessionState = [InitialSessionState]::CreateDefault2()
$runspacePool = [RunspaceFactory]::CreateRunspacePool($initialSessionState)
```

Any extra entries required in the InitialSessionState must either be added using the $initialSessionState variable before RunspacePool is created, or extra entries must be added using $runspacePool.InitialSessionState after RunspacePool is created. Changes cannot be made after RunspacePool has been opened.

If RunspacePool is created with InitialSessionState, the SetMinRunspaces and SetMaxRunspaces methods can be used to adjust the minimum and maximum number of threads. The default value for both the minimum and maximum is 1. The following example changes the maximum:

```
$runspacePool.SetMaxRunspaces(5)
```

The GetMinRunspaces and GetMaxRunspaces methods may be used to retrieve the current values.

RunspacePool is then used as shown in the *Using the RunspacePool object* section.

Using thread-safe objects

Several classes in .NET offer thread safety. This means that an instance of an object can be made accessible from runspaces that are, to a limited degree, synonymous with threads that share a common parent.

Thread-safe objects can be used with anything that makes use of runspaces, including jobs created by Start-ThreadJob, ForEach-Object -Parallel, event handlers, and runspaces.

The Start-Job command, as it is running in a separate process, cannot make use of the techniques explored here.

One of the simpler-to-use thread-safe objects is a hashtable. The hashtable is created using the Synchronized static method of the Hashtable type:

```
$synchronizedHashtable = [Hashtable]::Synchronized(@{
    Key = 'Value'
})
```

The synchronized hashtable can be added to an InitialSessionState object and then used within a script or command that is running in a runspace. The changes made to the hashtable within the runspace are visible outside:

```
using namespace System.Management.Automation.Runspaces
```

```
$variableEntry = [SessionStateVariableEntry]::new(
    'synchronizedHashtable',
    $synchronizedHashtable,
    ''
)
$runspace = [RunspaceFactory]::CreateRunspace(
    [InitialSessionState]::CreateDefault2()
)
$runspace.InitialSessionState.Variables.Add($variableEntry)
$psInstance = [PowerShell]::Create()
$psInstance.Runspace = $runspace
$runspace.Open()
$psInstance.AddScript(
    '$synchronizedHashtable.Add("NewKey", "NewValue")'
).Invoke()
```

After the script has completed, the key added by the script will be visible in the parent runspace in the current PowerShell session.

In addition to the runspace-synchronized hashtable, an `ArrayList` might be created in a similar manner, as follows:

```
[System.Collections.ArrayList]::Synchronized(
    [System.Collections.ArrayList]::new()
)
```

.NET also offers classes in the `System.Collections.Concurrent` namespace, which offers similar cross-runspace access as shown in the .NET reference: `https://learn.microsoft.com/dotnet/api/system.collections.concurrent`.

For example, the `ConcurrentStack` can be used as follows:

```
using namespace System.Collections.Concurrent
using namespace System.Management.Automation.Runspaces

$stack = [ConcurrentStack[object]]::new()
$stack.Push('Value')
$variableEntry = [SessionStateVariableEntry]::new(
    'stack',
    $stack,
    ''
)
$runspace = [RunspaceFactory]::CreateRunspace(
    [InitialSessionState]::CreateDefault2()
)
```

```
$runspace.InitialSessionState.Variables.Add($variableEntry)
$psInstance = [PowerShell]::Create()
$psInstance.Runspace = $runspace
$runspace.Open()
$psInstance.AddScript('
    $value = 0
    if ($stack.TryPop([ref]$value)) {
        $value
    }
').Invoke()
```

Use of this stack within ForEach-Object -Parallel or Start-ThreadJob is similar. The stack would be accessed via the $using modifier but the TryPop method is still used. In this case, the parallel block reads each of the 5 values from the stack:

```
using namespace System.Collections.Concurrent

$stack = [ConcurrentStack[int]]@(90, 1, 8, 6, 29)

1..5 | ForEach-Object -Parallel {
    Start-Sleep -Milliseconds (
        Get-Random -Minimum 0 -Maximum 500
    )
    $value = 0
    if (($using:stack).TryPop([ref]$value)) {
        'Iteration {0}, value {1}' -f $_, $value
    }
}
```

The random value for Start-Sleep causes the values to appear out of order, simulating a longer-running operation. Sample output is shown below:

```
Iteration 2, value 29
Iteration 5, value 6
Iteration 3, value 8
Iteration 4, value 90
Iteration 1, value 1
```

Each of the collection types in the System.Collections.Concurrent namespace offers similar Try methods to access elements.

Managing concurrent access

When writing code that runs asynchronously, it can be desirable to write to a resource that does not support concurrent access. For example, when writing to a log file, Windows will not allow two simultaneous write operations to a file.

Consider the following script. This script does nothing more than write a log file entry:

```
$script = {
    param (
        $Path,
        $RunspaceName
    )


    # Some long running activity


    $message = '{0:HH:mm:ss.fff}: Writing from runspace {1}' -f @(
        Get-Date
        $RunspaceName
    )
    [System.IO.File]::AppendAllLines(
        $Path,
        [string[]]$message
    )
}
```

The script uses the AppendAllLines method instead of a command like Add-Content as it better exposes an error that shows the problem with the script.

Before starting, ensure the runspace.log file does not exist:

```
Remove-Item runspace.log
```

When multiple instances of this script run, there are potentially attempts to simultaneously write to the file:

```
$jobs = for ($i = 0; $i -lt 5; $i++) {
    $instance = [PowerShell]::Create()
    $null = $instance.
        AddScript($script).
        AddParameters(@{
            Path         = Join-Path $pwd -ChildPath runspace.log
            RunspaceName = $instance.Runspace.Name
        })
```

```
    [PSCustomObject]@{
        Id          = $instance.InstanceId
        Instance    = $instance
        AsyncResult = $null
    } | Add-Member State -MemberType ScriptProperty -PassThru -Value {
        $this.Instance.InvocationStateInfo.State
    }
}

foreach ($job in $jobs) {
    $job.AsyncResult = $job.Instance.BeginInvoke()
}

while ($jobs.State -contains 'Running') {
    Start-Sleep -Seconds 5
}
```

In this example, the creation of the job and running `BeginInvoke` are split into separate loops to try and bring execution as close together as possible to trigger the problem.

When reviewing the log file, it will likely contain fewer lines than it should. For example, it may be like:

```
PS> Get-Content runspace.log


15:47:31.067: Writing from runspace Runspace2
15:47:31.081: Writing from runspace Runspace6
```

Reviewing the output streams from each instance should reveal the cause of the missing lines, with one or more repetitions of the error below:

```
PS> $jobs.Instance.Streams.Error


MethodInvocationException:
Line |
  16 |         [System.IO.File]::AppendAllLines(
     |         ~~~~~~~~~~~~~~~~~~~~~~~~~~~~~~~~~~~
     | Exception calling "AppendAllLines" with "2" argument(s): "The process
cannot access the file 'runspace.log' because it is being used by another
process."
```

There are a few possible solutions to this, but one of the more popular is to use a Mutex.

A Mutex can either be system-wide or local to the current process.

A system Mutex is appropriate when using `Start-Job`, where jobs are run in different processes. The Mutex instance is held by the operating system.

A local Mutex is appropriate when using a runspace, either directly or via a command-line `Start-ThreadJob`.

A local Mutex is simple to create:

```
$mutex = [System.Threading.Mutex]::new()
```

The script is adjusted to accept the Mutex as a parameter, then it calls the `WaitOne` method before accessing the file, and `ReleaseMutex` afterward. `WaitOne` will block the thread until all other threads have released the Mutex.

```
$script = {
    param (
        $Path,
        $RunspaceName,
        $Mutex
    )

    # Some long running activity

    $mutex.WaitOne()
    $message = '{0:HH:mm:ss.fff}: Writing from runspace {1}' -f @(
        Get-Date
        $RunspaceName
    )
    [System.IO.File]::AppendAllLines(
        $Path,
        [string[]]$message
    )
    $Mutex.ReleaseMutex()
}
```

When a script is finished, the Mutex should be disposed of. This `Dispose` step is highly important with a system Mutex.

```
$mutex.Dispose()
```

To try and ensure this happens, the job script makes use of `try`, `catch`, and `finally`. `try` statements are explored in more detail in *Chapter 22, Error Handling*.

```
try {
    $mutex = [System.Threading.Mutex]::new()

    $jobs = for ($i = 0; $i -lt 5; $i++) {
        $instance = [PowerShell]::Create()
        $null = $instance.
```

```
            AddScript($script).
            AddParameters(@{
                Path          = Join-Path $pwd -ChildPath runspace.log
                RunspaceName = $instance.Runspace.Name
                Mutex         = $mutex
            })

        [PSCustomObject]@{
            Id           = $instance.InstanceId
            Instance     = $instance
            AsyncResult = $null
        } | Add-Member State -MemberType ScriptProperty -PassThru -Value {
            $this.Instance.InvocationStateInfo.State
        }
    }
    foreach ($job in $jobs) {
        $job.AsyncResult = $job.Instance.BeginInvoke()
    }

    while ($jobs.State -contains 'Running') {
        Start-Sleep -Seconds 5
    }
} catch {
    Write-Error -ErrorRecord $_
} finally {
    $mutex.Dispose()
}
```

Because the script being run does not do anything except write the log line, this effectively makes this process synchronous. The WaitOne and ReleaseMutex methods should wrap around blocks of code that require exclusive access, not all the content of a script.

Once complete, the log file should contain entries from each of the instances, like the output below:

```
PS> Get-Content runspace.log

16:00:24.771: Writing from runspace Runspace3
16:01:14.292: Writing from runspace Runspace2
16:01:14.295: Writing from runspace Runspace3
16:01:14.297: Writing from runspace Runspace4
16:01:14.298: Writing from runspace Runspace5
16:01:14.299: Writing from runspace Runspace6
```

A system Mutex can also be created simply by giving a name to the Mutex. Each process that makes use of the Mutex creates one using the same name. This can be demonstrated by opening two PowerShell consoles.

Both consoles run the following command to create a Mutex named PSMutex:

```
# In both consoles
$mutex = [System.Threading.Mutex]::new($true, 'PSMutex')
```

In normal use, a better naming convention should be used—perhaps a value derived from a GUID as this applies to all processes.

In the first console, run:

```
# Inn the first console
$mutex.WaitOne()
```

This should return True. Then in the second console, run the same command. The command in the second console will block (not complete). There will not be any output from the command; it will continue to block (to wait).

In the first console, release the Mutex so the second process can make use of it:

```
# In the first console
$mutex.ReleaseMutex()
```

At this point, WaitOne in the second console should return True and will now have control of the Mutex.

In the second console, release the Mutex again:

```
# In the second console
$mutex.ReleaseMutex()
```

Then, in both consoles, run:

```
# In both consoles
$mutex.Dispose()
```

This mutex is system wide. If it is not disposed of, it will persist and be considered abandoned. Sharing system Mutex names across different applications can lead to very difficult problems to debug as it places an implicit wait dependency between applications.

Any system Mutex created and not correctly disposed of can be removed by restarting the operating system.

Summary

This chapter explored the job commands built into PowerShell; since they are built-in, they are a solid starting point for running asynchronous operations. Newer modules such as ThreadJob can be used to improve the efficiency of jobs.

You used event subscribers and commands to react to and work with events on .NET objects.

The final section detailed working with runspaces and runspace pools. These provide the greatest flexibility when working asynchronously.

Thread-safe types, such as those in the `System.Collections.Concurrent` namespaces, were demonstrated as a means of accessing and updating collections of objects across threads.

Finally, a Mutex was demonstrated as a means of safely gaining exclusive access to a resource when code is running asynchronously.

The next chapter explores the creation of graphical user interfaces in PowerShell.

Learn more on Discord

Read this book alongside other users, PowerShell experts, and the author himself. Ask questions, provide solutions to other readers, chat with the author via Ask Me Anything sessions, and much more.

Scan the QR code or visit the link to join the community.

`https://packt.link/SecNet`

16

Graphical User Interfaces

PowerShell is first and foremost a language built to work on the command line. Since PowerShell is based on .NET, it can use several different assemblies to create graphical user interfaces.

This chapter explores **Windows Presentation Foundation (WPF)**, a common choice for writing graphical user interfaces in Windows. WPF is not cross-platform; the content of this chapter will only work on Windows. WPF is used because much of the design of the interface is done using XML.

This chapter explores some of the basic controls (elements of the interface) in WPF, such as Label, TextBox, ComboBox, Button, Grid, and ListView. It explores positioning controls like StackPanel and DockPanel.

WPF comes with many built-in controls that there is not enough room to explore in this chapter, for example, TabControl, Calendar, Browser, and so on. The .NET reference can be used to view some of the possibilities: https://learn.microsoft.com/dotnet/api/system.windows.controls.

The most commonly used alternative UI framework in PowerShell is System.Windows.Forms. Many of the concepts and approaches applied to WPF here can be applied to Forms-based user interfaces. Forms-based user interfaces require significantly more code as each control must be defined and positioned in code rather than XML.

Avalonia is a possible choice for a cross-platform framework, but the use of it is unfortunately beyond the capacity of this chapter: http://avaloniaui.net/.

The following topics are explored in this chapter:

- About **Windows Presentation Foundation (WPF)**
- Designing a UI
- About XAML
- Displaying the UI
- Layout
- Naming and locating controls
- Handling events
- Responsive interfaces

Windows Presentation Foundation is available in both Windows PowerShell and PowerShell 7, although the interfaces it creates can only be used on Windows.

About Windows Presentation Foundation (WPF)

Windows Presentation Foundation, or **WPF**, is a user interface framework. The components of a user interface are referred to as controls and include Label, TextBox, Button, and so on.

Before WPF can be used, the PresentationFoundation assembly must be loaded. The assembly can be loaded using Add-Type. This command is required once in each PowerShell session that intends to use WPF:

```
Add-Type -AssemblyName PresentationFramework
```

A WPF user interface typically defines all or most of the visible components in an **Extensible Application Markup Language (XAML)** document.

Designing a UI

It is difficult, but not impossible, to design a user interface using code alone. This chapter focuses on a small number of simple UI elements, which can be combined to build a more complex user interface. The examples in this chapter do not require a visual designer.

There are several options available for visual designers:

- Visual Studio—free when using the Community edition: https://visualstudio.microsoft.com/vs/community/
- PoshGUI—web-based, requires a subscription: https://poshgui.com/
- PowerShell Pro Tools—Visual Studio Code extension, requires a subscription: https://ironmansoftware.com/powershell-pro-tools-for-visual-studio-code/

In the case of Visual Studio, it can be used to generate the XAML content in the designer, and that XAML content can be reused in PowerShell.

About XAML

XAML is an XML document. XAML is used to describe the components or elements of a user interface. The following example describes a 350-by-350-pixel Window containing a Label:

```
<?xml version="1.0" encoding="utf-8"?>
<Window
 xmlns="http://schemas.microsoft.com/winfx/2006/xaml/presentation"
 xmlns:x="http://schemas.microsoft.com/winfx/2006/xaml"
 Width="350" Height="350">
    <Label Content="Hello world" />
</Window>
```

The two namespace declarations in the xmlns and xmlns:x attributes are mandatory and cannot be omitted.

The document must first be read into an XmlDocument; the Xml type accelerator can be used for this. Then an XmlNodeReader is created by casting from an XmlDocument. Finally, the document is parsed using the XamlReader to create the user interface controls from the document:

```
$xaml = [xml]'<?xml version="1.0" encoding="utf-8"?>
<Window
 xmlns="http://schemas.microsoft.com/winfx/2006/xaml/presentation"
 xmlns:x="http://schemas.microsoft.com/winfx/2006/xaml"
 Width="350" Height="350">
    <Label Content="Hello world" />
</Window>'
$window = [System.Windows.Markup.XamlReader]::Load(
    [System.Xml.XmlNodeReader]$xaml
)
```

The $Window variable contains the Window and all child elements it implements. The Window can be explored and changed in PowerShell before it is displayed, or it can be displayed immediately.

Displaying the UI

The UI can be opened by using the ShowDialog method of the Window:

```
$Window.ShowDialog()
```

In each of the examples in each of the following sections, the following short function can be used to view the Window:

```
function Show-Window {
    param (
        [Xml]$Xaml
    )
    Add-Type -AssemblyName PresentationFramework
    $Window = [System.Windows.Markup.XamlReader]::Load(
        [System.Xml.XmlNodeReader]$Xaml
    )
    $Window.ShowDialog()
}
```

Examples and Show-Window

The preceding function is reused in the examples that follow. If it is not present in the PowerShell session, the examples will fail.

The function can be used with the first XAML example:

```
$xaml = '<?xml version="1.0" encoding="utf-8"?>
<Window
 xmlns="http://schemas.microsoft.com/winfx/2006/xaml/presentation"
 xmlns:x="http://schemas.microsoft.com/winfx/2006/xaml"
 Width="350" Height="350">
     <Label Content="Hello world" />
</Window>'
Show-Window $Xaml
```

If the first example has been added to the console, it will display as shown in *Figure 16.1*:

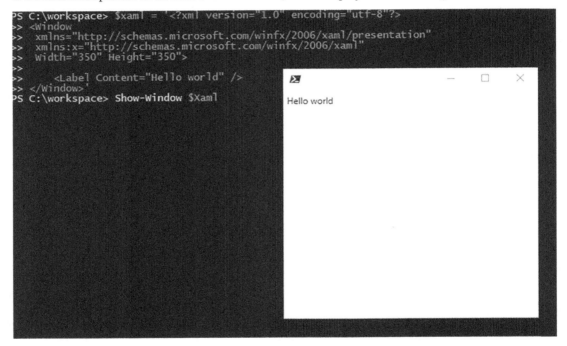

Figure 16.1: Showing the user interface

The properties and methods available for the Window are documented in the .NET reference: https://learn.microsoft.com/dotnet/api/system.windows.window.

In the preceding example, the Window contains a single Label. A Window can only directly contain a single child control, which is held in the Content property. The first few properties of the Label are shown here:

```
PS> $Window.Content

Target                         :
```

```
Content                        : Hello world
HasContent                     : True
ContentTemplate                :
ContentTemplateSelector        :
ContentStringFormat            :
BorderBrush                    :
BorderThickness                : 0,0,0,0
Background                     : #00FFFFFF
Foreground                     : #FF000000
```

WPF has a wide variety of layout controls that can be added to contain more controls. For example, a Grid control might be used to position Label and TextBox controls to create a simple form.

Layout

The layout of a WPF form is described by the elements it contains. Several controls are dedicated to positioning others. For example, a layout control may contain two Label controls.

Three different layout controls are explored:

- Grid
- StackPanel
- DockPanel

These three positioning controls can be used to create advanced layouts by specifying an absolute position for every single control by hand.

Layout controls such as those above can be nested inside one another to create more advanced interfaces.

A Grid can be used to arrange controls in rows and columns.

Using the Grid control

A Grid control can be added within the Window control in the XAML document:

```
$xaml = '<?xml version="1.0" encoding="utf-8"?>
<Window
 xmlns="http://schemas.microsoft.com/winfx/2006/xaml/presentation"
 xmlns:x="http://schemas.microsoft.com/winfx/2006/xaml">
    <Grid>
        <Label Content="Hello world" />
    </Grid>
</Window>'
Show-Window $xaml
```

By default, `Grid` has one row and one column: a single cell. To add a second control to the grid, either the number of columns or the number of rows must be increased (or both). Rows and columns are numbered from 0 in the `Grid` control. `Child` controls are, by default, placed in row 0, column 0.

The following example adds a second column; the two controls are placed side by side by using `Grid.Row` and `Grid.Column` to explicitly define where each should appear:

```
$xaml = '<?xml version="1.0" encoding="utf-8"?>
<Window
 xmlns="http://schemas.microsoft.com/winfx/2006/xaml/presentation"
 xmlns:x="http://schemas.microsoft.com/winfx/2006/xaml"
 Width="350" Height="350">
    <Grid>
        <Grid.ColumnDefinitions>
            <ColumnDefinition />
            <ColumnDefinition />
        </Grid.ColumnDefinitions>
        <Label Content="Row 1, Column 1"
         Grid.Row="0" Grid.Column="0" />
        <Label Content="Row 1, Column 2"
         Grid.Row="0" Grid.Column="1" />
    </Grid>
</Window>'
Show-Window $xaml
```

Rows can be added to the grid in a similar manner. The next code snippet adds a second row to the grid:

```
$xaml = '<?xml version="1.0" encoding="utf-8"?>
<Window
 xmlns="http://schemas.microsoft.com/winfx/2006/xaml/presentation"
 xmlns:x="http://schemas.microsoft.com/winfx/2006/xaml"
 Width="350" Height="350">
    <Grid>
        <Grid.ColumnDefinitions>
            <ColumnDefinition />
            <ColumnDefinition />
        </Grid.ColumnDefinitions>
        <Grid.RowDefinitions>
            <RowDefinition />
            <RowDefinition />
        </Grid.RowDefinitions>
        <Label Content="Row 1, Column 1"
         Grid.Row="0" Grid.Column="0" />
```

```
            <Label Content="Row 1, Column 2"
             Grid.Row="0" Grid.Column="1" />
            <Label Content="Row 2, Column 1"
             Grid.Row="1" Grid.Column="0" />
            <Label Content="Row 2, Column 2"
             Grid.Row="1" Grid.Column="1" />
        </Grid>
    </Window>'
    Show-Window $xaml
```

The rows and columns in the grid are equally distributed. The Width and Height of each column or row can be changed by setting those properties in the ColumnDefinition or the RowDefinition.

The UI created by the preceding XAML document is shown in *Figure 16.2*:

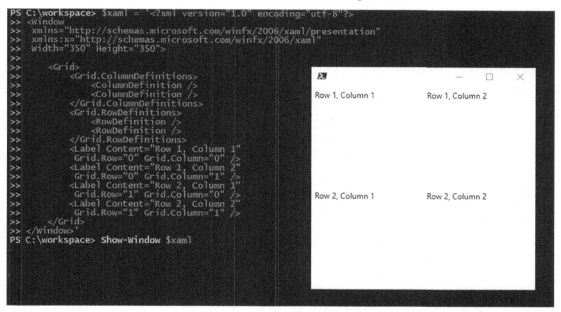

Figure 16.2: Grid with 2 columns and 2 rows

Column and row widths are defined in pixels or by fractional values based on the size of the parent (in this case, Window).

A fraction is described by following a numeric value with *. If * is used alone, the value is 1. In the following example, the first column takes three-quarters of the width, and the last column one-quarter. ShowGridLines has been enabled in the grid to show the effect of the width control more easily:

```
$xaml = '<?xml version="1.0" encoding="utf-8"?>
<Window
 xmlns="http://schemas.microsoft.com/winfx/2006/xaml/presentation"
```

```
    xmlns:x="http://schemas.microsoft.com/winfx/2006/xaml"
    Width="350" Height="350">
        <Grid ShowGridLines="True">
            <Grid.ColumnDefinitions>
                <ColumnDefinition Width="3*" />
                <ColumnDefinition Width="*" />
            </Grid.ColumnDefinitions>
            <Label Content="Row 1, Column 1"
             Grid.Row="0" Grid.Column="0" />
            <Label Content="Row 1, Column 2"
             Grid.Row="0" Grid.Column="1" />
        </Grid>
    </Window>'
    Show-Window $xaml
```

This creates the window shown in *Figure 16.3*:

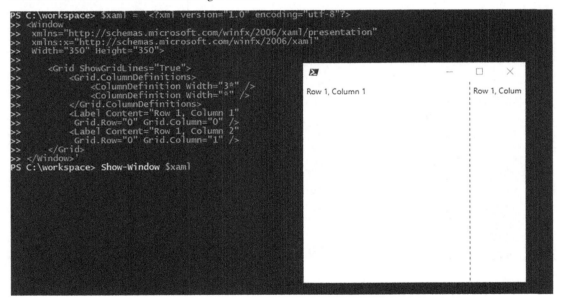

Figure 16.3: Grid control with fractional column width

The Grid control needs the number of rows and columns to be defined in advance. Each child control is placed within the grid using the Grid.Row and Grid.Column attributes, as shown in the preceding examples.

A StackPanel can be used to arrange controls in a vertical or horizontal stack.

Using the StackPanel control

A StackPanel control allows one control to be placed next to another. The StackPanel can be arranged horizontally or vertically. Controls can be added from left to right, or right to left. When the orientation is vertical, left to right is equivalent to top to bottom.

A StackPanel is an ideal choice for a list of controls, such as a list of buttons. In the following example, the buttons are arrays vertically (the default) within the StackPanel:

```
$xaml = '<?xml version="1.0" encoding="utf-8"?>
<Window
 xmlns="http://schemas.microsoft.com/winfx/2006/xaml/presentation"
 xmlns:x="http://schemas.microsoft.com/winfx/2006/xaml">
    <StackPanel>
        <Button Content="Button1" />
        <Button Content="Button2" />
        <Button Content="Button3" />
    </StackPanel>
</Window>'
Show-Window $xaml
```

The orientation can be changed with an attribute on the StackPanel element in the XAML document:

```
$xaml = '<?xml version="1.0" encoding="utf-8"?>
<Window
 xmlns="http://schemas.microsoft.com/winfx/2006/xaml/presentation"
 xmlns:x="http://schemas.microsoft.com/winfx/2006/xaml">
    <StackPanel Orientation="Horizontal">
        <Button Content="Button1" />
        <Button Content="Button2" />
        <Button Content="Button3" />
    </StackPanel>
</Window>'
Show-Window $xaml
```

If a Height or Width is set, the StackPanel will limit the size of the elements it contains. In the following example, the Width of the StackPanel is reduced to 50 pixels; it now only takes up a small part of the Window:

```
$xaml = '<?xml version="1.0" encoding="utf-8"?>
<Window
 xmlns="http://schemas.microsoft.com/winfx/2006/xaml/presentation"
 xmlns:x="http://schemas.microsoft.com/winfx/2006/xaml"
 Width="350" Height="350">
    <StackPanel Width="50">
```

```
            <Button Content="Button1" />
            <Button Content="Button2" />
            <Button Content="Button3" />
        </StackPanel>
</Window>'
Show-Window $xaml
```

The result of setting the width is shown next. As there is no code behind this user interface, pressing the buttons will have no effect. The resulting interface is shown in *Figure 16.4*.

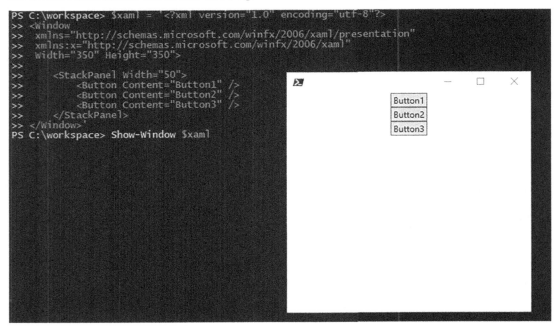

Figure 16.4: StackPanel positioned at the top center of a window

The default orientation for a StackPanel is vertical. The elements in the StackPanel may also be arranged horizontally:

```
$xaml = '<?xml version="1.0" encoding="utf-8"?>
<Window
 xmlns="http://schemas.microsoft.com/winfx/2006/xaml/presentation"
 xmlns:x="http://schemas.microsoft.com/winfx/2006/xaml"
 Width="350" Height="350">
    <StackPanel Orientation="Horizontal" Width="200" Height="40">
        <Button Content="Button1" />
        <Button Content="Button2" />
        <Button Content="Button3" />
    </StackPanel>
```

```
    </Window>'
    Show-Window $xaml
```

The result of this is shown in *Figure 16.5*.

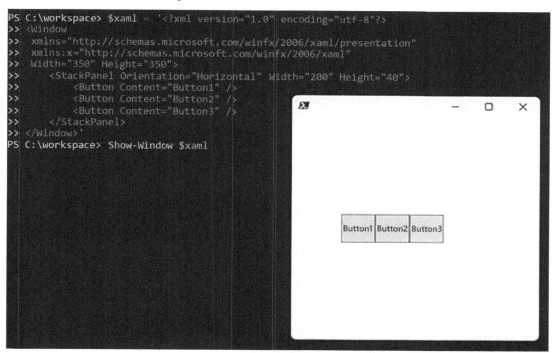

Figure 16.5: StackPanel with horizontal alignment

Elements within the StackPanel cannot exceed the Width and Height of that StackPanel.

The StackPanel is not especially useful where it is; the buttons are in the middle of the Window, which makes it hard to place more controls (Label, TextBox, Button, and so on). The StackPanel would be better placed within another control. A Grid is one option, but it is potentially difficult to arrange differently sized elements within a Grid. A DockPanel offers an easier alternative for putting together controls of different sizes.

Using the DockPanel control

A DockPanel is used to arrange elements around the edge of a rectangle. Each element is positioned using the DockPanel.Dock attribute, and the possible values are Top, Bottom, Left, and Right.

By default, the last control in the DockPanel uses up the rest of the available space. The StackPanel with the list of buttons might be positioned within a DockPanel, perhaps aligning it to the left, and a Label is added as a placeholder after this to use up the remaining space:

```
$xaml = '<?xml version="1.0" encoding="utf-8"?>
<Window
```

```
    xmlns="http://schemas.microsoft.com/winfx/2006/xaml/presentation"
    xmlns:x="http://schemas.microsoft.com/winfx/2006/xaml"
    Width="350" Height="350">
        <DockPanel>
            <StackPanel Width="50" DockPanel.Dock="Left">
                <Button Content="Button1" />
                <Button Content="Button2" />
                <Button Content="Button3" />
            </StackPanel>
            <Label />
        </DockPanel>
    </Window>'
    Show-Window $xaml
```

The outcome is shown in *Figure 16.6*:

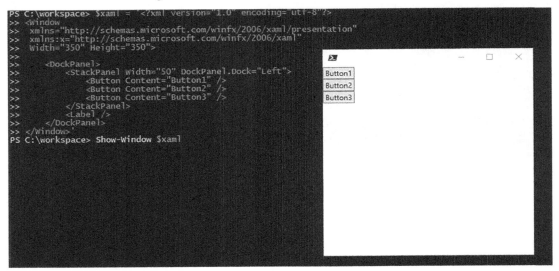

Figure 16.6: DockPanel and StackPanel

DockPanel allows elements to be arranged like a sliding puzzle. The following example includes each of the following elements:

1. A Label at the top
2. A StackPanel to the left
3. A ComboBox at the top

4. A `StackPanel` at the bottom
5. A `Label` to use up all remaining space

The order of the elements determines how much of the remaining space is available. The example below changes the background color of each element to better show the area it uses:

```
$xaml = '<?xml version="1.0" encoding="utf-8"?>
<Window
 xmlns="http://schemas.microsoft.com/winfx/2006/xaml/presentation"
 xmlns:x="http://schemas.microsoft.com/winfx/2006/xaml"
 Width="800" Height="500">
    <DockPanel>
        <Label Height="50" Background="Gainsboro"
         DockPanel.Dock="Top" />
        <StackPanel Background="LightBlue" Width="250"
         DockPanel.Dock="Left" />
        <ComboBox Margin="5" DockPanel.Dock="Top" />
        <StackPanel Height="30"
         Orientation="Horizontal"
         FlowDirection="RightToLeft"
         DockPanel.Dock="Bottom">
            <Button Content="Exit" Width="50" Margin="5" />
            <Button Content="Cancel" Width="50" Margin="5" />
            <Button Content="OK" Width="50" Margin="5" />
        </StackPanel>
        <Label Background="LightCoral" DockPanel.Dock="Top" />
    </DockPanel>
</Window>'
Show-Window $xaml
```

The top-most `Label` and `StackPanel` have a background color set to show how each of the elements takes up space. The final `Label` is also colored, highlighting the unused space in the interface.

The resulting interface is shown in *Figure 16.7*. As before, the user interface has no code behind it, so clicking the buttons will not have any effect.

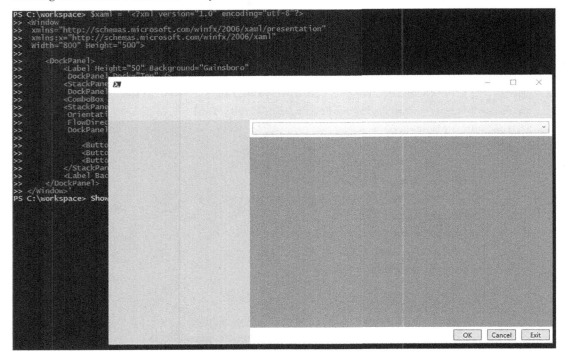

Figure 16.7: Multi-element docking

Each element of the user interface might be filled with different content.

The preceding example also makes use of several other layout properties, such as Margin and Padding.

About Margin and Padding

The Margin of a control is the space around the outside of that control. Most controls can use the Margin property. Notable exceptions include the RowDefinition and ColumnDefinition types. Margins for elements in a Grid must be defined on each nested element.

Margin and Padding are often used together to space out a user interface, preventing elements from running into each other, which results in a crowded user interface.

Padding is the space between the edge of a control and the Content. Controls like Button, Label, TextBox, and ComboBox all have a Padding property.

Both Padding and Margin can be defined on Left, Right, Top, and Bottom. Ultimately, this creates a System.Windows.Thickness object after the XAML has been read into PowerShell.

If a single value is used, as is the case with the ComboBox control used in the last example, the value will be applied to all four margins. The XAML element is shown here:

```
<ComboBox Margin="5" DockPanel.Dock="Top" />
```

It is possible to see the impact of this value by casting the Margin value to the Thickness type in PowerShell:

```
PS> [System.Windows.Thickness]'5'

Left Top Right Bottom
---- --- ----- ------
   5   5     5      5
```

The Thickness type is only available if the Add-Type command to load the PresentationFoundation assembly at the beginning of this section has been run in the PowerShell session.

If a control requires different margins, a comma-separated list of values can be set. For instance, if Margin is set as shown below, then only the top and bottom margins will be set:

```
<ComboBox Margin="0,5,0,5" DockPanel.Dock="Top" />
```

As before, the effect of these values can be tested by casting the comma-separated string to the Thickness type:

```
PS> [System.Windows.Thickness]'0,5,0,5'

Left Top Right Bottom
---- --- ----- ------
   0   5     0      5
```

The same approach used with Margin can be used with Padding values.

The following example attempts to show the impact of setting a Margin and Padding in a control:

```
$xaml = '<?xml version="1.0" encoding="utf-8"?>
<Window
 xmlns="http://schemas.microsoft.com/winfx/2006/xaml/presentation"
 xmlns:x="http://schemas.microsoft.com/winfx/2006/xaml"
 Width="350" Height="350">
    <Grid ShowGridLines="True">
        <Grid.RowDefinitions>
            <RowDefinition />
            <RowDefinition />
            <RowDefinition />
            <RowDefinition />
        </Grid.RowDefinitions>
        <TextBox Text="No margin, no padding"
         Grid.Row="0" />
        <TextBox Text="Margin, no padding" Margin="5"
```

```
        Grid.Row="1" />
      <TextBox Text="Padding, no margin" Padding="5"
      Grid.Row="2" />
      <TextBox Text="Padding and margin" Padding="5" Margin="5"
      Grid.Row="3" />
  </Grid>
</Window>'
Show-Window $xaml
```

A Grid is displayed with grid lines to show the boundary of each cell, and the TextBox is used as it has a border. The Margin is shown to affect the space around the outside of the TextBox, between the Grid cell edge and the TextBox edge. Padding is shown to affect the space between the TextBox edge and the text within the TextBox:

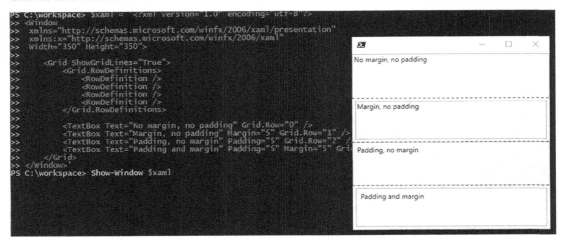

Figure 16.8: Margins and padding

The elements in the preceding XAML documents are only accessible by working down through the properties from the $Window variable.

Naming and locating controls

It is only possible to perform actions on controls in the UI if they can be located. None of the controls in the preceding examples have been given names. Locating one of the buttons in a StackPanel, for example, is difficult as it stands.

Returning to the StackPanel example, it has three buttons:

```
$xaml = [xml]'<?xml version="1.0" encoding="utf-8"?>
<Window
 xmlns="http://schemas.microsoft.com/winfx/2006/xaml/presentation"
 xmlns:x="http://schemas.microsoft.com/winfx/2006/xaml"
```

```
   Width="350" Height="350">
      <StackPanel Width="50">
          <Button Content="Button1" />
          <Button Content="Button2" />
          <Button Content="Button3" />
      </StackPanel>
</Window>'
$window = [System.Windows.Markup.XamlReader]::Load(
    [System.Xml.XmlNodeReader]$xaml
)
```

Accessing the Text property of Button3 as it stands requires the following relatively complex statement (in comparison to the complexity of the UI):

```
$button3 = $window.Content.Children[2].Content
```

This statement will potentially break if another button is added; it can therefore be said to be bad practice.

Instead of locating controls by position, a control can be given a name, and the name can be used to find that control in the UI:

```
$xaml = [xml]'<?xml version="1.0" encoding="utf-8"?>
<Window
 xmlns="http://schemas.microsoft.com/winfx/2006/xaml/presentation"
 xmlns:x="http://schemas.microsoft.com/winfx/2006/xaml"
 Width="350" Height="350">
      <StackPanel Width="50">
          <Button Name="Button1" Content="Button1" />
          <Button Name="Button2" Content="Button2" />
          <Button Name="Button3" Content="Button3" />
      </StackPanel>
</Window>'
$window = [System.Windows.Markup.XamlReader]::Load(
    [System.Xml.XmlNodeReader]$xaml
)
```

Now it has a name, each button (or any other named control) can be located by using a FindName method on any other element in the UI. For example:

```
PS> $button1 = $window.FindName('Button1')
PS> $button1.Name
Button1
PS> $button1.FindName('Button2').Name
Button2
```

FindName, when used in an event handler, can create difficult-to-resolve scoping problems in PowerShell; properties that are expected to be set may appear to be empty. Instead, each of the named controls can be gathered into a hashtable so each is easily accessible wherever it might be needed:

```
$xaml = [xml]'<?xml version="1.0" encoding="utf-8"?>
<Window
 xmlns="http://schemas.microsoft.com/winfx/2006/xaml/presentation"
 xmlns:x="http://schemas.microsoft.com/winfx/2006/xaml"
 Width="350" Height="350">
    <StackPanel Width="50">
        <Button Name="Button1" Content="Button1" />
        <Button Name="Button2" Content="Button2" />
        <Button Name="Button3" Content="Button3" />
    </StackPanel>
</Window>'
$window = [System.Windows.Markup.XamlReader]::Load(
    [System.Xml.XmlNodeReader]$xaml
)
$controls =  @{}
foreach ($control in $xaml.SelectNodes('//*[@Name]')) {
    $controls[$control.Name] = $Window.FindName($control.Name)
}
$controls['Button1']
```

The preceding SelectNodes method (used on the XmlDocument) finds all the elements in the XML document that have been given a name. It is therefore important to ensure that all names uniquely identify a single control.

A short function can be created to provide access to the top-level Window and all named child controls:

```
function Import-Xaml {
    param (
        [Xml]$Xaml
    )
    Add-Type -AssemblyName PresentationFramework
    $window = [System.Windows.Markup.XamlReader]::Load(
        [System.Xml.XmlNodeReader]$Xaml
    )
```

```
    $controls = @{}
    foreach ($control in $Xaml.SelectNodes('//*[@Name]')) {
        $controls[$control.Name] = $window.FindName($control.Name)
    }
    [PSCustomObject]@{
        MainWindow = $Window
        Controls   = $controls
    }
}
```

 Examples and Import-Xaml

The preceding function is reused in the examples that follow. If it is not present in the PowerShell session, the examples will fail.

The preceding function is shown below with the example used earlier in this section:

```
$xaml = '<?xml version="1.0" encoding="utf-8"?>
<Window
 xmlns="http://schemas.microsoft.com/winfx/2006/xaml/presentation"
 xmlns:x="http://schemas.microsoft.com/winfx/2006/xaml"
 Width="350" Height="350">
    <StackPanel Width="50">
        <Button Name="Button1" Content="Button1" />
        <Button Name="Button2" Content="Button2" />
        <Button Name="Button3" Content="Button3" />
    </StackPanel>
</Window>'
$ui = Import-Xaml $Xaml
```

The Controls property contains the three buttons used in the interface:

```
PS> $ui.Controls

Name                    Value
----                    -----
Button2                 System.Windows.Controls.Button: Button2
Button1                 System.Windows.Controls.Button: Button1
Button3                 System.Windows.Controls.Button: Button3
```

The `MainWindow` property can be used to access the `Window` itself and show the UI as shown in *Figure 16.9*:

```
PS C:\workspace> function Import-Xaml {
>>     param (
>>         [Xml]$Xaml
>>     )
>>
>>     Add-Type -AssemblyName PresentationFramework
>>
>>     $window = [System.Windows.Markup.XamlReader]::Load(
>>         [System.Xml.XmlNodeReader]$Xaml
>>     )
>>     $controls = @{}
>>     foreach ($control in $Xaml.SelectNodes('//*[@Name]')) {
>>         $controls[$control.Name] = $window.FindName($control.Name)
>>     }
>>
>>     [PSCustomObject]@{
>>         MainWindow = $window
>>         Controls   = $controls
>>     }
>> }
PS C:\workspace> $xaml = '<?xml version="1.0" encoding="utf-8"?>
>> <Window
>>   xmlns="http://schemas.microsoft.com/winfx/2006/xaml/presentation"
>>   xmlns:x="http://schemas.microsoft.com/winfx/2006/xaml"
>>   Width="350" Height="350">
>>
>>     <StackPanel Width="50">
>>         <Button Name="Button1" Content="Button1" />
>>         <Button Name="Button2" Content="Button2" />
>>         <Button Name="Button3" Content="Button3" />
>>     </StackPanel>
>> </Window>'
PS C:\workspace> $ui = Import-Xaml $Xaml
PS C:\workspace> $ui.MainWindow.ShowDialog()
```

Figure 16.9: Using Import-Xaml

The ability to locate individual elements in code allows changes to be made to individual elements, which is essential when working with event handlers.

Handling events

An event is raised in a UI when a button is pressed, when a selection changes, when a key is pressed, and so on.

To react to an event, an event handler must be created and attached to the control that raises the event.

Event handlers must be added before `ShowDialog` is run.

The list of possible events for the Window is extensive. The .NET reference lists the events and briefly describes each: https://learn.microsoft.com/dotnet/api/system.windows.window#events.

One possible event is pressing the Escape key while the UI has focus. It might be desirable to close the UI in this case. This is the KeyDown event and can be attached to the Window object.

For example, a KeyDown handler can be added to the following UI:

```
$xaml = '<?xml version="1.0" encoding="utf-8"?>
<Window
 xmlns="http://schemas.microsoft.com/winfx/2006/xaml/presentation"
 xmlns:x="http://schemas.microsoft.com/winfx/2006/xaml"
 Width="350" Height="350">
     <Label Content="Hello world" />
</Window>'
$ui = Import-Xaml $xaml
```

Event handlers are added by running a method named after the event. The method name is prefixed with add_. Get-Member can be used to show the methods, but the -Force parameter is required. For example:

```
PS> $ui.MainWindow | Get-Member add_KeyDown -Force


    TypeName: System.Windows.Window

Name          MemberType Definition
----          ---------- ----------
add_KeyDown   Method     void add_KeyDown(System.Windows.Input.K...
```

Two arguments are automatically made available to every event handler: the control that raised the event ($sender) and any event arguments ($eventArgs).

In the case of the KeyDown event, the $sender is the Window object, and $eventArgs includes the Key property describing which key was pressed.

Therefore, an event handler that allows the *Escape* key (*ESC*) to close the window can be added:

```
$ui.MainWindow.add_KeyDown({
    param ( $sender, $eventArgs )
    if ($eventArgs.Key -eq 'ESC') {
        $sender.Close()
    }
})
```

Adding the event handler alone like this has no visual impact. The change is only relevant when the UI is started.

With this event handler added, pressing *Escape* at any time after the UI has opened and with the UI having focus will close the UI:

```
$ui.MainWindow.ShowDialog()
```

This event handler is easy to implement as the only object it needs to act on is the Window itself. The Window is available in both the $Window variable and the $sender parameter; either variable can be used to run the Close method.

A similar approach can be taken to make an Exit button work.

Buttons and the Click event

The Click event on buttons can be used by adding an event handler. In the following example, the Exit button is used to close the parent window. First a UI is defined with an Exit button, and the button is given a name, allowing the control to be located:

```
$xaml = '<?xml version="1.0" encoding="utf-8"?>
<Window
 xmlns="http://schemas.microsoft.com/winfx/2006/xaml/presentation"
 xmlns:x="http://schemas.microsoft.com/winfx/2006/xaml"
 Width="350" Height="350">
    <Button Name="Button" Content="Exit" />
</Window>'
$ui = Import-Xaml $xaml
```

Once created, the event handler for Click is added to the Button:

```
$ui.Controls['Button'].add_Click({
    param ( $sender, $eventArgs )
    $ui.MainWindow.Close()
})
$ui.MainWindow.ShowDialog()
```

The controls in the UI are subject to default styling; moving the mouse over the button, for example, will cause the button to be highlighted. A detailed exploration of styling is beyond the scope of this chapter.

Controls in the UI can also read from and write to other controls.

In the following example, the Click event for the button is changed to update the content of another Label:

```
$xaml = '<?xml version="1.0" encoding="utf-8"?>
<Window
 xmlns="http://schemas.microsoft.com/winfx/2006/xaml/presentation"
 xmlns:x="http://schemas.microsoft.com/winfx/2006/xaml"
 Width="350" Height="350">
    <StackPanel>
        <Button Name="Button" Content="Run" />
        <Label Name="Label" />
    </StackPanel>
</Window>'
```

```
$ui = Import-Xaml $xaml
$ui.Controls['Button'].add_Click({
    param ( $sender, $eventArgs )
    $ui.Controls['Label'].Content = 'Hello world'
})
$ui.MainWindow.ShowDialog()
```

In the preceding example, the StackPanel is the only element without a name. In the case of this UI, it does not need a name as it is not referenced by any of the code.

The result of pressing the button in the UI is shown in the following example. Before the button is pushed, the area below the button will contain a blank Label:

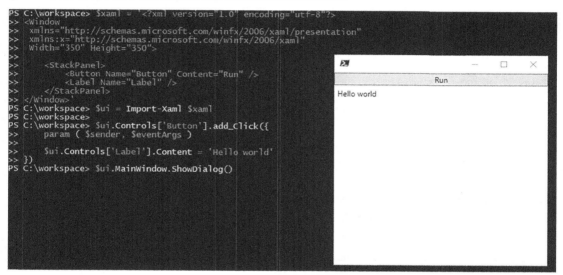

Figure 16.10: UI after pressing the Run button

Like Button, a ComboBox has specific events associated with the possible behavior of that control.

ComboBox and SelectionChanged

The SelectionChanged event can be used in a similar way to the Click event on a button. When the selection changes, the selection is available via the SelectedItem property of the ComboBox control.

The value in SelectedItem is a ComboBoxItem type; the actual value selected is held in the Content property of the item:

```
$xaml = '<?xml version="1.0" encoding="utf-8"?>
<Window
 xmlns="http://schemas.microsoft.com/winfx/2006/xaml/presentation"
 xmlns:x="http://schemas.microsoft.com/winfx/2006/xaml"
 Width="350" Height="350">
```

```
    <StackPanel>
        <ComboBox Name="ComboBox">
            <ComboBoxItem>Apple</ComboBoxItem>
            <ComboBoxItem>Orange</ComboBoxItem>
        </ComboBox>
        <Label Name="Label" />
    </StackPanel>
</Window>'
$ui = Import-Xaml $xaml
$ui.Controls['ComboBox'].add_SelectionChanged({
    param ( $sender, $eventArgs )
    $ui.Controls['Label'].Content = (
        'Selected a {0}' -f $sender.SelectedItem.Content
    )
})
$ui.MainWindow.ShowDialog()
```

Each control has different events available. The .NET reference and Get-Member can be used to explore the capabilities of that control.

Each of the values above has set a simple text value in the UI. If the content retrieved is more complex, dynamically creating controls to describe the output might be desirable.

Adding elements programmatically

One control might add more values to the UI when an event is triggered. For example, clicking a button might cause the results of a command to be displayed.

The previous examples can already deal with simple text output, but PowerShell rarely returns a simple string as the output from a command. A ListView control can be used to display more complex values.

The following Window is the starting point for this example:

```
$xaml = '<?xml version="1.0" encoding="utf-8"?>
<Window
 xmlns="http://schemas.microsoft.com/winfx/2006/xaml/presentation"
 xmlns:x="http://schemas.microsoft.com/winfx/2006/xaml"
 Width="350" Height="350">
    <DockPanel>
```

```
            <Button Name="Button" Content="Get-Process"
             DockPanel.Dock="Top" />
            <ListView Name="ListView">
                <ListView.View>
                    <GridView />
                </ListView.View>
            </ListView>
        </DockPanel>
    </Window>'
    $ui = Import-Xaml $xaml
```

The UI includes a button that will run a command. The Click event for the button updates the columns and items in the ListView:

```
$ui.Controls['Button'].add_Click({
    param ( $sender, $eventArgs )

    $data = Get-Process | Select-Object Name, ID
    $listView = $ui.Controls['ListView']

    # Clear any previous content
    $listView.View.Columns.Clear()
    foreach ($property in $data[0].PSObject.Properties) {
        $column = [System.Windows.Controls.GridViewColumn]@{
            DisplayMemberBinding = (
                [System.Windows.Data.Binding]$property.Name
            )
            Header               = $property.Name
        }
        $listView.View.Columns.Add($column)
    }
    $listView.ItemsSource = $data
})
$ui.MainWindow.ShowDialog()
```

When the UI is opened, and the button is clicked, the Name and ID of each running process will be displayed in the ListView.

The hidden member, PSObject, is used to dynamically discover the properties of whatever objects are held in the $data variable. In this case, those will only be Name and ID as Select-Object was used. The filtered output from the preceding example will be similar to that shown in *Figure 16.11*:

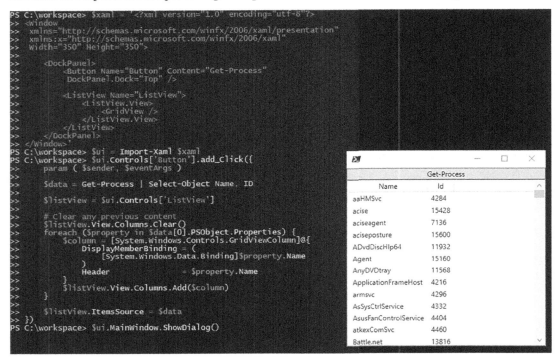

Figure 16.11: Updating ListView

The dynamically added content can be extended further to include an event handler that acts when a header is clicked, for example, to sort the list of processes.

Sorting a ListView

Adding column sorting to the UI is a useful example because it introduces an extra challenge.

The code used in this section is based on the example in the .NET reference: https://learn.microsoft.com/dotnet/desktop/wpf/controls/how-to-sort-a-gridview-column-when-a-header-is-clicked.

Two values need to be stored and tracked to allow sorting on multiple columns:

- The column which is currently being sorted
- The direction the column is sorted in

In addition to these, a visual clue needs to be added to the UI to show the sorted column and the direction. Two Unicode characters are used in this example:

```
PS> [char]0x25bc
▼
```

```
PS> [char]0x25b2
▲
```

It would easily be possible to store these values in script-scoped variables. However, an effort has been made to store information that is pertinent to the UI in the output from Import-Xaml. The following change to Import-Xaml adds a new State property, which can be used to hold arbitrary information about the UI in a single place:

```
function Import-Xaml {
    [CmdletBinding()]
    param (
        [Xml]$Xaml,

        [Hashtable]$State = @{}
    )

    Add-Type -AssemblyName PresentationFramework
    $window = [System.Windows.Markup.XamlReader]::Load(
        [System.Xml.XmlNodeReader]$Xaml
    )
    $controls = @{}
    foreach ($control in $Xaml.SelectNodes('//*[@Name]')) {
        $controls[$control.Name] = $window.FindName($control.Name)
    }
    [PSCustomObject]@{
        MainWindow = $Window
        Controls   = $controls
        State      = $State
    }
}
```

The layout of the UI has not changed from the previous example, but it must be imported using this new version of the Import-Xaml function. The State property is filled with values that are expected to be used:

```
$xaml = '<?xml version="1.0" encoding="utf-8"?>
<Window
 xmlns="http://schemas.microsoft.com/winfx/2006/xaml/presentation"
 xmlns:x="http://schemas.microsoft.com/winfx/2006/xaml"
 Width="350" Height="350">
    <DockPanel>
        <Button Name="Button" Content="Get-Process"
         DockPanel.Dock="Top" />
        <ListView Name="ListView">
```

```
                <ListView.View>
                    <GridView />
                </ListView.View>
            </ListView>
        </DockPanel>
    </Window>'
$ui = Import-Xaml $xaml -State @{
    LastSortDirection = $null
    LastSortedHeader  = $null
    Arrow             = @{
        Ascending  = [char]0x25b2
        Descending = [char]0x25bc
    }
}
```

Before attempting to set up the ListView, more code is required to:

1. Get the next direction value to sort in
2. Sort the content of the list view
3. Handle the Click event on a column header

The first two operations will be defined by functions. To simplify the code, each function implicitly accesses the $ui variable from a parent scope. This is the only non-local variable used by these functions.

First, a function is needed to get the next direction to sort in. This function accepts the column that was clicked using a parameter. The function outputs the next direction to sort in.

```
function Get-SortDirection {
    param (
        [System.Windows.Controls.GridViewColumnHeader]$Header
    )

    $lastSortDirection = $ui.State['LastSortDirection']
    $lastSortedHeader = $ui.State['LastSortedHeader']

    if ($null -eq $lastSortDirection -or -not $lastSortedHeader) {
        $direction = 'Ascending'
    } elseif (
        $lastSortedHeader -and
        $sender -ne $lastSortedHeader
    ) {
        $direction = 'Ascending'
    } else {
        # Swaps between Ascending and Descending (0 and 1)
```

```
        $direction = $lastSortDirection -bxor 1
    }
    [System.ComponentModel.ListSortDirection]$direction
}
```

The code above uses a comparison with $null and $lastSortDirection because the value of Ascending is 0, and therefore will evaluate as false.

The if statement below shows how the Ascending value is evaluated if there is no explicit comparison.

```
if ([System.ComponentModel.ListSortDirection]::Ascending) {
    Write-Host "Looks like true"
} else {
    Write-Host "Looks like false"
}
```

The example above will display Looks like false because the value is 0, and 0 is synonymous with false.

Sorting is performed on the default view of the ItemsSource collection; the collection contains the results of the Get-Process command. The view is acquired from the ListView control:

```
$listView = $ui.Controls['ListView']
$dataView = [System.Windows.Data.CollectionViewSource]::GetDefaultView(
    $listView.ItemsSource
)
```

This is added to a function that will be called from a click handler.

```
function Set-SortDirection {
    param (
        [string]
        $SortBy,

        [System.ComponentModel.ListSortDirection]
        $Direction
    )

    $listView = $ui.Controls['ListView']
    $dataView = [System.Windows.Data.CollectionViewSource]::GetDefaultView(
        $listView.ItemsSource
    )

    $dataView.SortDescriptions.Clear()

    $sortDescription = [System.ComponentModel.SortDescription]::new(
```

```
        $SortBy,
        $Direction
    )
    $dataView.SortDescriptions.Add($sortDescription)
    $dataView.Refresh()
}
```

The event handler that makes use of these functions needs to be defined. This event handler will be added to each column header as it is created. The handler is at this point a script block:

```
$headerClickHandler = {
    param ( $sender, $eventArgs )

    $lastSortedHeader = $ui.State['LastSortedHeader']

    $direction = Get-SortDirection -Header $sender

    # Update the last sorted values.
    $ui.State['LastSortedHeader'] = $sender
    $ui.State['LastSortDirection'] = $direction

    $indicator = $ui.State['Arrow'][$direction.ToString()]

    if ($lastSortedHeader) {
        $lastSortedHeader.Content = $lastSortedHeader.Name
    }
    $sender.Content = '{0} {1}' -f [char]$indicator, $sender.Name

    Set-SortDirection -SortBy $sender.Name -Direction $Direction
}
```

This runs each time any header is clicked. Any existing indicator on a header is removed each time before writing a new one.

Finally, the click handler created above needs to be added to a GridViewColumnHeader object when each GridViewColumn is created.

```
$ui.Controls['Button'].add_Click({
    param ( $sender, $eventArgs )

    $data = Get-Process | Select-Object Name, ID
    $listView = $ui.Controls['ListView']

    # Clear any previous content
    $listView.View.Columns.Clear()
```

```
        foreach ($property in $data[0].PSObject.Properties) {
            $header = [System.Windows.Controls.GridViewColumnHeader]@{
                Name    = $property.Name
                Content = $property.Name
            }
            $header.add_Click($headerClickHandler)

            $column = [System.Windows.Controls.GridViewColumn]@{
                DisplayMemberBinding = (
                    [System.Windows.Data.Binding]$property.Name
                )
                Header               = $header
            }
            $listView.View.Columns.Add($column)
        }
        $listView.ItemsSource = $data
    })
    $ui.MainWindow.ShowDialog()
```

The outcome of clicking **Sort** on the ID column is shown in *Figure 16.12*:

Figure 16.12: Adding column sorting to ListView

One of the biggest challenges when writing user interfaces in PowerShell is maintaining a responsive interface.

Responsive interfaces

The interfaces used in all the examples so far used short-running commands that have no significant impact on the user interface.

If an event handler in the user interface carries out a longer-running activity, the entire interface will freeze. This problem is simulated by using Start-Sleep in the following example:

```
$xaml = '<?xml version="1.0" encoding="utf-8"?>
<Window
 xmlns="http://schemas.microsoft.com/winfx/2006/xaml/presentation"
 xmlns:x="http://schemas.microsoft.com/winfx/2006/xaml"
 Width="350" Height="350">
     <Button Name="Button" Content="Start" />
</Window>'
$ui = Import-Xaml $xaml
$ui.Controls['Button'].add_Click({
     param ( $sender, $eventArgs )
     Start-Sleep -Seconds 10
})
$ui.MainWindow.ShowDialog()
```

Once the button is clicked, the user interface will freeze. It is not possible to move or close the window or interact with any of the controls until the script that is started by clicking the button completes.

This is clearly an undesirable problem; the UI appears to have crashed and it might leave anyone using the UI wondering what has gone wrong.

Solving this problem requires and extends upon the techniques used in *Chapter 15, Asynchronous Processing,* such as using runspaces, the InitialSessionState, and synchronized hashtables as a means of sharing data across runspaces.

Long-running actions must be moved into the background, and the task running in the background must update the user interface running in the foreground. A PowerShell runspace will be used to carry out long-running activities.

The first part of this is to provide a PowerShell runspace to execute the content of an event.

Import-Xaml and runspace support

The Import-Xaml function can be changed to better support UIs that run long-running commands. Support for State is retained in this version but will not be used in the examples that follow.

The following changes are going to be made to the Import-Xaml function:

- A runspace-synchronized hashtable is created holding each of the named controls
- An InitialSessionState is created to share the hashtable with the background runspace
- A PowerShell runspace is created and added as a property from the InitialSessionState

One final change to the function requires more of an explanation.

The background Runspace cannot directly interact with the UI, either to read properties from controls or to make changes. Interaction with the UI is performed via the Dispatcher property. The Dispatcher is available as a property on every single UI element and can be used to interact with elements of the UI in the UI thread.

For convenience, the Dispatcher property from the window is added to the Controls hashtable:

```
using namespace System.Management.Automation.Runspaces

function Import-Xaml {
    param (
        [Xml]$Xaml,

        [Hashtable]$State
    )
    Add-Type -AssemblyName PresentationFramework
    $window = [System.Windows.Markup.XamlReader]::Load(
        [System.Xml.XmlNodeReader]$Xaml
    )
    $controls = [Hashtable]::Synchronized(@{
        Dispatcher = $window.Dispatcher
    })
    foreach ($control in $Xaml.SelectNodes('//*[@Name]')) {
        $controls[$control.Name] = $window.FindName($control.Name)
    }
    $initialSessionState = [InitialSessionState]::CreateDefault2()
    $initialSessionState.Variables.Add(
        [SessionStateVariableEntry]::new(
            'ui',
            [PSCustomObject]@{ Controls = $controls },
            'UI controls'
        )
    )
    [PSCustomObject]@{
        MainWindow = $Window
```

```
        Controls    = $controls
        State       = @{}
        PSHost      = [PowerShell]::Create($initialSessionState)
    }
}
```

 Examples and Import-Xaml

This version of Import-Xaml replaces the previous version. The examples that follow expect to be able to use this version of the function.

The Dispatcher property can be used from a runspace to read from and write to the UI.

Introducing this extra runspace can make debugging more difficult.

Errors in the background

When running code in response to event handlers, output streams are not made visible in the console.

The PSHost object has access to each of the output streams from the nested runspace. The streams can be examined if the UI is not behaving as expected for possible errors.

Non-terminating errors are therefore accessible using the following:

```
$ui.PSHost.Streams.Error
```

Or, terminating errors using:

```
$ui.PSHost.InvocationStateInfo.Reason
```

Chapter 22, Error Handling, explores the difference between error types.

The PSHost makes use of the dispatcher to invoke in the UI thread.

Using the Dispatcher

As mentioned previously, the Dispatcher is used in the background thread to interact with the UI thread from the background.

The dispatcher expects a block of code known as a Delegate as an argument. This contains the code to execute in the UI thread.

A simple UI is required to start showing the different parts of this UI.

```
$xaml = '<?xml version="1.0" encoding="utf-8"?>
<Window
 xmlns="http://schemas.microsoft.com/winfx/2006/xaml/presentation"
 xmlns:x="http://schemas.microsoft.com/winfx/2006/xaml"
 Width="350" Height="350">
    <StackPanel>
```

```
            <Label Name="Status" />
            <Label Name="Output" />
            <Button Name="Button" Content="Start" />
        </StackPanel>
    </Window>'
```

This UI contains two labels and a button. The intent is to change the value of the output when the button is pressed. The status label will be used to provide feedback while testing.

A simple script that spends most of the time asleep can be used to simulate a slow command.

```
$script = {
    function Start-SlowCommand {
        Start-Sleep -Seconds 10
        'Hello world'
    }
    Start-SlowCommand
}
```

This ScriptBlock will be cast to a string shortly; the use of { } around the script allows syntax highlighting in an editor.

A Click event handler is added to the button. The button runs the PSHost script that was added to the output of Import-Xaml. This example requires the preceding code block that defines the value of $xaml:

```
$ui = Import-Xaml $xaml
$ui.Controls['Button'].add_Click({
    $ui.PSHost.Commands.Clear()
    $ui.PSHost.AddScript($script)
    $ui.PSHost.BeginInvoke()
})
```

This does not yet affect the state of the UI. Before starting any new command, the current command list for the PSHost is cleared, and the new script to run is added.

To affect the state of the UI, the script needs extending. More than one script can be run in the PSHost; each script is separated using the AddStatement method. This will be used to implement the following process:

1. Write to status and disable the button control.
2. Run the slow command.
3. Write to status and disable the button control.

Items 1 and 3 will be written directly into the event handler. However, the background PSHost cannot directly affect the content of the UI.

For example, running the following in another script is not enough:

```
$ui.Controls['Button'].Enabled = $false
```

This action must be invoked in the UI thread via the dispatcher.

```
$ui.Dispatcher.Invoke({
    $ui.Controls['Button'].Enabled = $false
})
```

Adding these actions changes the code as shown in the example below:

```
$ui = Import-Xaml $xaml
$ui.Controls['Button'].add_Click({
    $ui.PSHost.Commands.Clear()

    # Disable the button
    $ui.PSHost.AddScript({
        $ui.Controls['Dispatcher'].Invoke({
            $ui.Controls['Status'].Content = 'Running'
            $ui.Controls['Button']. IsEnabled = $false
        })
    }).AddStatement()

    $ui.PSHost.AddScript($script).AddStatement()

    # Enable the button
    $ui.PSHost.AddScript({
        $ui.Controls['Dispatcher'].Invoke({
            $ui.Controls['Status'].Content = 'Complete'
            $ui.Controls['Button'].IsEnabled = $true
        })
    })
    $ui.PSHost.BeginInvoke()
})
```

This so far causes the UI to update before the script starts and after it has completed, but no output from the script is visible.

The script is also updated to write back to the UI via the Dispatcher as shown below.

```
$script = {
    function Start-SlowCommand {
        Start-Sleep -Seconds 10
        'Hello world'
```

```
    }
    $output = Start-SlowCommand

    $ui.Controls['Dispatcher'].Invoke({
        $ui.Controls['Output'].Content = $output
    })
}
```

Note that the only thing executing in the UI thread is the update to the UI itself. The slow command is not pushed back into the UI thread.

The approach so far has been to significantly reduce the amount of work running in the UI thread. This in turn avoids freezing the entire UI. If the UI was being dragged around the screen at the exact point the UI updated, a momentary hang in the UI might be noticeable.

This momentary freeze is called by a callback between runspaces by the script blocks invoked via the dispatcher.

ScriptBlock runspace affinity

Script blocks created in PowerShell call back to the runspace they were created in to execute. This is known as runspace affinity. Runspace affinity is explored again in *Chapter 19, Classes and Enumerations*.

Runspace affinity can be stripped from a script block as follows:

```
$scriptBlock = { 'Hello world' }
$scriptBlock.Ast.GetScriptBlock()
```

The Ast property allows access to the **Abstract Syntax Tree.** This topic is explored in *Chapter 21, Testing*, as part of the static analysis topic.

Adding this approach to the Click event handler is shown below:

```
$ui.Controls['Button'].add_Click({
    $ui.PSHost.Commands.Clear()

    $ui.PSHost.AddScript({
        $ui.Controls['Dispatcher'].Invoke({
            $ui.Controls['Status'].Content = 'Running'
            $ui.Controls['Button'].IsEnabled = $false
        }.Ast.GetScriptBlock())
    }).AddStatement()

    $ui.PSHost.AddScript($script).AddStatement()

    $ui.PSHost.AddScript({
        $ui.Controls['Dispatcher'].Invoke({
```

```
            $ui.Controls['Status'].Content = 'Complete'
            $ui.Controls['Button'].IsEnabled = $true
        }.Ast.GetScriptBlock())
    })
    $ui.PSHost.BeginInvoke()
})
```

This method also needs adding to $script but doing so invalidates the use of the $output variable. That is, it introduces a scope problem that is not exhibited by the globally scoped $ui variable (in the context of the PSHost).

The scope of the variable could be changed, but it is more useful to explore getting output from and providing input to commands invoked like this.

Using the Action delegate

The System.Action can be used to write changes to a UI. An Action delegate returns no output but can accept arguments.

The code used in the examples above is equivalent to the use of an Action delegate that accepts no arguments.

The use of Invoke in the example below is equivalent to the examples above:

```
$ui.PSHost.AddScript([Action]{
    $ui.Controls['Dispatcher'].Invoke({
        $ui.Controls['Status'].Content = 'Running'
        $ui.Controls['Button'].IsEnabled = $false
    }.Ast.GetScriptBlock())
}).AddStatement()
```

This describes a delegate, a block of code that accepts no arguments and has no output.

If it were necessary to pass an argument to the delegate, the type of each argument would be defined. This also requires a different overload for the Invoke method.

For example, the change below accepts two arguments:

```
$ui.PSHost.AddScript({
    $content = 'Running'
    $enabled = $false

    $ui.Controls['Dispatcher'].Invoke(
        [Action[string,bool]]{
            param ( $content, $enabled )

            $ui.Controls['Status'].Content = $content
```

```
            $ui.Controls['Button'].IsEnabled = $enabled
        }.Ast.GetScriptBlock(),
        @($content, $enabled)
    )
}).AddStatement()
```

The type [Action[string,bool]] states that two parameters are expected: the first is a string, the second a Boolean. A param block is used inside the delegate to map those to variable names, and the values are passed to the delegate as an array.

This allows values to be explicitly passed to the delegate when the variable cannot be otherwise resolved.

This approach can be used to fix the problem with the content of the $script variable. In this case, the parameter type for the Action can simply be set to object.

```
$script = {
    function Start-SlowCommand {
        Start-Sleep -Seconds 10
        'Hello world'
    }
    $output = Start-SlowCommand

    $ui.Controls['Dispatcher'].Invoke(
        [Action[object]]{
            param ( $output )

            $ui.Controls['Output'].Content = $output
        }.Ast.GetScriptBlock(),
        @($output)
    )
}

$ui = Import-Xaml $xaml
$ui.Controls['Button'].add_Click({
    $ui.PSHost.Commands.Clear()

    $ui.PSHost.AddScript({
        $ui.Controls['Dispatcher'].Invoke({
            $ui.Controls['Status'].Content = 'Running'
            $ui.Controls['Button'].IsEnabled = $false
        }.Ast.GetScriptBlock())
    }).AddStatement()
```

```
    $ui.PSHost.AddScript($script).AddStatement()

    $ui.PSHost.AddScript({
        $ui.Controls['Dispatcher'].Invoke({
            $ui.Controls['Status'].Content = 'Complete'
            $ui.Controls['Button'].IsEnabled = $true
        }.Ast.GetScriptBlock())
    })
    $ui.PSHost.BeginInvoke()
})
$ui.MainWindow.ShowDialog()
```

Clicking the button in the GUI will immediately cause the status label to update, then, after 10 seconds, the status will change to Complete, and the output text will be written.

Reading values from a UI also requires a specific delegate type.

Using the Func delegate

The System.Func delegate can be used to both read values from the UI and write changes. It is used to describe a block of code that accepts zero or more arguments and returns an object of a specific type.

The current UI does not require reading from the UI as input for the code it executes. This last UI example implements a counter that repeatedly writes to the UI based on user-supplied values.

The Window implements the Label and TextBox controls for user input, making use of the controls introduced in this chapter. Output, as a counter value, is written to a single Label.

```
$xaml = '<?xml version="1.0" encoding="utf-8"?>
<Window
 xmlns="http://schemas.microsoft.com/winfx/2006/xaml/presentation"
 xmlns:x="http://schemas.microsoft.com/winfx/2006/xaml"
 Width="350" Height="350">
    <DockPanel>
        <Grid DockPanel.Dock="Top">
            <Grid.ColumnDefinitions>
                <ColumnDefinition Width="*" />
                <ColumnDefinition Width="2*" />
            </Grid.ColumnDefinitions>
            <Grid.RowDefinitions>
                <RowDefinition />
                <RowDefinition />
            </Grid.RowDefinitions>
            <Label Content="Start" Margin="5,5,5,0"
             Grid.Row="0" Grid.Column="0" />
```

```
                    <TextBox Name="TextBoxStart" Text="1" Margin="5,5,5,0"
                     Grid.Row="0" Grid.Column="1" />
                    <Label Content="End" Margin="5,5,5,0"
                     Grid.Row="1" Grid.Column="0" />
                    <TextBox Name="TextBoxEnd" Text="30" Margin="5,5,5,0"
                     Grid.Row="1" Grid.Column="1" />
                </Grid>
                <Button Name="Button" Margin="5" Padding="5"
                 Content="Go" DockPanel.Dock="Bottom" />
                <Label Name="Label"
                 Margin="5" HorizontalContentAlignment="Center"
                 VerticalContentAlignment="Center" FontSize="32"
                />
            </DockPanel>
        </Window>'
```

The Click event handler for the button is wired up as a single script block in this example.

The script block contains a slow command. Each execution of the command takes 1 second. The command acts in a pipeline. Pipeline support for scripts is explored in *Chapter 17, Scripts, Functions, and Script Blocks*. The script is shown below:

```
$script = {
    function Start-SlowCommand {
        process {
            Start-Sleep -Seconds 1
            $_
        }
    }

    $start..$end | Start-SlowCommand | ForEach-Object {
        $ui.Controls['Dispatcher'].Invoke(
            [Action[int]]{
                param ($number)

                $ui.Controls['Label'].Content = $number
            }.Ast.GetScriptBlock(),
            $_
        )
    }
}
```

The script makes use of the Action delegate type to accept a parameter, the output from the slow command, which is immediately written as a Label.

The Click method invokes the script, as well as making use of a Func delegate to read two values, one from each TextBox.

```
$ui = Import-Xaml $xaml
$ui.Controls['Button'].add_Click({
    $ui.PSHost.Commands.Clear()

    $ui.PSHost.AddScript({
        $ui.Controls['Dispatcher'].Invoke({
            $ui.Controls['Button'].IsEnabled = $false
        }.Ast.GetScriptBlock())
    }).AddStatement()

    $ui.PSHost.AddScript({
        $start, $end = $ui.Controls['Dispatcher'].Invoke([Func[object]]{
            $ui.Controls['TextBoxStart'].Text -as [int]
            $ui.Controls['TextBoxEnd'].Text -as [int]
        }.Ast.GetScriptBlock())
    }).AddStatement()

    $ui.PSHost.AddScript($script).AddStatement()

    $ui.PSHost.AddScript({
        $ui.Controls['Dispatcher'].Invoke({
            $ui.Controls['Button'].IsEnabled = $true
        }.Ast.GetScriptBlock())
    })

    $ui.PSHost.BeginInvoke()
})
$ui.MainWindow.ShowDialog()
```

The values read from the TextBox controls dictate the start and end values, and in turn the number of times Start-SlowCommand will run.

Implemented in this way, the UI will remain responsive. The preceding UI is shown in *Figure 16.13* after the Go button has been clicked:

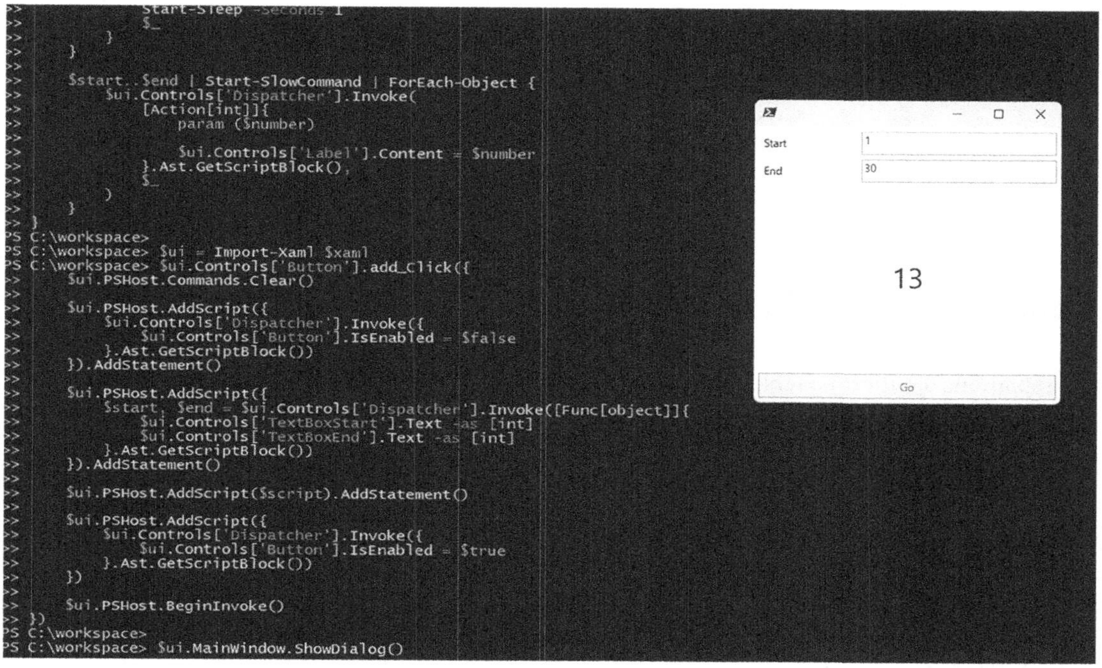

Figure 16.13: Counter UI

It is important to keep long-running activities outside of the code running in the Dispatcher.

The Dispatcher can be used on either side of the process to enable and disable controls, to write status messages and output, and so on.

Summary

User interfaces are a common requirement in PowerShell, and even though PowerShell is written to run as a shell, it is still possible to create advanced user interfaces.

WPF includes a wide variety of different controls that can be combined to build a user interface. The initial layout of a WPF UI can be described in a XAML document, reducing the amount of code required to create the interface. A designer can be used to help generate the XAML content if required.

Simple controls such as Grid, StackPanel, and DockPanel can be used to place controls without a need to resort to absolute or coordinate-based positioning within an interface.

Controls can be given names within the XAML document, allowing PowerShell to find controls to attach event handlers or change values at runtime.

Elements of the user interface can be added or changed in event handlers. A ListView control was used to demonstrate a dynamically created view of an object created in PowerShell.

Making a responsive user interface is challenging in PowerShell. The Dispatcher in WPF can be used to interact with the UI thread from a Runspace running in the background. The Dispatcher is used to read from and write to the user interface.

The next chapter explores scripts, functions, and script blocks.

Learn more on Discord

Read this book alongside other users, PowerShell experts, and the author himself. Ask questions, provide solutions to other readers, chat with the author via Ask Me Anything sessions, and much more.

Scan the QR code or visit the link to join the community.

https://packt.link/SecNet

17

Scripts, Functions, and Script Blocks

In PowerShell, scripts and functions are commands. They have overlapping capabilities and often only differ by common use.

Scripts tend to be used to implement well-defined processes; such scripts often run on a schedule of some kind. A script may include functions or run other scripts, and will often use commands from other modules. A script is convenient as it consists of a single `ps1` file.

Functions can be used to implement a single process in the same way as a script. A function might be part of a script, implementing a process, or part of a module. When automating a process, writing a module to host a function might be regarded as slightly less convenient and less simple than writing a script.

Whether a function is in a script or a module, the function should strive to be simple. It should aim to be great at one job and, if possible, reusable. Reusable or not, functions are a great way of isolating small chunks of complex logic. Functions are the building blocks of more complex code, including scripts and other functions.

A script block also has overlapping capabilities with scripts and functions. A script block is an anonymous or unnamed function (the `function` keyword is used to get a name to a script block); this is also known as lambda. Script blocks can therefore make use of `param` blocks and be invoked in a pipeline. They are used throughout PowerShell—for example, as parameters for `ForEach-Object`, `Where-Object`, `Invoke-Command`, and `Start-Job`.

The `Filter` keyword is briefly discussed in this chapter while exploring the named blocks, `begin`, `process`, and `end`.

This chapter explores the following topics:

- About style
- Capabilities of scripts, functions, and script blocks

- Parameters and the `param` block
- The `CmdletBinding` attribute
- The `Alias` attribute
- `begin`, `process`, `end`, and `clean`
- Managing output
- Working with long lines
- Comment-based help

Style in PowerShell is a very subjective topic, but an important one when writing code that will be maintained over a long period of time.

About style

Style in the context of a scripting language is all about aesthetics; it describes how variables are named, how code is indented, where opening and closing brackets are placed, and so on. Style is an easy thing to disagree with; the topic is full of opinions, many of which come down to what an individual feels is right.

PowerShell does not have an official style, nor does it have an official best practice.

PowerShell does have a set of guidelines for cmdlet development (commands typically written in a compiled language like C#): `https://learn.microsoft.com/powershell/scripting/developer/cmdlet/cmdlet-development-guidelines`.

It has been left to the community of PowerShell users and developers to provide further guidance. The community-created *PowerShell Practice and Style* repository describes many of the most widely accepted conventions: `https://github.com/poshcode/powershellpracticeandstyle`.

Many of these conventions (for example, warnings about the use of aliases in production code) are implemented in the `PSScriptAnalyzer` module. The `PSScriptAnalyzer` module is integrated with the PowerShell extension in Visual Studio Code and will show warnings as code is written:

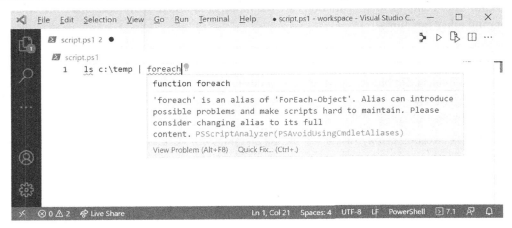

Figure 17.1: Warning from PSScriptAnalyzer in Visual Studio Code

A warning from PSScriptAnalyzer in Visual Studio Code often provides a link to fix the perceived problem. Not everyone will agree with all the rules, and this is fine. The PSScriptAnalyzer repository includes instructions for suppressing rules: https://github.com/PowerShell/PSScriptAnalyzer/blob/master/README.md.

The guidance on styling is therefore simple:

- Choose a style and use that style consistently. Remember that code will likely need to be maintained in the future.
- If contributing to a project started by somebody else, be considerate of any existing style; use that style in any changes.
- Personal style may change over time. This too is normal.

Establishing a style when writing code as a team can be difficult. Style choices can be a very personal topic. Compromise may be needed to find an approach that works. Having established something of a style, scripts and functions can be written, starting with an exploration of the capabilities of each. Ideally, the style chosen should be documented and enforced using the styling rules available with PSScriptAnalyzer.

Capabilities of scripts, functions, and script blocks

Scripts, functions, and script blocks share many of the same capabilities. These capabilities are explored during this and the next few chapters. Scripts, functions, and script blocks can each:

- Define parameters.
- Support pipeline input.
- Support common parameters, including support for Confirm and WhatIf.
- Allow other functions to be nested inside.

Scripts, but not functions or script blocks, support using statements. Scripts also support the Requires statement.

Scripts and using statements

using statements, introduced with PowerShell 5, were described in *Chapter 7, Working with .NET*. A short example of a using statement is shown here:

```
using namespace System.Xml.Linq
```

A function may benefit from using statements declared in a parent scope. The parent scope includes code run on the console, a script that contains a function, or a module (psm1 file) that contains a function.

The order in which the statements appear is not important, meaning the order of the commands in the previous example can be reversed with no change in the result. using namespace is a passive statement and is only important when code utilizing a shortened namespace is run.

Scripts and the Requires statement

The Requires statement is valid only in scripts and can be used to restrict a script from running if certain conditions are not met. For example, a script may require administrative rights or certain modules.

Requires statements are, by convention, placed on the first few lines of a script but, in practice, can appear anywhere in the script. A Requires statement may include more than one option or multiple Requires statements may be included.

An example of a Requires statement is shown below:

```
Requires -PSEdition Desktop -RunAsAdministrator
Requires -Modules @{ModuleName = 'TLS'; ModuleVersion = '2.0.0'}
```

Notice that there is no space between the comment character, #, and the Requires keyword.

Any modules required are loaded before the script starts.

PowerShell includes help for the Requires statement that describes the possible parameters:

```
Get-Help about_Requires
```

In a script, the Requires statement may be used to declare a need for administrative rights, a certain version of PowerShell, or the presence of certain modules.

Nesting functions

In the same way that a script can contain functions, a function can contain other functions. The following function contains two other functions; those functions are only available within the scope of the Outer function:

```
function Outer {
    param (
        $Parameter1
    )
    function Inner1 {
    }
    function Inner2 {
        function Inner3 {
        }
    }
    Write-Host 'Hello world'
}
```

Nested functions allow an author to isolate repeated sections of code with a function.

Nested functions must appear before they are used, but otherwise can appear anywhere in the body of the function.

The disadvantage of nesting a function is that it becomes harder to test and debug. The function only exists in the context of its parent function; it cannot be called and tested from the scope above that. This is an important consideration when developing a function as part of a larger work and it is therefore advisable to avoid nesting one function within another.

Script blocks and closures

A script block is an anonymous function. Script blocks are used a great deal in PowerShell; for example, they are used with:

- Where-Object as FilterScript
- ForEach-Object for the begin, process, and end parameters
- Select-Object as an Expression for a calculated property
- Sort-Object and Group-Object as calculated values for the Property parameter
- Code to execute with Invoke-Command and Start-Job

Like a function, when a script block is run, it can use variables from a parent scope. The following example will return the string first value, the value of the $string variable at the point in time it is run:

```
PS> $string = "first value"
PS> $scriptBlock = { $string }
PS> & $scriptBlock
first value
```

If the string changes before $scriptBlock is run, the output of $scriptBlock will change, in this case, to second value:

```
PS> $scriptBlock = { $string }
PS> $string = "second value"
PS> & $scriptBlock
second value
```

The GetNewClosure method can be used to copy the values of variables from the current session into the scriptBlock session. The following example will therefore return the value first value, despite the variable being updated afterward:

```
PS> $string = "first value"
PS> $scriptBlock = { $string }.GetNewClosure()
PS> $string = "second value"
PS> & $scriptBlock
first value
```

Closures are an interesting facet of script blocks in PowerShell, but it is difficult to find an instructive use that can be easily demonstrated without a great deal of design context.

The capabilities listed in this section are less frequently used than the following major features, such as our next topic on parameters.

Parameters and the param block

Parameters are used to describe and give names to the values a command is willing to accept when it is run. The list of parameters is separated by a comma.

Parameters can be defined as a block using the param keyword, which is the most popular approach as parameter blocks in PowerShell can become quite large. Using the param keyword is the only way to describe parameters for scripts and script blocks:

```
param (
    $Parameter1,
    $Parameter2
)
```

When used in a function, the param block is used as follows:

```
function New-Function {
    param (
        $parameter1,
        $parameter2
    )
}
```

The param block is required if CmdletBinding, Alias, or any other attributes are applied to the function. The CmdletBinding and Alias attributes are explored later in this chapter.

Functions also allow parameters to be defined immediately after the function name. For example:

```
function New-Function($Parameter1, $Parameter2) {
    # Function body
}
```

Either style may include line breaks:

```
function New-Function(
    $Parameter1,
    $Parameter2
) {
    # Function body
}
```

However, the inline style prevents the use of attributes such as CmdletBinding and Alias and is, therefore, not recommended.

When used, the param block must appear before all other code. An exception to this is using statements in a script, which must be written before param.

By default, parameters have the System.Object type. This means that any value type can be passed into a parameter. It may be desirable to restrict values to those of a specific type.

Parameter types

The type assigned to a parameter is written before the parameter name. The line break after the type is optional.

For example, if the function expects a string, the parameter type might be set to [string]:

```
param (
    [string]
    $Parameter1
)
```

Any value passed as an argument will be coerced into a string regardless of the original type.

When assigning a type to a parameter, the type persists until a new type is applied or the variable is removed (for example, with Remove-Variable). Any values assigned to $Parameter1 from the preceding example will be converted to a string.

This coercion of types was explored in *Chapter 3, Variables, Arrays, and Hashtables*.

Parameters that are given a type will be initialized with a default value or may be given an explicit default value.

Default values

Default values are used when a parameter value is not explicitly passed when calling the script, function, or script block.

Value types, such as Boolean or Int (Int32), and other numeric types are initialized with a default value for that type. A parameter of the Boolean type can never be null; it will be assigned a default value of false. Numeric values will default to 0, a string parameter will default to an empty string, and so on.

Conversely, parameters using types such as DateTime, TimeSpan, and Hashtable will default to null.

Parameters can be assigned default values in the param block. For example:

```
function Test-Parameter {
    param (
        [string]
        $Parameter1 = 'DefaultValue'
    )
}
```

If the assignment is the result of a command, the command must be placed in parentheses:

```
function Test-Parameter {
    param (
        [string]$ProcessName = (Get-Process -Id $PID |
            Select-Object -ExpandProperty Name)
    )
}
```

Assigning a default value was the basis for making parameters mandatory in PowerShell 1. The parameter would be assigned a throw statement by default. This is rarely seen in modern code. For example:

```
function Test-Parameter {
    param (
        [string]
        $Parameter1 = $(throw 'This parameter is mandatory')
    )
}
```

This method of making parameters mandatory was replaced in PowerShell 2 by the Mandatory property of the Parameter attribute. The Parameter attribute is used to define behavior for a parameter and is explored in detail in *Chapter 18, Parameters, Validation, and Dynamic Parameters*.

It is possible to provide a default value for a parameter based on the value of another within the param block.

Cross-referencing parameters

When using a param block, it is possible to cross-reference parameters. That is, the default value of a parameter can be based on the value of another parameter, as shown in the following example:

```
function Get-Substring {
    param (
        [string]
        $String,

        [int]
        $Start,

        [int]
        $Length = ($String.Length - $Start)
    )
    $String.Substring($Start, $Length)
}
```

The value of the Length parameter will use the default, derived from the first two parameters, unless the user of the function supplies their own value. The order of the parameters is important: the Start parameter must be declared in the param block before it can be used in the default value for Length.

Parameters in PowerShell are complex, and an exploration of their capabilities is covered in *Chapter 18, Parameters, Validation, and Dynamic Parameters*. This chapter focuses on the structure of strings and functions starting at the top with CmdletBinding.

The CmdletBinding attribute

The CmdletBinding attribute is used to turn a function into an advanced function and is placed immediately above a param block. The attribute is used to add extra functionality, such as access to common parameters, control over the impact level, and so on. Scripts are not referred to as advanced scripts, but the same principle applies.

CmdletBinding may be used to do the following:

*   Add common parameters, such as ErrorAction, Verbose, Debug, ErrorVariable, WarningVariable, and so on.
*   Enable the use of the built-in $PSCmdlet variable.
*   Declare support for WhatIf and Confirm and define the impact level of the command.

If a script or function has no parameters and wishes to make use of the capabilities provided by CmdletBinding, an empty param block must be declared:

```
function Test-EmptyParam {
    [CmdletBinding()]
    param ( )
}
```

One of the most important features added by CmdletBinding is the common parameters.

Common parameters

With CmdletBinding in place, a script or function may use common parameters. All the common parameters are listed here:

*   Debug
*   ErrorAction
*   ErrorVariable
*   InformationAction
*   InformationVariable
*   OutVariable
*   OutBuffer
*   PipelineVariable
*   ProgressAction
*   Verbose

- WarningAction
- WarningVariable

PowerShell provides a description of each of the common parameters in the about_CommonParameters help file:

```
Get-Help about_CommonParameters
```

The common parameters above can be listed in the console by using the CommonParameters static property of the PSCmdlet type:

```
[System.Management.Automation.PSCmdlet]::CommonParameters
```

For example, the Verbose parameter is made available when a function (or script) is advanced. The following function will display the verbose message when it is run with the Verbose parameter:

```
function Show-Verbose {
    [CmdletBinding()]
    param ( )
    Write-Verbose 'Verbose message'
}
```

That is, if the command below is run, the verbose message will display:

```
PS> Show-Verbose -Verbose
VERBOSE: Verbose message
```

In a similar way, parameters such as ErrorAction will affect Write-Error if it is used within the function.

CmdletBinding itself provides several properties used to influence the behavior of a function or script.

CmdletBinding properties

The full set of possible values that may be assigned can be viewed by creating an instance of the CmdletBinding object:

```
PS> [CmdletBinding]::new()

PositionalBinding        : True
DefaultParameterSetName  :
SupportsShouldProcess    : False
SupportsPaging           : False
SupportsTransactions     : False
ConfirmImpact            : Medium
HelpUri                  :
RemotingCapability       : PowerShell
TypeId                   : System.Management.Automation.CmdletBindingAttribute
```

For example, the output from the preceding command shows the existence of a PositionalBinding property. Setting this to false disables automatic position binding:

```
function Test-Binding {
    [CmdletBinding(PositionalBinding = $false)]
    param (
        $Parameter1
    )
}
```

When the preceding function is called and a value for Parameter1 is given by position, an error is thrown:

```
PS> Test-Binding 'value'
Test-Binding : A positional parameter cannot be found that accepts argument
'value'.
```

The command output also shows a HelpUri property. This property is used when a user makes use of Get-Help -Online to display help content on a web page.

Arguably the most widely used properties of CmdletBinding are SupportsShouldProcess and DefaultParameterSetName. DefaultParameterSetName is explored in *Chapter 18, Parameters, Validation, and Dynamic Parameters*. ShouldProcess and ShouldContinue offer support for WhatIf and confirmation prompting.

ShouldProcess and ShouldContinue

Setting the SupportsShouldProcess property of CmdletBinding enables the ShouldProcess parameters, Confirm and WhatIf. These two parameters are used in conjunction with the ShouldProcess method, which is exposed on the $PSCmdlet variable. $PSCmdlet is an automatically created variable available in the body of an advanced function or script.

Both the ShouldProcess and ShouldContinue methods of the $PSCmdlet variable become available when a script or function has the CmdletBinding attribute and the SupportsShouldProcess property is set.

The following example enables the SupportsShouldProcess setting:

```
function Enable-ShouldProcess {
    [CmdletBinding(SupportsShouldProcess)]
    param ( )
}
```

The ShouldProcess method is more commonly used than ShouldContinue.

ShouldProcess

ShouldProcess is used to support WhatIf and is responsible for raising confirmation prompts based on the impact level of a command.

The following example will display a message instead of running the `Write-Host` statement when the `WhatIf` parameter is used:

```
function Test-ShouldProcess {
    [CmdletBinding(SupportsShouldProcess)]
    param ( )
    if ($PSCmdlet.ShouldProcess('SomeObject')) {
        Write-Host 'Deleting SomeObject' -ForegroundColor Cyan
    }
}
```

When run using the `WhatIf` parameter, the command will show the following message:

```
PS> Test-ShouldProcess -WhatIf
What if: Performing the operation "Test-ShouldProcess" on target "SomeObject".
```

The name of the operation, which defaults to the command name, can be changed using a second overload for `ShouldProcess`:

```
function Test-ShouldProcess {
    [CmdletBinding(SupportsShouldProcess)]
    param ( )
    if ($PSCmdlet.ShouldProcess('SomeObject', 'delete')) {
        Write-Host 'Deleting SomeObject' -ForegroundColor Cyan
    }
}
```

Adding the second argument changes the message to the following:

```
PS> Test-ShouldProcess -WhatIf
What if: Performing the operation "delete" on target "SomeObject".
```

The whole message can be changed by adding one extra argument:

```
function Test-ShouldProcess {
    [CmdletBinding(SupportsShouldProcess)]
    param ( )
    if ($PSCmdlet.ShouldProcess(
            'Message displayed using WhatIf',
            'Warning: Deleting SomeObject',
            'Question: Are you sure you want to do continue?')
    ) {
        Write-Host 'Deleting SomeObject' -ForegroundColor Cyan
    }
}
```

Using the Confirm parameter instead of WhatIf forces the appearance of the second two messages and adds a prompt:

```
PS> Test-ShouldProcess -Confirm
Question: Are you sure you want to do continue?
Warning: Deleting SomeObject
[Y] Yes [A] Yes to All [N] No [L] No to All [S] Suspend [?] Help (default is
"Y"):
```

The different responses are automatically available without further code. If the request is within a loop, Yes to All may be used to bypass additional prompts. Replying Yes to All applies to all instances of ShouldProcess in the script or function:

```
function Test-ShouldProcess {
    [CmdletBinding(SupportsShouldProcess)]
    param ( )
    foreach ($value in 1..2) {
        if ($PSCmdlet.ShouldProcess(
                "Would delete SomeObject $value",
                "Warning: Deleting SomeObject $value",
                'Question: Are you sure you want to do continue?')
        ) {
            Write-Host "Deleting SomeObject $value" -ForegroundColor Cyan
        }
    }
}
```

Whether or not the confirmation prompt is displayed depends on the comparison between ConfirmImpact (Medium by default) and the value in the $ConfirmPreference variable, which is High by default.

If the impact of the function is raised to High, the prompt will display by default instead of on demand. This is achieved by modifying the ConfirmImpact property of the CmdletBinding attribute:

```
function Test-ShouldProcess {
    [CmdletBinding(SupportsShouldProcess, ConfirmImpact = 'High')]
    param ( )

    if ($PSCmdlet.ShouldProcess('SomeObject')) {
        Write-Host 'Deleting SomeObject' -ForegroundColor Cyan
    }
}
```

When the function is executed, the confirmation prompt will appear unless the user either uses -Confirm:$false or sets $ConfirmPreference to None.

ShouldContinue is available as an alternative to ShouldProcess.

ShouldContinue

The ShouldContinue method is also made available when the SupportsShouldProcess property is set in CmdletBinding.

ShouldContinue differs from ShouldProcess in that it always prompts. This technique is used by commands such as Remove-Item to force a prompt when attempting to delete a directory without supplying the Recurse parameter.

As the prompt for ShouldContinue is forced, it is rarely a better choice than ShouldProcess. It is available for cases where a function must have a confirmation prompt that cannot be bypassed. Using ShouldContinue may make it impossible to run a function without user interaction unless another means of bypassing the prompt is created.

The use of the ShouldContinue method is like the ShouldProcess method. The most significant difference is that the Yes to All and No to All options are not automatically implemented. The following example does not offer Yes to All and No to All options:

```
function Test-ShouldContinue {
    [CmdletBinding(SupportsShouldProcess)]
    param ( )

    if ($PSCmdlet.ShouldContinue(
            "Warning: Deleting SomeObject $value",
            'Question: Are you sure you want to do continue?')
    ) {
        Write-Host 'Deleting SomeObject' -ForegroundColor Cyan
    }
}
```

The prompt displayed is shown as follows:

```
PS> Test-ShouldContinue
Question: Are you sure you want to do continue?
Warning: Deleting SomeObject
[Y] Yes [N] No [S] Suspend [?] Help (default is "Y"): y
```

Adding support for Yes to All and No to All means using three extra arguments for the ShouldContinue method. The first of these new arguments, hasSecurityImpact, affects whether the default option presented is Yes (when hasSecurityImpact is false) or No (when hasSecurityImpact is true).

Boolean variables must be created to hold the Yes to All and No to All responses. These are passed as reference arguments to the ShouldContinue method, as shown in the following example:

```
function Test-ShouldContinue {
    [CmdletBinding(SupportsShouldProcess)]
    param ( )

    $yesToAll = $noToAll = $false
    if ($PSCmdlet.ShouldContinue(
            "Warning: Deleting SomeObject $value",
            'Question: Are you sure you want to do continue?',
            $false,
            [ref]$yesToAll,
            [ref]$noToAll)
    ) {
        Write-Host 'Deleting SomeObject' -ForegroundColor Cyan
    }
}
```

The confirmation prompt will now include the Yes to All and No to All options:

```
PS> Test-ShouldContinue
Question: Are you sure you want to do continue?
Warning: Deleting SomeObject
[Y] Yes [A] Yes to All [N] No [L] No to All [S] Suspend [?] Help (default is
"Y"):
```

It is possible to provide a means of bypassing the prompt by implementing another switch parameter. For example, a Force parameter might be added:

```
function Test-ShouldContinue {
    [CmdletBinding(SupportsShouldProcess)]
    param (
        [switch]$Force
    )
    $yesToAll = $noToAll = $false
    if ($Force -or $PSCmdlet.ShouldContinue(
            "Warning: Deleting SomeObject $value",
            'Question: Are you sure you want to do continue?',
            $false,
            [Ref]$yesToAll,
            [Ref]$noToAll)) {
        Write-Host 'Deleting SomeObject' -ForegroundColor Cyan
    }
}
```

As the value of Force is evaluated before ShouldContinue, the ShouldContinue method will not run if the Force parameter is supplied.

Other attributes can be added to the param block as required—for example, the Alias attribute.

The Alias attribute

Like CmdletBinding, the Alias attribute may be placed before the param block. It may be used before or after CmdletBinding; the ordering of attributes does not matter.

The Alias attribute is used to optionally create aliases for a function. A function can have one or more aliases; the attribute accepts either a single value or an array of values. For example, an alias gsm can be added to the Get-Something function by adding the Alias attribute:

```
function Get-Something {
    [CmdletBinding()]
    [Alias('gsm')]
    param ( )

    Write-Host 'Running Get-Something'
}
```

The alias is immediately available if the function is pasted into the console:

```
PS> gsm
Running Get-Something
```

The Get-Alias command will also show the alias has been created:

```
PS> Get-Alias gsm

CommandType        Name                          Version    Source
-----------        ----                          -------    ------
Alias              gsm -> Get-Something
```

The body of a function may use named blocks, such as begin, process, and end, to control how code executes.

begin, process, end, and clean

A script or function often begins with comment-based help followed by a param block. Following this, one or more named blocks may be used.

The named blocks are:

- begin
- process
- end

- dynamicparam
- clean

The dynamicparam block is explored in *Chapter 18, Parameters, Validation, and Dynamic Parameters*, as it is more complex and ties to more advanced parameter usage than covered by this chapter.

In a script or function, if none of these blocks are declared, content is in the end block.

The named blocks refer to a point in a pipeline and, therefore, make the most sense if the command is working on pipeline input.

In a filter, if none of these blocks are declared, content is in the process block. This is the only difference between a function and a filter.

This difference in a default block is shown in the following pipeline example. The function must explicitly declare a process block to use the $_ variable:

```
PS> function first { process { $_ } } # end block by default
PS> 1..2 | first                      # explicit process
1
2
```

The filter can leverage the default block:

```
PS> filter second { $_ }              # process block by default
PS> 1..2 | second                     # implicit process
1
2
```

Using named blocks is optional. If a command is not expected to work on a pipeline, the content can be left to fall into the default block.

begin

The begin block runs before pipeline processing starts. A pipeline that contains several commands will run each of the begin blocks for each command in turn before taking any further action.

The begin block will run for each command in a pipeline irrespective of piped values. That is, begin runs even when no values are passed between commands.

The following example shows a short function with a begin block:

```
function Show-Pipeline {
    begin {
        Write-Host 'Pipeline start'
    }
}
```

Pipeline input, or values from parameters accepting pipeline input, is not available within the begin block as pipeline input has not been passed into the function yet.

begin can be used to create things that are reused by the process block, setting up the initial conditions for a loop, perhaps.

process

The process block runs once for each value received from the pipeline. When there is no param block, the built-in variable $_ or $PSItem may be used to access objects in the pipeline within the process block. In the following example, the automatic variable $MyInvocation is used to show the position of the command in a pipeline:

```
function Show-Pipeline {
    begin {
        $position = $MyInvocation.PipelinePosition
        Write-Host "Pipeline position ${position}: Start"
    }

    process {
        Write-Host "Pipeline position ${position}: $_"
        $_
    }
}
```

When an object is passed to the pipeline, the start message will be shown before the numeric value:

```
PS> $result = 1..2 | Show-Pipeline
Pipeline position 1: Start
Pipeline position 1: 1
Pipeline position 1: 2
```

Adding Show-Pipeline to the end of the pipeline will show that begin executes twice before process runs:

```
PS> $result = 1..2 | Show-Pipeline | Show-Pipeline
Pipeline position 1: Start
Pipeline position 2: Start
Pipeline position 1: 1
Pipeline position 2: 1
Pipeline position 1: 2
Pipeline position 2: 2
```

The $result variable will contain the output of the last Show-Pipeline command.

end

The end block executes after the pipeline has finished. Like begin, end executes even if no values were passed in the pipeline.

In the end block, `$_` will be set to the last value received from a pipeline. Any other parameters that accept pipeline input will be filled with the last value from the process block:

```
function Show-Pipeline {
    begin {
        $position = $myinvocation.PipelinePosition
        Write-Host "Pipeline position ${position}: Start"
    }

    process {
        Write-Host "Pipeline position ${position}: $_"
        $_
    }

    end {
        Write-Host "Pipeline position ${position}: End"
    }
}
```

Running this command in a pipeline shows end executing after all items in the input pipeline have been processed:

```
PS> $result = 1..2 | Show-Pipeline
Pipeline position 1: Start
Pipeline position 1: 1
Pipeline position 1: 2
Pipeline position 1: End
```

Commands that make extensive use of the end block include Measure-Object, Sort-Object, ConvertTo-Html, and ConvertTo-Json. Such commands cannot return output until the end because the output is only valid when complete. The same is true of any other command that must gather input during a process block and output something on completion.

A simple command to count the number of elements in an input pipeline is shown here. The process block is unable to determine this; it must run again and again until the input pipeline is exhausted:

```
function Measure-Item {
    begin {
        $count = 0
    }

    process {
        $count++
    }
```

```
    end {
        $count
    }
}
```

The end block will run after all values in a pipeline have been received unless a terminating error is thrown by an earlier block.

clean

The clean block was added with PowerShell 7.3. The clean block addresses a long-standing problem when using pipelines with persistent streams or connections in PowerShell.

The following example is implemented in such a way that the Remove-Item command will occasionally fail:

```
using namespace System.IO

function Invoke-Something {
    begin {
        $fileStream = [File]::OpenWrite((
            Join-Path -Path $pwd -ChildPath NewFile.txt
        ))
        $count = 0
    }
    process {
        if ((++$count) -eq 3) {
            throw 'Unexpected error'
        }
    }
    end {
        $fileStream.Close()
    }
}

1..5 | Invoke-Something
Remove-Item NewFile.txt
```

Remove-Item fails because the $fileStream stream is not properly closed by the function unless the end block executes. The end block will not execute if a terminating error is raised inside the process block, prematurely stopping the command. .NET garbage collection must run to destroy the unreferenced file stream object before Remove-Item can act.

Restarting PowerShell will remove the open stream, allowing the file to be deleted.

The clean block addresses this problem as it will always run, even if a terminating error is raised during the normal operation of the command:

```
using namespace System.IO

function Invoke-Something {
    begin {
        $fileStream = [File]::OpenWrite((
            Join-Path -Path $pwd -ChildPath NewFile.txt
        ))
        $count = 0
    }

    process {
        if ((++$count) -eq 3) {
            throw 'Unexpected error'
        }
    }

    end {
        # Any actions end needs to perform
    }

    clean {
        $fileStream.Close()
    }
}
```

The clean block can therefore be used to properly close any open streams or connections, even if the command itself fails for some reason.

begin, process, and end can each emit values to the output pipeline. dynamicparam and clean cannot send values to an output pipeline.

The return keyword is sometimes mistaken as being capable of limiting the output of a command.

Named blocks and return

The return keyword is used to gracefully end the execution of a script block. It is often confused with return in C# (and other languages), where it explicitly returns an object from a method. In PowerShell, return has a slightly different purpose.

When a named block is executing, the return keyword may be used to end the execution of a script block immediately without stopping the rest of the pipeline.

For example, a return statement in the process block might be used to end early in certain cases. The end block will continue to execute as normal:

```
function Invoke-Return {
    process {
        if ($_ -gt 2 -and $_ -lt 9) {
            return
        }
        $_
    }

    end {
        'All done'
    }
}
```

When run, the process block will end early when the condition is met:

```
PS> 1..10 | Invoke-Return
1
2
9
10
All done
```

The return keyword may have a value to return; however, there is no effective difference between the two examples here:

```
function Test-Return { return 1 }
function Test-Return { 1; return }
```

In each case, 1 is sent to the output pipeline and then the function ends. return does not constrain or dictate the output from a function or a script.

begin, process, and end may all send output that has to be managed.

Managing output

PowerShell does not have a means of strictly enforcing the output from a script or function.

Any statement, composed of any number of commands, variables, properties, and method calls, may generate output. This output will be automatically sent to the output pipeline by PowerShell as it is generated. Unanticipated output can cause bugs in code.

The following function makes use of the StringBuilder type. Many of the methods in StringBuilder return the StringBuilder instance. This is shown here:

```
PS> using namespace System.Text
PS> $stringBuilder = [StringBuilder]::new()
PS> $stringBuilder.AppendLine('First')

Capacity    MaxCapacity    Length
--------    -----------    ------
      16     2147483647         7
```

This is useful in that it allows chaining to build up a more complex string in a single statement. The following function makes use of that chaining to build up a string:

```
using namespace System.Text

function Get-FirstService {
    $service = Get-Service | Select-Object -First 1
    $stringBuilder = [StringBuilder]::new()
    $stringBuilder.AppendFormat('Name: {0}', $service.Name).
        AppendLine().
        AppendFormat('Status: {0}', $service.Status).
        AppendLine().
        AppendLine()
    $stringBuilder.ToString()
}
```

When the function is run, both the StringBuilder object and the assembled string will be written to the output pipeline:

```
PS> Get-FirstService

Capacity    MaxCapacity    Length
--------    -----------    ------
      64     2147483647        37

Name: aciseagent
Status: Running
```

This example is contrived and writing the function slightly differently would resolve the problem of it emitting unwanted output. However, this problem is not unique to the type used here.

When writing a function or script, it is important to be aware of the output of the statements used. If a statement generates output and that output is not needed, it must be explicitly discarded. PowerShell will not automatically discard output from commands in functions and scripts.

There are several techniques available for dropping unwanted output; the following subsections show the common approaches.

The Out-Null command

The Out-Null command can be used at the end of a pipeline to discard the output from the preceding pipeline.

The Out-Null command is relatively unpopular in Windows PowerShell as it is slow. As a command in Windows PowerShell, it must still act on input passed to it (parameter binding), which has a processing cost.

In PowerShell 6 and 7, the speed issue is resolved; Out-Null is no longer quite what it seems. The Out-Null command acts as a keyword for the parser. When the parser encounters the keyword, any output piped to the command is discarded without invoking Out-Null as a command. This change in implementation makes Out-Null one of the fastest, if not *the* fastest, of the available options for discarding unwanted output.

Sticking with the StringBuilder example, the unwanted value might have dropped by appending Out-Null, as the following shows:

```
using namespace System.Text

$service = Get-Service | Select-Object -First 1

$stringBuilder = [StringBuilder]::new()
$stringBuilder.
    AppendFormat('Name: {0}', $service.Name).AppendLine().
    AppendFormat('Status: {0}', $service.Status).AppendLine().
    AppendLine() | Out-Null
$stringBuilder.ToString()
```

Piping output to Out-Null is a robust choice for discarding unwanted output. As a pipeline-style operation, values are not held in memory while the pipeline runs.

Alternatives to Out-Null include assigning output to the $null variable.

Assigning to null

Assigning a statement to the $null variable is a popular way of dropping unwanted output. It has the advantage of being obvious, in that it appears at the beginning of the statement:

```
using namespace System.Text

$service = Get-Service | Select-Object -First 1

$stringBuilder = [StringBuilder]::new()
$null = $stringBuilder.
    AppendFormat('Name: {0}', $service.Name).
    AppendLine().
```

```
    AppendFormat('Status: {0}', $service.Status).
    AppendLine().
    AppendLine()
$stringBuilder.ToString()
```

Assigning output to $null is reasonably fast in all versions of PowerShell. The downside when assigning to $null is that memory is allocated to the value on the right-hand side of the assignment; it is only released when the assignment completes.

Redirecting to null

Redirection to $null can be added at the end of a statement to discard output. An example of redirection is shown here:

```
using namespace System.Text

$service = Get-Service | Select-Object -First 1

$stringBuilder = [StringBuilder]::new()
$stringBuilder.
    AppendFormat('Name: {0}', $service.Name).AppendLine().
    AppendFormat('Status: {0}', $service.Status).AppendLine().
    AppendLine() > $null
$stringBuilder.ToString()
```

Redirection to $null is a relatively popular approach. Like assignment to $null, it will assign memory for an object before redirecting output.

Casting to void

It is possible to cast to System.Void to discard output. When using the StringBuilder example, this is a clean approach:

```
using namespace System.Text

$stringBuilder = [StringBuilder]::new()

[void]$stringBuilder.
    AppendFormat('Name: {0}', $service.Name).AppendLine().
    AppendFormat('Status: {0}', $service.Status).AppendLine().
    AppendLine()
$stringBuilder.ToString()
```

However, when used with a command, it requires the use of extra parentheses, which can make the option less appealing. This example uses Void to suppress the output from the Get-Command command:

```
[void](Get-Command Get-Command)
```

Like assignment and redirection, casting cannot take place until the command in the value being cast is completely assembled. Memory will be consumed by the statement until the cast is complete.

.NET garbage collection must also run for the consumed memory to be finally released. Although it should not be necessary, garbage collection can be run immediately using the following statement:

```
[GC]::Collect()
```

Any of the preceding methods of disposing of unwanted output used are viable, although, in PowerShell 6 and 7, Out-Null is the better approach. Personal preference often dictates which to use, especially for code intended to run in both Windows PowerShell and PowerShell 6 or 7.

Working with long lines

There are several techniques that can be used when writing scripts to avoid excessively long lines of code. The goal is to avoid needing to scroll to the right when reviewing code. A secondary goal is to avoid littering a script with the backtick (grave accent) character, ', which can be difficult to see for some.

This book continually makes use of these techniques to try and present examples without wrapping across lines. For example, one of the examples from ShouldProcess uses three arguments inside an if statement condition:

```
if ($PSCmdlet.ShouldProcess(
        'Message displayed using WhatIf',
        'Warning: Deleting SomeObject',
        'Question: Are you sure you want to do continue?')
) {
    Write-Host 'Deleting SomeObject' -ForegroundColor Cyan
}
```

This takes advantage of the ability to add a line break after (and ,. The example may be harder to read if all values are squashed onto a single line:

```
if ($PSCmdlet.ShouldProcess('Message displayed using WhatIf', 'Warning:
Deleting SomeObject', 'Question: Are you sure you want to do continue?')) {
    Write-Host 'Deleting SomeObject' -ForegroundColor Cyan
}
```

The most obvious use of line breaks is after opening bracket characters—for example, (, {, and even [. Line breaks after (and { have been used throughout this book to break code across multiple lines.

Adding extra line breaks is often a balancing act. Both too many and too few can make it harder to read a script.

Chapter 1, Introduction to PowerShell, introduced splatting as a means of dealing with commands that require more than a couple of parameters. It remains an important technique for avoiding excessively long lines.

Line break after a pipe

The most obvious technique is perhaps to add a line break after a pipe, for example:

```
Get-Process |
    Where-Object Name -match 'po?w(er)?sh(ell)?'
```

In PowerShell 7, the pipe can be placed at the start of the line, but only in scripts. Pasting the example below into the console will cause an error:

```
Get-Process
| Where-Object Name -match 'po?w(er)?sh(ell)?'
```

This is useful for long pipelines but may be considered unnecessary for short pipelines. For example, the following short pipeline ends with ForEach-Object. The statement is not necessarily long enough to need extra line breaks:

```
Get-Service | Where-Object Status -eq Running | ForEach-Object {
    # Do work on the service
}
```

A pipe is only one of many opportunities to add a line break without needing an escape character.

Line break after an operator

It is possible to add a line break after any of the operators. The most useful place for a line break is often after a logic operator is used to combine several comparisons, for example:

```
Get-Service | Where-Object {
    $_.Status -eq 'Running' -and
    $_.StartType -eq 'Manual'
}
```

One of the less obvious operators is the property dereference operator, ".". A line break may be added after calling a method of accessing a property. This is shown in the following example:

```
{ A long string in a script block }.
    ToString().
    SubString(0, 15).
    Trim().
    Length
```

It is not entirely common to find long chains of method calls within PowerShell. A more common scenario makes use of the array operator.

Using the array sub-expression operator to break up lines

The array sub-expression operator, @( ), can break up arrays that are used as arguments into operators, or values for parameters.

For example, the format operator, -f, may be used in place of sub-expressions or variable interpolation. @() may be used to define an array to hold the arguments for the operator. The following example shows two different ways of creating the same string:

```
$item = Get-Item C:\Windows\explorer.exe

# Sub-expressions and variable interpolation
"The file, $($item.Name), with path $item was last written on $($item.
LastWriteTime)"

# The format operator
'The file, {0}, with path {1} was last written on {2}' -f @(
    $item.Name
    $item
    $item.LastWriteTime
)
```

The same approach may be used for -replace operations that use particularly long regular expressions.

In *Chapter 9, Regular Expressions*, the (?x) modifier, which ignores white space and enables comments, was used to break long regular expressions across multiple lines. Another approach, which can be applied to any long string, is to make use of the array sub-expression operator and the -join operator.

The following -replace operation attempts to apply a standard format to a UK telephone number. The regular expression benefits from being on a new line:

```
$ukPhoneNumbers = '+442012345678', '0044(0)1234345678', '+44 (0) 20 81234567',
'01234 456789'
$ukPhoneNumbers -replace @(
    '^(?:(?:\+|00)\d{2})?[ -]*(?:\(?0\)?[ -]*)?([138]\d{1,3}|20)[ -]*(\d{3,4})[
-]*(\d{3,4})$'
    '+44 $1 $2 $3'
)
```

The preceding command converts each of the phone numbers into a consistent format, as shown below:

```
+44 20 1234 5678
+44 1234 345 678
+44 20 8123 4567
+44 1234 456 789
```

In the previous example, the string describing the regular expression itself is still extremely long. The approach may be extended further still to break up a complex string:

```
$ukPhoneNumbers = '+442012345678', '0044(0)1234345678', '+44 (0) 20 81234567',
'01234 456789'
$ukPhoneNumbers -replace @(
```

```
    -join @(
        '^(?:(?:\+|00)\d{2})?[ -]*'   # Country code
        '(?:\(?0\)?[ -]*)?'           # Area code prefix
        '([138]\d{1,3}|20)[ -]*'      # Area code
        '(\d{3,4})[ -]*(\d{3,4})$'    # Number
    )
    '+44 $1 $2 $3'
)
```

@() may also be used with arguments for commands, such as Select-Object:

```
Get-NetAdapter | Select-Object @(
    'Name'
    'Status'
    'MacAddress'
    'LinkSpeed'
    @{ Name = 'IPAddress'; Expression = {
        ($_ | Get-NetIPAddress).IPAddress
    }}
)
```

It is possible to add more line breaks to the Hashtable that describes the IPAddress property in the preceding example. Doing so may be beneficial if the Expression script is more complex.

Comment-based help

Comment-based help was introduced with PowerShell 2 and allows the author of a script or function to provide content for Get-Help without needing to understand and work with more complex MAML help files.

PowerShell includes help for authoring comment-based help:

```
Get-Help about_Comment_Based_Help
```

Comment-based help uses a series of keywords that match up to the different help sections. The following list shows the most common ones:

- .SYNOPSIS
- .DESCRIPTION
- .PARAMETER <Name>
- .EXAMPLE
- .INPUTS
- .OUTPUTS
- .NOTES
- .LINK

.SYNOPSIS and .DESCRIPTION are typically the minimum supplied when writing help.

.PARAMETER, followed by the name of a parameter, may be included once for each parameter.

.EXAMPLE may be used more than once, describing as many examples as desired.

The tag names are not case-sensitive; uppercase is shown here as it is one of the most widely adopted practices. Spelling mistakes in these section names may prevent help from appearing altogether; it is important to be careful when writing comment-based help.

Comment-based help may be used with scripts, functions, and filters and is often placed first before the param block in a script. The synopsis and description sections are shown in the following example:

```
<#
.SYNOPSIS
    Briefly describes the main action performed by script.ps1.

.DESCRIPTION
    A detailed description of the activities of script.ps1.
#>
```

In a function, help is often written inside the body of the function, before the param block:

```
function Get-Something {
    <#
    .SYNOPSIS
        Briefly describes the main action performed by
        Get-Something.

    .DESCRIPTION
        A detailed description of the activities of Get-Something.
    #>
}
```

Help for individual parameters can be defined in two different ways when using comment-based help.

Output help

The .OUTPUTS help entry can be set by making use of the OutputType attribute on the param block:

```
function Get-Something {
    <#
    .SYNOPSIS
        Synopsis text.
    #>
    [CmdletBinding()]
    [OutputType([string])]
```

```
    param ( )

    'string'
}
```

This value will be reflected as Get-Help -Full, as shown in the following truncated example:

```
PS> Get-Help Get-Something -Full
...
OUTPUTS
    System.String
```

The OutputType attribute is used by editors to provide tab completion for output values from the command.

The type used should be a scalar type, even if a function or script emits multiple values. For example:

```
function Get-Something {
    <#
    .SYNOPSIS
        Synopsis text.
    #>
    [CmdletBinding()]
    [OutputType([string])]
    param ( )

    [string[]]@(
        'first'
        'second'
    )
}
```

The exception to this is where a function or script expressly emits an unenumerated collection. For example:

```
function New-StringArray {
    <#
    .SYNOPSIS
        Synopsis text.
    #>
    [CmdletBinding()]
    [OutputType([string[]])]
    param ( )

    Write-Ouptut @('one', 'two') -NoEnumerate
}
```

This is added to the OUTPUTS section of help, as shown in the truncated example below:

```
PS> Get-Help New-StringArray -Full
...
OUTPUTS
    System.String[]
```

However, this is a rare and arguably advanced case.

Each parameter in a function may have help text.

Parameter help

Parameter help can be written using the .PARAMETER tag, as shown in the following example:

```
function Get-Something {
    <#
    .SYNOPSIS
        Synopsis text.

    .PARAMETER Parameter1
        Describes the purpose of Parameter1.

    .PARAMETER Parameter2
        Describes the purpose of Parameter2.
    #>
    param (
        $Parameter1,
        $Parameter2
    )
}
```

Help for a parameter may also be written as a comment above the parameter:

```
function Get-Something {
    <#
    .SYNOPSIS
        Synopsis text.
    #>
    param (
        # Describes the purpose of Parameter1.
        $Parameter1,

        # Describes the purpose of Parameter2.
        $Parameter2
```

```
    )
}
```

One possible advantage of the second approach is that it is easy to see which parameters have help and which do not.

Regardless of where help is written for a parameter, Get-Help will read the value:

```
PS> Get-Help Get-Something -Parameter Parameter1

-Parameter1 <Object>
    Describes the purpose of Parameter1.

    Required? false
    Position? 1
    Default value
    Accept pipeline input? false
    Accept wildcard characters? false
```

The help output shows several other fields that can be affected by attributes for a parameter in the param block.

Required, Position, and Accept pipeline input are all set based on the Parameter attribute, which will be explored in *Chapter 18, Parameters, Validation, and Dynamic Parameters*.

The Accept wildcard characters value is affected by including a SupportsWildcards attribute:

```
function Get-Something {
    <#
    .SYNOPSIS
        Synopsis text.
    #>
    param (
        # Describes the purpose of Parameter1.
        [SupportsWildcards()]
        $Parameter1
    )
}
```

The SupportsWildcards attribute is for documentation purposes only. It does not affect the value of the parameter.

PowerShell will attempt to read any assigned default value from an assignment. For example, if a default value is assigned to Parameter1, PowerShell will display this in the help text:

```
function Get-Something {
    <#
```

```
    .SYNOPSIS
        Synopsis text.
    #>
    param (
        # Describes the purpose of Parameter1.
        $Parameter1 = 1
    )
}
```

Running Get-Help will show the default value:

```
PS> Get-Help Get-Something -Parameter Parameter1


-Parameter1 <Object>
    Describes the purpose of Parameter1.

    Required?                    false
    Position?                    1
    Default value                1
    Accept pipeline input?       false
    Accept wildcard characters?  false
```

If the default value is too complex to be automatically discovered, for example, if the value is the result of a command:

```
$Path = (Get-Process -ID $PID).Path
```

Help will show the command itself. The PSDefaultValue attribute may be used to describe this value instead:

```
function Get-Something {
    <#
    .SYNOPSIS
        Synopsis text.
    #>
    param (
        # The path to the current PowerShell process.
        [PSDefaultValue(Help = 'pwsh.exe or powershell.exe')]
        $Path = (Get-Process -ID $PID).Path
    )
}
```

Examples of how to use a script or function are helpful, and more than one example can be added.

Examples

`Get-Help` expects examples to start with one or more lines of code followed by a description of the example, for example:

```
function Get-Something {
    <#
    .SYNOPSIS
        Synopsis text.

    .DESCRIPTION
        Description text.

    .EXAMPLE
        $something = Get-Something
        $something | Write-Host

        Gets something from somewhere and write it to the console.
    #>
    param (
        # Describes the purpose of Parameter1.
        $Parameter1,

        # Describes the purpose of Parameter2.
        $Parameter2
    )
}
```

The help parser is quite simple when it comes to comment-based help. All content above the first empty line is considered code. This can be demonstrated by exploring the object returned by `Get-Help` based on the preceding example:

```
PS> (Get-Help Get-Something -Examples).examples[0].example.code
$something = Get-Something
$something | Write-Host
```

The rest of the example is part of the remark.

Comment-based help is an important part of writing maintainable code and is simple to add to any function or script.

Summary

This chapter introduced writing scripts and functions, including brief guidance on establishing a style, followed by an exploration of the small differences between scripts, functions, and script blocks.

Parameters are used to accept user input for scripts, functions, and script blocks. The `param` block can be used to define the list of parameters.

Named blocks are used when acting on pipeline input. Each block executes at a different point in the pipeline lifecycle. The `function` and `filter` keywords use a different default named block but otherwise have identical functionality. The `begin` block in all commands in a pipeline executes before a pipeline starts, the `process` block executes once for each value passed from one function to another, and the end block executes once for each function after the last pipeline value is passed.

The `cleanup` block was very briefly introduced as an up-and-coming feature—hopefully, one that will make it into PowerShell 7 soon.

Output must be managed when writing code; it is important to appreciate that all statements that can generate output will send values to the output pipeline unless action is taken to prevent this. The `return` keyword was briefly explored as a means of ending a function or script early.

It is sometimes difficult, when writing code, to make a long statement easy to read. Several strategies for breaking up long lines of code were explored, such as using the array operator or adding a line break after an operator.

The final section covered the structure of commend-based help, including parameter help and examples. Documentation plays a vital role in writing maintainable code.

The next chapter builds on this chapter, exploring the extensive capabilities of the `param` block in much greater detail.

Learn more on Discord

Read this book alongside other users, PowerShell experts, and the author himself. Ask questions, provide solutions to other readers, chat with the author via Ask Me Anything sessions, and much more.

Scan the QR code or visit the link to join the community.

`https://packt.link/SecNet`

18

Parameters, Validation, and Dynamic Parameters

Parameters are used in PowerShell to accept arguments or user input for a command. Almost all commands accept parameters; there are only a few exceptions in the form of utility functions like those to change drive, such as the function `c:`.

PowerShell has an extensive parameter handling and validation system that can be used in scripts and functions. The system allows a developer to make parameters mandatory; to define what, if any, positional binding is allowed; to fill parameters from the pipeline; to describe different parameter sets; and to validate the values passed to a parameter. The wealth of options available makes parameter handling an incredibly involved subject.

This chapter explores the following topics:

- The `Parameter` attribute
- Validating input
- Pipeline input
- Defining parameter sets
- Argument completers
- Dynamic parameters

Parameters in PowerShell can make use of the `Parameter` attribute to define how the parameter should behave.

The Parameter attribute

The `Parameter` attribute is an optional attribute that you can use to define some of the behaviors of a parameter, such as making a parameter mandatory.

Creating an instance of the Parameter object shows the different properties that can be set:

```
PS> [Parameter]::new()

ExperimentName                      :
ExperimentAction                    : None
Position                            : -2147483648
ParameterSetName                    : __AllParameterSets
Mandatory                           : False
ValueFromPipeline                   : False
ValueFromPipelineByPropertyName     : False
ValueFromRemainingArguments         : False
HelpMessage                         :
HelpMessageBaseName                 :
HelpMessageResourceId               :
DontShow                            : False
TypeId                              : System.Management.Automation.Pa…
```

A few of these properties should be ignored as they are not intended to be set directly: HelpMessageBaseName, HelpMessageResourceId, and TypeId.

ExperimentName and ExperimentAction are for use with experimental features in PowerShell 7; the properties are not available in Windows PowerShell. These properties allow parameters to be made available on commands if a corresponding experimental feature is enabled. These properties do not appear to be in use at the time of writing.

Several other complex properties are explored later in this chapter, such as ParameterSetName, ValueFromPipeline, and ValueFromPipelineByPropertyName.

The Parameter attribute is placed before the parameter itself. The following example shows the simplest use of the Parameter attribute:

```
[CmdletBinding()]
param (
    [Parameter()]
    $Parameter
)
```

Using the Parameter attribute has the side effect of turning a basic function or script into an advanced function or script, even when the CmdletBinding attribute itself is missing. Get-Command can be used to explore whether CmdletBinding is present, for example, given the following function:

```
function Test-CmdletBinding {
    param (
        [Parameter()]
        $Parameter
```

```
    )
}
```

Get-Command can be used to get the state of CmdletBinding:

```
PS> Get-Command Test-CmdletBinding | Select-Object CmdletBinding

CmdletBinding
-------------
        True
```

This means that the common parameters, including Verbose and ErrorAction, are available to any function that uses the Parameter attribute (for any parameter).

Starting with PowerShell 3, Boolean properties, such as Mandatory and ValueFromPipeline, may be written without providing an explicit value. For example, Parameter1 is made mandatory in the following code:

```
function Test-Mandatory {
    [CmdletBinding()]
    param (
        [Parameter(Mandatory)]
        $Parameter
    )
}
```

Many scripts explicitly set Mandatory to false. However, this is unnecessary as it is the default state, and arguably can reduce readability. Someone reviewing the code might see the Mandatory property in a Parameter attribute, but could potentially miss an assignment of $false.

By default, parameters can be bound by position.

Position and positional binding

Position defaults to -2147483648, the smallest possible value for Int32 (see [Int32]::MinValue). Unless an explicit position is set, parameters may be bound in the order they are written in the parameter block. Setting the PositionalBinding property of CmdletBinding to false can disable this behavior.

Automatic positional binding is enabled by default and will be available for the function in the following example:

```
pfunction Test-Position {
    [CmdletBinding()]
    param (
        [Parameter()]
        $Parameter1,
```

```
        [Parameter()]
        $Parameter2
    )
    '{0}-{1}' -f $Parameter1, $Parameter2
}
```

When called, the command shows that `Parameter1` and `Parameter2` have been filled with the values supplied using `Position` only:

```
PS> Test-Position 1 2
1-2
```

Automatic positional binding is available by default; the `Parameter` attribute is not required. An explicit definition of position allows greater control and effectively disables automatic positional binding:

```
function Test-Position {
    param (
        [Parameter(Position = 1)]
        $Parameter1,

        $Parameter2
    )
}
```

Automatic positional binding is disabled when using parameter sets. Parameter sets are explored later in this chapter.

Exploring command metadata shows that positional binding is still enabled, but as this is an ordered operation; the default position no longer has meaning. The command metadata shows that positional binding is still enabled:

```
[System.Management.Automation.CommandMetadata](
    Get-Command Test-Position
)
```

The output from the preceding command is shown here:

```
Name                    : Test-Position
CommandType             :
DefaultParameterSetName :
SupportsShouldProcess   : False
SupportsPaging          : False
PositionalBinding       : True
SupportsTransactions    : False
HelpUri                 :
RemotingCapability      : PowerShell
```

```
ConfirmImpact              : Medium
Parameters                 : {[Parameter1, System.Management.Automation.
ParameterMetadata], [Parameter2,
System.Management.Automation.ParameterMetadata]}
```

Attempting to pass a value for Parameter2 by Position will raise an error:

```
PS> Test-Position 1 2
Test-Position: A positional parameter cannot be found that accepts argument
'2'.
```

PowerShell orders parameters based on the Position value. The value must be greater than -2147483648. It is possible, but may be confusing, to set Position to a negative value. A common practice for Position starts numbering at either 0 or 1; these starting values are simple and easily understood.

The DontShow property

The DontShow property can be used to hide a parameter from tab completion and IntelliSense. DontShow is rarely used but may occasionally be useful for recursive functions. The following function recursively calls itself, comparing MaxDepth and CurrentDepth. The CurrentDepth parameter is owned by the function and a user is never expected to supply a value:

```
function Show-Property {
    [CmdletBinding()]
    param (
        # Show the properties of the specified object.
        [Parameter(Mandatory)]
        [PSObject]
        $InputObject,

        # The maximum depth when expanding properties
        # of child objects.
        [int]
        $MaxDepth = 5,

        # Used to track the current depth during recursion.
        [Parameter(DontShow)]
        [int]
        $CurrentDepth = 0
    )

    $width = $InputObject.PSObject.Properties.Name |
        Sort-Object { $_.Length } -Descending |
        Select-Object -First 1 -ExpandProperty Length
```

```
    foreach ($property in $InputObject.PSObject.Properties) {
        '{0}{1}: {2}' -f @(
            ' ' * $CurrentDepth
            $property.Name.PadRight($width, ' ')
            $property.TypeNameOfValue
        )
        if ($CurrentDepth -lt $MaxDepth -and
            $property.Value -and
            -not $property.TypeNameOfValue.IsPrimitive) {
            $params = @{
                InputObject = $property.Value
                CurrentDepth = $CurrentDepth + 1
            }
            Show-Property @params
        }
    }
}
```

Marking a parameter as DontShow hides the parameter to a degree, but it does nothing to prevent a user from providing a value for the parameter. In this preceding case, a better approach might be to move the body of the function into a nested function. Alternatively, if the function is part of a module, the recursive code might be moved to a function that is not exported from a module and exposed by a second, tidier, function.

The ValueFromRemainingArguments property

Setting the ValueFromRemainingArguments property allows a parameter to consume any values not explicitly bound to a parameter of a command. This can be used to make an advanced function act in a similar way to a basic function.

For example, the basic function in the following example will fill the Parameter1 parameter with the first argument and ignore all others. The extra values are added to the $args automatic variable and are listed in the UnboundArguments property of the $MyInvocation automatic variable:

```
function Test-BasicBinding {
    param (
        $Parameter1
    )
    $MyInvocation.UnboundArguments
}
```

Calling the function with non-existent parameters will not raise an error. The additional values are added to the UnboundArguments array (and the $args variable):

```
PS> Test-BasicBinding -Parameter1 value1 -Parameter2 value2
-Parameter2
Value2
```

Without a declared parameter in the param block, Parameter2 is just another value; it is not parsed as the name of a parameter.

Advanced functions can accept arbitrary values in the same way if one parameter is set with the ValueFromRemainingArguments property. The following function will accept arbitrary values in the same way as the basic function in the last example:

```
function Test-AdvancedBinding {
    [CmdletBinding()]
    param (
        $Parameter1,

        [Parameter(ValueFromRemainingArguments)]
        $OtherArguments
    )
    $OtherArguments
}
```

If the $OtherArguments parameter is not for the normal use of the function, the DontShow property might be added to make it less obvious and intrusive.

The HelpMessage property

The HelpMessage property of the Parameter attribute is something of an odd feature in PowerShell.

The HelpMessage property is used to create a message that is only visible when:

1. A parameter is mandatory.
2. The user of a script or function does not provide a value for the parameter.
3. At the prompt for a mandatory value, the user enters ! ?.

This sequence is demonstrated here:

```
function Test-HelpMessage {
    param (
        [Parameter(
            Mandatory,
            HelpMessage = 'Help text for Parameter'
        )]
        $Parameter
    )
}
```

When the preceding function runs, a prompt will be raised for a missing mandatory parameter, and within that prompt, the !? sequence can be used to show the help message:

```
PS> Test-HelpMessage
cmdlet Test-HelpMessage at command pipeline position 1
Supply values for the following parameters:
(Type !? for Help.)
Parameter: !?
Help text for Parameter
Parameter1:
```

This makes it difficult to endorse HelpMessage as a useful tool. It is arguably far better to write comment-based help for a parameter than to use this. If used, it should only be used in addition to writing help content.

Comment-based help was explored in *Chapter 17, Scripts, Functions, and Script Blocks*.

Beyond making Parameter mandatory, the Parameter attribute does not control the values that can be used with a parameter. PowerShell offers attributes for validating parameter arguments.

Validating input

PowerShell provides a variety of different ways to tightly define the content for a parameter. Assigning a .NET type to a parameter is the first of these. If a parameter is set as [string], it will only ever hold a value of that type. PowerShell will attempt to coerce any values passed to the parameter into that type.

The PSTypeName attribute

The PSTypeName attribute can test the type name assigned to a custom object.

It is common in PowerShell to want to pass an object created in one command, as a PSObject (or PSCustomObject), to another.

Type names are assigned by setting (or adding) a value to the hidden PSTypeName property. There are several ways to tag PSCustomObject with a type name.

The simplest is to set a value for a PSTypeName property, shown as follows:

```
$object = [PSCustomObject]@{
    Property   = 'Value'
    PSTypeName = 'SomeTypeName'
}
```

The PSTypeName property does not exist on the resulting object, but Get-Member will now show the new type name:

```
PS> $object | Get-Member

    TypeName: SomeTypeName
```

```
Name            MemberType      Definition
----            ----------      ----------
Equals          Method          bool Equals(System.Object obj)
GetHashCode     Method          int GetHashCode()
GetType         Method          type GetType()
ToString        Method          string ToString()
Property        NoteProperty    string Property=Value
```

The type name will show at the top of the hidden PSTypeNames property:

```
PS> $object.PSTypeNames
SomeTypeName
System.Management.Automation.PSCustomObject
System.Object
```

It is also possible to add to the PSTypeNames array directly:

```
$object = [PSCustomObject]@{ Property = 'Value' }

# Add to the end of the existing List
$object.PSTypeNames.Add('SomeTypeName')

# Or add to the beginning of the List
$object.PSTypeNames.Insert(0, 'SomeTypeName')
```

Finally, Add-Member can add to the PSTypeNames array. If used, it adds the new type name at the top of the existing list:

```
$object = [PSCustomObject]@{ Property = 'Value' }
$object | Add-Member -TypeName 'SomeTypeName'
```

These tagged types may be tested using the PSTypeName attribute of a parameter, for example:

```
function Test-PSTypeName {
    [CmdletBinding()]
    param (
        [PSTypeName('SomeTypeName')]
        $InputObject
    )
}
```

This technique is used by many of the WMI-based commands implemented by Microsoft. For example, the Set-NetAdapter command uses a PSTypeName attribute for its InputObject parameter:

```
$command = Get-Command Set-NetAdapter
$command.Parameters['InputObject'].Attributes |
    Where-Object TypeId -eq ([PSTypeNameAttribute])
```

In the case of the WMI-based commands, this is used in addition to a .NET type name, an array of CimInstance. This type of parameter is like the following example:

```
function Test-PSTypeName {
    [CmdletBinding()]
    param (
        [Parameter(
            Mandatory,
            ValueFromPipeline,
            ParameterSetName = 'InputObject (cdxml)'
        )]
        [PSTypeName('Microsoft.Management.Infrastructure.CimInstance#MSFT_
NetAdapter')]
        [CimInstance[]]
        $InputObject
    )
}
```

This technique is incredibly useful when the .NET object type is not sufficiently detailed to restrict input, as is the case with the CimInstance type just used. This is true of the PSCustomObject input as much as the CimInstance array type used before.

Validation attributes

PowerShell offers several validation attributes to test the content of arguments passed to parameters. While the most common use is with variables used for parameters, validation attributes can be applied to any variable.

PowerShell includes a large range of built-in validation attributes:

- ValidateNotNull
- ValidateNotNullOrEmpty
- ValidateNotNullOrWhitespace
- ValidateCount
- ValidateLength
- ValidatePattern
- ValidateRange
- ValidateScript

- ValidateSet
- ValidateDrive
- ValidateUserDrive

It is also possible to add new validation attributes, a topic that is explored in *Chapter 19, Classes and Enumerations*.

Documentation for each of the validation attributes is available using Get-Help:

```
Get-Help about_Functions_Advanced_Parameters
```

Or, documentation is available in the PowerShell reference: https://learn.microsoft.com/powershell/module/microsoft.powershell.core/about/about_functions_advanced_parameters.

A validation attribute is placed before a variable and the type name is always followed by parentheses, indicating to PowerShell that this is an attribute. The parentheses may include any arguments the attribute requires. Discovering arguments will be explored later in this section.

ValidateNotNull is one of several attributes that does not require any arguments. This attribute is used to introduce some of the key behaviors associated with validation attributes in PowerShell.

The ValidateNotNull attribute

ValidateNotNull validates that a value, or an element in an array of values, is not null.

Note that ValidateNotNull and ValidateNotNullOrEmpty are not required for mandatory parameters.

In the following example, ValidateNotNull is used to test the state of a parameter argument:

```
function Test-ValidateNotNull {
    param (
        [ValidateNotNull()]
        $Parameter
    )
}
```

An attempt to pass an empty array or explicit null value when calling this function will cause an error to be raised.

```
PS> Test-ValidateNotNullOrEmpty -Parameter $null
Test-ValidateNotNullOrEmpty: Cannot validate argument on parameter 'Parameter'.
The argument is null or empty. Provide an argument that is not null or empty,
and then try the command again.
```

A similar message will be shown if a null value is included in an array:

```
PS> Test-ValidateNotNullOrEmpty -Parameter @(1, $null, 2)
Test-ValidateNotNullOrEmpty: Cannot validate argument on parameter 'Parameter'.
The argument is null, empty, or an element of the argument collection contains
a null value.
```

This shows that the validator is not just concerned about the argument only, that an array that is not empty was supplied, but that individual values within the array are tested.

Testing the content of collections is a common feature of validation attributes.

If the value is an empty array, a slightly different error will be shown:

```
PS> Test-ValidateNotNullOrEmpty -Parameter @()
Test-ValidateNotNullOrEmpty: Cannot validate argument on parameter 'Parameter'.
The argument is null, empty, or an element of the argument collection contains
a null value. Supply a collection that does not contain any null values and
then try the command again.
```

Validation attributes used with a variable apply for the lifetime of that variable. The validators assigned to the variable apply to any subsequent assignments.

```
PS> [ValidateNotNull()]$variable = 1
PS> $variable = $null
MetadataError: The variable cannot be validated because the value $null is not
a valid value for the variable variable.
```

Get-Variable can be used to show the presence of this validator on the variable:

```
PS> Get-Variable variable | ForEach-Object Attributes

TypeId
------
System.Management.Automation.ValidateNotNullAttribute
```

ValidateNotNull is one of several validators that do not require arguments. In the console, the need for arguments can be tested by looking at the constructors for the type.

```
PS> [ValidateNotNull]::new

OverloadDefinitions
-------------------
ValidateNotNull new()
```

Extra parentheses after the type name are not needed when getting the constructor.

ValidateNotNull does not apply to types that cannot be null, including string, bool, and numeric types. For example, it will not correctly validate the following case:

```
function Test-ValidateNotNull {
    [CmdletBinding()]
    param (
        [ValidateNotNull()]
        [string]
        $Parameter
```

```
    )
    Write-Host 'Parameter binding was successful'
}
```

Running the function with a null value for the parameter will not trigger the validator because the parameter type is a string, and type conversion runs before validation.

```
PS> Test-ValidateNotNull -Parameter $null
Parameter binding was successful
```

PowerShell immediately coerces the null value to a string, which will result in an empty string. This is a good case for the use of ValidateNotNullOrEmpty.

The ValidateNotNullOrEmpty attribute

ValidateNotNullOrEmpty extends ValidateNotNull to disallow null values, empty arrays, arrays containing empty values, empty strings, and arrays containing empty strings:

```
function Test-ValidateNotNullOrEmpty {
    [CmdletBinding()]
    param (
        [ValidateNotNullOrEmpty()]
        [string[]]
        $Parameter
    )
}
```

Like ValidateNotNull, errors will be raised if null values are passed. In addition, an explicit empty string or an array containing an empty string will also cause an error to be raised.

ValidateNotNullOrEmpty will permit a string consisting of white space (spaces, tabs, and line break characters) only.

The ValidateNotNullOrWhitespace attribute

ValidateNotNullOrWhitespace extends on ValidateNotNullOrEmpty to also disallow strings that consist of white space only.

The ValidateNotNullOrWhitespace attribute was added with PowerShell 7.4.

```
function Test-ValidateNotNullOrWhitespace {
    [CmdletBinding()]
    param (
        [ValidateNotNullOrWhitespace()]
        [string]
        $Parameter1
    )
}
```

ValidateCount is the first of the validation attributes to explore that requires arguments.

The ValidateCount attribute

ValidateCount can be used to test the size of an array supplied to a parameter. The attribute expects a minimum and maximum length for the array.

The need for arguments for this attribute can be shown by looking at the constructor:

```
PS> [ValidateCount]::new

OverloadDefinitions
-------------------
ValidateCount new(int minLength, int maxLength)
```

ValidateCount only has meaning when applied to an array-type parameter, for example:

```
function Test-ValidateCount {
    [CmdletBinding()]
    param (
        [ValidateCount(1, 1)]
        [string[]]
        $Parameter
    )
}
```

Variables cannot be used as the arguments for the ValidateCount attribute. Only numeric values and constants exposed as static properties are permitted. For example, the following statement permits any value between 10 and the maximum size of a byte.

```
function Test-ValidateCount {
    [CmdletBinding()]
    param (
        [ValidateCount(10, [byte]::MaxValue)]
        [string[]]
        $Parameter
    )
}
```

ValidateCount can be applied to any parameter that accepts a collection type, such as System.Collections.ArrayList or System.Collections.Generic.List.

The ValidateLength attribute

ValidateLength can be applied to a string parameter or a parameter that contains an array of strings. Each string will be tested against the minimum and maximum length:

```
function Test-ValidateLength {
    [CmdletBinding()]
    param (
        [ValidateLength(2, 6)]
        [string[]]
        $Parameter
    )
}
```

Any string with a length below the minimum or above the maximum will trigger an error; for example, using the preceding function with the value PowerShell:

```
PS> Test-ValidateLength -Parameter PowerShell
Test-ValidateLength: Cannot validate argument on parameter 'Parameter'. The
character length of the 10 argument is too long. Shorten the character length
of the argument so it is fewer than or equal to "6" characters, and then try
the command again.
```

Validating on length only is not common; it is frequently necessary to test the composition of a string as well.

The ValidatePattern attribute

ValidatePattern tests a value, or each of an array of values, against a regular expression.

The following example uses a simple regular expression:

```
function Test-ValidatePattern {
    [CmdletBinding()]
    param (
        [ValidatePattern('^Hello')]
        [string]
        $Parameter
    )
}
```

ValidatePattern requires a single argument, but can also accept the optional Options and, in Power-Shell 6 or higher, ErrorMessage parameters. It is possible to discover the presence of these additional parameters by looking at an instance of the validator:

```
PS> [ValidatePattern]::new('a')

RegexPattern    Options ErrorMessage TypeId
------------    ------- ------------ ------
a               IgnoreCase           System.Management.Automa...
```

The RegexPattern property is filled from the constructor. TypeId is present on all validators and cannot be changed, but Options and ErrorMessage can be.

The ability to set these values can be further demonstrated by looking at the output from Get-Member:

```
PS> [ValidatePattern]::new('a') | Get-Member -MemberType Property


    TypeName: System.Management.Automation.ValidatePatternAttribute


Name          MemberType Definition
----          ---------- ----------
ErrorMessage  Property   string ErrorMessage {get;set;}
Options       Property   System.Text.RegularExpressions.RegexOptions Options
{get;set;}
RegexPattern  Property   string RegexPattern {get;}
TypeId        Property   System.Object TypeId {get;}
```

The preceding output shows that both Options and ErrorMessage have set accessors, showing that the values may be changed.

For example, the Options parameter is used here:

```
function Test-ValidatePattern {
    [CmdletBinding()]
    param (
        [ValidatePattern('^Hello', Options = 'Multiline')]
        [string]
        $Parameter
    )
}
```

The possible values for Options are described by the System.Text.RegularExpressions.RegexOptions enumeration, which is documented in the .NET reference: https://learn.microsoft.com/dotnet/api/system.text.regularexpressions.regexoptions.

Further information on each option is available in the "Regular expression options" documentation: https://learn.microsoft.com/dotnet/standard/base-types/regular-expression-options.

More than one option can be set by using a comma-separated list. For example:

```
[ValidatePattern('^Hello', Options = 'IgnoreCase, Multiline')]
```

By default, the IgnoreCase option is set. If a pattern should be case sensitive, Options can be set to None:

```
[ValidatePattern('^Hello', Options = 'None')]
```

A criticism that was leveled against ValidatePattern is that there was no way to customize or define the error message in Windows PowerShell.

PowerShell 6 and above adds an optional `ErrorMessage` parameter to tackle this problem. The default error message written by `ValidatePattern` is shown as follows:

```
function Test-ValidatePattern {
    [CmdletBinding()]
    param (
        [ValidatePattern(
            '^[A-Z]',
            Options = 'None'
        )]
        [string]
        $Parameter
    )
}
```

The error message generated by the attribute is shown here:

```
PS> Test-ValidatePattern -Parameter 'hello Jim.'
Test-ValidatePattern: Cannot validate argument on parameter 'Parameter'. The
argument "hello Jim." does not match the "^[A-Z]" pattern. Supply an argument
that matches "^[A-Z]" and try the command again.
```

An alternative message may be set in PowerShell 6 and above:

```
function Test-ValidatePattern {
    [CmdletBinding()]
    param (
        [ValidatePattern(
            '^[A-Z]',
            Options      = 'None',
            ErrorMessage = 'Must start with a capital letter.'
        )]
        [string]
        $Parameter
    )
}
```

Running the new command with an invalid string shows the new error message:

```
PS> Test-ValidatePattern -Parameter 'hello Jim.'
Test-ValidatePattern: Cannot validate argument on parameter 'Greeting'. Must
start with a capital letter.
```

The new error message is far more user-friendly than showing a regular expression, even a relatively simple regular expression.

The ValidateRange attribute

ValidateRange tests whether a value, or an array of values, falls within a specified range. ValidateRange is most used to test numeric ranges. However, it is also able to test strings. For example, the z string can be said to be within the A to Z range. This approach is slightly harder to apply when testing strings as the Zz string is greater than Z.

The following example uses ValidateRange to test an integer value:

```
function Test-ValidateRange {
    [CmdletBinding()]
    param (
        [ValidateRange(1, 20)]
        [int]
        $Parameter
    )
}
```

If validation cannot be described by one of the more tightly defined validators, ValidateScript can be used to write an expression.

The ValidateScript attribute

ValidateScript allows the use of a ScriptBlock to validate an argument. If the argument is an array, each individual element is tested. The $_ or $PSItem variable is used to refer to the value being tested within the ScriptBlock.

One common use for ValidateScript is to test whether a path exists, for example:

```
function Test-ValidateScript {
    [CmdletBinding()]
    param (
        [ValidateScript( { Test-Path $_ -PathType Leaf } )]
        [string]
        $Parameter
    )
}
```

ValidateScript can contain a script of any length, although it might be wise to use call functions if the logic becomes overly complex.

In PowerShell 6 and above, ValidateScript gains an optional ErrorMessage parameter that replaces the default message, which repeats the failed script to the end user:

```
function Test-ValidateScript {
    [CmdletBinding()]
    param (
```

```
        [ValidateScript(
            { Test-Path $_ -PathType Leaf },
            ErrorMessage = 'Value must be an existing file'
        )]
        [string]
        $Parameter
    )
}
```

In Windows PowerShell, using throw within the script provides something of an equivalent to ErrorMessage:

```
function Test-ValidateScript {
    [CmdletBinding()]
    param (
        [ValidateScript({
            if (Test-Path $_ -PathType Leaf) {
                $true
            } else {
                throw 'Value must be an existing file'
            }
        })]
        [string]
        $Parameter
    )
}
```

If the preceding function is used with a path that does not exist or is not a file (leaf), the error will be displayed.

```
PS> Test-ValidateScript -Parameter c:\doesnotexist
Test-ValidateScript: Cannot validate argument on parameter 'Parameter'. Value
must be an existing file
```

If a value is one of a pre-defined set of values, the ValidateSet attribute can be used.

The ValidateSet attribute

ValidateSet tests whether the specified argument, or each element of an array of arguments, exists in a set of possible values. For example:

```
function Test-ValidateSet {
    [CmdletBinding()]
    param (
        [ValidateSet('One', 'Two', 'Three')]
        [string]
```

```
            $Paramter
    )
}
```

The set of values must be hardcoded in the attribute and cannot be derived from a variable or another command. This is so because ValidateSet is special; unlike the other validation attributes, ValidateSet also provides tab completion based on the set of values.

By default, the set is not case-sensitive. If desirable, the set can be case-sensitive by using the IgnoreCase parameter:

```
function Test-ValidateSet {
    [CmdletBinding()]
    param (
        [ValidateSet('One', 'Two', 'Three', IgnoreCase = $false)]
        [string]
        $Parameter
    )
}
```

Like ValidatePattern and ValidateSet, ValidateSet gains an optional ErrorMessage parameter in PowerShell 6 and above.

PowerShell 6 also added the ability to dynamically define the values that ValidateSet can use. The values are defined in a class that implements a GetValidValues method. An example of this class is available in the next chapter, *Chapter 19, Classes and Enumerations*.

The ValidateDrive attribute

ValidateDrive may be used to test the drive letter provided for a parameter that accepts a path. ValidateDrive handles both relative and absolute paths. A relative path is resolved to a full path before it is tested against the supplied drive letters. When using the ValidateDrive attribute, the parameter type must be string. The parameter cannot be omitted:

```
function Test-ValidateDrive {
    [CmdletBinding()]
    param (
        [ValidateDrive('C')]
        [string]
        $Parameter
    )
}
```

ValidateDrive cannot act on an array of paths; if the parameter type is an array, an error will be thrown stating that the path argument is invalid.

The ValidateUserDrive attribute

The ValidateUserDrive attribute is written for use within **Just Enough Administration (JEA)** configurations. The attribute validates that the specified drive is the User drive, as specified in a session configuration.

JEA was briefly explored in *Chapter 14, Remoting and Remote Management*. The User drive configuration is described in the PowerShell scripting reference: https://learn.microsoft.com/powershell/scripting/learn/remoting/jea/session-configurations.

ValidateUserDrive is used to validate that the root drive for a path is the JEA User drive:

```
function Test-ValidateDrive {
    [CmdletBinding()]
    param (
        [ValidateUserDrive()]
        [string]
        $Parameter1
    )
}
```

The ValidateUserDrive attribute is equivalent to using ValidateDrive with User as an argument:

```
[ValidateDrive('User')]
[string]
$Parameter
```

As noted previously, the definition of a User drive is part of the JEA session configuration.

The Allow attributes

The Allow attributes are most frequently used when a parameter is mandatory. If a parameter is mandatory, PowerShell will automatically disallow the assignment of empty values, that is, empty strings and empty arrays. The Allow attributes can be used to modify that behavior.

The following Allow attributes are available:

- AllowNull
- AllowEmptyString
- AllowEmptyCollection

The attributes make it possible to require a parameter but still allow empty values.

The AllowNull attribute

AllowNull is used to permit the explicit use of $null as a value for a Mandatory parameter:

```
function Test-AllowNull {
    [CmdletBinding()]
```

```
    param (
        [Parameter(Mandatory)]
        [AllowNull()]
        [object]
        $Parameter
    )
}
```

AllowNull is effective for array parameters and for parameters that use Object as a type. AllowNull is not effective for string parameters as the null value is cast to an empty string, and an empty string is still not permitted.

The AllowEmptyString attribute

AllowEmptyString fills the gap, allowing both null and empty values to be supplied for a mandatory string parameter. In both cases, the resulting assignment will be an empty string. It is not possible to distinguish between a value passed as null and a value passed as an empty string:

```
function Test-AllowEmptyString {
    [CmdletBinding()]
    param (
        [Parameter(Mandatory)]
        [AllowEmptyString()]
        [string]
        $Parameter
    )
}
```

Empty array arguments for parameters must use a different attribute.

The AllowEmptyCollection attribute

AllowEmptyCollection, as the name suggests, allows an empty array to be assigned to a mandatory parameter:

```
function Test-AllowEmptyCollection {
    [CmdletBinding()]
    param (
        [Parameter(Mandatory)]
        [AllowEmptyCollection()]
        [object[]]
        $Parameter
    )
}
```

This will allow the command to be called with an explicitly empty array:

```
Test-AllowEmptyCollection -Parameter @()
```

Validation in the param block is a valuable feature of PowerShell that greatly simplifies and standardizes handling input for functions and scripts.

PSReference parameters

Many of the object types used in PowerShell are reference types. When an object is passed to a function, any changes made to that object will be visible outside the function, irrespective of the output generated by the command. For example, the following function accepts an object as input and then changes the value of a property on that object:

```
function Set-Value {
    [CmdletBinding()]
    param (
        [PSObject]
        $Object
    )
    $Object.Value = 2
}
```

When the function is passed an object, the change can be seen on any other variables that reference that object:

```
PS> $myObject = [PSCustomObject]@{ Value = 1 }
PS> Set-Value $myObject
PS> $myObject.Value
2
```

Strings, numeric values, and dates, on the other hand, are all examples of value types. Changes made to a value type inside a function will not be reflected in variables that reference that value elsewhere; a new value is created.

Occasionally, it is desirable to make a function affect the content of a value type without either returning the value as output or changing the value of a property of an object. The PSReference type, [Ref], can be used to achieve this. The following function normally returns True or False depending on whether Get-Date successfully parsed the date string into a DateTime object:

```
function Test-Date {
    [CmdletBinding()]
    param (
        [string]
        $Date,

        [ref]
```

```
            $DateTime
    )
    if ($value = Get-Date $Date -ErrorAction SilentlyContinue) {
        if ($DateTime) {
            $DateTime.Value = $value
        }
        $true
    } else {
        $false
    }
}
```

When the function is run, a variable that holds an existing DateTime object might be passed as an optional reference. PowerShell can update the date via the reference, changing the value outside of the function:

```
PS> $dateTime = Get-Date
PS> Test-Date 01/01/2024 -DateTime ([Ref]$dateTime)
True
PS> $dateTime
01 January 2024 00:00:00
```

The same behavior can be seen with Boolean, string, and numeric types.

PowerShell offers a wide variety of attributes that help to validate user input without writing bespoke checks in the body of a function.

Moving back to the Parameter attribute again, the Parameter attribute can be used to define how a parameter behaves in a pipeline.

Pipeline input

Using the Parameter attribute to set either ValueFromPipeline or ValueFromPipelineByPropertyName sets a parameter up to fill from the input pipeline.

The pipeline is a complex topic and requires a background in the use of named blocks. Named blocks, along with a broader set of examples for pipeline usage, were discussed in *Chapter 17, Scripts, Functions, and Script Blocks*.

About ValueFromPipeline

ValueFromPipeline allows the entire object to be passed into a parameter from an input pipeline. The following function implements an InputObject parameter, which accepts a pipeline input by using the ValueFromPipeline property of the Parameter attribute:

```
function Get-InputObject {
    [CmdletBinding()]
```

```
    param (
        [Parameter(Mandatory, ValueFromPipeline)]
        $InputObject
    )
    process {
        'Input object was of type {0}' -f @(
            $InputObject.GetType().FullName
        )
    }
}
```

Remember that values read from an input pipeline are only available in the process block of a script or function. As the default type assigned to a parameter is Object, this will accept any kind of input that might be passed. This behaves in a similar manner to the InputObject parameter for Get-Member or Select-Object, for example.

Accepting null input

Commands such as Where-Object allow an explicit null value in the input pipeline. To allow null in an input pipeline, the [AllowNull()] attribute would be added to the InputObject parameter. There is a difference between supporting $null | Get-InputObject and implementing pipeline support originating from a command that returns nothing: AllowNull is only needed when an explicit null is in the input pipeline.

In the following example, the Get-EmptyOutput function has no body and will not return anything. This simulates a command that returns nothing because all the output is filtered out. The Get-InputObject function can take part in a pipeline with Get-EmptyOutput without using AllowNull:

```
function Get-EmptyOutput { }
function Get-InputObject {
    [CmdletBinding()]
    param (
        [Parameter(Mandatory, ValueFromPipeline)]
        $InputObject
    )
}
# No output, no error
Get-EmptyOutput | Get-InputObject
```

If Get-EmptyOutput were to explicitly return null, which is not a good practice, Get-InputObject would raise a parameter binding error:

```
PS> function Get-EmptyOutput { return $null }
PS> Get-EmptyOutput | Get-InputObject
Get-InputObject: Cannot bind argument to parameter 'InputObject' because it is
null.
```

Adding AllowNull would sidestep this error, but Get-InputObject would have to handle a null value internally:

```
function Get-EmptyOutput { return $null }
function Get-InputObject {
    [CmdletBinding()]
    param (
        [Parameter(Mandatory, ValueFromPipeline)]
        [AllowNull()]
        $InputObject
    )
    if ($InputObject) {
        # Do work
    }
}
# No output, no error
Get-EmptyOutput | Get-InputObject
```

If this were real output from a function, it may be better to consider the output from Get-EmptyOutput to be a bug and pass it through Where-Object to sanitize the input, which avoids the need to add AllowNull, for example:

```
Get-EmptyOutput | Where-Object { $_ } | Get-InputObject
```

Commands should not generally have to expect to deal with null input values so use of the AllowNull attribute is somewhat rare.

Input object types

If a type is defined for the InputObject variable, the command will only work if the input pipeline contains that object type. An error will be thrown when a different object type is passed. The following example modifies the command to accept pipeline input from Get-Process; it expects objects of the System.Diagnostics.Process type only:

```
function Get-InputObject {
    [CmdletBinding()]
    param (
        [Parameter(Mandatory, ValueFromPipeline)]
        [System.Diagnostics.Process]
        $InputObject
    )
    process {
        'Process name {0}' -f $InputObject.Name
    }
}
```

Attempting to pipe a value that is something other than a System.Diagnostics.Process value will result in an error:

```
PS> 1 | Get-InputObject
Get-InputObject: The input object cannot be bound to any parameters for the
command either because the command does not take pipeline input or the input
and its properties do not match any of the parameters that take pipeline input.
```

PowerShell attempts to bind as many values as possible to parameters that accept pipeline input.

Using ValueFromPipeline for multiple parameters

If more than one parameter uses ValueFromPipeline, PowerShell will attempt to provide values to each. The parameter binder can be said to be greedy in this respect. The following function can be used to show that both parameters are filled with the same value if the parameters accept the same type, or if the value can be coerced into that type:

```
function Test-ValueFromPipeline {
    [CmdletBinding()]
    param (
        [Parameter(ValueFromPipeline)]
        [int]
        $Parameter1,

        [Parameter(ValueFromPipeline)]
        [int]
        $Parameter2
    )
    process {
        'Parameter1: {0}:: Parameter2: {1}' -f @(
            $Parameter1
            $Parameter2
        )
    }
}
```

Providing an input pipeline for the command shows the values assigned to each parameter:

```
PS> 1..2 | Test-ValueFromPipeline
Parameter1: 1 :: Parameter2: 1
Parameter1: 2 :: Parameter2: 2
```

Filling variables is the job of the parameter binder in PowerShell. Using `Trace-Command` will show the parameter binder in action:

```
Trace-Command -PSHost -Name ParameterBinding -Expression {
    1 | Test-ValueFromPipeline
}
```

The `bind-pipeline` section will display messages that show that the value was successfully bound to each parameter. If the two parameters expect different types, the parameter binding will attempt to coerce the value into the requested type. If that is not possible, it will give up on the attempt to fill the parameter. The next example declares two different parameters; both accept values from the pipeline and neither is mandatory:

```
function Get-InputObject {
    [CmdletBinding()]
    param (
        [Parameter(ValueFromPipeline)]
        [System.Diagnostics.Process]
        $ProcessObject,

        [Parameter(ValueFromPipeline)]
        [System.ServiceProcess.ServiceController]
        $ServiceObject
    )
    process {
        if ($ProcessObject) {
            'Process: {0}' -f $ProcessObject.Name
        }
        if ($ServiceObject) {
            'Service: {0}' -f $ServiceObject.Name
        }
    }
}
```

The command will, at this point, accept pipeline input from both `Get-Process` and `Get-Service`. Each command will fill the matching parameter, `Get-Process` fills `ProcessObject`, and `Get-Service` fills `ServiceObject`.

This design is unusual and perhaps confusing; it is only demonstrated here because it is possible. A parameter set can be used to make sense of the pattern, which is explored in the *Defining parameter sets* section of this chapter.

About ValueFromPipelineByPropertyName

ValueFromPipelineByPropertyName attempts to fill a parameter from the property of an object in the input pipeline. When filling a value by property name, the name and type of the property is important, but not the object that implements the property.

For example, a function that accepts a string value from a Name property can be created:

```
function Get-Name {
    [CmdletBinding()]
    param (
        [Parameter(Mandatory, ValueFromPipelineByPropertyName)]
        [string]
        $Name
    )

    process {
        $Name
    }
}
```

Any command that returns an object that contains a Name property in a string is acceptable input for this function. Additional parameters might be defined, which would further restrict the input object type, assuming the new properties are mandatory:

```
function Get-Status {
    [CmdletBinding()]
    param (
        [Parameter(Mandatory, ValueFromPipelineByPropertyName)]
        [string]
        $Name,

        [Parameter(Mandatory, ValueFromPipelineByPropertyName)]
        [string]
        $Status
    )
    process {
        '{0}: {1}' -f $Name, $Status
    }
}
```

This new function would accept pipeline input from Get-Service, as the output from Get-Service has both Name and Status properties. Using Get-Member against Get-Service would show that the Status property is an enumeration value described by System.ServiceProcess.ServiceControllerStatus.

This value is acceptable to the Get-Status function as it can be coerced into a string, which satisfies the Status parameter.

The previous function is not limited to a specific input object type. A PSCustomObject can be created with properties to satisfy the parameters for the Get-Status function:

```
[PSCustomObject]@{ Name = 'Name'; Status = 'Running' } |
    Get-Status
```

As with the ValueFromPipeline input, the parameter binder will attempt to fill as many of the parameters as possible from the input pipeline. Trace-Command, as used when exploring ValueFromPipeline, shows the behavior of the parameter binder.

ValueFromPipelineByPropertyName and parameter aliases

Any parameter may be given one or more aliases using the Alias attribute, as shown in the following example:

```
function Get-InputObject {
    [CmdletBinding()]
    param (
        [Parameter(ValueFromPipelineByPropertyName)]
        [Alias('First', 'Second', 'Third')]
        $InputObject
    )
}
```

The alias name is considered when determining whether a property on an input object is suitable to fill a parameter when filling a parameter by property name.

One of the more common uses of this is to provide support for a Path parameter via a pipeline from Get-Item or Get-ChildItem. For example, the following pattern might be used to expose a Path parameter. This is used in the short helper function that imports JSON content from a file:

```
function Import-Json {
    [CmdletBinding()]
    param (
        [Parameter(Mandatory, ValueFromPipelineByPropertyName)]
        [Alias('PSPath')]
        [string]
        $Path
    )
    process {
        Get-Content $Path | ConvertFrom-Json
    }
}
```

The PSPath property of the object returned by Get-Item or Get-ChildItem is used to fill the Path parameter from a pipeline. FullName is a possible alternative to PSPath, depending on how the path is to be used.

> **Converting relative paths to full paths**
>
> When using a Path parameter, such as the one in the previous example, the following method can be used on the PSCmdlet object to ensure that a path is fully qualified, whether it exists or not:
>
> $Path = $PSCmdlet.GetUnresolvedProviderPathFromPSPath($Path)
>
> This technique is useful if working with .NET types, which require a path as these are not able to resolve PowerShell paths (either relative or via a PS drive).

The New-TimeSpan command is an example of an existing command that uses an alias to fill a parameter from the pipeline. The Start parameter has an alias of LastWriteTime. When Get-Item is piped into New-TimeSpan, the time since the file or directory was last written will be returned as a TimeSpan via the aliased parameter.

Defining parameter sets

A parameter set in PowerShell groups different parameters together. In some cases, this is used to change the output of a command; in others, it provides a different way of supplying a piece of information.

For example, the output from the Get-Process command changes if the Module parameter or, to a lesser extent, the IncludeUserName parameter is supplied.

The Get-ChildItem command also has two parameter sets: one that accepts a Path with wildcard support and another that accepts a LiteralPath that does not support wildcards.

Parameter sets are declared using the ParameterSetName property of the Parameter attribute.

The following example has two parameter sets; each parameter set contains a single parameter:

```
function Get-InputObject {
    [CmdletBinding()]
    param (
        [Parameter(ParameterSetName = 'FirstSetName')]
        $Parameter1,

        [Parameter(ParameterSetName = 'SecondSetName')]
        $Parameter2
    )
}
```

As neither parameter set is the default, attempting to run the command using a positional parameter only will result in an error:

```
PS> Get-InputObject value
Get-InputObject: Parameter set cannot be resolved using the specified named
parameters. One or more parameters issued cannot be used together or an
insufficient number of parameters were provided.
```

This can be resolved by setting a value for the DefaultParameterSetName property in the CmdletBinding attribute:

```
[CmdletBinding(DefaultParameterSetName = 'FirstSetName')]
```

Alternatively, an explicit position might be defined for one of the parameters; the set will be selected based on the explicit position:

```
[Parameter(Position = 1, ParameterSetName = 'FirstSetName')]
$Parameter1
```

The name of the parameter set within a function is visible using the ParameterSetName property of the PSCmdlet automatic variable, which is $PSCmdlet.ParameterSetName. The value of this property can be used to choose actions within the body of a function.

The following example shows a possible implementation that tests the value of ParameterSetName. The function accepts the name of a service as a string, a service object from Get-Service, or a service returned from the Win32_Service class. The function finds the process associated with that service or fails if the service is not running:

```
function Get-ServiceProcess {
    [CmdletBinding(DefaultParameterSetName = 'ByName')]
    param (
        [Parameter(
            Mandatory,
            Position = 1,
            ParameterSetName = 'ByName'
        )]
        [string]$Name,

        [Parameter(
            Mandatory,
            ValueFromPipeline,
            ParameterSetName = 'FromService'
        )]
        [System.ServiceProcess.ServiceController]$Service,

        [Parameter(
```

```
                Mandatory,
                ValueFromPipeline,
                ParameterSetName = 'FromCimService'
            )]
            [PSTypeName('Microsoft.Management.Infrastructure.CimInstance#root/cimv2/
Win32_Service')]
            [CimInstance]$CimService
        )
        process {
            if ($pscmdlet.ParameterSetName -eq 'FromService') {
                $Name = $Service.Name
            }
            if ($Name) {
                $params = @{
                    ClassName = 'Win32_Service'
                    Filter    = 'Name="{0}"' -f $Name
                    Property  = 'Name', 'ProcessId', 'State'
                }
                $CimService = Get-CimInstance @params
            }
            if ($CimService.State -eq 'Running') {
                Get-Process -Id $CimService.ProcessId
            } else {
                Write-Error ('The service {0} is not running' -f @(
                    $CimService.Name
                ))
            }
        }
    }
}
```

The previous function accepts several different parameters. Each parameter is ultimately used to get to a value for the $CimService variable (or parameter), which has a ProcessID property associated with the service.

Each of the examples so far has shown a parameter that is a member of a single explicitly declared set.

A parameter that does not describe a ParameterSetName is automatically part of every set.

In the following example, Parameter1 is part of every parameter set, while Parameter2 is in a named set only:

```
function Test-ParameterSet {
    [CmdletBinding(DefaultParameterSetName = 'Default')]
    param (
```

```
        [Parameter(Mandatory, Position = 1)]
        $Parameter1,

        [Parameter(ParameterSetName = 'NamedSet')]
        $Parameter2
    )
}
```

Get-Command may be used to show the syntax for the command; this shows that there are two different parameter sets, both of which require Parameter1:

```
PS> Get-Command Test-ParameterSet -Syntax

Test-ParameterSet [-Parameter1] <Object> [<CommonParameters>]
Test-ParameterSet [-Parameter1] <Object> [-Parameter2 <Object>]
[<CommonParameters>]
```

Parameters that do not use the Parameter attribute are also automatically part of all parameter sets.

A parameter may also be added to more than one parameter set. This is achieved by using more than one Parameter attribute:

```
function Test-ParameterSet {
    [CmdletBinding(DefaultParameterSetName = 'NamedSet1')]
    param (
        [Parameter(Mandatory)]
        $Parameter1,

        [Parameter(Mandatory, ParameterSetName = 'NamedSet2')]
        $Parameter2,

        [Parameter(Mandatory, ParameterSetName = 'NamedSet3')]
        $Parameter3,

        [Parameter(Mandatory, ParameterSetName = 'NamedSet2')]
        [Parameter(ParameterSetName = 'NamedSet3')]
        $Parameter4
    )
}
```

In the preceding example:

- Parameter1 is in all parameter sets.
- Parameter2 is in NamedSet2 only.
- Parameter3 is in NamedSet3 only.

- Parameter4 is mandatory in NamedSet2, and optional in NamedSet3.

This interplay of parameter sets is complex and difficult to describe without a complex command to use the parameters.

Many existing commands use complex parameter sets and their parameter sets may be explored. For example, the parameter block for the Get-Process command may be shown by running the following command:

```
[System.Management.Automation.ProxyCommand]::GetParamBlock((
    Get-Command Get-Process
))
```

Parameter sets are a powerful feature, allowing a command to handle different combinations of input values without resorting to complex logic in the body of a script or function.

Argument completers

The tab completion system uses argument completers to provide an argument for a parameter when Tab is pressed. For example, the Get-Module command cycles through module names when Tab is pressed after the command name.

Argument completers have been around in several different forms since PowerShell 2. This section focuses on the implementation of argument completers available in Windows PowerShell 5 and above.

An argument completer does not restrict the values that may be supplied for a parameter. It is used to offer values, to make it easier for an end user to figure out what to enter.

An argument completer is a script block; the script block can expect the following parameters (by position, in the order listed as follows):

- commandName
- parameterName
- wordToComplete
- commandAst
- fakeBoundParameter

Any of these parameters can be used in a completer, but the most frequently used is wordToComplete.

The following example suggests words from a fixed list:

```
{
    param (
        $commandName,
        $parameterName,
        $wordToComplete,
        $commandAst,
        $fakeBoundParameter
```

```
        )
        $possibleValues = 'Start', 'Stop', 'Create', 'Delete'
        $possibleValues -like "$wordToComplete*"
}
```

Notice that a wildcard, *, has been added to the end of wordToComplete. Tab completion expects the user to have typed part of a word, but a user would not normally include a wildcard character for matching against possible values.

Arguably, ValidateSet might be a better option in this case as it also implicitly provides tab completion. However, where ValidateSet enforces, ArgumentCompleter suggests.

The list of possible values used in an argument completer can be dynamic. That is, the list of possible values can be the result of running another command.

PowerShell provides different ways to assign an argument completer: the ArgumentCompleter attribute, the Register-ArgumentCompleter command, or by creating a class to describe a custom argument completer. Argument completer classes are demonstrated in *Chapter 19, Classes and Enumerations*.

The ArgumentCompleter attribute

The ArgumentCompleter attribute is used much like ValidateScript. You place the attribute before the parameter variable it is providing completion for.

The script block in the introduction is used as an argument for the attribute, as the following code shows:

```
function Test-ArgumentCompleter {
    [CmdletBinding()]
    param (
        [Parameter(Mandatory)]
        [ArgumentCompleter( {
            param (
                $commandName,
                $parameterName,
                $wordToComplete,
                $commandAst,
                $fakeBoundParameter
            )
            $possibleValues = 'Start', 'Stop', 'Create', 'Delete'
            $possibleValues -like "$wordToComplete*"
        } )]
        $Action
    )
}
```

When the user types Test-ArgumentCompleter and then presses *Tab*, the completer offers up each of the possible values with no filtering. If the user were to type Test-ArgumentCompleters, only Start and Stop would be offered when pressing Tab.

The Register-ArgumentCompleter command is an alternative to using the ArgumentCompleter attribute.

Using Register-ArgumentCompleter

The Register-ArgumentCompleter command provides an alternative to the ArgumentCompleter attribute. This can be used to register a single completer for more than one command parameter.

In addition to being able to add a completer to several commands, Register-ArgumentCompleter can create argument completers for native commands (.exe files).

For example, when used as an alternative to the ArgumentCompleter attribute, the command is used as follows:

```
function Test-ArgumentCompleter {
    [CmdletBinding()]
    param (
        [Parameter(Mandatory)]
        $Action
    )
}
$params = @{
    CommandName   = 'Test-ArgumentCompleter'
    ParameterName = 'Action'
    ScriptBlock   = {
        param (
            $commandName,
            $parameterName,
            $wordToComplete,
            $commandAst,
            $fakeBoundParameter
        )
        $possibleValues = 'Start', 'Stop', 'Create', 'Delete'
        $possibleValues -like "$wordToComplete*"
    }
}
Register-ArgumentCompleter @params
```

The CommandName parameter used for Register-ArgumentCompleter accepts an array of command names. In one step, the completer can be added to several different commands that share a parameter.

`Register-ArgumentCompleter` can also be used to add argument completion to native commands. The following example offers a user of the `wmic` command automatic alias completion:

```
Register-ArgumentCompleter -CommandName wmic -Native -ScriptBlock {
    param ( $wordToComplete, $commandAst, $cursorPosition )
    wmic /?:BRIEF |
        Where-Object { $_ -cmatch '^([A-Z]{2}\S+)+' } |
        ForEach-Object { $matches[1] } |
        Where-Object {
            $_ -notin 'CLASS', 'PATH', 'CONTEXT', 'QUIT/EXIT' -and
            $_ -like "$wordToComplete*"
        }
}
```

When using the `-Native` parameter, the arguments passed to the completer differ; the first argument becomes the word to complete.

An argument completer script typically returns one or more values. These are ultimately coerced to a `CompletionResult` object.

About CompletionResult

The `CompletionResult` object allows a value to be described in more detail, most notably offering the ability to add a tooltip message.

For example, the example that demonstrated the `ArgumentCompleter` attribute can be adjusted to include a tooltip:

```
function Test-ArgumentCompleter {
    [CmdletBinding()]
    param (
        [Parameter(Mandatory)]
        [ArgumentCompleter( {
            param (
                $commandName,
                $parameterName,
                $wordToComplete,
                $commandAst,
                $fakeBoundParameter
            )
            $possibleValues = @(
                @{ Value = 'Start'; ToolTip = 'The Start action' }
                @{ Value = 'Stop';  ToolTip = 'The Stop action' }
            )
            $possibleValues |
```

```
                    Where-Object Value -like "$wordToComplete*" |
                    ForEach-Object {
                        [CompletionResult]::new(
                            $_.Value, # completionText
                            $_.Value, # listItemText
                            [CompletionResultType]::ParameterValue,
                            $_.ToolTip
                        )
                    }
            } )]
            $Action
        )
    }
```

The ToolTip value will be displayed in editors that support completion, or it will be displayed when using the Control and spacebar to complete a value.

completionText is the value that appears after -Action in the following command line. listItemText is the selectable value that is displayed in the menu; this does not have to match the completionText value. The tooltip is displayed at the bottom as each option is highlighted.

The result of this is shown in *Figure 18.1*:

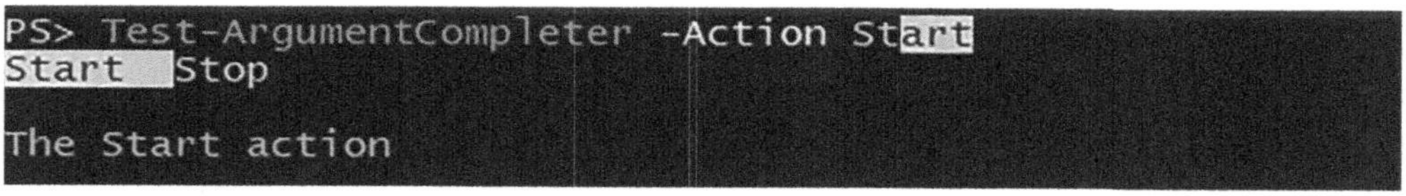

Figure 18.1: ArgumentCompleter tooltip

The Join-String command in PowerShell 7 uses a similar approach to generate a descriptive list for the Separator parameter, as shown in *Figure 18.2*:

Figure 18.2: ArgumentCompleter tooltip with the Seperator parameter

Join-String demonstrates that completionText does not have to be a literal value, the text does not have to be the exact bound value, and it can be the PowerShell code required to create that value.

Non-literal values

For the purpose of this exploration, values that are not directly equivalent to the value a parameter receives can be called non-literal values.

For example, if an argument completer were to return a path with spaces, the consumer of the function would not be able to directly use the value.

The simple argument completer emits strings that contain spaces:

```
function Test-ArgumentCompleter {
    [CmdletBinding()]
    param (
        [Parameter(Mandatory)]
        [ArgumentCompleter( {
            'C:\Program Files'
            'C:\Program Files (x86)'
        } )]
        $Path
    )
}
```

For simplicity, no attempt is made to compare with the $wordToComplete value.

A user using this completer will be presented with unquoted strings, for example, the first result:

```
Test-ArgumentCompleter -Path C:\Program Files
```

If the values returned by the completer are themselves quoted, the user of the completer will have a much more useful value:

```
function Test-ArgumentCompleter {
    [CmdletBinding()]
    param (
        [Parameter(Mandatory)]
        [ArgumentCompleter( {
            "'C:\Program Files'"
            "'C:\Program Files (x86)'"
        } )]
        $Path
    )
}
```

This completer is now emitting the PowerShell code required to create the string value. The PowerShell code in question is in this case very simple, a single-quoted string in each case.

The example could be extended to use a CompletionResult, this time creating a difference between the item in the completion list and the completed value to better describe the values:

```
function Test-ArgumentCompleter {
    [CmdletBinding()]
    param (
```

```
        [Parameter(Mandatory)]
        [ArgumentCompleter( {
            [CompletionResult]::new(
                "'C:\Program Files'",
                'C:\Program Files',
                'ParameterValue',
                '64-bit program files'
            )
            [CompletionResult]::new(
                "'C:\Program Files (x86)'",
                'C:\Program Files (x86)',
                'ParameterValue',
                '32-bit program files'
            )
        } )]
        $Path
    )
}
```

The described values will be incorrect if this is run in the 32-bit version of PowerShell as it is a primitive example.

Considering that the completer is potentially generating code to execute, a completer can return more complex expressions. This last argument completer generates syntax like that required by Select-Object when creating custom properties as an example of a completer generating code to execute.

```
function Test-ArgumentCompleter {
    param (
        [Parameter(Mandatory)]
        [object]
        $InputObject,

        [ArgumentCompleter({
            param (
                $commandName,
                $parameterName,
                $wordToComplete,
                $commandAst,
                $fakeBoundParameter
            )

            $object = $fakeBoundParameter['InputObject']
            $properties = $object.PSObject.Properties.Name
```

```
                foreach ($name in $properties) {
                    if ($name -notlike "$wordToComplete*") {
                        continue
                    }

                    $text = $name
                    if ($text -match '\s') {
                        $text = "'{0}'" -f $text
                    }
                    $text
                    "@{{ Name = '{0}'; Expression = '' }}" -f $name
                    "@{{ Name = '{0}'; Expression = {{ `$_.{1} }} }}" -f $name,
$text
                }
            })]
            $Property
        )
    }
```

The value assigned to `InputObject` in the command is read from the `fakeBoundParameters` dictionary in this example to generate a list of values that can be tabbed through.

If the following partial command is entered, the properties of the object are read and emitted:

```
$inputObject = [PSCustomObject]@{
    simple        = 1
    'with spaces' = 2
}
Test-ArgumentCompleter -InputObject $inputObject -Property
```

Typing the preceding command and pressing *Ctrl* and the *spacebar* after the `Property` parameter will show the possible completions shown in *Figure 18.3*.

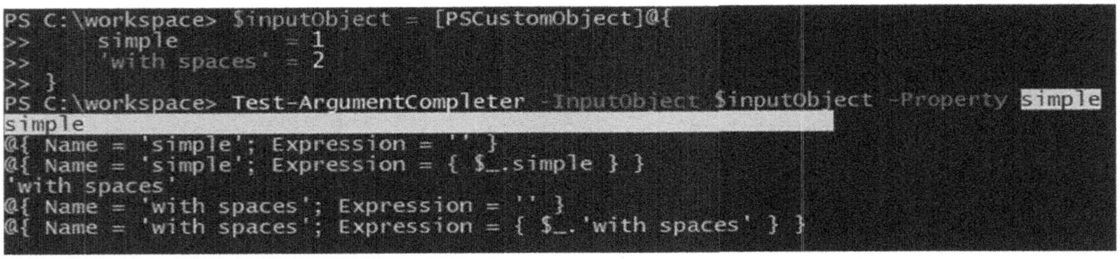

Figure 18.3: Argument completer options

Argument completers that have been added by `Register-ArgumentCompleter` are not trivially accessible.

Listing registered argument completers

While it is possible to register argument completers, PowerShell does not provide a way of listing them. This is somewhat frustrating as it makes exploration and finding examples more difficult.

The following script makes extensive use of reflection in .NET to explore classes that are not made publicly available, eventually getting to a property that holds the argument completers:

```powershell
using namespace System.Reflection

$localPipeline = [PowerShell].Assembly.GetType(
    'System.Management.Automation.Runspaces.LocalPipeline'
)
$getExecutionContextFromTLS = $localPipeline.GetMethod(
    'GetExecutionContextFromTLS',
    [BindingFlags]'Static, NonPublic'
)
$internalExecutionContext = $getExecutionContextFromTLS.Invoke(
    $null,
    [BindingFlags]'Static, NonPublic',
    $null,
    $null,
    $psculture
)


$internalExecutionContext.GetType().GetProperty(
    'CustomArgumentCompleters',
    [BindingFlags]'NonPublic, Instance'
).GetGetMethod(
    $true
).Invoke(
    $internalExecutionContext,
    [BindingFlags]'Instance, NonPublic, GetProperty',
    $null,
    @(),
    $PSCulture
)
```

Native argument completers are held in a different property and will not be shown by the previous snippet.

A more refined version of the previous snippet, which also supports the retrieval of native argument completers, is available in the book's example repository: https://github.com/PacktPublishing/ Mastering-PowerShell-Scripting-5E/blob/main/Chapter18/scripts/Get-ArgumentCompleter.ps1.

Argument completers are a fantastic way to suggest values for parameters without constraining the possible input values.

So far in this chapter, all the parameters have been explicitly defined in a param block, and any attributes have been explicitly added. In PowerShell, it is possible to define parameters dynamically.

Dynamic parameters

Dynamic parameters allow a developer to define the behavior of parameters when a function or script is run, rather than hardcoding that behavior in advance in a param block.

Dynamic parameters can be used to overcome some of the limitations inherent in a param block. For example, it is possible to change the parameters presented by a command based on the value of another parameter. It is also possible to dynamically write validation, such as dynamically assigning a value for the ValidateSet attribute.

Dynamic parameters remain unpopular in the PowerShell community. They are hard to define and difficult to troubleshoot, as they tend to silently fail rather than raise an error, and help cannot be provided using comment-based help.

Dynamic parameters have a named block: dynamicparam. If you use dynamicparam in a script or function, the implicit default blocks for a script or function cannot be used; all code must be contained within an explicitly named block.

Functions making use of dyamicparam must either include a CmdletBinding attribute or at least one statically defined parameter with a Parameter attribute. Dynamic parameters will silently fail to appear without the function explicitly being made advanced.

The following example includes an empty dynamicparam block as well as an end block, which would have been implicit if dynamicparam were not present:

```
function Test-DynamicParam {
    [CmdletBinding()]
    param ( )

    dynamicparam { }

    end {
        Write-Host 'Function body'
    }
}
```

If end or another named block declaration is missing around the code within the function, a syntax error will be displayed.

The following example will cause an error if pasted into the console or if the code is executed via an editor:

```
function Test-DynamicParam {
    [CmdletBinding()]
    param ( )

    dynamicparam { }

    Write-Host 'Function body'
}
```

In PowerShell 7, the first error message will explicitly state that Write-Host is unexpected and that a named block is expected:

```
ParserError:
Line |
   7 |         Write-Host 'Function body'
     |         ~~~~~~~~~~
     | unexpected token 'Write-Host', expected 'begin', 'process', 'end', or
'dynamicparam'.
```

Windows PowerShell is less clear; it states that a closing brace is missing:

```
At line:1 char:28
+ function Test-DynamicParam {
+                            ~
Missing closing '}' in statement block or type definition.
    + CategoryInfo          : ParserError: (:) [],
ParentContainsErrorRecordException
    + FullyQualifiedErrorId : MissingEndCurlyBrace
```

The dynamicparam block must create and return a RuntimeDefinedParameterDictionary object. The dictionary can contain zero or more RuntimeDefinedParameter objects.

Creating a RuntimeDefinedParameter object

A RuntimeDefinedParameter object describes a single parameter. The definition includes the name of the parameter, the parameter type, and any attributes that should be set for that parameter. PowerShell does not include type accelerators for creating RuntimeDefinedParameter; the full name, System. Management.Automation.RuntimeDefinedParameter, must be used.

The constructor for RuntimeDefinedParameter expects three arguments: a string, which is the parameter name, a .NET type for the parameter, and a collection or array of attributes that should be assigned. The attribute collection must contain at least one Parameter attribute to inform PowerShell which parameter sets the parameter can belong to.

The following example, which creates a parameter named Action, makes use of a using namespace statement to shorten the .NET type names:

```
using namespace System.Management.Automation

$parameter = [RuntimeDefinedParameter]::new(
    'Action',
    [string],
    [Attribute[]]@(
        [Parameter]@{ Mandatory = $true; Position = 1 }
        [ValidateSet]::new('Start', 'Stop', 'Create', 'Delete')
    )
)
```

The previous parameter is the equivalent of using the following in the param block:

```
param (
    [Parameter(Mandatory, Position = 1)]
    [ValidateSet('Start', 'Stop', 'Create', 'Delete')]
    [string]
    $Action
)
```

As the attributes are not being placed directly above a variable, each must be created as an independent object instance.

The shorthand used for the Parameter attribute in the param block cannot be used; expressions cannot be omitted when describing properties.

The ValidateSet attribute, and other validation attributes, must also be created as a new object rather than using the attribute syntax.

The Parameter attribute declaration takes advantage of the ability to assign property values to an object using a hashtable. This is feasible because a Parameter attribute can be created without supplying any arguments, that is, [Parameter]::new() can be used to create a Parameter attribute with default values. This technique cannot be used for ValidateSet, as it requires arguments. The ::new method or New-Object command must be used.

As with a normal parameter, RuntimeDefinedParameter can declare more than one Parameter attribute. Each Parameter attribute is added to the attribute collection:

```
using namespace System.Management.Automation

$parameter = [RuntimeDefinedParameter]::new(
    'Action',
    [string],
```

```
        [Attribute[]]@(
            [Parameter]@{
                Mandatory       = $true
                Position        = 1
                ParameterSetName = 'First'
            }
            [Parameter]@{
                ParameterSetName = 'Second'
            }
        )
    )
)
```

Any number of parameters can be created in this manner. Each parameter must have a unique name. Each parameter must be added to the RuntimeDefinedParameterDictionary.

Using RuntimeDefinedParameterDictionary

RuntimeDefinedParameterDictionary is the expected output from the dynamicparam block. The dictionary must contain all the dynamic parameters a function is expected to present.

The following example creates a dictionary and adds a single parameter:

```
using namespace System.Management.Automation

function Test-DynamicParam {
    [CmdletBinding()]
    param ( )

    dynamicparam {
        $parameters = [RuntimeDefinedParameterDictionary]::new()

        $parameter = [RuntimeDefinedParameter]::new(
            'Action',
            [string],
            [Attribute[]]@(
                [Parameter]@{ Mandatory = $true; Position = 1 }
                [ValidateSet]::new(
                    'Start',
                    'Stop',
                    'Create',
                    'Delete'
                )
            )
        )
```

```
            $parameters.Add($parameter.Name, $parameter)
            $parameters
    }
}
```

Dynamic parameters are not created as explicit variables within the function's scope. Values may be accessed in one of two ways: using PSBoundParameters or using the RuntimeDefinedParameterDic tionary instance.

Using dynamic parameters

Dynamic parameters are most often accessed using the PSBoundParameters variable within a function or script.

PSBoundParameters

The value of the Action parameter used in the previous examples must be retrieved by using Action as a key, as shown here:

```
using namespace System.Management.Automation

function Test-DynamicParam {
    [CmdletBinding()]
    param ( )

    dynamicparam {
        $parameters = [RuntimeDefinedParameterDictionary]::new()
        $parameter = [RuntimeDefinedParameter]::new(
            'Action',
            [string],
            [Attribute[]]@(
                [Parameter]@{ Mandatory = $true; Position = 1 }
                [ValidateSet]::new(
                    'Start',
                    'Stop',
                    'Create',
                    'Delete'
                )
            )
        )
        $parameters.Add($parameter.Name, $parameter)
        $parameters
    }
```

```
    end {
        Write-Host $PSBoundParameters['Action']
    }
}
```

As with parameters from the param block, the `$PSBoundParameters.ContainsKey` method may be used to find out whether a user has specified a value for the parameter.

A dynamic parameter that accepts pipeline input, like a normal parameter that accepts pipeline input, will only have a value within the process and end blocks. The end block will only see the last value in the pipeline. The following example demonstrates this:

```
using namespace System.Management.Automation

function Test-DynamicParam {
    [CmdletBinding()]
    param ( )

    dynamicparam {
        $parameters = [RuntimeDefinedParameterDictionary]::new()
        $parameter = [RuntimeDefinedParameter]::new(
            'InputObject',
            [string],
            [Attribute[]]@(
                [Parameter]@{
                    Mandatory         = $true
                    ValueFromPipeline = $true
                }
            )
        )
        $parameters.Add($parameter.Name, $parameter)
        $parameters
    }

    begin {
        'BEGIN: Input object is present: {0}' -f @(
            $PSBoundParameters.ContainsKey('InputObject')
        )
    }

    process {
        'PROCESS: Input object is present: {0}; Value: {1}' -f @(
            $PSBoundParameters.ContainsKey('InputObject')
```

```
                    $PSBoundParameters['InputObject']
            )
        }

    end {
        'END: Input object is present: {0}; Value: {1}' -f @(
            $PSBoundParameters.ContainsKey('InputObject')
            $PSBoundParameters['InputObject']
        )
    }
}
```

The function can be used with arbitrary input values, for example:

```
PS> 1..2 | Test-DynamicParam
BEGIN: Input object is present: False
PROCESS: Input object is present: True; Value: 1
PROCESS: Input object is present: True; Value: 2
END: Input object is present: True; Value: 2
```

Alternatively, values assigned to dynamic parameters may be accessed using the RuntimeDefinedPa
rameterDictionary.

RuntimeDefinedParameterDictionary

The RuntimeDefinedParameterDictionary created in the dynamicparam block may be used within
other named blocks. This approach has the advantage that any default value assigned to a dynamic
parameter can be read.

In the following example, a default value is assigned to the dynamic parameter:

```
using namespace System.Management.Automation

function Test-DynamicParam {
    [CmdletBinding()]
    param ( )

    dynamicparam {
        $parameters = [RuntimeDefinedParameterDictionary]::new()
        $parameter = [RuntimeDefinedParameter]::new(
            'Action',
            [string],
            [Attribute[]]@(
                [Parameter]@{ Position = 1 }
                [ValidateSet]::new(
```

```
                                'Start',
                                'Stop',
                                'Create',
                                'Delete'
                        )
                    )
                )
            $parameter.Value = 'Start'
            $parameters.Add($parameter.Name, $parameter)
            $parameters
        }

        end {
            $parameters['Action'].Value
        }
    }
}
```

The value assigned to the parameter may be read back from the parameter dictionary and used within the other named blocks.

The RuntimeDefinedParameter object, the value of $parameters['Action'] in the preceding example, also includes an IsSet property, which may be used to determine whether the parameter has a value at all.

Extending on this, the $parameter variable, which is used to define the parameter in the first place, may also be used. In the following truncated example, a more meaningful name is given to the parameter:

```
$actionParam = [RuntimeDefinedParameter]::new(
    'Action',
    [string],
    [Attribute[]]@(
        [Parameter]@{ Position = 1 }
        [ValidateSet]::new(
            'Start',
            'Stop',
            'Create',
            'Delete'
        )
    )
)
$actionParam.Value = 'Start'
```

The use of $actionParam.Value or $actionParam.IsSet within the body of the code would have a more obvious purpose with this renamed variable.

The $PSBoundParameters variable, and any other parameters, may be referenced inside the dynamicparam block.

Conditional parameters

One possible use of dynamic parameters is to change validation based on the value supplied for another parameter. Another use is to change which parameters are available, again based on the value of another parameter.

The following example changes validValues into ValidateSet depending on the value supplied for the Type parameter:

```
using namespace System.Management.Automation
function Test-DynamicParam {
    [CmdletBinding()]
    param (
        [Parameter(Mandatory, Position = 1)]
        [ValidateSet('Service', 'Process')]
        [string]
        $Type,

        [Parameter(Mandatory, Position = 3)]
        [string]
        $Name
    )

    dynamicparam {
        $parameters = [RuntimeDefinedParameterDictionary]::new()
        [String[]]$validValues = switch ($Type) {
            'Service' { 'Get', 'Start', 'Stop', 'Restart' }
            'Process' { 'Get', 'Kill' }
        }
        $parameter = [RuntimeDefinedParameter]::new(
            'Action',
            [String],
            [Attribute[]]@(
                [Parameter]@{ Mandatory = $true; Position = 2 }
                [ValidateSet]::new($validValues)
            )
        )
        $parameters.Add($parameter.Name, $parameter)
        $parameters
    }
}
```

Changing validation in this manner is entirely reliant on the user having typed a value for the Type parameter before attempting to type Action. Other comparisons can be made in dynamic parameter blocks; for example, a parameter might only appear when a certain condition is met. RuntimeDefine dParameterDictionary is valid even if it is empty and no extra parameters need to be added.

Summary

Attributes can be set on parameters in PowerShell to quickly and easily define behavior, acceptable values, and usage for a parameter. These attributes greatly simplify the validation that may be required in the body of a script or function.

PowerShell comes with a wide range of built-in validators, and each of the existing validators is briefly demonstrated in this chapter. As well as validation, extra controls can be placed around the content of a parameter, such as whether empty strings or collections may be used as a value.

The Parameter attribute is incredibly important in PowerShell as it allows pipeline input support to be declared for a parameter, and for parameters to be placed in different parameter sets.

Argument completers have changed a great deal as PowerShell has progressed through each version. In PowerShell 5 and above, you can use the ArgumentCompleter attribute and the Register-ArgumentCompleter command to add tab completion support to a parameter.

Dynamic parameters are an interesting feature of PowerShell, although it is a feature that should be used with care as it is easy to break. The examples in this chapter presented the creation of dynamic parameters using the simplest syntax possible.

The next chapter explores the features available to classes that were introduced with PowerShell 5.

Learn more on Discord

Read this book alongside other users, PowerShell experts, and the author himself. Ask questions, provide solutions to other readers, chat with the author via Ask Me Anything sessions, and much more.

Scan the QR code or visit the link to join the community.

`https://packt.link/SecNet`

19

Classes and Enumerations

PowerShell 5 introduced support for creating classes and enumerations within PowerShell directly. Prior to this, classes had to be created in a language such as C#, or dynamically created using the complex dynamic assembly types in the System.Reflection namespace.

Classes and enumerations have only changed a little in PowerShell 6 and 7. There are numerous enhancement issues open in the PowerShell project on GitHub, but they have been slow to make their way into PowerShell. Examples include support for writing interfaces and the ability to define getters and setters for properties.

This chapter explores the following topics:

- Defining an enumeration
- Creating a class
- Classes and runspace affinity
- Transformation, validation, and completion
- Classes and DSC

Defining an enumeration

An enumeration is a set of named, numeric constants that provides a relatively simple introduction to creating types. .NET is full of examples of enumerations. For example, the System.Security. AccessControl.FileSystemRights enumeration describes all of the numeric values that are used to define access rights for files or directories.

Enumerations are also used by PowerShell. For example, System.Management.Automation. ActionPreference contains the values for the preference variables, such as ErrorActionPreference and DebugPreference.

Enumerations are created by using the enum keyword followed by a list of names and values:

```
enum MyEnum {
    First  = 1
```

```
        Second = 2
        Third  = 3
    }
```

Each name must be unique within the enumeration and must start with a letter or an underscore. The name may contain numbers after the first character. The name cannot be quoted and cannot contain the hyphen character.

The value does not have to be unique. One or more names in an enumeration can share a single value:

```
    enum MyEnum {
        One    = 1
        First  = 1
        Two    = 2
        Second = 2
    }
```

By default, enumeration values are Int32, which is the underlying type.

Enum and underlying types

In languages such as C#, enumerations can be given an underlying type, such as Byte or Int64. In PowerShell 5 and PowerShell Core 6.1 and older, the enumeration type is fixed to Int32:

```
    enum MyEnum {
        First = 1
    }
```

This type is shown using the following command:

```
PS> [MyEnum].GetEnumUnderlyingType()


IsPublic    IsSerial    Name     BaseType
--------    --------    ----     --------
True        True        Int32    System.ValueType
```

In PowerShell 7, the value type can be specified for an enumeration:

```
    enum MyEnum : ulong {
        First = 0
        Last  = 18446744073709551615
    }
```

Any integer type can be used as the value type, including Byte, short (Int16), ushort (UInt16), int, uint (UInt32), long (Int64), and ulong (UInt64). BigInt is not a permissible value type.

An enumeration value may be cast to its underlying type to reveal the number behind the name:

```
    [int][MyEnum]::First
```

Alternatively, the -as operator can be used:

```
[MyEnum]::First -as [MyEnum].GetEnumUnderlyingType()
```

The numeric value is also accessible using the value__ property:

```
PS> [MyEnum]::First.value__
0
```

The preceding example enumerations have explicit values defined for each name. Enumerations support automatic numbering, as the next section shows.

Automatic value assignment

An enumeration may be created without defining a value for a name. PowerShell will automatically allocate a sequence of values starting from 0. In the following example, the names Zero and One are automatically created with the values 0 and 1, respectively:

```
enum MyEnum {
    Zero
    One
}
```

If a value is assigned to a name, the sequence will continue from that point. The following example starts with the value 5. The name Six will automatically be given the value 6:

```
enum MyEnum {
    Five = 5
    Six
}
```

Automatic value assignment is always based on the previous value; an explicit assignment can be made at any point. The following example demonstrates both restarting a sequence and skipping values in a sequence:

```
enum MyEnum {
    One   = 1
    Two
    Five  = 5
    Six
    First = 1
    Second
}
```

The value of Second in this enumeration can be shown to be 2:

```
PS> [MyEnum]::Second.value__
2
```

The previous example mixes two potentially different name sets in a single enumeration to demonstrate restarting the numeric sequence. It is rarely desirable to mix names and values in this manner. If a distinct set of constant names is needed for a set of names, a second enumeration is a better approach.

Enumerations can be used to restrict arguments for parameters in a similar manner to the ValidateSet attribute.

Enum or ValidateSet

It is common to create functions or scripts with parameters that accept a fixed set of values. ValidateSet can be used to limit the possible arguments for a parameter.

The following example uses the values Absent and Present for a parameter named Ensure. This parameter and these values are commonly used when writing **Desired State Configuration (DSC)** resources, which are explored further at the end of this chapter:

```
function Test-ParameterValue {
    param (
        [Parameter(Mandatory)]
        [ValidateSet('Absent', 'Present')]
        [string]
        $Ensure
    )
}
```

The ValidateSet attribute used in the preceding example restricts the parameter to one of the two different values. As many values as required can be used with ValidateSet.

Using an enumeration instead has the benefit that the same set of values can be shared across several different functions in a script or module.

The following enumeration describes the same possible values used in ValidateSet in the previous example:

```
enum Ensure {
    Absent
    Present
}
function Test-ParameterValue {
    param (
        [Parameter(Mandatory)]
        [Ensure]
        $Ensure
    )
}
```

In some cases, the numeric value may be irrelevant, which can be true of the values for preference variables in PowerShell, for instance. The value of a preference variable can be numeric but it is far more common to use a string. For example, the following two preference variable assignments are equivalent:

```
$VerbosePreference = 'Continue'
$VerbosePreference = 2
```

The origin of the numeric value used above is shown in the following line of code:

```
[System.Management.Automation.ActionPreference]::Continue.value__
```

The GetEnumNames method or the GetEnumValues method can be used to see all possible names or values, respectively. Here's an example using GetEnumValues:

```
PS> using namespace System.Management.Automation
PS> [ActionPreference].GetEnumValues()
SilentlyContinue
Stop
Continue
Inquire
Ignore
Suspend
Break
```

The numeric value may be considered important again when it has a parallel with another value type. In the case of the Ensure enumeration, it is most logical to have Absent represented by 0 and Present by 1.

The enumerations used previously are used as single values. The name used with the parameter is either Absent or Present, never a combination of the two. Enumerations that support more than one name being used are created using the Flags attribute.

The Flags attribute

Flags enumerations are used to express multiple values using a single number.

This type of value is known as a bit field. Meaning is ascribed to each individual bit in the value. For example, a 32-bit integer can be used to describe 32 individual flags. Bits can be toggled on or off to enable (or disable) a specific value in the field.

For example, let's look at the first few values of the FileSystemRights enumeration, which is used to describe rights for filesystem permissions:

```
using namespace System.Security.AccessControl

$names = [FileSystemRights].GetEnumNames() |
    Select-Object -First 5
foreach ($name in $names) {
```

```
    $value = $name -as [FileSystemRights] -as [int]
    [PSCustomObject]@{
        Name    = $name
        Value   = $value
        Binary  = [Convert]::ToString($value, 2).PadLeft(4, '0')
    }
}
```

The loop above will display the output below:

```
Name            Value Binary
----            ----- ------
ReadData            1 0001
ListDirectory       1 0001
WriteData           2 0010
CreateFiles         2 0010
AppendData          4 0100
```

Values are duplicated in the enumeration because the bits can have different meanings depending on context (rights on a file or rights on a folder). Each of these values represents a single bit or flag.

Bit fields are extremely efficient. They take a minimal amount of space (in bytes), which makes them ideal for contexts where size is a consideration. Bit fields are frequently used in network protocols, where the amount of data to transport over a network is important.

In *Chapter 10, Files, Folders, and the Registry*, the FileSystemRights enumeration was used to describe access rights. Access rights are described as a combination of several bits. The names given to those bits were written as a comma-separated list.

An enumeration that uses the Flags attribute allows more than one name to describe a value. For example:

```
[System.Security.AccessControl.FileSystemRights]'ReadData, Delete'
```

This is only possible because the enumeration has the Flags attribute set:

```
PS> $enumType = [System.Security.AccessControl.FileSystemRights]
PS> $enumType.CustomAttributes.AttributeType.Name
FlagsAttribute
```

The Flags attribute can be used when creating enumerations in PowerShell. The attribute is placed before the enum keyword, as shown here:

```
[Flags()]
enum MyEnum {
    First  = 1
    Second = 2
```

```
    Third  = 4
}
```

Each numeric value in the enumeration has a distinct combination of (binary) bits set to make the value unique:

```
[Flags()]
enum MyEnum {
    First  = 1 # 001
    Second = 2 # 010
    Third  = 4 # 100
}
```

The value of the flag will therefore double each time: 1, 2, 4, 8, 16, 32, 64, 128, and so on. Enumeration values, especially flags, might be written in hexadecimal:

```
[Flags()]
enum MyEnum {
    First  = 0x001  # 1 or  000001
    Second = 0x002  # 2 or  000010
    Third  = 0x004  # 4 or  000100
    Fourth = 0x008  # 8 or  001000
    Fifth  = 0x010  # 16 or 010000
    Sixth  = 0x020  # 32 or 100000
}
```

In many respects, it is easier to read the value in hexadecimal. The unique values are always 1, 2, 4, and 8, with a shift in position each time the value appears: 0x001 the first time, 0x002 the second, 0x004 the third, and so on.

As each number doubles, automatic value assignment does not create useful values (beyond the 1 and 2) if the Flags attribute is used.

PowerShell will cast a numeric value into a set of names if it can be matched in a Flags enumeration. A value of 6 can be used to represent the Second and Third flags, for example:

```
PS> [MyEnum]6
Second, Third
```

Several enumerations that use the Flags attribute also provide named composite values. For example, System.Security.AccessControl.FileSystemRights defines several permissions as combinations of other values. The ReadAndExecute right is made up of the individual ReadData, ReadExendedAttributes, and ReadPermissions flags. The following function can be used to reveal these individual flag values from a combined or composite value:

```
function Get-FlagName {
    [CmdletBinding()]
```

```
    param (
        $Value
    )
    $enumType = $Value.GetType()
    $i = 0
    do {
        $bit = $Value -as [Int64] -band 1 -shl $i++
        if ($bit) {
            [PSCustomObject]@{
                Name        = $bit -as $enumType
                Integer     = $bit
                Hexadecimal = '0x{0:X8}' -f $bit
                BitPosition = $i
            }
        }
    } until (1 -shl $i -ge $value)
}
```

The function works by taking the value 1 and then bit-shifting it one place to the left with each iteration of the loop. That is, it compares the value 1, then 2, 4, 8, 16, and so on. If that exact bit in the composite value is set, the custom object describing that value is returned.

Running the function with the ReadAndExecute enumeration value shows the individual flags that make up the composite value:

```
PS> using namespace System.Security.AccessControl
PS> Get-FlagName -Value ([FileSystemRights]::ReadAndExecute)

                 Name Integer Hexadecimal BitPosition
                 ---- ------- ----------- -----------
             ReadData       1 0x00000001            1
ReadExtendedAttributes     8 0x00000008            4
          ExecuteFile      32 0x00000020            6
       ReadAttributes     128 0x00000080            8
      ReadPermissions  131072 0x00020000           18
```

Composite values can be created in a PowerShell enumeration by setting a value that has more than one flag set. For example, the tweak to the example enumeration adds a composite value for the First and Third flags:

```
[Flags()]
enum MyEnum {
    First      = 1 # 001
    Second     = 2 # 010
```

```
    Third         = 4 # 100
    FirstAndThird = 5 # 101
}
```

As FirstAndThird explicitly matches the value 5, any value the enumeration converts will use the FirstAndThird name instead of the individual values:

```
PS> [MyEnum]7
Second, FirstAndThird
PS> [MyEnum]'First, Second, Third'
Second, FirstAndThird
```

The preceding function can be used on the tweaked enumeration to show the individual values:

```
PS> Get-FlagName -Value ([MyEnum]::FirstAndThird)

 Name Integer Hexadecimal BitPosition
 ---- ------- ----------- -----------
First       1 0x00000001            1
Third       4 0x00000004            3
```

As enumerations associate a name with a number, enumerations can be used to convert different related names.

Using enumerations to convert a value

Enumerations are lists of names, each assigned a numeric value. A pair of enumerations can be used to convert between two lists of names linked by a common number.

The following example defines two enumerations. The first is a list of values the end user will see; the second holds the internal name required by the code. This simulates, in part, the type of aliasing performed by the wmic command:

```
enum AliasName {
    OS
    Process
}
enum ClassName {
    Win32_OperatingSystem
    Win32_Process
}
```

A function can use the AliasName enumeration, as shown here:

```
function Get-CimAliasInstance {
    [CmdletBinding()]
    param (
```

```
            [Parameter(Mandatory, Position = 1)]
            [AliasName]
            $AliasName
        )
        Get-CimInstance -ClassName ([ClassName]$AliasName)
}
```

The command may now be used with the OS argument for the AliasName parameter, as demonstrated in the following trimmed output:

```
PS> Get-CimAliasInstance -AliasName OS


SystemDirectory         Organization BuildNumber
---------------         ------------ -----------
C:\WINDOWS\system32                  19042
```

This will be converted to Win32_OperatingSystem by way of the enumeration. Get-CimInstance handles converting that value into a string.

An enumeration is a simple type with the specific intent of describing numbers. Classes, on the other hand, allow a lot more flexibility.

Creating a class

Classes were first introduced in *Chapter 7, Working with .NET*. A class was described as the recipe used to define a type; it is used to describe an object. This may be any object, which means that a class in PowerShell might be used for any purpose.

Classes in PowerShell are created using the class keyword. The following class describes a type that contains a single property:

```
class MyClass {
    [string] $Value = 'My value'
}
```

An instance of a type (defined by a class) can be explicitly created by using either the New-Object command or the ::new() method:

```
PS> New-Object MyClass


Value
-----
My Value


PS> [MyClass]::new()


Value
```

```
- - - - -
My Value
```

The type can also be implicitly created by casting a dictionary. For example, a hashtable is used below:

```
# Do not change any default property values
[MyClass]@{}
# Or set a new value for the Value property
[MyClass]@{ Value = 'New value' }
```

It is also possible to create instances from a PSCustomObject:

```
$customObject = [PSCustomObject]@{ Value = 'New value' }
[MyClass]$customObject
```

The extra assignment in the example above is not required; it is present only to show that the cast to MyClass does not have to be in the same statement.

In the examples above, the value of the single property in the class is changed. If it is not changed it, maintains the default value.

Properties

The properties defined in a class may define a .NET type and may have a default value, if required. The following class has a single property with the string type:

```
class MyClass {
    [string] $Value = 'My value'
}
```

PowerShell automatically adds hidden get and set methods used to access the property; these cannot be overridden or changed at this time (within the class itself). The get and set methods may be viewed using Get-Member with the Force parameter:

```
PS> [MyClass]::new() | Get-Member get_*, set_* -Force


    TypeName: MyClass

Name        MemberType    Definition
----        ----------    ----------
get_Value   Method        string get_Value()
set_Value   Method        void set_Value(string )
```

The property of MyClass may be accessed using an instance of the class:

```
PS> $instance = [MyClass]::new()
PS> $instance.Value
My value
```

Classes are created with a default constructor that requires no arguments unless a constructor is explicitly defined.

Constructors

A constructor is executed when either New-Object or ::new is used to create an instance of a class. The implicit or default constructor does not require arguments.

An explicit constructor may be created to handle more complex actions when creating an object.

The constructor has the same name as the class. The reserved $this variable is used to refer to properties and methods within the class. The following constructor sets a value for Value when an instance of the class is created:

```
class MyClass {
    [string]$Value
    MyClass() {
        $this.Value = 'Hello world'
    }
}
```

The constructor may require arguments to create an instance of the class. The following example requires a string, updates the value, then sets it as the value of the Value property:

```
class MyClass {
    [string]$Value
    MyClass(
        [string] $Argument
    ) {
        $culture = Get-Culture
        $this.Value = $culture.TextInfo.ToTitleCase(
            $Argument
        )
    }
}
```

The argument for the constructor is passed when creating the instance of the object. The result is:

```
PS> [MyClass]::new('hello world')

Value
-----
Hello World
```

The preceding ToTitleCase method has capitalized the first characters of each word in the string before assigning it to the Value property.

So far, it can be said that:

- Default values may be assigned to properties as required.
- If work is required to fill a property (or properties) when an object is created, a constructor with no arguments can be used.
- If work is required to fill a property (or properties), and an argument should be supplied by the consumer (end user, or another piece of code) of the class, a constructor can be created that accepts arguments.

Constructors may be overloaded to allow the class to accept different arguments or combinations of arguments when the class is created.

The following example has two constructors. The first is a default constructor that sets a default value for the Value property. The second constructor allows the consumer of the class to define a value:

```
class MyClass {
    [string] $Value

    MyClass() {
        $this.Value = 'Hello world'
    }

    MyClass(
        [string] $Argument
    ) {
        $culture = Get-Culture
        $this.Value = $culture.TextInfo.ToTitleCase(
            $Argument
        )
    }
}
```

Each constructor must have a unique signature. The signature for the constructor is based on the number of arguments and the types (such as string, as used above) of those arguments.

Methods are created within classes to expose the ability to change an object to a user and to enclose shared functionality or complex logic.

Methods

A method causes a change to the object. This may be an internal change, such as opening a connection or stream, or it may take the object and change it into a different form, as is the case with the ToString method.

With MyClass <code style>, if ToString is called, the name of the class is returned:

```
class MyClass {
    [string]$Value = 'Hello world'
}
```

The output of the string method is shown below:

```
PS> [MyClass]::new().ToString()
MyClass
```

This is the default implementation for the ToString method. The method can be replaced in the class so that it returns the value of the property (or any other value):

```
class MyClass {
    [string] $Value = 'Hello world'

    [string] ToString() {
        return $this.Value
    }
}
```

Running the ToString method this time shows the value of the Value property:

```
PS> [MyClass]::new().ToString()
Hello world
```

When working with methods, and unlike functions in PowerShell, the return keyword is mandatory. Methods do not return output by default. An error will be raised if a method has an output type declared and it does not return output from each code path.

Methods can accept arguments in the same way as constructors. Methods can also be overloaded. For example, the ToString method might be overloaded, providing support for output formatting. An example of this is shown here:

```
class MyClass {
    [string] $Value = 'Hello world'

    [string] ToString() {
        return '{0} on {1}' -f @(
            $this.Value
            (Get-Date).ToShortDateString()
        )
    }
```

```
    [string] ToString(
        [string] $dateFormat
    ) {
        return '{0} on {1}' -f @(
            $this.Value
            Get-Date -Format $dateformat
        )
    }
}
```

The arguments supplied will dictate which method implementation (overload) is being used.

Properties and methods in a class can be hidden from casual viewing using the hidden modifier.

The Hidden modifier

The hidden modifier can be used to hide a property or method from tab completion and Get-Member.

Members marked as hidden can still be seen if the Force parameter is used with Get-Member and hidden members may still be accessed or invoked. In many respects, hidden is like the DontShow property of the Parameter attribute.

In the following example, the Initialize method is hidden:

```
class MyClass {
    [string]$Property
    MyClass() {
        $this.Initialize()
    }
    hidden [void] Initialize() {
        $this.Property = 'defaultValue'
    }
}
```

As mentioned above, the Force parameter of Get-Member will show hidden members:

```
PS> [MyClass]::new() | Get-Member Initialize -Force


    TypeName: MyClass


Name          MemberType     Definition
----          ----------     ----------
Initialize    Method         void Initialize()
```

The properties and methods in the classes demonstrated so far require an instance of the type to be created before they can be used.

The static modifier

All of the members demonstrated so far have required the creation of an instance of a type using either New-Object or ::new().

Static members can be accessed or executed without creating an instance of a type (based on a class).

Classes may implement static properties and static methods using the static modifier keyword:

```
class MyClass {
    static [string] $Property = 'Property value'

    static [string] Method() {
        return 'Method return'
    }
}
```

The static members are accessed or used as follows:

```
[MyClass]::Property
[MyClass]::Method()
```

The hidden modifier may be used in conjunction with the static modifier. The modifiers may be used in either order.

Classes can inherit properties and methods from other classes.

Inheritance

Classes in PowerShell can inherit from other classes, from classes in PowerShell and .NET. The properties and methods in a base class are available to an inheriting class.

The following example defines two classes – the second inherits from the first:

```
class MyBaseClass {
    [string] $BaseProperty = 'baseValue'
}


class MyClass : MyBaseClass {
    [string] $Property = 'Value'
}
```

The BaseProperty property is made available on instances of the child class:

```
PS> [MyClass]::new()


Property       BaseProperty
--------       ------------
Value          baseValue
```

Members may be overridden by redeclaring the member on the inheriting class. The `GetString` method implementation from the base class is overridden in the following example:

```
class MyBaseClass {
    [string] GetString() { return 'default' }
}
class MyClass : MyBaseClass {
    [string] GetString() { return 'new' }
}
```

When overriding members, the return type of a method can be changed. For example, the return type of `GetValue` may be changed in the child class:

```
class MyBaseClass {
    [string] GetValue() { return 'default' }
}

class MyClass : MyBaseClass {
    [int] GetValue() { return 1 }
}
```

However, the value type of properties cannot be changed. The example below attempts to do so. The class definition will not raise an error:

```
class MyBaseClass {
    [string] $Property = 'default'
}

class MyClass : MyBaseClass {
    [int] $Property = 1
}
```

However, attempting to create an instance of `MyClass` will raise an error:

```
PS> [MyClass]::new()
OperationStopped: Ambiguous match found for 'MyClass Int32 Property'.
```

This limitation applies to instance properties only; static properties are not affected.

Each class can only inherit from one other class, but there is no limit to how deep inheritance can go.

Constructors are also accessible via inherited classes, but each constructor must be defined in a child class. Constructor inheritance is not entirely automatic.

Constructors and inheritance

Constructors in an inheritance hierarchy are not overridden but are instead executed in sequence.

In the following example, both classes have a default constructor (a constructor that does not require any arguments):

```
class ParentClass {
    ParentClass() {
        Write-Host 'Default parent constructor'
    }
}

class ChildClass : ParentClass {
    ChildClass() {
        Write-Host 'Default child constructor'
    }
}
```

When an instance of ChildClass is created, the constructor on the parent class implicitly executes first, followed by the constructor on the child class:

```
PS> $instance = [ChildClass]::new()
Default parent constructor
Default child constructor
```

If an overload is added to the constructor on ChildClass, PowerShell will run the new constructor and the default constructor on ParentClass. The changed classes are as follows:

```
class ParentClass {
    ParentClass() {
        Write-Host 'Default parent constructor'
    }
}
class ChildClass : ParentClass {
    ChildClass() {
        Write-Host 'Default child constructor'
    }

    ChildClass([string]$value) {
        Write-Host 'Overloaded child constructor'
    }
}
```

Creating an instance of ChildClass shows that both constructors are called:

```
PS> $instance = [ChildClass]::new('value')
Parent constructor
Overloaded child constructor
```

Automatic execution of the default constructor in an inherited class works provided the inherited class has a default constructor. In the following example, the default constructors are removed from both classes:

```
class ParentClass {
    ParentClass(
        [string] $value
    ) {
        Write-Host 'Overloaded parent constructor'
    }
}


class ChildClass : ParentClass {
    ChildClass(
        [string] $value
    ) {
        Write-Host 'Overloaded child constructor'
    }
}
```

Attempting to create a new instance of ChildClass will now result in an error. PowerShell expects to be able to invoke the default constructor in ParentClass and that no longer exists:

```
PS> $instance = [ChildClass]::new('value')
MethodException:
Line |
   2 |         ChildClass([string]$value) {
     |                           ~
     | Cannot find an overload for "new" and the argument count: "0".
```

Without the default constructor, ChildClass must be told how it is to build an instance of ParentClass. The base keyword is used to achieve this:

```
class ParentClass {
    ParentClass(
        [string] $value
    ) {
        Write-Host 'Non-default parent constructor'
    }
```

```
    }

    class ChildClass : ParentClass {
        ChildClass(
            [string] $value
        ) : base(
            $value
        ) {
            Write-Host 'Non-default child constructor'
        }
    }
}
```

Creating an instance of ChildClass this time shows both constructors run again:

```
PS> $instance = [ChildClass]::new('value')
Non-default parent constructor
Non-default child constructor
```

In the previous example, the $value variable is accepted by the constructor on the ChildClass and explicitly passed as an argument to the constructor in ParentClass.

Extending on the preceding example, the constructor in the ChildClass can be changed again: this time, removing the argument. The base keyword is used with a string to invoke the constructor in ParentClass:

```
class ParentClass {
    ParentClass(
        [string] $value
    ) {
        Write-Host 'Non-default parent constructor'
    }
}
class ChildClass : ParentClass {
    ChildClass() : base(
        'Any string value'
    ) {
        Write-Host 'Default child constructor'
    }
}
```

Once again, creating an instance of ChildClass shows which constructors are being used:

```
PS> $instance = [ChildClass]::new()
Non-default parent constructor
Default child constructor
```

The constructor in the parent class is matched by the names and types of arguments for the base keyword.

Using this, it can be said that:

- By default, all constructors in a child class call the default constructor in a parent class.
- If a default constructor does not exist in a parent class, the base keyword must be used with every constructor in a child class to specify a constructor in the parent class.

The base keyword cannot be applied to methods in classes. A different technique must be used when invoking methods of the same name in a parent class.

Calling methods in a parent class

Methods declared in a child class override the method defined in a parent class. Methods in a parent class are not implicitly called.

It is possible to invoke methods in a child class by casting to the parent class type. This is useful if, for example, the method in the child class adds more specialized functionality than the original method:

```
class ParentClass {
    [string] GetString() {
        return 'Hello world'
    }
}


class ChildClass : ParentClass {
    [string] GetString() {
        $string = ([ParentClass]$this).GetString()

        return '{0} on {1}' -f @(
            $string
            Get-Date -Format 'dddd'
        )
    }
}
```

The method is invoked on an instance of ChildClass:

```
PS> [ChildClass]::new().GetString()
Hello world on Sunday
```

If the cast to ParentClass were omitted, the method would start an infinite loop.

Interfaces can be used to support specific functionalities such as comparisons, equality, and many others. The inheritance notation can be used to implement an interface.

Working with interfaces

An interface is a set of instructions for implementing a specific behavior in a class. .NET includes many different interfaces; two of the more common examples are IComparable and IEquatable.

Implementing IComparable defines how an instance of a class should be compared using the -gt, -ge, -lt, and -le operators. IComparable also provides support for sorting.

Implementing IEquatable defines how an instance of a class should be compared using the -eq and -ne operators. While, at first glance, the two might seem to overlap, the sections that follow show this is not the case.

Declaring support for an interface uses the same notation as inheritance; however, unlike class inheritance, a class can implement more than one interface.

To demonstrate these interfaces, a simple class with a single property that has a numeric value is used:

```
class MyClass {
    [int] $Number
}
```

The numeric value will be used as the basis for the comparisons used below. The choice of value (and value type) is otherwise arbitrary.

Each interface defines the methods a class must implement to support that interface.

Implementing IComparable

As mentioned above, the IComparable interface makes it possible to usefully compare two instances of a class using -gt, -ge, -lt, and -le. It also makes it possible to sort instances of a class without naming a property to sort on.

IComparable must be implemented as described in the .NET reference: https://learn.microsoft.com/dotnet/api/system.icomparable.

Classes implementing IComparable must therefore define a CompareTo method that returns a single integer value. Typically, the values are limited to 1, -1, or 0.

The .NET reference includes a second version of IComparable, IComparable<T>. Limitations in the class implementation in PowerShell make the two indistinguishable, so the simpler version is used.

Support for IComparable in the class is therefore added as shown here:

```
class MyClass : IComparable {
    [int] $Number

    [int] CompareTo(
        [object] $object
    ) {
        if ($this.Number -gt $object.Number) {
```

```
        return 1
    } elseif ($this.Number -lt $object.Number) {
        return -1
    } else {
        return 0
    }
}
}
```

As the comparison above depends on a comparison between int values, the comparison might be performed by calling CompareTo on the Number property:

```
class MyClass : IComparable {
    [int] $Number

    [int] CompareTo(
        [object] $object
    ) {
        return $this.Number.CompareTo($object.Number)
    }
}
```

Once the method and the interface declaration exist, one instance of the class can be compared to another:

```
PS> $first = [MyClass]@{ Number = 1 }
PS> $second = [MyClass]@{ Number = 2 }
PS> $first -lt $second
True
PS> $first -gt $second
False
```

If the value of the Number property in both instances of the class is the same, then -ge and -le will return true:

```
PS> $first = [MyClass]@{ Number = 1 }
PS> $second = [MyClass]@{ Number = 1 }
PS> $first -ge $second
True
PS> $first -le $second
True
```

However, because IComparable does not specifically allow the testing of equality, using the -eq operator will return false. The CompareTo method defined in the class is not used for the equality comparison:

```
PS> $first -eq $second
False
```

The IEquatable interface is used to support equality comparisons.

Implementing IEquatable

The IEquatable interface can be used to support equality expressions using -eq and -ne.

The .NET reference shows IEquatable with a type argument, indicated by the <T> in the type name:

https://learn.microsoft.com/dotnet/api/system.iequatable-1.

The documentation shows that any class implementing the IEquatable interface must implement an Equals method that returns a Boolean value and a GetHashCode method.

The type used is expected to be the same type as the IEquatable class is being implemented for. That is, an implementation of IEquatable would normally expect to start as follows:

```
class MyClass : IEquatable[MyClass] {
```

PowerShell is not able to support this. The following error will be shown if the preceding approach is used:

```
ParentContainsErrorRecordException: An error occurred while creating the
pipeline.
```

To allow PowerShell to create the class, we'll use [object] as the type in place of the more specific MyClass. This is shown in the following example, which also implements GetHashCode.

GetHashCode should provide a unique value describing the object. As the basis for all comparisons with this object is the value of the Number property, the value of the property is also used as the hash code. The number 1, after all, uniquely identifies the number 1 when compared with all other numbers.

GetHashCode is a complex and involved topic. The .NET reference material dives into far greater detail: https://learn.microsoft.com/dotnet/api/system.object.gethashcode#remarks.

This example extends the existing class that supports IComparable to support IEquatable. Note that IEquatable uses [object] instead of [MyClass]:

```
class MyClass : IComparable, IEquatable[object] {
    [int] $Number

    [int] CompareTo([object] $object) {
        if ($this.Number -gt $object.Number) {
            return 1
        } elseif ($this.Number -lt $object.Number) {
            return -1
```

```
            } else {
                return 0
            }
        }

    [int] GetHashCode() {
        return $this.Number
    }

    [bool] Equals(
        [object] $equalTo
    ) {
        return $this.Number -eq $equalTo.Number
    }
}
```

Note that the argument type for the `Equals` method must be `[object]` in the preceding example; it must match the type used in `IEquatable[object]`.

Once the interface has been implemented, two instances of the class may be compared using the `-eq` operator:

```
PS> $first = [MyClass]@{ Number = 1 }
PS> $second = [MyClass]@{ Number = 1 }
PS> $first -eq $second
True
```

Classes can support casting in several different ways.

Supporting casting

The simplest way to support casting between PowerShell classes is to create a constructor that will accept the incoming type.

For example, it is possible to cast from `Int` to `MyClass` by implementing a constructor that accepts `Int` as an argument:

```
class MyClass {
    [int] $Number

    MyClass() { }

    MyClass([int] $value) {
        $this.Number = $value
    }
}
```

With the constructor in place, PowerShell will allow Int32 values to be cast to the class:

```
PS> [MyClass]1

Number
------
     1
```

If PowerShell can convert a value into Int32, then the assignment will succeed. Therefore, short (Int16), byte, and other values smaller than Int32 will succeed.

Attempting to cast larger types, long (Int64), will fail:

```
PS> [MyClass][long]1
InvalidArgument: Cannot convert the "1" value of type "System.Int64" to type
"MyClass".
```

PowerShell is also capable of coercing a value to a type using a Parse static method. In the following example, the method accepts any object, and if it can coerce that to Int32, it will return an instance of MyClass:

```
class MyClass {
    [int] $Number

    static [MyClass] Parse(
        [object] $value
    ) {
        if ($value -as [int]) {
            return [MyClass]@{ Number = $value }
        } else {
            throw 'Unsupported value'
        }
    }
}
```

As this version parses values of type [object] (or anything), it will accept larger value types, if the actual value can be reduced into an Int32:

```
PS> [MyClass][long]2312

Number
------
  2312
```

The preceding methods support casting from a specific value to an instance of MyClass. It is possible for the class to support casting to another type by implementing an implicit conversion operator. The operator is implemented as a static method named op_Implicit:

```
class NewClass {
    [string] $DayOfWeek
}

class MyClass {
    [int] $Number

    hidden static [NewClass] op_Implicit(
        [MyClass] $instance
    ) {
        return [NewClass]@{
            DayOfWeek = [DayOfWeek]$instance.Number
        }
    }
}
```

The advantage of this approach is that the conversion logic is part of MyClass. NewClass does not have to know anything about MyClass or how to perform the conversion:

```
PS> [NewClass][MyClass]@{ Number = 1 }

DayOfWeek
---------
Monday
```

The disadvantage of this approach is that a maximum of two op_Implicit methods can be added. Each method requires a unique signature (name and arguments), and the return type is not part of that signature.

A second signature can be added by changing the argument type to [object]; in this case, it supports casting to the [DayOfWeek] enumeration:

```
class NewClass {
    [string] $DayOfWeek
}

class MyClass {
    [int] $Number

    hidden static [NewClass] op_Implicit(
        [MyClass] $instance
```

```
    ) {
        return [NewClass]@{
            DayOfWeek = [DayOfWeek]$instance.Number
        }
    }

    hidden static [DayOfWeek] op_Implicit(
        [object] $instance
    ) {
        return [DayOfWeek]$instance.Number
    }
}
```

Instances of classes created in PowerShell will, by default, have affinity with the session state they were created within.

Classes and runspace affinity

Classes in PowerShell have affinity with the runspace the instance of a class was created within. This means that any method call made in a different runspace is queued to run in the original runspace.

This affinity can be shown by inspecting the runspace ID. In a script executed within a newly created PowerShell runspace, each ID will be different:

```
1..5 | ForEach-Object {
    [PowerShell]::Create().
        AddScript('[Runspace]::DefaultRunspace.Id').
        Invoke()
}
```

The command above will show the individual runspace IDs like those shown below:

```
2
3
4
5
6
```

In the example below, a class is defined, then an instance is created. The instance of the class is passed as an argument to a newly created runspace to execute the method. Each execution of the Run method will show the value 1 if the class instance is created in the interactive runspace:

```
class WithAffinity {
    [void] Run() {
        [Console]::WriteLine([Runspace]::DefaultRunspace.Id)
    }
}
```

```
}

1..5 | ForEach-Object {
    $instance = [WithAffinity]::new()
    [PowerShell]::Create().
        AddScript('$args[0].Run()').
        AddArgument($instance).
        Invoke()
}
```

This feature introduces two potentially significant problems:

- Cross-runspace method calls may cause session state corruption and deadlock.
- Operations will run serially because each must wait for the original runspace to execute.

The first of these is difficult to demonstrate. When it is encountered, the PowerShell process will hang. PowerShell will not respond to user input or to cancellation using Control and C.

The second point, while less serious, is much easier to demonstrate. The previous example showed that the executing runspace ID in the method was 1. Making the invocation asynchronous and adding console output in the method can be used to show each block runs serially rather than in parallel.

Start-Sleep is used in the example below to simulate a long-running method, which makes the issue of serial execution more apparent:

```
class WithAffinity {
    [void] Run() {
        [Console]::WriteLine(
            'Runspace: {0}; Time: {1:HH:mm:ss.fff}' -f @(
                [Runspace]::DefaultRunspace.Id
                Get-Date
            )
        )
        Start-Sleep -Seconds 2
    }
}

1..5 | ForEach-Object {
    $instance = [WithAffinity]::new()
    [PowerShell]::Create().
        AddScript('$args[0].Run()').
        AddArgument($instance).BeginInvoke() | Out-Null
}
```

The expected output from this is like the snippet below. The times will differ, but each should show the method runs in runspace 1. Importantly, it also shows an approximate delay of two seconds between each method starting:

```
Runspace: 1; Time: 12:43:30.671
Runspace: 1; Time: 12:43:32.685
Runspace: 1; Time: 12:43:34.693
Runspace: 1; Time: 12:43:36.702
Runspace: 1; Time: 12:43:38.710
```

PowerShell 7.3 introduces a new attribute, NoRunspaceAffinity, which can be used with a class to remove affinity. This causes the method to run in the new runspace rather than the creator's runspace.

The class above has been modified to include this attribute in the example below, which repeats the timed test:

```
[NoRunspaceAffinity()]
class NoAffinity {
    [void] Run() {
        [Console]::WriteLine(
            'Runspace: {0}; Time: {1:HH:mm:ss.fff}' -f @(
                [Runspace]::DefaultRunspace.Id
                Get-Date
            )
        )
        Start-Sleep -Seconds 2
    }
}

1..5 | ForEach-Object {
    $instance = [NoAffinity]::new()
    [PowerShell]::Create().
        AddScript('$args[0].Run()').
        AddArgument($instance).BeginInvoke() | Out-Null
}
```

When executing this version, the console output will show each method starting almost simultaneously, or as fast as ForEach-Object can complete. The output from the above is expected to be like the below, with little or no delay between each method start:

```
Runspace: 6; Time: 12:47:40.839
Runspace: 2; Time: 12:47:40.839
Runspace: 5; Time: 12:47:40.839
Runspace: 4; Time: 12:47:40.839
Runspace: 3; Time: 12:47:40.839
```

The `NoRunspaceAffinity` attribute is an important addition that increases the flexibility of class instances across different runspaces in PowerShell.

Classes can be used for a variety of existing purposes in PowerShell. Classes can be used to implement parameter transformation and validation.

Transformation, validation, and completion

PowerShell offers attributes to transform or validate values of variables, parameters, and class properties in PowerShell.

In addition to these, PowerShell also offers argument completer attributes, which were explored in *Chapter 18, Parameters, Validation, and Dynamic Parameters*.

In addition to the built-in validators, each of these transformation, validation, and completion attributes can be implemented using classes in PowerShell.

Argument transformation attributes are used to transform values being assigned to a variable, parameter, or property before validation and binding.

Argument transformation attribute classes

An argument-transformation attribute is used to convert the value of an argument for a variable. The transformation operation is carried out before PowerShell completes the assignment to the variable (or binding to a parameter or property), giving the opportunity to change the value.

Classes for argument transformation must implement a `Transform` method. The `Transform` method must accept two arguments, a `System.Object` and a `System.Management.Automation.EngineIntrinsics`. The argument names are arbitrary; the names used follow the example in the .NET reference: `https://learn.microsoft.com/dotnet/api/system.management.automation.argumenttransformationattribute.transform`.

The class must therefore inherit from `System.Management.Automation.ArgumentTransformationAttribute`.

Abstract classes such as the `ArgumentTransformationAttribute` type are somewhat like interfaces. However, while a class may implement one or more interfaces, a class can only inherit from one abstract type. In essence, this ensures that the class implements the required functionality.

The following example is an argument-transformation attribute that converts a date string in the format `yyyyMMddHHmmss` to `DateTime` before the assignment to the parameter is completed:

```
using namespace System.Management.Automation

class DateTimeStringTransformationAttribute :
    ArgumentTransformationAttribute {

    [object] Transform(
        [EngineIntrinsics] $engineIntrinsics,
```

```
        [object]                $inputData
    ) {
        if ($inputData -is [DateTime]) {
            return $inputData
        }
        $date = Get-Date
        $isValidDate = [DateTime]::TryParseExact(
            $inputData,
            'yyyyMMddHHmmss',
            $null,
            'None',
            [ref]$date
        )
        if ($isValidDate) {
            return $date
        }
        throw 'Unexpected date format'
    }
}
```

The class does not need to contain anything other than the Transform method implementation. If the transformation is more complex, it may implement other helper methods. The following example moves [DateTime]::TryParseExact into a new method:

```
using namespace System.Management.Automation

class DateTimeStringTransformationAttribute :
    ArgumentTransformationAttribute {

    hidden [DateTime] $date

    hidden [bool] tryParseExact(
        [string] $value
    ) {
        $parsedDate = Get-Date
        $parseResult = [DateTime]::TryParseExact(
            $value,
            'yyyyMMddHHmmss',
            $null,
            'None',
            [Ref]$parsedDate
        )
```

```
                $this.date = $parsedDate
                return $parseResult
        }


        [object] Transform(
            [EngineIntrinsics] $engineIntrinsics,
            [object]           $inputData
        ) {
            if ($inputData -is [DateTime]) {
                return $inputData
            }
            if ($this.tryParseExact($inputData)) {
                return $this.date
            }
            throw 'Unexpected date format'
        }
    }
}
```

The new class may be used with a parameter, as shown here. Note that the Attribute string at the end of the class name may be omitted when it is used:

```
function Test-Transform {
    param (
        [DateTimeStringTransformation()]
        [DateTime]
        $Date
    )

    Write-Host $Date
}
```

With this attribute in place, the function can be passed a date and time in a format that would not normally convert:

```
PS> Test-Transform -Date '20210102090000'
02/01/2021 09:00:00
```

Classes can also be used to implement customized validation.

Validation attribute classes

PowerShell classes can be used to build custom validation attributes. This offers an alternative to ValidateScript.

Validation attributes must inherit from either `ValidateArgumentsAttribute` or `ValidateEnumerate` `dArgumentsAttribute`.

Validators are most often used with parameters in scripts and functions, but they may be used with any variable.

ValidateArgumentsAttribute

Validators inheriting from `ValidateArgumentsAttribute`, such as `ValidateCount`, test the entirety of a value. Most validators only test individual elements in arrays.

Classes that implement `ValidateArgumentsAttribute` must inherit from `System.Management.` `Automation.ValidateArgumentsAttribute`. The class must implement a `Validate` method that is marked as abstract in the `ValidateArgumentsAttribute` class.

The `Validate` method accepts two arguments with the `System.Object` and `System.Management.` `Automation.EngineIntrinsics` types. This is shown in the .NET reference: `https://learn.microsoft.` `com/dotnet/api/system.management.automation.validateargumentsattribute.validate`.

For example, it may be desirable to validate that an array of values is in a specific order. Testing order requires visibility of the whole array of values. This case, if obscure, is a reasonable candidate for using `ValidateArgumentsAttribute`.

The attribute below tests that a set of strings provided as an argument is in alphabetical order:

```
using namespace System.Management.Automation

class ValidateAlphabeticalOrder : ValidateArgumentsAttribute {
    [void] Validate(
        [object]              $arguments,
        [EngineIntrinsics] $engineIntrinsics
    ) {
        $values = @($arguments)
        for ($i = 1; $i -lt $values.Count; $i++) {
            if ($values[$i] -lt $values[$i - 1]) {
                throw 'Arguments must be in alphabetical order.'
            }
        }
    }
}
```

The attribute is placed on top of a parameter and will run for every assignment statement:

```
function Test-Validate {
    [CmdletBinding()]
    param (
        [ValidateAlphabeticalOrder()]
```

```
        [string[]]
        $Value
    )
}
```

If the array is in alphabetical order, no error is thrown and the argument successfully validates:

```
Test-Validate -Value 'a', 'c', 'f'
```

However, if the array is not in alphabetical order, an error will be raised:

```
PS> Test-Validate -Value 'a', 'f', 'a'
Test-Validate: Cannot validate argument on parameter 'Value'. Arguments must be
in alphabetical order.
```

It is relatively rare to need to evaluate an array of values; a more common scenario is to validate each element individually.

ValidateEnumeratedArgumentsAttribute

Classes that inherit from ValidateEnumeratedArgumentsAttribute (in the System.Management. Automation namespace) can test each of the elements in an array (when associated with an array-based parameter), or a single item (when associated with a scalar parameter).

The class must implement a ValidateElement method that is marked as abstract in the ValidateEnu meratedArgumentsAttribute class.

The ValidateElement method accepts one argument with the System.Object type. This method is shown in the .NET reference: https://learn.microsoft.com/dotnet/api/system.management. automation.validateenumeratedargumentsattribute.validateelement.

The ValidateElement method does not return any output; it either runs successfully or throws an error. The error will be displayed to the end user.

The next code block validates that an IP address used as an argument falls in a private address range.

There are many different methods for determining if an address range is private. The following class tests the first three octets of the IP address. For instance, if the first octet is 10, the address is private. If the first octet is 172 and the second is between 16 and 31, the address is private, and so on.

If the address is not part of a private range or not a valid IP address, the ValidateElement method will throw an error:

```
using namespace System.Management.Automation
class ValidatePrivateIPAddressAttribute :
        ValidateEnumeratedArgumentsAttribute {

    hidden [bool] IsPrivateIPAddress(
        [IPAddress] $address
    ) {
```

```
        $bytes = $address.GetAddressBytes()
        $isPrivateIPAddress = switch ($null) {
            { $bytes[0] -eq 10 } { $true; break }
            { $bytes[0] -eq 172 -and
              $bytes[1] -ge 16 -and
              $bytes[1] -le 31 } { $true; break }
            { $bytes[0] -eq 192 -and
              $bytes[1] -eq 168 } { $true; break }
            default { $false }
        }
        return $isPrivateIPAddress
    }


    [void] ValidateElement(
        [object] $element
    ) {
        $ipAddress = $element -as [IPAddress]
        if (-not $ipAddress) {
            throw '{0} is an invalid IP address format' -f @(
                $element
            )
        }
        if (-not $this.IsPrivateIPAddress($element)) {
            throw '{0} is not a private IP address' -f @(
                $element
            )
        }
    }
}
```

The attribute created by the example above can be used with any parameter to validate IP addressing, as shown in the following short function:

```
function Test-Validate {
    [CmdletBinding()]
    param (
        [ValidatePrivateIPAddress()]
        [IPAddress]
        $IPAddress
    )

    Write-Host $IPAddress
}
```

When used, the function will only allow the address as an argument for the parameter if it is in one of the reserved private ranges:

```
PS> Test-Validate -IPAddress 10.0.0.11
10.0.0.11
```

When a public IP address is specified, binding will fail:

```
PS> Test-Validate -IPAddress 50.0.0.11
Test-Validate: Cannot validate argument on parameter 'IPAddress'. 50.0.0.11 is
not a private IP address
```

If something other than an IP address is supplied, the error will state that the IP address is invalid:

```
PS> Test-Validate -IPAddress someString
Test-Validate: Cannot process argument transformation on parameter 'IPAddress'.
Cannot convert value "someString" to type "System.Net.IPAddress". Error: "An
invalid IP address was specified."
```

Validation like this can be implemented with ValidateScript, which also inherits from ValidateEnumeratedArgumentsAttribute. ValidateScript can call functions, centralizing the validation code where necessary.

ValidateSet value generator

ValidateSet in Windows PowerShell will test the value assigned to a variable (often a parameter) against a hard-coded list of values.

In PowerShell 7, ValidateSet can be used with a type to dynamically determine the values to validate against. This is achieved by writing a class that implements the IValidateSetValuesGenerator interface: https://learn.microsoft.com/dotnet/api/system.management.automation.ivalidatesetvaluesgenerator.

The interface requires the class to implement a GetValidValues method, which should return an array of strings. The class can use any method it needs to generate the list of values. In the following example, the list is derived from the list of environment variable names in the current process:

```
using namespace System.Management.Automation

class EnvironmentVariable : IValidateSetValuesGenerator {
    [string[]] GetValidValues() {
        return Get-ChildItem env: -Name
    }
}
```

The set generator can use the class for tab completion and to validate the values for a parameter of a function:

```
function Get-EnvironmentVariable {
    [CmdletBinding()]
    param (
        [Parameter(Mandatory)]
        [ValidateSet([EnvironmentVariable])]
        [string]
        $Name
    )

    Get-Item env:$Name
}
```

The preceding classes are mostly used with parameters, but they can be used with any variable, including properties in classes. Argument completers, on the other hand, are exclusively written for parameters.

Argument completers

Argument completers were explored in *Chapter 18, Parameters, Validation, and Dynamic Parameters*, using script blocks for the ArgumentCompleter attribute.

An argument completer can be created by writing a class that inherits from IArgumentCompleter.

IArgumentCompleter

IArgumentCompleter requires a CompleteArgument method. The CompleteArgument must return IEnumerable[CompletionResult] and must accept the following arguments:

- commandName (string)
- parameterName (string)
- wordToComplete (string)
- commandAst (System.Management.Automation.Language.CommandAst)
- fakeBoundParameters (IDictionary)

These arguments are used in the same way as the examples in *Chapter 18, Parameters, Validation, and Dynamic Parameters*.

One of the simpler completers made use of the following script block:

```
{
    param (
        $commandName,
        $parameterName,
        $wordToComplete,
```

```
        $commandAst,
        $fakeBoundParameter
    )
    $possibleValues = 'Start', 'Stop', 'Create', 'Delete'
    $possibleValues -like "$wordToComplete*"
}
```

This script block can be converted into a CompleteArgument method as shown below. This example cannot be used as it stands; it requires a class around it:

```
[Ienumerable[CompletionResult]] CompleteArgument(
    [string]      $commandName,
    [string]      $parameterName,
    [string]      $wordToComplete,
    [CommandAst]  $commandAst,
    [Idictionary] $fakeBoundParameters
) {
    $possibleValues = 'Start', 'Stop', 'Create', 'Delete'
    $values = $possibleValues -like "$wordToComplete*"
    return $values -as [CompletionResult[]]
}
```

The implementation in the class is much stricter than the script block. The arguments for the method must be given the correct type and the method must return an array of CompletionResult.

A type implementing IArgumentCompleter can be created to make use of the method above:

```
using namespace System.Collections
using namespace System.Collections.Generic
using namespace System.Management.Automation
using namespace System.Management.Automation.Language

class ActionCompleter : IArgumentCompleter {
    [IEnumerable[CompletionResult]] CompleteArgument(
        [string]      $commandName,
        [string]      $parameterName,
        [string]      $wordToComplete,
        [CommandAst]  $commandAst,
        [IDictionary] $fakeBoundParameters
    ) {
        $possibleValues = 'Start', 'Stop', 'Create', 'Delete'
        $values = $possibleValues -like "$wordToComplete*"
        return $values -as [CompletionResult[]]
    }
}
```

This definition makes use of four using namespace statements. If pasted into the console, only the last of these will act. If you're testing in the console, put all the using namespace statements on the same line separated by a semicolon.

A parameter making use of this type must use it as an argument for the ArgumentCompleter attribute. The function below has no output but demonstrates the placement of the completer type:

```
function Test-ArgumentCompleter {
    [CmdletBinding()]
    param (
        [Parameter(Mandatory)]
        [ArgumentCompleter([ActionCompleter])]
        $Action
    )
}
```

If it were desirable to pass arguments to this completer, for example, with the values hard-coded as possibleValues, then a second class is required.

IArgumentCompleterFactory

A type that inherits from IArgumentCompleterFactory can be used to create instances of an argument completer with specific arguments.

To reduce repetition in this section, the following using namespace statements are assumed to be present for each example:

```
using namespace System.Collections
using namespace System.Collections.Generic
using namespace System.Management.Automation
using namespace System.Management.Automation.Language
```

To support this, a constructor must be added to the completer created in the previous section:

```
class ActionCompleter : IArgumentCompleter {
    [string[]] $PossibleValues

    ActionCompleter(
        [string[]] $possibleValues
    ) {
        $this.PossibleValues = $possibleValues
    }

    [IEnumerable[CompletionResult]] CompleteArgument(
        [string]      $commandName,
        [string]      $parameterName,
```

```
            [string]      $wordToComplete,
            [CommandAst]  $commandAst,
            [IDictionary] $fakeBoundParameters
        ) {
            $values = $this.PossibleValues -like "$wordToComplete*"
            return $values -as [CompletionResult[]]
        }
    }
```

This constructor allows custom values to be passed. However, the ArgumentCompleter attribute used in the last example function does not offer the ability to accept arguments.

A new class inheriting from ArgumentCompleterAttribute and implementing the IArgumentCompleterFactory interface must be created. The class must implement a Create method that returns instances of the original class.

This second class also needs a constructor to accept arguments that are ultimately passed on to ActionCompleter.

To make naming clear, the new class is called CustomActionsCompleter; this class is used to create instances of the updated ActionCompleter type:

```
class CustomActionsCompleter : ArgumentCompleter,
    IArgumentCompleterFactory {

    [string[]] $PossibleValues

    CustomActionsCompleter(
        [string[]] $possibleValues
    ) {
        $this.PossibleValues = $possibleValues
    }

    [IArgumentCompleter] Create() {
        return [ActionCompleter]::new($this.PossibleValues)
    }
}
```

Finally, the new completer is added to the example function along with the arguments that will be used:

```
function Test-ArgumentCompleter {
    [CmdletBinding()]
    param (
        [Parameter(Mandatory)]
        [CustomActionsCompleter((
```

```
                'Start',
                'Stop',
                'Create',
                'Delete'
            ))]
            $Action
    )
}
```

Argument completers are complex, but the ability to define and customize them in PowerShell directly is very valuable.

Microsoft Desired State Configuration is perhaps the most important use for classes in PowerShell.

Classes and Microsoft Desired State Configuration

Microsoft DSC, or **Desired State Configuration**, is one of several different configuration management systems available. Individual items are configured idempotently; that is, they only change when change is required.

Classes in PowerShell exist because of DSC. DSC resources written as PowerShell classes are very succinct; they avoid the repetition inherent in a script-based resource. Script-based resources must at least duplicate a param block.

Class-based DSC resources in a module must be explicitly exported using the DscResourcesToExport key in a module manifest document.

The class must include a DscResource attribute. Each property a user is expected to set must have a DscProperty attribute. At least one property must be the Key property of the DscProperty attribute set. The class must implement the Get, Set, and Test methods.

Class-based resources may use inheritance to simplify an implementation as required; this is especially useful if a group of resources uses the same code to act out changes.

A basic DSC resource is defined as follows:

```
enum Ensure {
    Absent
    Present
}

[DscResource()]
class MyResource {
    [DscProperty(Key)]
    [Ensure] $Ensure

    [MyResource] Get() { return $this }
```

```
    [void] Set() { }

    [bool] Test() { return $true }
}
```

This resource implements all the required methods, but it performs no actions.

Like a good function, a good DSC resource should strive to be good at one thing and one thing only. If a particular item has a variety of configuration options, it is often better to have a set of similar resources than a single resource that attempts to do it all.

The sections that follow will focus on the creation of a short resource that sets the computer description.

This resource will need to make a change to a single registry value. The computer description is set under the HKLM:\SYSTEM\CurrentControlSet\Services\LanmanServer\Parameters key using the svrcomment string value.

The starting point, a framework for a resource, with expected properties is shown below:

```
enum Ensure {
    Absent
    Present
}

[DscResource()]
class ComputerDescription {
    [DscProperty(Key)]
    [Ensure]$Ensure

    [DscProperty()]
    [string]$Description

    hidden $path = 'HKLM:\SYSTEM\CurrentControlSet\Services\LanmanServer\
Parameters'
    hidden $valueName = 'svrcomment'

    [ComputerDescription] Get() { return $this }

    [void] Set() { }

    [bool] Test() { return $true }
}
```

Two of the values are hidden; they are used internally, but users of the class are not expected to change the values.

The methods implemented in this framework should be replaced with those demonstrated in the following sections.

Implementing Get

The Get method should evaluate the current state of the resource. The registry key will exist, but the registry value may be incorrect or may not exist.

The Get method will act as follows:

- If the value is present, it will set the Ensure property to Present and update the value of the Description property.
- If the value is not present, it will set the Ensure property to Absent only.

The following snippet implements these actions:

```
class ComputerDescription {
    [ComputerDescription] Get() {
        $key = Get-Item $this.Path
        if ($key.GetValueNames() -contains $this.valueName) {
            $this.Ensure = 'Present'
            $this.Description = $key.GetValue($this.valueName)
        } else {
            $this.Ensure = 'Absent'
        }
        return $this
    }
}
```

If the properties from the class framework at the start of this section are added, the Get method can be invoked. The output from the method is shown below:

```
PS> [ComputerDescription]::new().Get() | Format-List

Ensure      : Absent
Description :
```

The Get method can either return the existing instance, return $this, or generate a new instance, for example, by returning a hashtable:

```
class ComputerDescription {
    [ComputerDescription] Get() {
        $properties = @{}
```

```
                $key = Get-Item $this.Path
            if ($key.GetValueNames() -contains $this.valueName) {
                $properties.Ensure = 'Present'
                $properties.Description = $key.GetValue(
                    $this.valueName
                )
            } else {
                $properties.Ensure = 'Absent'
            }
            return $properties
        }
    }
```

The hashtable returned by the preceding function is automatically cast to the class, creating a new instance.

The Get method is only used when explicitly invoked. It is not mandatorily used by either Set or Test. Get might be used if it creates a new instance because it should return the current state of the resource.

Implementing Set

The Set method deals with making a change if a change is required. Set will ordinarily assume that Test has been run and, therefore, that a change is required.

As the resource allows a user to ensure a value is either present or absent, it must handle the creation and deletion of the value:

```
class ComputerDescription {
    [void] Set() {
        $commonParams = @{
            Path = $this.path
            Name = $this.valueName
        }
        if ($this.Ensure -eq 'Present') {
            $newParams = @{
                Value = $this.Description
                Type  = 'String'
                Force = $true
            }
            New-ItemProperty @newParams @commonParams
        } else {
            $key = Get-Item $this.Path
            if ($key.GetValueNames() -contains $this.valueName) {
                Remove-ItemProperty @commonParams
```

```
            }
        }
    }
}
```

This method can be used to replace the existing method in the framework. The method can be invoked by creating an instance of the class. Running Set will attempt to change the current computer description value:

```
$resource = [ComputerDescription]@{
    Description = 'New description'
}
$resource.Set()
```

The Set method does not have any output, but the method above will fail unless the shell is being run as the administrator.

This version of Set uses the Force parameter of New-ItemProperty to overwrite any existing values of the same name. Using Force also handles cases where the value exists but the value type is incorrect.

Implementing Test

The Test method is used to determine whether Set should be run. DSC invokes Test before Set. The Test method returns a Boolean value.

The Test method must perform the following tests to ascertain the state of this configuration item:

- When Ensure is present, fail if the value does not exist.
- When Ensure is present, fail if the value exists but the description does not match the requested value.
- When Ensure is absent, fail if the value name exists.
- Otherwise, pass.

The following snippet implements these tests:

```
class ComputerDescription {
    [bool] Test() {
        $key = Get-Item $this.Path
        if ($this.Ensure -eq 'Present') {
            if (
                $key.GetValueNames() -notcontains $this.valueName
            ) {
                return $false
            }
            return $key.GetValue($this.valueName) -eq
                $this.Description
        } else {
```

```
            return $key.GetValueNames() -notcontains
                $this.valueName
        }
        return $true
    }
}
```

Again, the method can be copied back into the framework example and then invoked:

```
$resource = [ComputerDescription]@{
    Description = 'New description'
}
```

If the description is already set, the Test method will output True; otherwise, it will output False:

```
PS> $resource.Test()
False
```

Each of these methods must be copied back into the resource class.

Using the resource

Making use of this resource has a couple of considerations:

- If you're making use of the DSC commands, such as Get-DscResource and Invoke-DscResource, Windows PowerShell must be used. Note that PowerShell 7 will load PSDesiredStateConfiguration using implicit remoting (the compatibility session).
- If you're directly interacting with the class, both editions of PowerShell can be used.

The complete class, ComputerDescription, incorporating each of the preceding methods is shown here:

```
enum Ensure {
    Absent
    Present
}

[DscResource()]
class ComputerDescription {
    [DscProperty(Key)]
    [Ensure] $Ensure

    [DscProperty()]
    [string] $Description
    $path = 'HKLM:\SYSTEM\CurrentControlSet\Services\LanmanServer\Parameters'

    $valueName = 'svrcomment'
```

```
[ComputerDescription] Get() {
    $key = Get-Item $this.Path
    if ($key.GetValueNames() -contains $this.valueName) {
        $this.Ensure = 'Present'
        $this.Description = $key.GetValue($this.valueName)
    } else {
        $this.Ensure = 'Absent'
    }
    return $this
}

[void] Set() {
    $commonParams = @{
        Path = $this.path
        Name = $this.valueName
    }
    if ($this.Ensure -eq 'Present') {
        $newParams = @{
            Value = $this.Description
            Type  = 'String'
            Force = $true
        }
        New-ItemProperty @newParams @commonParams
    } else {
        $key = Get-Item $this.Path
        if ($key.GetValueNames() -contains $this.valueName) {
            Remove-ItemProperty @commonParams
        }
    }
}

[bool] Test() {
    $key = Get-Item $this.Path
    if ($this.Ensure -eq 'Present') {
        if (
            $key.GetValueNames() -notcontains $this.valueName
        ) {
            return $false
        }
        return $key.GetValue($this.valueName) -eq
```

```
                        $this.Description
            } else {
                return $key.GetValueNames() -notcontains
                    $this.valueName
            }
            return $true
        }
    }
}
```

DSC will only find the class using `Get-DscResource` if the following are true:

* The class is saved in a module.
* The module exports the DSC resource.
* The module is in one of the paths in `$env:PSMODULEPATH` for Windows PowerShell.
* The module path is system-wide and accessible by the **Local Configuration Manager** (**LCM**).

The following script creates the files and folders required to achieve under `Program Files`. The module is installed in a path used by Windows PowerShell. The script will require administrative rights:

```
$modulePath = 'C:\Program Files\WindowsPowerShell\Modules'
$newItemParams = @{
    Path     = Join-Path $modulePath 'LocalMachine\1.0.0\LocalMachine.psm1'
    ItemType = 'File'
    Force    = $true
}
New-Item @newItemParams
$joinPathParams = @{
    Path      = $modulePath
    ChildPath = 'LocalMachine\1.0.0\LocalMachine.psd1'
}
$newModuleManifestParams = @{
    Path                = Join-Path @joinPathParams
    RootModule          = 'LocalMachine.psm1'
    ModuleVersion       = '1.0.0'
    DscResourcesToExport = 'ComputerDescription'
}
New-ModuleManifest @newModuleManifestParams
```

The `LocalMachine.psm1` file should be edited, adding the `Ensure` enumeration and the `ComputerDescription` class.

Once this is done, Get-DscResource can be used in Windows PowerShell:

```
PS> Get-DscResource ComputerDescription

ImplementedAs Name                     ModuleName   Version Propertie
------------- ----                     ----------   ------- ----------
PowerShell    ComputerDescription LocalMachine 1.0.0   {Ensure,...
```

Invoke-DscResource, which interacts with the LCM, can also be used. The example below calls the Get method. This can only be used in Windows PowerShell when it is being run as administrator:

```
$params = @{
    Name = 'ComputerDescription'
    ModuleName = 'LocalMachine'
    Method     = 'Get'
    Property = @{
        Ensure = 'Present'
        Description = 'New description'
    }
}
Invoke-DscResource @params
```

If the command above completes successfully, it will provide the output shown below:

```
ConfigurationName    :
DependsOn            :
ModuleName           : LocalMachine
ModuleVersion        : 1.0.0
PsDscRunAsCredential :
ResourceId           :
SourceInfo           :
Description          : New description
Ensure               : Absent
PSComputerName       : localhost
```

Alternatively, the class can be directly used with the using module command. Note that the module only exists in the Windows PowerShell module path if the steps above were followed. The module can be copied to C:\Program Files\PowerShell\Modules if required:

```
using module LocalMachine

$class = [ComputerDescription]@{
    Ensure      = 'Present'
    Description = 'Computer description'
}
```

Individual methods may be invoked; for example, Get can be run:

```
PS> $class.Get()

Ensure    Description
------    -----------
Absent    Computer description
```

Classes provide a concise way of implementing DSC resources and can be used outside of the context of DSC by making use of using module.

Summary

Enumerations in PowerShell are useful for defining customized lists of constant values for use within a script, function, or module. The values in the enumeration can be used if required, or the enumeration can be used as little more than a list of names.

Flag-based enumerations are used when managing flag-based fields. The FileSystemRights enumeration was used as a basis for demonstrating capabilities.

Classes in PowerShell can be used to describe any object. Classes include members such as properties and methods. The hidden keyword can be used to hide either properties or methods from view.

Class inheritance is a vital part of working with classes. One class can inherit properties and methods from another, allowing a layered approach to class implementation with shared code in underlying classes.

Inheritance-style notation is the basis for implementing interfaces from .NET in a class in PowerShell. The IComparable and IEquatable interfaces and the operator support that interfaces can add were demonstrated.

Casting and coercing types in PowerShell is a complex process. Constructors and the Parse static method allow PowerShell to cast from a fixed type to a class defined in PowerShell. The implicit conversion operator can be implemented as a static method named op_Implicit in a PowerShell class to allow casting to one or two other types.

The new NoRunspaceAffinity attribute introduced in PowerShell 7.3 was discussed; it is an important tool for classes that expect to be used across runspaces.

Classes in PowerShell can be used to implement custom argument transformation and validation attributes. The validation and transformation classes are derived from abstract classes in the System.Management.Automation namespace.

In PowerShell 6, ValidateSet gained the ability to use a dynamic set provided by a class implementing the IValidateSetValuesGenerator interface. The creation and use of the validator were demonstrated.

Argument completers can be written using classes, offering the ability to define arguments that should be passed to a completer.

Microsoft Desired State Configuration is one of the driving forces behind the existence of classes in PowerShell. A simple DSC resource that allows a computer description to be set via the registry was created and demonstrated.

Functions and classes are pulled together in the next chapter, which explores building modules.

Online Chapter

Chapter 20 is an online-only chapter that explores the key concepts of creating modules in PowerShell.

Scan this QR code or visit the link to access the chapter:

`https://static.packt-cdn.com/downloads/9781805120278_Chapter_20.pdf`

Learn more on Discord

Read this book alongside other users, PowerShell experts, and the author himself. Ask questions, provide solutions to other readers, chat with the author via Ask Me Anything sessions, and much more.

Scan the QR code or visit the link to join the community.

`https://packt.link/SecNet`

21

Testing

The goal of testing in PowerShell is to ensure that the code works as intended. Automatic testing ensures that this continues to be the case as code is changed over time.

Testing often begins before code is ready to execute. PSScriptAnalyzer can look at code and provide advice on possible best practices that help prevent common mistakes. PSScriptAnalyzer uses what is known as static analysis.

Unit testing, the testing of the smallest units of code, starts when the code is ready to execute. Tests can be created before the code when following practices such as **Test-Driven Development (TDD)**. A unit test focuses on the smallest parts of a module, the functions, and classes. A unit test strives to validate the inner workings of a unit of code, ensuring that conditions evaluate correctly, that it terminates or returns where it should, and so on.

Testing might extend into systems and acceptance testing, although this often requires a test environment to act against. Acceptance testing may include black-box testing, which is used to verify that a command accepts known parameters and generates an expected set of results. Black-box testing, as the name suggests, does not concern itself with understanding how a block of code arrives at a result.

This chapter makes use of Pester, a PowerShell module that provides a framework for authoring tests.

This chapter covers the following topics:

- Static analysis
- Testing with Pester

This chapter makes use of several modules that must be installed; let's cover those first.

Technical requirements

The following modules are used in this chapter:

- PSScriptAnalyzer 1.21.1
- ShowPSAst 1.0
- Pester 5.5.0

PSScriptAccnalyzer and ShowPSAst are used when exploring static analysis.

Static analysis

Static analysis is the process of evaluating code without executing it. As mentioned in the introduction, PSScriptAnalyzer uses static analysis.

In PowerShell, static analysis most often makes use of an **Abstract Syntax Tree (AST)**: a tree-like representation of a piece of code. In PowerShell, an element of a script is represented by a node in the syntax tree. AST was introduced with PowerShell 3.

The largest elements represent the script itself, the root of the tree in effect. Each element added to the script is represented by a child node. For example, the parameter block is described by a ParamBlockAst object, an individual parameter by a ParameterAst, and so on.

A simple script block can be used as an example:

```
$scriptBlock = {
    param ( $String )
    Write-Host $String
}
```

This simple script block contains the nodes shown in *Figure 21.1*:

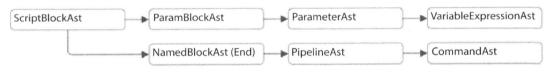

Figure 21.1: AST nodes

If the script had more than one parameter, more ParameterAst nodes would be linked to the ParamBlockAst.

If the script had more than one command, additional PipelineAst nodes would be added.

Commands running in a pipeline, conditions expressed with if, loops, and so on would all add extra nodes to the diagram.

Evaluating elements of the AST is the basis for many of the rules implemented in PSScriptAnalyzer.

PSScriptAnalyzer

The PSScriptAnalyzer module is used to run a series of rules against a file or string containing a script. PSScriptAnalyzer can be installed using the following code:

```
Install-Module PSScriptAnalyzer
```

PSScriptAnalyzer inspects a script with the `Invoke-ScriptAnalzyer` command. For example, the tool will raise one error and one warning for the following script:

```
@'
[CmdletBinding()]
param (
    [Parameter(Mandatory)]
    [String]$Password
)
$credential = [PSCredential]::new(
    '.\user',
    ($Password | ConvertTo-SecureString -AsPlainText -Force)
)
$credential.GetNetworkCredential().Password
'@ | Set-Content Show-Password.ps1
```

When `Invoke-ScriptAnalyzer` is run on the file, two rule violations are shown—one for the use of `ConvertTo-SecureString` and one for the `$Password` parameter using plain text:

```
PS> Invoke-ScriptAnalyzer .\Show-Password.ps1 | Format-List


RuleName : PSAvoidUsingConvertToSecureStringWithPlainText
Severity : Error
Line     : 9
Column   : 18
Message  : File 'Show-Password.ps1' uses ConvertTo-SecureString
           with plaintext. This will expose secure information.
           Encrypted standard strings should be used instead.
RuleName : PSAvoidUsingPlainTextForPassword
Severity : Warning
Line     : 3
Column   : 5
Message  : Parameter '$Password' should use SecureString,
           otherwise this will expose sensitive information. See
           ConvertTo-SecureString for more information.
```

This is one of many best practice style rules that can be used to test a script.

Configurable rules

PSScriptAnalyzer includes many default rules. Most of these rules are automatically evaluated when a script is analyzed. Several rules require configuration before they can be used; these are not enabled by default.

The following command shows the rules that must be explicitly configured before they can be applied:

```
Get-ScriptAnalyzerRule | Where-Object {
    $_.ImplementingType.BaseType.Name -eq 'ConfigurableRule'
}
```

Conversely, the rules that are evaluated by default (without extra configuration) are shown with the following command:

```
Get-ScriptAnalyzerRule | Where-Object {
    $_.ImplementingType.BaseType.Name -ne 'ConfigurableRule'
}
```

Configurable rules may be configured using either a settings file or a hashtable that describes the configuration for a rule. The following example shows how to use the PSUseCorrectCasing rule against a script read from a string:

```
$params = @{
    ScriptDefinition = 'get-process'
    Settings = @{
        Rules = @{
            PSUseCorrectCasing = @{
                Enable = $true
            }
        }
    }
}
Invoke-ScriptAnalyzer @params
```

Once the configuration for the rule is added, the rule will execute according to the settings for that rule. The settings for the rule are documented in the PSScriptAnalyzer repository. The documentation for PSUseCorrectCasing can be found here: https://github.com/PowerShell/PSScriptAnalyzer/blob/master/docs/Rules/UseCorrectCasing.md.

Note that the rule documentation omits the PS prefix on the rule name. Several other rules, such as PlaceOpenBrace, require configuration in a similar manner.

PSScriptAnalyzer includes several built-in settings files, which will tab complete when using the Settings parameter. For example:

```
Invoke-ScriptAnalyzer .\Show-Password.ps1 -Settings CodeFormatting
```

The settings used by each are not documented in Help for the module, but the content of each file can be viewed in the module directory. These files can be used as they are, or as an example to build a customized settings file.

The settings files shipped with PSScriptAnalyzer can be viewed on GitHub: https://github.com/ PowerShell/PSScriptAnalyzer/tree/master/Engine/Settings.

It is sometimes hard to meet the requirements of all the rules in PSScriptAnalyzer. Rules can be suppressed globally in the settings file, or rules can be suppressed in code.

Suppressing rules

It is rarely realistic to expect any significant piece of code to pass all the tests that PSScriptAnalyzer will throw at it.

Individual tests can be suppressed at the function, script, or class level. The following demonstrative function creates a PSCustomObject:

```
@'
function New-Message {
    [CmdletBinding()]
    param (
        $Message
    )

    [PSCustomObject]@{
        Name  = 1
        Value = $Message
    }
}
'@ | Set-Content New-Message.ps1
```

Running PSScriptAnalyzer against a file containing the function will show the following warning:

```
PS> Invoke-ScriptAnalyzer -Path .\New-Message.ps1 | Format-List


RuleName  : PSUseShouldProcessForStateChangingFunctions
Severity  : Warning
Line      : 1
Column    : 10
Message   : Function 'New-Message' has verb that could change
            system state. Therefore, the function has to support
            'ShouldProcess'.
```

Given that this function creates a new object in memory and does not change the system state, the message might be suppressed. This is achieved by adding a SuppressMessage attribute before a param block:

```
function New-Message {
    [Diagnostics.CodeAnalysis.SuppressMessage(
```

```
        'PSUseShouldProcessForStateChangingFunctions',
        ''
    )]
    [CmdletBinding()]
    param (
        $Message
    )

    [PSCustomObject]@{
        Name  = 1
        Value = $Message
    }
}
```

PSScriptAnalyzer leverages an existing class from .NET to express suppressed rules. Visual Studio Code will offer to create an attribute when "suppress" is typed. The second argument, set to an empty string in the preceding example, is required.

The empty string used in the example above can be filled in to limit what a suppression applies to. The value can be filled with a RuleSuppressionId from a triggered rule.

In the following example, the PSReviewUnusedParameter rule will trigger for both the Message and PassThru parameters:

```
$script = @'
function Send-Message {
    [CmdletBinding()]
    param (
        $Message,

        $PassThru
    )
}
'@


Invoke-ScriptAnalyzer -ScriptDefinition $script
```

The example below shows the output of running the rule and includes the RuleSuppressionID. In this case, it is simply the parameter name:

```
Invoke-ScriptAnalyzer -ScriptDefinition $script |
    Format-List Message, RuleName, RuleSuppressionID
```

The command above will show the triggered rules shown below:

```
Message           : The parameter 'Message' has been declared but not used.
RuleName          : PSReviewUnusedParameter
RuleSuppressionID : Message

Message           : The parameter 'PassThru' has been declared but not used.
RuleName          : PSReviewUnusedParameter
RuleSuppressionID : PassThru
```

If there is a good reason to accept but not use a specific parameter, the rule can be suppressed for just that one parameter. The rule is suppressed for the Message parameter in the example below:

```
function Send-Message {
    [Diagnostics.CodeAnalysis.SuppressMessage(
        'PSReviewUnusedParameter',
        'Message'
    )]
    [CmdletBinding()]
    param (
        $Message,

        $PassThru
    )
}
```

The rule will continue to trigger for the PassThru parameter.

Any suppression attribute can optionally include a Justification message. Justification is a named argument for SuppressMessage, as shown in the example below:

```
function Send-Message {
    [Diagnostics.CodeAnalysis.SuppressMessage(
        'PSReviewUnusedParameter',
        'Message',
        Justification = 'Accepted, but not used'
    )]
    [CmdletBinding()]
    param (
        $Message,

        $PassThru
    )
}
```

AST is the basis for most of the rules used by `PSScriptAnalyzer`.

Using AST

The AST in PowerShell is available for any script block; an example is as follows:

```
PS> { Write-Host 'content' }.Ast

Attributes          : {}
UsingStatements     : {}
ParamBlock          :
BeginBlock          :
ProcessBlock        :
EndBlock            : Write-Host 'content'
DynamicParamBlock   :
ScriptRequirements  :
Extent              : { Write-Host 'content' }
Parent              : { Write-Host 'content' }
```

The object returned describes each of the elements of the script (or script block in this case). It shows that the command in the script block is in the end block, the default block.

The script block that defines a function can be retrieved via `Get-Command`:

```
function Write-Content { Write-Host 'content' }

(Get-Command Write-Content).ScriptBlock
```

The script block defining a function can be retrieved using `Get-Item`:

```
function Write-Content { Write-Host 'content' }

(Get-Item function:\Write-Content).ScriptBlock
```

The preceding approaches have one thing in common: PowerShell is immediately parsing the script and will stop if there are any parser errors. The impact of this can be seen if an error is inserted into a script block; the syntax tree will not be accessible:

```
PS> {
    Write-Host
    --String--
}
ParserError:
Line |
   3 |        --String--
     |            ~
     | Missing expression after unary operator '--'.
```

To allow access to the AST, regardless of errors in the script, the Parser class can be used to read content either from a file or from a string.

The Parser class is accessed under the System.Management.Automation.Language namespace. The following example uses the ParseInput method to read PowerShell content from a string:

```
using namespace System.Management.Automation.Language

$script = @'
Write-Host
--String--
'@
$ast = [Parser]::ParseInput($script,  [ref]$null, [ref]$null)
```

The ParseFile method can be used in place of ParseInput. The same arguments are used but the string containing the script can be replaced for a path to a file (a full path, not a relative path).

Two of the method arguments to the ParseInput method in the previous example are set as references to $null. This essentially means they are ignored at this point. Ordinarily, the first would be used to fill an existing array of tokens, and the second, an array of errors. Tokens are explored in more detail later in this section.

The errors array reference can be used to capture parse-time errors, such as the error shown when attempting to create the script block:

```
using namespace System.Management.Automation.Language

$errors = $tokens = @()
$script = @'
Write-Host
--String—
'@
$ast = [Parser]::ParseInput($script,  [ref]$tokens, [ref]$errors)
```

The content of the array can be viewed after the ParseInput method has completed:

```
PS> $errors | Format-List


Extent          :
ErrorId         : MissingExpressionAfterOperator
Message         : Missing expression after unary operator '--'.
IncompleteInput : False
Extent          : String--
ErrorId         : UnexpectedToken
Message         : Unexpected token 'String--' in expression or statement.
IncompleteInput : False
```

The original script block only showed one error, but parsing stopped at the first error. This approach shows all syntax errors. If attempting to fix such errors, a top-down approach is required; one syntax error can easily cause another.

Returning to the AST object, the object represents a tree; therefore, it is possible to work down the list of properties to get to more specific elements of the script. Each element has a different type. The following example includes ScriptBlockAst, StatementAst, NamedBlockAst, PipelineAst, and CommandAst (and more as the more detailed elements of the script are explored).

The following example gets the CommandAst for the Get-Process command. That is the part of the script that represents just Get-Process -ID $PID:

```
$ast = { Get-Process -ID $PID | Select-Object Name, Path }.Ast
$ast.EndBlock.Statements[0].PipelineElements[0]
```

All named blocks, such as the EndBlock here, can contain zero or more statements. Each statement can contain one or more pipeline elements. The Select-Object command in this example is in index 1 of the PipelineElements property.

ShowPSAst can be used to visualize the tree; the module uses Windows Forms to draw a GUI and is therefore only compatible with Windows systems.

Visualizing the AST

The ShowPSAst module, available in the PowerShell Gallery, may be used to visualize the AST tree. Install the module with:

```
Install-Module ShowPSAst -Scope CurrentUser
```

Once installed, the Show-Ast command can be used on a string, a function, a module, a script block, and so on. Running the following command will show the AST tree in an **Ast Explorer** window:

```
Show-Ast 'Get-Process -ID $PID | Select-Object Name, Path'
```

Figure 21.2 shows the **Ast Explorer** window:

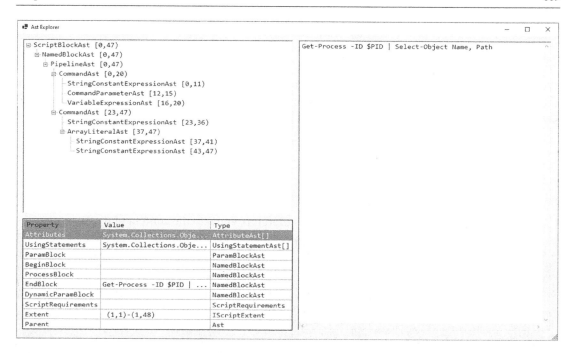

Figure 21.2: The Ast Explorer window

This tiny script with just one short line of code has 12 separate nodes in the AST. Attempting to access individual elements of a script by expanding each property and array index quickly becomes impractical in large scripts.

It is possible to search the AST tree using the Find and FindAll methods on any AST node.

Searching the AST

Searches against the AST can use the Find, which finds the first match only, and FindAll methods of any AST node. The methods find descendant nodes of the current node. Therefore, a search on a PipelineAst instance will only find results beneath that node.

An earlier example found the CommandAst for Get-Process by expanding properties in the AST:

```
$ast = { Get-Process -ID $PID | Select-Object Name, Path }.Ast
$ast.EndBlock.Statements[0].PipelineElements[0]
```

This can be rewritten to use the Find method instead. The key to the Find method is a predicate. The predicate is a script block that returns true or false. Each node is tested against the predicate and is output if the result is true.

Therefore, the simplest predicate is as follows:

```
$predicate = { $true }
```

When used with the Find method, the first matching node is returned. This will be the ScriptBlockAst, the top-most node in the tree. The second argument states whether the Find (or FindAll) method should search nested script blocks. More on this shortly:

```
using namespace System.Management.Automation.Language


$ast = { Get-Process -ID $PID | Select-Object Name, Path }.Ast
$predicate = { $true }
```

Find will show the ScriptBlockAst object and is therefore equal to the content of the $ast variable:

```
PS> $ast.Find($predicate, $true)

Attributes          : {}
UsingStatements     : {}
ParamBlock          :
BeginBlock          :
ProcessBlock        :
EndBlock            : Get-Process -ID $PID | Select-Object Name, Path
DynamicParamBlock   :
ScriptRequirements  :
Extent              : { Get-Process -ID $PID | Select-Object Name,
                      Path }
Parent              : { Get-Process -ID $PID | Select-Object Name,
                      Path }
```

Finding the node for the Get-Process command requires a more complex predicate. Each node in the AST is passed as an argument into the predicate. This can either be accessed using $args[0] or by defining a parameter to accept that value (as the following code shows). The AST type required is CommandAst. CommandAst has a GetCommandName method, which can be used to separate the command name from the arguments. Here is the updated predicate:

```
using namespace System.Management.Automation.Language


$ast = { Get-Process -ID $PID | Select-Object Name, Path }.Ast
$predicate = {
    param ( $node )
    $node -is [CommandAst] -and
    $node.GetCommandName() -eq 'Get-Process'
}
```

This time, the result of the search is the node describing Get-Process:

```
PS> $ast.Find($predicate, $true)


CommandElements     : {Get-Process, ID, $PID}
InvocationOperator  : Unknown
DefiningKeyword     :
Redirections        : {}
Extent              : Get-Process -ID $PID
Parent              : Get-Process -ID $PID | Select-Object Name, Path
```

As shown in the preceding example, each AST node returns an Extent property. The Extent property describes information about the position of a node within the larger script, such as where it begins and ends:

```
PS> $ast.Find($predicate, $true).Extent

File                :
StartScriptPosition : System.Management.Automation.Language.Int...
EndScriptPosition   : System.Management.Automation.Language.Int...
StartLineNumber     : 1
StartColumnNumber   : 10
EndLineNumber       : 1
EndColumnNumber     : 30
Text                : Get-Process -ID $PID
StartOffset         : 9
EndOffset           : 29
```

Line and column numbers may vary depending on the source script.

This information can potentially be used to selectively edit a script if required. This technique is used by several commands in the PSKoans module (https://github.com/vexx32/PSKoans) to replace or update content in existing scripts.

As mentioned at the start of this section, searches like this are the basis for many of the rules in PSScriptAnalyzer. PSScriptAnalyzer supports a second type of rule, one based on tokens within a script.

Tokenizer

In addition to the AST, PowerShell can also convert a script into a series of tokens, each representing an element of a script with no hierarchy.

One of the advantages of the tokenizer is that it will return tokens representing comments, whereas the AST ignores comments entirely:

```
using namespace System.Management.Automation.Language

$errors = $tokens = @()
$script = @'
# A short script
Write-Host 'Hello world'
'@
$ast = [Parser]::ParseInput($script,  [ref]$tokens, [ref]$errors)
```

Once executed, the tokens that make up the script can be examined. The first two tokens are shown here:

```
PS> $tokens | Select-Object -First 2

Text       : # A short script
TokenFlags : ParseModeInvariant
Kind       : Comment
HasError   : False
Extent     : # A short script

Text       :
TokenFlags : ParseModeInvariant
Kind       : NewLine
HasError   : False
Extent     :
```

Tokens are less useful than the AST when it comes to defining rules. The lack of context makes it more difficult to relate one token to another beyond the order in the array. Tokens might be used in a rule to validate the content of comments if necessary.

The AST and tokens are used by PSScriptAnalyzer to implement rules.

Custom script analyzer rules

PSScriptAnalyzer allows custom rules to be defined and used. Custom rules might be used to test for personal or organization-specific conventions when striving for a consistent style; such conventions may not necessarily be widely adopted best practices, but instead locally established best practices.

Script analyzer rules must be defined in a module psm1 file. The path to the module file may be passed in by using the CustomRulePath parameter or may be defined in a script analyzer configuration file.

Creating a custom rule

A script analyzer rule is a function within a module. The PSScriptAnalyzer module allows rules to be written to evaluate AST nodes or tokens.

The name of the function is arbitrary. The community examples use the verb measure; however, the use of this verb is not mandatory and does not affect discovery. The community example is linked here for reference: https://learn.microsoft.com/powershell/utility-modules/psscriptanalyzer/create-custom-rule.

The following examples use a much more lightweight format. This does not sacrifice functionality.

The script analyzer engine examines each function in the custom rule module, looking for parameters with a particular naming style. If a parameter is found, the function is deemed to be a rule.

If a rule is expected to act based on an AST node, the first parameter name must end with ast. The parameter must use one of the AST types, such as System.Management.Automation.Language. ScriptBlockAst.

If a rule is expected to act based on a token, the first parameter name must end with token and must accept an array of tokens.

AST-based rules

Script analyzer rules are often simple; it is not always necessary for a rule to perform complex AST searches.

The following example evaluates the named blocks dynamicparam, begin, process, and end. If one of the blocks is declared in a function, script, or script block and it is empty, the rule will respond.

The rule only accepts NamedBlockAst nodes, the smallest scope for the rule to effectively evaluate the script. The script analyzer only passes nodes of that type to the rule; therefore, the rule itself does not have to worry about handling other node types or performing searches itself.

The rule simply looks to see if the number of statements in the block is 0. If it is 0, then the rule triggers.

The following rule is expected to be placed in a psm1 file. For the sake of this example, that file can be named CustomRules.psm1:

```
Set-Content CustomRules.psm1 -Value @'
using namespace Microsoft.Windows.PowerShell.ScriptAnalyzer.Generic
using namespace System.Management.Automation.Language

function PSAvoidEmptyNamedBlocks {
    [CmdletBinding()]
    param (
        [NamedBlockAst]
        $ast
    )
```

```
    if ($ast.Statements.Count -eq 0) {
        [DiagnosticRecord]@{
            Message  = 'Empty {0} block.' -f $ast.BlockKind
            Extent   = $ast.Extent
            RuleName = $MyInvocation.MyCommand.Name
            Severity = 'Warning'
        }
    }
}
'@
```

The rule returns DiagnosticRecord when it is triggered. The record is returned by the script analyzer provided the rule is not suppressed. The next command shows the rule in action:

```
@'
[CmdletBinding()]
param ( )

begin { }

process { }

end {
    Write-Host 'Hello world'
}
'@ | Set-Content script.ps1

$params = @{
    Path           = 'script.ps1'
    CustomRulePath = '.\CustomRules.psm1'
}
Invoke-ScriptAnalyzer @params
```

The output from the command flags the begin and process blocks as they are empty:

```
PS> Invoke-ScriptAnalyzer @params


RuleName                   Severity ScriptName Line Message
--------                   -------- ---------- ---- -------
PSAvoidEmptyNamedBlocks Warning  script.ps1 4    Empty Begin ...
PSAvoidEmptyNamedBlocks Warning  script.ps1 5    Empty Process...
```

Token-based rules are written in a similar manner.

Token-based rules

Rules based on tokens evaluate an array of tokens. The following example looks for empty single-line comments in a block of code. Comments are not a part of the syntax tree, so using tokens is the only option. This new rule can be added to the CustomRules.psm1 file created in the previous section:

```
using namespace Microsoft.Windows.PowerShell.ScriptAnalyzer.Generic
using namespace System.Management.Automation.Language

function PSAvoidEmptyComments {
    [CmdletBinding()]
    param (
        [Token[]]
        $token
    )

    $ruleName = $MyInvocation.MyCommand.Name
    $token | Where-Object {
        $_.Kind -eq 'Comment' -and
        $_.Text.Trim() -eq '#'
    } | ForEach-Object {
        [DiagnosticRecord]@{
            Message   = 'Empty comment.'
            Extent    = $_.Extent
            RuleName  = $ruleName
            Severity  = 'Information'
        }
    }
}
```

As the name suggests, the rule will trigger when it encounters an empty line comment. This is demonstrated by the following example:

```
@'
[CmdletBinding()]
param ( )
#
# Comment
Write-Host 'Hello world'
'@ | Set-Content script.ps1
```

The output from `Invoke-ScriptAnalyzer` shows the line that failed:

```
$params = @{
    Path            = 'script.ps1'
    CustomRulePath = '.\CustomRules.psm1'
}
Invoke-ScriptAnalyzer @params
```

The script will trigger the new rule about avoiding empty comments, as shown below:

```
RuleName              Severity     ScriptName Line  Message
--------              --------     ---------- ----  -------
PSAvoidEmptyComments  Information  script.ps1 4     Empty comment.
```

> **More custom rules**
>
> For more examples of custom rules, please see:
>
> https://github.com/indented-automation/Indented.ScriptAnalyzerRules.

`PSScriptAnalyzer` is a fantastic tool that can attempt to enforce a specific style or help fix common problems.

Testing with Pester

Pester is a framework for executing tests. It includes tools to define and execute test cases against anything that can be written in PowerShell.

This part of the chapter focuses on Pester 5, the latest major release. Pester 5 is not installed by default; Windows ships with Pester 3.4. This pre-installed version can be ignored. If Pester is already installed, `Force` must be used and the publisher check must be skipped. Otherwise, the two additional parameters below can be ignored:

```
Install-Module Pester -Force -SkipPublisherCheck
```

The `SkipPublisherCheck` parameter is required as Pester has changed maintainer since the version shipped with Windows was released. The certificate issued to the pre-installed version differs from the certificate issued to the current version.

Pester can be used to write tests for code, systems, and everything in between. Pester is implemented as what is known as a **Domain-Specific Language (DSL)**. It has specific functions that are implemented to behave like language keywords. For example, *function* is a language-specific keyword. Pester tests are written using PowerShell, but for the most part, the language, keywords, and so on, are defined by and specific to Pester.

The following example creates a test that asserts that PowerShell 7 or greater should be in use. If the test runs in Windows PowerShell, the test will fail, and the results of that failure will be displayed to someone running the test. Pester tests are most often saved to a file before running `Invoke-Pester`:

```
@'
Describe 'PS developer workstation' {
    It 'PowerShell 7 is installed' {
        $PSVersionTable.PSVersion |
            Should -BeGreaterOrEqual 7.0.0
    }

    It 'Workspace must exist' {
        'C:\workspace' | Should -Exist
    }
}
'@ | Set-Content workstation.tests.ps1
Invoke-Pester -Path workstation.tests.ps1
```

The outcome of running the test is displayed in the console, although the results of the test are summarized by default. Times to perform discovery and execute tests may vary:

```
PS> Invoke-Pester -Path workstation.tests.ps1
Starting discovery in 1 files.
Discovery finished in 5ms.
[+] C:\workspace\workstation.tests.ps1 91ms (2ms|86ms)
Tests completed in 93ms
Tests Passed: 1, Failed: 0, Skipped: 0 NotRun: 0
```

Tests may also be run directly in the console by creating a PesterContainer:

```
$container = New-PesterContainer -ScriptBlock {
    Describe 'PS developer workstation' {
        It 'PowerShell 7 is installed' {
            $PSVersionTable.PSVersion |
                Should -BeGreaterOrEqual 7.0.0
        }

        It 'Workspace must exist' {
            'C:\workspace' | Should -Exist
        }
    }
}
Invoke-Pester -Container $container
```

Setting the Output parameter to Detailed will show the results of each of the tests performed in the script:

```
PS> Invoke-Pester -Path workstation.tests.ps1 -Output Detailed
Pester v5.5.0

Starting discovery in 1 files.
Discovery found 2 tests in 12ms.
Running tests.

Running tests from 'C:\workspace\workstation.tests.ps1'
Describing PS developer workstation
  [+] PowerShell 7 is installed 13ms (4ms|9ms)
  [+] Workspace must exist 5ms (4ms|0ms)
Tests completed in 53ms
Tests Passed: 2, Failed: 0, Skipped: 0 NotRun: 0
```

This section focuses on test file content and not on the process of saving that content to a file. Test content should be saved to a file and run in the same manner as the preceding examples.

Note that the Invoke-Pester command specifically looks for .tests.ps1 in filenames by default.

The previous example uses three of the major keywords used in Pester:

- Describe: Groups tests for a particular subject together
- It: Defines a single test that should be executed
- Should: Asserts what the value or result of an expression should be

The condition used with the Should keyword simply states that the major version number should be 7 or greater.

Testing methodologies

Testing is a complex topic; it encompasses a wide range of different methodologies and concepts. The majority of these are beyond the scope of this chapter. Further reading is available on sites such as Wikipedia: https://en.wikipedia.org/wiki/Software_testing.

Two methodologies are of interest in this chapter. They are:

- Acceptance testing
- Unit testing

Acceptance testing is used to validate that the subject of the tests conforms to a pre-defined state. The test for the version of PowerShell at the start of this section might be part of an acceptance test for a developer workstation.

Acceptance testing in relation to PowerShell development strives to test the outcome of actions performed by a command (or script) without having any knowledge of how that script works. Therefore, acceptance testing is a form of black-box testing and requires a system that code can be run against.

Unit testing aims to test the smallest units of code and is a form of white-box testing. The author of a unit test must be familiar with the inner workings of the subject of the test.

Unit testing is most relevant in PowerShell when testing that the components of a module behave as they are expected to behave: that the different paths through a function, based on `if` statements and loops, are used correctly. Unit testing does not require a live service to act on. External calls are mocked, and a fake response is returned. Mocking is explored later in this chapter.

The advantage of putting tests in code is that they can be run whenever the state of the subject changes. It is possible to continue to prove that the subject of a set of tests is working as expected.

One of the most challenging aspects of any testing process is figuring out what should be tested.

What to test

When testing systems, or performing acceptance testing, the following are rough examples of things that might be tested:

- Installed software packages
- Filesystem paths or environment variables
- Application or service configuration
- Responses from remote systems that the subject is expected to interact with
- Network access and network configuration

When testing a module, or performing unit testing, consider testing the following:

- `Parameters` (and parameter binding)
- Any complex conditions and branches (conditional statements and loops) in the code
- Acceptance of different input or expected values, including complex parameter validation
- Exit conditions, especially raised errors or exceptions

When writing a unit test, resist the temptation to test other functions or commands called by the unit of code. A unit test is not responsible for making sure that every command that it calls works.

How extensive tests should be is debatable. Enough to ensure the functionality of a given script or module is perhaps the only real definition.

Code coverage is one of the measures that is often used. This is the percentage of code that is visited when executing a set of tests. Pester is capable of measuring code coverage. The details of this are shown later in this section. However, while this is an interesting indicator, it does not prove that code has been effectively tested.

Perhaps the most important keywords in Pester are `Describe`, `It`, and `Should`. They are the backbone of any set of tests.

Describing tests

Pester includes keywords that are used to enclose and group tests together. This section explores the keywords that are used to enclose tests. They are:

- `Describe`
- `Context`
- `It`

The `Describe` and `Context` keywords are both used to enclose or group sets of tests. The tests themselves are defined within an `It` statement.

All test documents will include the `Describe` keyword and one or more `It` statements.

About the Describe and Context keywords

`Describe` is the most-used keyword in a test document. It most often describes the subject of the tests.

`Context` is essentially the same as `Describe`. It has the same capabilities and will contain one or more `It` statements. `Context` is typically used under `Describe` to group together small sets of tests, typically where the tests have a similar purpose or require similar start conditions.

A test document might have a broadly defined subject and several more specifically defined components. For example, a set of tests might be developed to describe the expected state of a developer workstation. The tests are broken down into more detailed subsections:

```
Describe 'PS developer workstation' {
    Context 'PowerShell' {
    }

    Context 'Packages' {
    }
}
```

The use of `Context` will become clear as tests grow in complexity and unit tests against PowerShell code are introduced later in this chapter.

`Describe`, or each `Context`, can include one or more `It` blocks, which describe the expected outcome.

About the It keyword

The `It` keyword is used to define a single test. The test title should describe the purpose and, potentially, the expected outcome of the test:

```
Describe 'PS developer workstation' {
    Context 'PowerShell' {
        It 'PowerShell 7 is installed' {
        }
```

```
        }

    Context 'Packages' {
        It 'git is installed' {
        }

        It 'Terraform is installed' {
        }
    }
}
```

The It keyword will contain one or more assertions using the Should keyword.

Should and assertions

The Should keyword is used to assert the state of the thing it is testing.

Should has 26 different parameter sets, one for each of the assertions it supports. The different assertions are documented in the Pester wiki along with an example: https://pester.dev/docs/assertions/.

The example used at the start of this section uses one of the possible assertions, the BeGreaterOrEqual assertion. Assertions have unsurprising options for the most part. If testing a Boolean value, BeTrue or BeFalse are appropriate.

Comparisons are achieved using Be, BeLessThan, BeLessOrEqual, BeGreaterThan, BeGreaterOrEqual, and so on.

The first of the tests, the test for the installation of PowerShell 7, can be changed to allow it to run in Windows PowerShell as well. The point is to prove that the system is in the expected state, not that the current runtime is PowerShell 7. The second Context is temporarily removed to focus on this one assertion:

```
Describe 'PS developer workstation' {
    Context 'PowerShell' {
        It 'PowerShell 7 is installed' {
            Get-Command pwsh -ErrorAction Ignore |
                ForEach-Object Version |
                Should -BeGreaterOrEqual '7.0.0'
        }
    }
}
```

Testing for errors is perhaps one of the most complex assertions and benefits from more extensive exploration. The Should -Throw assertion can be used to test whether a specific error is raised (or not) when running a command.

Testing for errors

The Throw assertion is used to test whether a block of code throws a terminating error such as one raised when ErrorAction is set to Stop or when the throw keyword is used.

The assertion can be used for several of the tests above, but for the sake of variety, it is only used to test for the installation of Chocolatey, a package manager for Windows:

```
Describe 'PS developer workstation' {
    Context 'PowerShell' {
        It 'PowerShell 7 is installed' {
            Get-Command pwsh -ErrorAction Ignore |
                ForEach-Object Version |
                Should -BeGreaterOrEqual '7.0.0'
        }
    }

    Context 'Packages' {
        It 'Chocolatey is installed' {
            { Get-Command choco -ErrorAction Stop } |
                Should -Not -Throw
        }
    }
}
```

Notice how the expression being tested is defined as a script block, and that the script block is piped to the Should keyword.

The assertion used in the preceding example expects there to be no error. Therefore, there is no need to test anything else about the error.

If an error is expected to be thrown, then further tests might be beneficial. For example, attempting to divide 1 by 0 will raise an error:

```
Describe Division {
    It 'Throws an error when 1 is divided by 0' {
        { 1/0 } | Should -Throw
    }
}
```

This type of test is not specific; it does not differentiate between the actual problem and any other error that might occur. Changing the assertion, as the following shows, will still correctly identify that an error is thrown, but the error is no longer consistent with the descriptive name for the It statement:

```
Describe Division {
    It 'Throws an error when 1 is divided by 0' {
```

```
            { throw } | Should -Throw
        }
    }
```

The tests for division can be run in a `PesterContainer`:

```
$container = New-PesterContainer -ScriptBlock {
    Describe Division {
        It 'Throws an error when 1 is divided by 0' {
            { throw } | Should -Throw
        }
    }
}
Invoke-Pester -Container $container
```

Adding the `-ExpectedMessage` parameter is one way to tackle this. Testing for a specific message will greatly improve the accuracy of the test:

```
Describe Division {
    It 'Throws an error when 1 is divided by 0' {
        { 1/0 } | Should -Throw -ExpectedMessage 'Attempted to divide by zero.'
    }
}
```

For the preceding exception, testing the message is potentially as good as it gets. However, since error messages are often written in a user's language, testing the message is a weak test as it demands that the tests are run in a specific culture.

The `-Throw` assertion allows both the error type and the fully qualified error ID to be tested instead. These are far more robust if the expression raising the error reveals them. The following example tests the fully qualified error ID:

```
Describe ErrorID {
    It 'Raises an error with a fully-qualified error ID' {
        { Write-Error error -ErrorID SomeErrorID -ErrorAction Stop } |
            Should -Throw -ErrorId SomeErrorID
    }
}
```

This type of testing is far more accurate; it may be possible to attribute the `ErrorID` to a single statement in the code being tested rather than testing for any error anywhere.

It is frequently necessary to perform setup actions prior to executing tests. Pester includes several named blocks for this purpose.

Iteration with Pester

It is often desirable to repeat the same test or tests for a different subject. Pester offers the ForEach parameter on Describe, Context, and It.

The ForEach parameter on an It statement has an alias of TestCases; the use of the parameter is identical to the use of TestCases in older versions of Pester.

The ForEach parameter for an It statement allows a single test to be executed against a set of pre-defined cases.

Using the ForEach parameter

The Packages context of the "PS developer workstation" acceptance tests is a good candidate for making use of the ForEach parameter. A few packages were listed in the example context. The following tests assert that each of these should have been installed using Chocolatey, a package manager for Windows that can be downloaded from https://chocolatey.org.

With Chocolatey, the installation of a package can be tested using the following command:

```
choco list -e terraform -l -r
```

If the exact package name (-e) is installed locally (-l), it will be included in the output from the command. The -r parameter is used to limit output to essential information only—in this case, just the package name and version.

The version of the installed package is not relevant as far as the following tests are concerned. The tests might be extended to ensure a specific version in a real-world implementation:

```
Describe 'PS developer workstation' {
    Context 'Packages' {
        It 'Chocolatey is installed' {
            { Get-Command choco -ErrorAction Stop } |
                Should -Not -Throw
        }

        It '<Name> is installed' -ForEach @(
            @{ Name = 'terraform' }
            @{ Name = 'git' }
        ) -Test {
            choco list -e $Name -l -r | Should -Match $Name
        }
    }
}
```

Values for ForEach are frequently defined as hashtables. When this is done, a variable is created for each key in the hashtable, as used in the example above.

The keys in the hashtable can be used in the It description by enclosing the name in < >.

The $_ variable may also be used to access the value from ForEach:

```
Describe 'PS developer workstation' {
    Context 'Packages' {
        It 'Chocolatey is installed' {
            { Get-Command choco -ErrorAction Stop } |
                Should -Not -Throw
        }

        It '<_> is installed' -ForEach @(
            'terraform'
            'git'
        ) -Test {
            choco list -e $Name -1 -r | Should -Match $_
        }
    }
}
```

The value of the case can be used in the It description by using an underscore instead of a key name, as shown in the example above.

Pester allows the expansion of properties of values in the description. For instance, using <Name.Length> from the first example (or <_.Length> from the second) in the description would show the length of the string. Not a very practical use in this case.

The outcome of running the tests can be viewed by saving the previous example to a file or making use of New-PesterContainer, such as workstation.tests.ps1, and using Invoke-Pester:

```
PS> Invoke-Pester -Path .\workstation.tests.ps1 -Output Detailed
Running tests from 'C:\workspace\workstation.tests.ps1'
Describing PS developer workstation
 Context Packages
   [+] Chocolatey is installed 20ms (15ms|5ms)
   [+] terraform is installed 802ms (799ms|3ms)
   [+] git is installed 786ms (786ms|1ms)
Tests completed in 1.79s
Tests Passed: 3, Failed: 0, Skipped: 0 NotRun: 0
```

The preceding tests are executed against a single subject, the local machine. The ForEach parameter of Describe or Context can be used to run a set of tests against more than one subject.

ForEach with Describe and Context

The ForEach parameter can be used to execute either a Describe or Context block against an array of values. Continuing with the theme of acceptance testing, it might be desirable to run a set of tests against several different servers.

The following tests assert that the DNS service exists on a set of Windows servers. The names of the servers are made up. The tests will potentially work if a meaningful set of names is provided:

```powershell
Describe "DNS servers" -ForEach @(
    'dns01'
    'dns02'
) {
    It 'The DNS service is running on <_>' {
        $params = @{
            ClassName    = 'Win32_Service'
            Filter       = 'Name="dns"'
            ComputerName = $_
        }
        Get-CimInstance @params | Should -Not -BeNullOrEmpty
    }
}
```

As with the use of ForEach with It, the <_> value in the description above is used to display the name of a specific computer.

Using a hashtable will bind variables based on keys for each of the values in ForEach, which is useful when making use of ForEach on more than one nested block:

```powershell
Describe "DNS servers" -ForEach @(
    @{ ComputerName = 'dns01' }
    @{ ComputerName = 'dns02' }
) {
    It 'The DNS service is running on <ComputerName>' {
        $params = @{
            ClassName    = 'Win32_Service'
            Filter       = 'Name="dns"'
            ComputerName = $ComputerName
        }
        Get-CimInstance @params | Should -Not -BeNullOrEmpty
    }
}
```

Get-CimInstance is used in the preceding example but Invoke-Command and Get-Service might be used instead if appropriate. Tests should be implemented in a way that is appropriate to the environment in which the test executes.

All the tests used in this section have the potential to fail and raise errors that are not handled within the test. In the cases of the tests using choco, the tests will raise an error if Chocolatey is not actually installed. In the case of the last example, the tests will raise an error if the server does not exist or Get-CimInstance fails for any other reason.

Problems of this kind can potentially be handled by skipping tests or marking a test as inconclusive.

Conditional testing

There are two possible approaches for dealing with tests that cannot be executed:

- The result of It can be forcefully set by using Set-ItResult.
- The test can be skipped entirely using the Skip parameter.

Set-ItResult can be used with the <Name> is installed test, enabling the test to account for situations where the choco command is not available.

Using Set-ItResult

The Set-ItResult command can be used inside any It statement. In the following example, it is used to change the result of the It statement based on the availability of the choco command:

```
Describe 'PS developer workstation' {
    Context 'Packages' {
        It '<_> is installed' -TestCases @(
            'terraform'
            'git'
        ) -Test {
            if (-not (Get-Command choco -ErrorAction Ignore)) {
                Set-ItResult -Skipped
            }

            choco list -e $_ -l -r | Should -Match $Name
        }
    }
}
```

The name of the test is changed in the result to show it has been skipped if the choco command is not available:

```
PS> Invoke-Pester -Path .\workstation.tests.ps1 -Output Detailed
Starting discovery in 1 files.
Discovering in C:\workspace\workstation.tests.ps1.
Found 2 tests. 27ms
Discovery finished in 31ms.
Running tests from 'C:\workspace\workstation.tests.ps1'
Describing PS developer workstation
 Context Packages
   [!] terraform is installed is skipped 14ms (9ms|5ms)
   [!] git is installed is skipped 2ms (1ms|1ms)
Tests completed in 217ms
Tests Passed: 0, Failed: 0, Skipped: 2 NotRun: 0
```

Set-ItResult allows the result to be set to Inconclusive, Pending, or Skipped.

The advantage of using Set-ItResult, in this case, is that the test cases are still processed. The Name value is expanded in the output of the tests. The -Skip parameter will stop Pester from expanding this value.

The Skip parameter can be used on any It block that is not using TestCases.

Using Skip

Skip, a switch parameter, can be used to bypass one or more tests.

An explicit value can be set for the parameter such as a value based on a variable. The following example changes the test for the installation of Chocolatey. It will be skipped if the current operating system is not Windows:

```
Describe 'PS developer workstation' {
    Context 'Packages' {
        It 'Chocolatey is installed' -Skip:(-not $IsWindows) {
            { Get-Command choco -ErrorAction Stop } |
                Should -Not -Throw
        }
    }
}
```

The $IsWindows, $IsMacOS, and $IsLinux variables are all automatically available in PowerShell 6 and above.

Values used with the Skip parameter must be available during the Discovery phase in Pester.

Pester phases

Pester 5 introduces the concept of different phases when executing tests. This is visible in the output of the tests run in this section:

```
Starting discovery in 1 files.
Discovering in C:\workspace\workstation.tests.ps1.
Found 2 tests. 27ms
Discovery finished in 31ms.
Running tests from 'C:\workspace\workstation.tests.ps1'
Describing PS developer workstation
```

First, the Discovery phase is run. During the Discovery phase, Pester attempts to find all the tests it will be running. Each test is defined by an It statement.

The Run phase will execute only those tests found during the Discovery phase.

This concept is new in Pester 5; it means that everything used to define what will be tested must be in place before discovery occurs, which affects the dynamic creation of tests.

Pester provides a BeforeDiscovery block, which may be placed either before or inside Describe. The code in BeforeDiscovery is, as the name suggests, executed before the Discovery run starts.

The last example used the predefined $IsWindows variable. As this is built-in, it is automatically available during the Discovery phase.

If the tests were instead to be executed based on a user-defined variable, this variable would need to be created in BeforeDiscovery. The same limitation applies to any test cases used with the TestCases parameter, and any arrays used with ForEach parameters.

An earlier example used ForEach to attempt to execute tests on an array of server names. If the server names had to be read from an external system, then that discovery action would be placed in the BeforeDiscovery block.

The following example uses the Get-ADComputer command from the ActiveDirectory module to get the list of servers to query. These tests will only succeed if the ActiveDirectory module is installed and it is able to find server names to test:

```
BeforeDiscovery {
    $dnsServers = Get-ADComputer -Filter 'name -like "dns*"'
}

Describe 'DNS servers' -ForEach $dnsServers -Fixture {
    It 'The DNS service is running on <_.Name>' {
        $params = @{
            ClassName    = 'Win32_Service'
            Filter       = 'Name="dns"'
            ComputerName = $_.DnsHostName
```

```
        }
        Get-CimInstance @params | Should -Not -BeNullOrEmpty
    }
}
```

BeforeDiscovery is therefore useful to ensure that the values needed to define which tests are present are in place when Pester is attempting to discover which tests are going to be executed.

Pester provides other named blocks to execute code at certain points during the Run phase. These can be used to define variables and set up conditions for tests. They should avoid defining which tests are executed.

Before and After blocks

Pester offers several blocks that can be used to perform actions before and after tests execute. Such blocks may be used to set up an environment or tear it down afterward.

The blocks are:

- BeforeAll
- BeforeEach
- AfterAll
- AfterEach

The All blocks execute once, before (or after) any of the tests in that block. The Each blocks execute before (or after) individual It blocks.

Each block can exist once in any Describe or Context block. If a Describe block contains BeforeAll, and a nested Context also contains BeforeAll, then both blocks will be executed (the Describe instance first, then the Context instance).

The BeforeAll and BeforeEach blocks are frequently used when defining a Mock for a command in unit testing.

Mocking commands

Mocking is used to reduce the scope of a set of tests and is a vital part of unit testing. Mocking allows the implementation of a command to be replaced with one defined in a test. Mocked commands are created using the Mock keyword.

The Mock keyword may be used in BeforeAll, BeforeEach, or It.

When mocking, it is important to consider the context. Mocks must be created in the right scope to be effective. When testing scripts, no specific action is required here, but when testing modules, the ModuleName parameter must be used. The ModuleName parameter describes the scope in which the mock is to be created, not the module that owns the mocked command.

As module testing tends to be more common, the examples that follow all make use of the ModuleName parameter.

The following command reads a CSV file, then either starts or stops a service based on whether that service matches the state in the file:

```
@'
function Set-ServiceState {
    [CmdletBinding()]
    param (
        [string]
        $Path
    )
    Import-Csv $Path | ForEach-Object {
        $service = Get-Service $_.Name
        if ($service.Status -ne $_.ExpectedStatus) {
            if ($_.ExpectedStatus -eq 'Stopped') {
                Stop-Service -Name $_.Name
            } else {
                Start-Service -Name $_.Name
            }
        }
    }
}
'@ | Set-Content -Path ServiceState.psm1
```

Place this function in a file named ServiceState.psm1; it will be used as the subject of the first set of unit tests.

To effectively test this command, the system running the tests would need to have all the services listed in the CSV file, and it would have to be possible to change the state of those services.

Instead, depending on a complete system to execute on, the results of the code can be tested by mocking each of the commands external to the function.

Two of the commands (Import-Csv and Get-Service) must return information, and two (Start-Service and Stop-Service) return nothing at all.

Using Mock for Start-Service and Stop-Service is therefore straightforward but, because this is a module, the ModuleName parameter must be used to create the mock inside the session state of the module being tested:

```
Mock Start-Service -ModuleName ServiceState
Mock Stop-Service -ModuleName ServiceState
```

If the subject of the tests were a script, ModuleName would not be required.

The output from `Import-Csv` and `Get-Service` needs to resemble the output from those real commands. The output can be simplified depending on what the command is expecting to do with that.

`Import-Csv` is expected to output an object with a `Name` and `ExpectedStatus` property:

```
Mock Import-Csv -ModuleName ServiceState {
    [PSCustomObject]@{
        Name = 'service1'
        ExpectedStatus = 'Running'
    }
}
```

`Get-Service` is expected to return an object with a `Status` property, but no other properties from `Get-Service` are used. Mocking `Get-Service` allows the tests to run even if the current computer does not have the service being tested:

```
Mock Get-Service -ModuleName ServiceState {
    [PSCustomObject]@{
        Status = 'Stopped'
    }
}
```

The name of the service is a parameter value for `Get-Service` and it is not used by the function. The name of the service can therefore be ignored in the object the mock emits.

Given the outputs that have been defined above, the expectation is that when running `Set-ServiceStatus`, the `Start-Service` command will be used to start `service1`.

Execution of the mock can be tested by using a `Should -Invoke` assertion. This example also includes a splat to reduce the repetition of the `ModuleName` parameter:

```
@'
BeforeDiscovery {
    Import-Module .\ServiceState.psm1 -Force
}

Describe Set-ServiceState {
    BeforeAll {
        $module = @{ ModuleName = 'ServiceState' }

        Mock Get-Service @module {
            [PSCustomObject]@{
                Status = 'Stopped'
            }
        }
        Mock Import-Csv @module {
```

```
            [PSCustomObject]@{
                Name          = 'service1'
                ExpectedStatus = 'Running'
            }
        }
    }
    Mock Start-Service @module
    Mock Stop-Service @module
}

It 'When ExpectedStatus is running, starts the service' {
    Set-ServiceState -Path file.csv

    Should -Invoke Start-Service @module
}
}
'@ | Set-Content ServiceState.tests.ps1
```

The previous command saves the tests in a `Set-ServiceState.tests.ps1` file. The content of this file is modified during this section; the size of the file prohibits repeating the content in full for each change.

As `Import-Csv` is being mocked in the tests, the name used for the file (the `Path` parameter) is not relevant and a made-up value can be used.

The result of running the tests is shown here:

```
PS> Invoke-Pester -Path .\ServiceState.tests.ps1
Starting discovery in 1 files.
Discovery finished in 10ms.
[+] C:\workspace\ServiceState.tests.ps1 127ms (16ms|102ms)
Tests completed in 130ms
Tests Passed: 1, Failed: 0, Skipped: 0 NotRun: 0
```

In this function, there are three possible paths through the code for each service:

- The service is in the expected state. `Start-Service` and `Stop-Service` should not run.
- The service state is stopped but was expected to be running. `Start-Service` should run.
- The service state is running but was expected to be stopped. `Stop-Service` should run.

Parameter values passed to mocks are bound to variables that can be used in the body of the `Mock`.

Parameter variables

The mock for `Get-Service` created in the example above can directly access any parameter values it has been passed by variable name:

```
Mock Get-Service @module {
    [PSCustomObject]@{
```

```
        Name    = $Name
        Status = 'Stopped'
    }
}
```

When writing functions in PowerShell, it is possible to determine whether a variable has been supplied or not by making use of the PSBoundParameters variable. For example:

```
function Test-BoundParameter {
    param (
        [string]
        $Name
    )
    $PSBoundParameters.ContainsKey('Name')
}
```

If Name is used with the function above, $PSBoundParameters.ContainsKey will return true—otherwise, false.

$PSBoundParameters cannot be effectively used inside Mock so Pester provides an alternative, $PesterBoundParameters. This has been added to the example below, although, in this case, the parameter is always supplied:

```
Mock Get-Service @module {
    if ($PesterBoundParameters.ContainsKey('Name')) {
        [PSCustomObject]@{
            Name    = $Name
            Status = 'Stopped'
        }
    }
}
```

A parameter filter for the Get-Service mock can be created to allow a different output based on the service name, which will allow each of the paths to be tested.

Parameter filtering

Parameter filters can be used to define when a specific Mock is used or to assert that a Mock has been called with specific parameters.

Parameter filters are added using the ParameterFilter parameter for Mock or Should -Invoke. The parameter filter is a script block that is most often used to test parameter values.

First, the mock for Import-Csv can be extended by adding two more services:

```
Mock Import-Csv @module {
    [PSCustomObject]@{
```

```
            Name            = 'service1'
            ExpectedStatus = 'Running'
        }
        [PSCustomObject]@{
            Name            = 'service2'
            ExpectedStatus = 'Running'
        }
        [PSCustomObject]@{
            Name            = 'service3'
            ExpectedStatus = 'Stopped'
        }
    }
}
```

Then, the original mock for Get-Service is replaced with three new mocks. Each uses a ParameterFilter and tests a different service name:

```
Mock Get-Service @module -ParameterFilter {
    $Name -eq 'service1'
} {
    [PSCustomObject]@{
        Status = 'Running'
    }
}
Mock Get-Service @module -ParameterFilter {
    $Name -eq 'service2'
} -MockWith {
    [PSCustomObject]@{
        Status = 'Stopped'
    }
}
Mock Get-Service @module -ParameterFilter {
    $Name -eq 'service3'
} -MockWith {
    [PSCustomObject]@{
        Status = 'Running'
    }
}
```

Note that $PesterBoundParameters can also be used in the ParameterFilter script block.

Finally, the It block is adjusted. For this version, Start-Service will run once, and Stop-Service will run once. The previous assertion simply stated that Start-Service would run, which implicitly means it runs one or more times:

```
It 'Ensures all services are in the desired state' {
    Set-ServiceState -Path file.csv

    Should -Invoke Start-Service -Times 1 -Exactly @module
    Should -Invoke Stop-Service -Times 1 -Exactly @module
}
```

Similarly, it is possible to test that a mock was called with specific parameters. In this example, the separate mocks are removed again to demonstrate that the parameter filter with Should -Invoke is independent of parameter filtering for Mock.

```
Mock Get-Service @module {
    [PSCustomObject]@{
        Status = 'Running'
    }
}
```

This mock means that all services will report status as running. The mock of Stop-Service will therefore be called once for service3 only.

This time, the Should -Invoke assertions are changed to include a parameter filter:

```
It 'Ensures all services are in the desired state' {
    Set-ServiceState -Path file.csv

    Should -Invoke Stop-Service @module -ParameterFilter {
        $Name -eq 'service3'
    }
}
```

Once the changes are made to the tests file, the single test will pass. However, while this test passes, it remains difficult to explicitly relate cause to effect. A failure in any one or more of the comparisons will cause the preceding tests to fail, but it will not indicate which value caused the failure.

An alternative to using ParameterFilter might be to use Context to change the values provided by Import-Csv or the values returned by Get-Service.

Overriding mocks

Mock can be used in either It or a Context (or Describe) block to override an existing mock or create new mocks that are specific to a specific branch of code. Mock is scoped to the block it is created in; therefore, a Mock created in It only applies to that single It block.

Generally, the safest approach is to define default mocks under a BeforeAll in Describe, and then override those as needed. The presence of the default mocks acts as a safeguard. Running the subject of the tests (Set-ServiceState, in the following example) will only ever call a mocked command. It will never accidentally call the real command because something has been missed from a specific context:

```
@'
BeforeDiscovery {
    Import-Module .\ServiceState.psm1 -Force
}
Describe Set-ServiceState {
   BeforeAll {
        $module = @{ ModuleName = 'ServiceState' }

        Mock Get-Service @module {
            [PSCustomObject]@{
                Status = 'Running'
            }
        }
        Mock Import-Csv @module {
            [PSCustomObject]@{
                Name           = 'service1'
                ExpectedStatus = 'Running'
            }
        }
        Mock Start-Service @module
        Mock Stop-Service @module
    }
}
'@ | Set-Content Set-ServiceState.tests.ps1
```

The first path through the code, when the service is already in the expected state and neither Start-Service nor Stop-Service will be called, can be tested using the default mocks established above. The It block can explicitly assert that Start-Service and Stop-Service were not called:

```
It 'Service is running, expected running' {
    Set-ServiceState -Path file.csv

    Should -Not -Invoke Start-Service @module
    Should -Not -Invoke Stop-Service @module
}
```

The second path, when the service is stopped and should be started, can be achieved by overriding the mock for Get-Service. Note that the Set-ServiceState command is called again after overriding the mock:

```
It 'Service is stopped, expected running' {
    Mock Get-Service @module {
        [PSCustomObject]@{
            Status = 'Stopped'
        }
    }

    Set-ServiceState -Path file.csv

    Should -Invoke Start-Service @module
    Should -Not -Invoke Stop-Service @module
}
```

Finally, the last path runs when the service is running but the expected state is stopped. This time, the mock for Import-Csv is replaced:

```
It 'Service is running, expected stopped' {
    Mock Import-Csv @module {
        [PSCustomObject]@{
            Name           = 'service1'
            ExpectedStatus = 'Stopped'
        }
    }

    Set-ServiceState -Path file.csv

    Should -Not -Invoke Start-Service @module
    Should -Invoke Stop-Service @module
}
```

These new tests should be added to the Describe block of Set-ServiceState.tests.ps1. Once added, the tests file can be run with detailed output:

```
$params = @{
    Path   = '.\ServiceState.tests.ps1'
    Output = 'Detailed'
}
Invoke-Pester @params
```

Running the command above will show the output below:

```
Starting discovery in 1 files.
Discovering in C:\workspace\ServiceState.tests.ps1.
Found 3 tests. 11ms
Discovery finished in 16ms.
Running tests from 'C:\workspace\ServiceState.tests.ps1'
Describing Set-ServiceState
  [+] Service is running, expected running 16ms (13ms|3ms)
  [+] Service is stopped, expected running 15ms (15ms|1ms)
  [+] Service is running, expected stopped 24ms (22ms|1ms)
Tests completed in 188ms
Tests Passed: 3, Failed: 0, Skipped: 0 NotRun: 0
```

These new tests provide a granular view of the different behaviors of the function. If a test fails, it is extremely easy to attribute cause to effect without having to spend extra time figuring out where either the tests or the subject failed.

The examples used to demonstrate mocking so far assume that the command being mocked is available on the current system. Commands that are not locally installed cannot be mocked.

Mocking non-local commands

If a command is not available on the system running tests, the attempt to create a mock will fail.

It is possible to work around this limitation with a small part of the command required by the tests. This can be referred to as a stub and typically consists of a function with only a parameter block.

The stub is used to provide something to mock, and the mock is used to track the execution of the function and ensure that a subject behaves as intended.

For example, consider a function that creates and configures a DNS zone with a predefined set of parameter values:

```
function New-DnsZone {
    [CmdletBinding()]
    param (
        [Parameter(Mandatory)]
        [string]
        $Name
    )
    $params = @{
        Name             = $Name
        DynamicUpdate    = 'Secure'
        ReplicationScope = 'Domain'
    }
```

```
        $zone = Get-DnsServerZone $Name -ErrorAction SilentlyContinue
    if (-not $zone) {
        Add-DnsServerPrimaryZone @params
    }
}
```

It may not be desirable to install the DnsServer tools on a development system to run unit tests. To mock and verify that Add-DnsServerPrimaryZone is called, a function must be created first:

```
Describe CreateDnsZone {
    BeforeAll {
        function Get-DnsServerZone { }
        function Add-DnsServerPrimaryZone { }

        Mock Get-DnsServerZone
        Mock Add-DnsServerPrimaryZone
    }
    It 'When the zone does not exist, creates a zone' {
        New-DnsZone -Name name
        Should -Invoke Add-DnsServerPrimaryZone
    }
}
```

Creating the function as shown here is enough to satisfy the tests, but the approach is basic. The test will pass even if parameter names are incorrect or missing.

A more advanced function to mock may be created by visiting a system with the command installed and retrieving the param block. The ProxyCommand type includes a method to get the param block from a command. The example below gets the param block from the Add-DnsServerPrimaryZone command in the DnsServer module. The module must already be installed for the command to succeed:

```
using namespace System.Management.Automation

$command = Get-Command Add-DnsServerPrimaryZone
[ProxyCommand]::GetParamBlock(
    $command
)
```

For Add-DnsServerPrimaryZone, the result is long. A command such as Select-Object has a simpler param block and is, therefore, easier to view:

```
using namespace System.Management.Automation
[ProxyCommand]::GetParamBlock((Get-Command Select-Object))
```

The first parameters from Select-Object created by the command above are shown below:

```
    [Parameter(ValueFromPipeline=$true)]
```

```
    [psobject]
    ${InputObject},

    [Parameter(ParameterSetName='DefaultParameter', Position=0)]
    [Parameter(ParameterSetName='SkipLastParameter', Position=0)]
    [System.Object[]]
    ${Property},
```

This technique can be used to create a stub of many modules, allowing tests to run even if the module is not locally installed.

The following snippet combines the GetParamBlock with GetCmdletBindingAttribute to create an accurate copy of the basics of the module to use as the basis for mocking a command:

```
using namespace System.Management.Automation

$moduleName = 'DnsServer'
Get-Command -Module $moduleName | ForEach-Object {
    $param = [ProxyCommand]::GetParamBlock($command)
    $param = $param -split '\r?\n' -replace '^\s{4}', '$0$0'
    'function {0} {{' -f $_.Name
    '    {0}' -f [ProxyCommand]::GetCmdletBindingAttribute($_)
    '    param ('
    $param
    '    )'
    '}'
    ''
} | Set-Content "$moduleName.psm1"
```

This approach works for the DnsServer module because the module is based on CIM classes; it only depends on assemblies that are already available in PowerShell.

Adding a copy of a module will improve the overall quality of the tests for a command. Tests will fail if a non-existent parameter is used or if an invalid parameter combination is used.

Each of the mocks used so far has emitted a PSCustomObject, and in many cases, a PSCustomObject is enough to use within a set of tests.

Mocking objects

Mocking allows the result of running another command to be faked. The examples in the previous section have returned a PSCustomObject where output is required.

It is not uncommon for a command to expect to work with the properties and methods of another object. This might be a value returned by another command, or it might be the value of a parameter the test subject requires.

The ability to mock objects or a specific type or objects that implement methods is important in testing.

Two approaches can be taken when testing:

- Methods can be added to a PSCustomObject.
- .NET types can be disarmed and returned.

PowerShell includes many modules that are based on CIM classes. These modules often expect CIM instances as input to work. Testing code that uses CIM-based commands may need to create values that closely resemble the real command output.

Methods can be added to a PSCustomObject, allowing code that uses those methods to be tested without needing to use a more specific .NET type.

Adding methods to PSCustomObject

Objects with specific properties can be simulated by creating a PSCustomObject object:

```
[PSCustomObject]@{
    Property = "Value"
}
```

If the subject of a test takes the result of a mocked command and invokes a method, it will fail unless the method is available. Methods can be added to a PSCustomObject using Add-Member:

```
$object = [PSCustomObject]@{} |
    Add-Member MethodName -MemberType ScriptMethod -Value { }
$object
```

If the method used already exists, such as the ToString method, then the -Force parameter must be used:

```
$object = [PSCustomObject]@{}
$object |
    Add-Member ToString -MemberType ScriptMethod -Force -Value { }
$object
```

As many methods as needed can be added to the PSCustomObject as required.

The method added to the PSCustomObject may return nothing (as in the preceding examples), return a specific value, or set a variable in the script scope that can be tracked or tested. This idea is explored when disarming an existing .NET object.

Disarming .NET types

A piece of code being tested may interact with a specific .NET type. The .NET type may (by default) need to interact with other systems in a way that is not desirable when testing.

The following simple function expects to receive an instance of a `SqlConnection` object and expects to be able to call the `Open` method:

```
using namespace System.Data.SqlClient

function Open-SqlConnection {
    [CmdletBinding()]
    param (
        [Parameter(Mandatory)]
        [SqlConnection]$SqlConnection
    )

    if ($sqlConnection.State -eq 'Closed') {
        $SqlConnection.Open()
    }
}
```

As the value of the `SqlConnection` parameter is explicitly set to accept an instance of `System.Data.SqlClient.SqlConnection`, a `PSCustomObject` cannot be used as a substitute.

When running the function in a test, an instance of `SqlConnection` must be created to pass to the function.

The following `It` block creates such an instance and passes it to the function:

```
It 'Opens an SQL connection' {
    $connection = [System.Data.SqlClient.SqlConnection]::new()
    Open-SqlConnection -SqlConnection $connection
}
```

This `It` block does not contain any assertions yet. It can assert that no errors should be thrown, but the test can only succeed if the computer running the tests is running a SQL server instance. By extension, the test can only fail if the computer running the tests is not a SQL server.

Each of the following tests can be added to a `sql.tests.ps1` file. The `Describe` block has been omitted from the examples to reduce indentation. The following command creates the tests file. All the content of the `Describe` block should be replaced with each example:

```
@'
BeforeAll {
functionOpen-SqlConnection {
    [CmdletBinding()]
    param (
        [Parameter(Mandatory)]
        [System.Data.SqlClient.SqlConnection]
```

```
        $SqlConnection
    )
    if ($sqlConnection.State -eq 'Closed') {
        $SqlConnection.Open()
    }
}
}
Describe Open-SqlConnection {

}
'@ | Set-Content sql.tests.ps1
```

PowerShell code will prefer to call a ScriptMethod on an object over a Method provided by the .NET type. Therefore, a disarmed version of the SqlConnection object could be created, and the Open method overridden using Add-Member:

```
BeforeAll {
    $connection = [System.Data.SqlClient.SqlConnection]::new()
    $connection |
        Add-Member Open -MemberType ScriptMethod -Value { } -Force
}

It 'Opens an SQL connection' {
    Open-SqlConnection -SqlConnection $connection
}
```

This step solves the problem of needing a SQL server to run Open, but it does not solve the problem of testing whether Open was called. After all, the command does not return the connection object; there is no output to test.

Pester solves this problem by providing the New-MockObject command. The New-MockObject command provides two benefits:

- It completely disarms any .NET object.
- It allows mocked method usage to be tracked.

For example, the implementation of the Open method is replaced in the example below:

```
BeforeAll {
    $connection = New-MockObject System.Data.SqlClient.SqlConnection
-Properties @{
        State = 'Closed'
    } -Methods @{
        Open = { }
    }
}
```

When the Open method is called, Pester attaches an _Open property to the mocked object, which includes details about how the method was called:

```
It 'Opens an SQL connection' {
    Open-SqlConnection -SqlConnection $connection

    $connection._Open | Should -HaveCount 1
}
```

The _Open property is an array that contains the details of each invocation of the Open method, including the arguments that were passed (if any). This allows for quite detailed testing.

The techniques used in the previous examples can be applied to a wide variety of .NET objects. CimInstance objects are a special case when it comes to mocking.

Mocking CIM objects

Many modules in PowerShell are based on CIM classes. For example, the Net modules, such as NetAdapter, NetSecurity, and NetTCPIP, are all based on CIM classes.

The commands in these modules either return CIM instances or include parameters that require a specific CIM instance as an argument.

For example, the following function uses two of the commands in a pipeline. Any tests would have to account for the CIM classes when mocking commands:

```
function Enable-PhysicalAdapter {
    Get-NetAdapter -Physical | Enable-NetAdapter
}
```

When these commands act in a pipeline, Enable-NetAdapter fills the InputObject parameter from the pipeline. Get-Help shows that the parameter accepts an array of CimInstance from the pipeline:

```
PS> Get-Help Enable-NetAdapter -Parameter InputObject

-InputObject <CimInstance[]>
    Specifies the input to this cmdlet. You can use this parameter, or you can
pipe the input to this cmdlet.
    Required?                    true
    Position?                    named
    Default value
    Accept pipeline input?       true (ByValue)
    Accept wildcard characters?  false
```

However, this is not the whole story. The parameter value is further constrained by a PSTypeName attribute. This can be seen using Get-Command:

```
$command = (Get-Command Enable-NetAdapter)
$parameter = $command.Parameters['InputObject']
$attribute = $parameter.Attributes |
    Where-Object TypeId -match 'PSTypeName'
$attribute.PSTypeName
```

The result is the PSTypeName the command expects to receive from the pipeline:

```
Microsoft.Management.Infrastructure.CimInstance#MSFT_NetAdapter
```

Any mock for Get-NetAdapter must therefore return an MSFT_NetAdapter CimInstance object. Before the instance can be created, one final piece of information is required: the namespace of the CIM class.

The namespace can be taken from any object returned by Get-NetAdapter:

```
PS> Get-NetAdapter | Select-Object CimClass -First 1

CimClass
--------
ROOT/StandardCimv2:MSFT_NetAdapter
```

Finally, the CimInstance object can be created using the New-CimInstance command, as shown here:

```
$params = @{
    ClassName  = 'MSFT_NetAdapter'
    Namespace  = 'ROOT/StandardCimv2'
    ClientOnly = $true
}
New-CimInstance @params
```

This instance can be added to a mock for Get-NetAdapter when testing the Enable-PhysicalAdapter command:

```
BeforeDiscovery {
    function Script:Enable-PhysicalAdapter {
        Get-NetAdapter -Physical | Enable-NetAdapter
    }
}
Describe Enable-PhysicalAdapter {
    BeforeAll {
        Mock Enable-NetAdapter
        Mock Get-NetAdapter {
            $params = @{
                ClassName  = 'MSFT_NetAdapter'
```

```
                    Namespace  = 'ROOT/StandardCimv2'
                    ClientOnly = $true
                }
                New-CimInstance @params
            }
        }
    It 'Enables a physical network adapter' {
        { Enable-PhysicalAdapter } | Should -Not -Throw

        Should -Invoke Enable-NetAdapter
    }
}
```

The commands used in each of the tests in this section are expected to be available in the global scope so that Pester can mock and run the commands. Pester is also able to test commands and classes that are not exported from a module.

InModuleScope

The InModuleScope command and the ModuleName parameter of Should and Mock are important features of Pester. The command and parameters allow access to content that is normally in the module scope and inaccessible outside.

The following two commands were first introduced in *Chapter 20, Building Modules*:

```
@'
function GetRegistryParameter {
    [CmdletBinding()]
    param ( )
    @{
        Path = 'HKLM:\SYSTEM\CurrentControlSet\Services\LanmanServer\
Parameters'
        Name = 'srvcomment'
    }
}
function Get-ComputerDescription {
    [CmdletBinding()]
    param ( )
    $getParams = GetRegistryParameter
    Get-ItemPropertyValue @getParams
}
Export-ModuleMember Get-ComputerDescription
'@ | Set-Content LocalMachine.psm1
```

The function `GetRegistryParameter` can be tested in Pester by using `InModuleScope`:

```
@'
BeforeDiscovery {
    Import-Module .\LocalMachine.psm1 -Force
}
Describe GetRegistryParameter {
    It 'Returns a hashtable' {
        InModuleScope -ModuleName LocalMachine {
            GetRegistryParameter
        } | Should -BeOfType [Hashtable]
    }
}
'@ | Set-Content GetRegistryParameter.tests.ps1
```

If the `InModuleScope` command is omitted, the test will fail and the `GetRegistryParameter` function is not exported from the module and is, therefore, not normally accessible.

The result of running the tests is shown here:

```
PS> Invoke-Pester -Script .\GetRegistryParameter.tests.ps1
Starting discovery in 1 files.
Discovery finished in 227ms.
Running tests.
[+] C:\workspace\GetRegistryParameter.tests.ps1 1.04s (152ms|702ms)
Tests completed in 1.06s
Tests Passed: 1, Failed: 0, Skipped: 0 NotRun: 0
```

In the same way, if it were desirable to mock that command when testing the `Get-ComputerDescription` command, the -ModuleName parameter is required for the `Mock` keyword:

```
BeforeAll {
    Mock GetRegistryParameter -ModuleName LocalMachine
}
```

`InModuleScope` can be used to access anything in the module scope, including private commands, classes, enumerations, and any module-scoped variables.

Pester in scripts

Using `InModuleScope` can add complexity when running Invoke-Pester from a script.

When `Invoke-Pester` is run from a global scope, `ModuleName` is only required to access private components of a module.

When `Invoke-Pester` is run from a script, problems may surface because the script scope breaks Pester's scoping.

Consider the following tests:

```
$container = New-PesterContainer -ScriptBlock {
    BeforeDiscovery {
        Import-Module .\LocalMachine.psm1 -Force
    }
    Describe Get-ComputerDescription {
        BeforeAll {
            Mock Get-ItemPropertyValue {
                'Mocked description'
            }
        }
        It 'Returns the mocked description' {
            Get-ComputerDescription |
                Should -Be 'Mocked description'
            Should -Invoke Get-ItemPropertyValue
        }
    }
}
```

When `Invoke-Pester` is run from the console, the tests pass provided the `LocalMachine` module was successfully imported:

```
PS> Invoke-Pester -Container $container
Starting discovery in 1 files.
Discovery finished in 7ms.
[+] C:\workspace\Get-ComputerDescription.tests.ps1 98ms (6ms|86ms)
Tests completed in 99ms
Tests Passed: 1, Failed: 0, Skipped: 0 NotRun: 0
```

If, instead, the `Invoke-Pester` command is put in a script and the script is run, the mock is completely ignored:

```
@'
Invoke-Pester -Path .\Get-ComputerDescription.tests.ps1
'@ | Set-Content script.ps1
```

This is shown here when running the script:

```
PS> .\script.ps1
Starting discovery in 1 files.
Discovery finished in 7ms.
[-] Get-ComputerDescription.Returns the mocked description 5ms (4ms|1ms)
 PSArgumentException: Property srvcomment does not exist at path HKEY_LOCAL_
MACHINE\SYSTEM\CurrentControlSet\Services\LanmanServer\Parameters.
```

```
 at Get-ComputerDescription, C:\workspace\LocalMachine.psm1:16
 at <ScriptBlock>, C:\workspace\Get-ComputerDescription.tests.ps1:12
Tests completed in 117ms
Tests Passed: 0, Failed: 1, Skipped: 0 NotRun: 0
```

To work around this problem, the `ModuleName` parameter must be added to all `Mock` commands and all `Should -Invoke` assertions. In the following example, a splat is used:

```
Describe Get-ComputerDescription {
    BeforeAll {
        $module = @{
            ModuleName = 'LocalMachine'
        }
        Mock Get-ItemPropertyValue @module {
            'Mocked description'
        }
    }
    It 'Returns the mocked description' {
        Get-ComputerDescription |
            Should -Be 'Mocked description'
        Should -Invoke Get-ItemPropertyValue @module
    }
}
```

In all cases, the module name is the scope the mock should be created in, In all cases, the value of `ModuleName` must be the scope the mock is created within. That is, the module which is the subject of the tests, not the module the mocked command belongs to.

With this in place, `Invoke-Pester` can be run from a script:

```
PS> .\script.ps1
Starting discovery in 1 files.
Discovery finished in 23ms.
[+] C:\workspace\Get-ComputerDescription.tests.ps1 135ms (25ms|88ms)
Tests completed in 137ms
Tests Passed: 1, Failed: 0, Skipped: 0 NotRun: 0
```

Pester is a wonderful tool for writing tests for a variety of different purposes. The tools above offer an introduction to the capabilities of the module.

Summary

This chapter explored the complex topic of testing in PowerShell.

Static analysis is one part of testing and is the approach used by modules like `PSScriptAnalyzer`. Static analysis makes use of the AST and tokenizers in PowerShell.

The AST describes the content of a block of code as a tree of different elements, starting with a `ScriptBlockAst` at the highest level. The `ParseInput` and `ParseFile` methods of the `Parser` type can be used to get either an instance of the AST for a piece of code or the tokens that make up a script that includes comments.

The `ShowPSAst` module can be used to visualize and explore the AST tree. `ShowPSAst` is a useful tool when starting to work with AST as the tree can quickly become complex.

`PSScriptAnalyzer` uses either the AST or tokens to define rules. Rules can be used to test and enforce personal or organization-specific practices.

Pester is a testing framework and this chapter explores both acceptance and unit testing.

Acceptance testing is commonly used to assess the state of systems and services. Pester can be used to define tests that can be saved and shared. Such tests can be used to validate that a system is configured or behaving as it should be.

Pester is a rich tool that supports iteration with the `ForEach` or `TestCases` parameters. Conditional testing can be achieved using the `Set-ItResult` or `Skip` parameter.

Mocking is an exceptionally useful feature of Pester and is often used when writing unit tests to reduce the amount of code that must be tested when the subject is a single command.

The next chapter explores error handling in PowerShell, including terminating and non-terminating errors and the use of `try`, `catch`, `finally`, and the `trap` statement.

Learn more on Discord

Read this book alongside other users, PowerShell experts, and the author himself. Ask questions, provide solutions to other readers, chat with the author via Ask Me Anything sessions, and much more.

Scan the QR code or visit the link to join the community.

`https://packt.link/SecNet`

22

Error Handling

Errors communicate unexpected conditions and exceptional circumstances. Errors often contain useful information that can be used to diagnose a problem.

PowerShell has two different types of errors, terminating and non-terminating, and several different ways to raise and handle them.

Error handling in PowerShell is a complex topic, which is not helped by incorrect assertions in help documentation surrounding terminating errors. These challenges are explored in this chapter.

Self-contained blocks of code are described as scripts in this chapter. That is, functions, script blocks, and scripts can be considered interchangeable in the context of error handling.

This chapter covers the following topics:

- Error types
- Error actions
- Raising errors
- Catching errors

The two different types of error will be explored first.

Error types

As mentioned above, PowerShell defines two different types of errors: terminating and non-terminating errors.

Each command in PowerShell may choose to raise either of these, depending on the operation.

Terminating errors

Terminating errors are used to stop a script in the event of a problem, or to stop an operation from continuing.

Terminating errors are split in two, depending on how the error is raised; this leads to some inconsistent behavior, which is explored in the *Raising errors* recipe later in this chapter.

A terminating error stops a script once an error is thrown. No further commands will execute after the error is thrown.

When running the following command, the second Write-Host statement will never execute:

```
function Stop-Command {
    Write-Host 'First'
    throw 'Error'
    Write-Host 'Second'
}
```

Running the function will show that the second Write-Host command does not execute:

```
PS> $ErrorActionPreference = 'Continue'
PS> Stop-Command
First
Exception:
Line |
   3 |         throw 'Error'
     |         ~~~~~~~~~~~~~
     | Error
```

The assertion that the second statement will never run has a caveat—terminating errors raised by throw are affected by the ErrorActionPreference variable. This is the reason to ensure that $ErrorActionPreference is set to Continue before running the last example.

Setting the $ErrorActionPreference to SilentlyContinue shows that the script continues without showing the error:

```
PS> $ErrorActionPreference = 'SilentlyContinue'

PS> Stop-Command
First
Second
```

This contradicts the statements in the PowerShell documentation:

- Get-Help about_Throw asserts that the throw keyword causes a terminating error.
- Get-Help about_Preference_Variables asserts that the ErrorActionPreference variable and ErrorAction parameter do not affect terminating errors.

Exactly how this affects code and how to create code that behaves consistently are explored in this chapter.

$ErrorActionPreference should be reset to the default value, or the console should be restarted:

```
$ErrorActionPreference = 'Continue'
```

If an operation can continue when an error occurs, a non-terminating error should be used.

Non-terminating errors

A non-terminating error, a type of informational output, is written without stopping a script. Non-terminating errors exist to allow a command to continue in the event of a partial failure. For example, if a command acts on a pipeline and one item fails, the command can write an error and continue to process the remaining items.

Non-terminating errors can be written using the `Write-Error` command, although a deeper analysis of this approach and alternatives are explored later in this chapter.

The following example demonstrates how a non-terminating error can be used in a function accepting pipeline input:

```
function Update-Value {
    [CmdletBinding()]
    param (
        [Parameter(Mandatory, ValueFromPipeline)]
        [string]$Value
    )

    process {
        if ($Value.Length -lt 5) {
            Write-Error ('The value {0} is unacceptable' -f
                $Value
            )
        } else {
            'Updated value: {0}' -f $Value
        }
    }
}
```

When executed on a pipeline containing words, the command will write an error and continue every time it encounters a word with a length of less than 5:

```
PS> 'value', 'val', 'longvalue' | Update-Value
Updated value: value
Update-Value: The value val is unacceptable
Updated value: longvalue
```

Scenarios like this are why non-terminating errors exist. It is then up to the consumer of the command to decide if a script should continue.

Non-terminating errors should be used when a script acts on more than one input, and an error for a single item does not affect the success or failure of subsequent items.

Before exploring raising errors in PowerShell, the `ErrorActionPreference` variable and `ErrorAction` parameter should be introduced.

Error actions

The ErrorAction parameter and the ErrorActionPreference variable are used to control what happens when a non-terminating error is encountered, subject to the previous notes about throw.

The ErrorAction parameter is made available on advanced functions, script blocks, and scripts when either the CmdletBinding attribute is used or more parameters in a script use the Parameter attribute.

By default, ErrorAction is set to Continue. Non-terminating errors will be displayed, but a script will continue to run.

ErrorActionPreference is a scoped variable, which can be used to affect all commands in a particular scope and any child scopes. By default, ErrorActionPreference is set to Continue. The variable can be overridden in child scopes (such as a function inside a script).

All errors in a session are implicitly added to the reserved variable Error unless the error action is set to Ignore. The Error variable is an ArrayList and contains each error in the session, with the newest first (at index 0).

If ErrorAction is set to SilentlyContinue, errors will still be added to the $Error automatic variable, but the error will not be displayed in the host.

The following function writes a non-terminating error using Write-Error:

```
function Start-Task {
    [CmdletBinding()]
    param ( )


    Write-Error 'Something went wrong'
}
Start-Task -ErrorAction SilentlyContinue
```

The error is not displayed in the host or console; it can be viewed as the latest entry in the Error variable:

```
PS> $Error[0]
Start-Task: Something went wrong
```

If the error action is set to Stop, a non-terminating error becomes a terminating error. In the console, the output in either case is similar. However, a terminating error is displayed differently when viewing $Error[0]:

```
PS> Start-Task -ErrorAction Stop
Start-Task: Something went wrong


PS> $Error[0]


ErrorRecord                       : Something went wrong
```

```
WasThrownFromThrowStatement : False
TargetSite                  : System.Collections.ObjectModel.Coll
                              ection`1[System.Management.Automati
                              on.PSObject] Invoke(System.Collecti
                              ons.IEnumerable)
StackTrace                  :    at System.Management.Automation.
                              Runspaces.PipelineBase.Invoke(IEnum
                              erable input)
                                 at System.Management.Automation.
                              Runspaces.Pipeline.Invoke()
                                 at Microsoft.PowerShell.Executor
                              .ExecuteCommandHelper(Pipeline
                              tempPipeline, Exception&
                              exceptionThrown, ExecutionOptions
                              options)
Message                     : The running command stopped
                              because the preference variable
                              "ErrorActionPreference" or common
                              parameter is set to Stop:
                              Something went wrong
Data                        : {System.Management.Automation.Inter
                              preter.InterpretedFrameInfo}
InnerException              :
HelpLink                    :
Source                      : System.Management.Automation
HResult                     : -2146233087
```

The content of the object is difficult to read, especially in a narrow console.

PowerShell 7 includes a Get-Error command, which can be used to explore errors that have been raised in greater detail.

About Get-Error

The Get-Error command was introduced with PowerShell 7. When used without any parameters, it gets the latest error from the Error variable and provides a summary of the content of that error.

If the Start-Task function above is executed, Get-Error can be used to explore the details of the error it raised.

The output differs between terminating and non-terminating errors; more information is shown for terminating errors.

Figure 22.1 shows the output of the command when a non-terminating error has been written; the content does not display well in a narrow console:

```
 C:\Program Files\PowerShell\7\pwsh.exe

PS C:\> function Start-Task {
>>      [CmdletBinding()]
>>      param ( )
>>
>>      Write-Error 'Something went wrong'
>> }
PS C:\> Start-Task
Start-Task: Something went wrong
PS C:\> Get-Error

Exception               :
    Type     : Microsoft.PowerShell.Commands.WriteErrorException
    Message  : Something went wrong
    HResult  : -2146233087
CategoryInfo            : NotSpecified: (:) [Write-Error], WriteErrorException
FullyQualifiedErrorId   : Microsoft.PowerShell.Commands.WriteErrorException,Start-Task
InvocationInfo          :
    MyCommand         : Start-Task
    ScriptLineNumber  : 1
    OffsetInLine      : 1
    HistoryId         : 12
    Line              : Start-Task
    PositionMessage   : At line:1 char:1
                        + Start-Task
                        + ~~~~~~~~~~
    InvocationName    : Start-Task
    CommandOrigin     : Internal
ScriptStackTrace        : at Start-Task, <No file>: line 5
                          at <ScriptBlock>, <No file>: line 1
PipelineIterationInfo   :
```

Figure 22.1: Get-Error command

Get-Error can be used to view the last error, a user-defined number of the newest errors, and a specific error using ErrorRecord.

For example, if $Error contained 10 errors, and only one of those from the middle of the set was of interest, Get-Error would accept one or more errors as pipeline input:

```
$Error[4] | Get-Error
```

If there were fewer than five (indexing from zero) errors, another error would be written.

When writing scripts, it is often desirable to write or raise an error.

Raising errors

When writing a script, it may be desirable to use errors to notify the person running the script of a problem. The severity of the problem will dictate whether an error is non-terminating or terminating.

If a script makes a single change to many diverse, unrelated objects, a terminating error might be frustrating for anyone using the script.

On the other hand, if a script fails to read a critical configuration file or fails some advanced parameter validation, a terminating error is likely the right choice.

Error records

When an error is raised in PowerShell, an ErrorRecord object is created (explicitly or implicitly).

An ErrorRecord object contains several fields that are useful for diagnosing an error. ErrorRecord can be explored by using the Get-Member or the Get-Error command.

For example, an ErrorRecord will be generated when attempting to divide by 0:

```
100 / 0
$record = $Error[0]
```

The ErrorRecord object that was generated has a ScriptStackTrace property. The property includes the script names that were called and the position where an error occurred. ScriptTrackTrace is extremely useful when debugging problems in larger scripts:

```
PS> $record.ScriptStackTrace
at <ScriptBlock>, <No file>: line 1
```

A bespoke ErrorRecord can be created within a script to describe a problem more clearly to the user. The error record might include additional information to assist with debugging.

For example, if the values for a division operation were dynamically set, an ErrorRecord might be created to include those values in the TargetObject to assist with debugging:

```
using namespace System.Management.Automation

$numerator = 10
$denominator = 0
try {
    $numerator / $denominator
} catch {
    $errorRecord = [ErrorRecord]::new(
        [Exception]::new($_.Exception.Message),
        'InvalidDivision',    # ErrorId
        'InvalidOperation',   # ErrorCategory
        [PSCustomObject]@{    # TargetObject
            Numerator   = $numerator
            Denominator = $denominator
        }
    )
    Write-Error -ErrorRecord $errorRecord
}
```

The example above makes use of a try, catch statement, which is explored in more detail later in this chapter. Within catch, the $_ refers to the error that caused catch to trigger.

The ErrorRecord object and the constructor in the preceding example are described in the .NET reference: https://learn.microsoft.com/dotnet/api/system.management.automation.errorrecord.-ctor #System_Management_Automation_ErrorRecord__ctor_System_Exception_System_String_System_Management_Automation_ErrorCategory_System_Object_.

The values added to the ErrorRecord can be viewed by exploring the TargetObject property:

```
PS> $Error[0].TargetObject


Numerator    Denominator
---------    -----------
       10              0
```

The try-catch statement used in the previous example is covered in detail when we explore try, catch, and finally later in this chapter.

Raising non-terminating errors

The Write-Error command can be used to write a non-terminating error message.

The Write-Error command can display a simple message:

```
Write-Error -Message 'Message'
```

Alternatively, the error might include additional information, such as a category and error ID to aid diagnosis by the person using the script:

```
$params = @{
    Message  = 'Message'
    Category = 'InvalidOperation'
    ErrorID  = 'UniqueID'
}
Write-Error @params
```

The following example shows a non-terminating error that was raised while running a loop:

```
function Test-Error {
    [CmdletBinding()]
    param ( )

    for ($i = 0; $i -lt 3; $i++) {
        Write-Error -Message "Iteration: $i"
    }
}
```

When the function runs, an error is displayed three times without stopping execution:

```
PS> Test-Error
Test-Error: Iteration: 0
Test-Error: Iteration: 1
Test-Error: Iteration: 2
```

Setting the value of ErrorAction to Stop will cause Write-Error to throw a terminating error, ending the function within the first iteration of the loop:

```
PS> Test-Error -ErrorAction Stop
Test-Error: Iteration: 0
```

Alternatively, the error can be silenced (SilentlyContinue) or ignored (Ignore), depending on the importance of the error to the user of the function.

The behavior of the non-terminating error can be demonstrated by making a function from the division operation in the previous section. The error generated has been simplified to shorten the example code:

```
function Invoke-Divide {
    [CmdletBinding()]
    param (
        [Parameter(Mandatory)]
        [int]
        $Numerator,

        [Parameter(Mandatory)]
        [int]
        $Denominator
    )

    try {
        $Numerator / $Denominator
    } catch {
        Write-Error -ErrorRecord $_
    }
}
```

When this function is used, it will only raise an error for a failing operation:

```
1, 0, 2 | ForEach-Object {
    Invoke-Divide -Numerator 2 -Denominator $_
}
```

This will show an error between two successful values, as shown below:

```
2
Invoke-Divide:
Line |
   2 |        Invoke-Divide -Numerator 2 -Denominator $_
     |        ~~~~~~~~~~~~~~~~~~~~~~~~~~~~~~~~~~~~~~~~~~~~~
     | Attempted to divide by zero.
1
```

One disadvantage of using the `Write-Error` command is that it does not set the value of the automatic variable `$?` unless `ErrorAction` is set to `Stop`. The variable `$?` is set to `True` if the last command was successful, or `False` if the last command failed:

```
PS> Test-Error
Test-Error: Iteration: 0
Test-Error: Iteration: 1
Test-Error: Iteration: 2

PS> $?
True
```

The `WriteError` method of the `$PSCmdlet` automatic variable can be used as an alternative to the `Write-Error` command.

Using the WriteError method

The `WriteError` method is used by binary commands and can optionally be used by scripts (and functions or script blocks), provided the script is advanced.

The presence of the `CmdletBinding` attribute makes the `$PSCmdlet` variable available for use within a script. The `$PSCmdlet` variable provides access to the `WriteError` method.

The `WriteError` method requires an `ErrorRecord` as an argument, as shown in the following example:

```
using namespace System.Management.Automation

function Test-Error {
    [CmdletBinding()]
    param ( )

    for ($i = 0; $i -lt 3; $i++) {
        $errorRecord = [ErrorRecord]::new(
            [Exception]::new('Iteration {0}' -f $i),
            'InvalidOperation',
            'InvalidOperation',
```

```
            $i
        )
        $PSCmdlet.WriteError($errorRecord)
    }
}
```

When running the command, the value of $? correctly reflects that one or more errors occurred in the last command:

```
PS> Test-Error
Test-Error: Iteration 0
Test-Error: Iteration 1
Test-Error: Iteration 2
```

The value of $? will be false, indicating the command was not successful:

```
PS> $?
False
```

The WriteError method otherwise only differs from the Write-Error command in the CategoryInfo associated with the error. The function below can be used to show this difference:

```
function Test-WriteError {
    [CmdletBinding()]
    param (
        [switch]
        $UseMethod
    )
    $errorRecord = [ErrorRecord]::new(
        [Exception]::new('Error occurred'),
        'InvalidOperation',
        'InvalidOperation',
        $null
    )
    if ($UseMethod) {
        $PSCmdlet.WriteError($errorRecord)
    } else {
        Write-Error -ErrorRecord $errorRecord
    }
}
```

By default, `Write-Error` is used to raise the non-terminating error. This is reflected in the `Activity` property of the `CategoryInfo` property in the error:

```
PS> Test-WriteError
Test-WriteError: Error occurred
PS> Get-Error | ForEach-Object CategoryInfo


Category    : InvalidOperation
Activity    : Write-Error
Reason      : Exception
TargetName  :
TargetType  :
```

When the `WriteError` method is used instead, the `Activity` shows the executing function name:

```
PS> Test-WriteError -UseMethod
Test-WriteError: Error occurred
PS> Get-Error | ForEach-Object CategoryInfo


Category    : InvalidOperation
Activity    : Test-WriteError
Reason      : Exception
TargetName  :
TargetType  :
```

Terminating errors can be raised by setting `ErrorAction` to `Stop` when using the `Write-Error` command. However, it is often more appropriate to explicitly raise a terminating error.

Raising terminating errors

The throw keyword raises a terminating error, as shown in the following example:

```
throw 'Error message'
```

Existing exception types are documented in .NET Framework; each is ultimately derived from the `System.Exception` type found in the .NET reference: https://learn.microsoft.com/dotnet/api/system.exception.

throw can be used with a string or a message, as shown previously. throw can also be used with an exception object:

```
throw [ArgumentException]::new('Unsupported value')
```

Alternatively, throw can be used with an `ErrorRecord`:

```
using namespace System.Management.Automation
```

```
throw [ErrorRecord]::new(
    [InvalidOperationException]::new('Invalid operation'),
    'AnErrorID',
    [ErrorCategory]::InvalidOperation,
    $null
)
```

Commands in binary modules cannot use throw; it has a different meaning in the languages that might be used to author a cmdlet (such as C#, VB, or F#). Cmdlets use the ThrowTerminatingError method instead.

Using the ThrowTerminatingError method

Like the WriteError method, ThrowTerminatingError is made available to advanced scripts via the PSCmdlet variable.

The ThrowTerminatingError method requires an ErrorRecord object, as shown in the following example:

```
using namespace System.Management.Automation

function Invoke-Something {
    [CmdletBinding()]
    param ( )

    $errorRecord = [ErrorRecord]::new(
        [InvalidOperationException]::new('Failed'),
        'AnErrorID',
        [ErrorCategory]::OperationStopped,
        $null
    )
    $PSCmdlet.ThrowTerminatingError($errorRecord)
}
```

Running the command will show this simple error message:

```
PS> Invoke-Something
Invoke-Something: Failed
```

More detailed error information can be viewed using the Get-Error command.

An error may only exist to communicate a problem to an end user, but it is common to capture and handle errors in another script.

Catching errors

Capturing an error so that a script can react to it depends on the error type:

- Non-terminating errors can be captured by using the ErrorVariable parameter.
- Terminating errors can be captured by using either a try, catch, and finally statement, or by using a trap statement.

Although trap can be used to handle terminating errors, exploring trap is deferred until later in this chapter because it is infrequently used for that task.

The ErrorVariable parameter can be used to create a scoped alternative to the Error variable.

ErrorVariable

The Error variable is a collection (ArrayList) of handled and unhandled errors raised in the Power-Shell session.

The ErrorVariable parameter can be used to name a specific variable that should be used for a command. The ErrorVariable accepts the name of a variable and is created as an ArrayList.

The following function writes a single error using the Write-Error command:

```
function Invoke-Something {
    [CmdletBinding()]
    param ( )

    Write-Error 'Invoke-Something Failed'
}
```

The command can be run using the -ErrorVariable parameter. The -ErrorAction parameter below is used to suppress the normal error output:

```
$params = @{
    ErrorVariable = 'MyErrorVariable'
    ErrorAction   = 'SilentlyContinue'
}
Invoke-Something @params
```

Nothing is displayed in the console, but the error is added to the MyErrorVariable variable:

```
PS> $MyErrorVariable
Invoke-Something: Invoke-Something Failed
```

Error messages written to an ErrorVariable are duplicated in Error.

If no errors occur, an ErrorVariable variable will still be created as an ArrayList, but the list will contain no elements.

The Count property might be inspected to see if any errors occurred:

```
$MyErrorVariable.Count -eq 0
```

A single ErrorVariable can be shared by several different scripts; by default, the content of the variable is overwritten. If + is added to the beginning of the variable name, then new errors will be added without overwriting the content of the variable. The following command is run twice; the first run creates a new error variable, and the second adds to that existing variable:

```
Invoke-Something -ErrorVariable MyErrorVariable
Invoke-Something -ErrorVariable +MyErrorVariable
```

Once the two commands have finished, the MyErrorVariable variable will contain two errors, one from each command.

Terminating errors are most frequently handled using try, catch, and finally.

try, catch, and finally

PowerShell 2.0 introduced try, catch, and finally as a means of handling terminating errors.

try statements are used to enclose a region of code that may raise an error. A try statement must include a catch block, a finally block, or both. The example describes the generalized layout of a try statement:

```
try {
    <# Code that may raise an error #>
} catch {
    <# Optional handling for errors #>
} finally {
    <# Optional code to always run try, regardless of errors. #>
}
```

In this section, Write-Host is frequently used in catch to explore different behaviors. This is a bad practice in most cases, as it hides information from the consumer. Errors should ideally be rich enough to debug a problem and, therefore, should avoid hiding error information unless the problem is extremely tightly defined.

As a best practice, return rich errors that include positional information, which can be used to debug. For example, use the ErrorRecord parameter with Write-Error in a catch block, instead of the Exception or Message parameter:

```
try {
    1/0
} catch {
    Write-Error -ErrorRecord $_
}
```

try cannot be used alone; it must be used with either catch, finally, or both.

The most common statement is a try, followed by a single catch:

```
try {
    throw 'An error'
} catch {
    Write-Host 'Caught an error'
}
```

The catch block only executes if an error is raised; a terminating error will stop the script enclosed by try at the point the error is thrown.

Inside the catch block, $_ (or $PSItem) is set to the ErrorRecord that caused catch to trigger. This is important if a command such as ForEach-Object is used; the original pipeline variable is not accessible inside the catch block.

The ErrorRecord has an Exception property, and the Exception has a Message property. These values were seen when looking at the output from Get-Error. These values, and any other properties of the ErrorRecord, can be accessed by using $_ , as the following code shows:

```
try {
    1/0
} catch {
    Write-Host $_.Exception.Message
}
```

In this example, the catch statement reacts if any exception type is thrown. The statement is equivalent to the following:

```
try {
    1/0
} catch [Exception] {
    Write-Host $_.Exception.Message
}
```

catch can be used to react to a more specific exception type instead:

```
try {
    throw [ArgumentException]::new('Invalid argument')
} catch [ArgumentException] {
    Write-Host 'Caught an argument exception'
}
```

More than one catch statement can be supplied, allowing different reactions to different types of errors:

```
try {
    throw [ArgumentException]::new('Invalid argument')
```

```
} catch [InvalidOperationException] {
    Write-Host 'Caught an invalid operation exception'
} catch [ArgumentException] {
    Write-Host 'Caught an argument exception'
}
```

The `catch` statements are evaluated in the order they are written. The most specific handlers should be written before more general error types:

```
try {
    throw [ArgumentException]::new('Invalid argument')
} catch [ArgumentException] {
    Write-Host 'Caught an argument exception'
} catch {
    Write-Host 'Something else went wrong'
}
```

Each `catch` statement can be triggered by one or more exception types:

```
try {
    throw [ArgumentException]::new('Invalid argument')
} catch [InvalidOperationException], [ArgumentException] {
    Write-Host 'Argument or InvalidOperation exception'
}
```

The `finally` block can be used either alongside or instead of `catch`. The `finally` block always executes, even if an error occurred during `try`; it is an ideal place to clean up anything that might otherwise cause a problem, including open connections and streams.

In the following example, `finally` is used to close a potentially open connection to an SQL server:

```
using namespace System.Data.SqlClient

$connectionString = 'Data Source=dbServer;Initial Catalog=dbName'
try {
    $sqlConnection = [SqlConnection]::new($connectionString)
    $sqlConnection.Open()
    $sqlCommand = $sqlConnection.CreateCommand()
    $sqlCommand.CommandText = 'SELECT * FROM Employee'
    $reader = $sqlCommand.ExecuteReader()
} finally {
    if ($sqlConnection.State -eq 'Open') {
        $sqlConnection.Close()
    }
}
```

When catch is used with finally, the content of finally is executed before errors are returned but after the body of catch has executed. This is demonstrated by the following example:

```
try {
    Write-Host "Try"
    throw 'Error'
} catch {
    Write-Host "Catch, after Try"
    throw
} finally {
    Write-Host "Finally, after Catch, before the exception"
}
```

An error raised in try can be repeated in a catch block.

Rethrowing errors

Errors may be caught using try and then thrown again (or rethrown) in a catch block. This technique can be useful if a try block performs several dependent steps in a sequence where one or more might fail.

Rethrowing an error raised by a script can be as simple as using throw in a catch block:

```
try {
    'Statement1'
    throw 'Statement2'
    'Statement3'
} catch {
    throw
}
```

The previous example will display Statement1, and then the error. Statement3 will never run in this case.

The ThrowTerminatingError method can be used to emit the error record that catch handles:

```
function Invoke-Something {
    [CmdletBinding()]
    param ( )

    try {
        'Statement1'
        throw 'Statement2'
        'Statement3'
    } catch {
        $PSCmdlet.ThrowTerminatingError($_)
    }
}
```

When an error is rethrown in the manner shown above, the second instance of the error (within the catch block) is not written to either $Error or a user-defined error variable. If the error is not modified, this is not a problem.

If information is added to the error before it is rethrown, such as an error ID, the modified error record will not be available to error variables. This is shown in the following example:

```
try {
    throw 'Error'
} catch {
    $params = @{
        Exception = $_.Exception
        ErrorID   = 'SomeErrorID'
        Category  = 'InvalidOperation'
    }
    Write-Error @params
}
```

Get-Error can be used to show that the category and ErrorID are not set as defined in the catch block for the last error raised:

```
Get-Error |
    Select-Object CategoryInfo, FullyQualifiedErrorId |
    Format-List
```

This command will show the selected properties, as shown below:

```
CategoryInfo          : OperationStopped: (Error:String) [],
                        RuntimeException
FullyQualifiedErrorId : Error
```

The preceding problem can be resolved by creating a new error record, with the original exception as an inner exception:

```
try {
    throw 'Error'
} catch {
    $params = @{
        Exception = [InvalidOperationException]::new(
            $_.Exception.Message,
            $_.Exception
        )
        ErrorID   = 'SomeErrorID'
        Category  = 'InvalidOperation'
    }
    Write-Error @params
}
```

In the case of the preceding exception and most exception types, the first argument of the constructor is a message, and the second (optional) argument is an inner exception.

Inner exception types cannot be used with catch statements in PowerShell except when a MethodInvocationException is raised.

A MethodInvocationException is a generic error that is raised when PowerShell executes a method on a .NET type or object:

```
[DateTime]::DaysInMonth(2019, 13)
Get-Error | ForEach-Object {
    $_.Exception.GetType().Name
}
```

PowerShell can react to the MethodInvocationException type:

```
using namespace System.Management.Automation

try {
    [DateTime]::DaysInMonth(2019, 13)
} catch [MethodInvocationException] {
    Write-Host 'Caught a method invocation exception'
}
```

However, this exception type is not particularly useful. In the case of a MethodInvocationException, PowerShell can catch the inner exception—in this case, an ArgumentOutOfRange exception:

```
try {
    [DateTime]::DaysInMonth(2019, 13)
} catch [ArgumentOutOfRangeException] {
    Write-Host 'Out of range'
}
```

When a command raises an error, the actual problem may be nested under one or more inner exceptions. When only the inner exception is interesting, the InnerException property of $_.Exception can be used to access that. In the following example, the property is used to access the ArgumentException of the thrown error:

```
try {
    throw [InvalidOperationException]::new(
        'OuterException',
        [ArgumentException]::new(
            'IntermediateException',
            [UnauthorizedAccessException]::new('InnerException')
        )
    )
```

```
} catch {
    Write-Host $_.Exception.InnerException.Message
}
```

The Exception class (and all derived classes) include a GetBaseException method. This method provides simple access to the innermost exception and is useful when the number of nested exceptions is unknown:

```
try {
    throw [InvalidOperationException]::new(
        'OuterException',
        [ArgumentException]::new(
            'IntermediateException',
            [UnauthorizedAccessException]::new('InnerException')
        )
    )
} catch {
    Write-Host $_.Exception.GetBaseException().Message
}
```

In cases where the exception type is not sufficient, the catch block can be expanded to include if or switch statements, allowing decisions to be made based on values like the message in an exception.

As error messages might be localized, it is often worth trying to find some unique facet of an error, such as the FullyQualifiedErrorID, or status codes in an exception, falling back on the error message as a last resort.

Inconsistent error handling

The different methods PowerShell exposes to create a terminating error are not consistent and can be extremely confusing.

The behavior of the different types of error is explored in detail in an issue in the PowerShell Docs repository: https://github.com/MicrosoftDocs/PowerShell-Docs/issues/1583.

Unfortunately, the content of the thread has yet to find a home in the released documentation.

When throw is used to raise a terminating error, the current script, and anything that called the current script, is stopped. The preceding link refers to errors raised by throw as a script-terminating error.

A script-terminating error is shown in the following example:

```
$ErrorActionPreference = 'Continue'

function caller {
    first
    second
}
```

```
function first {
    throw 'Failed'
    'first'
}

function second {
    'second'
}
```

The error raised in the function named first stops all commands in the chain. The function named second is never executed. This is shown when the function caller is run:

```
PS> caller
Exception:
Line |
   2 |         throw 'Failed'
     |         ~~~~~~~~~~~~~~~
     | Failed
```

This differs from the behavior when ThrowTerminatingError is called. ThrowTermatingError is used by binary modules that want to stop execution; this introduces a rift in error handling between the script and binary modules.

The URL at the beginning of this subsection refers to an error raised by ThrowTerminatingError as a statement-terminating error:

```
using namespace System.Management.Automation

function caller {
    first
    second
}

function first {
    [CmdletBinding()]
    param ( )

    $errorRecord = [ErrorRecord]::new(
        [Exception]::new('Failed'),
        'ID',
        'OperationStopped',
        $null
    )
```

```
        $PSCmdlet.ThrowTerminatingError($errorRecord)
        'first'
}

function second {
    'second'
}
```

Running the function `first` shows a different result to the version that used a `throw` statement instead:

```
PS> caller
first:
Line |
   2 |        first
     |        ~~~~~
     | Failed
Second
```

The `ThrowTerminatingError` statement stops the function `first` from completing, but it does not stop the function `caller` from continuing.

This second version is, therefore, consistent with a script that runs a command from a binary module. In the following example, `ConvertFrom-Json` raises a terminating error but does not stop the function that called it from executing:

```
function caller {
    ConvertFrom-Json -InputObject '{{'
    second
}
function second {
    'second'
}
```

The output when running `caller` is:

```
PS> caller
ConvertFrom-Json:
Line |
   2 |        ConvertFrom-Json -InputObject '{{'
     |        ~~~~~~~~~~~~~~~~~~~~~~~~~~~~~~~~~~~~
     | Conversion from JSON failed with error: Invalid property identifier
character: {. Path '', line 1, position 1.
second
```

The same behavior is seen when calling .NET methods. The static method, IPAddress.Parse, will raise an exception because the use of the method is not valid. The function continues from this error and calls the function second:

```
function caller {
    [IPAddress]::Parse('this is not an IP')
    second
}
function second {
    'second'
}
caller
```

Not only do errors raised by throw differ from those raised by ThrowTerminatingError, but throw statements are also influenced by the error action preference.

throw and ErrorAction

The throw keyword raises a terminating error; terminating errors are described in about_Preference_Variables as not being affected by the ErrorActionPreference.

Unfortunately, errors raised by throw are affected by ErrorAction when ErrorAction is set to SilentlyContinue. This behavior is an important consideration when designing commands for others to use.

The following function throws a terminating error; the second statement should never run:

```
function Invoke-Something {
    [CmdletBinding()]
    param ( )

    throw 'Error'
    Write-Host 'No error'
}
```

Running the function with an error action set to the default, Continue, shows that the error is thrown and the second command does not execute:

```
PS> Invoke-Something
Exception:
Line |
   5 |        throw 'Error'
     |        ~~~~~~~~~~~~~
     | Error
```

If ErrorAction is set to SilentlyContinue or Ignore, throw will be ignored:

```
PS> Invoke-Something -ErrorAction SilentlyContinue
No error
```

The same problem exists if the ErrorActionPreference variable is set in the parent scope:

```
PS> $ErrorActionPreference = 'SilentlyContinue'
PS> Invoke-Something
No error
```

A throw statement can still be used in a script, but because it does not behave as described in the documentation, it must be used with care.

Enclosing a throw statement in a try block will cause it to trigger catch, ending the script as it should regardless of the ErrorAction setting:

```
function Invoke-Something {
    [CmdletBinding()]
    param ( )

    try {
        throw 'Error'
        Write-Host 'No error'
    } catch {
        Write-Host 'An error occurred'
    }
}
```

When the function is called, the content of the catch block executes as it should:

```
PS> Invoke-Something -ErrorAction SilentlyContinue
An error occurred
```

The problem described here also applies when throw is used within the catch block, although, in this case, the script still terminates.

The following script should result in an error being displayed as the error terminates; however, no error is displayed if ErrorAction is set to SilentlyContinue. The error raised in try still prevents the script from progressing to the Write-Host command:

```
function Invoke-Something {
    [CmdletBinding()]
    param ( )

    try {
        throw 'Error'
```

```
        Write-Host 'No error'
    } catch {
        throw 'An error occurred'
    }
}
```

In this version, any statements that appear after the throw statement in the catch block will not execute. When ErrorAction is set to SilentlyContinue, this function runs and returns nothing at all. The only evidence of an error is in the Error variable:

```
PS> $Error.Clear()
PS> Invoke-Something -ErrorAction SilentlyContinue
PS> $Error[0]

Exception:
Line |
   9 |              throw 'An error occurred'
     |              ~~~~~~~~~~~~~~~~~~~~~~~~~~
     | An error occurred
```

For scripts that use the CmdletBinding attribute, ThrowTerminatingError can be used. The ThrowTerminatingError method is not affected by the ErrorAction parameter or the ErrorActionPreference variable:

```
function Invoke-Something {
    [CmdletBinding()]
    param ( )

    try {
        throw 'Error'
        Write-Host 'No error'
    } catch {
        $PSCmdlet.ThrowTerminatingError($_)
    }
}
```

Running the command shows will reliably show the error. The error can be handled by using a try statement in the script, calling this command:

```
PS> Invoke-Something -ErrorAction SilentlyContinue
Exception: Error
```

When using the ErrorAction parameter, the action to be taken applies to the child scope of Invoke-Something; it does not change how the caller's script behaves. The behavior of terminating errors in the caller's scope is explored later in this section.

To establish consistent behavior, the following recommendations can be made:

- Prefer to use `CmdletBinding` with functions, scripts, and script blocks.
- When using `throw`, only use `throw` inside the `try` block.
- Use the `ThrowTerminatingError` method to stop a script from executing.
- Prefer the `WriteError` method when creating non-terminating errors, as this correctly sets the value for `$?`.
- Any script that calls another that may raise an error should expect and handle errors using a `try` block.

The `try` statement can be nested to provide more granular error handling in a script.

Terminating errors in child scopes

The function used in the previous section raises a terminating error within the scope of the function. The function has been modified to include code after the command ended:

```
function Invoke-Something {
    [CmdletBinding()]
    param ( )

    try {
        throw 'Error'
    } catch {
        $PSCmdlet.ThrowTerminatingError($_)
    }
}
```

When a caller invokes this function as part of a script, and `ErrorActionPreference` is `Continue`, `SilentlyContinue`, or `Ignore`, the terminating error will not cause the script to end. The terminating error is raised with respect to the function; it does not tear down all parent scopes:

```
& {
    $ErrorActionPreference = 'Continue'
    Invoke-Something
    'After Invoke-Something'
}
```

This will show that the last statement runs:

```
Exception:
Line |
   3 |         Invoke-Something
     |         ~~~~~~~~~~~~~~~~
     | Error
After Invoke-Something
```

If the caller encloses all statements in try, the error raised by Invoke-Something will trigger catch:

```
& {
    $ErrorActionPreference = 'Continue'
    try {
        Invoke-Something
        'After Invoke-Something'
    } catch {
        throw
    }
}
```

Running the script above will show an error; the After Invoke-Something statement will not run, as shown below:

```
Exception:
Line |
   4 |            Invoke-Something
     |            ~~~~~~~~~~~~~~~~~
     |  Error
```

A similar effect can be achieved by setting $ErrorActionPreference to Stop in the caller scope:

```
& {
    $ErrorActionPreference = 'Stop'
    Invoke-Something
    'After Invoke-Something'
}
```

The error will display, and the script will not continue. The error is shown below.

```
Exception:
Line |
   3 |        Invoke-Something
     |        ~~~~~~~~~~~~~~~~~
     |  Error
```

This shows the importance of considering error handling in every scope rather than depending on globally set preferences.

Nesting try, catch, and finally

One try statement can be inside another to provide granular error handling of small operations.

A script that performs setup actions and then works on several objects in a loop is a good example of a script that might benefit from more than one try statement. The script should terminate cleanly if something goes wrong during setup, but it might only notify if an error occurs within the loop.

The following functions can be used as a working example of such a script. The setup actions might include connecting to a management server or a data source of some kind:

```
function Connect-Server {}
```

Once the connection is established, a set of objects might be retrieved:

```
function Get-ManagementObject {
    1..10 | ForEach-Object {
        [PSCustomObject]@{
            Name     = $_
            Property = "Value$_"
        }
    }
}
```

These objects might be modified by another function, which occasionally goes wrong:

```
function Set-ManagementObject {
    [CmdletBinding()]
    param (
        [Parameter(Mandatory, ValueFromPipeline)]
        $Object,

        $Property
    )
    process {
        try {
            if (Get-Random -Maximum 2) {
                throw 'something went wrong!'
            }
            $Object.Property = $Property
        } catch {
            $PSCmdlet.ThrowTerminatingError($_)
        }
    }
}
```

The following script uses the previous functions. If a terminating error is raised during either the Connect or Get commands, the script will stop. If a terminating error is raised when executing the Set command, the script writes a non-terminating error and moves on to the next object:

```
try {
    Connect-Server
    Get-ManagementObject | ForEach-Object {
```

```
        try {
            $_ | Set-ManagementObject -Property 'NewValue'
        } catch {
            Write-Error -ErrorRecord $_
        }
    }
} catch {
    throw
}
```

A throw is used in the catch block of the statement above, as it does not include a CmdletBinding attribute and a param block.

Before try, catch, and finally were introduced, handling exceptions in PowerShell required the use of a trap statement.

About trap

All the way back in PowerShell 1.0, a trap statement was the only way to handle terminating errors in a script.

As trap very occasionally finds its way into modern scripts, it is beneficial to understand the use of the statement. One possible use in modern scripts might be to log unhandled or unanticipated errors in a script.

trap is used to catch errors raised anywhere within the scope of the trap declaration, that is, the current scope and any child scopes.

The PowerShell engine finds trap statements anywhere within a script before beginning the execution of the script. It deviates from the line-by-line approach you might expect when running a PowerShell script. When PowerShell was first released, this made trap quite confusing to use.

trap is one of the statements within PowerShell that are read when a script is parsed and before it is run. Such statements are not affected by their position within the script. Other examples of parse-time statements include class, enum, and #Requires statements.

Using trap

A trap statement is declared in a similar manner to the catch block. A trap statement can be created to handle any exception type:

```
trap {
    Write-Host 'An error occurred'
}
```

A trap statement can also be created to handle a specific exception type:

```
trap [ArgumentException] {
```

```
        Write-Host 'Argument exception'
    }
```

A script may contain more than one trap statement, for example:

```
trap [InvalidOperationException] {
    Write-Host 'An invalid operation'
}
trap {
    Write-Host 'Catch all other exceptions'
}
```

The ordering of the preceding trap statements does not matter; the statement with the most specific error type is always used to handle a given error.

The following example uses a trap statement at the end of the script to illustrate that the location of the statement is unimportant:

```
& {
    Write-Host 'Statement1'
    throw 'Statement2'
    Write-Host 'Statement3'

    trap { Write-Host 'An error occurred' }
}
```

The error raised by throw causes the trap statement to execute, and then the execution stops; Statement3 is never written.

trap, scope, and continue

By default, if an error is handled by trap, the script execution stops.

The continue keyword can be used to resume a script at the next statement.

The following example handles the error raised by throw and continues onto the next statement:

```
& {
    Write-Host 'Statement1'
    throw 'Statement2'
    Write-Host 'Statement3'

    trap {
        Write-Host 'An error occurred'
        continue
    }
}
```

The behavior of continue is dependent on the scope that the trap statement is written in. In the preceding example, continue moves on to writing Statement3 as the trap statement, and the statements that are executed are in the same scope.

The following script declares a function that throws an error. trap is declared in the parent scope of the function:

```
& {
    function Invoke-Something {
        Write-Host 'Statement1'
        throw 'Statement2'
        Write-Host 'Statement3'
    }

    Invoke-Something
    Write-Host 'Done'

    trap {
        Write-Host 'An error occurred'
        continue
    }
}
```

When the code above runs, the output shown below is displayed:

```
Statement1
An error occurred
Done
```

The continue keyword is used, but Statement3 is not displayed. Execution can only continue in the same scope as the trap statement.

Summary

Error handling in PowerShell is a complex topic, perhaps made more so by inconsistencies in the documentation that can trip up new and experienced PowerShell users.

PowerShell includes the concept of non-terminating errors. Non-terminating errors allow a script, such as one acting on a pipeline, to carry on in the event of an error.

It is not always true that a problem that prevents an action from continuing will be described as a terminating error. The reverse is also true: not all actions that allow an action to continue are described as non-terminating errors. Therefore, care must be taken when writing code to correctly handle error conditions.

Non-terminating errors should be used when writing commands that expect to act on more than one object, if an error is restricted to that one object and does not prevent a broader activity from completing.

Terminating errors can be used when execution absolutely cannot continue.

PowerShell includes several different ways to raise both terminating and non-terminating errors. `Write-Error`, `$PSCmdlet.WriteError`, `throw`, and `$PSCmdlet.ThrowTerminatingError` were all introduced in this chapter.

The problems associated with the use of `throw` were explored, and there were general recommendations that `throw` should be confined to `try` and `$PSCmdlet.ThrowTerminatingError` should be used to end a script in the event of a terminal problem.

Finally, `trap` statements were demonstrated. `trap` has been available since PowerShell 1 and is rarely used in modern scripts. `trap` has largely been superseded by `try`, `catch`, and `finally`, which were introduced with PowerShell 2.

The next chapter explores the debugging options available in PowerShell.

Learn more on Discord

Read this book alongside other users, PowerShell experts, and the author himself. Ask questions, provide solutions to other readers, chat with the author via Ask Me Anything sessions, and much more.

Scan the QR code or visit the link to join the community.

`https://packt.link/SecNet`

23

Debugging

Debugging is the art of discovering, isolating, and fixing bugs in code. The complexity of debugging increases with the complexity of the code.

To a degree, the need to debug complex scripts can be reduced by adopting certain development strategies:

- Scripts should be broken down into discreet units by using functions.
- Each unit of code should strive to excel at one thing only.
- Each unit of code should strive to be as short as it can reasonably be without sacrificing clarity.
- Tests should be developed to ensure that each unit of code acts as it should.
- Use commands such as `Write-Verbose` or `Write-Debug` to write identifiable messages, perhaps including values of variables.

Debugging is an inevitable part of the development process. Fortunately, the debugger itself is not difficult to use.

This chapter explores the following topics:

- Common problems
- Debugging in the console
- Debugging in Visual Studio Code
- Debugging other PowerShell processes

Before looking at specific debugging tools, some of the more common problems can be explored.

Common problems

When supporting PowerShell development, some problems appear again and again. No one is immune from writing a bug into code, no matter how experienced. All experience brings is the ability to find and fix bugs more quickly.

This section explores the following relatively common problems:

- Dash characters
- Operator usage
- Use of named blocks
- Problems with variables

The dash character is a relatively common problem when a piece of code is copied from a blog article or when any code has been corrected by a word processor.

Dash characters

In PowerShell, a hyphen is used to separate the verb from the noun in command names and is also used to denote a parameter name after a command.

When looking for examples on the internet, it is common to bump into PowerShell code that has been formatted into rich text—that is, where the hyphen character has been replaced by a dash character, such as an em or en dash.

In printed text, this problem is difficult to show, which is why it is a problem in the first place.

This command may appear ordinary:

```
Get-Process | Where-Object WorkingSet64 -gt 100MB
```

If the command is pasted into the PowerShell console, the dash characters disappear, and PowerShell will complain that the command does not exist:

Figure 23.1: Pasting into a console

If the command is run in either ISE (under PowerShell 5.1) or the Visual Studio integrated terminal, the dash character stays, but PowerShell still raises an error about the command name. This error message is even less useful because the dash is still present, and the command name appears correct:

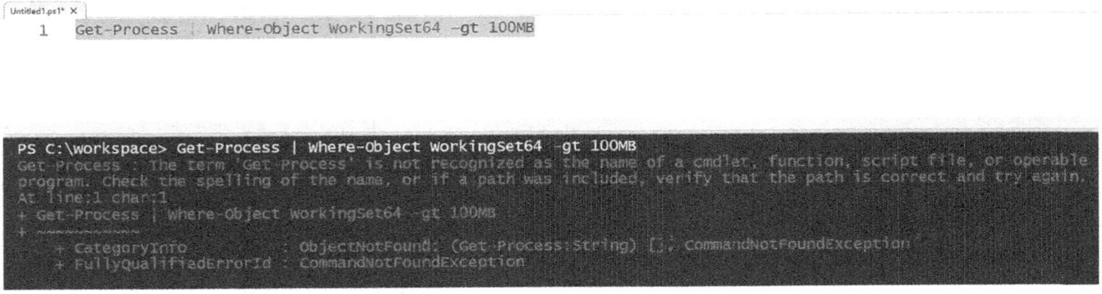

Figure 23.2: Error when running a selection in ISE

The same error shows in Visual Studio Code. This time, the code is executed in PowerShell 7.1.3:

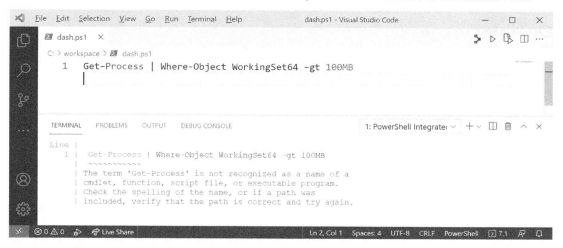

Figure 23.3: Error when running a selection in Visual Studio Code

The syntax highlighter in Visual Studio Code hints at the problem. The Get-Process command in the script has two different colors (the actual colors will depend on which themes are enabled). The Get-Process command should have the same highlighting as the Where-Object command in this example.

The color difference is because the dash character used is not a hyphen—it is an en dash—and this confuses PowerShell, new and old.

Fixing the dash in the Get-Process command (by retyping the character) fixes the Get-Process command, but despite the filter appearing to be correct, the filter will still fail to apply.

The same dash appears again in the -gt parameter, and it must also be fixed for the code to work as intended.

If the problem described previously does not show when pasting the preceding example, the example can be recreated from the following string:

```
"Get$([char]8211)Process | Where-Object WorkingSet64 $([char]8211)gt 100MB"
```

It takes a sharp eye to spot a problem based only on a tiny difference in the length of a dash character. Syntax highlighting helps a lot, but this does not clearly point out that there is a problem.

PSScriptAnalyzer

The default rules in PSScriptAnalyzer do not warn about this problem, but it is possible to create a rule. My module, Indented.ScriptAnalyzerRules, includes a rule for this problem, AvoidDashCharacters:

https://github.com/indented-automation/Indented.ScriptAnalyzerRules.

Operators in PowerShell are another opportunity for bugs to creep into code.

Operator usage

Bugs in code can easily be caused by the incorrect usage of an operator. This can be a logical error, such as using -gt, where -ge was a better choice (or vice versa).

Operators were explored in detail in *Chapter 5, Operators*.

Problems can also be caused if = is accidentally used instead of -eq.

Assignment instead of equality

Accidentally using the assignment operator, =, in place of the equality operator, -eq, is a common problem.

When an assignment operation is enclosed in brackets, PowerShell performs the assignment and returns the value that was assigned—for example:

```
PS> ($variable = $true)
True
```

The same applies if the assignment statement is part of an if statement:

```
if ($variable = $true) {
    Write-Host 'The condition is true'
} else {
    Write-Host 'The condition is false'
}
```

In this example, the variable will always have the value $true because of the assignment inside the if statement.

PowerShell will not highlight this assignment as being an error. It is a legitimate use of the assignment operator. The following example captures the output from the Get-Process command at the same time as testing it:

```
$params = @{
    Name         = 'notepad'
    ErrorAction = 'SilentlyContinue'
}
if ($process = Get-Process @params) {
    Write-Host "$($process.Name) is running, ID is $($process.ID)"
} else {
    Write-Host "$($params.name) is not running"
}
```

It would be easy to argue that this is not a good practice to adopt. However, there is a difference between what is possible and what might be considered a good practice.

PSScriptAnalyzer includes a run that attempts to warn about possible incorrect use of assignment in a condition.

Comparison operators are not the only type of operator that can occasionally cause confusion.

-or instead of -and

The logical operators -and and -or are occasionally easy to confuse. This is typically seen when converting a thought in a natural language directly into code.

For example, the following statement can be translated into code:

```
I want all names which do not start with a or b.
```

The expectation is that the output does not include names starting with a and does not include names starting with b.

When writing the code to implement the statement, it is tempting to use the same logical expression as used in natural language; in this case, that is or:

```
@(
    'Anna'
    'Ben'
    'Chris'
    'David'
) | Where-Object { $_ -notlike 'a*' -or 'b*' }
```

In this case, all the names will be returned. There are two distinct comparisons above, and the second, b*, will always be considered true as it is not an empty string.

Realizing this, and extending the expression to include a second explicit comparison, will still result in unintended values appearing:

```
@(
    'Anna'
    'Ben'
    'Chris'
    'David'
) | Where-Object { $_ -notlike 'a*' -or $_ -notlike 'b*' }
```

Each comparison is evaluated without considering the other. The preceding code will return Anna, because Anna does not start with the letter b, and it will return Ben, because Ben does not begin with the letter a.

Using -and in place of -or will fix the problem in the code, as shown here:

```
@(
    'Anna'
    'Ben'
```

```
        'Chris'
        'David'
) | Where-Object { $_ -notlike 'a*' -and $_ -notlike 'b*' }
```

The filter above will return two names only, as shown below:

```
Chris
David
```

A less common problem can be seen when using a comparison operator on an array.

Negated array comparisons

Each of the comparison operators includes a negated version, that is, -eq and -ne, -match and -notmatch, and so on.

When performing a comparison on an array, it can be tempting to use the negative version of the operator to make an assertion.

In this example, the -notmatch operator is erroneously used to assert that there are no names in the array that start with a or b:

```
$array = @(
    'Anna'
    'Ben'
    'Chris'
    'David'
)
if ($array -notmatch '^[ab]') {
    Write-Host "No names starting A or B"
}
```

When the example above runs, the body of the if statement will execute, and the message will be written as shown below:

```
No names starting A or B
```

When acting on an array, the comparison operator does not return a simple $true or $false; it returns the elements in the array that satisfy the comparison. In the preceding example, the result of the comparison is the strings Chris and David.

If the -not operator is used in conjunction with the -match operator instead, the statement in the body of the if statement becomes more accurate:

```
$array = @(
    'Anna'
    'Ben'
    'Chris'
```

```
    'David'
)
if (-not ($array -match '^[ab]')) {
    Write-Host "No names starting A or B"
}
```

It is easy to make a mistake with a comparison operator and, at times, it can be difficult to spot such problems. Testing is an important part of any development process.

PowerShell uses named blocks to support pipeline operations.

Use of named blocks

The named blocks begin, process, and end are used to support pipeline operations in PowerShell. Named blocks are also used if dynamic parameters are in use.

Named blocks are explored in *Chapter 17*, *Scripts, Functions, and Script Blocks*.

Dynamic parameters are explored in *Chapter 18*, *Parameters, Validation, and Dynamic Parameters*.

When a named block is used, all code must be placed inside named blocks.

Code outside of a named block

Placing code outside of a named block when named blocks are in use can result in several different errors.

In the following example, a verbose statement has erroneously been placed before the process block. The function uses a brace style where the opening brace is placed on the line after the statement:

```
function Get-Something
{
    [CmdletBinding()]
    param
    (
        [Parameter(ValueFromPipeline)]
        [string]
        $InputObject
    )
    Write-Verbose 'Starting Get-Something'

    process
    {
        Write-Verbose "Working on $InputObject"
    }
}
```

It would be easy to expect an editor to regard this script as invalid; however, it is not. When it is run, the following happens:

1. The `Write-Verbose` statement will run (showing a message using -Verbose).
2. A list of processes will be displayed.
3. The script block containing the second `Write-Verbose` statement will be emitted, but not executed.

These actions happen because the first statement after param defines the block that is used. `Write-Verbose` means all content is placed in the end block (the default for the function).

The process statement is considered a command and implicitly aliased to `Get-Process`. PowerShell attempts to find and run a `Get-` command for all bare words that do not explicitly resolve to another command; for example, running the service will cause `Get-Service` to execute.

If the braces were placed on the same line as the preceding statement, the outcome would be slightly different:

```powershell
function Get-Something {
    [CmdletBinding()]
    param (
        [Parameter(ValueFromPipeline)]
        [string]
        $InputObject
    )

    Write-Verbose 'Starting Get-Something'

    process {
        Write-Verbose "Working on $InputObject"
    }
}
```

This time, when the function is run, the output is as follows:

1. The `Write-Verbose` statement will run (showing a message using -Verbose).
2. `Get-Process` attempts to run, but an error is thrown because the script block containing `Write-Verbose` is not a valid parameter.

The error when this function runs is shown below:

```
PS> Get-Something
Get-Process:
Line |
  10 |         process {
     |                 ~
```

```
    | Cannot evaluate parameter 'Name' because its argument is specified as a
script block and there is no input. A script block cannot be evaluated without
input.
```

When one named block is used, all code must be placed inside a named block. Moving the initial Write-Verbose statement into a begin block will fix the problem with the function.

If no blocks are defined, PowerShell uses the default block. For functions, scripts, and script blocks, the default block is end. For functions created using the filter keyword, the default block is process.

Pipeline without process

Functions can be created with parameters that accept pipeline input. If the body of the function is not placed inside a named block, then PowerShell will use the default block, end.

When a pipeline parameter is added to a function that only implements an end block, the body of the function will only ever be able to use the last value in the pipeline:

```
function Write-Number {
    [CmdletBinding()]
    param (
        [Parameter(ValueFromPipeline)]
        [int]
        $Number
    )
    Write-Host $Number
}
```

When running in a pipeline, only the last of the input values will be displayed:

```
PS> 1..5 | Write-Number
5
```

Moving the body of the function into a process block will allow it to act on all values from the input pipeline:

```
function Write-Number {
    [CmdletBinding()]
    param (
        [Parameter(ValueFromPipeline)]
        [int]
        $Number
    )

    process {
        Write-Host $Number
    }
}
```

When the function is used, it will correctly display each of the numbers read from the pipeline because the process block is correctly implemented:

```
PS> 1..5 | Write-Number
1
2
3
4
5
```

Perhaps one of the most obvious causes of bugs is a problem with a variable.

Problems with variables

Variables are a critical part of almost every script. Potential problems with variables include:

- Typing errors
- Incorrectly assigned types
- Accidental use of reserved variables

It is difficult to solve the problems above using tools; context plays a large part in determining what is correct. Understanding context often requires a human actor. Humans are particularly good at spotting patterns, while computers must be taught based on large sample sets.

One possible technical solution that can be used to reduce the risk impact of typing errors is strict mode in PowerShell.

About strict mode

Strict mode in PowerShell is used to add several additional parser rules when evaluating scripts. Strict mode is enabled using the Set-StrictMode command. The mode is applied to the current scope and all child scopes.

Set-StrictMode can be used in a module without affecting the global scope or any other modules.

Strict mode can be set to one of three (effective) values:

- 1.0
- 2.0
- Latest

For example, the following command sets strict mode to Latest:

```
Set-StrictMode -Version Latest
```

The effect of each of these modes is described in the help file for Set-StrictMode. When Latest is used as the mode, the effect in PowerShell is that it:

- Prohibits the use of uninitialized variables
- Prohibits references to non-existent properties of objects

- Prohibits function calls that use the syntax for calling methods
- Prohibits out-of-bounds or unresolvable array indexes

For example, when enabled in the following function, strict mode causes an error because of the mistake in a variable name:

```
function Test-StrictMode {
    Set-StrictMode -Version Latest

    $names = 'pwsh', 'powershell'
    foreach ($name in $naems) {
        Write-Host $name
    }
}
```

When the function runs, an error relating to the variable name is displayed:

```
PS> Test-StrictMode
InvalidOperation:
Line |
   5 |        foreach ($name in $naems) {
     |                          ~~~~~~~
     | The variable '$naems' cannot be retrieved because it has not been set.
```

It is important to note that Set-StrictMode does not enforce scope, so if, for some reason, the $naems variable were to exist in a parent scope, the error would not be displayed.

Set-StrictMode has a mixed reputation in the PowerShell community. On the one hand, it offers some small protection against errors. On the other hand, it prohibits certain simple patterns, for instance, testing for a non-existent property on an object.

Most important of all, the protection strict mode brings is only displayed at runtime.

As a developer, the problem with the variable ideally needs to be shown in an editor when writing code. By the time a script is handed to someone else to run, it is far too late to show errors about variable usage.

Without strict mode, it is possible to test for a null, empty, false, or non-existent property in an if statement, as the following shows:

```
$object = [PSCustomObject]@{
    ValueA = 1
}
if ($object.ValueB) {
    Write-Host "ValueB is set"
}
```

Enabling strict mode will instead show an error:

```
Set-StrictMode -Version Latest
if ($object.ValueB) {
    Write-Host "ValueB is set"
}
```

The statement above will show the error shown below:

```
PropertyNotFoundException:
Line |
   2 |   if ($object.ValueB) {
     |        ~~~~~~~~~~~~~~~
     | The property 'ValueB' cannot be found on this object. Verify that the
property exists.
```

To accommodate strict mode, the condition must become much more complex, making use of the hidden PSObject member of objects in PowerShell:

```
Set-StrictMode -Version Latest

$object = [PSCustomObject]@{
    ValueA = 1
}
if ($object.PSObject.Properties['ValueB'] -and
    $object.ValueB
) {
    Write-Host "ValueB is set"
}
```

Strict mode can be disabled at any time by using the following command:

```
Set-StrictMode -Off
```

It is up to each developer to decide whether strict mode is appropriate.

Beyond typing mistakes, one of the most common errors with variables is caused by assigning a type to a variable.

Variables and types

Variables in PowerShell may be assigned a type on creation by placing the type on the left-hand side of the variable. For example, the variable in the following code is defined as having a string type:

```
[string]$string = 'Hello world'
```

Any subsequent assignment to the variable will be coerced into a string:

```
PS> $string = @{}
PS> $string
System.Collections.Hashtable
```

The GetType method can be used to show that the value is a string, regardless of the assignment:

```
PS> $string.GetType()

IsPublic IsSerial Name       BaseType
-------- -------- ----       --------
True     True     String     System.Object
```

The type applies to all assignments made to that variable until either another type is assigned (on the left-hand side of the variable) or the variable is destroyed using the Remove-Variable command.

This is most commonly a problem where a parameter for a command is created with a type, and an attempt is made to reuse the variable in the body script or function.

Assigning a type to a variable can have interesting consequences when applied to an automatic variable.

Types and reserved variables

PowerShell includes many built-in variables; these variables are described in the about_automatic_ variables help file:

```
Get-Help about_automatic_variables
```

Several of these variables only exist in a specific context. For example, the $foreach variable only exists inside a foreach loop.

Accidental use of reserved variables as parameters with a type constraint can cause errors.

For example, the following switch statement will act on either true or false:

```
switch ($true) {
    $true  { 'The value is true' }
    $false { 'The value is false' }
}
```

If a type is erroneously assigned to a variable called $switch, the statement will no longer function as the iterator it requires is broken. Instead, an error will be displayed:

```
[switch]$Switch = $true
switch ($true) {
    $true  { 'The value is true' }
    $false { 'The value is false' }
}
```

The following `System.SZArrayEnumerator` error is the type the `$switch` variable should have but no longer does because of the previous assignment statement:

```
MetadataError:
Line |
   2 |   switch ($true) {
     |          ~~~~~
     | Cannot convert value "System.ArrayEnumerator" to type "System.
Management.Automation.SwitchParameter". Boolean parameters accept only Boolean
values and numbers, such as $True, $False, 1 or 0.
```

Windows PowerShell will display a slightly different error, this time referencing the `System.Array+SZArrayEnumerator` type.

PowerShell will not prevent this from happening; it is up to a developer to prevent this problem in the first place.

The problem with `switch` in the preceding example will persist until either PowerShell is restarted or the variable is removed:

```
Remove-Variable switch
```

It is important to be mindful of and avoid using automatic variables in code.

Being aware of potential problems avoids the need for extensive debugging. When the problem is less obvious, the debugger can be used.

Debugging in the console

The PowerShell debugger allows code execution to be paused and the state of a script to be analyzed at a specific point.

These points are known as breakpoints and are set using the `Set-PSBreakpoint` command.

PowerShell describes the following operations in the about_Debuggers help file:

```
Get-Help about_Debuggers
```

The `Set-PSBreakpoint` command can be used to set a breakpoint when a command is run, when a variable is used, or on a specific line in a saved script.

Setting a command breakpoint

Setting a breakpoint on a command will trigger the debugger when that command is run.

In the next example, a breakpoint is created that triggers when the `Get-Process` command runs. As `Get-Process` is inside a loop, it will be possible to inspect the state of variables inside the loop in the debugger:

```
Set-PSBreakpoint -Command Get-Process
$names = 'powershell', 'pwsh', 'code'
```

```
foreach ($name in $names) {
    Get-Process $name -ErrorAction SilentlyContinue
}
```

When the example is run, the DBG prompt will appear:

```
Hit Command breakpoint on 'Get-Process'
At line:2 char:5
+       Get-Process $name -ErrorAction SilentlyContinue
+       ~~~~~~~~~~~~~~~~~~~~~~~~~~~~~~~~~~~~~~~~~~~~~~~~~~
[DBG]: PS C:\workspace>>
```

Pressing ? in the DBG prompt will show the possible debug actions. The output is shown in *Figure 23.4*:

```
PS C:\workspace> foreach ($name in $names) {
>>      Get-Process $name -ErrorAction SilentlyContinue
>> }
Entering debug mode. Use h or ? for help.

Hit Command breakpoint on 'Get-Process'

At line:2 char:5
+       Get-Process $name -ErrorAction SilentlyContinue
+       ~~~~~~~~~~~~~~~~~~~~~~~~~~~~~~~~~~~~~~~~~~~~~~~~~~
[DBG]: PS C:\workspace>> ?

 s, stepInto          Single step (step into functions, scripts, etc.)
 v, stepOver          Step to next statement (step over functions, scripts, etc.)
 o, stepOut           Step out of the current function, script, etc.

 c, continue          Continue operation
 q, quit              Stop operation and exit the debugger
 d, detach            Continue operation and detach the debugger.

 k, Get-PSCallStack Display call stack

 l, list              List source code for the current script.
                      Use "list" to start from the current line, "list <m>"
                      to start from line <m>, and "list <m> <n>" to list <n>
                      lines starting from line <m>

 <enter>              Repeat last command if it was stepInto, stepOver or list

 ?, h                 displays this help message.

For instructions about how to customize your debugger prompt, type "help about_prompt".
```

Figure 23.4: Error when running a selection in Visual Studio Code

In addition to these actions, any variable values may be inspected at this point in the loop simply by typing the variable name into the prompt:

```
[DBG]: PS C:\workspace>> $name
powershell
```

The current script may be displayed using the list command inside the debug prompt. By default, it will list the entire script. A range of lines may be displayed by specifying optional start and end line numbers for the list command:

```
[DBG]: PS C:\workspace>> list 1 2
    1:   foreach ($name in $names) {
    2:*      Get-Process $name -ErrorAction SilentlyContinue
```

If the end line is not specified, the command will display all script lines from the start to the end of the script.

Pressing c, to continue, will move to the next iteration in the loop. If any of the processes are not running, an error will be displayed by Get-Process. This time, the $name variable will show the second item in the loop:

```
[DBG]: PS C:\workspace>> $name
pwsh
```

If the process is running, the process objects will be returned. Once the script completes, the debug prompt will close.

Breakpoints in a session can be viewed using the Get-PSBreakpoint command, and any existing breakpoint can be removed using Remove-PSBreakpoint. The following command removes all breakpoints in the session:

```
Get-PSBreakpoint | Remove-PSBreakpoint
```

Breakpoints may also be set on variables.

Using variable breakpoints

When a breakpoint is set on a variable, it will, by default, only trigger when the variable is set (written to).

Writing to a variable means changing the value held by the variable. In the following example, the value of the $newValue variable is set five times, once per iteration of the loop:

```
foreach ($value in 1..5) {
    $newValue = $value
}
```

Setting a breakpoint based on this variable will therefore cause the debugger to pause execution five times:

```
Set-PSBreakpoint -Variable newValue
foreach ($value in 1..5) {
    $newValue = $value
}
```

If a variable holds a collection, such as a hashtable, it is important to note that adding a key is not a write operation with respect to the variable. In this example, the debugger will only trigger when $values is created:

```
Set-PSBreakpoint -Variable values
$values = @{}
foreach ($value in 1..5) {
    $values[$value] = $value
}
```

The operation to add a key to the hashtable is performed on the value of the variable, which is read from the variable object.

The -Mode parameter, which has the default value Write, may be used to trigger the debugger when a variable is read by setting the argument to either Read or ReadWrite.

If the last breakpoint is removed, and a new breakpoint added, the debugger will trigger five times again:

```
Set-PSBreakpoint -Variable values -Mode Read
$values = @{}
foreach ($value in 1..5) {
    $values[$value] = $value
}
```

The most common use of the debugger is a line breakpoint.

Setting a line breakpoint

A line breakpoint can only be set if a script is saved to a file. The debugger will trigger when the line in the script is executed. The debugger may be used to explore the current state:

```
@'
$names = 'powershell', 'pwsh', 'code'
foreach ($name in $names) {
    Get-Process $name -ErrorAction SilentlyContinue
}
'@ | Set-Content script.ps1
Set-PSBreakpoint -Script script.ps1 -Line 3
.\script.ps1
```

When accessing script variables inside the debugger, several automatic variables cannot be viewed:

- $Args
- $Input
- $MyInvocation
- $PSBoundParameters

These variables are used by the debugger and are therefore overwritten by the debugger, hiding any values the script might use.

The value of an automatic variable should be assigned to another named variable in the script to view the content of that variable. For example, the $PSBoundParameters variable value is assigned to another variable in the following example:

```
@'
param (
    [string[]]$Name
)


$boundParameters = $PSBoundParameters
foreach ($processName in $Name) {
    Get-Process $name -ErrorAction SilentlyContinue
}
'@ | Set-Content script.ps1
Set-PSBreakpoint -Script script.ps1 -Line 7
```

When the debugger starts, the value of the $boundParameters variable can be inspected, but the value of $PSBoundParameters is not available. This is shown in the following snippet:

```
PS C:\workspace> .\script.ps1 -Name 'pwsh'
Hit Line breakpoint on 'C:\workspace\script.ps1:7'
At C:\workspace\script.ps1:7 char:5
+     Get-Process $name
+     ~~~~~~~~~~~~~~~~~~
```

In the debug prompt, $PSBoundParameters will be null:

```
[DBG]: PS C:\workspace>> $PSBoundParameters
```

The assigned $boundParameters will be available:

```
[DBG]: PS C:\workspace>> $boundParameters

Key   Value
---   -----
Name  {pwsh}
```

Setting breakpoints using line numbers in the console is possible but is not the easiest way to work with the debugger.

The Visual Studio Code editor includes a debugger interface, which is a lot easier to work with than the command line.

Debugging in Visual Studio Code

Visual Studio Code and other interactive editors greatly simplify working with the debugger. The debugger is accessed via a button on the left-hand side of the editor.

Using the debugger

The debugging options in Visual Studio Code, by default, will run a script and stop at any defined breakpoint.

The `param` block is removed from `script.ps1` for this example, making the content:

```
$names = 'powershell', 'pwsh', 'code'
foreach ($name in $names) {
    Get-Process $name -ErrorAction SilentlyContinue
}
```

Breakpoints can be added to a script by clicking to the left of the line number. A breakpoint has been added to `script.ps1`, as shown in *Figure 23.5*:

Figure 23.5: Debugging in Visual Studio Code

The breakpoint appears as a red dot next to the line. When the **Run and Debug** button is pressed, Visual Studio Code will execute the script. The script in this case is run in PowerShell 7.1 based on the version in the bottom-left corner of the editor.

When run, the **VARIABLES** and **CALL STACK** boxes will fill as shown in *Figure 23.6*:

Figure 23.6: Accessible variables in the debugger

The icons in the bar at the top of the window present the different options for the debugger:

Figure 23.7: Debugger controls

Pressing the left-most icon, *Continue*, will move on to the next breakpoint.

The **VARIABLES** box on the left-hand side shows the state of each of the variables in PowerShell at the point the debugger stopped. The values of the $name and $names variables are visible and can be inspected.

Viewing CALL STACK

CALL STACK is used to record the path taken to a specific point in code. **CALL STACK** includes a record of each command, script, or script block that was called.

A script that contains a single command with a breakpoint, such as the following script, will only contain itself in **CALL STACK**:

```
Write-Host 'Hello world'
```

This is shown in *Figure 23.8*:

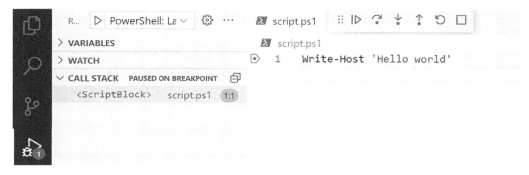

Figure 23.8: Viewing CALL STACK

Each script, function, or script block that is called to get to the breakpoint is added to **CALL STACK**. In the following script, getting to the breakpoint means calling the first function, then the second, and then the third:

```
function first {
    second
}
function second {
    third
}
function third {
    Write-Host 'Hello world'
}
first
```

Each time a function is called from inside an existing function (or script, or script block), a new value is added to **CALL STACK**:

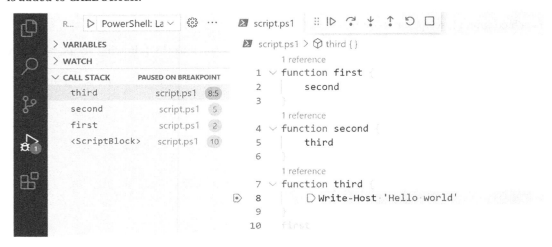

Figure 23.9: Viewing CALL STACK with nested functions

Clicking on each of the entries in **CALL STACK** will show what was called to get to the breakpoint. The final entry in **CALL STACK** will highlight line **10**.

This allows a developer to follow the path to the breakpoint even if a script is more complex.

The functions in the previous example do not make use of any variables. The **Auto** section of the **VARIABLES** window is therefore empty.

Using launch configurations

A launch configuration is a JSON file that describes how debugging should be performed. Launch configurations are valuable if a script requires arguments. Without a launch configuration, the script would have to be edited, removing any required arguments.

Launch configurations are only available when Visual Studio Code has a directory open. If the editor was used to open a file path, the **Run and Debug** option will show the need to open a folder:

Figure 23.10: Opening a folder dialog

Selecting open a folder will offer a prompt for the directory containing the current script. Clicking **OK** will open that directory, and the **Explorer** option will contain all the files in that folder.

Returning to the **Run and Debug** option will now offer an option to **create a launch .json file**:

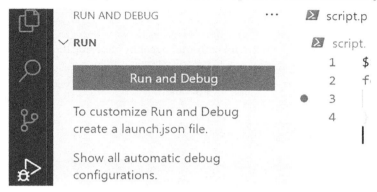

Figure 23.11: Creating a launch configuration

Clicking on the new option will open a new menu. Selecting **Launch Current File** will create a launch. json file in a .vscode folder in the current directory.

The launch.json file can be edited, adding a configuration that can be used to run a specific script.

Each configuration is written in JSON. In the following example, the existing entry is copied and used to create a new launch configuration. The configuration includes the args property, and a value is set to satisfy the script:

```
{
    "version": "0.2.0",
    "configurations": [
        {
            "name": "PowerShell: Launch Current File",
            "type": "PowerShell",
            "request": "launch",
            "script": "${file}",
            "cwd": "${file}"
        },
        {
            "name": "PowerShell: Launch with arguments",
            "type": "PowerShell",
            "request": "launch",
            "script": "${file}",
            "cwd": "${file}",
            "args": [
```

```
                "-Name pwsh"
            ]
        }
    ]
}
```

A script requiring arguments can now be run in the debugger by choosing the new **PowerShell: Launch with arguments** configuration:

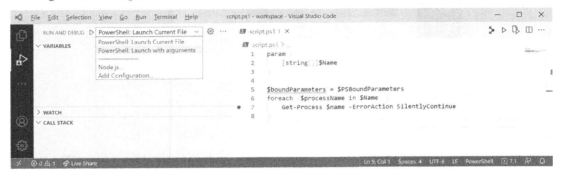

Figure 23.12: Launch with arguments

Debugging modules also requires another step.

Debugging modules

Breakpoints may be used anywhere in a module, but the module must be invoked by a script.

A script module in a psm1 file cannot be directly invoked. Attempting to run the debugging on a psm1 file will open an editor instead of running content.

A script to import and then run the module code is required to visit the breakpoints within the module.

In *Chapter 20, Building Modules*, a LocalMachine module was created. The module can easily be edited in Visual Studio and the debugger is used via a script to run specific commands.

The harness script and the breakpoint are shown in *Figure 23.13*.

Figure 23.13: Breakpoint in module

A complex script or module may include many variables. This can make attempting to track values using the **VARIABLES** window difficult.

Using WATCH

You can use the **WATCH** window to track a smaller number of variables or expressions as breakpoints are triggered.

The next example script sets two variables with every iteration of a loop:

```
$AValue = $ZValue = 0
for ($i = 0; $i -lt 10; $i++) {
    $AValue = $i
    $ZValue = $i * 2
}
```

The names of the variables mean they will appear at opposite ends of the **VARIABLES** window.

Each variable can be added to the **WATCH** window and the debugger will show the current value of those variables. Before the debugger runs, the value is shown as not available:

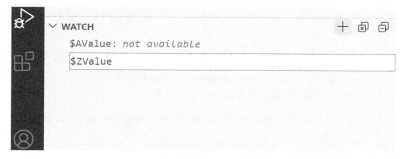

Figure 23.14: WATCH expressions

Once the debugger is started, the variables will be given their initial values as defined by the script. Then, each time **Continue** is pressed, the values will update to reflect that iteration of the loop.

For example, after the fifth press of **Continue**, the updated state of the variables is as follows:

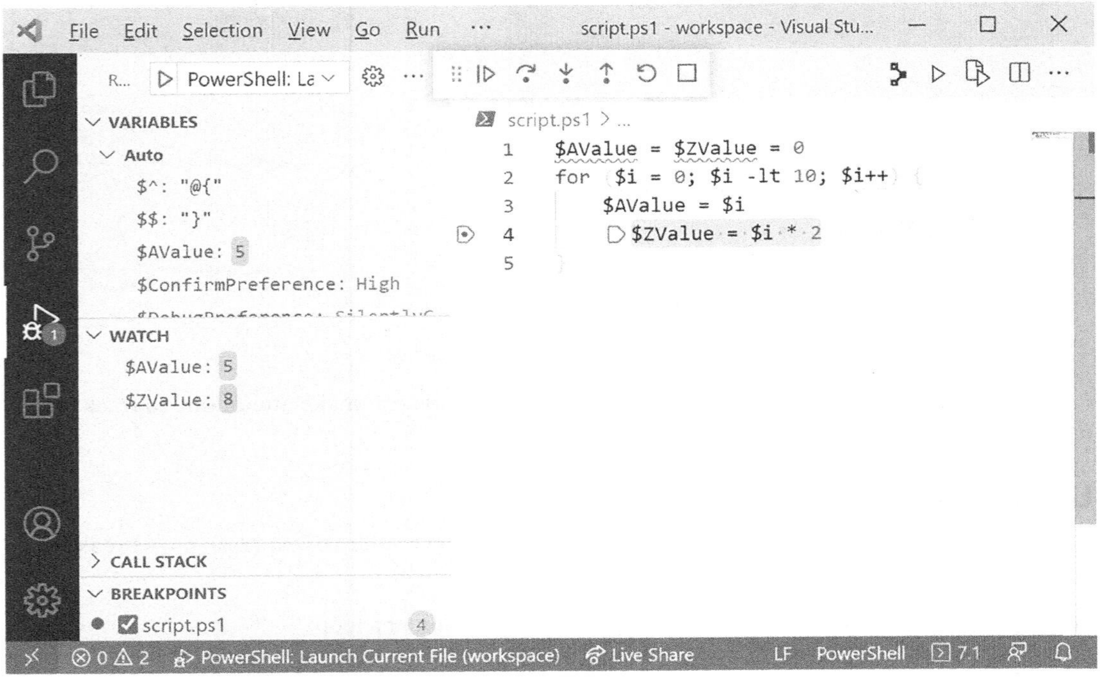

Figure 23.15: WATCH in action

The expression added to **WATCH** can be any command or statement that returns a simple value. Complex values, such as custom objects, will not display well in the **WATCH** window.

The debugging in Visual Studio Code is an especially useful tool that simplifies debugging complex scripts.

Debugging other PowerShell processes

A PowerShell developer can make use of Enter-PSHostProcess to debug a script running in a different PowerShell process.

The Enter-PSHostProcess command creates a remote runspace inside an existing PowerShell process.

Demonstrating use requires two PowerShell processes. The first PowerShell process is started, and for convenience, the PID of that process is shown.

A simple infinite loop is started after setting the window title to show the current PID:

```
$host.UI.RawUI.WindowTitle = 'Script runner: {0}' -f $PID
$i = 0
```

```
while ($true) {
    Write-Host "Working on $i"
    $i++
    Start-Sleep -Seconds 30
}
```

In the example that follows, the first process showed a PID of 14504 and is used to connect to that process. This PID will be different in each case.

A second process is started and the Enter-PSHostProcess command is used to connect to the original PID. The prompt will change to reflect the connection to the remote process.

```
[Process:14504]: PS>
```

The Get-Runspace command can be used to list runspaces in use in the remote host. Note that two runspaces are shown in this example. The first, Runspace1, is the running the loop, and the second is the remote connection to the process:

```
[Process:14504]: PS> Get-Runspace

Id Name         ComputerName    Type    State     Availability
-- ----         ------------    ----    -----     ------------
 1 Runspace1    localhost       Local   Opened    Busy
 2 RemoteHost   localhost       Local   Opened    Busy
```

Since Runspace1 is running the loop, it is desirable to debug that runspace.

The Debug-Runspace command can be used with the BreakAll switch to start the debugging when the next statement in the script runs.

```
Debug-Runspace -BreakAll
```

Note that the script may be sleeping, the debugger will not interrupt a running command, it will stop on the next line of PowerShell code.

The prompt will change again, this time showing DBG as shown in *Figure 23.16*.

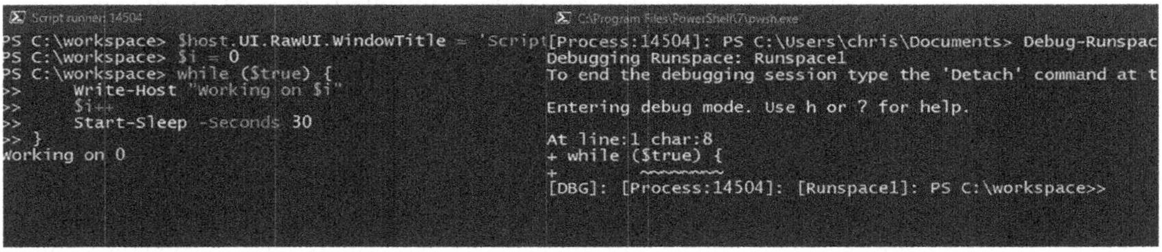

Figure 23.16: Remote process debug prompt

At this point, the debugger may be used in the same way as when exploring usage in the console. The current value of any variables may be explored, and the call stack is accessible using the Get-PSCallStack command.

Running the Detach command disconnects the debugger:

```
Detach
```

Once the debugger has stopped, the loop will continue.

Summary

Some errors in PowerShell come up again and again, and being able to spot and identify such errors can reduce the amount of time spent attempting to isolate a problem. Several common problems were introduced based on real-world bugs.

Not every bug can be attributed to a common error, and sometimes a more extensive investigation is required. PowerShell includes a debugger that can be used from either the command line or an editor to isolate bugs.

Visual Studio is a PowerShell editor that simplifies using the PowerShell debugger. It makes it easier for a developer to use line-based debugging.

This chapter brings this book to a close. PowerShell is full of rabbit holes to dive down and explore, more than is possible to include in this book.

Perhaps one of the most prominent features of PowerShell is consistency. Each command, each module, is presented consistently, and each has help immediately available or downloadable using Update-Help.

The move to .NET Core and open source has opened interesting avenues for exploring the inner workings of PowerShell, fixing bugs, and extending the language.

Each new release of PowerShell includes new features, fixes, and sometimes new bugs to explore. For example, the upcoming 7.5 release has several new features: https://learn.microsoft.com/powershell/scripting/whats-new/what-s-new-in-powershell-75.

Few of the major third-party modules were explicitly demonstrated in this book and favor a task-oriented approach depending on interest and responsibilities. Third-party in this case includes those developed by the wider Microsoft organization, anyone outside the PowerShell team.

Modules like the Microsoft ActiveDirectory module are notorious for confusing filter syntax, a complex topic on its own. Similarly, the Microsoft Graph modules are extremely popular and can be difficult to learn.

Utilizing more features from .NET is a huge area to explore, again with a task-oriented approach. Similarly, extending into developing modules in compiled languages like C# was beyond the scope of this book, but you may wish to look into this as you continue on your learning journey.

PowerShell is supported by a fantastic friendly community, willing to help and chat regardless of experience level. User groups exist in many parts of the world, and the virtual PowerShell user group is always available: https://poshcode.org/.

All these things combine to make PowerShell a fun language to learn and use.

Learn more on Discord

Read this book alongside other users, PowerShell experts, and the author himself. Ask questions, provide solutions to other readers, chat with the author via Ask Me Anything sessions, and much more.

Scan the QR code or visit the link to join the community.

https://packt.link/SecNet

packt.com

Subscribe to our online digital library for full access to over 7,000 books and videos, as well as industry leading tools to help you plan your personal development and advance your career. For more information, please visit our website.

Why subscribe?

- Spend less time learning and more time coding with practical eBooks and Videos from over 4,000 industry professionals
- Improve your learning with Skill Plans built especially for you
- Get a free eBook or video every month
- Fully searchable for easy access to vital information
- Copy and paste, print, and bookmark content

At www.packt.com, you can also read a collection of free technical articles, sign up for a range of free newsletters, and receive exclusive discounts and offers on Packt books and eBooks.

Other Books You May Enjoy

If you enjoyed this book, you may be interested in these other books by Packt:

Windows Server Automation with PowerShell Cookbook - Fifth Edition

Thomas Lee

ISBN: 9781804614235

- Perform key admin tasks on Windows Server
- Keep your organization secure with JEA, group policies, logs, and Windows Defender
- Use .NET Framework for administrative scripting
- Manage data and storage on Windows, including disks, volumes, and filesystems
- Report system performance using built-in cmdlets and WMI to obtain single measurements
- Apply the right tools and modules to troubleshoot and debug Windows Server
- Create, manage, and back up a second VM using the subnetwork in Azure
- Learn how to set up a VPN in Azure with PowerShell

Mastering Microsoft Intune - Second Edition

Christiaan Brinkhoff, Per Larsen

ISBN: 9781835468517

- Simplify the deployment of Windows in the cloud with Windows 365 Cloud PCs
- Deliver next-generation security features with Intune Suite
- Simplify Windows Updates with Windows Autopatch
- Configure advanced policy management within Intune
- Discover modern profile management and migration options for physical and Cloud PCs
- Harden security with baseline settings and other security best practices
- Find troubleshooting tips and tricks for Intune, Windows 365 Cloud PCs, and more
- Discover deployment best practices for physical and cloud-managed endpoints

Packt is searching for authors like you

If you're interested in becoming an author for Packt, please visit authors.packtpub.com and apply today. We have worked with thousands of developers and tech professionals, just like you, to help them share their insight with the global tech community. You can make a general application, apply for a specific hot topic that we are recruiting an author for, or submit your own idea.

Share your thoughts

Now you've finished *Mastering PowerShell Scripting, Fifth Edition*, we'd love to hear your thoughts! Scan the QR code below to go straight to the Amazon review page for this book and share your feedback or leave a review on the site that you purchased it from.

https://packt.link/r/1805120271

Your review is important to us and the tech community and will help us make sure we're delivering excellent quality content.

Index

A

About_* help files 14, 15
Abstract Syntax Tree (AST) 509, 660
  searching 669-671
  using 666-668
  visualizing 668, 669
acceptance testing 659, 678, 679
Access Control Entries (ACEs) 282, 325
  adding 288
  filesystem rights 288-290
  registry rights 290
  removing 286, 287
Access Control List (ACL) 282
  numeric values 290-292
access mask 286
access modifiers 107-109
Action delegate 510
  using 510-512
Adapted Type Systems (ATS) 106
  reference link 106
add and assign operator 187
Add-Content command 272
addition operator 162, 163
Add-Member command 115
  and custom objects 116, 117
Alias attribute 532
Allow attributes 573
AllowEmptyCollection attribute 574, 575
AllowEmptyString attribute 574
AllowNull attribute 573, 574
and operator 179
ArgumentCompleter attribute 588, 589
argument completers 587, 588, 644
ArgumentList parameter 412, 413
argument-transformation attribute 637
argument-transformation attribute classes 637-639

ArgumentTypeConverterAttribute type 253-256
arithmetic operators 161
  addition 162, 163
  decrement 165-167
  division 164
  increment 165-167
  multiplication 164
  remainder 165
  subtraction 163, 164
Array.Reverse Method
  reference link 249
arrays 80, 81
  ArrayList 85, 86
  creating 82, 83
  creating, by assignment 81, 82
  elements, adding to 83, 84
  elements, removing 89
  elements, removing by index 90
  elements, selecting from 86-89
  element values, modifying 89
  jagged arrays 92
  List 84, 85
  multi-dimensional arrays 91
  variables, filling from 90, 91
  with type 83
array sub-expression operator 159, 160
  using, to break up lines 543-545
as operator 190, 191
assembly 232, 233
assignment operators 186
  add and assign 187
  assign 186
  divide-and-assign 188
  multiply and assign 188
  remainder-and-assign 188
  subtract and assign 188
assign operator 186
automatic testing 659

B

background operator 205, 442

bad SSL site
  URL 380

band (Bitwise AND) operator 182

basic authentication 385

begin block 533

binary operator 160

bitwise operators 180, 181
  band (Bitwise AND) 182
  bnot (Bitwise NOT) 183
  bor (Bitwise OR) 182
  bxor (Bitwise eXclusive OR) 182
  shl (Shift left) 183
  shr (Shift right) 183

black-box testing 659

bnot (Bitwise NOT) operator 183

BOM values
  reference link 194

bor (Bitwise OR) operator 182

boxing 256

break keyword 224

breakpoints 760

bxor (Bitwise eXclusive OR) operator 182

Byte Order Mark (BOM) 274

C

call operator 197, 198

CALL STACK
  viewing 767, 768

Cascading Style Sheet (CSS) 332

casting
  supporting 631-633

catch block 727-729, 742

CertificatePolicy 380

certificate validation 380

CIM commands 301
  associated classes 309
  Get-CimClass command 302, 303
  Get-CimInstance command 301, 302
  Invoke-CimMethod command 303-305
  New-CimInstance command 306

Remove-CimInstance command 307

CIM objects
  mocking 705-707

CIM sessions 430, 431
  using 432
  working with 308

classes 236, 616, 617, 648
  constructors 618, 619
  hidden modifier 621
  inheritance 622, 623
  methods 619, 620
  properties 617
  runspace affinity 634-637
  static modifier 622

clean block 536, 537

Clear-Variable command 73

closures 521

CmdletBinding attribute 525
  common parameters 525, 526
  properties 526, 527
  ShouldContinue 527, 530, 531
  ShouldProcess 527-529

code coverage 679

command breakpoint
  setting 760-762

command line 3, 4

commands 15
  aliases 17, 18
  finding 16, 17
  mocking 690-693
  nouns 16
  verbs 15, 16

comma operator 196

comment-based help 545, 546
  examples 551
  output help 546-548
  parameter help 548-550

Common Information Model (CIM) 301, 430

common issues 747
  dash character 748, 749
  named blocks, usage 753
  operator usage 750
  with variables 756

Common Language Infrastructure (CLI) 145

Compare-Object command 139-141

comparison operators 167
  arrays 170-172
  case sensitivity 170
  comparisons to null 172
  contains 173
  eq 167, 168
  greater than 169
  in 173
  less than 169
  like 168
  ne 167, 168
  notlike 168
CompletionResult object 590, 591
composite formatting
  reference link 198
concurrent access
  managing 467-471
conditional parameters 604, 605
conditional statement 207
conditional testing 687
console
  debugging 760
constructors 243, 244, 618, 619
  inheritance 624-627
contains operator 173
content
  reading 271, 272
  reading, from pipeline 271
  writing 271-273
  writing, in pipeline 271
Context keyword 680
continue keyword 224, 743, 744
ConvertFrom-Json command 366-369
  AsHashtable 369
  NoEnumerate 370
Convert-Path command 266
ConvertTo-Html command 331-334
  HTML content, modifying 335, 336
  multiple tables 332
  style, adding 332, 333
ConvertTo-Json command 363, 364
  AsArray 365
  EnumsAsStrings 364, 365
  EscapeHandling 365, 366
ConvertTo-Xml command 341, 342

Copy-Item command 416
CredSSP 429
custom script analyzer rules 672, 673

D

dash characters 748, 749
debugger
  using 765, 766
debugging 747
debugging modules 770, 771
decrement operator 165-167
default file encoding 194
default values 523, 524
  parameters, cross-referencing 524, 525
Describe keyword 680
Desired State Configuration (DSC) 331
Desired State Configuration (DSC) resources 610
  using 653-657
Discretionary Access Control List (DACL) 283
Distributed Component Object Model (DCOM) API 300
Distributed Management Task Force (DMTF) standard DSP0004 300
divide-and-assign operator 188
division operator 164
DockPanel control
  using 483-486
Document Type Definition (DTD) 337, 338
Domain-Specific Language (DSL) 331, 676
DontShow property 557, 558
double-hop problem 428, 429
do-until loop 220
do-while loop 220
drives 34, 35
dynamic parameters 596, 597, 600

E

editors 4
elseif statement 208
else statement 208
end block 534, 535
Enter-PSSession command 406, 407

enumerating 118

enumerations 236, 607
automatic value assignment 609, 610
Flags attribute 611-615
underlying types 608, 609
used, for converting value 615, 616
ValidateSet 610, 611

eq operator 167, 168

ErrorAction parameter 716, 736-738

ErrorActionPreference variable 716

error records 719

errors 713
catching 726
non-terminating errors 715
raising 718
rethrowing 730-733
terminating errors 713, 714

Error variable 726

ErrorVariable parameter 726, 727

event handlers 492

event handling 492, 493
Buttons and Click event 494, 495
ComboBox 495
elements, adding programmatically 496, 497
ListView, sorting 498-503
SelectionChanged event 495, 496

events 492
reacting to 445

experimental features 41, 42

Export-Clixml command 145, 146

Export-Csv command 141-143

exporting commands 148

Export-PSSession 416

Extended Type Systems (ETS) 106
reference link 106

Extensible Application Markup
Language (XAML) 474, 475

Extensible Markup Language (XML) 331, 336, 337
attributes 337
elements 337
namespaces 337
schemas 338

F

file attributes
adding 276, 277
removing 276, 277

file catalog commands 294
New-FileCatalog 294
Test-FileCatalog 295-297

File Integrity Monitoring (FIM) 294

files
downloading 378

filesystem paths
testing 268

FileSystem provider
properties 275

finally block 727, 729, 730, 742

Find-Module command
using, in modules 53, 54

flags enumerations 611-615

fluent interface 247, 248

foreach loop 217
foreach alias 217
foreach keyword 217

ForEach-Object command 118
Begin and End parameters 119, 120
MemberName parameter 122
Parallel parameter 120-122

ForEach parameter
using 684, 685
with Describe and Context 686, 687

for loop 218-220

Format-List command 149, 150

format-only properties 152-155

format operator 198-200

Format-Table command 148, 149

formatting commands 148

Func delegate 512
using 512-514

functions 517
capabilities 519

G

generics 256
  classes 256, 257
  methods 257-259
Get-ChildItem command 262, 264, 280
Get-CimClass command 302, 303
Get-CimInstance command 301, 302
Get-CimSession 432
Get-Content command 262, 271, 272
Get-Error command 717, 718, 731
Get-Event command 446, 447
Get-EventSubscriber command 449, 450
Get-Help command 6-8
  Detailed switch parameter 11
  example 9
  Full switch parameter 11
  parameter 10
  syntax 9
Get-Item command 262, 264
Get-ItemProperty command 275
Get-Job command 438
Get-Member command 105, 106
Get method
  implementing 650, 651
Get-Module command
  using, in modules 46
Get-PSSession command 415
Get-Unique 128
Get-Variable command 69, 70
GitHub REST API 385
Global Assembly Cache (GAC) 234
greater than operator 169
Grid control
  using 477-480
grouping operator 158
Group-Object command 134-137

H

hard link 270
hashing 294

hashtables 67, 92, 93
  creating 93
  enumerating 97, 98
  keys, adding 93
  keys, modifying 94
  keys, removing 94
  using, to filter 94-97
HEAD method 378
HelpMessage property 559, 560
help system 6
  About_* help files 14, 15
  Get-Help command 7, 8
  Save-Help command 12, 13
  updatable help 6, 7
  Update-Help command 13, 14
hidden modifier 621
HTTP methods 376
  DELETE 376
  GET 376
  HEAD 376
  OPTIONS 376
  POST 376
  PUT 376
  reference link 376
HTTPS (HTTP over Secure Sockets Layer (SSL)) 379
Hypertext Transfer Protocol (HTTP) 376

I

IArgumentCompleter 644-646
IArgumentCompleterFactory 646, 647
IComparable interface
  implementing 628-630
IEquatable interface
  implementing 630, 631
if statement 208
  assignment 209
Implicit Boolean 209
Import-Clixml command 145, 146
Import-Csv command 143-145
Import-Module command
  using, in modules 47, 48
Import-PSSession 416
inconsistent error handling 733-735
increment operator 165-167

index operator 196, 197

inheritance 622, 623

InitialSessionState object 459, 460
functions, adding 462, 463
modules, adding 460, 461
snap-ins, adding 460, 461
variables, adding 461, 462

inline output command 150-152

InModuleScope command 707, 708

in operator 173

input object types 578, 579

input validation 560

Install-Module command
using, in modules 54

interfaces
IComparable 628-630
IEquatable 630, 631
working with 628

Invoke-CimMethod command 303-305

Invoke-Command 407, 408
ArgumentList parameter 412, 413
local functions and remote sessions 411
parallel execution 409
remoting failures, catching 410, 411
using scope modifier 413, 414

Invoke-Item command 275

Invoke-RestMethod command 383, 384

Invoke-WebRequest 377, 378, 401

isnot operator 191

is operator 191

items 265
creating 270, 271
invoking 275
properties 275
removing 275
searching 280, 281
testing 267

It keyword 680

J

jagged arrays 92

JavaScript Object Notation (JSON) 331, 363

jobs
batching 443-445
using scope modifier, using 441, 442
working with 437

join operator 200

junction 270

Just Enough Administration (JEA) 432, 573
reference link 433
role capabilities 434, 435
session configuration 433, 434

L

labels 224, 225

Language Integrated Query (LINQ) 356

launch configurations
using 768-770

layout controls, WPF 477
DockPanel control 483-486
Grid control 477-480
Margin 486-488
Padding 486-488
StackPanel control 481-483

less than operator 169

like operator 168

line breakpoint
setting 763, 764

Local Configuration Manager (LCM) 655

logical operators 179
and 179
not 179, 180
or 179
xor 180

long lines
line break, after operator 543
line break, after pipe 543
working with 542

loops 207, 217
break 222, 223
continue 222, 223
do-until loop 220
do-while loop 220
foreach loop 217
for loop 218-220
queues, using 225-228
stacks, using 225-228
while loop 221

M

match operator 174

MD5 hashing 294

Measure-Object command 134, 137-139

members 104, 242
  constructors 243, 244
  methods 246, 247
  property 244, 245
  static properties 250, 251

methods 246, 247, 619, 620
  argument types 112, 113
  calling, in parent class 627
  fluent interface 247, 248
  new() method 250
  return types 112, 113
  static methods 248, 249
  using 110-112

methods, StringBuilder type
  reference link 246

Microsoft Desired State Configuration 648

Microsoft .NET 231

Microsoft.PowerShell.PSResourceGet 55
  repositories 56
  version ranges 56, 57

mocking 690

Mock keyword 690

mocks
  overriding 696-699

modules 45, 46
  content 49, 50
  finding 52
  Find-Module command, using 53, 54
  Get-Module command, using 46
  Import-Module command, using 47, 48
  installing 52
  Install-Module command, using 54
  PSModulePath 48, 49
  Remove-Module command, using 48
  Save-Module command, using 55
  Update-Module command, using 54

multi-dimensional arrays 91

multiplication operator 164

multiply and assign operator 188

Mutex 468
  local Mutex 469
  system Mutex 468

N

named blocks
  begin 532
  begin block 533
  clean block 536, 537
  code, placing outside 753-755
  end block 534-536
  pipeline, adding without process 755, 756
  process block 534
  return keyword 537, 538
  usage 753

namespace 237
  documentation link 237

ne operator 167, 168

nesting functions 520

.NET types
  disarming 702-705

New-CimInstance command 306

New-CimSession command 431

New-FileCatalog command 294

New-Item command 262, 270

new() method 250

New-Object command 115

New-PSSession command 414

New-PSSessionConfigurationFile command 433

New-TemporaryFile command 274

Newtonsoft JSON 363

New-Variable command 70, 71

New-WebServiceProxy command 394

non-literal values 591-594

non-local commands
  mocking 699-701

non-local scoped variables
  in scripts and functions 76

non-standard output 103

non-terminating errors 715
  raising 720-722

notlike operator 168

notmatch operator 174

not operator 179, 180

NuGet repositories 58

null coalescing assignment operator 201

null coalescing operator 200, 201

null conditional operator 202, 203

null input
   accepting 577, 578

O

OAuth 385, 390
   access token, requesting 392
   application, creating 390
   authorization code, obtaining 390, 391
   HTTP listener, implementing 391, 392
   token, using 392

Object pipeline 104

object properties
   accessing 106, 107

objects
   creating 113
   mocking 701
   modifying 113

Only Stdout 194

operator precedence 158

operators 195
   arithmetic 161
   array sub-expression 159, 160
   assignment 186
   background 205
   binary 160
   bitwise 180, 181
   call 197, 198
   comma 196
   comparison 167
   format 198-200
   grouping 158
   index 196, 197
   join 200
   logical 179
   null coalescing 200, 201
   null coalescing assignment 201
   null conditional 202, 203
   pipeline chain 203-205

range 197
redirection 191, 192
regular expression-based 173
sub-expression 159
ternary 161
type 190
unary 160

operator usage 750
   assignment operator, using instead of
      equality operator 750, 751
   negated array comparisons 752, 753
   -or, using instead of -and 751, 752

Ordered 98, 99, 240-242

OrderedDictionary 98, 99

or operator 179

Out-Null command 540

output managing 538, 539
   casting, to void 541, 542
   Out-Null command 540
   redirecting, to null 541
   statement, to null 540

Out-String command 334

overloads 244

P

paging
   working with 388, 389

param block 522, 523

parameter aliases 582

Parameter attribute 553-555
   DontShow property 557, 558
   HelpMessage property 559, 560
   Position 555-557
   positional binding 555-557
   ValueFromRemainingArguments property 558, 559

parameter filtering 694-696

parameters 20
   common parameters 25, 26
   Confirm 26
   ConfirmPreference 26-29
   Force parameter 30
   mandatory parameters 21
   mandatory positional parameters 21, 22
   optional parameters 20

optional positional parameters 21
PassThru parameter 31
sets 24, 25
switch parameters 22, 23
types 523
using 522
values 23
WhatIf 26, 29
WhatIfPreference 30
parameter sets
defining 583-587
parameter variables 693, 694
parent class
methods, calling in 627
parser modes 40
paths 266, 267
path type
testing 269, 270
permissions
working with 321
permissions, sharing 322
Access Control Entry (ACE), adding 325
security descriptor, obtaining 323, 324
security descriptor, setting 326
shared history, creating 322
Pester 676
After block 690
Before block 690
in scripts 708-710
iteration with 684
phases, for executing tests 689, 690
pipeline 102
Object pipeline 103, 104
rules 104
pipeline chain operators 203-205
pipeline input 576
Pop-Location command 264
positional parameter 120
PowerShell 1-3
PowerShell 7.3.5 231
PowerShell editors 4-6
PowerShell Extension 5
PowerShell Gallery 52, 53

PowerShell processes
debugging 772-774
PowerShell Pro Tools 6
PowerShell Remoting Protocol (PSRP) 417
PowerShell repositories 57
NuGet repositories 58
SMB repository 57
private variables 79
process block 534
profile scripts 19, 20
properties 244-246, 617
reference link 244
property set 129
providers 32, 33
drives 265
Get-Item command 264
Set-Location command 263
working with 262, 263
provider variables 63
PSBoundParameters 600-602
PSControl Class
reference link 153
PSCustomObject 240-242
methods, adding to 702
using 113-115
PSKoans module
reference link 671
PSMemberTypes Enum
reference link 243
PSModulePath 48, 49
PSReadLine 3
PSReference parameters 575, 576
PSScriptAnalyzer 659-661, 676, 749
configurable rules 661-663
suppressing rules 663-665
PSSessions 414
disconnected sessions 415, 416
Export-PSSession 416
Get-PSSession 415
Import-PSSession 416
New-PSSession 414
PSTypeName attribute 560-562

PSUseCorrectCasing
  reference link 662
PSWriteHtml module 331
Push-Location command 264

Q

queues 225

R

range operator 197
Receive-Job command 438-440
redirection
  to file 192, 193
  to null 195
redirection operators 191, 192
reflection 251
  reference link 251
Register-ArgumentCompleter command 589, 590
registered argument completers
  listing 595
Register-ObjectEvent command 446, 447
  Action parameter 447
  EventArgs parameter 448
  Event parameter 447
  MessageData parameter 448, 449
registry paths
  testing 268, 269
registry values 277-279
  and environment variables 279, 280
regular expression-based operators
  match 174
  notmatch 174
  replace 175-177
  split 177, 178
regular expressions 173
relative paths 266
remainder-and-assign operator 188
remainder operator 165
remote commands
  Enter-PSSession 406, 407
  executing 405, 406
  Invoke-Command 407, 408

remote session
  credentials, passing into 430
remoting
  and SSL 418-421
  configuring 417
  connection, from Linux to Windows 426-428
  connection, from Windows to Linux 425
  enabling 417
  on Linux 423, 424
  over SSH 424
Remove-Item command 275
Remove-Job command 438, 439
Remove-Module command
  using, in modules 48
Remove-Variable command 72
replace operator 175-177
Representational State Transfer (REST) 375, 383
  requests with arguments 386, 387
  simple requests 384
requests
  with arguments 385, 387
Requires statement 520
reserved variables 759, 760
Resolve-Path command 266
responsive interfaces 504
  Action delegate, using 510-512
  background errors 506
  dispatcher, using 506-509
  Func delegate, using 512-514
  Import-Xaml and runspace support 504-506
  ScriptBlock runspace affinity 509, 510
return keyword 537, 538
runspaces and runspace pools, using 450
  BeginInvoke method 452-454
  InitialSessionState object, using 459, 460, 464
  InvocationStateInfo property 455, 456
  Invoke method 452-454
  multiple instances, running 457, 458
  PowerShell instance, creating 451, 452
  RunspacePool object, using 458, 459, 464
  Streams property 455, 456
RuntimeDefinedParameterDictionary 602, 603
  using 599, 600
RuntimeDefinedParameter object
  creating 597-599

S

Save-Help command 12, 13
Save-Module command
  using, in modules 55
scope modifier 76
script analyzer rules 672, 673
  AST-based rules 673, 674
  token-based rules 675, 676
script block 517, 521
  capabilities 519
scripts 517
  capabilities 519
Security Descriptor Definition
    Language (SDDL) 328, 329
security protocols 379
Select-Object command 123-125, 150-152
  calculated properties 126, 127
  ExpandProperty parameter 127
  property set 129, 130
  Unique parameter 128, 129
Select-Xml command 338, 339
  namespaces 340, 341
selenium-powershell module
  reference link 378
Send-MailMessage command 333, 334
ServicePointManager
  reference link 379
Set-Content command 262, 271, 272
Set-ItemProperty command 275
Set-ItResult command
  using 687, 688
Set-Location command 262, 263
Set method
  implementing 651, 652
Set-Variable command 72
SHA1 294
shl operator 184-186
ShouldContinue 530, 531
Should keyword 681
ShouldProcess 528, 529
shr operator 184-186
Simple Object Access Protocol (SOAP) 375, 393, 417

Skip parameter
  using 688
SMB repository
  creating 57
SmbShare module 322
snap-ins 58
SOAP, in PowerShell 7 399
  methods and enumerations 399, 401
  methods, running 401-403
  WSDL document, obtaining 399
SOAP, in Windows PowerShell 394
  methods 395
  methods and enumerations 396, 397
  methods and SOAP objects 397
  New-WebServiceProxy 394
  services, overlapping 398, 399
SOAP service
  finding 393
Software Development Kits (SDKs) 234
software testing
  reference link 678
Sort-Object command 123, 130-133
  Unique parameter 133
splatting 35
  conditional use of parameters 38
  positional parameters 39, 40
  used, for avoiding long lines 36, 37
  used, for avoiding repetition 38, 39
split operator 177, 178
SSL errors
  capturing 382, 383
StackPanel control
  using 481-483
stacks 225
standard output (stdout) 102, 194
Start-Job command 437
Start-ThreadJob command 443
statements
  assigning, to variables 189
static analysis 660
static methods 248, 249
static modifier 622

static properties 250, 251

streams
    redirecting, to standard output 194

strict mode 756-758

StringBuilder class
    reference link 243

StringBuilder Constructors 243

Structured Query Language (SQL) 310

style 518, 519

styling
    guidelines 519

sub-expression operator 159

subtract and assign operator 188

subtraction operator 163, 164

switch statement 210
    break 215-217
    continue 215-217
    enums, using 214, 215
    Regex parameter 212
    script block cases 212-214
    using, on arrays 210, 211
    using, on files 211
    Wildcard parameter 211

symbolic link 270

System Access Control List (SACL) 283

System Center Configuration Manager (SCCM) 310

System.IO Namespace
    documentation link 237

System.Object array 80

System.Xml.Linq namespace 356
    documents, creating 358, 359
    documents, opening 356, 357
    element and attribute values, modifying 360
    nodes, adding 361
    nodes, removing 361
    nodes, selecting 357
    schema validation 362, 363
    working with 359

System.Xml namespace 342
    element and attribute values, modifying 348, 349
    elements, adding 349, 350
    elements and attributes, removing 350
    nodes, copying between documents 350, 351
    schema, inferring 353-355

schema validation 351-353
SelectNodes method 344
working with 345, 346
XmlDocument 343, 344
XML documents, creating 346, 347
XML type accelerator 342, 343
XPath 343, 344
XPathNodeList object 344

T

Tee-Object command 146, 147

temporary files 274

terminating errors 713, 714
    in child scopes 739, 740
    raising 724, 725

ternary operator 161

Test-Connection 410

Test-Driven Development (TDD) 659

Test-FileCatalog command 295-297

testing 659
    considerations 679
    for errors 682, 683
    methodologies 678, 679

Test-Json command 370-372

Test method
    implementing 652, 653

Test-Path command 267

tests
    describing 680

text file encoding 273, 274

ThreadJob module 443

thread-safe objects
    using 464-466

Throw assertion 682, 683

throw keyword 736-738

ThrowTerminatingError method
    using 725

tokenizer 672

tokens 672

transactions 293

trap statement 742-744
    using 742, 743

trusted hosts 422, 423

try statement 727, 740
type 235
    describing, as objects in PowerShell 236
type accelerators 240
    Ordered 240-242
    PSCustomObject 240-242
TypeAccelerators type 252, 253
type descriptions
    as objects 236
type operators 190
    as 190, 191
    is 191
    isnot 191
types variables 759, 760

U

unary operator 160
Uniform Resource Identifier (URI) 340
unit testing 659, 679
Unregister-Event command 450
Update-Help command 6, 7, 13, 14
Update-Module command
    using, in modules 54
User Account Control (UAC) 421, 422
user interface (UI), WPF
    designing 474
    displaying 475, 477
using assembly statement 239
using keyword 237
using namespace statement 238, 239
using scope modifier 413, 414, 441, 442
using statements 519

V

ValidateArgumentsAttribute 640, 641
ValidateCount attribute 566
ValidateDrive attribute 572
ValidateEnumeratedArgumentsAttribute 641-643
ValidateLength attribute 566, 567
ValidateNotNull attribute 563-565
ValidateNotNullOrEmpty attribute 565

ValidateNotNullOrWhitespace attribute 565, 566
ValidatePattern attribute 567-569
ValidateRange attribute 570
ValidateScript attribute 570, 571
ValidateSet attribute 571, 572
ValidateSet value generator 610, 643, 644
ValidateUserDrive attribute 573
validation attribute classes 639
validation attributes 562, 563
ValueFromPipeline 576
    using, for multiple parameters 579, 580
ValueFromPipelineByPropertyName 581-583
ValueFromRemainingArguments property 558, 559
variable breakpoints
    using 762, 763
variable commands 69
    Clear-Variable 73
    Get-Variable 69, 70
    New-Variable 70, 71
    Remove-Variable 72
    Set-Variable 72
variable provider 73, 74
variables 61
    accessing 75, 76
    creating 62
    filling, from arrays 90, 91
    in strings 63, 64
    issues 756
    naming 62
    private variables 79
    provider variables 63
    reserved variable 759, 760
    scope modifiers 76
    statements, assigning to 189
    strict mode 756-758
    types, assigning to 758, 759
    types variable 759, 760
variable scope 74, 75
    numeric scope 77, 78
variable types 64, 65
    assignment with types, on left 66
    assignment with types, on right 65
    conversion 68, 69
    reference type 66

value type 66, 67

Visual Studio Code
debugging 765
URL 5

W

Wait-Job command 440, 441

WATCH window
using 771, 772

web-based Application Programming
    Interface (API) 375

web pages
parsing 377

web requests 376

Where-Object command 122, 123

while loop 221

Windows Management Instrumentation (WMI) 299
classes 299
commands 300
working with 299

Windows permissions 282, 283
access and audit 283
ACEs, adding 288
ACEs, removing 286, 287
inheritance and propagation flags 285, 286
lists and entries, copying 287, 288
numeric values, in ACL 290-292
ownership 292
rule protection 283, 284

Windows PowerShell 231
certificate validation 380, 381

Windows PowerShell modules
using, in PowerShell 7 50, 51

Windows Presentation Foundation (WPF) 473, 474
layout 477
naming and locating controls 488-492
user interface, designing 474
user interface, displaying 475-477

WMI permissions 327
access mask 327, 328
security descriptor, obtaining 327

WMI Query Language (WQL) 302, 310
associated classes 314, 315
ASSOCIATORS OF, using 316, 317

comparison operators 312
escape sequences 311, 312
filter, with dates 312
FROM keyword 310
logic operators 313
SELECT keyword 310
values, quoting 313, 314
WHERE keyword 310
wildcards 311, 312
WMI object paths 315

WMI type accelerators 317
associated classes 321
dates, working with 318
instances, creating 321
methods, calling 319, 320
wmiclass accelerator 319
wmisearcher type accelerator 317

Write-Error command 720

WriteError method
using 722-724

Write-Host command 150-152, 192

WS-Management 417

WSMan drive 418

X

xor operator 180
XPath 339

Download a free PDF copy of this book

Thanks for purchasing this book!

Do you like to read on the go but are unable to carry your print books everywhere?

Is your eBook purchase not compatible with the device of your choice?

Don't worry, now with every Packt book you get a DRM-free PDF version of that book at no cost.

Read anywhere, any place, on any device. Search, copy, and paste code from your favorite technical books directly into your application.

The perks don't stop there, you can get exclusive access to discounts, newsletters, and great free content in your inbox daily.

Follow these simple steps to get the benefits:

1. Scan the QR code or visit the link below:

https://packt.link/free-ebook/9781805120278

2. Submit your proof of purchase.
3. That's it! We'll send your free PDF and other benefits to your email directly.

Made in the USA
Las Vegas, NV
13 December 2024